Principles and Practice of
AMERICAN
POLITICS

Principles and Practice of
AMERICAN POLITICS
CLASSIC AND CONTEMPORARY READINGS

Third Edition

Edited by

Samuel Kernell
University of California, San Diego

Steven S. Smith
Washington University, St. Louis

CQ PRESS

A Division of Congressional Quarterly Inc.
Washington, D.C.

CQ Press
1255 22nd Street, NW, Suite 400
Washington, DC 20037

Phone: 202-729-1900; toll-free, 1-866-427-7737 (1-866-4CQ-PRESS)

Web: www.cqpress.com

Cover design: Malcolm McGaughy
Cover photos: Top photo, Digital Vision/Tom Brakefield; Bottom photo, AP Images

⊗ The paper used in this publication exceeds the requirements of the American National Standard for Information Sciences--Permanence of Paper for Printed Library Materials, ANSI Z39.48-1992.

Printed and bound in the United States of America

10   09   08   07   06   1   2   3   4   5

LIBRARY OF CONGRESS CATALOGING-IN-PUBLICATION DATA

Principles and practice of American politics : classic and contemporary readings / edited by Samuel Kernell, Steven S. Smith. -- 3rd ed.
      p. cm.
   Includes bibliographical references.
   ISBN 1-933116-72-2 (alk. paper)
   1. United States--Politics and government. 2. Political culture--United States. I. Kernell, Samuel, 1945- II. Smith, Steven S., 1953- III. Title.

JK21.P76 2007
320.973--dc22

                              2006018287

CONTENTS

Chapter 3. Federalism   77

Nobel laureate economist James M. Buchanan makes a case for federalism based on a "market" model of governments.

Donald F. Kettl explores the lessons of Hurricane Katrina for understanding the ever-evolving division of power and responsibility between the state and federal governments.

Chapter 4. Civil Rights   107

Taeku Lee reminds us that the state of minority relations over the next decades will reflect as much the criteria with which different ethnic and racial groups in America define themselves as with changing Census counts.

Nathan Glazer looks at how both the government and the people are redefining race in America's increasingly multiracial society.

Chapter 5. Civil Liberties   134

Gerald N. Rosenberg examines the political and legal environment surrounding abortion policy, still a source of conflict thirty years after *Roe v. Wade*.

These noted scholars tackle the ageless yet timely question for republican democracy: Do the demands of war endanger the citizenry's liberties?

In this landmark case on the protection of Fifth Amendment rights, the Supreme Court outlines procedures to be followed by police officers and prosecutors.

Chapter 8. The Bureaucracy   327

Chapter 9. The Judiciary   378

Chapter 10. Public Opinion   448

Chapter 11. Voting, Campaigns, and Elections   511

Chapter 12. Political Parties   566

PREFACE

ASSEMBLING THIS SET of readings for students of American politics has been a pleasure and a challenge. The pleasure has come in discovering so many articles that illuminate American politics. The challenge has come in finding far more than can be contained in a single volume. Consequently, despite its heft, *Principles and Practice* represents a small sampling of the literature.

The selection of articles has been guided by our shared perspective on politics. Political actors pursue goals informed by self-interest. This perspective does not require one to abandon all hope that politics can result in public policy that serves the common interests of the public today and for future generations. It says simply that to understand politics we need to understand what the different political actors want and how this leads them to engage in various strategies to achieve their goals. For government actors these goals will largely reflect the offices they serve in, the constituents they represent, and their constitutional and other legal obligations and opportunities. Other major actors—the public, the news media, and activists in political parties and interest groups—are similarly motivated by self-interest. They do not occupy offices of government, and so their behavior is regulated by a different constellation of opportunities and limitations. Each chapter's readings introduce the interests, rules, and strategic contexts of political action in a major forum of national politics.

Given the extraordinary changes that have occurred in American politics since 9/11, we have again included selections that assess the impact of war on politics and governance. Other recent events—most notably, the government's response to Hurricane Katrina—have provided their own unfortunate lessons, which we take into account in this revision. Other new selections reflect the changing composition of the Supreme Court and the intensification of fights over Court nominations, the debate over the polarization of the American electorate and the place of parties and interest groups in our polity, the ever-evolving state of civil liberties (including the press' asserted rights to protect sources), and the role of television in campaigns and governance.

We have chosen the readings to serve two audiences. Many instructors will employ *Principles and Practice* as a supplement to an introductory American politics textbook. For others, this book may constitute the core reading material for the course. For the former, we looked to readings that will animate the institutional processes described in the text. For the latter, we have sought readings that do not assume more than an elementary knowledge of America's government and politics.

Some of the selections are classics that all instructors will recognize; others address contemporary political developments or proposals for reform and may be unfamiliar. Each article adds emphasis and depth to textbook coverage and illustrates an important theme; most introduce an important writer on American politics. We hope students' understanding of American politics is enriched by them all.

We have taken care to include as much of each original source as possible. In the interest of making them appropriate for use in the classroom, we have edited some of the pieces. Ellipses indicate where material has been excised, and brackets enclose editorial interpolations. Other changes are explained in the source note for the reading.

We wish to thank the editorial staff of CQ Press for its expertise, energy, and patience in helping us bring this project to completion. Brenda Carter, James Headley, and Charisse Kiino provided essential encouragement and guidance throughout the effort. Nancy Geltman and Anne Stewart provided superb editorial assistance, and Dwain Smith and Hans Manzke demonstrated persistence in gaining permission to reprint the selections. Several anonymous reviewers and the following political scientists provided very helpful comments on our plans for this third edition: Adam Berinsky, Massachusetts Institute of Technology; Jamie Carson, University of Georgia; Donald Davidson, Rollins College; Michele Deegan, Moravian College; Erik Engstrom, University of North Carolina, Chapel Hill; Gerard J. Fitzpatrick, Ursinus College; James Huffman, Purdue University; Mark Kemper, Bridgewater State College; Jason MacDonald, Kent State University; Alan Wiseman, Ohio State University; and McGee Young, Marquette University.

Samuel Kernell
Steven S. Smith

ABOUT THE EDITORS

Samuel Kernell is professor of political science at the University of California, San Diego, where he has taught since 1977. He taught previously at the University of Mississippi and the University of Minnesota and served as a senior fellow at the Brookings Institution. Kernell's research interests focus on the presidency, political communication, and American political history. His recent books include *Going Public: New Strategies of Presidential Leadership*, 4th edition (forthcoming); an edited collection of essays, *James Madison: The Theory and Practice of Republican Government*; and *The Logic of American Politics*, 3rd edition, coauthored with Gary C. Jacobson. He and Erik J. Engstrom are currently writing *Manufactured Responsiveness*, an analysis of the effects of 19th-century state electoral laws on national politics.

Steven S. Smith is professor of political science and director of the Weidenbaum Center at Washington University in St. Louis. He has taught at the University of Minnesota, Northwestern University, and George Washington University and has served as a senior fellow at the Brookings Institution. His research interests include American politics, congressional politics, Russian politics, positive theories of politics, and theories of institutional development. He is author or coauthor of *Politics or Principle: Filibustering in the United States; Committees in Congress*, 3rd edition; *The American Congress; Call to Order: Floor Politics in the House and Senate; Managing Uncertainty in the House of Representatives;* and *The Politics of Institutional Choice: The Formation of the Russian State Duma.*

Chapter 1

Designing Institutions

1-1

from *The Logic of Collective Action*

Mancur Olson Jr.

With the publication of The Logic of Collective Action *in 1965, Mancur Olson introduced the fundamental dilemma of collective action to all who study politics. When members of a group agree to work together to achieve a collective goal, each member as an individual faces powerful disincentives, Olson showed, that can frustrate the efforts of the group as a whole. For example, when each can foresee that his or her relatively small contribution to a collective enterprise will not affect its overall success, many will fail to contribute—a phenomenon known as free riding—and leave to everyone else the burden of supplying the collective good. As a consequence, collective enterprises based on cooperation, and supported by the entire collectivity, nevertheless often fail.*

IT IS OFTEN taken for granted, at least where economic objectives are involved, that groups of individuals with common interests usually attempt to further those common interests. Groups of individuals with common interests are expected to act on behalf of their common interests much as single individuals are often expected to act on behalf of their personal interests. This opinion about

Source: Mancur Olson Jr., *The Logic of Collective Action: Public Goods and the Theory of Groups* (Cambridge: Harvard University Press, 1971), 1–19.

group behavior is frequently found not only in popular discussions but also in scholarly writings. Many economists of diverse methodological and ideological traditions have implicitly or explicitly accepted it. This view has, for example, been important in many theories of labor unions, in Marxian theories of class action, in concepts of "countervailing power," and in various discussions of economic institutions. It has, in addition, occupied a prominent place in political science, at least in the United States, where the study of pressure groups has been dominated by a celebrated "group theory" based on the idea that groups will act when necessary to further their common or group goals. Finally, it has played a significant role in many well-known sociological studies.

The view that groups act to serve their interests presumably is based upon the assumption that the individuals in groups act out of self-interest. If the individuals in a group altruistically disregarded their personal welfare, it would not be very likely that collectively they would seek some selfish common or group objective. Such altruism is, however, considered exceptional, and self-interested behavior is usually thought to be the rule, at least when economic issues are at stake; no one is surprised when individual businessmen seek higher profits, when individual workers seek higher wages, or when individual consumers seek lower prices. The idea that groups tend to act in support of their group interests is supposed to follow logically from this widely accepted premise of rational, self-interested behavior. In other words, if the members of some group have a common interest or objective, and if they would all be better off if that objective were achieved, it has been thought to follow logically that the individuals in that group would, if they were rational and self-interested, act to achieve that objective.

But it is *not* in fact true that the idea that groups will act in their self-interest follows logically from the premise of rational and self-interested behavior. It does *not* follow, because all of the individuals in a group would gain if they achieved their group objective, that they would act to achieve that objective, even if they were all rational and self-interested. Indeed, unless the number of individuals in a group is quite small, or unless there is coercion or some other special device to make individuals act in their common interest, *rational, self-interested individuals will not act to achieve their common or group interests.* In other words, even if all of the individuals in a large group are rational and self-interested, and would gain if, as a group, they acted to achieve their common interest or objective, they will still not voluntarily act to achieve that common or group interest. The notion that groups of individuals will act to achieve their common or group interests, far from being a logical implication of the assumption that the individuals in a group will rationally further their individual interests, is in fact inconsistent with that assumption. . . .

A Theory of Groups and Organizations

The Purpose of Organization

Since most (though by no means all) of the action taken by or on behalf of groups of individuals is taken through organizations, it will be helpful to consider organizations in a general or theoretical way.[1] The logical place to begin any systematic study of organizations is with their purpose. But there are all types and shapes and sizes of organizations, even of economic organizations, and there is then some question whether there is any single purpose that would be characteristic of organizations generally. One purpose that is nonetheless characteristic of most organizations, and surely of practically all organizations with an important economic aspect, is the furtherance of the interests of their members. That would seem obvious, at least from the economist's perspective. To be sure, some organizations may out of ignorance fail to further their members' interests, and others may be enticed into serving only the ends of the leadership.[2] But organizations often perish if they do nothing to further the interests of their members, and this factor must severely limit the number of organizations that fail to serve their members.

The idea that organizations or associations exist to further the interests of their members is hardly novel, nor peculiar to economics; it goes back at least to Aristotle, who wrote, "Men journey together with a view to particular advantage, and by way of providing some particular thing needed for the purposes of life, and similarly the political association seems to have come together originally, and to continue in existence, for the sake of the *general* advantages it brings."[3] More recently Professor Leon Festinger, a social psychologist, pointed out that "the attraction of group membership is not so much in sheer belonging, but rather in attaining something by means of this membership."[4] The late Harold Laski, a political scientist, took it for granted that "associations exist to fulfill purposes which a group of men have in common."[5]

The kinds of organizations that are the focus of this study are *expected* to further the interests of their members.[6] Labor unions are expected to strive for higher wages and better working conditions for their members; farm organizations are expected to strive for favorable legislation for their members; cartels are expected to strive for higher prices for participating firms; the corporation is expected to further the interests of its stockholders;[7] and the state is expected to further the common interests of its citizens (though in this nationalistic age the state often has interests and ambitions apart from those of its citizens).

Notice that the interests that all of these diverse types of organizations are expected to further are for the most part *common* interests: the union members'

common interest in higher wages, the farmers' common interest in favorable legislation, the cartel members' common interest in higher prices, the stockholders'
common interest in higher dividends and stock prices, the citizens' common
interest in good government. It is not an accident that the diverse types of organizations listed are all supposed to work primarily for the *common* interests of
their members. Purely personal or individual interests can be advanced, and usually advanced most efficiently, by individual, unorganized action. There is obviously no purpose in having an organization when individual, unorganized action
can serve the interests of the individual as well as or better than an organization;
there would, for example, be no point in forming an organization simply to play
solitaire. But when a number of individuals have a common or collective interest—when they share a single purpose or objective—individual, unorganized
action (as we shall soon see) will either not be able to advance that common
interest at all, or will not be able to advance that interest adequately. Organizations can therefore perform a function when there are common or group interests, and though organizations often also serve purely personal, individual interests, their characteristic and primary function is to advance the common
interests of groups of individuals.

The assumption that organizations typically exist to further the common
interests of groups of people is implicit in most of the literature about organizations, and two of the writers already cited make this assumption explicit: Harold
Laski emphasized that organizations exist to achieve purposes or interests which
"a group of men have in common," and Aristotle apparently had a similar notion
in mind when he argued that political associations are created and maintained
because of the "general advantages" they bring. . . . As Arthur Bentley, the
founder of the "group theory" of modern political science, put it, "there is no
group without its interest."[8] The social psychologist Raymond Cattell was
equally explicit, and stated that "every group has its interest."[9] This is also the
way the word "group" will be used here.

Just as those who belong to an organization or a group can be presumed to
have a common interest,[10] so they obviously also have purely individual interests,
different from those of the others in the organization or group. All of the members of a labor union, for example, have a common interest in higher wages, but
at the same time each worker has a unique interest in his personal income, which
depends not only on the rate of wages but also on the length of time that he
works.

Public Goods and Large Groups

The combination of individual interests and common interests in an organization suggests an analogy with a competitive market. The firms in a perfectly

competitive industry, for example, have a common interest in a higher price for the industry's product. Since a uniform price must prevail in such a market, a firm cannot expect a higher price for itself unless all of the other firms in the industry also have this higher price. But a firm in a competitive market also has an interest in selling as much as it can, until the cost of producing another unit exceeds the price of that unit. In this there is no common interest; each firm's interest is directly opposed to that of every other firm, for the more other firms sell, the lower the price and income for any given firm. In short, while all firms have a common interest in a higher price, they have antagonistic interests where output is concerned. . . .

For these reasons it is now generally understood that if the firms in an industry are maximizing profits, the profits for the industry as a whole will be less than they might otherwise be.[11] And almost everyone would agree that this theoretical conclusion fits the facts for markets characterized by pure competition. The important point is that this is true because, though all the firms have a common interest in a higher price for the industry's product, it is in the interest of each firm that the other firms pay the cost—in terms of the necessary reduction in output—needed to obtain a higher price.

About the only thing that keeps prices from falling in accordance with the process just described in perfectly competitive markets is outside intervention. Government price supports, tariffs, cartel agreements, and the like may keep the firms in a competitive market from acting contrary to their interests. Such aid or intervention is quite common. It is then important to ask how it comes about. How does a competitive industry obtain government assistance in maintaining the price of its product?

Consider a hypothetical, competitive industry, and suppose that most of the producers in that industry desire a tariff, a price-support program, or some other government intervention to increase the price for their product. To obtain any such assistance from the government, the producers in this industry will presumably have to organize a lobbying organization; they will have to become an active pressure group.[12] This lobbying organization may have to conduct a considerable campaign. If significant resistance is encountered, a great amount of money will be required.[13] Public relations experts will be needed to influence the newspapers, and some advertising may be necessary. Professional organizers will probably be needed to organize "spontaneous grass roots" meetings among the distressed producers in the industry, and to get those in the industry to write letters to their congressmen.[14] The campaign for the government assistance will take the time of some of the producers in the industry, as well as their money.

There is a striking parallel between the problem the perfectly competitive industry faces as it strives to obtain government assistance, and the problem it faces in the marketplace when the firms increase output and bring about a fall in price. *Just as it was not rational for a particular producer to restrict his output in order that there might be a higher price for the product of his industry, so it would not be rational for him to sacrifice his time and money to support a lobbying organization to obtain government assistance for the industry. In neither case would it be in the interest of the individual producer to assume any of the costs himself. A lobbying organization, or indeed a labor union or any other organization, working in the interest of a large group of firms or workers in some industry, would get no assistance from the rational, self-interested individuals in that industry.* This would be true even if everyone in the industry were absolutely convinced that the proposed program was in their interest (though in fact some might think otherwise and make the organization's task yet more difficult).

Although the lobbying organization is only one example of the logical analogy between the organization and the market, it is of some practical importance. There are many powerful and well-financed lobbies with mass support in existence now, but these lobbying organizations do not get that support because of their legislative achievements. . . .

Some critics may argue that the rational person will, indeed, support a large organization, like a lobbying organization, that works in his interest, because he knows that if he does not, others will not do so either, and then the organization will fail, and he will be without the benefit that the organization could have provided. This argument shows the need for the analogy with the perfectly competitive market. For it would be quite as reasonable to argue that prices will never fall below the levels a monopoly would have charged in a perfectly competitive market, because if one firm increased its output, other firms would also, and the price would fall; but each firm could foresee this, so it would not start a chain of price-destroying increases in output. In fact, it does not work out this way in a competitive market; nor in a large organization. When the number of firms involved is large, no one will notice the effect on price if one firm increases its output, and so no one will change his plans because of it. Similarly, in a large organization, the loss of one dues payer will not noticeably increase the burden for any other one dues payer, and so a rational person would not believe that if he were to withdraw from an organization he would drive others to do so.

The foregoing argument must at the least have some relevance to economic organizations that are mainly means through which individuals attempt to obtain the same things they obtain through their activities in the market. Labor unions, for example, are organizations through which workers strive to get the same things they get with their individual efforts in the market—higher wages, better working conditions, and the like. It would be strange indeed if the workers did not confront some of the same problems in the union that they meet in the market, since their efforts in both places have some of the same purposes.

However similar the purposes may be, critics may object that attitudes in organizations are not at all like those in markets. In organizations, an emotional or ideological element is often also involved. Does this make the argument offered here practically irrelevant?

A most important type of organization—the national state—will serve to test this objection. Patriotism is probably the strongest non-economic motive for organizational allegiance in modern times. This age is sometimes called the age of nationalism. Many nations draw additional strength and unity from some powerful ideology, such as democracy or communism, as well as from a common religion, language, or cultural inheritance. The state not only has many such powerful sources of support; it also is very important economically. Almost any government is economically beneficial to its citizens, in that the law and order it provides is a prerequisite of all civilized economic activity. But despite the force of patriotism, the appeal of the national ideology, the bond of a common culture, and the indispensability of the system of law and order, no major state in modern history has been able to support itself through voluntary dues or contributions. Philanthropic contributions are not even a significant source of revenue for most countries. Taxes, *compulsory* payments by definition, are needed. Indeed, as the old saying indicates, their necessity is as certain as death itself.

If the state, with all of the emotional resources at its command, cannot finance its most basic and vital activities without resort to compulsion, it would seem that large private organizations might also have difficulty in getting the individuals in the groups whose interests they attempt to advance to make the necessary contributions voluntarily.[15]

The reason the state cannot survive on voluntary dues or payments, but must rely on taxation, is that the most fundamental services a nation-state provides are, in one important respect, like the higher price in a competitive market: they must be available to everyone if they are available to anyone. The basic and most elementary goods or services provided by government, like defense and police protection, and the system of law and order generally, are such that they go to everyone or practically everyone in the nation. It would obviously not be feasible, if indeed it were possible, to deny the protection provided by the military services, the police, and the courts to those who did not voluntarily pay their share of the costs of government, and taxation is accordingly necessary. The common or collective benefits provided by governments are usually called "public goods" by economists, and the concept of public goods is one of the oldest and most important ideas in the study of public finance. A common, collective, or public good is here defined as any good such that, if any person X_i in a group $X_l, \ldots, X_i, \ldots, X_n$ consumes it, it cannot feasibly be withheld from the others in that group.[16] In other words, those who do not purchase or pay for any of the public or collective good cannot be excluded or kept from sharing in the consumption of the good, as they can where noncollective goods are concerned.

Students of public finance have, however, neglected the fact that *the achievement of any common goal or the satisfaction of any common interest means that a public or collective good has been provided for that group.*[17] The very fact that a goal or purpose is *common* to a group means that no one in the group is excluded from the benefit or satisfaction brought about by its achievement. As the opening paragraphs of this chapter indicated, almost all groups and organizations have the purpose of serving the common interests of their members. As R. M. MacIver puts it, "Persons . . . have common interests in the degree to which they participate in a cause . . . which indivisibly embraces them all."[18] It is of the essence of an organization that it provides an inseparable, generalized benefit. It follows that the provision of public or collective goods is the fundamental function of organizations generally. A state is first of all an organization that provides public goods for its members, the citizens; and other types of organizations similarly provide collective goods for their members.

And just as a state cannot support itself by voluntary contributions, or by selling its basic services on the market, neither can other large organizations support themselves without providing some sanction, or some attraction distinct from the public good itself, that will lead individuals to help bear the burdens of maintaining the organization. The individual member of the typical large organization is in a position analogous to that of the firm in a perfectly competitive market, or the taxpayer in the state: his own efforts will not have a noticeable effect on the situation of his organization, and he can enjoy any improvements brought about by others whether or not he has worked in support of his organization.

There is no suggestion here that states or other organizations provide *only* public or collective goods. Governments often provide noncollective goods like electric power, for example, and they usually sell such goods on the market much as private firms would do. Moreover . . . large organizations that are not able to make membership compulsory *must also* provide some noncollective goods in order to give potential members an incentive to join. Still, collective goods are the characteristic organizational goods, for ordinary noncollective goods can always be provided by individual action, and only where common purposes or collective goods are concerned is organization or group action ever indispensable.[19]

NOTES

1. Economists have for the most part neglected to develop theories of organizations, but there are a few works from an economic point of view on the subject. See, for example, three papers by Jacob Marschak, "Elements for a Theory of Teams," *Management Science,* I (January 1955), 127–137, "Towards an Economic Theory of Organization and Information," in *Decision*

Processes, ed. R. M. Thrall, C. H. Combs, and R. L. Davis (New York: John Wiley, 1954), pp. 187–220, and "Efficient and Viable Organization Forms," in *Modern Organization Theory,* ed. Mason Haire (New York: John Wiley, 1959), pp. 307–320; two papers by R. Radner, "Application of Linear Programming to Team Decision Problems," *Management Science,* V (January 1959), 143–150, and "Team Decision Problems," *Annals of Mathematical Statistics,* XXXIII (September 1962), 857–881; C. B. McGuire, "Some Team Models of a Sales Organization," *Management Science,* VII (January 1961), 101–130; Oskar Morgenstern, *Prolegomena to a Theory of Organization* (Santa Monica, Calif.: RAND Research Memorandum 734, 1951); James G. March and Herbert A. Simon, *Organizations* (New York: John Wiley, 1958); Kenneth Boulding, *The Organizational Revolution* (New York: Harper, 1953).

2. Max Weber called attention to the case where an organization continues to exist for some time after it has become meaningless because some official is making a living out of it. See his *Theory of Social and Economic Organization,* trans. Talcott Parsons and A. M. Henderson (New York: Oxford University Press, 1947), p. 318.

3. *Ethics* viii.9.1160a.

4. Leon Festinger, "Group Attraction and Membership," in *Group Dynamics,* ed. Dorwin Cartwright and Alvin Zander (Evanston, Ill.: Row, Peterson, 1953), p. 93.

5. *A Grammar of Politics,* 4th ed. (London: George Allen & Unwin, 1939), p. 67.

6. Philanthropic and religious organizations are not necessarily expected to serve only the interests of their members; such organizations have other purposes that are considered more important, however much their members "need" to belong, or are improved or helped by belonging. But the complexity of such organizations need not be debated at length here, because this study will focus on organizations with a significant economic aspect. The emphasis here will have something in common with what Max Weber called the "associative group"; he called a group associative if "the orientation of social action with it rests on a rationally motivated agreement." Weber contrasted his "associative group" with the "communal group," which was centered on personal affection, erotic relationships, etc., like the family. (See Weber, pp. 136–139, and Grace Coyle, *Social Process in Organized Groups,* New York: Richard Smith, Inc., 1930, pp. 7–9.) The logic of the theory developed here can be extended to cover communal, religious, and philanthropic organizations, but the theory is not particularly useful in studying such groups. See Olson, pp. 61n17, 159–162.

7. That is, its members. This study does not follow the terminological usage of those organization theorists who describe employees as "members" of the organization for which they work. Here it is more convenient to follow the language of everyday usage instead, and to distinguish the members of, say, a union from the employees of that union. Similarly, the members of the union will be considered employees of the corporation for which they work.

8. Arthur Bentley, *The Process of Government* (Evanston, Ill.: Principia Press, 1949), p. 211. David B. Truman takes a similar approach; see his *The Governmental Process* (New York: Alfred A. Knopf, 1958), pp. 33–35. See also Sidney Verba, *Small Groups and Political Behavior* (Princeton, N.J.: Princeton University Press, 1961), pp. 12–13.

9. Raymond Cattell, "Concepts and Methods in the Measurement of Group Syntality," in *Small Groups,* ed. A. Paul Hare, Edgard F. Borgatta, and Robert F. Bales (New York: Alfred A. Knopf, 1955), p. 115.

10. Any organization or group will of course usually be divided into subgroups or factions that are opposed to one another. This fact does not weaken the assumption made here that

organizations exist to serve the common interests of members, for the assumption does not imply that intragroup conflict is neglected. The opposing groups within an organization ordinarily have some interest in common (if not, why would they maintain the organization?), and the members of any subgroup or faction also have a separate common interest of their own. They will indeed often have a common purpose in defeating some other subgroup or faction. The approach used here does not neglect the conflict within groups and organizations, then, because it considers each organization as a unit only to the extent that it does in fact attempt to serve a common interest, and considers the various subgroups as the relevant units with common interests to analyze the factional strife.

11. For a fuller discussion of this question see Mancur Olson, Jr., and David McFarland, "The Restoration of Pure Monopoly and the Concept of the Industry," *Quarterly Journal of Economics,* LXXVI (November 1962), 613–631.

12. Robert Michels contends in his classic study that "democracy is inconceivable without organization," and that "the principle of organization is an absolutely essential condition for the political struggle of the masses." See his *Political Parties,* trans. Eden and Cedar Paul (New York: Dover Publications, 1959), pp. 21–22. See also Robert A. Brady, *Business as a System of Power* (New York: Columbia University Press, 1943), p. 193.

13. Alexander Heard, *The Costs of Democracy* (Chapel Hill: University of North Carolina Press, 1960), especially note 1, pp. 95–96. For example, in 1947 the National Association of Manufacturers spent over $4.6 million, and over a somewhat longer period the American Medical Association spent as much on a campaign against compulsory health insurance.

14. "If the full truth were ever known . . . lobbying, in all its ramifications, would prove to be a billion dollar industry." U.S. Congress, House, Select Committee on Lobbying Activities, *Report,* 81st Cong., 2nd Sess. (1950), as quoted in the *Congressional Quarterly Almanac,* 81st Cong., 2nd Sess., VI, 764–765.

15. Sociologists as well as economists have observed that ideological motives alone are not sufficient to bring forth the continuing effort of large masses of people. Max Weber provides a notable example:

> All economic activity in a market economy is undertaken and carried through by individuals for their own ideal or material interests. This is naturally just as true when economic activity is oriented to the patterns of order of corporate groups. . . .
>
> Even if an economic system were organized on a socialistic basis, there would be no fundamental difference in this respect. . . . The structure of interests and the relevant situation might change; there would be other means of pursuing interests, but this fundamental factor would remain just as relevant as before. It is of course true that economic action which is oriented on purely ideological grounds to the interest of others does exist. But it is even more certain that the mass of men do not act this way, and it is an induction from experience that they cannot do so and never will. . . .
>
> In a market economy the interest in the maximization of income is necessarily the driving force of all economic activity. (Weber, pp. 319–320)

Talcott Parsons and Neil Smelser go even further in postulating that "performance" throughout society is proportional to the "rewards" and "sanctions" involved. See their *Economy and Society* (Glencoe, Ill.: Free Press, 1954), pp. 50–69.

16. This simple definition focuses upon two points that are important in the present context. The first point is that most collective goods can only be defined with respect to some spe-

cific group. One collective good goes to one group of people, another collective good to another group; one may benefit the whole world, another only two specific people. Moreover, some goods are collective goods to those in one group and at the same time private goods to those in another, because some individuals can be kept from consuming them and others can't. Take for example the parade that is a collective good to all those who live in tall buildings overlooking the parade route, but which appears to be a private good to those who can see it only by buying tickets for a seat in the stands along the way. The second point is that once the relevant group has been defined, the definition used here, like Musgrave's, distinguishes collective good in terms of infeasibility of excluding potential consumers of the good. This approach is used because collective goods produced by organizations of all kinds seem to be such that exclusion is normally not feasible. To be sure, for some collective goods it is physically possible to practice exclusion. But, as Head has shown, it is not necessary that exclusion be technically impossible; it is only necessary that it be infeasible or uneconomic. Head has also shown most clearly that nonexcludability is only one of two basic elements in the traditional understanding of public goods. The other, he points out, is "jointness of supply." A good has "jointness" if making it available to one individual means that it can be easily or freely supplied to others as well. The polar case of jointness would be Samuelson's pure public good, which is a good such that additional consumption of it by one individual does not diminish the amount available to others. By the definition used here, jointness is not a necessary attribute of a public good. As later parts of this chapter will show, at least one type of collective good considered here exhibits no jointness whatever, and few if any would have the degree of jointness needed to qualify as pure public goods. Nonetheless, most of the collective goods to be studied here do display a large measure of jointness. On the definition and importance of public goods, see John G. Head, "Public Goods and Public Policy," *Public Finance,* vol. XVII, no. 3 (1962), 197–219; Richard Musgrave, *The Theory of Public Finance* (New York: McGraw-Hill, 1959); Paul A. Samuelson, "The Pure Theory of Public Expenditure," "Diagrammatic Exposition of A Theory of Public Expenditure," and "Aspects of Public Expenditure Theories," in *Review of Economics and Statistics,* XXXVI (November 1954), 387–390, XXXVII (November 1955), 350–356, and XL (November 1958), 332–338. For somewhat different opinions about the usefulness of the concept of public goods, see Julius Margolis, "A Comment on the Pure Theory of Public Expenditure," *Review of Economics and Statistics,* XXXVII (November 1955), 347–349, and Gerhard Colm, "Theory of Public Expenditures," *Annals of the American Academy of Political and Social Science,* CLXXXIII (January 1936), 1–11.

17. There is no necessity that a public good to one group in a society is necessarily in the interest of the society as a whole. Just as a tariff could be a public good to the industry that sought it, so the removal of the tariff could be a public good to those who consumed the industry's product. This is equally true when the public-good concept is applied only to governments; for a military expenditure, or a tariff, or an immigration restriction that is a public good to one country could be a "public bad" to another country, and harmful to world society as a whole.

18. R. M. MacIver in *Encyclopaedia of the Social Sciences,* VII (New York: Macmillan, 1932), 147.

19. It does not, however, follow that organized or coordinated group action is *always* necessary to obtain a collective goal.

1-2

The Tragedy of the Commons

Garrett Hardin

In this seminal article, Garrett Hardin identifies another class of collective action problems, the "tragedy of the commons." The concept—a "tragedy" because of the inevitability with which public goods, or the "commons," will be exploited—is generally applied to study cases in which natural resources are being misused. Unlike the problems we have already encountered, which concern the production of public goods, the tragedy of the commons affects their conservation. Because public goods are freely available, members of the community will be tempted to overly consume them—to overfish, to overuse national parks, to pollute public water or air—even as they realize their behavior and that of their neighbors is destroying the goods. Hardin discusses social arrangements that can substitute for the commons, or public ownership of scarce resources, and argues that the tragedy of the commons is becoming a more pressing concern as the population increases. As with the problem of free riding described by Mancur Olson, government authority offers one solution extricating participants from their bind.

AT THE END of a thoughtful article on the future of nuclear war, Wiesner and York concluded that: "Both sides in the arms race are . . . confronted by the dilemma of steadily increasing military power and steadily decreasing national security. *It is our considered professional judgment that this dilemma has no technical solution. If the great powers continue to look for solutions in the area of science and technology only, the result will be to worsen the situation.*" [1]

I would like to focus your attention not on the subject of the article (national security in a nuclear world) but on the kind of conclusion they reached, namely that there is no technical solution to the problem. An implicit and almost universal assumption of discussions published in professional and semipopular scientific journals is that the problem under discussion has a technical solution. A technical solution may be defined as one that requires a change only in the techniques of the natural sciences, demanding little or nothing in the way of change in human values or ideas of morality.

Source: Garrett Hardin, "The Tragedy of the Commons," *Science,* December 3, 1968, 1243–1248.

In our day (though not in earlier times) technical solutions are always welcome. . . . [Yet of the] class of human problems which can be called "no technical solution problems" . . . [i]t is easy to show that [it] is not a null class. Recall the game of tick-tack-toe. Consider the problem, "How can I win the game of tick-tack-toe?" It is well known that I cannot, if I assume (in keeping with the conventions of game theory) that my opponent understands the game perfectly. Put another way, there is no "technical solution" to the problem. I can win only by giving a radical meaning to the word "win." I can hit my opponent over the head; or I can drug him; or I can falsify the records. Every way in which I "win" involves, in some sense, an abandonment of the game, as we intuitively understand it. (I can also, of course, openly abandon the game—refuse to play it. This is what most adults do.)

The class of "No technical solution problems" has members. My thesis is that the "population problem," as conventionally conceived, is a member of this class. How it is conventionally conceived needs some comment. It is fair to say that most people who anguish over the population problem are trying to find a way to avoid the evils of overpopulation without relinquishing any of the privileges they now enjoy. They think that farming the seas or developing new strains of wheat will solve the problem—technologically. I try to show here that the solution they seek cannot be found. The population problem cannot be solved in a technical way, any more than can the problem of winning the game of tick-tack-toe.

What Shall We Maximize?

Population, as Malthus said, naturally tends to grow "geometrically," or, as we would now say, exponentially. In a finite world this means that the per capita share of the world's goods must steadily decrease. Is ours a finite world?

A fair defense can be put forward for the view that the world is infinite; or that we do not know that it is not. But, in terms of the practical problems that we must face in the next few generations with the foreseeable technology, it is clear that we will greatly increase human misery if we do not, during the immediate future, assume that the world available to the terrestrial human population is finite. "Space" is no escape.[2]

A finite world can support only a finite population; therefore, population growth must eventually equal zero. . . . When this condition is met, what will be the situation of mankind? Specifically, can [Jeremy] Bentham's goal of "the greatest good for the greatest number" be realized? . . .

The . . . reason [why not] springs directly from biological facts. To live, any organism must have a source of energy (for example, food). This energy is utilized for two purposes: mere maintenance and work. For man, maintenance of life requires about 1600 kilocalories a day ("maintenance calories"). Anything that he does over and above merely staying alive will be defined as work, and is supported by "work calories" which he takes in. Work calories are used not only for what we call work in common speech; they are also required for all forms of enjoyment, from swimming and automobile racing to playing music and writing poetry. If our goal is to maximize population it is obvious what we must do: We must make the work calories per person approach as close to zero as possible. No gourmet meals, no vacations, no sports, no music, no literature, no art. . . . I think that everyone will grant, without argument or proof, that maximizing population does not maximize goods. Bentham's goal is impossible. . . .

The optimum population is, then, less than the maximum. The difficulty of defining the optimum is enormous; so far as I know, no one has seriously tackled this problem. Reaching an acceptable and stable solution will surely require more than one generation of hard analytical work—and much persuasion. . . .

We can make little progress in working toward optimum population size until we explicitly exorcize the spirit of Adam Smith in the field of practical demography. In economic affairs, *The Wealth of Nations* (1776) popularized the "invisible hand," the idea that an individual who "intends only his own gain," is, as it were, "led by an invisible hand to promote . . . the public interest."[3] Adam Smith did not assert that this was invariably true, and perhaps neither did any of his followers. But he contributed to a dominant tendency of thought that has ever since interfered with positive action based on rational analysis, namely, the tendency to assume that decisions reached individually will, in fact, be the best decisions for an entire society. If this assumption is correct it justifies the continuance of our present policy of laissez-faire in reproduction. If it is correct we can assume that men will control their individual fecundity so as to produce the optimum population. If the assumption is not correct, we need to reexamine our individual freedoms to see which ones are defensible.

Tragedy of Freedom in a Commons

The rebuttal to the invisible hand in population control is to be found in a scenario first sketched in a little-known pamphlet in 1833 by a mathematical amateur named William Forster Lloyd (1794–1852).[4] We may well call it "the tragedy of the commons," using the word "tragedy" as the philosopher Whitehead used it: "The essence of dramatic tragedy is not unhappiness. It resides in the solemnity of the remorseless working of things."[5] He then goes on to say, "This inevitableness of destiny can only be illustrated in terms of human life by incidents which in fact involve unhappiness. For it is only by them that the futility of escape can be made evident in the drama."

The tragedy of the commons develops in this way. Picture a pasture open to all. It is to be expected that each herdsman will try to keep as many cattle as possible on the commons. Such an arrangement may work reasonably satisfactorily for centuries because tribal wars, poaching, and disease keep the numbers of both man and beast well below the carrying capacity of the land. Finally, however, comes the day of reckoning, that is, the day when the long-desired goal of social stability becomes a reality. At this point, the inherent logic of the commons remorselessly generates tragedy.

As a rational being, each herdsman seeks to maximize his gain. Explicitly or implicitly, more or less consciously, he asks, "What is the utility *to me* of adding one more animal to my herd?" This utility has one negative and one positive component.

1. The positive component is a function of the increment of one animal. Since the herdsman receives all the proceeds from the sale of the additional animal, the positive utility is nearly +1.
2. The negative component is a function of the additional overgrazing created by one more animal. Since, however, the effects of overgrazing are shared by all the herdsmen, the negative utility for any particular decision-making herdsman is only a fraction of –1.

Adding together the component partial utilities, the rational herdsman concludes that the only sensible course for him to pursue is to add another animal to his herd. And another. . . . But this is the conclusion reached by each and every rational herdsman sharing a commons. Therein is the tragedy. Each man is locked into a system that compels him to increase his herd without limit—in a world that is limited. Ruin is the destination toward which all men rush, each pursuing his own best interest in a society that believes in the freedom of the commons. Freedom in a commons brings ruin to all.

Some would say that this is a platitude. Would that it were! In a sense, it was learned thousands of years ago, but natural selection favors the forces of psychological denial.[6] The individual benefits as an individual from his ability to deny the truth even though society as a whole, of which he is a part, suffers. Education can counteract the natural tendency to do the wrong thing, but the inexorable succession of generations requires that the basis for this knowledge be constantly refreshed.

A simple incident that occurred a few years ago in Leominster, Massachusetts, shows how perishable the knowledge is. During the Christmas shopping season the parking meters downtown were covered with plastic bags that bore tags reading: "Do not open until after Christmas. Free parking courtesy of the mayor and city council." In other words, facing the prospect of an increased demand for already scarce space, the city fathers reinstituted the system of the commons. (Cynically, we suspect that they gained more votes than they lost by this retrogressive act.)

In an approximate way, the logic of the commons has been understood for a long time, perhaps since the discovery of agriculture or the invention of private property in real estate. But it is understood mostly only in special cases which are not sufficiently generalized. Even at this late date, cattlemen leasing national land on the western ranges demonstrate no more than an ambivalent understanding, in constantly pressuring federal authorities to increase the head count to the point where overgrazing produces erosion and weed-dominance. Likewise, the oceans of the world continue to suffer from the survival of the philosophy of the commons. Maritime nations still respond automatically to the shibboleth of the "freedom of the seas." Professing to believe in the "inexhaustible resources of the oceans," they bring species after species of fish and whales closer to extinction.[7]

The National Parks present another instance of the working out of the tragedy of the commons. At present, they are open to all, without limit. The parks themselves are limited in extent—there is only one Yosemite Valley— whereas population seems to grow without limit. The values that visitors seek in the parks are steadily eroded. Plainly, we must soon cease to treat the parks as commons or they will be of no value to anyone.

What shall we do? We have several options. We might sell them off as private property. We might keep them as public property, but allocate the right to enter them. The allocation might be on the basis of wealth, by the use of an auction system. It might be on the basis of merit, as defined by some agreed-upon standards. It might be by lottery. Or it might be on a first-come, first-served basis, administered to long queues. These, I think, are all the reasonable possibilities. They are all objectionable. But we must choose—or acquiesce in the destruction of the commons that we call our National Parks.

Pollution

In a reverse way, the tragedy of the commons reappears in problems of pollution. Here it is not a question of taking something out of the commons, but of putting something in—sewage, or chemical, radioactive, and heat wastes into water; noxious and dangerous fumes into the air; and distracting and unpleasant advertising signs into the line of sight. The calculations of utility are much the same as before. The rational man finds that his share of the cost of the wastes he discharges into the commons is less than the cost of purifying his wastes before releasing them. Since this is true for everyone, we are locked into a system of "fouling our own nest," so long as we behave only as independent, rational, free-enterprisers.

The tragedy of the commons as a food basket is averted by private property, or something formally like it. But the air and waters surrounding us cannot readily be fenced, and so the tragedy of the commons as a cesspool must be prevented by different means, by coercive laws or taxing devices that make it cheaper for the polluter to treat his pollutants than to discharge them untreated. We have not progressed as far with the solution of this problem as we have with the first. Indeed, our particular concept of private property, which deters us from exhausting the positive resources of the earth, favors pollution. The owner of a factory on the bank of a stream—whose property extends to the middle of the stream—often has difficulty seeing why it is not his natural right to muddy the waters flowing past his door. The law, always behind the times, requires elaborate stitching and fitting to adapt it to this newly perceived aspect of the commons.

The pollution problem is a consequence of population. It did not much matter how a lonely American frontiersman disposed of his waste. "Flowing water purifies itself every 10 miles," my grandfather used to say, and the myth was near enough to the truth when he was a boy, for there were not too many people. But as population became denser, the natural chemical and biological recycling processes became overloaded, calling for a redefinition of property rights.

How to Legislate Temperance?

Analysis of the pollution problem as a function of population density uncovers a not generally recognized principle of morality, namely: *the morality of an act is a function of the state of the system at the time it is performed.*[8] Using the commons as a cesspool does not harm the general public under frontier conditions, because there is no public; the same behavior in a metropolis is unbearable. A hundred and fifty years ago a plainsman could kill an American bison, cut out only the tongue for his dinner, and discard the rest of the animal. He was not in any important sense being wasteful. Today, with only a few thousand bison left, we would be appalled at such behavior.

In passing, it is worth noting that the morality of an act cannot be determined from a photograph. One does not know whether a man killing an elephant or setting fire to the grassland is harming others until one knows the total system in which his act appears. "One picture is worth a thousand words," said an ancient Chinese; but it may take 10,000 words to validate it. It is as tempting to ecologists as it is to reformers in general to try to persuade others by way of the photographic shortcut. But the essence of an argument cannot be photographed: it must be presented rationally—in words.

That morality is system-sensitive escaped the attention of most codifiers of ethics in the past. "Thou shalt not . . ." is the form of traditional ethical directives which make no allowance for particular circumstances. The laws of our society follow the pattern of ancient ethics, and therefore are poorly suited to governing a complex, crowded, changeable world. Our epicyclic solution is to augment statutory law with administrative law. Since it is practically impossible to spell out all the conditions under which it is safe to burn trash in the back yard or to run an automobile without smog-control, by law we delegate the details to bureaus. The result is administrative law, which is rightly feared for an ancient reason—*Quis custodiet ipsos custodes?*—"Who shall watch the watchers themselves?" John Adams said that we must have "a government of laws and not men." Bureau administrators, trying to evaluate the morality of acts in the total system, are singularly liable to corruption, producing a government by men, not laws.

Prohibition is easy to legislate (though not necessarily to enforce); but how do we legislate temperance? Experience indicates that it can be accomplished best through the mediation of administrative law. We limit possibilities unnecessarily if we suppose that the sentiment of *Quis custodiet* denies us the use of administrative law. We should rather retain the phrase as a perpetual reminder of fearful dangers we cannot avoid. The great challenge facing us now is to invent the corrective feedbacks that are needed to keep custodians honest. We must find ways to legitimate the needed authority of both the custodians and the corrective feedbacks.

Freedom to Breed Is Intolerable

The tragedy of the commons is involved in population problems in another way. In a world governed solely by the principle of "dog eat dog"—if indeed there ever was such a world—how many children a family had would not be a matter of public concern. Parents who bred too exuberantly would leave fewer descendants, not more, because they would be unable to care adequately for their children. David Lack and others have found that such a negative feedback demonstrably controls the fecundity of birds.[9] But men are not birds, and have not acted like them for millenniums, at least.

If each human family were dependent only on its own resources; *if* the children of improvident parents starved to death; *if,* thus, overbreeding brought its own "punishment" to the germ line—*then* there would be no public interest in controlling the breeding of families. But our society is deeply committed to the welfare state,[10] and hence is confronted with another aspect of the tragedy of the commons.

In a welfare state, how shall we deal with the family, the religion, the race, or the class (or indeed any distinguishable and cohesive group) that adopts over-breeding as a policy to secure its own aggrandizement?[11] To couple the concept of freedom to breed with the belief that everyone born has an equal right to the commons is to lock the world into a tragic course of action.

Unfortunately this is just the course of action that is being pursued by the United Nations. In late 1967, some 30 nations agreed to the following: "The Universal Declaration of Human Rights describes the family as the natural and fundamental unit of society. It follows that any choice and decision with regard to the size of the family must irrevocably rest with the family itself, and cannot be made by anyone else."[12] It is painful to have to deny categorically the validity of this right; denying it, one feels as uncomfortable as a resident of Salem, Massachusetts, who denied the reality of witches in the 17th century. At the present time, in liberal quarters, something like a taboo acts to inhibit criticism of the United Nations. There is a feeling that the United Nations is "our last and best hope," that we shouldn't find fault with it; we shouldn't play into the hands of the archconservatives. However, let us not forget what Robert Louis Stevenson said: "The truth that is suppressed by friends is the readiest weapon of the enemy." If we love the truth we must openly deny the validity of the Universal Declaration of Human Rights, even though it is promoted by the United Nations. We should also join with Kingsley Davis in attempting to get Planned Parenthood–World Population to see the error of its ways in embracing the same tragic ideal.[13] . . .

. . . The argument has here been stated in the context of the population problem, but it applies equally well to any instance in which society appeals to an individual exploiting a commons to restrain himself for the general good—by means of his conscience. To make such an appeal is to set up a selective system that works toward the elimination of conscience from the race.

Pathogenic Effects of Conscience

It is a mistake to think that we can control the breeding of mankind in the long run by an appeal to conscience. . . . If we ask a man who is exploiting a commons to desist "in the name of conscience," what are we saying to him? What does he hear?—not only at the moment but also in the wee small hours of the night when, half asleep, he remembers not merely the words we used but also the

nonverbal communication cues we gave him unawares? Sooner or later, consciously or subconsciously, he senses that he has received two communications,
and that they are contradictory: (i) (intended communication) "If you don't do
as we ask, we will openly condemn you for not acting like a responsible citizen";
(ii) (the unintended communication) "If you *do* behave as we ask, we will secretly
condemn you for a simpleton who can be shamed into standing aside while the
rest of us exploit the commons." ...

To conjure up a conscience in others is tempting to anyone who wishes to
extend his control beyond the legal limits. Leaders at the highest level succumb
to this temptation. Has any President during the past generation failed to call
on labor unions to moderate voluntarily their demands for higher wages, or to
steel companies to honor voluntary guidelines on prices? I can recall none. The
rhetoric used on such occasions is designed to produce feelings of guilt in
noncooperators.

For centuries it was assumed without proof that guilt was a valuable, perhaps
even an indispensable, ingredient of the civilized life. Now, in this post-Freudian
world, we doubt it.

Paul Goodman speaks from the modern point of view when he says: "No good
has ever come from feeling guilty, neither intelligence, policy, nor compassion.
The guilty do not pay attention to the object but only to themselves, and not even
to their own interests, which might make sense, but to their anxieties."[14]

One does not have to be a professional psychiatrist to see the consequences of
anxiety. We in the Western world are just emerging from a dreadful two-
centuries-long Dark Ages of Eros that was sustained partly by prohibition laws,
but perhaps more effectively by the anxiety-generating mechanisms of education. Alex Comfort has told the story well in *The Anxiety Makers;* it is not a pretty
one.[15]

Since proof is difficult, we may even concede that the results of anxiety may
sometimes, from certain points of view, be desirable. The larger question we
should ask is whether, as a matter of policy, we should ever encourage the use of
a technique the tendency (if not the intention) of which is psychologically path-
ogenic. We hear much talk these days of responsible parenthood; the coupled
words are incorporated into the titles of some organizations devoted to birth
control. Some people have proposed massive propaganda campaigns to instill
responsibility into the nation's (or the world's) breeders. But what is the meaning of the word responsibility in this context? Is it not merely a synonym for the
word conscience? When we use the word responsibility in the absence of substantial sanctions are we not trying to browbeat a free man in a commons into
acting against his own interest? Responsibility is a verbal counterfeit for a substantial *quid pro quo.* It is an attempt to get something for nothing.

If the word responsibility is to be used at all, I suggest that it be in the sense Charles Frankel uses it.[16] "Responsibility," says this philosopher, "is the product of definite social arrangements." Notice that Frankel calls for social arrangements—not propaganda.

Mutual Coercion, Mutually Agreed Upon

The social arrangements that produce responsibility are arrangements that create coercion, of some sort. Consider bank-robbing. The man who takes money from a bank acts as if the bank were a commons. How do we prevent such action? Certainly not by trying to control his behavior solely by a verbal appeal to his sense of responsibility. Rather than rely on propaganda we follow Frankel's lead and insist that a bank is not a commons; we seek the definite social arrangements that will keep it from becoming a commons. That we thereby infringe on the freedom of would-be robbers we neither deny nor regret.

The morality of bank-robbing is particularly easy to understand because we accept complete prohibition of this activity. We are willing to say "Thou shalt not rob banks," without providing for exceptions. But temperance also can be created by coercion. Taxing is a good coercive device. To keep downtown shoppers temperate in their use of parking space we introduce parking meters for short periods, and traffic fines for longer ones. We need not actually forbid a citizen to park as long as he wants to; we need merely make it increasingly expensive for him to do so. Not prohibition, but carefully biased options are what we offer him. A Madison Avenue man might call this persuasion; I prefer the greater candor of the word coercion.

Coercion is a dirty word to most liberals now, but it need not forever be so. As with the four-letter words, its dirtiness can be cleansed away by exposure to the light, by saying it over and over without apology or embarrassment. To many, the word coercion implies arbitrary decisions of distant and irresponsible bureaucrats; but this is not a necessary part of its meaning. The only kind of coercion I recommend is mutual coercion, mutually agreed upon by the majority of the people affected.

To say that we mutually agree to coercion is not to say that we are required to enjoy it, or even to pretend we enjoy it. Who enjoys taxes? We all grumble about them. But we accept compulsory taxes because we recognize that voluntary taxes would favor the conscienceless. We institute and (grumblingly) support taxes and other coercive devices to escape the horror of the commons.

An alternative to the commons need not be perfectly just to be preferable. With real estate and other material goods, the alternative we have chosen is the institution of private property coupled with legal inheritance. Is this system perfectly just? As a genetically trained biologist I deny that it is. It seems to me that, if there are to be differences in individual inheritance, legal possession should be perfectly correlated with biological inheritance—that those who are biologically more fit to be the custodians of property and power should legally inherit more. But genetic recombination continually makes a mockery of the doctrine of "like father, like son" implicit in our laws of legal inheritance. An idiot can inherit millions, and a trust fund can keep his estate intact. We must admit that our legal system of private property plus inheritance is unjust—but we put up with it because we are not convinced, at the moment, that anyone has invented a better system. The alternative of the commons is too horrifying to contemplate. Injustice is preferable to total ruin.

It is one of the peculiarities of the warfare between reform and the status quo that it is thoughtlessly governed by a double standard. Whenever a reform measure is proposed it is often defeated when its opponents triumphantly discover a flaw in it. As Kingsley Davis has pointed out,[17] worshippers of the status quo sometimes imply that no reform is possible without unanimous agreement, an implication contrary to historical fact. As nearly as I can make out, automatic rejection of proposed reforms is based on one of two unconscious assumptions: (i) that the status quo is perfect; or (ii) that the choice we face is between reform and no action; if the proposed reform is imperfect, we presumably should take no action at all, while we wait for a perfect proposal.

But we can never do nothing. That which we have done for thousands of years is also action. It also produces evils. Once we are aware that the status quo is action, we can then compare its discoverable advantages and disadvantages with the predicted advantages and disadvantages of the proposed reform, discounting as best we can for our lack of experience. On the basis of such a comparison, we can make a rational decision which will not involve the unworkable assumption that only perfect systems are tolerable.

Recognition of Necessity

Perhaps the simplest summary of this analysis of man's population problems is this: the commons, if justifiable at all, is justifiable only under conditions of low-population density. As the human population has increased, the commons has had to be abandoned in one aspect after another.

First we abandoned the commons in food gathering, enclosing farm land and restricting pastures and hunting and fishing areas. These restrictions are still not complete throughout the world.

Somewhat later we saw that the commons as a place for waste disposal would also have to be abandoned. Restrictions on the disposal of domestic sewage are widely accepted in the Western world; we are still struggling to close the commons to pollution by automobiles, factories, insecticide sprayers, fertilizing operations, and atomic energy installations.

In a still more embryonic state is our recognition of the evils of the commons in matters of pleasure. There is almost no restriction on the propagation of sound waves in the public medium. The shopping public is assaulted with mindless music, without its consent. Our government is paying out billions of dollars to create supersonic transport which will disturb 50,000 people for every one person who is whisked from coast to coast 3 hours faster. Advertisers muddy the airwaves of radio and television and pollute the view of travelers. We are a long way from outlawing the commons in matters of pleasure. Is this because our Puritan inheritance makes us view pleasure as something of a sin, and pain (that is, the pollution of advertising) as the sign of virtue?

Every new enclosure of the commons involves the infringement of somebody's personal liberty. Infringements made in the distant past are accepted because no contemporary complains of a loss. It is the newly proposed infringements that we vigorously oppose; cries of "rights" and "freedom" fill the air. But what does "freedom" mean? When men mutually agreed to pass laws against robbing, mankind became more free, not less so. Individuals locked into the logic of the commons are free only to bring on universal ruin; once they see the necessity of mutual coercion, they become free to pursue other goals. I believe it was Hegel who said, "Freedom is the recognition of necessity."

The most important aspect of necessity that we must now recognize, is the necessity of abandoning the commons in breeding. No technical solution can rescue us from the misery of overpopulation. Freedom to breed will bring ruin to all. At the moment, to avoid hard decisions many of us are tempted to propagandize for conscience and responsible parenthood. The temptation must be resisted, because an appeal to independently acting consciences selects for the disappearance of all conscience in the long run, and an increase in anxiety in the short.

The only way we can preserve and nurture other and more precious freedoms is by relinquishing the freedom to breed, and that very soon. "Freedom is the recognition of necessity"—and it is the role of education to reveal to all the necessity of abandoning the freedom to breed. Only so, can we put an end to this aspect of the tragedy of the commons.

NOTES

1. J. B. Wiesner and H. F. York, *Sci. Amer.* 211 (No. 4), 27 (1964).
2. G. Hardin, *J. Hered.* 50, 68 (1959); S. von Hoernor, *Science* 137, 18 (1962).

3. A. Smith, *The Wealth of Nations* (Modern Library, New York, 1937), p. 423.

4. W. F. Lloyd, *Two Lectures on the Checks to Population* (Oxford Univ. Press, Oxford, England, 1833), reprinted (in part) in *Population, Evolution, and Birth Control,* G. Hardin, Ed. (Freeman, San Francisco, 1964), p. 37.

5. A. N. Whitehead, *Science and the Modern World* (Mentor, New York, 1948), p. 17.

6. G. Hardin, Ed. *Population, Evolution and Birth Control* (Freeman, San Francisco, 1964), p. 56.

7. S. McVay, *Sci. Amer.* 216 (No. 8), 13 (1966).

8. J. Fletcher, *Situation Ethics* (Westminster, Philadelphia, 1966).

9. D. Lack, *The Natural Regulation of Animal Numbers* (Clarendon Press, Oxford, 1954).

10. H. Girvetz, *From Wealth to Welfare* (Stanford Univ. Press, Stanford, Calif., 1950).

11. G. Hardin, *Perspec. Biol. Med.* 6, 366 (1963).

12. U. Thant, *Int. Planned Parenthood News,* No. 168 (February 1968), p. 3.

13. K. Davis, *Science* 158, 730 (1967).

14. P. Goodman, *New York Rev. Books* 10(8), 22 (23 May 1968).

15. A. Comfort, *The Anxiety Makers* (Nelson, London, 1967).

16. C. Frankel, *The Case for Modern Man* (Harper, New York, 1955), p. 203.

17. J. D. Roslansky, *Genetics and the Future of Man* (Appleton-Century-Crofts, New York, 1966), p. 177.

1-3

The Prosperous Community

SOCIAL CAPITAL AND PUBLIC LIFE

Robert D. Putnam

The solutions to all of the problems presented in this chapter require participants to cooperate—to pay their taxes, to refrain from overfishing, to fix their polluting vehicles, and the like—even as each participant recognizes that he or she would be rewarded by failing to cooperate. This situation not only endangers a community's ability to achieve its collective goals but also engenders mutual suspicion and hostility among community members. In the article that follows, Robert Putnam argues persuasively that successful cooperation breeds success in the future. If we trust our neighbors to follow through on their commitments, then we are more likely to do the same.

> Your corn is ripe today; mine will be so tomorrow. 'Tis profitable for us both, that I should labour with you today, and that you should aid me tomorrow. I have no kindness for you, and know you have as little for me. I will not, therefore, take any pains upon your account; and should I labour with you upon my own account, in expectation of a return, I know I should be disappointed, and that I should in vain depend upon your gratitude. Here then I leave you to labour alone; You treat me in the same manner. The seasons change; and both of us lose our harvests for want of mutual confidence and security.
>
> —DAVID HUME

THE PREDICAMENT of the farmers in Hume's parable is all too familiar in communities and nations around the world:

- Parents in communities everywhere want better educational opportunities for their children, but collaborative efforts to improve public schools falter.
- Residents of American ghettos share an interest in safer streets, but collective action to control crime fails.
- Poor farmers in the Third World need more effective irrigation and marketing schemes, but cooperation to these ends proves fragile.

Source: Robert D. Putnam, "The Prosperous Community: Social Capital and Public Life," *The American Prospect,* March 21, 1993.

- Global warming threatens livelihoods from Manhattan to Mauritius, but joint action to forestall this shared risk founders.

Failure to cooperate for mutual benefit does not necessarily signal ignorance or irrationality or even malevolence, as philosophers since Hobbes have underscored. Hume's farmers were not dumb, or crazy, or evil; they were trapped. Social scientists have lately analyzed this fundamental predicament in a variety of guises: the tragedy of the commons; the logic of collective action; public goods; the prisoners' dilemma. In all these situations, as in Hume's rustic anecdote, everyone would be better off if everyone could cooperate. In the absence of coordination and credible mutual commitment, however, everyone defects, ruefully but rationally, confirming one another's melancholy expectations.

How can such dilemmas of collective action be overcome, short of creating some Hobbesian Leviathan? Social scientists in several disciplines have recently suggested a novel diagnosis of this problem, a diagnosis resting on the concept of *social capital*. By analogy with notions of physical capital and human capital—tools and training that enhance individual productivity—"social capital" refers to features of social organization, such as networks, norms, and trust, that facilitate coordination and cooperation for mutual benefit. Social capital enhances the benefits of investment in physical and human capital.

Working together is easier in a community blessed with a substantial stock of social capital. This insight turns out to have powerful practical implications for many issues on the American national agenda—for how we might overcome the poverty and violence of South Central Los Angeles, or revitalize industry in the Rust Belt, or nurture the fledgling democracies of the former Soviet empire and the erstwhile Third World....

How does social capital undergird good government and economic progress? First, networks of civic engagement foster sturdy norms of generalized reciprocity: I'll do this for you now, in the expectation that down the road you or someone else will return the favor. "Social capital is akin to what Tom Wolfe called the 'favor bank' in his novel *The Bonfire of the Vanities*," notes economist Robert Frank. A society that relies on generalized reciprocity is more efficient than a distrustful society, for the same reason that money is more efficient than barter. Trust lubricates social life.

Networks of civic engagement also facilitate coordination and communication and amplify information about the trustworthiness of other individuals. Students of prisoners' dilemmas and related games report that cooperation is most easily sustained through repeat play. When economic and political dealing is embedded in dense networks of social interaction, incentives for opportunism and malfeasance are reduced. This is why the diamond trade, with its extreme possibilities for fraud, is concentrated within close-knit ethnic enclaves. Dense social ties facilitate gossip and other valuable ways of cultivating reputation—an essential foundation for trust in a complex society.

Finally, networks of civic engagement embody past success at collaboration, which can serve as a cultural template for future collaboration. The civic traditions of north-central Italy provide a historical repertoire of forms of cooperation that, having proved their worth in the past, are available to citizens for addressing new problems of collective action.

Sociologist James Coleman concludes, "Like other forms of capital, social capital is productive, making possible the achievement of certain ends that would not be attainable in its absence. . . . In a farming community . . . where one farmer got his hay baled by another and where farm tools are extensively borrowed and lent, the social capital allows each farmer to get his work done with less physical capital in the form of tools and equipment." Social capital, in short, enables Hume's farmers to surmount their dilemma of collective action.

Stocks of social capital, such as trust, norms, and networks, tend to be self-reinforcing and cumulative. Successful collaboration in one endeavor builds connections and trust—social assets that facilitate future collaboration in other, unrelated tasks. As with conventional capital, those who have social capital tend to accumulate more—them as has, gets. Social capital is what the social philosopher Albert O. Hirschman calls a "moral resource," that is, a resource whose supply increases rather than decreases through use and which (unlike physical capital) becomes depleted if *not* used.

Unlike conventional capital, social capital is a "public good," that is, it is not the private property of those who benefit from it. Like other public goods, from clean air to safe streets, social capital tends to be underprovided by private agents. This means that social capital must often be a by-product of other social activities. Social capital typically consists in ties, norms, and trust transferable from one social setting to another. . . .

Social Capital and Economic Development

Social capital is coming to be seen as a vital ingredient in economic development around the world. Scores of studies of rural development have shown that a vigorous network of indigenous grassroots associations can be as essential to growth as physical investment, appropriate technology, or (that nostrum of neoclassical economists) "getting prices right." Political scientist Elinor Ostrom has explored why some cooperative efforts to manage common pool resources, like grazing grounds and water supplies, succeed, while others fail. Existing stocks of social capital are an important part of the story. Conversely, government interventions that neglect or undermine this social infrastructure can go seriously awry.

Studies of the rapidly growing economies of East Asia almost always emphasize the importance of dense social networks, so that these economies are sometimes said to represent a new brand of "network capitalism." These networks, often based on the extended family or on close-knit ethnic communities like the overseas Chinese, foster trust, lower transaction costs, and speed information and innovation. Social capital can be transmuted, so to speak, into financial capital: In novelist Amy Tan's *Joy Luck Club*, a group of mah-jong–playing friends evolves into a joint investment association. China's extraordinary economic growth over the last decade has depended less on formal institutions than on *guanxi* (personal connections) to underpin contracts and to channel savings and investment. ...

Bill Clinton's proposals for job-training schemes and industrial extension agencies invite attention to social capital. The objective should not be merely an assembly-line injection of booster shots of technical expertise and work-related skills into individual firms and workers. Rather, such programs could provide a matchless opportunity to create productive new linkages among community groups, schools, employers, and workers, without creating costly new bureaucracies. Why not experiment with modest subsidies for training programs that bring together firms, educational institutions, and community associations in innovative local partnerships? The latent effects of such programs on social capital accumulation could prove even more powerful than the direct effects on technical productivity.

Conversely, when considering the effects of economic reconversion on communities, we must weigh the risks of destroying social capital. Precisely because social capital is a public good, the costs of closing factories and destroying communities go beyond the personal trauma borne by individuals. Worse yet, some government programs themselves, such as urban renewal and public housing projects, have heedlessly ravaged existing social networks. The fact that these collective costs are not well measured by our current accounting schemes does not mean that they are not real. Shred enough of the social fabric and we all pay.

Social Capital and America's Ills

Fifty-one deaths and 1 billion dollars in property damage in Los Angeles . . . put urban decay back on the American agenda. Yet if the ills are clear, the prescription is not. Even those most sympathetic to the plight of America's ghettos are not persuaded that simply reviving the social programs dismantled in the last decade or so will solve the problems. The erosion of social capital is an essential and under-appreciated part of the diagnosis.

Although most poor Americans do not reside in the inner city, there is something qualitatively different about the social and economic isolation experienced by the chronically poor blacks and Latinos who do. Joblessness, inadequate education, and poor health clearly truncate the opportunities of ghetto residents. Yet so do profound deficiencies in social capital.

Part of the problem facing blacks and Latinos in the inner city is that they lack "connections" in the most literal sense. Job-seekers in the ghetto have little access, for example, to conventional job referral networks. Labor economists Anne Case and Lawrence Katz have shown that, regardless of race, inner-city youth living in neighborhoods blessed with high levels of civic engagement are more likely to finish school, have a job, and avoid drugs and crime, controlling for the individual characteristics of the youth. That is, of two identical youths, the one unfortunate enough to live in a neighborhood whose social capital has eroded is more likely to end up hooked, booked, or dead. Several researchers seem to have found similar neighborhood effects on the incidence of teen pregnancy, among both blacks and whites, again controlling for personal characteristics. Where you live and whom you know—the social capital you can draw on—helps to define who you are and thus to determine your fate.

Racial and class inequalities in access to social capital, if properly measured, may be as great as inequalities in financial and human capital, and no less portentous. Economist Glenn Loury has used the term "social capital" to capture the fundamental fact that racial segregation, coupled with socially inherited differences in community networks and norms, means that individually targeted "equal opportunity" policies may not eliminate racial inequality, even in the long run. Research suggests that the life chances of today's generation depend not only on their parents' social resources, but also on the social resources of their parents' ethnic group. Even workplace integration and upward mobility by successful members of minority groups cannot overcome these persistent effects of inequalities in social capital. William Julius Wilson has described in tragic detail how the exodus of middle-class and working-class families from the ghetto has eroded the social capital available to those left behind. The settlement houses that nurtured sewing clubs and civic activism a century ago, embodying community as much as charity, are now mostly derelict.

It would be a dreadful mistake, of course, to overlook the repositories of social capital within America's minority communities. . . . Historically, the black church has been the most bounteous treasure-house of social capital for African Americans. The church provided the organizational infrastructure for political mobilization in the civil rights movement. Recent work on American political participation by political scientist Sidney Verba and his colleagues shows that the church is a uniquely powerful resource for political engagement among blacks—an arena in which to learn about public affairs and hone political skills and make connections.

In tackling the ills of America's cities, investments in physical capital, financial capital, human capital, and social capital are complementary, not competing alternatives. Investments in jobs and education, for example, will be more effective if they are coupled with reinvigoration of community associations.

Some churches provide job banks and serve as informal credit bureaus, for example, using their reputational capital to vouch for members who may be ex-convicts, former drug addicts, or high school dropouts. In such cases the church does not merely provide referral networks. More fundamentally, wary employers and financial institutions bank on the church's ability to identify parishioners whose formal credentials understate their reliability. At the same time, because these parishioners value their standing in the church, and because the church has put its own reputation on the line, they have an additional incentive to perform. Like conventional capital for conventional borrowers, social capital serves as a kind of collateral for men and women who are excluded from ordinary credit or labor markets. In effect, the participants pledge their social connections, leveraging social capital to improve the efficiency with which markets operate.

The importance of social capital for America's domestic agenda is not limited to minority communities. Take public education, for instance. The success of private schools is attributable, according to James Coleman's massive research, not so much to what happens in the classroom nor to the endowments of individual students, but rather to the greater engagement of parents and community members in private school activities. Educational reformers like child psychologist James Comer seek to improve schooling not merely by "treating" individual children but by deliberately involving parents and others in the educational process. Educational policymakers need to move beyond debates about curriculum and governance to consider the effects of social capital. Indeed, most commonly discussed proposals for "choice" are deeply flawed by their profoundly individualist conception of education. If states and localities are to experiment with voucher systems for education or child care, why not encourage vouchers to be spent in ways that strengthen community organization, not weaken it? Once we recognize the importance of social capital, we ought to be able to design programs that creatively combine individual choice with collective engagement.

Many people today are concerned about revitalizing American democracy. Although discussion of political reform in the United States focuses nowadays on such procedural issues as term limits and campaign financing, some of the ills that afflict the American polity reflect deeper, largely unnoticed social changes.

"Some people say that you usually can trust people. Others say that you must be wary in relations with people. Which is your view?" Responses to this question, posed repeatedly in national surveys for several decades, suggest that social trust in the United States has declined for more than a quarter century. By contrast, American politics benefited from plentiful stocks of social capital in earlier times. Recent historical work on the Progressive Era, for example, has uncovered evidence of the powerful role played by nominally non-political associations (such as women's literary societies) precisely because they provided a dense social network. Is our current predicament the result of a long-term erosion of social capital, such as community engagement and social trust?

Economist Juliet Schorr's discovery of "the unexpected decline of leisure" in America suggests that our generation is less engaged with one another outside the marketplace and thus less prepared to cooperate for shared goals. Mobile, two-career (or one-parent) families often must use the market for child care and other services formerly provided through family and neighborhood networks. Even if market-based services, considered individually, are of high quality, this deeper social trend is eroding social capital. There are more empty seats at the PTA and in church pews these days. While celebrating the productive, liberating effects of fuller equality in the workplace, we must replace the social capital that this movement has depleted.

Our political parties, once intimately coupled to the capillaries of community life, have become evanescent confections of pollsters and media consultants and independent political entrepreneurs—the very antithesis of social capital. We have too easily accepted a conception of democracy in which public policy is not the outcome of a collective deliberation about the public interest, but rather a residue of campaign strategy. The social capital approach, focusing on the indirect effects of civic norms and networks, is a much-needed corrective to an exclusive emphasis on the formal institutions of government as an explanation for our collective discontents. If we are to make our political system more responsive, especially to those who lack connections at the top, we must nourish grass-roots organization.

Classic liberal social policy is designed to enhance the opportunities of *individuals,* but if social capital is important, this emphasis is partially misplaced. Instead we must focus on community development, allowing space for religious organizations and choral societies and Little Leagues that may seem to have little to do with politics or economics. Government policies, whatever their intended effects, should be vetted for their indirect effects on social capital. If, as some suspect, social capital is fostered more by home ownership than by public or private tenancy, then we should design housing policy accordingly. Similarly, as Theda Skocpol has suggested, the direct benefits of national service programs might be dwarfed by the indirect benefits that could flow from the creation of social networks that cross class and racial lines. In any comprehensive strategy for improving the plight of America's communities, rebuilding social capital is as important as investing in human and physical capital. . . .

Wise policy can encourage social capital formation, and social capital itself enhances the effectiveness of government action. From agricultural extension services in the last century to tax exemptions for community organizations in this one, American government has often promoted investments in social capital, and it must renew that effort now. A new administration that is, at long last, more willing to use public power and the public purse for public purpose should not overlook the importance of social connectedness as a vital backdrop for effective policy.

Students of social capital have only begun to address some of the most important questions that this approach to public affairs suggests. What are the actual trends in different forms of civic engagement? Why do communities differ in their stocks of social capital? What *kinds* of civic engagement seem most likely to foster economic growth or community effectiveness? Must specific types of social capital be matched to different public problems? Most important of all, how is social capital created and destroyed? What strategies for building (or rebuilding) social capital are most promising? How can we balance the twin strategies of exploiting existing social capital and creating it afresh? The suggestions scattered throughout this essay are intended to challenge others to even more practical methods of encouraging new social capital formation and leveraging what we have already.

We also need to ask about the negative effects of social capital, for like human and physical capital, social capital can be put to bad purposes. Liberals have often sought to destroy some forms of social capital (from medieval guilds to neighborhood schools) in the name of individual opportunity. We have not always reckoned with the indirect social costs of our policies, but we were often right to be worried about the power of private associations. Social inequalities may be embedded in social capital. Norms and networks that serve some groups may obstruct others, particularly if the norms are discriminatory or the networks socially segregated. Recognizing the importance of social capital in sustaining community life does not exempt us from the need to worry about how that community is defined—who is inside and thus benefits from social capital, and who is outside and does not. Some forms of social capital can impair individual liberties, as critics of communitarianism warn. Many of the Founders' fears about the "mischiefs of faction" apply to social capital. Before toting up the balance sheet for social capital in its various forms, we need to weigh costs as well as benefits. This challenge still awaits.

Progress on the urgent issues facing our country and our world requires ideas that bridge outdated ideological divides. Both liberals and conservatives agree on the importance of social empowerment, as E. J. Dionne recently noted ("The Quest for Community (Again)," *TAP,* Summer 1992). The social capital approach provides a deeper conceptual underpinning for this nominal convergence. Real progress requires not facile verbal agreement, but hard thought and ideas with high fiber content. The social capital approach promises to uncover new ways of combining private social infrastructure with public policies that work, and, in turn, of using wise public policies to revitalize America's stocks of social capital.

Chapter 2

The Constitutional Framework

2-1

The Founding Fathers: A Reform Caucus in Action

John P. Roche

Textbook consideration of the Constitution's Framers reverentially casts them as political philosophers conveying to future generations timeless laws of proper civic relations. Students of the era delve into arguments of The Federalist and other source materials to detect the intellectual roots of the Framers in the political theories of Locke, Montesquieu, Hume, and even Machiavelli. In this essay Roche reminds us that we should not forget that these were politicians charged with proposing a reform that had to win the endorsement of at least nine states before it became more than the collective ruminations of thirty-nine delegates. The Framers were certainly conversant with the leading political thought of their era—so conversant, indeed, that they exhibited great versatility in invoking these theorists in behalf of whatever scheme they were endorsing. Roche makes a persuasive case that the Constitution reflects the at times brilliant but always pragmatic choices of Framers ever mindful of the preferences of their constituents. Consequently, the Constitution was, in Roche's assessment, a "patch-work sewn together under the pressure of both time and events."

Source: John P. Roche, "The Founding Fathers: A Reform Caucus in Action," *American Political Science Review* 55, no. 4 (December 1961): 799–816. Some notes appearing in the original have been deleted.

OVER THE LAST CENTURY and a half, the work of the Constitutional Convention and the motives of the Founding Fathers have . . . undergone miraculous metamorphoses: at one time acclaimed as liberals and bold social engineers, today they appear in the guise of sound Burkean conservatives. . . . The implicit assumption is that if James Madison were among us, he would be President of the Ford Foundation, while Alexander Hamilton would chair the Committee for Economic Development.

The "Fathers" have thus been admitted to our best circles; the revolutionary ferocity which confiscated all Tory property in reach and populated New Brunswick with outlaws has been converted by . . . American historians into a benign dedication to "consensus" and "prescriptive rights." The Daughters of the American Revolution have . . . at last found ancestors worthy of their descendants. It is not my purpose here to argue that the "Fathers" were, in fact, radical revolutionaries; that proposition has been brilliantly demonstrated by Robert R. Palmer in his *Age of the Democratic Revolution.* My concern is with the further position that not only were they revolutionaries, but also they were democrats. Indeed, . . . they were first and foremost superb democratic politicians. I suspect that in a contemporary setting, James Madison would be Speaker of the House of Representatives and Hamilton would be the *eminence grise* dominating . . . the Executive Office of the President. They were, with their colleagues, *political men* . . . and as recent research into the nature of American polities in the 1780s confirms,[1] they were committed (perhaps willy-nilly) to working within the democratic framework, within a universe of public approval. Charles Beard *and* the filiopietists to the contrary notwithstanding, the Philadelphia Convention was not a College of Cardinals or a council of Platonic guardians working within a manipulative, predemocratic framework; it was a *nationalist* reform caucus which had to operate with great delicacy and skill in a political cosmos full of enemies to achieve the one definitive goal-popular approbation.

Perhaps the time has come, to borrow Walton Hamilton's fine phrase, to raise the Framers from immortality to mortality, to give them credit for their magnificent demonstration of the art of democratic politics. The point must be reemphasized; they *made* history and did it within the limits of consensus. There was nothing inevitable about the future in 1787. . . . What they did was to hammer out a pragmatic compromise which would both bolster the "National interest" and be acceptable to the people. What inspiration they got came from their collective experience as professional politicians in a democratic society. As John Dickinson put it to his fellow delegates on August 13, "Experience must be our guide. Reason may mislead us."

In this context, let us examine the problems they confronted and the solutions they evolved. The Convention has been described picturesquely as a counter-revolutionary junta and the Constitution as a *coup d'etat*,[2] but this has been accomplished by withdrawing the whole history of the movement for constitutional reform from its true context. No doubt the goals of the constitutional elite were "subversive" to the existing political order, but it is overlooked that their subversion could only have succeeded if the people of the United States endorsed it by regularized procedures. Indubitably they were "plotting" to establish a much stronger central government than existed under the Articles, but only in the sense in which one could argue equally well that John F. Kennedy was, from 1956 to 1960, "plotting" to become President. In short, on the fundamental *procedural* level, the Constitutionalists had to work according to the prevailing rules of the game. . . .

I

When the Constitutionalists went forth to subvert the Confederation, they utilized the mechanisms of political legitimacy. And the roadblocks which confronted them were formidable. At the same time, they were endowed with certain potent political assets. The history of the United States from 1786 to 1790 was largely one of a masterful employment of political expertise by the Constitutionalists as against bumbling, erratic behavior by the opponents of reform. Effectively, the Constitutionalists had to induce the states, by democratic techniques of coercion, to emasculate themselves. To be specific, if New York had refused to join the new Union, the project was doomed; yet before New York was safely in, the reluctant state legislature had *sua s'ponte* to take the following steps: (1) agree to send delegates to the Philadelphia Convention; (2) provide maintenance for these delegates (these were distinct stages: New Hampshire was early in naming delegates, but did not provide for their maintenance until July); (3) set up the special *ad hoc* convention to decide on ratification; and (4) concede to the decision of the *ad hoc* convention that New York should participate. New York admittedly was a tricky state, with a strong interest in a *status quo* which permitted her to exploit New Jersey and Connecticut, but the same legal hurdles existed in every state. And at the risk of becoming boring, it must be reiterated that the *only* weapon in the Constitutionalist arsenal was an effective mobilization of public opinion.

The group which undertook this struggle was an interesting amalgam of a few dedicated nationalists with the self-interested spokesmen of various parochial bailiwicks. The Georgians, for example, wanted a strong central authority to provide military protection for their huge, underpopulated state against the Creek Confederacy; Jerseymen and Connecticuters wanted to escape from economic bondage to New York; the Virginians hoped to establish a system which would give that great state its rightful place in the councils of the republic. The dominant figures in the politics of these states therefore cooperated in the call for the Convention. . . . There was, of course, a large element of personality in the affair: there is reason to suspect that Patrick Henry's opposition to the Convention and the Constitution was founded on his conviction that Jefferson was behind both, and a close study of local politics elsewhere would surely reveal that others supported the Constitution for the simple (and politically quite sufficient) reason that the "wrong" people were against it.

To say this is not to suggest that the Constitution rested on a foundation of impure or base motives. It is rather to argue that in politics there are no immaculate conceptions, and that in the drive for a stronger general government, motives of all sorts played a part. Few men in the history of mankind have espoused a view of the "common good" or "public interest" that militated against their private status; even Plato with all his reverence for disembodied reason managed to put philosophers on top of the pile. Thus it is not surprising that a number of diversified private interests joined to push the nationalist public interest; what would have been surprising was the absence of such a pragmatic united front. And the fact remains that, however motivated, these men did demonstrate a willingness to compromise their parochial interests in behalf of an ideal which took shape before their eyes and under their ministrations.

. . . [W]hat distinguished the leaders of the Constitutionalist caucus from their enemies was a "Continental" approach to political, economic and military issues. To the extent that they shared an institutional base of operations, it was the Continental Congress (thirty-nine of the delegates to the Federal Convention had served in Congress), and this was hardly a locale which inspired respect for the state governments. . . . [M]embership in the Congress under the Articles of Confederation worked to establish a continental frame of reference, that a Congressman from Pennsylvania and one from South Carolina would share a universe of discourse which provided them with a conceptual common denominator *vis-à-vis* their respective state legislatures. This was particularly true with respect to external affairs: the average state legislator was probably about as concerned with foreign policy then as he is today, but Congressmen were constantly forced to take the broad view of American prestige, were compelled to listen to the reports of Secretary John Jay and to the dispatches and pleas from their frustrated envoys in Britain, France and Spain. From considerations such as these, a "Continental" ideology developed which seems to have demanded a revision of our domestic institutions primarily on the ground that only by invigorating our general government could we assume our rightful place in the international arena. Indeed, an argument with great force-particularly since Washington was its incarnation-urged that our very survival in the Hobbesian jungle of world politics depended upon a reordering and strengthening of our national sovereignty.[3]

. . . [T]he great achievement of the Constitutionalists was their ultimate success in convincing the elected representatives of a majority of the white male population that change was imperative. A small group of political leaders with a Continental vision and essentially a consciousness of the United States' *international* impotence provided the matrix of the movement. To their standard other leaders rallied with their own parallel ambitions. Their great assets were (1) the presence in their caucus of the one authentic American "father figure," George Washington, whose prestige was enormous;[4] (2) the energy and talent of their leadership (in which one must include the towering intellectuals of the time, John Adams and Thomas Jefferson, despite their absence abroad), and their communications "network," which was far superior to anything on the opposition side;[5] (3) the preemptive skill which made "their" issue The Issue and kept the locally oriented opposition permanently on the defensive; and (4) the subjective consideration that these men were spokesmen of a new and compelling credo: *American* nationalism, that ill-defined but nonetheless potent sense of collective purpose that emerged from the American Revolution.

Despite great institutional handicaps, the Constitutionalists managed in the mid-1780s to mount an offensive which gained momentum as years went by. Their greatest problem was lethargy, and paradoxically, the number of barriers in their path may have proved an advantage in the long run. Beginning with the initial battle to get the Constitutional Convention called and delegates appointed, they could never relax, never let up the pressure. In practical terms, this meant that the local "organizations" created by the Constitutionalists were perpetually in movement building up their cadres for the next fight. (The word organization has to be used with great caution: a political organization in the United States—as in contemporary England—generally consisted of a magnate and his following, or a coalition of magnates. This did not necessarily mean that it was "undemocratic" or "aristocratic," in the Aristotelian sense of the word: while a few magnates such as the Livingstons could draft their followings, most exercised their leadership without coercion on the basis of popular endorsement. The absence of organized opposition did not imply the impossibility of competition any more than low public participation in elections necessarily indicated an undemocratic suffrage.)

The Constitutionalists got the jump on the "opposition" . . . at the outset with the demand for a Convention. Their opponents were caught in an old political trap: they were not being asked to approve any specific program of reform, but only to endorse a meeting to discuss and recommend needed reforms. If they took a hard line at the first stage, they were put in the position of glorifying the *status quo* and of denying the need for *any* changes. Moreover, the Constitutionalists could go to the people with a persuasive argument for "fair play"—"How can you condemn reform before you know precisely what is involved?" Since the state legislatures obviously would have the final say on any proposals that might emerge from the Convention, the Constitutionalists were merely reasonable men asking for a chance. Besides, since they did not make any concrete proposals at that stage, they were in a position to capitalize on every sort of generalized discontent with the Confederation.

Perhaps because of their poor intelligence system, perhaps because of over-confidence generated by the failure of all previous efforts to alter the Articles,[6] the opposition awoke too late to the dangers that confronted them in 1787. Not only did the Constitutionalists manage to get every state but Rhode Island . . . to appoint delegates to Philadelphia, but when the results were in, it appeared that they dominated the delegations. Given the apathy of the opposition, this was a natural phenomenon: in an ideologically nonpolarized political atmosphere those who get appointed to a special committee are likely to be the men who supported the movement for its creation. Even George Clinton, who seems to have been the first opposition leader to awake to the possibility of trouble, could not prevent the New York legislature from appointing Alexander Hamilton-though he did have the foresight to send two of his henchmen to dominate the delegation. Incidentally, much has been made of the fact that the delegates to Philadelphia were not elected by the people; some have adduced this fact as evidence of the "undemocratic" character of the gathering. But put in the context of the time, this argument is wholly specious: the central government under the Articles was considered a creature of the component states and in all the states but Rhode Island, Connecticut and New Hampshire, members of the national Congress were chosen by the state legislatures. This was not a consequence of elitism or fear of the mob; it was a logical extension of states'-rights doctrine to guarantee that the national institution did not end-run the state legislatures and make direct contact with the people.[7]

II

With delegations safely named, the focus shifted to Philadelphia. While waiting for a quorum to assemble, James Madison got busy and drafted the so-called Randolph or Virginia Plan with the aid of the Virginia delegation. This was a political master-stroke. Its consequence was that once business got underway, the framework of discussion was established on Madison's terms. There was no interminable argument over agenda; instead the delegates took the Virginia Resolutions—"just for purposes of discussion"—as their point of departure. And along with Madison's proposals, many of which were buried in the course of the summer, went his major premise: a new start on a Constitution rather than piece-meal amendment. This was not necessarily revolutionary—a little exegesis could demonstrate that a new Constitution might be formulated as "amendments" to the Articles of Confederation—but Madison's proposal that this "lump sum" amendment go into effect after approval by nine states (the Articles required unanimous state approval for any amendment) was thoroughly subversive.[8]

Standard treatments of the Convention divide the delegates into "nationalists" and "states'-righters" with various improvised shadings ("moderate national-ists," etc.), but these are *a posteriori* categories which obfuscate more than they clarify. What is striking to one who analyzes the Convention as a case-study in democratic politics is the lack of clear-cut ideological divisions in the Conven-tion. Indeed, I submit that the evidence—Madison's *Notes,* the correspondence of the delegates, and debates on ratification—indicates that this was a remarkably homogeneous body on the ideological level. Yates and Lansing, Clinton's two chaperones for Hamilton, left in disgust on July 10. (Is there anything more tedious than sitting through endless disputes on matters one deems fundamen-tally misconceived? It takes an iron will to spend a hot summer as an ideological *agent provocateur.*) Luther Martin, Maryland's bibulous narcissist, left on Septem-ber 4 in a huff when he discovered that others did not share his self-esteem; oth-ers went home for personal reasons. But the hard core of delegates accepted a grinding regimen throughout the attrition of a Philadelphia summer precisely because they shared the Constitutionalist goal.

Basic differences of opinion emerged, of course, but these were not ideologi-cal; they were *structural.* If the so-called "states'-rights" group had not accepted the fundamental purposes of the Convention, they could simply have pulled out and by doing so have aborted the whole enterprise. Instead of bolting, they returned day after day to argue and to compromise. An interesting symbol of this basic homogeneity was the initial agreement on secrecy: these professional politicians did not want to become prisoners of publicity; they wanted to retain that freedom of maneuver which is only possible when men are not forced to take public stands in the preliminary stages of negotiation.[9] There was no legal means of binding the tongues of the delegates: at any stage in the game a dele-gate with basic principled objections to the emerging project could have taken the stump (as Luther Martin did after his exit) and denounced the convention to the skies. Yet Madison did not even inform Thomas Jefferson in Paris of the course of the deliberations[10] and available correspondence indicates that the del-egates generally observed the injunction. Secrecy is certainly uncharacteristic of any assembly marked by strong ideological polarization. This was noted at the time: the *New York Daily Advertiser,* August 14, 1787, commented that the " . . . profound secrecy hitherto observed by the Convention [we consider] a happy omen, as it demonstrates that the spirit of party on any great and essential point cannot have arisen to any height." [11]

Commentators on the Constitution who have read *The Federalist* in lieu of reading the actual debates have credited the Fathers with the invention of a sublime concept called "Federalism." Unfortunately *The Federalist* is probative evidence for only one proposition: that Hamilton and Madison were inspired propagandists with a genius for retrospective symmetry. Federalism, as the theory is generally defined, was an improvisation which was later promoted into a political theory. Experts on "federalism" should take to heart the advice of David Hume, who warned in his *Of the Rise and Progress of the Arts and Sciences* that " . . . there is no subject in which we must proceed with more caution than in [history], lest we assign causes which never existed and reduce what is merely contingent to stable and universal principles." In any event, the final balance in the Constitution between the states and the nation must have come as a great disappointment to Madison, while Hamilton's unitary views are too well known to need elucidation.

It is indeed astonishing how those who have glibly designated James Madison the "father" of Federalism have overlooked the solid body of fact which indicates that he shared Hamilton's quest for a unitary central government. To be specific, they have avoided examining the clear import of the Madison-Virginia Plan,[12] and have disregarded Madison's dogged inch-by-inch retreat from the bastions of centralization. The Virginia Plan envisioned a unitary national government effectively freed from and dominant over the states. The lower house of the national legislature was to be elected directly by the people of the states with membership proportional to population. The upper house was to be selected by the lower and the two chambers would elect the executive and choose the judges: The national government would be thus cut completely loose from the states.[13]

The structure of the general government was freed from state control in a truly radical fashion, but the scope of the authority of the national sovereign as Madison initially formulated it was breathtaking. . . . The national legislature was to be empowered to disallow the acts of state legislatures, and the central government was vested, in addition to the powers of the nation under the Articles of Confederation, with plenary authority wherever " . . . the separate States are incompetent or in which the harmony of the United States may be interrupted by the exercise of individual legislation." [14] Finally, just to lock the door against state intrusion, the national Congress was to be given the power to use military force on recalcitrant states.[15] This was Madison's "model" of an ideal national government, though it later received little publicity in *The Federalist*.

The interesting thing was the reaction of the Convention to this militant program for a strong autonomous central government. Some delegates were startled, some obviously leery of so comprehensive a project of reform,[16] but nobody set off any fireworks and nobody walked out. Moreover, in the two weeks that followed, the Virginia Plan received substantial endorsement *en principe*; the initial temper of the gathering can be deduced from the approval "without debate or dissent," on May 31, of the Sixth Resolution which granted Congress the authority to disallow state legislation "... contravening *in its opinion* the Articles of Union." Indeed, an amendment was included to bar states from contravening national treaties.[17]

The Virginia Plan may therefore be considered, in ideological terms, as the delegates' Utopia, but as the discussions continued and became more specific, many of those present began to have second thoughts. After all, they were not residents of Utopia or guardians in Plato's Republic who could simply impose a philosophical ideal on subordinate strata of the population. They were practical politicians in a democratic society, and no matter what their private dreams might be, they had to take home an acceptable package and defend it—and their own political futures—against predictable attack. On June 14 the breaking point between dream and reality took place. Apparently realizing that under the Virginia Plan, Massachusetts, Virginia and Pennsylvania could virtually dominate the national government—and probably appreciating that to sell this program to "the folks back home" would be impossible—the delegates from the small states dug in their heels and demanded time for a consideration of alternatives. One gets a graphic sense of the inner politics from John Dickinson's reproach to Madison: "You see the consequences of pushing things too far. Some of the members from the small States wish for two branches in the General Legislature and are friends to a good National Government; but we would sooner submit to a foreign power than ... be deprived of an equality of suffrage in both branches of the Legislature, and thereby be thrown under the domination of the large States." [18] ...

III

According to the standard script, at this point the "states'-rights" group intervened in force behind the New Jersey Plan, which has been characteristically portrayed as a reversion to the *status quo* under the Articles of Confederation with but minor modifications. A careful examination of the evidence indicates that only in a marginal sense is this an accurate description. It is true that the New Jersey Plan put the states back into the institutional picture, but one could argue that to do so was a recognition of political reality rather than an affirmation of states'-rights. A serious case can be made that the advocates of the New Jersey Plan, far from being ideological addicts of states'-rights, intended to substitute for the Virginia Plan a system which would both retain strong national power and have a chance of adoption in the states. The leading spokesman for the project asserted quite clearly that his views were based more on counsels of expediency than on principle; said Paterson on June 16: "I came here not to speak my own sentiments, but the sentiments of those who sent me. Our object is not such a Government as may be best in itself, but such a one as our Constituents have authorized us to prepare, and as they will approve." . . . With a shrewd eye, Paterson queried:

> Will the Operation and Force of the [central] Govt. depend upon the mode of Representn.—No—it will depend upon the Quantum of Power lodged in the leg. ex. and judy. Departments—Give [the existing] Congress the same Powers that you intend to give the two Branches, [under the Virginia Plan] and I apprehend they will act with as much Propriety and more Energy . . .[19]

In other words, the advocates of the New Jersey Plan concentrated their fire on what they held to be the *political liabilities* of the Virginia Plan—which were matters of institutional structure—rather than on the proposed scope of national authority. Indeed, the Supremacy Clause of the Constitution first saw the light of day in Paterson's Sixth Resolution; the New Jersey Plan contemplated the use of military force to secure compliance with national law; and finally Paterson made clear his view that under either the Virginia or the New Jersey systems, the general government would ". . . act on individuals and not on states." [20] From the states'-rights viewpoint, this was heresy: the fundament of that doctrine was the proposition that any central government had as its constituents the states, not the people, and could only reach the people through the agency of the state government.

Paterson then reopened the agenda of the Convention, but he did so within a distinctly nationalist framework. Paterson's position was one of favoring a strong central government in principle, but opposing one which in fact *put the big states in the saddle.* (The Virginia Plan, for all its abstract merits, did very well by Virginia.) As evidence for this speculation, there is a curious and intriguing proposal among Paterson's preliminary drafts of the New Jersey Plan:

> Whereas it is necessary in Order to form the People of the U. S. of America in to a Nation, that the States should be consolidated, by which means all the Citizens thereof will become equally intitled to and will equally participate in the same Privileges and Rights . . . it is therefore resolved, that all the Lands contained within the Limits of each state individually, and of the U. S. generally be considered as constituting one Body or Mass, and be divided into thirteen or more integral parts.
>
> Resolved, That such Divisions or integral Parts shall be styled Districts.[21]

This makes it sound as though Paterson was prepared to accept a strong unified central government along the lines of the Virginia Plan if the existing states were eliminated. He may have gotten the idea from his New Jersey colleague Judge David Brearley, who on June 9 had commented that the only remedy to the dilemma over representation was " . . . that a map of the U. S. be spread out, that all the existing boundaries be erased, and that a new partition of the whole be made into 13 equal parts." [22] According to Yates, Brearley added at this point " . . . then a government on the present [Virginia Plan] system will be just." [23]

This proposition was never pushed—it was patently unrealistic—but one can appreciate its purpose: it would have separated the men from the boys in the large-state delegations. How attached would the Virginians have been to their reform principles if Virginia were to disappear as a component geographical unit (the largest) for representational purposes? Up to this point, the Virginians had been in the happy position of supporting high ideals with that inner confidence born of knowledge that the "public interest" they endorsed would nourish their private interest. Worse, they had shown little willingness to compromise. Now the delegates from the small states announced that they were unprepared to be offered up as sacrificial victims to a "national interest" which reflected Virginia's parochial ambition. Caustic Charles Pinckney was not far off when he remarked sardonically that " . . . the whole [conflict] comes to this": "Give N. Jersey an equal vote, and she will dismiss her scruples, and concur in the Natil. system." [24] What he rather unfairly did not add was that the Jersey delegates were not free agents who could adhere to their private convictions; they had to take back, sponsor and risk their reputations on the reforms approved by the Convention—and in New Jersey, not in Virginia.

Paterson spoke on Saturday, and one can surmise that over the weekend there was a good deal of consultation, argument, and caucusing among the delegates. One member at least prepared a full length address: on Monday Alexander Hamilton, previously mute, rose and delivered a six-hour oration.[25] It was a remarkably apolitical speech; the gist of his position was that *both* the Virginia and New Jersey Plans were inadequately centralist, and he detailed a reform program which was reminiscent of the Protectorate under the Cromwellian *Instrument of Government* of 1653. It has been suggested that Hamilton did this in the best political tradition to emphasize the moderate character of the Virginia Plan,[26] to give the cautious delegates something *really* to worry about; but this interpretation seems somehow too clever. Particularly since the sentiments Hamilton expressed happened to be completely consistent with those he privately—and sometimes publicly—expressed throughout his life. He wanted, to take a striking phrase from a letter to George Washington, a "strong well mounted government";[27] in essence, the Hamilton Plan contemplated an elected life monarch, virtually free of public control, on the Hobbesian ground that only in this fashion could strength and stability be achieved. The other alternatives, he argued, would put policy-making at the mercy of the passions of the mob; only if the sovereign was beyond the reach of selfish influence would it be possible to have government in the interests of the whole community.[28]

From all accounts, this was a masterful and compelling speech, but (aside from furnishing John Lansing and Luther Martin with ammunition for later use against the Constitution) it made little impact. Hamilton was simply transmitting on a different wavelength from the rest of the delegates; the latter adjourned after his great effort, admired his rhetoric, and then returned to business.[29] It was rather as if they had taken a day off to attend the opera. Hamilton, never a particularly patient man or much of a negotiator, stayed for another ten days and then left, in considerable disgust, for New York.[30] Although he came back to Philadelphia sporadically and attended the last two weeks of the Convention, Hamilton played no part in the laborious task of hammering out the Constitution. . . .

IV

On Tuesday morning, June 19, the vacation was over. James Madison led off with a long, carefully reasoned speech analyzing the New Jersey Plan which, while intellectually vigorous in its criticisms, was quite conciliatory in mood. "The great difficulty," he observed, "lies in the affair of Representation; and if this could be adjusted, all others would be surmountable." [31] (As events were to demonstrate, this diagnosis was correct.) When he finished, a vote was taken on whether to continue with the Virginia Plan as the nucleus for a new constitution: seven states voted "Yes"; New York, New Jersey, and Delaware voted "No"; and Maryland, whose position often depended on which delegates happened to be on the floor, divided. Paterson, it seems, lost decisively; yet in a fundamental sense he and his allies had achieved their purpose: from that day onward, it could never be forgotten that the state governments loomed ominously in the background and that no verbal incantations could exorcise their power. Moreover, nobody bolted the convention: Paterson and his colleagues took their defeat in stride and set to work to modify the Virginia Plan, particularly with respect to its provisions on representation in the national legislature. Indeed, they won an immediate rhetorical bonus; when Oliver Ellsworth of Connecticut rose to move that the word "national" be expunged from the Third Virginia Resolution ("Resolved that a *national* Government ought to be established consisting of a *supreme* Legislative, Executive and Judiciary" [32]), Randolph agreed and the motion passed unanimously.[33] The process of compromise had begun.

For the next two weeks, the delegates circled around the problem of legislative representation. The Connecticut delegation appears to have evolved a possible compromise quite early in the debates, but the Virginians and particularly Madison (unaware that he would later be acclaimed as the prophet of "federalism") fought obdurately against providing for equal representation of states in the second chamber. There was a good deal of acrimony and at one point Benjamin Franklin—of all people—proposed the institution of a daily prayer; practical politicians in the gathering, however, were meditating more on the merits of a good committee than on the utility of Divine intervention. On July 2, the ice began to break when through a number of fortuitous events[34]—and one that seems deliberate[35]—the majority against equality of representation was converted into a dead tie. The Convention had reached the stage where it was "ripe" for a solution (presumably all the therapeutic speeches had been made), and the South Carolinians proposed a committee. Madison and James Wilson wanted none of it, but with only Pennsylvania dissenting, the body voted to establish a working party on the problem of representation.

The members of this committee, one from each state, were elected by the delegates—and a very interesting committee it was. Despite the fact that the Virginia Plan had held majority support up to that date, neither Madison nor Randolph was selected (Mason was the Virginian) and Baldwin of Georgia, whose shift in position had resulted in the tie, was chosen. From the composition, it was clear that this was not to be a "fighting" committee: the emphasis in membership was on what might be described as "second-level political entrepreneurs." On the basis of the discussions up to that time, only Luther Martin of Maryland could be described as a "bitter-ender." Admittedly, some divination enters into this sort of analysis, but one does get a sense of the mood of the delegates from these choices—including the interesting selection of Benjamin Franklin, despite his age and intellectual wobbliness, over the brilliant and incisive Wilson or the sharp, polemical Gouverneur Morris, to represent Pennsylvania. His passion for conciliation was more valuable at this juncture than Wilson's logical genius, or Morris' acerbic wit.

There is a common rumor that the Framers divided their time between philosophical discussions of government and reading the classics in political theory. Perhaps this is as good a time as any to note that their concerns were highly practical, that they spent little time canvassing abstractions. A number of them had some acquaintance with the history of political theory (probably gained from reading John Adams' monumental compilation *A Defense of the Constitutions of Government*,[36] the first volume of which appeared in 1786), and it was a poor rhetorician indeed who could not cite Locke, Montesquieu, or Harrington *in support* of a desired goal. Yet up to this point in the deliberations, no one had expounded a defense of states'-rights or the "separation of powers" on anything resembling a theoretical basis. It should be reiterated that the Madison model had no room either for the states or for the "separation of powers": effectively *all* governmental power was vested in the national legislature. The merits of Montesquieu did not turn up until *The Federalist;* and although a perverse argument could be made that Madison's ideal was truly in the tradition of John Locke's *Second Treatise of Government,*[37] the Locke whom the American rebels treated as an honorary president was a pluralistic defender of vested rights,[38] not of parliamentary supremacy.

It would be tedious to continue a blow-by-blow analysis of the work of the delegates; the critical fight was over representation of the states and once the Connecticut Compromise was adopted on July 17, the Convention was over the hump. Madison, James Wilson, and Gouverneur Morris of New York (who was there representing Pennsylvania!) fought the compromise all the way in a last-ditch effort to get a unitary state with parliamentary supremacy. But their allies deserted them and they demonstrated after their defeat the essentially opportunist character of their objections—using "opportunist" here in a non-pejorative sense, to indicate a willingness to swallow their objections and get on with the business. Moreover, once the compromise had carried (by five states to four, with one state divided), its advocates threw themselves vigorously into the job of strengthening the general government's substantive powers—as might have been predicted, indeed, from Paterson's early statements. It nourishes an increased respect for Madison's devotion to the art of politics, to realize that this dogged fighter could sit down six months later and prepare essays for *The Federalist* in contradiction to his basic convictions about the true course the Convention should have taken.

V

Two tricky issues will serve to illustrate the later process of accommodation. The first was the institutional position of the Executive. Madison argued for an executive chosen by the National Legislature and on May 29 this had been adopted with a provision that after his seven-year term was concluded, the chief magistrate should not be eligible for reelection. In late July this was reopened and for a week the matter was argued from several different points of view. A good deal of desultory speech-making ensued, but the gist of the problem was the opposition from two sources to election by the legislature. One group felt that the states should have a hand in the process; another small but influential circle urged direct election by the people. There were a number of proposals: election by the people, election by state governors, by electors chosen by state legislatures, by the National Legislature (James Wilson, perhaps ironically, proposed at one point that an Electoral College be chosen by lot from the National

Legislature!), and there was some resemblance to three-dimensional chess in the dispute because of the presence of two other variables, length of tenure and reeligibility. Finally, after opening, reopening, and re-reopening the debate, the thorny problem was consigned to a committee for resolution.

The Brearley Committee on Postponed Matters was a superb aggregation of talent and its compromise on the Executive was a masterpiece of political improvisation. (The Electoral College, its creation, however, had little in its favor as an *institution*—as the delegates well appreciated.) The point of departure for all discussion about the presidency in the Convention was that in immediate terms, the problem was non-existent; in other words, everybody present knew that under any system devised, George Washington would be President. Thus they were dealing in the future tense and to a body of working politicians the merits of the Brearley proposal were obvious: everybody got a piece of cake. (Or to put it more academically, each viewpoint could leave the Convention and argue to its constituents that it had *really* won the day.) First, the state legislatures had the right to determine the mode of selection of the electors; second, the small states received a bonus in the Electoral College in the form of a guaranteed minimum of three votes while the big states got acceptance of the principle of proportional power; third, if the state legislatures agreed (as six did in the first presidential election), the people could be involved directly in the choice of electors; and finally, if no candidate received a majority in the College, the right of decision passed to the National Legislature with each state exercising equal strength. (In the Brearley recommendation, the election went to the Senate, but a motion from the floor substituted the House; this was accepted on the ground that the Senate already had enough authority over the executive in its treaty and appointment powers.)

This compromise was almost too good to be true, and the Framers snapped it up with little debate or controversy. No one seemed to think well of the College as an *institution;* indeed, what evidence there is suggests that there was an assumption that once Washington had finished his tenure as President, the electors would cease to produce majorities and the chief executive would usually be chosen in the House. George Mason observed casually that the selection would be made in the House nineteen times in twenty and no one seriously disputed this point. The vital aspect of the Electoral College was that it got the Convention over the hurdle and protected everybody's interests. The future was left to cope with the problem of what to do with this Rube Goldberg mechanism.

In short, the Framers did not in their wisdom endow the United States with a College of Cardinals—the Electoral College was neither an exercise in applied Platonism nor an experiment in indirect government based on elitist distrust of the masses. It was merely a jerry-rigged improvisation which has subsequently been endowed with a high theoretical content. When an elector from Oklahoma in 1960 refused to cast his vote for Nixon (naming Byrd and Goldwater instead) on the ground that the Founding Fathers intended him to exercise his great independent wisdom, he was indulging in historical fantasy. If one were to indulge in counter-fantasy, he would be tempted to suggest that the Fathers would be startled to find the College still in operation—and perhaps even dismayed at their descendants' lack of judgment or inventiveness.[39]

The second issue on which some substantial practical bargaining took place was slavery. The morality of slavery was, by design, not at issue;[40] but in its other concrete aspects, slavery colored the arguments over taxation, commerce, and representation. The "Three-Fifths Compromise," that three-fifths of the slaves would be counted both for representation and for purposes of direct taxation (which was drawn from the past—it was a formula of Madison's utilized by Congress in 1783 to establish the basis of state contributions to the Confederation treasury) had allayed some Northern fears about Southern overrepresentation (no one then foresaw the trivial role that direct taxation would play in later federal financial policy), but doubts still remained. The Southerners, on the other hand, were afraid that Congressional control over commerce would lead to the exclusion of slaves or to their excessive taxation as imports. Moreover, the Southerners were disturbed over "navigation acts," *i.e.*, tariffs, or special legislation providing, for example, that exports be carried only in American ships; as a section depending upon exports, they wanted protection from the potential voracity of their commercial brethren of the Eastern states. To achieve this end, Mason and others urged that the Constitution include a proviso that navigation and commercial laws should require a two-thirds vote in Congress.

These problems came to a head in late August and, as usual, were handed to a committee in the hope that, in Gouverneur Morris' words, " . . . these things may form a bargain among the Northern and Southern states." [41] The Committee reported its measures of reconciliation on August 25, and on August 29 the package was wrapped up and delivered. What occurred can best be described in George Mason's dour version (he anticipated Calhoun in his conviction that permitting navigation acts to pass by majority vote would put the South in economic bondage to the North—it was mainly on this ground that he refused to sign the Constitution):

> The Constitution as agreed to till a fortnight before the Convention rose was such a one as he would have set his hand and heart to. . . . [Until that time] The 3 New England States were constantly with us in all questions . . . so that it was these three States with the 5 Southern ones against Pennsylvania, Jersey and Delaware. With respect to the importation of slaves, [decision-making] was left to Congress. This disturbed the two Southernmost States

who knew that Congress would immediately suppress the importation of slaves. Those two States therefore struck up a bargain with the three New England States. If they would join to admit slaves for some years, the two Southern-most States would join in changing the clause which required the 2/3 of the Legislature in any vote [on navigation acts]. It was done.[42]

On the floor of the Convention there was a virtual love-feast on this happy occasion. Charles Pinckney of South Carolina attempted to overturn the committee's decision, when the compromise was reported to the Convention, by insisting that the South needed protection from the imperialism of the Northern states. But his Southern colleagues were not prepared to rock the boat and General C. C. Pinckney arose to spread oil on the suddenly ruffled waters; he admitted that:

> It was in the true interest of the S[outhern] States to have no regulation of commerce; but considering the loss brought on the commerce of the Eastern States by the Revolution, their liberal conduct towards the views of South Carolina [on the regulation of the slave trade] and the interests the weak Southn. States had in being united with the strong Eastern states, he thought it proper that no fetters should be imposed on the power of making commercial regulations; *and that his constituents, though prejudiced against the Eastern States, would be reconciled to this liberality.* He had himself prejudices agst the Eastern States before he came here, but would acknowledge that he had found them as liberal and candid as any men whatever. (Italics added)[43]

Pierce Butler took the same tack, essentially arguing that he was not too happy about the possible consequences, but that a deal was a deal.[44] . . .

VI

Drawing on their vast collective political experience, utilizing every weapon in the politician's arsenal, looking constantly over their shoulders at their constituents, the delegates put together a Constitution. It was a makeshift affair; some sticky issues (for example, the qualification of voters) they ducked entirely; others they mastered with that ancient instrument of political sagacity, studied ambiguity (for example, citizenship), and some they just overlooked. In this last category, I suspect, fell the matter of the power of the federal courts to determine the constitutionality of acts of Congress. When the judicial article was formulated (Article III of the Constitution), deliberations were still in the stage where the legislature was endowed with broad power under the Randolph formulation, authority which by its own terms was scarcely amenable to judicial review. In essence, courts could hardly determine when " . . . the separate States are incompetent or . . . the harmony of the United States may be interrupted"; the National Legislature, as critics pointed out, was free to define its own jurisdiction. Later the definition of legislative authority was changed into the form we know, a series of stipulated powers, *but the delegates never seriously reexamined the jurisdiction of the judiciary under this new limited formulation.*[45] All arguments on the intention of the Framers in this matter are thus deductive and a *posteriori*, though some obviously make more sense than others.

The Framers were busy and distinguished men, anxious to get back to their families, their positions, and their constituents, not members of the French Academy devoting a lifetime to a dictionary. They were trying to do an important job, and do it in such a fashion that their handiwork would be acceptable to very diverse constituencies. No one was rhapsodic about the final document, but it was a beginning, a move in the right direction, and one they had reason to believe the people would endorse. In addition, since they had modified the impossible amendment provisions of the Articles (the requirement of unanimity which could always be frustrated by "Rogues Island") to one demanding approval by only three-quarters of the states, they seemed confident that gaps in the fabric which experience would reveal could be rewoven without undue difficulty. . . .

Madison, despite his reservations about the Constitution, was the campaign manager in ratification. His first task was to get the Congress in New York to light its own funeral pyre by approving the "amendments" to the Articles and sending them on to the state legislatures. Above all, momentum had to be maintained. The anti-Constitutionalists, now thoroughly alarmed and no novices in politics, realized that their best tactic was attrition rather than direct opposition. Thus they settled on a position expressing qualified approval but calling for a second Convention to remedy various defects (the one with the most demagogic appeal was the lack of a Bill of Rights). Madison knew that to accede to this demand would be equivalent to losing the battle, nor would he agree to conditional approval (despite wavering even by Hamilton). This was an all-or-nothing proposition: national salvation or national impotence with no intermediate positions possible. Unable to get congressional approval, he settled for second best: a unanimous resolution of Congress transmitting the Constitution to the states for whatever action they saw fit to take. The opponents then moved from New York and the Congress, where they had attempted to attach amendments and conditions, to the states for the final battle.

At first the campaign for ratification went beautifully: within eight months after the delegates set their names to the document, eight states had ratified. Only in Massachusetts had the result been close (187-168). Theoretically, a ratification by one more state convention would set the new government in motion, but in fact until Virginia and New York acceded to the new Union, the latter was a fiction. New Hampshire was the next to ratify; Rhode Island was involved in its characteristic political convulsions (the Legislature there sent the Constitution out to the towns for decision by popular vote and it got lost among a series of local issues); North Carolina's convention did not meet until July and then postponed a final decision. This is hardly the place for an extensive analysis of the conventions of New York and Virginia. Suffice it to say that the Constitutionalists clearly outmaneuvered their opponents, forced them into impossible political positions, and won both states narrowly. The Virginia Convention could serve as a classic study in effective floor management: Patrick Henry had to be contained, and a reading of the debates discloses a standard two-stage technique. Henry would give a four- or five-hour speech denouncing some section of the Constitution on every conceivable ground (the federal district, he averred at one point, would become a haven for convicts escaping from state authority!);[46] when Henry subsided, "Mr. Lee of Westmoreland" would rise and literally poleaxe him with sardonic invective (when Henry complained about the militia power, "Lighthorse Harry" really punched below the belt: observing that while the former Governor had been sitting in Richmond during the Revolution, *he* had been out in the trenches with the troops and thus felt better qualified to discuss military affairs).[47] Then the gentlemanly Constitutionalists (Madison, Pendleton and Marshall) would pick up the matters at issue and examine them in the light of reason.

Indeed, modern Americans who tend to think of James Madison as a rather desiccated character should spend some time with this transcript. Probably Madison put on his most spectacular demonstration of nimble rhetoric in what might be called "The Battle of the Absent Authorities." Patrick Henry in the course of one of his harangues alleged that Jefferson was known to be opposed to Virginia's approving the Constitution. This was clever: Henry hated Jefferson, but was prepared to use any weapon that came to hand. Madison's riposte was superb: First, he said that with all due respect to the great reputation of Jefferson, he was not in the country and therefore could not formulate an adequate judgment; second, no one should utilize the reputation of an outsider—the Virginia Convention was there to think for itself; third, if there were to be recourse to outsiders, the opinions of George Washington should certainly be taken into consideration; and finally, he knew from privileged personal communications from Jefferson that in fact the latter *strongly favored* the Constitution.[48] To devise an assault route into this rhetorical fortress was literally impossible.

VII

The fight was over; all that remained now was to establish the new frame of government in the spirit of its framers. And who were better qualified for this task than the Framers themselves? Thus victory for the Constitution meant simultaneous victory for the Constitutionalists; the anti-Constitutionalists either capitulated or vanished into limbo—soon Patrick Henry would be offered a seat on the Supreme Court[49] and Luther Martin would be known as the Federalist "bulldog." [50] And irony of ironies, Alexander Hamilton and James Madison would shortly accumulate a reputation as the formulators of what is often alleged to be our political theory, the concept of "federalism." . . .

Thus we can ask what the Framers meant when they gave Congress the power to regulate interstate and foreign commerce, and we emerge, reluctantly perhaps, with the reply that . . . they may not have known what they meant, that there may not have been any semantic consensus. The Convention was not a seminar in analytic philosophy or linguistic analysis. Commerce was *commerce*— and if different interpretations of the word arose, later generations could worry about the problem of definition. The delegates were in a hurry to get a new government established; when definitional arguments arose, they characteristically took refuge in ambiguity. If different men voted for the same proposition for varying reasons, that was politics (and still is); if later generations were unsettled by this lack of precision, that would be their problem.

There was a good deal of definitional pluralism with respect to the problems the delegates did discuss, but when we move to the question of extrapolated intentions, we enter the realm of spiritualism. When men in our time, for instance, launch into elaborate talmudic exegesis to demonstrate that federal aid to parochial schools is (or is not) in accord with the intentions of the men who established the Republic and endorsed the Bill of Rights, they are engaging in historical Extra-Sensory Perception. (If one were to join this E. S. P. contingent for a minute, he might suggest that the hard-boiled politicians who wrote the Constitution and Bill of Rights would chuckle scornfully at such an invocation of authority: obviously a politician would chart his course on the intentions of the living, not of the dead, and count the number of Catholics in his constituency.)

The Constitution, then, was not an apotheosis of "constitutionalism," a triumph of architectonic genius; it was a patch-work sewn together under the pressure of both time and events by a group of extremely talented democratic politicians. They refused to attempt the establishment of a strong, centralized sovereignty on the principle of legislative supremacy for the excellent reason that the people would not accept it. They risked their political fortunes by opposing the established doctrines of state sovereignty because they were convinced that the existing system was leading to national impotence and probably foreign domination. For two years, they worked to get a convention established. For over three months, in what must have seemed to the faithful participants an endless process of give-and-take, they reasoned, cajoled, threatened, and bargained amongst themselves. The result was a Constitution which the people, in fact, by democratic processes, did accept, and a new and far better national government was established.

Beginning with the inspired propaganda of Hamilton, Madison and Jay, the ideological build-up got under way. *The Federalist* had little impact on the ratification of the Constitution, except perhaps in New York, but this volume had enormous influence on the image of the Constitution in the minds of future generations, particularly on historians and political scientists who have an innate fondness for theoretical symmetry. Yet, while the shades of Locke and Montesquieu *may* have been hovering in the background, and the delegates *may* have been unconscious instruments of a transcendent *telos,* the careful observer of the day-to-day work of the Convention finds no over-arching principles. The "separation of powers" to him seems to be a by-product of suspicion, and "federalism" he views as a *pis aller,* as the farthest point the delegates felt they could go in the destruction of state power without themselves inviting repudiation.

To conclude, the Constitution was neither a victory for abstract theory nor a great practical success. Well over half a million men had to die on the battlefields of the Civil War before certain constitutional principles could be defined—a baleful consideration which is somehow overlooked in our customary tributes to the farsighted genius of the Framers and to the supposed American talent for "constitutionalism." The Constitution was, however, a vivid demonstration of effective democratic political action, and of the forging of a national elite which literally persuaded its countrymen to hoist themselves by their own boot straps. American pro-consuls would be wise not to translate the Constitution into Japanese, or Swahili, or treat it as a work of semi-Divine origin; but when students of comparative politics examine the process of nation-building in countries newly freed from colonial rule, they may find the American experience instructive as a classic example of the potentialities of a democratic elite.

NOTES

1. The view that the right to vote in the states was severely circumscribed by property qualifications has been thoroughly discredited in recent years. See Chilton Williamson, *American Suffrage from Property to Democracy, 1760–1860* (Princeton, 1960). The contemporary position is

that John Dickinson actually knew what he was talking about when he argued that there would be little opposition to vesting the right of suffrage in freeholders since "The great mass of our Citizens is composed at this time of freeholders, and will be pleased with it." Max Farrand, *Records of the Federal Convention*, Vol. 2, p. 202 (New Haven, 1911). (Henceforth cited as *Farrand*.)

2. The classic statement of the *coup d'etat* theory is, of course, Charles A. Beard, *An Economic Interpretation of the Constitution of the United States* (New York, 1913). . . .

3. "[T]he situation of the general government, if it can be called a government, is shaken to its foundation, and liable to be overturned by every blast. In a word, it is at an end; and, unless a remedy is soon applied, anarchy and confusion will inevitably ensue." Washington to Jefferson, May 30, 1787, *Farrand*, III, 31. See also Irving Brant, *James Madison, The Nationalist* (New York, 1948), ch. 25.

4. The story of James Madison's cultivation of Washington is told by Brant, *op. cit.*, pp. 394–97.

5. The "message center" being the Congress; nineteen members of Congress were simultaneously delegates to the Convention. One gets a sense of this coordination of effort from Broadus Mitchell, *Alexander Hamilton, Youth to Maturity* (New York, 1957), ch. 22.

6. The Annapolis Convention, called for the previous year, turned into a shambles: only five states sent commissioners, only three states were legally represented, and the instructions to delegates named varied quite widely from state to state. Clinton and others of his persuasion may have thought this disaster would put an end to the drive for reform. See Mitchell, *op. cit.*, pp. 362–67; Brant, *op. cit.*, pp. 375–87.

7. The terms "radical" and "conservative" have been bandied about a good deal in connection with the Constitution. This usage is nonsense if it is employed to distinguish between two economic "classes"—*e.g.,* radical debtors versus conservative creditors, radical farmers versus conservative capitalists, etc.—because there was no polarization along this line of division; the same types of people turned up on both sides. And many were hard to place in these terms: does one treat Robert Morris as a debtor or a creditor? or James Wilson? See Robert E Brown, *Charles Beard and the Constitution* (Princeton, 1956), passim. The one line of division that holds up is between those deeply attached to states'-rights and those who felt that the Confederation was bankrupt. Thus, curiously, some of the most narrow-minded, parochial spokesmen of the time have earned the designation "radical" while those most willing to experiment and alter the *status quo* have been dubbed "conservative"! See Cecelia Kenyon, "Men of Little Faith," *William and Mary Quarterly*, Vol. 12, p. 3 (1955).

8. Yet, there was little objection to this crucial modification from any quarter—there almost seems to have been a gentlemen's agreement that Rhode Island's *liberum veto* had to be destroyed.

9. See Mason's letter to his son, May 27, 1787, in which he endorsed secrecy as "a proper precaution to prevent mistakes and misrepresentation until the business shall have been completed, when the whole may have a very different complexion from that in which the several crude and indigested parts might in their first shape appear if submitted to the public eye." *Farrand*, III, 28.

10. See Madison to Jefferson, June 6, 1787, *Farrand*, III, 35.

11. Cited in Charles Warren, *The Making of the Constitution* (Boston, 1928), p. 138.

12. "I hold it for a fundamental point, that an individual independence of the states is utterly irreconcilable with the idea of an aggregate sovereignty," Madison to Randolph, cited in Brant, *op. cit.*, p. 416.

13. The Randolph Plan was presented on May 29, see *Farrand*, I, 18–23; the state legislatures retained only the power to *nominate* candidates for the upper chamber. Madison's view of the appropriate position of the states emerged even more strikingly in Yates' record of his speech on June 29: "Some contend that states are sovereign when in fact they are only political societies. There is a gradation of power in all societies, from the lowest corporation to the highest sovereign. The states never possessed the essential rights of sovereignty. . . . The states, at present, are only great corporations, having the power of making by-laws, and these are effectual only if they are not contradictory to the general confederation. The states ought to be placed under the control of the general government—at least as much so as they formerly were under the king and British parliament." *Farrand*, I, 471. Forty-six years later, after Yates' "Notes" had been published, Madison tried to explain this statement away as a misinterpretation: he did not flatly deny the authenticity of Yates' record, but attempted a defense that was half justification and half evasion. Madison to W. C. Rives, Oct. 21, 1833. *Farrand*, III, 521–24.

14. Resolution 6.

15. *Ibid.*

16. See the discussions on May 30 and 31. "Mr. Charles Pinkney wished to know of Mr. Randolph whether he meant to abolish the State Governts. Altogether . . . Mr. Butler said he had not made up his mind on the subject and was open to the light which discussion might throw on it . . . Genl. Pinkney expressed a doubt . . . Mr. Gerry seemed to entertain the same doubt." *Farrand*, I, 33–34. There were no denunciations—though it should perhaps be added that Luther Martin had not yet arrived.

17. *Farrand*, I, 54. (Italics added.)

18. *Ibid.*, p. 242. Delaware's delegates had been instructed by their general assembly to maintain in any new system the voting equality of the states. *Farrand*, III, 574.

19. *Ibid.*, pp. 275–76.

20. "But it is said that this national government is to act on individuals and not on states; and cannot a federal government be so framed as to operate in the same way? It surely may." *Ibid.*, pp. 182–83; also *ibid.* at p. 276.

21. *Farrand*, III, 613.

22. *Farrand*, I, 177.

23. *Ibid.*, p. 182.

24. *Ibid.*, p. 255.

25. J. C. Hamilton, cited *ibid.*, p. 293.

26. See, *e.g.*, Mitchell, *op. cit.*, p. 381.

27. Hamilton to Washington, July 3, 1787, *Farrand*, III, 53.

28. A reconstruction of the Hamilton Plan is found in *Farrand*, III, 617–30.

29. Said William Samuel Johnson on June 21: "A gentleman from New-York, with boldness and decision, proposed a system totally different from both [Virginia and New Jersey]; and though he has been praised by every body, he has been supported by none." *Farrand*, I, 363.

30. See his letter to Washington cited *supra* note 43.

31. *Farrand*, I, 321.

32. This formulation was voted into the Randolph Plan on May 30, 1787, by a vote of six states to none, with one divided. *Farrand*, I, 30.

33. *Farrand*, I, 335–36. In agreeing, Randolph stipulated his disagreement with Ellsworth's rationale, but said he did not object to merely changing an "expression." Those who subject

the Constitution to minute semantic analysis might do well to keep this instance in mind; if Randolph could so concede the deletion of "national," one may wonder if any word changes can be given much weight.

34. According to Luther Martin, he was alone on the floor and cast Maryland's vote for equality of representation. Shortly thereafter, Jenifer came on the floor and "Mr. King, from Massachusetts, valuing himself on Mr. Jenifer to divide the State of Maryland on this question . . . requested of the President that the question might be put again; however, the motion was too extraordinary in its nature to meet with success." Cited from "The Genuine Information, . . ." *Farrand,* III, 188.

35. Namely Baldwin's vote *for* equality of representation which divided Georgia—with Few absent and Pierce in New York fighting a duel, Houston voted against equality and Baldwin shifted to tie the state. Baldwin was originally from Connecticut and attended and tutored at Yale, facts which have led to much speculation about the pressures the Connecticut delegation may have brought on him to save the day (Georgia was the last state to vote) and open the way to compromise. To employ a good Russian phrase, it was certainly not an accident that Baldwin voted the way he did. See *Warren,* p. 262.

36. For various contemporary comments, see *Warren,* pp. 814–18. On Adams' technique, see Zoltan Haraszti, "The Composition of Adams' *Defense,*" in *John Adams and the Prophets of Progress* (Cambridge, 1952), ch. 9. In this connection it is interesting to check the Convention discussions for references to the authority of Locke, Montesquieu and Harrington, the theorists who have been assigned various degrees of paternal responsibility. There are no explicit references to James Harrington; one to John Locke (Luther Martin cited him on the state of nature, *Farrand,* I, 437); and seven to Montesquieu, only one of which related to the "separation of powers" (Madison in an odd speech, which he explained in a footnote was given to help a friend rather than advance his own views, cited Montesquieu on the separation of the executive and legislative branches, *Farrand,* II, 34). This, of course, does not prove that Locke and Co. were without influence; it shifts the burden of proof, however, to those who assert ideological causality. See Benjamin F. Wright, "The Origins of the Separation of Powers in America," *Economica,* Vol. 13 (1933), p. 184.

37. I share Willmoore Kendall's interpretation of Locke as a supporter of parliamentary supremacy and majoritarianism; see Kendall, *John Locke and the Doctrine of Majority Rule* (Urbana, 1941). Kendall's general position has recently received strong support in the definitive edition and commentary of Peter Laslett, *Locke's Two Treatises of Government* (Cambridge, 1960).

38. The American Locke is best delineated in Carl Becker, *The Declaration of Independence* (New York, 1948).

39. See John P. Roche, "The Electoral College: A Note on American Political Mythology," *Dissent* (Spring, 1961), pp. 197–99. The relevant debates took place July 19–26, 1787, *Farrand,* II, 50–128, and September 5–6, 1787, *ibid.,* pp. 505–31.

40. See the discussion on August 22, 1787, *Farrand,* II, 366–75; King seems to have expressed the sense of the Convention when he said, "the subject should be considered in a political light only." *Ibid.* at 373.

41. *Farrand,* II, 374. Randolph echoed his sentiment in different words.

42. Mason to Jefferson, cited in *Warren,* p. 584.

43. August 29, 1787, *Farrand,* II, 449–50.

44. *Ibid.*, p. 451. The plainest statement of the matter was put by the three North Carolina delegates (Blount, Spaight and Williamson) in their report to Governor Caswell, September 18, 1787. After noting that "no exertions have been wanting on our part to guard and promote the particular interest of North Carolina," they went on to explain the basis of the negotiations in cold-blooded fashion: "While we were taking so much care to guard ourselves against being over reached and to form rules of Taxation that might operate in our favour, it is not to be supposed that our Northern Brethren were Inattentive to their particular Interest. A navigation Act or the power to regulate Commerce in the Hands of the National Government . . . is what the Southern States have given in Exchange for the advantages we Mentioned." They concluded by explaining that while the Constitution did deal with other matters besides taxes—"there are other Considerations of great Magnitude involved in the system"—they would not take up valuable time with boring details! *Farrand*, III, 83–84.

45. The Committee on Detail altered the general grant of legislative power envisioned by the Virginia Plan into a series of specific grants; these were examined closely between August 16 and August 23. One day only was devoted to the Judicial Article, August 27, and since no one raised the question of judicial review of *Federal* statutes, no light was cast on the matter. A number of random comments on the power of the judiciary were scattered throughout the discussions, but there was another variable which deprives them of much probative value: the proposed Council of Revision which would have joined the Executive with the judges in *legislative* review. Madison and Wilson, for example, favored this technique—which had nothing in common with what we think of as judicial review except that judges were involved in the task.

46. See *Elliot's Debates on the Federal Constitution* (Washington, 1836), Vol. 3, pp. 436–38.

47. This should be quoted to give the full flavor: "Without vanity, I may say I have had different experience of [militia] service from that of [Henry]. It was my fortune to be a soldier of my country. . . . I saw what the honorable gentleman did not see—our men fighting. . . ." *Ibid.*, p. 178,

48. *Ibid.*, p. 329.

49. Washington offered him the Chief Justiceship in 1796, but he declined; Charles Warren, *The Supreme Court in United States History* (Boston, 1947), Vol. 1, p. 139.

50. He was a zealous prosecutor of seditions in the period 1798–1800; with Justice Samuel Chase, like himself an alleged "radical" at the time of the Constitutional Convention, Martin hunted down Jeffersonian heretics. See James M. Smith, *Freedom's Fetters* (Ithaca, 1956), pp. 342–43.

2-2

Federalist No. 10

James Madison
November 22, 1787

*When one reads this tightly reasoned, highly conceptual essay, it is easy to for-
get that it was published in a New York newspaper with the purpose of persuading that state's ratification convention to endorse the Constitution.
Although after ratification this essay went unnoticed for more than a century,
today, it stands atop virtually every scholar's ranking of* The Federalist
papers. *Written in November 1787, it was James Madison's first contribution
to the ratification debate, and it develops a rationale for a large, diverse republic that he had employed several times at the Convention. His allies admired
the inventive way it rebutted opponents' arguments that only small republics
were safe. The modern reader can appreciate how it resonates with the
nation's diversity of interests in the twenty-first century. And everyone, then
and now, can admire the solid logic employed by this smart man, who begins
with a few unobjectionable assumptions and derives from them the counter-
intuitive conclusion that the surest way to avoid the tyranny of faction is to
design a political system in which factions are numerous and none can dominate. This essay repays careful reading.*

AMONG THE NUMEROUS advantages promised by a well-constructed Union, none
deserves to be more accurately developed than its tendency to break and control
the violence of faction. The friend of popular governments never finds himself
so much alarmed for their character and fate, as when he contemplates their
propensity to this dangerous vice. He will not fail, therefore, to set a due value
on any plan which, without violating the principles to which he is attached, provides a proper cure for it. The instability, injustice, and confusion introduced into
the public councils, have, in truth, been the mortal diseases under which popular governments have everywhere perished; as they continue to be the favorite
and fruitful topics from which the adversaries to liberty derive their most specious declamations. The valuable improvements made by the American constitutions on the popular models, both ancient and modern, cannot certainly be too
much admired; but it would be an unwarrantable partiality, to contend that they
have as effectually obviated the danger on this side, as was wished and expected.

Complaints are everywhere heard from our most considerate and virtuous citizens, equally the friends of public and private faith, and of public and personal liberty, that our governments are too unstable, that the public good is disregarded in the conflicts of rival parties, and that measures are too often decided, not according to the rules of justice and the rights of the minor party, but by the superior force of an interested and overbearing majority. However anxiously we may wish that these complaints had no foundation, the evidence, of known facts will not permit us to deny that they are in some degree true. It will be found, indeed, on a candid review of our situation, that some of the distresses under which we labor have been erroneously charged on the operation of our governments; but it will be found, at the same time, that other causes will not alone account for many of our heaviest misfortunes; and, particularly, for that prevailing and increasing distrust of public engagements, and alarm for private rights, which are echoed from one end of the continent to the other. These must be chiefly, if not wholly, effects of the unsteadiness and injustice with which a factious spirit has tainted our public administrations.

By a faction, I understand a number of citizens, whether amounting to a majority or a minority of the whole, who are united and actuated by some common impulse of passion, or of interest, adversed to the rights of other citizens, or to the permanent and aggregate interests of the community.

There are two methods of curing the mischiefs of faction: the one, by removing its causes; the other, by controlling its effects. There are again two methods of removing the causes of faction: the one, by destroying the liberty which is essential to its existence; the other, by giving to every citizen the same opinions, the same passions, and the same interests.

It could never be more truly said than of the first remedy, that it was worse than the disease. Liberty is to faction what air is to fire, an aliment without which it instantly expires. But it could not be less folly to abolish liberty, which is essential to political life, because it nourishes faction, than it would be to wish the annihilation of air, which is essential to animal life, because it imparts to fire its destructive agency.

The second expedient is as impracticable as the first would be unwise. As long as the reason of man continues fallible, and he is at liberty to exercise it, different opinions will be formed. As long as the connection subsists between his reason and his self-love, his opinions and his passions will have a reciprocal influence on each other; and the former will be objects to which the latter will attach themselves. The diversity in the faculties of men, from which the rights of property originate, is not less an insuperable obstacle to a uniformity of interests. The protection of these faculties is the first object of government. From the protection of different and unequal faculties of acquiring property, the possession of different degrees and kinds of property immediately results; and from the influence of these on the sentiments and views of the respective proprietors, ensues a division of the society into different interests and parties.

The latent causes of faction are thus sown in the nature of man; and we see them everywhere brought into different degrees of activity, according to the different circumstances of civil society. A zeal for different opinions concerning religion, concerning government, and many other points, as well of speculation as of practice; an attachment to different leaders ambitiously contending for preeminence and power; or to persons of other descriptions whose fortunes have been interesting to the human passions, have, in turn, divided mankind into parties, inflamed them with mutual animosity, and rendered them much more disposed to vex and oppress each other than to co-operate for their common good. So strong is this propensity of mankind to fall into mutual animosities, that where no substantial occasion presents itself, the most frivolous and fanciful distinctions have been sufficient to kindle their unfriendly passions and excite their most violent conflicts. But the most common and durable source of factions has been the various and unequal distribution of property. Those who hold and those who are without property have ever formed distinct interests in society. Those who are creditors, and those who are debtors, fall under a like discrimination. A landed interest, a manufacturing interest, a mercantile interest, a moneyed interest, with many lesser interests, grow up of necessity in civilized nations, and divide them into different classes, actuated by different sentiments and views. The regulation of these various and interfering interests forms the principal task of modern legislation, and involves the spirit of party and faction in the necessary and ordinary operations of the government.

No man is allowed to be a judge in his own cause, because his interest would certainly bias his judgment, and, not improbably, corrupt his integrity. With equal, nay with greater reason, a body of men are unfit to be both judges and parties at the same time; yet what are many of the most important acts of legislation, but so many judicial determinations, not indeed concerning the rights of single persons, but concerning the rights of large bodies of citizens? And what are the different classes of legislators but advocates and parties to the causes which they determine? Is a law proposed concerning private debts? It is a question to which the creditors are parties on one side and the debtors on the other. Justice ought to hold the balance between them. Yet the parties are, and must be, themselves the judges; and the most numerous party, or, in other words, the most powerful faction must be expected to prevail. Shall domestic manufactures be encouraged, and in what degree, by restrictions on foreign manufactures? are questions which would be differently decided by the landed and the manufacturing classes, and probably by neither with a sole regard to justice and the public good. The apportionment of taxes on the various descriptions of property is an act which seems to require the most exact impartiality; yet there is, perhaps, no legislative act in which greater opportunity and temptation are given to a predominant party to trample on the rules of justice. Every shilling with which they overburden the inferior number, is a shilling saved to their own pockets.

It is in vain to say that enlightened statesmen will be able to adjust these clashing interests, and render them all subservient to the public good. Enlightened statesmen will not always be at the helm. Nor, in many cases, can such an adjustment be made at all without taking into view indirect and remote considerations, which will rarely prevail over the immediate interest which one party may find in disregarding the rights of another or the good of the whole. The inference to which we are brought is, that the causes of faction cannot be removed, and that relief is only to be sought in the means of controlling its effects.

If a faction consists of less than a majority, relief is supplied by the republican principle, which enables the majority to defeat its sinister views by regular vote. It may clog the administration, it may convulse the society; but it will be unable to execute and mask its violence under the forms of the Constitution. When a majority is included in a faction, the form of popular government, on the other hand, enables it to sacrifice to its ruling passion or interest both the public good and the rights of other citizens. To secure the public good and private rights against the danger of such a faction, and at the same time to preserve the spirit and the form of popular government, is then the great object to which our inquiries are directed. Let me add that it is the great desideratum by which this form of government can be rescued from the opprobrium under which it has so long labored, and be recommended to the esteem and adoption of mankind.

By what means is this object attainable? Evidently by one of two only. Either the existence of the same passion or interest in a majority at the same time must be prevented, or the majority, having such coexistent passion or interest, must be rendered, by their number and local situation, unable to concert and carry into effect schemes of oppression. If the impulse and the opportunity be suffered to coincide, we well know that neither moral nor religious motives can be relied on as an adequate control. They are not found to be such on the injustice and violence of individuals, and lose their efficacy in proportion to the number combined together, that is, in proportion as their efficacy becomes needful.

From this view of the subject it may be concluded that a pure democracy, by which I mean a society consisting of a small number of citizens, who assemble and administer the government in person, can admit of no cure for the mischiefs of faction. A common passion or interest will, in almost every case, be felt by a majority of the whole; a communication and concert result from the form of government itself; and there is nothing to check the inducements to sacrifice the weaker party or an obnoxious individual. Hence it is that such democracies have ever been spectacles of turbulence and contention; have ever been found incompatible with personal security or the rights of property; and have in general been as short in their lives as they have been violent in their deaths. Theoretic politicians, who have patronized this species of government, have erroneously supposed that by reducing mankind to a perfect equality in their political rights, they would, at the same time, be perfectly equalized and assimilated in their possessions, their opinions, and their passions.

A republic, by which I mean a government in which the scheme of representation takes place, opens a different prospect, and promises the cure for which we are seeking. Let us examine the points in which it varies from pure democracy, and we shall comprehend both the nature of the cure and the efficacy which it must derive from the Union.

The two great points of difference between a democracy and a republic are: first, the delegation of the government, in the latter, to a small number of citizens elected by the rest; secondly, the greater number of citizens, and greater sphere of country, over which the latter may be extended. The effect of the first difference is, on the one hand, to refine and enlarge the public views, by passing them through the medium of a chosen body of citizens, whose wisdom may best discern the true interest of their country, and whose patriotism and love of justice will be least likely to sacrifice it to temporary or partial considerations. Under such a regulation, it may well happen that the public voice, pronounced by the representatives of the people, will be more consonant to the public good than if pronounced by the people themselves, convened for the purpose. On the other hand, the effect may be inverted. Men of factious tempers, of local prejudices, or of sinister designs, may, by intrigue, by corruption, or by other means, first obtain the suffrages, and then betray the interests, of the people. The question resulting is, whether small or extensive republics are more favorable to the election of proper guardians of the public weal; and it is clearly decided in favor of the latter by two obvious considerations.

In the first place, it is to be remarked that, however small the republic may be, the representatives must be raised to a certain number, in order to guard against the cabals of a few; and that, however large it may be, they must be limited to a certain number, in order to guard against the confusion of a multitude. Hence, the number of representatives in the two cases not being in proportion to that of the two constituents, and being proportionally greater in the small republic, it follows that, if the proportion of fit characters be not less in the large than in the small republic, the former will present a greater option, and consequently a greater probability of a fit choice.

In the next place, as each representative will be chosen by a greater number of citizens in the large than in the small republic, it will be more difficult for unworthy candidates to practice with success the vicious arts by which elections are too often carried; and the suffrages of the people being more free, will be more likely to centre in men who possess the most attractive merit and the most diffusive and established characters.

It must be confessed that in this, as in most other cases, there is a mean, on both sides of which inconveniences will be found to lie. By enlarging too much the number of electors, you render the representatives too little acquainted with all their local circumstances and lesser interests; as by reducing it too much, you render him unduly attached to these, and too little fit to comprehend and pursue great and national objects. The federal Constitution forms a happy combination in this respect; the great and aggregate interests being referred to the national, the local and particular to the State legislatures.

The other point of difference is, the greater number of citizens and extent of territory which may be brought within the compass of republican than of democratic government; and it is this circumstance principally which renders factious combinations less to be dreaded in the former than in the latter. The smaller the society, the fewer probably will be the distinct parties and interests composing it; the fewer the distinct parties and interests, the more frequently will a majority be found of the same party; and the smaller the number of individuals composing a majority, and the smaller the compass within which they are placed, the more easily will they concert and execute their plans of oppression. Extend the sphere, and you take in a greater variety of parties and interests; you make it less probable that a majority of the whole will have a common motive to invade the rights of other citizens; or if such a common motive exists, it will be more difficult for all who feel it to discover their own strength, and to act in unison with each other. Besides other impediments, it may be remarked that, where there is a consciousness of unjust or dishonorable purposes, communication is always checked by distrust in proportion to the number whose concurrence is necessary.

Hence, it clearly appears, that the same advantage which a republic has over a democracy, in controlling the effects of faction, is enjoyed by a large over a small republic,—is enjoyed by the Union over the States composing it. Does the advantage consist in the substitution of representatives whose enlightened views and virtuous sentiments render them superior to local prejudices and schemes of injustice? It will not be denied that the representation of the Union will be most likely to possess these requisite endowments. Does it consist in the greater security afforded by a greater variety of parties, against the event of any one party being able to outnumber and oppress the rest? In an equal degree does the increased variety of parties comprised within the Union, increase this security.

Does it, in fine, consist in the greater obstacles opposed to the concert and accomplishment of the secret wishes of an unjust and interested majority? Here, again, the extent of the Union gives it the most palpable advantage.

The influence of factious leaders may kindle a flame within their particular States, but will be unable to spread a general conflagration through the other States. A religious sect may degenerate into a political faction in a part of the Confederacy; but the variety of sects dispersed over the entire face of it must secure the national councils against any danger from that source. A rage for paper money, for an abolition of debts, for an equal division of property, or for any other improper or wicked project, will be less apt to pervade the whole body of the Union than a particular member of it; in the same proportion as such a malady is more likely to taint a particular county or district, than an entire State.

In the extent and proper structure of the Union, therefore, we behold a republican remedy for the diseases most incident to republican government. And according to the degree of pleasure and pride we feel in being republicans, ought to be our zeal in cherishing the spirit and supporting the character of Federalists.

2-3

Federalist No. 51

James Madison
February 8, 1788.

Where Federalist No. 10 *finds solution to tyranny in the way society is organized, No. 51 turns its attention to the Constitution. In a representative democracy citizens must delegate authority to their representatives. But what is to prevent these ambitious politicians from feathering their own nests or usurping power altogether at their constituencies' expense? The solution, according to James Madison, is to be found in "pitting ambition against ambition," just as the solution in No. 10 lay in pitting interest against interest. In this essay, Madison explains how the Constitution's system of checks and balances will accomplish this goal.*

TO WHAT EXPEDIENT, then, shall we finally resort, for maintaining in practice the necessary partition of power among the several departments, as laid down in the Constitution? The only answer that can be given is, that as all these exterior provisions are found to be inadequate, the defect must be supplied, by so contriving the interior structure of the government as that its several constituent parts may, by their mutual relations, be the means of keeping each other in their proper places. Without presuming to undertake a full development of this important idea, I will hazard a few general observations, which may perhaps place it in a clearer light, and enable us to form a more correct judgment of the principles and structure of the government planned by the convention.

In order to lay a due foundation for that separate and distinct exercise of the different powers of government, which to a certain extent is admitted on all hands to be essential to the preservation of liberty, it is evident that each department should have a will of its own; and consequently should be so constituted that the members of each should have as little agency as possible in the appointment of the members of the others. Were this principle rigorously adhered to, it would require that all the appointments for the supreme executive, legislative, and judiciary magistracies should be drawn from the same fountain of authority, the people, through channels having no communication whatever with one another. Perhaps such a plan of constructing the several departments would be less difficult in practice than it may in contemplation appear. Some difficulties, however, and some additional expense would attend the execution of it. Some deviations, therefore, from the principle must be admitted. In the constitution of the judiciary department in particular, it might be inexpedient to insist rigorously on the principle: first, because peculiar qualifications being essential in the members, the primary consideration ought to be to select that mode of choice which best secures these qualifications; secondly, because the permanent tenure by which the appointments are held in that department, must soon destroy all sense of dependence on the authority conferring them.

It is equally evident, that the members of each department should be as little dependent as possible on those of the others, for the emoluments annexed to their offices. Were the executive magistrate, or the judges, not independent of the legislature in this particular, their independence in every other would be merely nominal.

But the great security against a gradual concentration of the several powers in the same department, consists in giving to those who administer each department the necessary constitutional means and personal motives to resist encroachments of the others. The provision for defense must in this, as in all other cases, be made commensurate to the danger of attack. Ambition must be made to counteract ambition. The interest of the man must be connected with the constitutional rights of the place. It may be a reflection on human nature, that such devices should be necessary to control the abuses of government. But what is government itself, but the greatest of all reflections on human nature? If men were angels, no government would be necessary. If angels were to govern men, neither external nor internal controls on government would be necessary. In framing a government which is to be administered by men over men, the great difficulty lies in this: you must first enable the government to control the governed; and in the next place oblige it to control itself. A dependence on the people is, no doubt, the primary control on the government; but experience has taught mankind the necessity of auxiliary precautions.

This policy of supplying, by opposite and rival interests, the defect of better motives, might be traced through the whole system of human affairs, private as well as public. We see it particularly displayed in all the subordinate distributions of power, where the constant aim is to divide and arrange the several offices in such a manner as that each may be a check on the other; that the private interest of every individual may be a sentinel over the public rights. These inventions of prudence cannot be less requisite in the distribution of the supreme powers of the State.

But it is not possible to give to each department an equal power of self-defense. In republican government, the legislative authority necessarily predominates. The remedy for this inconveniency is to divide the legislature into different branches; and to render them, by different modes of election and different principles of action, as little connected with each other as the nature of their common functions and their common dependence on the society will admit. It may even be necessary to guard against dangerous encroachments by still further precautions. As the weight of the legislative authority requires that it should be thus divided, the weakness of the executive may require, on the other hand, that it should be fortified. An absolute negative on the legislature appears, at first view, to be the natural defense with which the executive magistrate should be armed. But perhaps it would be neither altogether safe nor alone sufficient. On ordinary occasions it might not be exerted with the requisite firmness, and on extraordinary occasions it might be perfidiously abused. May not this defect of an absolute negative be supplied by some qualified connection between this weaker department and the weaker branch of the stronger department, by which the latter may be led to support the constitutional rights of the former, without being too much detached from the rights of its own department? . . .

2-4

Showdown: The Election of 1800

James MacGregor Burns

Constitutions are contracts. For each officeholder, they identify a network of rights and obligations. And they specify the terms that entitle a given politician to occupy an office. Like all contracts, constitutions can be broken if one "party" reneges on its obligations when it finds its interest better served by doing so. Therefore one of the most critical tests of a constitution arises the first time those who control the government must surrender power to their opponents. In this sense, the election of 1800 was a critical event, a kind of behavioral ratification of the U.S. Constitution. The following excerpt from James MacGregor Burns's broader investigation into the Constitution's early development conveys the palpable tension felt by all participants to the first serious challenge to the governing Federalist political party. When to the surprise of nearly everyone the Republicans won control of the presidency and both houses of Congress, a true constitutional crisis was at hand. Federalist politicians worried that if the "radical" Republicans were allowed to assume control, they would import the French Revolution to America. Republican politicians worried that the Federalists would try some subterfuge to change the outcome of the election or simply refuse to surrender power. Many people feared that "ballots would give way to bullets." That the Federalists, despite their deep concerns, surrendered control of government, just as the Constitution prescribed, reinforced future generations' confidence that the Constitution was a contract opposing politicians would live by.

ON THE EVE of the last year of the century, American leaders were intent more on political prospects than moral. The looming national elections were tending to focus their minds. The decisive figure in this election would be Thomas Jefferson. But Jefferson hardly appeared decisive at the time. His political course during the late 1790s had mirrored the political uncertainties and party gropings of those years. Tentatively he looked for some kind of North-South combination.

"If a prospect could be once opened upon us of the penetration of truth into the eastern States; if the people there, who are unquestionably republicans, could discover that they have been duped into the support of measures calculated to

Source: James MacGregor Burns, *The Vineyard of Liberty* (New York: Vintage Books, 1983), 144–155.

sap the very foundations of republicanism, we might still hope for salvation," Jefferson had written Aaron Burr some weeks after Adams' inauguration in 1797. ". . . But will that region ever awake to the true state of things? Can the middle, Southern and Western States hold on till they awake?" He asked Burr for a "comfortable solution" to these "painful questions."

Immensely flattered, Burr requested an early meeting with the Vice-President in Philadelphia. Jefferson now became more active as party leader, working closely with Madison in Virginia and with Gallatin in the House of Representatives. Following the election setbacks to Republicans in 1798, he redoubled his efforts especially as a party propagandist. He asked every man to "lay his purpose & his pen" to the cause; coaxed local Republican leaders into writing pamphlets and letters to editors; stressed the issues of peace, liberty, and states' rights; turned his office into a kind of clearinghouse for Republican propaganda. "The engine is the press," he told Madison.

Hundreds of other men too were busy with politics, but like Jefferson earlier, in an atmosphere of uncertainty and suspense. Intellectual leaders—clergymen, editors, and others—were still preaching against the whole idea of an open, clear-cut party and election battle. Party formations were still primitive in many areas. Even fiercer than the conflict between Federalists and Republicans was the feuding between factions within the parties—especially between the Adams following and the Hamilton "cabal." Certain high Federalists were hinting at the need for armed repression of the opposition, particularly in the event of war, and Jefferson and Madison were openly pushing the Kentucky and Virginia resolutions—a strategy of nullification and even secession still in flat contradiction to the idea of two-party opposition and rotation in power. All these factors enhanced the most pressing question of all—could the American republic, could any republic, survive a decisive challenge by the "outs" to the "ins"? Or would ballots give way to bullets?

Not intellectual theorizing but heated issues, fierce political ambitions, and the practical need to win a scheduled national election compelled the political testing of 1800.

In Philadelphia, John Adams contemplated the coming test with apprehension and anger. Political and personal affairs had gone badly for him since the euphoria of '98. Abigail was ill a good part of the time, and his beloved son Charles, a bankrupt and an alcoholic, was dying in New York. As proud, captious, sensitive, and sermonizing as ever, he hated much of the day-to-day business of the presidency, and he longed to take sanctuary in Quincy; but he desperately wanted to win in 1800, to confound his enemies, to complete his work. He tried to lend some direction and unity to the Federalists, but he was handicapped by his concept of leadership as a solitary search for the morally correct course, regardless of day-to-day pressures from factions and interests. He sensed, probably correctly, that his party should take a more centrist course to win in 1800. But his own moderate positions on foreign and domestic policy left him isolated between high Federalists and moderate Republicans.

The Fries "rebellion" epitomized his difficulty. A direct federal tax on land and houses, enacted by Congress in 1798, touched off the next winter an uprising by several hundred Pennsylvanians—and especially by the women, who poured scalding water on assessors who came to measure their windows. John Fries, a traveling auctioneer, led a band of men to Bethlehem, where they forced the release of others jailed for resisting the tax. The President promptly labeled the act treasonable and ordered Fries and his band arrested. Unlucky enough to be tried before Justice Samuel Chase, the auctioneer was convicted of treason and, amid great hubbub, sentenced to die. Later the President, without consulting his Cabinet, pardoned Fries—only to arouse the fury of high Federalists. Not the least of these was Alexander Hamilton, who, his biographer says, would have preferred to load the gibbets of Pennsylvania with Friesians and viewed the pardon as one more example of Adams' petulant indecisiveness.

By the spring of 1800 Adams' wrath against the Hamiltonians in his Cabinet—especially Pickering and McHenry—was about to burst out of control. Politically the President faced a dilemma: he wished to lead the Federalists toward the center of the political spectrum, in order to head off any Republican effort to preempt the same ground, but he feared to alienate the high Federalists and disrupt his party when unity was desperately needed. His uncertainty and frustration only exacerbated his anger. One day, as he was talking with McHenry about routine matters, his anger boiled over. He accused the frightened McHenry to his face of being subservient to Hamilton—a man, he went on, who was the "greatest intriguant in the world—a man devoid of every moral principle—a bastard and as much a foreigner as Gallatin." Adams accepted McHenry's resignation on the spot. A few days later he demanded that Pickering quit. When the Secretary of State refused, Adams summarily sacked him. Oddly, he did not fire Secretary of the Treasury Wolcott, who was Hamilton's main conduit to the high Federalists in Adams' administration.

Thomas Jefferson, watching these events from his vice-presidential perch, had the advantage of being close to the government, if not inside it, with little of the burden of power and none of the responsibility. By early 1800 he was emerging clearly as the national leader of the Republicans. Gone were the doubts and vacillations of earlier days. He was eager to take on the "feds," as he called them, to vanquish their whole philosophy and practice of government, to establish his party and himself in control of Congress and the presidency. He consciously assumed leadership of his party. Unable to campaign across the country—

stumping was contrary to both his own nature and the custom of the day—he cast political lines into key areas through letters and friends.

His meeting with Burr paid off handsomely. The dapper little New Yorker set to work uniting New York Republicans against the divided Federalists. Then he organized his lieutenants tightly on a ward-by-ward basis; had the voters' names card-indexed, along with their political background, attitudes, and need for transportation on election day; set up committees for house-to-house canvassing for funds; pressed more affluent Republicans for bigger donations; organized rallies; converted Tammany into a campaign organization; debated Hamilton publicly; and spent ten hours straight at the polls on the last day of the three-day state election. He won a resounding victory in the election of state assemblymen—and got full credit for it from Republican leaders in Philadelphia.

The New York victory buoyed Jefferson's hopes. He recognized the critical role of the central states, and how they hung together. "If the *city* election of N York is in favor of the Republican ticket, the issue will be republican," he had instructed Madison; "if the federal ticket for the city of N York prevails, the probabilities will be in favor of a federal issue, because it would then require a republican vote both from Jersey and Pennsylva to preponderate against New York, on which we could not count with any confidence." What Jefferson called the "Political arithmetic" looked so good after the New York victory that he shrugged off the Federalist "lies" about him. He would not try to answer them, "for while I should be engaged with one, they would publich twenty new ones." He had confidence in the voters' common sense. "Thirty years of public life have enabled most of those who read newspapers to judge of one for themselves."

Doubtless Jefferson was too optimistic. The Federalists in 1800 were still a formidable party. While they were losing some of the vigorous younger men to the Republicans, they were still the party of Washington and Adams and Jay and Pinckney and Hamilton, and the vehicle of a younger generation represented by men like John Marshall and Fisher Ames. The Federalists had never been a purely mercantile or urban party; their strength lay also in rural areas and along the rivers and other avenues of commerce into the hinterland, such as the Connecticut Valley. Adams as President had immense national prestige, if not always popularity, and his "move toward the middle" broadened the party's appeal. Stung by losses in New York, the Federalists rallied their forces in other states. In New Jersey, where women were not expressly barred from voting, they "marched their wives, daughters, and other qualified 'females' to the polls," in one historian's words, and won the state's seven electoral votes.

Not only was the parties' popular support crucial, but also the manner in which that support was translated into presidential electoral votes. The selection of presidential electors was not designed for accurate translation. For one thing, state legislatures set selection of electors on a statewide basis or on a district basis, or took on the task themselves, according to a guess by the party dominating the legislature as to which system would help that party's candidate. More and more legislatures moved to choose electors themselves, rather than by popular vote. Electors were supposed to exercise some independent judgment. But more important in 1800, the electoral system was still so novel as to be open to flagrant rigging, such as changing the method of choosing electors. Broaching to John Jay such a scheme for New York, Hamilton said that "in times like these in which we live, it will not do to be over-scrupulous." It was permissible to take such a step to "prevent an atheist in religion, and a fanatic in politics, from getting possession of the helm of state." Jay was not impressed.

And so the presidential campaign proceeded, in its noisy, slightly manipulated, but nonviolent way. During the summer candidates for state legislatures toured the districts and talked to crowds where they could find them—"even at a horse race—a cock fight—or a Methodist quarterly meeting." . . .

. . . By fall the presidential race was reaching a climax. Slander on both sides was uncontained—and the politicos of the day were masters at it. Adams was called a would-be dictator and a "monocrat" who would make the country a monarchy and his children successors to the throne. Even Adams could smile at a story that he had sent a United States frigate to England to procure mistresses for himself. The Federalists gave even better than they got. Jefferson was an infidel, a "howling" atheist, an "intellectual voluptuary" who would "destroy religion, introduce immorality, and loosen all the bonds of society" at home. The Jacobin leader was the real debauchee, Federalists whispered, having sired mulatto children at Monticello. Somehow the voters groped their way through the invective to a sense of the genuine issues. They faced a real choice. Jefferson was still silent as a candidate, but he had repeatedly made clear his stands for a frugal government, a small Navy and Army, states' rights, the Bill of Rights liberties, a small diplomatic establishment. The Federalists had made their positions clear through legislation they had passed, or tried to pass. The election would be a showdown between men, platforms, and ideologies.

Slowly the returns came in as electors met and voted in their states. The Federalists had a moment of euphoria as Adams picked up some unexpected support. By late November the two parties were running neck and neck. For a time Federalist hopes were pinned on South Carolina, on whether Charles Cotesworth Pinckney, Adams' running mate, could deliver that state's eight electoral votes. But Pinckney could not even deliver all the Pinckneys, least of all Charles Pinckney, leader of the Republican branch of the family, who through generous offers of jobs under a Republican administration, managed to persuade enough members of the state legislature to choose a pro-Jefferson slate of electors.

By late December the total vote was in. It was Jefferson over Adams, 73 to 65. But it was also Burr over Pinckney, 73 to 64, with one of Pinckney's votes diverted to John Jay.

The Republicans had won, but Jefferson had not been elected. Burr had an equal constitutional claim to the presidency. Something new and extraordinary had happened in American politics: the parties had disciplined their ranks enough to produce the same total (73) for the two Republican running mates and an almost equal tally (65 to 64) for the two Federalists. In order to prevent votes from being thrown away, each party caucus had pledged equal support to both candidates on the ticket. To do this was to run the risk that, under the Constitution, a presidential tie vote would go to the House of Representatives for decision. Both parties knowingly ran that risk. But the politics of the lower chamber would be quite different from the politics of the electoral groups meeting separately in the state capitols. The presidential race would now be focused in the nation's capitol; it would take place in a lame-duck, Federalist-dominated House of Representatives; and each state delegation in the House, whether large or small, would have a single vote.

The remarkable result was that the Federalists had lost the presidency, but in the Congress they had the power to throw the election to either Jefferson or Burr, or possibly stall indefinitely. What would they do with this exquisite consolation prize? Most of the congressional Federalists feared Jefferson the ideologue more than they hated Burr the opportunist. "They consider Burr as actuated by ordinary ambition, Jefferson by that & the pride of the Jacobinic philosophy," high Federalist George Cabot wrote Hamilton. "The former may be satisfied by power & property, the latter must see the roots of our Society pulled up & a new course of cultivation substituted." If Burr was ambitious, slippery, and even venal, well, perhaps the Federalists could make use of such qualities; "they loved Burr for his vices," John Miller has noted. Other Federalists disagreed. No matter how much they hated Jefferson, they were not going to put into the presidency a man they considered a knave and a blackguard.

The competing forces were so counterpoised that the House of Representatives went through thirty-five ballotings, all resulting in a vote of eight states for Jefferson, six for Burr, and two divided. The stalemate lasted as long as the representatives stuck to their convictions, or biases; it ended when three men—Jefferson, Burr, and Hamilton—acted out of character. Jefferson, no longer the relaxed and diffident philosopher, responded to the looming crisis with anger, but also with decisiveness and determination. He began to act like the President-elect as soon as the unofficial returns were in; thus he wrote Robert R. Livingston to ask him to serve as Secretary of the Navy—the New Yorker declined—and incidentally to discuss the bones of a mammoth that had been found near New

York. He wrote Burr, congratulating him on the election results but implying ever so delicately that Jefferson expected him to serve as Vice-President. He wrote Burr again to warn that the "enemy" would try to "sow tares between us," and branding as a forgery a letter purportedly by Jefferson that criticized Burr. At the same time Jefferson subtly let out word that, while he would not make deals—he knew that Burr could outdeal him—he could be counted on to act moderately as President, to be "liberal and accommodating."

Hamilton had no time for subtleties. His clear hierarchy of animosities—he resented Adams, hated Jefferson, and despised Burr—helped him to decide early that if the choice lay between Jefferson and Burr, he would thwart the latter. While Jefferson was only a "contemptible hypocrite," crafty, unscrupulous, and dishonest, Hamilton told his Federalist friends, Burr was a "most unfit and dangerous man," a Jacobin who would overthrow the fiscal system, a rogue who would "employ the rogues of all parties to overrule the good men of all parties," and above all a Catiline who would take over the government as Napoleon had just done in France. Hamilton had little influence with the Federalist "high-flyers" (as Jefferson called them) in Congress, but his principled view that his party must not bargain with the likes of Aaron Burr carried weight with national Federalist leaders such as John Jay.

Burr played a waiting game. He assured Jefferson and his friends so convincingly that he would not deal with the enemy and balk the real will of the people that Jefferson confided to his daughter: "The Federalists were confident, at first, they could debauch Col. B from his good faith by offering him their vote to be President," but his "conduct has been honorable and decisive, and greatly embarrasses them." Burr's behavior was curious all the way through. He evidently did spurn a deal with the Federalists, but he did not take the honorable course of simply withdrawing; he never made perfectly clear that he would not serve as President if elected; he apparently allowed some of his friends to put out feelers on his behalf, and his best strategy in any event would have been inaction, since the Federalist bloc in Congress was cemented to his cause as a result of their hatred and fear of Jefferson. Still, the long-drawn-out constitutional crisis afforded Burr countless opportunities to undercut Jefferson and perhaps to win the presidency—but he remained in Albany, attending to his law practice.

Twelve weeks passed as Jefferson remained resolute, Hamilton busy, Burr inactive, and the election stalemated. There is no record of all that happened in the last confused, crisis-ridden days; in particular we know little of the role of less visible but influential politicians. John Marshall evidently angled for his own selection as President should the deadlock persist. But this much seems clear: during the final weeks the nation veered toward disunion and civil war, as Republicans threatened to bring in state militias from Pennsylvania and Virginia if the

Federalists further thwarted the "popular will." The crisis revealed not merely two parties in combat but four party factions: Jeffersonians, Burrites, high Federalists mainly centered in Congress, and a group of moderate Federalists led on this occasion by Hamilton and nurtured in the nationalist, moderate leadership of George Washington.

As March 4, 1801, approached and tension mounted two developments staved off a constitutional and perhaps military debacle. Jefferson, all the while asserting that he would not "receive the government" on capitulation, that he would not go into it "with my hands tied," told a Federalist intermediary that the public credit would be safe, the Navy increased, and lesser federal jobholders left in their places. And ingenious mediators worked out an artifice that enabled Jefferson to be elected President without a single Federalist voting for him. A number of Federalists cast blank ballots, and a single congressman from Vermont now cast his state's vote for Jefferson. That congressman was "Spitting Matt" Lyon.

The crisis was over—Thomas Jefferson was elected President of the United States. Much would be made in later years of this unprecedented example of a peaceful shift from one party to another, of the avoidance of violence and bloodshed, of the example Americans had set for other constitutional republics. But it had been a close-run thing. If Jefferson had not been firm in his ambition, Hamilton not principled in his hatred, Burr not inactive; if moderates in both parties had not been in control, or if fewer politicians had respected the Constitution, the American republic probably would have lived a briefer life than many republics before and since. Perhaps most decisive in the whole episode was the willingness of state and local leaders, Federalist and Republican, to wait for the crisis to be resolved rather than break into local magazines, gather arms, and march on the Capitol. Once again "followers" had acted as leaders.

The suspense of the election quickly changed into excitement over the coming of a new President, a new party, a new government, a new program. Later Jefferson would argue that the "Revolution of 1800 was as real a revolution in the principles of our government as that of 1776 was in its form." . . .

Chapter 3

Federalism

3-1

Federalism as an Ideal Political Order and an Objective for Constitutional Reform

James M. Buchanan

In this essay Nobel laureate economist James M. Buchanan makes a case for federalism. Buchanan, a market-oriented economist, arrives at a solution to the threat of concentrated power nearly opposite to that proposed by Madison. Whereas Madison thought that the nation would be safe from such a threat if power were reposed in an inherently factious and weak national majority, Buchanan prefers a more decentralized approach. He would give states greater authority and let market mechanisms regulate them—as in the residence decisions of a mobile citizenry, the subject of the excerpt below.

MY AIM HERE is to discuss federalism, as a central element in an inclusive political order, in two, quite different, but ultimately related, conceptual perspectives. First, I examine federalism as an ideal type, as a stylized component of a constitutional structure of governance that might be put in place ab initio, as emergent from agreement among citizens of a particular community before that community, as such, has experienced its own history. Second, the discussion shifts dramatically toward reality, and the critical importance of defining the historically

Source: James Buchanan, "Federalism as an Ideal Political Order and an Objective for Constitutional Reform," *Publius: The Journal of Federalism* 25 (spring 1995): 19–27.

determined status quo is recognized as a necessary first step toward reform that may be guided by some appreciation of the federalist ideal.

Ideal Theory

Federalism as an Analogue to the Market

An elementary understanding and appreciation of political federalism is facilitated by a comparable understanding and appreciation of the political function of an economy organized on market principles. Quite apart from its ability to produce and distribute a highly valued bundle of "goods," relative to alternative regimes, a market economy serves a critically important political role. To the extent that allocative and distributive choices can be relegated to the workings of markets, the necessity for any politicization of such choices is eliminated.

But why should the politicization of choices be of normative concern? Under the standard assumptions that dominated analysis before the public choice revolution, politics is modeled as the activity of a benevolently despotic and monolithic authority that seeks always and everywhere to promote "the public interest," which is presumed to exist independently of revealed evaluations and which is amenable to discovery or revelation. If this romantic image of politics is discarded and replaced by the empirical reality of politics, any increase in the relative size of the politicized sector of an economy must carry with it an increase in the potential for exploitation.[1] The well-being of citizens becomes vulnerable to the activities of politics, as described in the behavior of other citizens as members of majoritarian coalitions, as elected politicians, and as appointed bureaucrats.

This argument must be supplemented by an understanding of why and how the market, as the alternative to political process, does not also expose the citizen-participant to comparable exploitation. The categorical difference between market and political interaction lies in the continuing presence of an effective exit option in market relationships and in its absence in politics. To the extent that the individual participant in market exchange has available effective alternatives that may be chosen at relatively low cost, any exchange is necessarily voluntary. In its stylized form, the market involves no coercion, no extraction of value from any participant without consent. In dramatic contrast, politics is inherently coercive, independently of the effective decision rules that may be operative.

The potential for the exercise of individual liberty is directly related to the relative size of the market sector in an economy. A market organization does not, however, emerge spontaneously from some imagined state of nature. A market economy must, in one sense, be "laid on" through the design, construction, and implementation of a political-legal framework (i.e., an inclusive constitution) that protects property and enforces voluntary contracts. As Adam Smith emphasized, the market works well only if these parameters, these "laws and institutions," are in place.[2]

Enforceable constitutional restrictions may constrain the domain of politics to some extent, but these restrictions may not offer sufficient protection against the exploitation of citizens through the agencies of governance. That is to say, even if the market economy is allowed to carry out its allocational-distributional role over a significant relative share of the political economy, the remaining domain of actions open to politicization may leave the citizen, both in person and property, vulnerable to the expropriation of value that necessarily accompanies political coercion.

How might the potential for exploitation be reduced or minimized? How might the political sector, in itself, be constitutionally designed so as to offer the citizen more protection?

The principle of federalism emerges directly from the market analogy. . . . Under a federalized political structure, persons, singly and / or in groups, would be guaranteed the liberties of trade, investment, and migration across the inclusive area of the economy. Analogously to the market, persons retain an exit option; at relatively low cost, at least some persons can shift among the separate political jurisdictions. Again analogously to the market, the separate . . . state governments would be forced to compete, one with another, in their offers of publicly provided services. The federalized structure, through the forces of interstate competition, effectively limits the power of the separate political units to extract surplus value from the citizenry.

Principles of Competitive Federalism

The operating principles of a genuinely competitive federalism can be summarized readily.[3] As noted, the central or federal government would be constitutionally restricted in its domain of action, severely so. Within its assigned sphere, however, the central government would be strong, sufficiently so to allow it to enforce economic freedom or openness over the whole of the territory. The separate states would be prevented, by federal authority, from placing barriers on the free flow of resources and goods across their borders.

The constitutional limits on the domain of the central or federal government would not be self-enforcing, and competition could not be made operative in a manner precisely comparable to that which might restrict economic exploitation by the separate states. If the federal (central) government, for any reason, should move beyond its constitutionally dictated mandate of authority, what protection might be granted—to citizens individually or to the separate states—against the extension of federal power?

The exit option is again suggested, although this option necessarily takes on a different form. The separate states, individually or in groups, must be constitutionally empowered to secede from the federalized political structure, that is, to form new units of political authority outside of and beyond the reach of the existing federal government. Secession, or the threat thereof, represents the only means through which the ultimate powers of the central government might be held in check. Absent the secession prospect, the federal government may, by overstepping its constitutionally assigned limits, extract surplus value from the citizenry almost at will, because there would exist no effective means of escape.[4]

With an operative secession threat on the part of the separate states, the federal or central government could be held roughly to its assigned constitutional limits, while the separate states could be left to compete among themselves in their capacities to meet the demands of citizens for collectively provided services. . . .

We should predict, of course, that the separate states of a federal system would be compelled by the forces of competition to offer tolerably "efficient" mixes of publicly provided goods and services, and, to the extent that citizens in the different states exhibit roughly similar preferences, the actual budgetary mixes would not be predicted to diverge significantly, one from the other. However, the point to be emphasized here (and which seems to have been missed in so much of the discussion about the potential European federalism) is that any such standardization or regularization as might occur, would itself be an emergent property of competitive federalism rather than a property that might be imposed either by constitutional mandate or by central government authority.

The Path Dependency of Constitutional Reform

From Here to There: A Schemata

The essential principle for meaningful discourse about constitutional-institutional reform (or, indeed, about any change) is the recognition that reform involves movement from some "here" toward some "there." The evaluative comparison of alternative sets of rules and alternative regimes of political order, as discussed above in the first section, aims exclusively at defining the "there," the idealized objective toward which any change must be turned. But the direction for effective reform also requires a definition of the "here." Any reform, constitutional or otherwise, commences from some "here and now," some status quo that is the existential reality. History matters, and the historical experience of a political community is beyond any prospect of change; the constitutional-institutional record can neither be ignored nor rewritten. The question for reform is, then: "How do we get there from here?"

These prefatory remarks are necessary before any consideration of federalism in discussion of practical reform. The abstracted ideal—a strong but severely limited central authority with the capacity and the will to enforce free trade over the inclusive territory, along with several separate "states," each one of which stands in a competitive relationship with all other such units—of this ideal federal order may be well-defined and agreed upon as an objective for change. However, until and unless the "here," the starting point, is identified, not even the direction of change can be known.

A simple illustration may be helpful. Suppose that you and I agree that we want to be in Washington, D.C. But, suppose that you are in New York and I am in Atlanta. We must proceed in different directions if we expect to get to the shared or common objective.

Constitutional reform aimed toward an effective competitive federalism may reduce or expand the authority of the central government relative to that of the separate state governments. . . . If the status quo is described as a centralized and unitary political authority, reform must embody devolution, a shift of genuine political power from the center to the separate states. On the other hand, if the status quo is described by a set of autonomous political units that may perhaps be geographically contiguous but which act potentially in independence one from another, reform must involve a centralization of authority, a shift of genuine power to the central government from the separate states.

Figure 1 offers an illustrative schemata. Consider a well-defined territory that may be organized politically at any point along the abstracted unidimensional spectrum that measures the extent to which political authority is centralized. At the extreme left of this spectrum, the territory is divided among several fully autonomous political units, each one of which possesses total "sovereignty," and among which any interaction, either by individuals or by political units, must be subjected to specific contractual negotiation and agreement. At the extreme right of this spectrum, the whole of the territory is organized as an inclusive political community, with this authority centralized in a single governmental unit. Individuals and groups may interact, but any such interaction must take place within the uniform limits laid down by the monolithic authority.

An effective federal structure may be located somewhere near the middle of the spectrum, between the regime of fully autonomous localized units on the one hand and the regime of fully centralized authority on the other. This simple illustration makes it easy to see that constitutional reform that is aimed toward the competitive federal structure must be characterized by some increase in centralization, if the starting point is on the left, and by some decrease in centralization, if the starting point is on the right.

The illustration prompts efforts to locate differing regimes at differing places in their own separate histories on the unidimensional scalar. In 1787, James

Figure 1. A Constitutional Reform Schemata

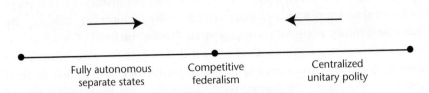

Fully autonomous   Competitive   Centralized
separate states   federalism   unitary polity

Madison, who had observed the several former British colonies that had won their independence and organized themselves as a confederation, located the status quo somewhere to the left of the middle of the spectrum, and he sought to secure an effective federalism by establishing a stronger central authority, to which some additional powers should be granted. Reform involved a reduction in the political autonomy of the separate units. In the early post–World War II decades, the leaders of Europe, who had observed the terrible nationalistic wars, located their status quo analogously to Madison. They sought reform in the direction of a federalized structure—reform that necessarily involved some establishment of central authority, with some granting of power independently of that historically claimed by the separate nation-states.

By comparison and contrast, consider the United States in 1995, the history of which is surely described as an overshooting of Madison's dreams for the ideal political order. Over the course of two centuries, and especially after the demise of any secession option, as resultant from the great Civil War of the 1860s, the U.S. political order came to be increasingly centralized. The status quo in 1995 lies clearly to the right of the spectrum, and any reform toward a federalist ideal must involve some devolution of central government authority and some increase in the effective independent power of the several states. . . .

Constitutional reform in many countries, as well as the United States, would presumably involve devolution of authority from the central government to the separate states.

Constitutional Strategy and the Federalist Ideal

The simple construction of Figure 1 is also helpful in suggesting that it may be difficult to achieve the ideal constitutional structure described as competitive federalism. Whether motivated by direct economic interest, by some failure to understand basic economic and political theory, or by fundamental conservative instincts, specific political coalitions will emerge to oppose any shift from the status quo toward a federal structure, no matter what the starting point. If, for example, the status quo is described by a regime of fully autonomous units (the nation-states of Europe after World War II), political groups within each of these units will object to any sacrifice of national sovereignty that might be required by a shift toward federalism. . . .

Similar comments may be made about the debates mounted from the opposing direction. If a unitary centralized authority describes the status quo ante, its supporters may attempt to and may succeed in conveying the potential for damage through constitutional collapse into a regime of autonomous units, vulnerable to economic and political warfare. The middle way offered by devolution to a competitive federalism may, in this case, find few adherents.[5] . . .

As the construction in Figure 1 also suggests, however, the fact that the federalist structure is, indeed, "in the middle," at least in the highly stylized sense discussed here, may carry prospects for evolutionary emergence in the conflicts between centralizing and decentralizing pressures. Contrary to the poetic pessimism of William Butler Yeats, the "centre" may hold, if once attained, not because of any intensity of conviction, but rather due to the location of the balance of forces.[6]

Federalism and Increasing Economic Interdependence

In the preceding discussion, I have presumed that the economic benefits of a large economic nexus, defined both in territory and membership, extend at least to and beyond the limits of the political community that may be constitutionally organized anywhere along the spectrum in Figure 1, from a regime of fully autonomous political units to one of centralized political authority. Recall that Adam Smith emphasized that economic prosperity and growth find their origins in the division (specialization) of labor and that this division, in turn, depends on the extent of the market. Smith placed no limits on the scope for applying this principle. But we know that the economic world of 1995 is dramatically different from that of 1775. Technological development has facilitated a continuing transformation of local to regional to national to international interactions among economic units. Consistently with Smith's insights, economic growth has been more rapid where and when political intrusions have not emerged to prevent entrepreneurs from seizing the advantages offered by the developing technology.

Before the technological revolution in information processing and communication, however, a revolution that has occurred in this half-century, politically motivated efforts to "improve" on the workings of market processes seemed almost a part of institutional reality. In this setting, it seemed to remain of critical economic importance to restrict the intrusiveness of politics, quite apart from the complementary effects on individual liberties. Political federalism, to the extent that its central features were at all descriptive of constitutional history, did serve to facilitate economic growth.

The modern technological revolution in information processing and communications may have transformed, at least to some degree, the setting within which politically motivated obstructions may impact on market forces. This technology may, in itself, have made it more difficult for politicians and governments, at any and all levels, to check or to limit the ubiquitous pressures of economic interdependence.[7] When values can be transferred worldwide at the speed of light and when events everywhere are instantly visible on CNN, there are elements of competitive federalism in play, almost regardless of the particular constitutional regimes in existence.

Finally, the relationship between federalism, as an organizing principle for political structure, and the freedom of trade across political boundaries must be noted. An inclusive political territory, say, the United States or Western Europe, necessarily places limits on its own ability to interfere politically with its own internal market structure to the extent that this structure is, itself, opened up to the free workings of international trade, including the movement of capital. On the other hand, to the extent that the internal market is protected against the forces of international competition, other means, including federalism, become more essential to preserve liberty and to guarantee economic growth.

Conclusion

The United States offers an illustrative example. The United States prospered mightily in the nineteenth century, despite the wall of protectionism that sheltered its internal markets. It did so because political authority, generally, was held in check by a constitutional structure that did contain basic elements of competitive federalism. By comparison, the United States, in this last decade of the twentieth century, is more open to international market forces, but its own constitutional structure has come to be transformed into one approaching a centralized unitary authority.

Devolution toward a competitive federal structure becomes less necessary to the extent that markets are open to external opportunities. However, until and unless effective constitutional guarantees against political measures to choke off external trading relationships are put in place, the more permanent constitutional reform aimed at restoring political authority to the separate states offers a firmer basis for future economic growth along with individual liberty. . . .

NOTES

1. James M. Buchanan, "Politics without Romance: A Sketch of Positive Public Choice Theory and Its Normative Implications," Inaugural Lecture, Institute for Advanced Studies, Vienna, Austria, *IHS Journal, Zeitschrift des Instituts für Höhere Studien* 3 (1979): B1–B11.

2. Adam Smith, *The Wealth of Nations* (1776; Modern Library ed.; New York: Random House, 1937).

3. See Geoffrey Brennan and James M. Buchanan, *The Power to Tax: Analytical Foundations of a Fiscal Constitution* (New York: Cambridge University Press, 1980), pp. 168–186, for more comprehensive treatment.

4. For formal analysis of secession, see James M. Buchanan and Roger Faith, "Secession and the Limits of Taxation: Towards a Theory of Internal Exit," *American Economic Review* 5 (December 1987): 1023–1031; for a more general discussion, see Allen Buchanan, *Secession: The Morality of Political Divorce from Fort Sumter to Lithuania and Quebec* (Boulder, Colo.: Westview, 1991).

5. The theory of agenda-setting in public choice offers analogies. If the agenda can be manipulated in such fashion that the alternatives for choice effectively "bracket" the ideally preferred position, voters are confronted with the selection of one or the other of the extreme alternatives, both of which may be dominated by the preferred option. See Thomas Romer and Howard Rosenthal, "Political Resource Allocation, Controlled Agendas, and the Status Quo," *Public Choice* 33 (Winter 1978): 27–43.

6. William Butler Yeats, "The Second Coming," *The Collected Works of W. B. Yeats*, vol. 1, *The Poems*, Ed. Richard J. Finneran (New York: Macmillan, 1989), p. 187.

7. Richard McKenzie and Dwight Lee, *Quicksilver Capital: How the Rapid Movement of Wealth Has Changed the World* (New York: Free Press, 1991).

Federalism: Battles on the Front Lines of Public Policy

Donald F. Kettl

The phrase "separation of powers" refers to the division of authority across the institutions of the national government; "federalism" refers to the vertical division of authority and responsibility between Washington and the states. The Constitution keeps state authority separate and distinct, but its Framers did not build walls separating these governments into exclusive domains of policy. Instead American federalism, like separation of powers, is a system of shared powers. During the twentieth century, power and responsibility have undoubtedly shifted to the national (or, as it is commonly called, "federal") government. Yet the states remain key participants, meaning that successful programs involve continuous coordination across these levels of government. Mostly the arrangement works reasonably well. But as Hurricane Katrina taught us in 2005, America's federalism is anything but a finely tuned machine. In the following essay, Donald Kettl, one of the nation's authorities on the subject, finds the difficult lessons this disaster taught the public and policymakers.

IN THE EYES of many sad observers, Hurricane Katrina's assault on the Gulf Coast over Labor Day weekend 2005 was not only a stunning reminder of just how far the nation still must go to resolve deep racial and class divisions in American society. It also marked a collapse—both political and administrative—of American federalism. Thousands of New Orleans residents found themselves marooned at the tattered Superdome. CNN got its cameras there, but neither the city, the state, nor the federal government could seem to get food, water, or medicine to the trapped residents. The military and an armada of buses finally arrived to take the trapped refugees to safety, but not before people died in the chaos.

Standing in front of the St. Louis Cathedral in New Orleans just days after the Superdome evacuation, President Bush applauded the work of government officials. Nevertheless, he admitted, "the system, at every level of government, was not well coordinated and was overwhelmed in the first few days." He stunned

Source: This piece is an original essay commissioned for this volume. Some of the material in this reading first appeared in the author's "Potomac Chronicle" column, which is featured every other month in *Governing* magazine, a publication for state and local governments.

state and local officials with what came next. "It is now clear," he said, "that a challenge on this scale requires greater federal authority and a broader role for the armed forces—the institution of our government most capable of massive logistical operations on a moment's notice." [1] The glaring headlines and searing pictures had painted a portrait of the failure of federalism. The initial chaos quickly gave way to finger-pointing, with federal officials saying they were awaiting clear requests, submitted in the proper form, from state and local officials. Louisiana Governor Kathleen Blanco, in her first phone call to the president, asked for "all federal firepower." She continued, "I meant everything. Just send it. Give me planes, give me boats. . . ." [2]

New Orleans Mayor Ray Nagin sent out his own plea: "I need everything." He criticized federal officials and said, "They're thinking small, man. And this is a major, major, major deal. And I can't emphasize it enough, man. This is crazy." When top federal officials told them help was on the way, Nagin countered, "They're not here." Frustrated, he added, "Now get off your asses and do something, and let's fix the biggest goddamn crisis in the history of this country." [3] But help was painfully slow in coming.

Challenging Federalism

Mayor Nagin was stuck for four days in the battered Hyatt Hotel, with no air conditioning in the sweltering, late summer heat. The mayor and his staff found their temporary headquarters in shambles. Not only had the storm isolated them, but it spun off a tornado that ripped away part of the hotel. For the first two days, Nagin had no communication with the outside world except through press releases to CNN reporters. One of his technology aides then remembered that he had established an Internet phone account. The mayor's technology aides eventually found a working Internet connection in one of the hotel's conference rooms and managed to get eight lines hooked up just in time to get a call from President Bush in *Air Force One*. Conditions were brutal. When a gang tried to break into the hotel and steal their small supply of food, the mayor and his small party had to evacuate from the fourth to the 27th floor. The phones they were using worked only if the caller leaned over the balcony into the indoor atrium. "This was when the last parts of the government were about to come undone," explained Greg Meffert, New Orleans's chief technology officer. "It felt like the Alamo—we were surrounded and had only short bursts of communication." [4]

It was little wonder that the president considered a larger role for the military in disaster response. Katrina literally and figuratively swamped the ability of state and local governments to respond. But although the nation's governors saw an important federal role, they rejected the idea of federal control. A month after the storm hit, *USA Today* published a survey of the governors. A total of thirty-eight governors had responded. Only two supported the president's plan. Mississippi Governor Haley Barbour, a Republican who had once headed the party, whose state took a direct hit from Katrina, said the states might need some federal help. "But we don't need them coming and running things," said the governor's spokesman. Michigan Governor Jennifer Granholm, a Democrat, was blunter. "Whether a governor is a Republican or Democrat, I would expect the response would be, 'Hell no,'" she said.[5]

Lurking behind the terrible difficulty in marshaling an effective response to Katrina's devastation was a more subtle political battle over how to manage the inevitable political fallout. Shortly after the storm overwhelmed news coverage on television sets around the nation, the Pew Research Center for the People and the Press surveyed Americans about how they viewed government's response to the storm. The survey revealed an enormous gulf with enormous implications for federalism: When asked whether President Bush had done all he could, 53 percent of Republicans agreed. However, 85 percent of Democrats and 71 percent of independents believed he could have done more. When asked about the response of state and local governments, there was little partisan difference in the answers. Among Republicans, 54 percent rated the response of state and local governments as only "fair" or "poor." For Democrats the figure was 51 percent, and for independents, 52 percent.[6]

There were big partisan divisions in Americans' assessment of the federal government's response to the disaster. Top Republicans quickly calculated that conversations about what went wrong at the federal level—whether the Federal Emergency Management Agency (FEMA) could or should have acted differently, for example—could only go in the wrong direction, from President Bush's point of view. So they resisted calls for a national commission to examine the government's response and instead relied on the polls to point to a different interpretation: that state and local governments should have responded better and had failed their citizens. In part, that explains President Bush's suggestion about a stronger military role in responding to disasters. His underlying argument was that when the crisis occurred, state and local governments could not rise to the challenge. Only the federal government—at least, the federal military—could respond effectively. Coming from a former governor, the argument might have seemed strange. But for a president facing devastating performance by his own emergency response agency and equally devastating findings in public opinion polls, it made sense to deflect blame to state and local governments and to rely on the military's response to deflect criticism of his actions.

Wilma's Test

Soon after Katrina's floodwaters subsided, another enormous storm, Hurricane Wilma, flared up in the Gulf of Mexico. This time the storm struck at southern Florida. Although the devastation was not nearly as brutal as that from Katrina's blow at New Orleans and southern Mississippi, Wilma left hundreds of thousands of residents without food, water, or electric power for days.

The storm got much less attention from the news media, but government officials and administrators put planning and response under a microscope. Before Wilma hit, Florida Governor Jeb Bush firmly told members of Congress, "I can say with certainty that federalizing emergency response to catastrophic events would be a disaster as bad as Hurricane Katrina." In fact, he concluded, "If you federalize, all the innovation, creativity, and knowledge at the local level would subside." [7] If the storm did its worst, the state's Division of Emergency Management promised, residents would have ice, food, and water within twenty-four hours. The storm hit hard, but it stopped short of Category 5. Six million residents found themselves without ice, food, water, or electricity. Long lines snaked around the few operating gasoline pumps. A three-star army general called state officials to say he wanted to fly in and take command. According to later reports, Governor Bush told federal Department of Homeland Security officials that the federal takeover effort was "insulting" to him personally.

Florida officials launched a clever countercoup. Craig Fugate, Florida's emergency manager, seized the Department of Homeland Security's National Incident Management System. In principle, every incident must have a single commander, to prevent battles over who is in charge of what. "I'd now like to introduce the incident commander," Fugate told federal officials during a videoconference. To the stunned surprise of the feds from the Department of Homeland Security, he pulled in Governor Bush. Under the federal government's own rules, federal officials were required to support the incident commander, and Fugate's maneuver had outflanked them. One of Fugate's first acts was to seize control of 300 satellite phones that the federal department had sent to Florida for the use of its officials and give them to local emergency workers instead. FEMA sent in a large team of workers, but its employees ended up working under the overall authority of state officials.

Governor Bush said the state was responsible for the problems that developed, but everyone had basic supplies within seventy-two hours. And if state officials did not meet their twenty-four-hour response target, they nevertheless retained control of the operation—and overall command of the federal response. When big storms hit, Fugate—a rabid University of Florida fan—puts on a weather-beaten, orange Gators cap. When the crisis ebbs, he switches to a clean blue one.

Within days of Wilma's assault on southern Florida, Fugate was wearing his blue Gators cap again.

Federalism's Arenas

In the storms, federalism played itself out in a host of complex ways. In part the issue was a political one: With so many different players at all levels involved in the difficult process, finger-pointing and blame-shifting became inevitable. In part it was fiscal: Given the enormity of the damage, who ought to pay for—and control decisions about—rebuilding the region? And in part it was administrative: Why did the federal, state, and local governments find it so difficult to provide a coordinated, effective response?

And as with everything else in federalism, complicated issues became entangled with each other. In mid-2005, America's governors had pushed hard for fundamental changes in the Medicaid program, the nation's most important program for providing medical and nursing home care for the poor, including the poor elderly. From 1998 to 2003, Medicaid spending increased 62 percent, compared with a 36 percent increase for Medicare, the federal program that pays doctor and hospital bills for seniors. Experts estimated that over the next fifteen years Medicaid's cost would grow 145 percent, an annual growth rate of 8.2 percent for the states.[8] For most governors, Medicaid was the fastest-growing item in the budget, and they looked for help in funding a program that, after all, was mostly federal. "Governors believe that Medicaid reform must be driven by good public policy and not by the federal budget process," the National Governors Association concluded in a 2005 report.[9]

The secretary of the federal Department of Health and Human Services, Michael Leavitt, created a special commission to study Medicaid and strategies for putting it on a sounder financial footing. The commission proposed giving states more flexibility in managing the program, including new options for reducing the cost of prescription drugs. It also argued for making it harder for individuals to transfer their assets to others so as to qualify sooner for Medicaid benefits (which have strict limits on recipients' income, savings, and other assets). The commission, however, did not solve the biggest problems: dealing with the rising cost of long-term care, especially in nursing homes, and as the commission put it, "expanding the number of people covered with quality care while recognizing budget constraints."[10]

The governors hoped that their work, coupled with the special commission's, would build momentum for fundamental reform. The two projects, they thought, could come together in President Bush's budget address early in 2006 and set the stage for sweeping changes. But the rising costs of the war in Iraq, coupled with the enormous, uncounted costs of federal assistance for the Gulf Coast, torpedoed that plan. Thus, in addition to the administrative, financial, and political implications of the hurricanes, the states had to reckon with significant collateral damage: The storms blew away what governors hoped would be their best chance for Medicaid reform. No one in Washington had the resources or the energy for a major assault on such a difficult set of questions, so the states concluded they might well end up having to attack the problems piecemeal and on their own.

Federalism behaved, at once, exactly as the Founders designed it—and precisely as some of them feared it would stumble in crisis. However, the Founders never intended this American invention of "federalism" to be a bold, sweeping innovation. They were supremely practical men (women were not invited to Philadelphia to help frame the new nation) with a supremely practical problem. Northern states did not trust southern states. Farmers did not trust merchants. Most of all, larger states did not trust smaller states and vice versa. The fledgling nation's army had won independence from Great Britain, but the notables gathered in Philadelphia in 1787 needed to find some glue to hold the new country together. If they had failed, the individual states would have been too small to endure—and would surely have proved easy pickings for European nations eager to expand.

It is not surprising, therefore, that the nation's Founders relied on a supremely pragmatic strategy for solving the practical problem of how to balance power among the states. They made the national[11] government supreme, but they also created the Tenth Amendment to the Constitution to remind everyone that the states retained any power not explicitly given to the national government. Except for forbidding the states from interfering with commerce between them, the Constitution allowed the states to govern themselves.

The system of federalism that the Founders created had few rules and fewer fixed boundaries. As federalism has developed over the centuries, however, two important facts about the system have become clear. First, federalism's very strength comes from its enormous flexibility—its ability to adapt to new problems and political cross-pressures. Second, it creates alternative venues for political action. Interests that fight and lose at the state level have been able to find clever ways of taking their battles to the national government. Losers at the national level have been able to refight their wars in the states.

Throughout American history, we have frequently looked on federalism as a rather sterile scheme for determining who is in charge of what in our governmental system. But that misses most of what makes federalism important and exciting. It makes far more sense to view federalism as an ever-evolving, flexible system for creating arenas for political action. Americans have long celebrated their basic document of government as a "living Constitution." No part of it has lived more—indeed, changed more—than that involving the relationship between the national and the state governments and the relationships among the states. This can be seen clearly in the rich variations on the three themes that Katrina highlighted: political, fiscal, and administrative federalism.

Political Federalism

In the 1990s some South Carolina business owners launched the *Tropic Sea* as a casino boat for "cruises to nowhere." However, the enterprise soon became a cruise to a very important somewhere by raising the question, Just how far can—and should—federal power intrude on the prerogatives of the states?

This balance-of-power question is as old as the American republic and in fact predates the Constitution. When the colonies declared their independence from King George III, they formed a loose confederation. It proved barely strong enough to win the war and not nearly strong enough to help govern the new nation. Problems with the country's Articles of Confederation led the nation's leaders to gather in Philadelphia to draft a new constitution. At the core of their debate was the question of how much power to give the national government and how much to reserve to the states. The Founders followed a time-honored tradition in resolving such tough issues—they sidestepped it. The Constitution is silent on the question, and the Tenth Amendment simply reinforces the obvious: The national government has only the powers that the Constitution gives it. By leaving the details vague, the authors of the Constitution avoided a wrenching political battle. They also ensured that generations of Americans after them would refight the same battles—most often with legal stratagems in the nation's courts, but sometimes, as in the Civil War, with blood.

A Cruise to Somewhere?

The *Tropic Sea* sailed into an ongoing struggle in South Carolina politics. Although developers loved gambling ships such as the *Tropic Sea,* which lured tourists to the state, several legislators and local officials did not, and they had been actively campaigning against the ships. As a result, when the *Tropic Sea* asked permission to dock at Charleston's State Ports Authority (SPA) Pier, the SPA said no. The boat ended up at anchor in the harbor while its owners sought help from the Federal Maritime Commission (FMC). The FMC sided with the boat owners but was overturned by a federal appeals court. The case eventually ended up in the U.S. Supreme Court.

South Carolina argued that, as a state government, it wasn't subject to the FMC's jurisdiction, and in a bitter five-to-four decision at the end of its 2002 term, the Supreme Court agreed. Writing for the majority, Justice Clarence Thomas looked past the usual foundation of political struggles over state power, the Tenth Amendment, and instead built his argument on the little-noticed Eleventh Amendment, ratified in 1798, which specifies that the judicial power of the United State does not extend to the states. This amendment supported the notion of "dual federalism"—separate spheres of federal and state action. In the decades after its ratification, however, the dual federalism argument gradually eroded, especially after 1868, under the weight of the "equal protection" clause of the Fourteenth Amendment. That amendment asserts that all citizens have the right to equal treatment under the law. In establishing a national standard, the Fourteenth Amendment gave the courts power to enforce national policy over state objections. That pushed away the dual federalism concept and helped shift the balance of power to the national government. After William Rehnquist became chief justice in 1986, however, dual federalism resurfaced and surged ahead again.

In ruling for South Carolina, Justice Thomas admitted that there was little textual evidence to support his position. Rather, he said, dual federalism was "embedded in our constitutional structure." The concept helped uphold the "dignity" of the states as dual sovereigns. That, he said, was the core of the decision.[12]

Asserting the dignity of the states is a new constitutional standard. The Eleventh Amendment explicitly applies to federal courts, not federal administrators, such as employees of the FMC. Conservatives, of course, had long criticized liberals for making law from the bench. In this case, however, it was the conservatives on the Court who crafted a new principle, which they used to push back the scope of the national government's power.

Federalism Means War

The Supreme Court under Rehnquist gradually chipped away at national power and aggressively worked to strengthen the role of the states. The major federalism decisions have all been by votes of five to four, built on the conservative bloc of Rehnquist, Thomas, Anthony Kennedy, Sandra Day O'Connor, and Antonin Scalia. The disputes, on the Court as well as off, have become increasingly intense. As *New York Times* reporter Linda Greenhouse put it, "These days, federalism means war."[13]

The battles became so sharp that candidates' views on federalism were critical in the battles over new appointments to the Supreme Court, especially those of Chief Justice John Roberts and Justice Samuel Alito. Given the ages of several other justices, more appointment battles are certain—and so are questions about the Court's role in reframing federalism. Will the Court remain on its dual federalism course? Staying that course raises two very difficult questions.

First, just how far is the Court prepared to go in pursuing dual federalism? In the past it has ruled that workers cannot sue states for discrimination under federal age and disability standards. It has also protected states from suits by people who claimed unfair competition from state activities in the marketplace, such as photocopying by state universities. Bit by bit the Court has extended state power at the expense of the national government's jurisdiction.

At some point, however, the pursuit of state "dignity" will collide with national standards for equal protection. At some point, state protection against national labor standards will crash into national protection of civil rights and civil liberties. That point might come in debates over family leave or prescription drugs, over voting rights or transportation of nuclear waste. But a collision is certain. From the Fourteenth Amendment, there is a long tradition of asserting national power over the states. From the Rehnquist court, there is a new legal argument for reasserting state power.

Neither argument is an absolute. In some issues (such as civil rights) there is a strong case for national preeminence. In other issues (such as the states' own systems of law) there is a strong case for state preeminence. Still other issues, however (such as gambling boats), rest squarely in the middle. The nation then has to determine how best to balance competing policy goals and constitutional principles. Sometimes those battles are fought out in the legislative and executive branches, but most often they are contested in the courts.

Since the dawn of Roosevelt's New Deal in the 1930s, national power has grown at the expense of the states. Now, with an uncommon purpose, the conservatives on the Supreme Court are pushing that line back. The Roberts Court can continue the campaign to reassert the power of the states, but clearly at some point it will have to hold national interests paramount. What is less clear is where and how the Court will draw that line.

The second question that the Court's pro-dual federalism course raises is even tougher: How far can the Court advance state-centered federalism without running headlong into the new campaign for homeland security, which demands a strong national role? It is one thing for the Court to pursue the principles of state sovereignty and dignity. But beefing up homeland security inevitably means strengthening federal power. There is a vital national interest in ensuring that state and local governments protect critical infrastructure, such as water systems and harbors. The nation needs not only a strong intelligence apparatus but also a powerful emergency response system.

Federalism and the Living Constitution

It may be that relatively few Americans care about whether a gambling boat can dock at a South Carolina port. But the basic issue—where to draw the line between national and state power, and who ought to draw it—is an issue that all Americans care about, even if they spend little time thinking about it in those terms. It has been the stuff of bloody battles and endless debate. As political scientist Howard Gillman told the *New York Times*, federalism has become "the biggest and deepest disagreement about the nature of our constitutional system." [14] The equal protection and homeland security issues will only intensify that disagreement as we wade deeper into the real meaning of the states' "dignity."

These issues are scarcely ones that the Founders could have anticipated when they wrote the Constitution and the Bill of Rights. Few present-day Americans, after all, had heard the phrase "homeland security" before September 11, 2001. The genius of the Founders was that they recognized the importance of federalism, that they put broad boundaries around it but did not try to resolve it for all time, and that they created a mechanism for Americans in subsequent generations to adjust the balance, subtly and continually.

It was no easy matter to recognize the key questions out of thousands that engaged the members of the Constitutional Convention in Philadelphia. It was even tougher to resolve the questions just sufficiently to win the Constitution's adoption, without pushing so hard as to deepen the divisions. And it was quite remarkable to do so in a way that has allowed us to reshape the balance in our time.

Fiscal Federalism

These grand debates are what most Americans think of when they think of "federalism." They are the stuff of high school civics classes and the enduring classics of American history. For national, state, and local policymakers, however, the soft underbelly of federalism is much more often the question of who pays for what.

That has not always been the case. But in the 1950s, as the nation—and the national government—became much more ambitious about domestic policy, fiscal federalism became increasingly important. During that period, citizens and national policymakers wanted the country to undertake new, large-scale projects, such as building a national network of highways and tearing down decaying slums. State and local governments could not, or would not, move ahead on such matters. Often they simply did not have the funds to do so; sometimes local political forces opposed the policies. Even without those impediments, state and local governments almost always lacked the ability to coordinate the creation of such complex systems as effective high-speed highways with other jurisdictions. (Who would want to drive on a modern, four-lane road only to hit a two-lane gravel path at the state line?) Therefore citizens and national policymakers pressed to empower the national government to undertake the projects.

National Goals through Intergovernmental Grants

The national government tackled the problem of getting local and state governments to do what it wanted done by offering them grants. If local governments lacked the resources to tear down dilapidated housing, the national government could create an "urban renewal" program and provide the money, thus avoiding the constitutional problem that would have come with national coercion. The national government did not *make* local governments accept the money or tear down the slums. But few local officials could resist a national program that helped them do what they, too—or at least many of their constituents—wanted done.

The same was true at the state level. In the 1950s Americans were buying cars in record numbers, but they found the roads increasingly clogged. Long-distance driving often proved a special chore because road systems did not connect well and the quality of the roads fell far below the performance ability of the cars driving on them. During the Eisenhower administration the national government decided to tackle that problem by creating a new program—the interstate highway system—and inducing states to join it by funding 90 percent of the construction costs. With motorists demanding better roads, the offer was too good to refuse. Since this was occurring amid the hottest moments of the cold war, President Dwight D. Eisenhower reinforced the idea of a national interest by arguing that the system served both transportation and defense goals—it would allow troops to move quickly to wherever they might be needed. (Wags have since joked that the system could best serve the national defense by luring Russian tanks onto the [Beltway around Washington, D.C.,] and challenging them to cope with the traffic and find the right exit.)[15]

The strategy continued to be used through the 1960s. When Lyndon B. Johnson announced his War on Poverty, he decided to fight it primarily through national grants to state and local governments. He created the Model Cities program, which provided aid to local communities trying to uproot poverty and rebuild urban neighborhoods, and established other programs to provide better housing for poor Americans. He founded Medicaid, which provided grants to state governments so that they, in turn, could provide health care to the poor. More grants followed, to support job training, criminal justice, public health, and a host of other national goals.

It was a clever strategy in a number of ways. For one, it sidestepped constitutional limitations on national interference in state and local issues: The national government did not force state and local governments to join the programs; it simply made them financially irresistible. No state or local officials wanted to have to explain to constituents why they left cheap money on the table, especially when their neighbors were benefiting from the programs.

This approach sidestepped another tough constitutional problem as well: the national government's dealing directly with local governments. Through long-standing constitutional interpretation and practice, local governments are considered creatures of the states, not the national government. The states created the national government, so constitutionally the national government must deal with the states. Hence the states alone have the power to control what local governments can—and cannot—do. Before Johnson's program, local governments struggled with increasing problems of poverty, substandard housing, and other human needs. They often found themselves without power or enough money to attack the problems. Few state governments themselves had adequate resources to address these serious issues, and in many states, political forces prevented the creation of new programs that might have helped.

Many analysts concluded that the only solution was to create a direct link between the national and local governments—a link that bypassed the states. But given both constitutional limits and political conflicts, how could such a link be established? Federal grants to local governments proved the answer. Across the nation, state governments gave permission for local governments to receive the money. If the national government agreed to take on the problems and keep state officials out of the process, the programs seemed an attractive proposition to state and local officials alike.

From the 1950s through the 1970s, these intergovernmental aid programs became increasingly popular and important. They not only grew in size but also became ever more vital elements of state and local government financing. In 1938 federal aid had amounted to just 8.7 percent of state and local revenue. It surged to 22 percent—more than one out of every five dollars raised by state and local governments—in 1978, at the high-water mark of federal aid.

As the national government used its funds to support state and local governments and to induce them to do things they might not have done otherwise, federal aid became not only an increasingly important part of the policy system but also something on which those governments became ever more dependent. When the national government began tightening its fiscal belt in the late 1970s, state and local governments felt the effects keenly. In 1980, federal aid was 40 percent of all spending by state and local governments from their own sources. By

2002 it had dropped to 29 percent.[16] Few federal programs were abolished, however. Rather, the national government simply cut back support—leaving state and local governments to deal with ongoing commitments and, in many cases, powerful supporters who fought hard to keep the programs alive. In the federal highway program, federal support mostly provided aid for construction, not maintenance. As highways aged, state governments found themselves with huge bills for repairing crumbling bridges and old roadbeds.

When recession hit in 2002, state and local governments looked expectantly to Washington for some hope—and help.

No News Was Bad News

The nation's governors, in particular, were hoping for good news when President George W. Bush began 2003 by announcing his plans for a $670 billion tax cut. They hoped the speech would contain at least some help for their ailing budgets. Except for a modest proposal on unemployment insurance, however, they found themselves left out in the January cold.

With their budgets in the biggest crisis since World War II, governors had been lobbying hard for national help. They hoped for a short-term resuscitation of revenue sharing, the federal government's program of distributing broad grants to state and local governments to use as they wished. The program ended in 1982, but they wanted to bring it back. Failing that, they pressed for at least some tinkering with the formula for reimbursing Medicaid spending, the fastest-growing program in many state budgets and one, as noted earlier, that was originally launched through the incentive of national grants. Changes in the Medicaid formulas, the governors hoped, would ease their budget worries.

Ignoring most of the states' pleas, Bush instead advanced a bold stroke to restructure the national tax system. The administration did suggest some changes to Medicaid, but the changes proposed would have reduced aid (or increased costs) for the poor, and they immediately incited opposition from groups struggling to protect the program. The states were left on their own with a $90 billion budget shortfall that threatened to soak up all of the short-term economic stimulus Bush was proposing, and more. The net effect promised to be an economic wash surrounded by political conflict.

Who is at fault here? The feds, for failing to extend a helping hand when the states needed it most? Or the states, for digging themselves into the hole and whining when Bush refused to help them out? As with most questions of fault, the answer is, both.

If Bush truly had been interested in jump-starting the economy, pumping money through the states would quickly have done just that. But the president was concerned more with long-term revision of the tax code than with short-term economic stimulus, especially through the states. As for the states, their fault lies in having hitched their spending to the booming economy of the 1990s. They forgot "Stein's Law," derived by the late Herbert Stein, once chairman of the president's Council of Economic Advisers: "Things that can't go on forever— won't." [17] When the boom collapsed, the states found themselves hooked on spending increases they could not support.

Exploding Health Care Costs

In the 1990s national aid to state and local governments had actually resumed its upward course (see Figure 1), but not because the national government had decided to resume its generosity to state and local governments. Rather, the reason was that national aid for payments to individuals—mostly through Medicaid—suddenly accelerated, as the benefits became more generous and health care costs began to grow rapidly. Grants for all other purposes had leveled off or shrunk, but national aid for health care had swung quickly upward, as had state governments' own spending for their matching share of the costs. In 1960 federal grants for payments to individuals amounted to 31 percent of all grants. By 2009, budget experts estimate, the figure will swell to 71 percent (see Figure 2). There will little federal aid for anything but payments to individuals, most of which will be Medicaid.

As the new century began, health care costs, particularly under Medicaid, exploded at precisely the same moment that state revenues collapsed. Spending for doctor visits, hospital care, and especially prescription drugs swelled at the highest rate in a decade, growing to 30 percent of state spending, and it could not have come at a worse time for state governments. It has swamped the states' efforts to control the rest of their budgets and aggravated their financial hemorrhage. The monster in the states' budgetary basement has become health care: treating the uninsured, providing long-term care for the elderly, and buying prescription drugs. With the baby boomers reaching retirement age, the budgetary problem promises to get worse.

State spending pegged to unsustainable revenue growth and the sudden increase in health care costs threaten a continuing, profound crisis for state policymakers. Aggravating it is the projection by most economists that economic growth will not proceed fast enough to bail out the states any time soon. It's little wonder that in some states Democrats were quietly rooting for Republican governors to make the hard budgetary decisions, and vice versa. If the states are the laboratories of democracy, the lurching of budgetary Frankensteins could litter broken test tubes across the floor. This is a long way from the salad days of national-state relations in the 1960s and early 1970s. The feds then saw state and

Figure 1. Federal Aid to State and Local Governments

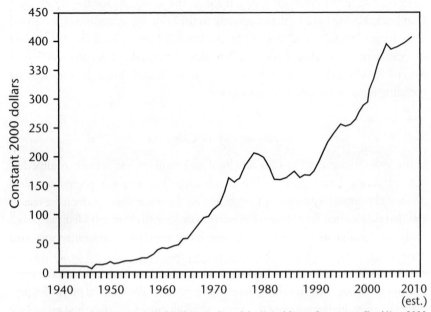

Source: U.S. Office of Management and Budget, *Budget of the United States Govenment, Fiscal Year 2005: Historical Tables* (Table 12.1), www.gpoaccess.gov/usbudget/fy05/hist.html (accessed January 21, 2006). Figures for fiscal years 2004–2009 are estimates.

local problems as their own. Democrats and Republicans joined together to provide national funds to leverage state and local action. The partnership might have been paternalistic, but it shaped policy for decades. When budget cuts hit in the late 1970s and early 1980s, national-state ties became increasingly frayed. They unraveled further with the Bush administration's 2002 loosening of air pollution regulations, which complicated the job many states faced in meeting pollution standards, and frayed some more with the administration's capital gains tax plan.

The states can—indeed, they have to—deal with some of these problems by putting their spending back into balance with a realistic view of their revenues. They need to update their revenue systems. But they cannot solve their fundamental fiscal problems without a new partnership between the states and the feds. And that will be hard to realize as long as the two groups move in such different orbits that the fundamental problems they share never come together.

Figure 2. Grants for Payments to Individuals as a Share of All Grants

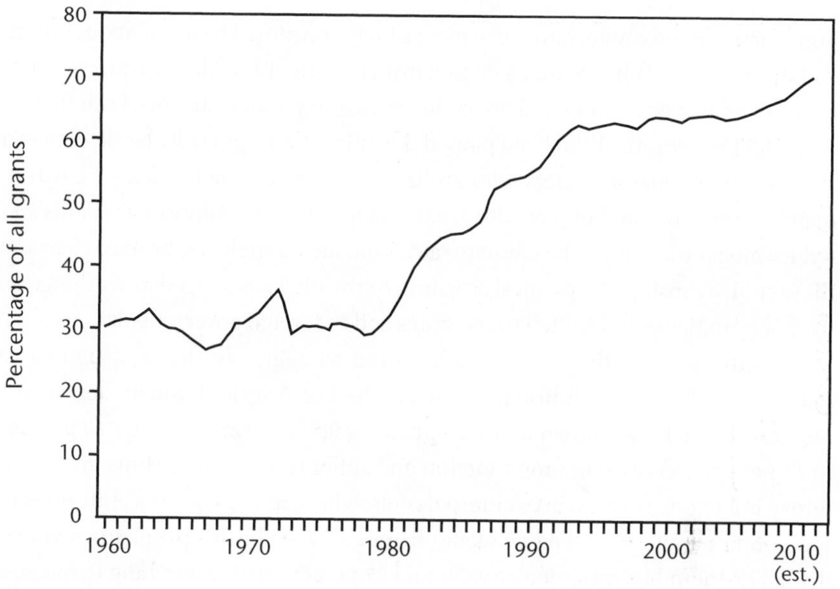

Source: U.S. Office of Management and Budget, *Budget of the United States Government, Fiscal Year 2005: Historical Tables* (Table 12.1), http://www.gpoaccess.gov/usbudget/fy05/hist.html (accessed January 21, 2006). Figures for fiscal years 2004–2009 are estimates.

Administrative Federalism

A close corollary of the rise of fiscal federalism has been the growing importance of state and local governments as administrative agents of national programs. As close observers of Washington politics know, the national government has increased its spending without increasing (in fact, while decreasing) the number of bureaucrats. The reason it has been able to do so? The national government has leveraged the activity of state and local governments as agents to do much of its work. As is the case in fiscal federalism, the states usually have discretion about whether to enlist as national agents, but the construction of programs typically leaves them little choice. Consider, for example, the case of environmental policy. Under national environmental laws, state governments have substantial responsibility for issuing permits and monitoring emissions.

The Environmental Protection Agency (EPA) relies heavily on state governments for much of the frontline work. In the process, however, some states have used that role to set their own policies, which often have been far broader than those of the EPA. In a peculiar, up-from-the-bottom style of federalism, that has meant that some states have, in practice, set policy for the entire nation.

Policymaking for the Nation—in Sacramento

Top officials in the capital have been increasingly consumed by a war about the air, and there is a good chance that a decade from now the EPA administrator will not be setting much environmental policy. Recent agency administrators, both Republican and Democratic, have been pinned down in a fierce guerrilla battle between some congressional members who are trying to lighten the burden of environmental regulations and others who are trying to toughen pollution standards and reduce global warming. The administrator's job increasingly has been to chart the EPA's course through the political crossfire. As the melee has raged in Washington, the policy initiative has shifted to the states and to foreign governments.

It is little wonder that California has been so aggressive in campaigning to reduce air pollution. Pollution problems in the Los Angeles basin are legendary. Medical research has shown that kids growing up in the area suffer a 10 percent to 15 percent decrease in lung function and suffer more from asthma and respiratory infections than their counterparts elsewhere in the country. Autopsies of 152 young people who died suddenly from crime or health problems revealed that all of them had inflamed airways and 27 percent had severe lung damage.

The state has set tougher standards than federal regulations required, and in the past twenty-five years the results have been remarkable. The number of health advisories for high levels of ozone shrank from 166 in 1976 to just fifteen in 2001.

In July 2002 California took another tough step. The legislature passed a bill requiring that all cars sold in California after 2009 meet tough standards for greenhouse gases, the carbon-based emissions scientists believe promote global warming. In signing the bill, Governor Gray Davis chided the national government for "failing to ratify the Kyoto treaty on global warming." They "missed their opportunity to do the right thing," Davis said. "So it is left to California, the nation's most populous state and the world's fifth largest economy, to take the lead." California was proud to "join the long-standing and successful effort of European nations against global warming." [18]

With its legislation, California rendered moot President Bush's March 2001 decision to withdraw the United States from the Kyoto treaty, at least with respect to carbon dioxide pollution from cars. Carmakers had waged a fierce battle against the California bill, but in the end they could not beat the forces of environmentalists and citizens worried about public health. They found themselves trooping off to Sacramento to haggle over the details of the new regulations.

No automaker can afford to ignore California and its huge market, as was clear after the state's earlier decision to mandate cleaner gas and catalytic converters. When California mandated catalytic converters to scrub auto exhaust, it soon became impossible to buy cars in Wisconsin or Texas that did not contain the device as well. As California goes, at least in air pollution, so goes the nation.

For California regulators, the aggressive antipollution campaign has not been a one-way street. The new California law requires regulators to reduce not only smog but also greenhouse gases, such as carbon dioxide. New-generation diesel engines are more fuel efficient than many gasoline-powered engines. That means less fuel and fewer carbon dioxide emissions. And that, in turn, has brought California regulators into close negotiations with automakers about encouraging production of diesel-powered cars.

For those who have long seen diesels as blue-smoke-belching behemoths, the idea that diesel power might be a pollution-reducing strategy may seem preposterous. It may seem even more unlikely that government would be encouraging a shift to diesel engines or that government regulators would be in conversations with automakers hammering out deals to do so. Above all, it may seem incredible that the government taking the action would be a state government. But that is exactly what is happening in California.

All this, in turn, has led to budding ties between state regulators and the European Union (EU). European nations have been working as hard and as long on global warming as anyone. The EU's aggressive efforts to reduce greenhouse gases have stimulated new diesel technologies. So California regulators find themselves steering in the same direction as their counterparts abroad. Put together, this means that American policy for auto emissions is subtly shifting course, driven by activities at the state and international levels.

State governments have long prided themselves on being the nation's policy laboratories, and healthy competition among them might produce new breakthroughs. But there is also a profound risk that the nation could find its policy strategies increasingly evolving through accidental bits and bumps, without a national debate about what is truly in the national interest. The trend is already briskly under way. General Electric chief executive Jeffrey Immelt has said that 99 percent of all new regulations the company faces are, over time, coming not from the national government but from the European Union.[19] The states are vigorously developing new pollution standards. Meanwhile, as Washington policymakers focus on the interest group battles that constantly consume them, they risk fighting more and more about less and less.

Conclusion

If James Madison today rode his horse to Washington, down the interstate from his Virginia estate at Montpelier, would he recognize the system of federalism he helped to craft? He would undoubtedly be stunned at the very idea of using federalism to work out problems of ship-based gambling, health care for the poor, or global warming. However, on a few moments' reflection—and perhaps after a bit of conversation to get up to speed on the stunning policy predicaments of the twenty-first century—he would see in these puzzles echoes of the issues he and his colleagues dealt with at the end of the eighteenth century. He would surely recognize the tough battles that raged in the days after the fierce hurricanes of 2005. They were little different in tone from the ones he and his colleagues waged in Philadelphia.

The glue holding together America's special—and peculiar—democratic system comes from a unique blending of federal, state, and local responsibilities. Early Americans faced a fundamental, dramatic choice: to assign those responsibilities clearly to different levels of government and then write rules for governments to coordinate their inevitable differences, or to allow governments to share responsibilities and then to negotiate their differences through a political process. The latter is the cornerstone of American federalism.

Thus federalism is a much-revered constitutional principle, rooted deeply in the American tradition, which draws its life from political bargaining. It is tempting to read the Constitution, think of the stirring rhetoric of the Founders, and celebrate federalism as a set of rules. In reality, federalism is a set of political action arenas. It is far less an institution than a living organism, one that breathes, grows, shrinks, and changes in response to the forces pressing upon it.

Federalism has helped Americans survive the pressures that led to the Civil War, and it has often made possible programs and policies that might not otherwise have existed. It would be hard, for example, to imagine the national government itself taking on the job of building the massive interstate highway system. Only through federalism did this crucial system come into being, as federalism introduced the possibility of a political, fiscal, and administrative partnership that made possible a program no one government alone could have produced. By the same means, federalism has transformed American cities (for better or worse) through urban renewal, launched a war on poverty, helped clean the environment, and produced a health care program for the nation's poor.

Of course, this partnership has not always been a happy or peaceful one. Governors are never convinced that the national government provides enough money, and national policymakers constantly find it difficult to corral fifty different states—and tens of thousands of local governments—into a coherent policy system. When Hurricane Katrina devastated the Gulf Coast, federalism created a series of roadblocks that vastly complicated the job of getting critical relief to suffering citizens. New Orleans's mayor blamed Louisiana's governor. The governor called on the federal government to send everything it had, but the feds said that the governor had not requested the information in the right way. When the process of rebuilding began, New Orleans residents complained that the feds were slow in providing everything from new maps of the flood plain to trailers for displaced residents. Louisiana residents complained that citizens in Mississippi, the state next door, received more money per capita.

In the storm's wake, study after study pointed to failures of leadership and coordination. It is no exaggeration to conclude that the struggle to coordinate the intergovernmental system cost some people their lives. When quick, coordinated governmental response is needed, federalism has sometimes proved slow and disjointed. It is a system far better equipped to broaden participation in the political process than to produce efficient government.

Of course, if we had wanted that kind of government, we would long ago have sided with Alexander Hamilton in his effort to bring energy to the executive and to strengthen presidential power. Other Founders rejected his argument, and the resulting political system has proved remarkably resilient. The system's flexibility has not only made it possible to work out accommodations for the tough issues but also created arenas in which Americans with many different points of view can continue to contest the future of the nation's public policy. But the new challenges of homeland security and Katrina-like disasters raise tough questions about how to ensure that the quest for responsiveness does not prove administratively chaotic.

NOTES

1. George W. Bush, "Address to the Nation," September 15, 2005, www.whitehouse.gov/news/releases/2005/09/2005915-8.html (accessed January 19, 2006).

2. CNN, *American Morning,* September 2, 2005, http://transcripts.cnn.com/TRANSCRIPTS/0509/02/ltm.03.html (accessed January 19, 2006).

3. CNN.com, "Transcript of Radio Interview with Mayor Nagin," September 2, 2005, www.cnn.com/2005/US/09/02/nagin.transcript/ (accessed January 19, 2006).

4. Christopher Rhoads and Peter Grant, "City Officials Struggled to Keep Order with Crisis," *Wall Street Journal,* September 9, 2005, A1.

5. Bill Nichols and Richard Benedetto, "Govs to Bush: Relief Our Job," *USA Today,* October 2, 2005, www.usatoday.com/news/washington/2005-10-02-gov-survey_x.htm (accessed January 19, 2006).

6. Pew Research Center for the People and the Press, "Two-in-Three Critical of Bush's Relief Efforts," September 8, 2005, http://people-press.org/reports/display.php3?ReportID=255 (accessed January 20, 2006).

7. The facts and quotations in this discussion come from Robert Block and Amy Schatz, "Local and Federal Authorities Battle to Control Disaster Relief," *Wall Street Journal,* December 8, 2005, A1.

8. Bipartisan Commission on Medicaid Reform, "The Medicaid Commission," September 1, 2005, 8.

9. National Governors Association, "Medicaid Reform: A Preliminary Report," June 15, 2005, 1, www.nga.org/Files/pdf/0506medicaid.pdf (accessed January 21, 2006).

10. Ibid., 14.

11. Throughout this chapter, I will use *national* to refer to what most people call the *federal* government. To use *federal* in discussing *federalism* often causes endless confusion, so I am resorting to the less-common usage to maintain clarity. Readers who find that in itself confusing can simply substitute *federal* for *national* wherever it appears.

12. *Federal Maritime Commission v. South Carolina Ports Authority*, No. 01-46. See Linda Greenhouse, "Justices Expand States' Immunity in Federalism Case," *New York Times*, May 29, 2002, sec. A.

13. Linda Greenhouse, "The Nation: 5-to-4, Now and Forever; At the Court, Dissent over States' Rights Is Now War," *New York Times*, June 9, 2002, sec. 4.

14. Ibid.

15. For a map of the system, see www.fhwa.dot.gov/hep10/nhs.

16. U.S. Census Bureau, *Statistical Abstract of the United States, 2006* (Washington, D.C.: Government Printing Office), Table 421.

17. Herbert Stein, interview with the author.

18. Gray Davis, "California Takes on Air Pollution," *Washington Post*, July 22, 2002, sec. A.

19. Brandon Mitchener, "Increasingly, Rules of Global Economy Are Set in Brussels," *Wall Street Journal*, April 23, 2002, sec. A.

Chapter 4

Civil Rights

4-1

Immigration and the Future of Identity Politics in the United States

Taeku Lee

Considering the same demographic trends pondered in the last essay, Taeku Lee asks how race and ethnicity will influence American society and politics a decade from now. Answering this question is not a simple matter of projecting population trends. Lee argues that the answer lies in how Americans define themselves and their place in relation to others in our multiracial, multicultural society. Race, ethnicity, class, and a more subjective quality that Lee calls "nation" combine in several ways to create alternative vignettes of the future.

MUCH HAS BEEN made of the dramatic influx of immigration to the United States since the mid-1960s. According to federal statistics, immigrants and their children make up nearly one in four American residents. More than 34 million foreign-born persons and almost 32 million second generation immigrants lived in the United States in 2002 (U.S. Census Bureau 2002). The so-called Fourth Wave of immigration has swept in a sea change in the racial and ethnic composition of the United States. Up until the first decade of the twentieth century, about 90 percent of new migrants to the United States set sail from European shores. By the 1990s the proportion had dwindled to about 15 percent, and more than 80

Source: Adapted from the article originally appearing in *Perspectives on Politics,* 2003, Volume 3, Issue 3, pp. 557–561.

percent of new migrants came from Asia and the Americas (U.S. Immigration and Naturalization Service 2002).

Much too has been made of the changes in how the U.S. government classifies and counts by race and ethnicity. In 1977 the Office of Management and Budget (OMB) issued its Directive No. 15, requiring all federal agencies to collect data for at least five groups—American Indians and Alaska Natives, Asians and Pacific Islanders, non-Hispanic blacks, non-Hispanic whites, and Hispanics. OMB then revised the directive in 1997 to include the instruction to "mark one or more" responses, thus allowing people to identify themselves with multiple races or ethnicities (Perlmann and Waters 2002). As a result of the changes, the U.S. government today formally recognizes sixty-three distinct "races" and 126 unique ethno-racial combinations.

The face of America is changing before us and, with it, the names and categories we use to identify ourselves. These changes have emboldened some scholars to conjure Panglossian reveries of a multiracial city on the hill, while others portend the rise of Manichean "race wars," "culture wars," and the end of our national identity as we know it. Several pointed questions prefigure these debates, however. Will Asians increasingly be "honorary whites"? Will Latinos increasingly be racialized, assimilated, or fragmented? Will African Americans remain relatively unified, or will they find themselves increasingly divided by class, political ideology, or something else? What effect will the multiracial population of America have on these trends? Lastly, what can the work of social science tell us about the likely configuration of race and ethnic politics over a finite future, say, ten years hence?[1]

Demography as Destiny

A fine line separates forecasting from fortune-telling in a domain as complex and dynamic as racial and ethnic politics, but some predictions seem obvious. Foremost among them is that current demographic trends will persist. In the coming decade we can expect the foreign-born population—and the proportion of Asians and Latinos in the United States—to continue to rise (Bean and Stevens 2003). Sometime in this century, we are told, whites (as conventionally defined) will no longer be a majority of the voting-age population. Based on the last two Censuses, moreover, the migration of Asians and Latinos to the United States is likely to spread well beyond gateway cities like New York, Los Angeles, and Miami into more geographically dispersed locales (Frey 2002). Thus in ten years fewer Americans will be able to claim no direct encounter with an Asian or Latino person.

A second prediction is that the population of Americans who identify themselves with more than one race and ethnic group is likely to increase by 2015. This is likely for several reasons, first among them being our greater familiarity with the option of identifying ourselves as multiracial. Another reason is the continuing increase in the number of interracial marriages, with Asian Americans in particular being likelier to marry outside the group than African Americans or, to a lesser extent, Latinos (Bean and Stevens 2003). Third, the best evidence suggests that only a small fraction of the Americans who might have identified with more than one race did so in 2000 (Goldstein and Morning 2000). That conclusion is buttressed by the fact that modest changes in how we ask people to self-identify ethno-racially can produce dramatic increases in the estimated population of multiracial Americans.[2] Finally, the trend of growing social acceptance of interracial families and political legitimacy of multiracial identity will likely continue, amplifying each of the other factors leading to greater multiracial identification (Schuman et al. 1997).

These predictions about demographic change, however, do not translate neatly into predictions about the likely effect on race relations and politics. We commonly think of politics as a game of numbers. Perhaps, then, their increasing numbers will fuel a high-octane Latino and Asian political power in America. Such expectations have thus far been dashed. Asian Americans and Latinos are less likely to be citizens, less likely to register to vote, and less likely to engage in all realms of politics (voting or otherwise) than their white and African American counterparts (Ramakrishnan 2005). Moreover, the politics of these new Americans is characterized by the relative absence of party mobilization, the salience of dual citizenship and transnational political ties, the persistence of language barriers, little discretionary time, the instability and uncertainty of social and political group identities, and other impediments to full incorporation and greater participation (DeSipio 1996, Jones-Correa 1998, Wong 2005).

In civic and economic realms it is similarly far from clear whether the influx of new ethnic Americans will herald the formation of harmonious, multiracial, multiethnic coalitions or portend the activation of invidious interethnic conflicts and competition. That diversity is a boon is a widely held belief. It enriches our social and cultural lives and enhances the kind of creative, adaptive, collective decision making that U.S. businesses need to compete and prevail in a globalized economy. Some evidence does tell us that—under conditions of equal status, mutual interdependence, common goals, and strong leadership—the fact of diversity tempers deep-rooted prejudices and fosters interracial harmony and tolerance (Allport 1954). Yet other studies tell us that a changing demography—especially under conditions of economic scarcity and competition—preconditions race riots, hate crimes, heightened intolerance and distrust, and the general outbreak of incivility and ill-will between fellow Americans (Blalock 1967, Bobo and Hutchings 1996, Green, Strolovich, and Wong 1998).

The prospect of a growing multiracial population in America too yields no clear story about the future. Some scholars see the growing recognition of our multiple racial lineages and envisage a radical transformation of how we conceive of families (DaCosta 2003). Some see the mounting tendency of groups to lobby and contest how our government categorizes and counts its population and contemplate the possibility of a groundswell of politics organized around multiracial identity (Williams 2006). Some see the rise in immigration and interracial marriages and fret about the emergence of a *mestizo* nation and a *mestizaje* politics (Huntington 2004). Many envision the abandonment of existing ethnoracial categories altogether but differ about what follows: Some think such categories would be replaced with a renewed interest in ancestry (Glazer 2002); others, with a renewed interest in pigmentation (Hochschild 2005). Yet others suggest that although the categories we use may vanish, "race" as an organizing principle in American life will remain intact (Hollinger 2003).

Beyond Black-White

What then can we say beyond merely that growth and complexity will continue? We might, alternatively, presume that the past is prologue and work as though past trends and current realities will morph mechanically into future projections. This approach typically leads to the conclusion that our current racial order will be recapitulated, putting whites on top, blacks at the bottom, and Asians and Latinos somewhere in between. Pressed further, we might also extrapolate that Asians will grow indistinct from ethnic whites and that Latinos and African Americans will continue to share the common lot of economic hardship, social segregation, and political marginalization. Moreover, we might expect Asians and Latinos to continue to become immersed in, and integrated into, the fabric of American society through processes of assimilation and incorporation that are segmented and uneven across the multiple contexts of immigrant life (Portes and Zhou 1993, Bean and Stevens 2003).

Such predictions, however, are often as indiscriminate and incomplete as they are unsurprising. For one thing, we often miss crucial diversity within groups when we focus reflexively on differences between groups. Historically, for instance, immigrants of European descent, such as Irish, Italian, and Jewish Americans, were not always categorized as "white," nor were the attendant privileges of "whiteness" easily obtained (Roediger 1991). Today the material conditions facing Southeast Asians are discernibly worse than those facing other Asians; the economic and political power of Florida's Cuban American community is substantial compared with that of other Latinos; and the persecution facing Muslims, Arabs, and South Asians since the terrorist attacks of September 11, 2001, is more acute than that facing other immigrants in America. Even within the supposedly homogeneous African American community, there is considerable (and, by some accounts, growing) ideological diversity, economic division, and conflict across gender, sexual orientation, and immigrant identities (Dawson 2001, Wilson 1978, Cohen 1999, Rogers 2006).

More important, especially given the speed and scope of the changes that are occurring, it is far from obvious that the best way to understand a dynamic phenomenon like race and immigration in the United States is by using static tools and theories wrought from the past. Viewing race through a black-white lens or immigration through an assimilation-racialization lens is only helpful if it fits with our current circumstances. It is far from clear, for instance, why current U.S. Census classification treats distinct populations that share a common Asian national origin—Chinese, Filipino, Japanese, and so on—as separate "races" (but not ethnicities), while it treats populations of distinct Latin American national origins as a single "ethnicity" (but not race). More on this in a moment.

I propose that we think about our future prospects quite differently. The approach I have in mind starts by digging deeper into existing black-white and assimilation-racialization frameworks and identifying the root dimensions that Americans use to define themselves. I suggest that when most Americans ask themselves the question, Who am I? their answer reflects one or a combination of four durable, overlapping dimensions of "identity"—race, ethnicity, class, and nation (Smith 2003; Lie 2004). These dimensions also serve as the basis for organizing, perpetuating, and contesting much of the existing powers and privileges of contemporary American society. It is crucial, as many scholars have noted, to understanding race as separate from, and not reducible to, ethnicity, class, and nation (e.g., Omi and Winant 1994). But it is it is equally crucial to note that that these dimensions are not independent of one another. Rather, they overlap and reinforce each other and are sure to continue to do so in the foreseeable future. So in asking the question, What will race and immigration look like ten years from now? I propose that we consider how these root dimensions currently stack up and how they may be rearranged in the future. Specifically, let us consider three vignettes in which race pairs with class, ethnicity, and nation, respectively. For each, I give a rendition of how Asian Americans, African Americans, Latinos, and whites are currently situated relative to one another and then briefly speculate on how the relation might change in the next decade or so. The first two vignettes enlist current, standard definitions of "race" and "ethnicity," and in the third I consider race in its more subjective and ideologically nuanced sense. To preview, the purpose of this exercise is to demonstrate that how we currently think of whites, blacks, Asians, and Latinos vis-à-vis one another depends on which root dimensions we employ. How the four primary ethno-racial groups might relate to one another in the future will likely depend on whether and how the root dimensions are rearranged and become most salient to a person's identity

Vignette 1: Race and Class

The first vignette depicts the standard black-white paradigm on which contemporary debates over racial progress and racial attitudes are typically founded. Here race and class trump all other potentially defining features of a person's identity. The emergence of a black middle class, some say, implies the declining significance of race (Wilson 1978). The political failures of race-based affirmative action policies, others say, necessitate a move to class-based education and employment policies (Wilson 1987). We are all too familiar with such arguments, where race and class are spoken of as two sides of the same coin.

In the diagram in Figure 1, race and class, taken together, situate whites and blacks at the antipodes with respect to each other.[3] Both dimensions inform the everyday experiences of African Americans, whereas white Americans typically ignore race as an integral aspect of their lives. Racial considerations are more easily rendered invisible to white Americans, it is argued, because of the prevailing belief among many whites in individualism and meritocracy. That is, they tend to believe that opportunities to succeed are equal between blacks and whites and that whites are better off than blacks simply because they work with greater spirit and industry to avail themselves of those opportunities. That core division between blacks and whites has been such a durable and defining characteristic of America's racial order that it is unlikely to change over the next ten years.

What about Asians and Latinos? If we hew narrowly to the current government definitions of Asian or Pacific Islander "races" and Latino "ethnicity," Asians and Latinos, too, are situated opposite one another in the two-dimensional space depicted in Figure 1. That Asians and Latinos enter the twenty-first century facing quite different socioeconomic conditions would appear uncontroversial. The material circumstances of Asian Americans are comparable to those of whites and quite unlike those of Latinos (especially Mexicans), who continue to function in the U.S. economy as its principal source of low-wage labor (Massey, Durand, and Malone 2002). In 2004 the per capita incomes of non-Hispanic whites and Asian Americans were $27,414 and $26,217, respectively. For African Americans and Latinos the comparable figures were $16,035 and $14,106 (DeNavas-Walt, Proctor, and Lee 2005). It is important to note that the different

Figure 1. Mapping Class Identity onto Racial Identity

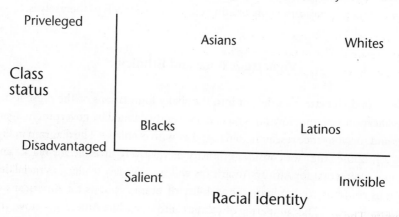

national origin groups among Asians and Latinos are not equally well off. For instance, whereas the poverty rate for Asian Americans in 1999 was 12.6 percent (very close to the national average of 12.4 percent), the proportion of Asians living below the poverty line ranged from 6.3 percent for Filipinos, to 29.3 percent for Cambodians, and 37.8 percent for Hmongs (Reeves and Bennett 2004).

Racially, Asians are given a high salience, and Latinos a low salience in part because government agencies such as the Census Bureau consider Asian Americans a "racial" group and Latinos an "ethnic" group. In addition, the relatively greater salience of race for Asians is suggested by the fact that Asian Americans are about as likely to report being discriminated against on account of race as Latinos—a rather striking result given that Asian Americans enjoy substantially greater material advantages than Latino Americans (Lee 2000). Many will likely balk at such a claim. From the standpoint of Asians as a "race," some have noted that the differences in class mobility among national origin groups likely work against the development of a durable pan-ethnic solidarity. For Latinos, second generation immigrants are much likelier to view their experiences in a racial light than are their first generation counterparts (Portes and Rumbaut 2001), so this representation of Asians and Latinos as in opposite situations may not hold for long. In 1990 and 2000, more than 40 percent of Americans who identified themselves as Latino on the Census Bureau's "ethnicity" identifier also identified racially as "Other race"; conversely, 97 percent of those who identified as "Other race" were Americans who also identified as Latino (Lopez 2005). It is hard to interpret these outcomes as anything other than an explicit rejection of the deracialization of Latino identity. They may say more about the ironies of the present-day ethno-racial classification system than about any real differences in how ordinary Americans apply existing ethnic/racial labels to themselves.

Vignette 2: Race and Ethnicity

The second vignette goes deeper into the shaky foundations of the present-day classification system. How does race, as currently defined by government agencies and social science research, join together with ethnicity? The diagram in Figure 2 proposes that we consider ethnicity as relatively invisible for blacks and whites. Doing that for African Americans will surprise few readers, as racial definitions continue to dominate the viability of ethnic options for Americans of African descent.[4] The laundering of ethnic claims for white Americans, however, may evoke protest from readers who would point to the seas of green that flood Boston, Chicago, and other cities every Saint Patrick's Day or the many "Little Italy's" that continue to thrive across the American urban landscape. Yet as sociologists have shown, while ethnic claims are perhaps more readily accessible for whites than for blacks, the era of European national ancestry as a defining identity for white Americans is largely in its twilight, coming to light only episodically in symbolic celebrations like Saint Patrick's Day parades, Oktoberfests, and tulip festivals (Alba 1990, Waters 1990). By contrast, there is significant evidence that for Asians and Latinos ethnicity is a substantive, instrumental identity. Beyond ritual celebrations of Cinco de Mayo, Lunar New Year, Diwali, and the like, ethnic ties and ethnic discrimination are instrumental in defining where Latinos and Asians live, the civic and religious associations they belong to, and even, at times, whether and when they are politically mobilized (Espiritu 1992, Jones-Correa 1998, Bobo et al. 2000).

If this way of thinking about how race and ethnicity come together holds up, one outcome is that whites and Asians stand opposite each another. This result contrasts starkly against the prevailing views that whites and Asians are more alike than different and that whites and Asians growing ever-closer over time.

One might object that I have managed to situate whites and Asians opposite one another by using an ethno-racial classification scheme that simply fails to capture the complexity of our times. One might also object that the classification scheme that the Office of Management and Budget and the Census Bureau currently use has no scientific basis and is the result of political compromises. Note, for instance, that in other contexts, such as current Equal Employment Opportunity Commission affirmative action guidelines, Latinos, Asians, and Native Americans are rather seamlessly included in the same administrative class as African Americans (Skrentny 2002). More generally, other scholars have noted

Figure 2. Mapping Ethnic Identity onto Racial Identity

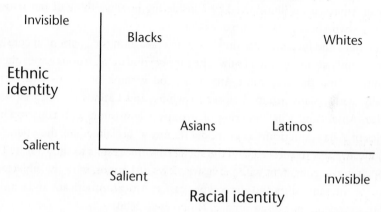

the ubiquity of a "one-hate rule," in which whites are singled out as distinct from nonwhites and in which all kinds of white racism are treated as equivalent regardless of the group against which it is directed (Hollinger 2005).

These are valid contentions. They point to the absurdity of current governmental definitions of race and ethnicity. Bureaucratic illogics are often a generative force for change, and one likely future is that the way race and ethnicity are currently defined will change. Government actors (professors, too) are not simply "consumers" of predetermined racial/ethnic names and labels (Omi and Winant 1994; Smith 2003). They are producers as well. So, too, increasingly, are the diverse and proliferating citizen groups that seek recognition, representation, and the right to be named. In fact, most of the recent changes to governmental definitions of race and ethnicity—the separation of Latino "ethnicity" from non-Latino "races," the fragmentation of nationally specific Asian and Pacific Islander "races," the creation of a hybrid multiracial identity—have been the result of such interest group mobilization. Thus the future is likely to bring new ethnoracial classification systems, most likely ones that try to bring emerging groups such as Asians and Latinos more in line with a black-white racial hierarchy.

Vignette 3: Race and Nation

What should not be lost in the rush to change the way we classify people to better fit preconceived notions of "race" is the fact that the experiences of Asians and Latinos are in crucial respects distinct from those of both whites and African

Americans. The palpable divide separating Asians and Latinos from whites and African Americans is illuminated by considering how we think of our national identity—who belongs and who does not.

The third and final vignette thus considers race alongside nation. In considering race and nation together, I now take race beyond incongruous governmental definitions and the way most Americans today think of Asians and Latinos racially, with Asians grouped closer to whites and Latinos grouped closer to African Americans. That ordering of groups is consistent with contemporary stories of Asian Americans as a "model minority" acclaimed for their penchant for industry, zeal to succeed, and the socioeconomic results to show for it (Tuan 1999). It is also consistent with pervasive views of Latinos, who are subjected to many of the same slurs and stereotypes cast at African Americans and similarly severe socioeconomic disadvantages (Bobo et al. 2000).

What then groups Asians together with Latinos and apart from both whites and African Americans? As Figure 3 illustrates, the differentiation occurs on the axis of national belonging. As newcomers to America, both Asians and Latinos are commonly viewed as outsiders whose cultures are unassimilable and whose loyalties are suspect. Evidence for this includes the stubborn belief that most Latinos are undocumented "aliens" and the fear that the continued influx of Mexicans into the United States will lead to balkanization and the demise of the nation's core Anglo-Protestant culture (Huntington 2004). With respect to Asian Americans, the evidence includes a long history in which the loyalties of U.S. citizens of Asian descent have been presumed to be to their Asian home countries and not to the United States—a history that ranges from the forced internment of Japanese Americans during World War II, to contemporary cases like the alleged foreign influence peddling of Asian American donors in the 1996 presidential election and alleged espionage by Dr. Wen Ho Lee, a Taiwanese American nuclear scientist working at Los Alamos (see, e.g., Kim 1999). Especially in post-9/11 America, there is a bright line of national belonging that separates immigrant-based ethnic groups such as Asians, Latinos, and Arabs from whites and African Americans.

This vignette reveals a third possible ordering. As Figure 3 shows, whites and Latinos are now at the antipodes of the main diagonal axis, with blacks and Asians opposite each other on the "off-diagonal" axis. Thus one upshot of the three vignettes is that any group—blacks, Latinos, or Asians—might be situated opposite to whites, depending on how "race" is defined and which overlapping identity classes are paired with it. A second upshot is that the pairings of race with class, ethnicity, and nationhood are not equally likely to be durable over the next decade. Class and race are likely to continue to go hand in hand, as a group's socioeconomic attainments are likely to match their status in America's racial

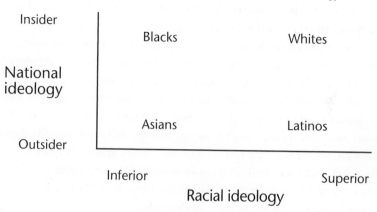

Figure 3. Mapping National Ideology onto Racial Ideology

hierarchy in the foreseeable future. That racial hierarchy, however, is an uncomfortable fit with the current government system of classifying people into racial and ethnic categories. Moreover, if the post-9/11 drumbeat for patriotism and national identity continues with greater force and urgency, the relative status of whites, blacks, Asians, and Latinos in the American landscape may shift yet again away from strictly race-based hierarchies and toward a more ethnocentric view of national belonging.

Two Steps Back

At this point, the vignettes sputter and clang like a jalopy, implying conclusions without the benefit of testable premises. That said, however, in the spirit of taking risks rather than hedging bets, I close by being even more specific about [what] can be predicted for the next decade or so. First, as suggested earlier, we are not likely to grin and bear the current ethno-racial classification system for long. In particular, the current convention—most evident in the Census—that only ethnicity distinguishes Hispanics from non-Hispanics, while assorted Asian-national-origin groups are defined as separate "races," is untenable and likely to change in the near future.

Such a prospect is often taken to imply a gradual decline of the primacy of race in American life. In my view, such a prediction is either naïvely optimistic or willfully blind. The ubiquity of race/ethnicity, class, and nationhood is likely to continue into the near future. This is especially so given the social and political environment in which we currently live—one characterized by Republican control of all branches of the federal government, with nativist vigilantes policing the United States-Mexico border, sustained efforts to unmake the racial progress of the 1960s and remake the "wall of separation" dividing religion and politics, public embrace of ethno-religious criminal profiling, and other spectacles of nostalgia and jingoism. The names and labels used to describe and categorize individuals in America may change, but the use of social and political constructions that divide a people into us and them, insider and outsider, citizen and alien, or deserving and undeserving, and so on, will continue.

What does this mean, really? It means that the adaptation and inclusion of immigrants into American life, if they are Afro-Caribbean, Arab, Asian, or Latino, will remain a clash of fates—success with scorn, hope with despair. Immigrants who come matched to skills in demand in the U.S. economy will continue to enjoy the material fruits of their labor, but never without the thorns of social ostracism and ethno-national chauvinism. Similarly, it means that a select few blacks will continue to move onward and upward in America, but never without sobering reminders that—in a society that presently privileges the principle of color-blindness as a goal over the unfulfilled reality of color-blindness in the antidiscriminatory practices of our institutions—the success of the few will only come at the expense of the abject failure of the many. With or without affirmative action, deep-rooted formal and informal practices will leave African Americans conspicuously underrepresented in most privileged and powerful walks of American life into the future.

Finally, the prospects for communities of color seizing their own destinies by engaging in multiracial politics are dim. To be fair, there have been intermittent glimmers of hope, as in the elections of Harold Washington as mayor of Chicago in 1983, Gary Locke as governor of Washington in 1996, and Antonio Villaraigosa as mayor of Los Angeles in 2005. But our current milieu is one in which the political labors that bear fruit are seemingly the labors of working "within the system," as seen in the appointments of Colin Powell, Condoleeza Rice, Alberto Gonzalez, Elaine Chao, Norman Mineta, Carlos Gutierrez, and others by the current administration.[5] These gestures of the Republican Party to reach out to blacks, Asians, and Latinos may be purely symbolic, or they may be genuine, but over the short duration of a decade their greatest effect (especially for Asians and Latinos) is likely to be the increased dispersion of votes across party lines. Barring some restoration of the left, the Democratic Party's historic hold on the partisan loyalties (if not actual votes) of communities of color will likely continue to attenuate. We have already seen this in the higher proportion of Latino and Asian American Republican voters in the 2004 presidential election. Good or bad, this dispersion of votes is quite likely to further weaken the ability of blacks, Asians, and Latinos to demand and achieve substantive policy representation. Here again, ours is an era that favors the few haves over the many have-nots.

This view into the future is decidedly bleak. To adapt Donald Rumsfeld's poetics to present circumstances, it is created from "known knowns" and "known unknowns." But there are "unknown unknowns" that too may adjudicate between the soothsayer and sophist in this essay. Ultimately, time (and perhaps our will to make a difference) will tell that tale.

NOTES

1. Given the economy of space in these essays, I do not discuss the racial positioning of Native Americans. This is a regrettable omission not just because a corner of the "ethno-racial pentagon" is abandoned, but more so because it has been a transformative space, with the dramatic political and demographic "resurgence of the native" in the last several decades (but see, e.g., Nagel 1997).

2. A 2003 survey of Californians, for example, found that more than one in four respondents identified multiracially when asked to self-identify using "identity points," a substantially greater proportion than the one in twenty Californians who identified multiracially under the "Mark one or more" format of the 2000 Census (Lee 2006).

3. These figures are used purely for illustrative purposes and are not intended imply the specific placement of any group—e.g., that race is equally salient for Asians as for blacks.

4. Important exceptions here are the salience of ethnic claims of African or Afro-Caribbean immigrants and cultural strands of underlying Afro-centrism and the Black Muslim movement in America.

5. Colin Powell was U.S. secretary of state from 2001 to 2004; Condoleeza Rice was national security adviser from 2001 to 2004 and has been secretary of state since 2005; Alberto Gonzalez was White House counsel from 2001 to 2004 and has been attorney general since 2005; Elaine Chao has been secretary of labor since 2001; Norman Mineta has been secretary of transportation since 2001; Carlos Gutierrez has been secretary of commerce since 2005.

REFERENCES

Alba, Richard D. 1990. *Ethnic Identity: The Transformation of White America*. New Haven: Yale University Press.

Allport, Gordon. 1954. *The Nature of Prejudice*. Cambridge, Mass.: Addison-Wesley.

Bean, Frank D., and Gillian Stevens. 2003. *America's Newcomers and the Dynamics of Diversity*. New York: Russell Sage.

Blalock, Hubert. 1967. *Toward a Theory of Minority-Group Relations*. New York: Wiley.

Bobo, Lawrence, and Vincent Hutchings. 1996. "Perceptions of Racial Group Competition." *American Sociological Review* 61(6): 951–972.

Bobo, Lawrence, Melvin Oliver, James Johnson Jr., and Abel Valenzuela Jr., eds. 2000. *Prismatic Metropolis: Inequality in Los Angeles*. New York: Russell Sage.

Cohen, Cathy. 1999. *Boundaries of Blackness: AIDS and the Breakdown of Black Politics.* Chicago: University of Chicago Press.

DaCosta, Kimberly McClain. 2003. "Multiracial Identity: From Personal Problem to Public Issue." In *New Faces in a Changing America,* ed. Loretta Winters and Herman DeBose. Thousand Oaks, Calif.: Sage.

Dawson, Michael C. 2001. *Black Visions.* Chicago: University of Chicago Press.

DeNavas-Walt, Carmen, Bernadette D. Proctor, and Cheryl Hill Lee. 2005. *Income, Poverty, and Health Insurance Coverage in the United States: 2004.* U.S. Census Bureau, Current Population Reports, 60-229. Washington, D.C.: U.S. Government Printing Office.

DeSipio, Louis. 1996. *Counting on the Latino Vote: Latinos as a New Electorate.* Charlottesville: University of Virginia Press.

Espiritu, Yen Le. 1992. *Asian American Panethnicity.* Philadelphia: Temple University Press.

Frey, William H. 2002. *Census 2000 Reveals New Native-Born and Foreign-Born Shifts across U.S.* PSC Research Report 02-520. Ann Arbor, Mich.: Population Studies Center, Institution for Social Research.

Glazer, Nathan. 2002. "Do We Need the Census Race Question?" *Public Interest,* Fall, 21–31.

Goldstein, Joshua, and Ann Morning. 2000. "The Multiple-Race Population of the United States: Issues and Estimates." *Proceedings of the National Academy of Sciences* 97 (11): 6230–6235.

Green, Donald Philip, Dara Strolovich, and Janelle Wong. 1998. "Defended Neighborhoods, Integration, and Racially Motivated Crime." *American Journal of Sociology* 104 (2): 372–403.

Hochschild, Jennifer. 2005. "Looking Ahead: Racial Trends in the United States." *Daedalus,* Winter, 70–81.

Hollinger, David. 2003. "Amalgamation and Hypodescent: The Question of Ethnoracial Mixture in the History of the United States." *American Historical Review* 108 (5): 1363–1390.

———. 2005. "The One Drop Rule and the One Hate Rule." *Daedalus,* Winter, 18–28.

Huntington, Samuel P. 2004. *Who Are We? The Challenges to America's National Identity.* New York: Simon and Schuster.

Jones-Correa, Michael. 1998. *Between Two Nations: The Political Predicament of Latinos in New York City.* Ithaca, N.Y.: Cornell University Press.

Kim, Claire Jean. 1999. *Bitter Fruit: The Politics of Black-Korean Conflict in New York City.* New Haven: Yale University Press.

Lee, Taeku. 2000. "Racial Attitudes and the Color Line(s) at the Close of the Twentieth Century." In *The State of Asian Pacific Americans: Transforming Race Relations,* ed. Paul Ong. Los Angeles: LEAP/UCLA Asian Pacific American Public Policy Institute.

———. 2006. "Between Social Theory and Social Science Practice: Towards a New Approach to the Survey Measurement of Race." In *Identity as a Variable: A Guide to Conceptualization and Measurement of Identity,* ed. Rawi Abdelal, Yoshiko Herrera, Alastair Iain Johnston, and Rose McDermott. New York: Cambridge University Press.

Lie, John. 2004. *Modern Peoplehood.* Cambridge, Mass.: Harvard University Press.

Lopez, Ian Haney. 2005. "Race on the 2010 Census: Hispanics and the Shrinking White Majority." *Daedalus,* Winter, 42–52.

Massey, Douglas S., Jorge Durand, and Nolan J. Malone. 2002. *Beyond Smoke and Mirrors: Mexican Immigration in an Era of Economic Integration.* New York: Russell Sage.

Nagel, Joane. 1997. *American Indian Ethnic Renewal: Red Power and the Resurgence of Identity and Culture*. New York: Oxford University Press.

Omi, Michael, and Howard Winant. 1994. Rev. ed. *Racial Formation in the United States*. New York: Routledge.

Perlmann, J., and Mary J. Waters, eds. 2002. *The New Race Question: How the Census Counts Multi-racial Individuals*. New York: Russell Sage.

Portes, Alejandro, and Min Zhou. 1993. "The New Second Generation: Segmented Assimilation and its Variants." *Annals of the American Academy of Political and Social Science* 530:74–97.

Portes, Alejandro, and Rubén G. Rumbaut. 2001. *Legacies: The Story of the Immigrant Second Generation*. Berkeley: University of California Press.

Ramakrishnan, Karthick. 2005. *Democracy in Immigrant America*. Palo Alto, Calif.: Stanford University Press.

Reeves, Terrance, and Claudette Bennett. 2004. *We the People: Asians in the United States*. U.S. Census Bureau, Census 2000 Special Reports, CENSR-17. Washington, D.C.: U.S. Government Printing Office.

Roediger, David. 1991. *Wages of Whiteness: Race and the Making of the American Working Class*. London: Verso.

Rogers, Reuel. 2006. *Afro-Caribbean Immigrants and the Politics of Incorporation: Ethnicity, Exception, and Exit*. New York: Cambridge University Press.

Schuman, Howard, Charlotte Steeh, Lawrence Bobo, and Maria Krysan. 1997. *Racial Attitudes in America*, rev. ed. Cambridge, Mass.: Harvard University Press.

Skrentny, John D. 2002. *The Minority Rights Revolution*. Cambridge, Mass.: Harvard University Press.

Smith, Rogers. 2003. *Stories of Peoplehood: The Politics and Morals of Political Membership*. New York: Cambridge University Press.

Tuan, Mia. 1999. *Forever Foreigners or Honorary Whites?* New Brunswick, N.J.: Rutgers University Press.

U.S. Census Bureau. 2002. *Current Population Survey: Monthly Demographic File*. March. Washington, D.C.: U.S. Census Bureau.

U.S. Immigration and Naturalization Service. 2002. *2000 INS Statistical Yearbook*. Washington, D.C.: Government Printing Office.

Waters, Mary C. 1990. *Ethnic Options: Choosing Identities in America*. Berkeley: University of California Press.

Williams, Kim. 2006. *Race Counts: American Multiracialism and Civil Rights Policies*. Ann Arbor: University of Michigan Press.

Wilson, William Julius. 1978. *The Declining Significance of Race: Blacks and Changing American Institutions*. Chicago: University of Chicago Press.

———. 1987. *The Truly Disadvantaged: The Inner City, the Underclass, and Public Policy*. Chicago: University of Chicago Press.

Wong, Janelle. 2005. *Democracy's Promise: Immigrants and American Civic Institutions*. Ann Arbor, Mich.: University of Michigan Press.

4-2

American Diversity and the 2000 Census

Nathan Glazer

Since the earliest days of the republic, race has proved a difficult issue for each generation of politicians to resolve. While the problem began with slavery, it did not, of course, end with the institution's eradication during the Civil War. Throughout the nineteenth and twentieth centuries, the core issues of "white over black" never receded far from the surface of America's politics. As the country has entered the twenty-first century there have been signs of change in the racial picture, change that has been occurring for some time but has suddenly become manifest. For one, Hispanics have now eclipsed African Americans as the nation's largest racial minority. In this essay, Nathan Glazer ponders a couple of fundamental, yet easily overlooked, issues of race for this next century. They concern how the government defines race and, more importantly, how in our increasingly multiracial and at the same time assimilated society we define ourselves.

THE 2000 CENSUS, on which the Census Bureau started issuing reports in March and April of 2001, reflected, in its structure and its results, the two enduring themes of American racial and ethnic diversity, present since the origins of American society in the English colonies of the Atlantic coast: first, the continued presence of what appears to be an almost permanent lower caste composed of the black race; and second, the ongoing process of immigration of races and peoples from all quarters of the globe, who seem, within a few generations, to merge into a common American people.

To make two such large generalizations is admittedly a bold move. Undoubtedly, as further data from the census is released, we will have evidence of the continuing progress of American blacks in education, occupational diversity, and income. We will have grounds for arguing that the effects of integration into a common people can be seen, at long last, among American blacks. And when it comes to the new waves of immigration of the past few decades, some will question whether the process of assimilation and incorporation, which has swallowed

Source: Nathan Glazer, "American Diversity and the 2000 Census," *Public Interest* 144 (summer 2001): 3–18.

up so many groups and races and religions into a common American people, will continue to work its effects on the new groups now gathered together under the terms "Hispanic" and "Asian." Yet I believe it can be argued that this large distinction in the processes of assimilation and integration that has persisted during the three- or four-century history of American diversity—the distinction between blacks and others—still shows itself, and still poses some of the most difficult questions for American society.

The First Census

The distinction makes itself evident in the very history and structure of the census, and in the character of the data that it first presents to the public today. In the first census of 1790, required for purposes of apportionment [seats in the House of Representatives] by the U.S. Constitution adopted in 1787, the separation between blacks and whites was already made. Indeed, that separation was itself foreshadowed by the Constitution, which, in a famous compromise, decreed that "Representatives . . . shall be apportioned among the several states . . . according to their respective numbers, which shall be determined by adding to the whole number of free persons . . . three-fifths of all other persons." Those "other persons" were slaves. The "three-fifths" was a compromise between excluding all slaves for purposes of apportionment (which would have reduced the weight of the Southern slave states in the union) or counting them simply as persons (which would have given the slave states too great weight).

The census could have fulfilled the requirements of the Constitution by counting only slaves. But what was to be done with free blacks? There were, even then, free blacks, but their civil status was sharply below that of whites. It was apparently decided that they could not be simply numbered among the "free persons" referred to in the Constitution but had to be clearly distinguished from whites. So the first census went beyond the Constitution: It counted "free white males and females" as one category, "slaves" as another, but then added a category of "all other free persons." The count of "other persons"—slaves—and "all other free persons"—free blacks—produced the total number of blacks. Thus from the beginning, white could be differentiated from black. That has remained the most enduring distinction in the U.S. census.

In that first census, following the apportionment provision of the Constitution, "Indians not taxed" were also excluded. Over time, this simple scheme has been extended to cover other races and ethnic groups as they entered the new nation through immigration, to a degree which is possibly unique among national censuses, and which we will explore below. But the census begins crucially with the distinction between white and black. As Clara Rodriguez writes in her book *Changing Race:*

> Between the drafting of the Constitution of 1787 and the taking of the first census in 1790, the term white became an explicit part of [the free population]. . . . Theoretically, those in political charge could have chosen another definition for the [free population]. . . . They could have chosen "free English-speaking males over sixteen" or "free males of Christian descent" or "of European descent." But they chose color. Having named the central category "white" gave a centrality and power to color that has continued throughout the history of the census.

But of course this reflected the centrality of the black-white distinction in American society and the American mind. Rodriguez goes on to note that on occasion in the pre-Civil War censuses "aliens and foreigners not naturalized," separately numbered, are combined in one table with native whites and citizens in a table of "total white." "In the 1850 census, the category 'free whites' is changed to simply 'whites,' which suggests by this time it was evident that all the people in this category were free."

The Color Line

Color—race—has since been elaborated to a remarkable degree in the U.S. census. The most striking aspect of the American census of 2000—as of the few before—is that the short form, which goes to all American households, consists mostly of questions on race and "Hispanicity." Two large questions ask for the respondent's race, and whether the respondent is of "Spanish/Hispanic" origin, and both go into considerable detail in trying to determine just what race, and just what kind of "Hispanic," the respondent is. The race question lists many possibilities to choose from, including, to begin with, "white" and "black," and going on to "Indian (Amer.)," with an additional request to list the name of the tribe, "Eskimo," or "Aleut." And then under the general heading "Asian or Pacific Islander (API)," it lists as separate choices Chinese, Filipino, Hawaiian, Korean, Vietnamese, Japanese, Asian Indian, Samoan, Guamanian, "Other API," and finally "Other race (print name)." In the 2000 census, it was possible for the first time for the respondent to check more than one race. This change was made after an extended discussion in the 1990s about how to account for those with parents of different race, who wanted to check off both, or perhaps more than two.

The question on whether one is Spanish/Hispanic also goes on to list a range of possibilities: "Mexican, Mexican-Am. [for "American"], or Chicano" (to account for the fact that Mexican Americans choose different terms to describe themselves), "Puerto Rican," "Cuban," and "other Spanish/Hispanic," with again the request to write in one group. In the 1990 census, a host of examples—"Argentinean, Colombian, Dominican, Nicaraguan, Salvadoran, Spaniard, and so on," was offered.

The observant and conscientious citizen may note that many other matters of interest to the census and the polity—whether one is of foreign birth or not, a citizen or not, and one's education, occupation, income, housing status, etc.—are all relegated to the long form, which goes to a large sample of citizens. And he may also ask why the census pays such great and meticulous attention to race and ethnicity (or rather one kind of ethnicity, that of Spanish-Hispanic background).

Many answers, going back to the first census of 1790, and before that, to the Constitution that prescribed a regular decennial census, and before that, to the first arrival of black slaves in the English colonies in the early seventeenth century, are available to explain why the first statistics the census makes available today, along with the raw number of the population in each state and locality, are those describing race and ethnicity. But there is also an immediate and proximate answer of much more recent currency: Congress requires that ethnic and racial statistics be available within a year of the census for the purpose of redrawing the boundaries of congressional districts, and the other electoral districts for state legislative assemblies, and for city and county elected officials.

Ethnic and racial statistics have become so significant for redistricting because of the Civil Rights Act of 1964, the Voting Rights Acts of 1965, and the latter's amendments of 1970, 1975, and 1982. . . . The right enshrined in the Voting Rights statute, to the free exercise of the vote, has been extended through litigation and administrative and judicial rule-making to cover rights to the drawing of congressional and other district boundaries in such a way as to protect or enhance the ability of minority groups, blacks in particular, but others too, to elect representatives of their own group. If blacks are to be protected from discrimination . . . then detailed statistics of how a race is distributed are necessary.

That is why the first statistics that come out of the census are those that make it possible to redraw district lines immediately on the basis of the new census, and for various groups to challenge the new district lines if they are aggrieved. . . . For those with the responsibility of drawing up the new districts—the state legislatures primarily—the central concern is generally the maximization of the number of representatives of the party in power in the state legislature. A second concern is to maintain for the incumbents of the favored party district boundaries that secure their return. But overlaying these historic political reasons for drawing district lines, which courts accept in some measure as legitimate, is a new imperative, the protection of minority groups.

The Four "Official" Minorities

"Portrait of a Nation" is the title of a major story on the first results of the census in the *New York Times,* and it is accompanied by elaborate colored maps. The colors provide information on the distribution of the minority population—blacks, Hispanics, Asians, American Indians.

To explain how these have become the American minorities—to the exclusion of many other possible minorities—and why their numbers and distribution are in every newspaper report considered the most important information to look for in the census, would require a precis of American history. It is hardly necessary to explain why blacks are the first of the minority groups. They have been a significant presence in the United States and its predecessor colonies from the beginning. Our greatest national trauma—the Civil War—was directly occasioned by the problem of black slavery, and the most significant amendments to the Constitution became part of that quasi-sacred document in order to deal with the consequences of black slavery.

American Indians were there even before the beginning but were considered outside the society and polity unless they individually entered into non-Indian-American society, as many have, through intermarriage and assimilation. Their status has changed over time, from outside the polity as semi-sovereign foreign nations, to subjects almost without rights, to a population confined on reservations, to one that now increasingly becomes part of the society. Indeed, today, to be able to claim an American-Indian heritage is a plus for one's social status. This is too complex a history to be reviewed here. There is good reason to maintain a separate count of Indians, though there are great complexities in doing so.

"Hispanics," too, were there from before the beginning, if we take into account the Spaniards and Creoles moving up from Mexico who had already established colonial settlements in northern Mexico—what is now the Southwest of the United States—before the first English colonists had established permanent settlements on the Atlantic coast. Of course, they were not "Hispanics" then. Two hundred and fifty years later, this mixed population became part of the United States as a result of the annexation of the northern part of Mexico after the Mexican-American war. But it contained then a small population of Mexicans and Indians, and interestingly enough, despite the sense of racial difference felt by the Anglo-Americans, and despite the prejudice against Mexicans, they were not differentiated in the census as a separate group until 1930. Until then, one presumes, they were "white." In that year, Clara Rodriguez notes, a census publication, responding to the increase in immigration from Mexico as a result of the revolutionary wars and troubles of the 1920s, reported that "persons of Mexican birth or parentage who were not definitely reported as white or Indian were designated

Mexican" and included in "other races." In 1940, this policy was changed, and Mexicans became white again. By 1950, added to the growing number of Mexicans in the Southwest, as a result of immigration in the previous decades, was a large number of Puerto Ricans in New York City, migrants from the island of Puerto Rico, which had been annexed after the Spanish-American war of 1898. In that census year, the two were combined in the census—along with smaller numbers of other groups—into a "Spanish-surnamed" group.

In the wake of Castro's victory in Cuba, a third large group of Latin Americans emigrated to the United States. Whether or not one could make a single meaningful category out of Mexicans, Puerto Ricans, and Cubans, separated as they are by culture, history, and to some extent by racial characteristics, they were so combined, with a host of other Spanish-speaking groups, into a "Hispanic" category in the census of 1970. The creation of the category was a response to political pressure from Mexican Americans. It now includes large numbers of Nicaraguans, Guatemalans, Salvadorans, Dominicans, Colombians, Ecuadorians, and others fleeing the political and economic troubles of their homelands.

Racial and ethnic groups are conventionally described today as "constructed," but it is worth noting that this "construction" is not simply the result of white determinations—it is also the result of group insistence, at least to some degree. As Peter Skerry tells us in his book *Counting on the Census:*

> The finalized questionnaires for the 1970 census were already at the printers when a Mexican American member of the U.S. Interagency Committee on Mexican American affairs demanded that a specific Hispanic-origin question be included. . . . Over the opposition of Census Bureau officials, who argued against inclusion of an untested question so late in the process, [President] Nixon ordered the secretary of commerce and the census director to add the question.

And so "Hispanics" were born. The pressure to maintain the category, with all its subdistinctions, persists. The distinguished demographer Stanley Lieberson has written about a well-intentioned intervention at a conference preparatory to the 1990 census:

> I naively suggested that there was no reason to have an Hispanic question separate from the ethnic ancestry question [an ancestry question has been part of the long form since 1980] since the former . . . could be classified as a subpart of the latter. Several participants from prominent Hispanic organizations were furious at such a proposal. They were furious, by the way, not at me (just a naive academic), rather it was in the form of a warning to census personnel of the consequences that would follow were this proposal to be taken seriously.

The last of the four minorities distinguished in the census is the "Asian," a creation—or construction—that has as complex a history as that of the Hispanic. Chinese and Japanese individuals were undoubtedly present in the United States before they were first listed as "races" in 1870—by then there was a substantial population of Chinese in California, and they were already the subject of racist legislation. In 1930, "Filipino," "Hindu" [sic], and "Korean" were added as separate races, and it became the pattern to add a new "race" for each Asian immigrant group as it became numerous. Eventually, we have the complex category of "Asian and Pacific Islander" (API), with all its listed subgroups.

As in the case of the Mexicans, the initial discrimination that made each of these a separate group was undoubtedly racist and reflected a sense of white superiority. The Asian groups were all subjected to discriminatory legislation. One could be naturalized as a citizen only if one were "white" (or, after the Civil War, black). All sorts of restrictions, from land ownership to the pursuit of certain professions or occupations, were imposed on them by various states because they were noncitizens. But Asian immigrants were denied because of race the right of becoming citizens. These groups were indeed nonwhite, but their separate classification was more than a matter of keeping neat statistics. An identity was being selected for a group felt to be inferior. This identity may well have been the one the members of the group would have chosen, but it was not they who decided they should be numbered aside from the dominant whites. . . .

A Melting Pot?

These then are the four "official" minorities, though no law names these and only these as minorities. But what has happened then to all those others once considered "minorities," ethnic groups that were in the first quarter of the twentieth century in the eye of public attention because of the recency of their immigration, their lower social and economic status, and the concern that they could not be assimilated? Immigration was largely cut off by law in the 1920s because of these concerns. The United States has been a country of immigration since its origins, and by some measures the immigration of the first two decades of the twentieth century was much greater than the immigration of the last three decades, which has swelled the numbers of the new minorities. Had one picked up a book on American minorities and race relations in the 1950s, Jews might have been presented as the typical minority: Much of the social theory and social psychology on minority status was formulated with the position of Jews in mind. Jews were a major element in the mass immigration that preceded the present one, from the 1880s to the 1920s. Other major components of this immigration were Italians,

Poles, Hungarians, Czechs, Slovaks, Slovenes, Croats, Serbs, Greeks, Armenians, Lebanese, Syrians, and many other peoples of Eastern and Southern Europe and the Near East. Are they no longer included in the story of American minorities?

One can go further back and ask, what has happened to the Irish, the Germans, the Swedes, Norwegians, and Danes, and the host of immigrants who came earlier and were also once sharply distinguished as separate groups, different from the founding group, the English? Does not the story of American diversity include all these too? How has the palette become restricted to the four minorities that play so large a role in the current census?

The simple answer is that integration and assimilation reduce over time the differences that distinguish one group from another, or from the original settler group, what Tocqueville called the "Anglo-Americans." We have no good term for this group. WASP ("White Anglo-Saxon Protestant") has been used in recent decades, ironically or derisively, for the founding element and their descendants. But aside from the necessity to distinguish such a group historically, no term is currently really necessary: Immigrants merge in two or three generations into a common American people, and ethnic distinctions become less and less meaningful. Ethnicity becomes symbolic, a matter of choice, to be noted on the basis of name or some other signifier on occasion, of little matter for most of one's life.

At one time, the census distinguished the foreign-born by place of birth, and the foreign-born parents of the native-born by place of birth, permitting us to track ethnic groups (somewhat uncertainly, owing to the lack of fit between ethnicity and national boundaries) for two generations. The rest of the population was classed as natives of native parentage, not further distinguishable, at least in the census, on the basis of their ethnicity. In 1980, the question on birthplace of parents was dropped, to the distress of sociologists and students of ethnicity. A new question on "ancestry" was added, which, in theory, would permit us to connect people to ethnic groups in the third generation and beyond. But the amount of mixture among groups, through marriage, is today such that the answers to the ancestry question, if one is not an immigrant or the child of an immigrant with a clear sense of ancestry, are not helpful in distinguishing an ethnic group much beyond the second generation. The answers then become so variable, so dependent on cues from the census itself—such as the examples the census form gives to the respondent regarding what is intended by the term "ancestry," which is by no means clear to many people—as to be hardly meaningful. It is a question that permits some 40 million Americans, seven times the population of Ireland, to declare that they are of "Irish" ancestry.

There are indeed differences of some significance based on ethnicity among the native white population, and sometimes these become evident—when home countries are involved in conflict, for example—or even paramount. This is particularly evident for Jews, who are marked not only as a religion (but the census rigorously refrains from asking any question or accepting any response on religion) but also by ethnicity (but to the census, Jews are not an ethnic group but a religion). The exceptional history that resulted in the killing of most of the Jews of Europe, and the creation of a regularly imperiled State of Israel, ties Jews to their past and to their co-religionists abroad much more than other ethnic groups. They are not to be found in any census count—they are not a "race" and not even, for the census, an "ancestry," even though that answer would make sense for most Jews.

Sociologists and political scientists can plumb for differences among the native white population, and they will find not insignificant differences in income, occupation, political orientation, and so on. Jews, for example, are exceptional among "whites" for their regular overwhelming support for Democrats. Indeed, the differences among native whites, ethnically distinguished, may be greater than those among the official minority groups or between any of them and the native white population. Yet from the point of view of public opinion and official notice, these differences are not significant. The ethnic groups of the great immigrations of the nineteenth and early twentieth century have sunk below the horizon of official attention. They have merged into the "white" population, become integrated and assimilated, and only emerge as a special interest on occasion, stimulated by a conflict or crisis involving the home country.

"Whiteness Theory"

Recently, this somewhat benign view of American history, one in which immigrant groups steadily assimilate to, and become part of, the common American people, has been challenged by historians who argue that this was a strictly limited process, available only to whites, and, further, that many of those who were eventually included as full Americans had to overcome a presumption that they were not "really" white. In other words, race is crucial, both at its beginning and, by implication, throughout American history, for full inclusion. To take one powerful and clear statement of this position:

> The saga of European immigration has long been held up as proof of the openness of American society, the benign and absorptive powers of American capitalism, and the robust health of American democracy. "Ethnic inclusion," "ethnic mobility," and "ethnic assimilation" on the European model set the standard upon which "America," as an ideal, is presumed to work; they provide the normative experience against which others are measured. But this pretty story suddenly fades once one recognizes how crucial Europeans' racial status as "free white persons" was to their gaining entrance in the first

place; how profoundly dependent their racial inclusion was upon the racial exclusion of others; how racially accented the native resistance was even to their inclusion for something over half a century. [Matthew Frye Jacobsen, in *Whiteness of a Different Color.*] The implication of this point of view is that the present minorities as commonly understood exist not only because of the recency of their immigration but primarily because of color: They are not white. Their ability to become full and equal participants in American society is thereby limited because of America's racist character.

But I believe these "whiteness theorists" are wrong. The racist character of the past is clear, and a degree of racism in the present is also evident, despite radical changes in public opinion and major changes in law and legal enforcement. But there has been a striking and irreversible change between the 1920s—when immigration from Eastern and Southern Europe was sharply reduced and immigration from Asia was banned entirely—and the postwar decades and, in particular, the period since the 1960s. Public institutions and significant private institutions today may only take account of race for the purpose of benefiting minorities.

The whiteness theorists may have a story to tell about the past, but it is one that has limited bearing on the present. The new immigrant groups are for the most part distinguished by race or quasi-racial characteristics from the population of European white origin. Yet it seems likely they progress pretty much at the same rate, affected by the same factors—their education and skills, their occupations, the areas of the country in which they settle, and the like—as the European immigrants of the past.

They merge into the common population at the same rate too. We will soon have analyses of marriages between persons of different race and ethnicity, to the extent the census makes possible, but we already know that the number and percentage of intermarriages between persons from the minorities and the majority has grown greatly in recent decades. One analysis of the 1990 census, reported by David T. Canon in his *Race, Redistricting and Representation*, shows that "for married people between the ages of twenty-five and thirty-four, 70 percent of Asian women and 39 percent of Hispanic women have white [*sic*] husbands." But only 2 percent of black women in the same age group were married to white men. The theme of black difference contrasted with the intermixture and merger of other groups is clearly sounded in these and other statistics.

The End of "Race"?

The first studies conducted by independent analysts of the 2000 census statistics brought up sharply the degree to which blacks are still distinguished from other minorities or subgroups in the United States by residential segregation. "Analysis of Census Finds Segregation Along With Diversity," reads one headline. "Segregation" in this analysis is measured by the diversity of census tracts, as experienced by the "average" person of a given group or race. The average white person lives in a tract that is 80 percent white, down from 85 percent in 1990; the average black person lives in a tract that is 51 percent black, down from 56 percent in 1990; the average Hispanic is less "segregated" by this measure—his tract is 45 percent Hispanic, and increased from 43 percent in 1990. But one may explain this degree of segregation and its rise since 1990 by the huge increase, based on immigration, much of it illegal, of the Hispanic population. The average Asian lives in a tract that is not particularly Asian—18 percent, as against 15 percent in 1990. This rise reflects to some degree the 50 percent increase of the Asian population, mostly through immigration, in the decade.

Local reporting focused on the relative proportions of the minority groups in each community, and also on the degree of segregation. Integration proceeds, but slowly. There are black census tracts in Boston with almost no whites and white tracts with almost no blacks. We calculate these figures every census, as if watching a fever report. The overall picture is that the segregation of blacks is great, the segregation of Hispanic groups, despite the recency of their immigration and their foreign tongue, is rather less, and little segregation is noted among Asians.

The big news of the census was that "Hispanics" had for the first time surpassed blacks in number, but that was only the case if one excluded from the black population those individuals who had chosen the race "black" along with another race. Hispanics rose to 35.3 million, a 61 percent increase in 10 years; blacks rose by about 16 percent to 34.7 million, or 36.4 million if one added those who chose more than one race. Blacks are 12.3 percent of the population, about the same percentage they have maintained for the past century. The increase in Hispanics was much greater than expected: It was generally agreed that one reason for this increase was a larger number of illegal immigrants than had been previously calculated, 9 million according to one demographer instead of 7, perhaps as much as 11 million according to another demographer.

Making the comparison between the two largest minorities was complicated by the fact that respondents could choose more than one race for the first time, and 7 million did so. Analysis of these mixed-race choices, even reporting on them, is not easy. A reporter writes: "Five percent of blacks, 6 percent of Hispanics, 14 percent of Asians and 2.5 percent of whites identified themselves as multi-racial." But why are these multi-race choosers labeled "black" or "Asian"? Is the "one drop" rule once used by the southern states operating here? If someone chooses "American Indian" and another race, do we include that person in the count of American Indians? If we do, that would increase the number of

American Indians by more than 50 percent. The Office of Management and Budget oversees the race and ethnic statistics compiled by federal agencies, and it has determined that for their purposes (affirmative-action monitoring and the like) all multi-race choosers who chose white and a minority race are to be counted as being part of the minority, a decision that has pleased minority advocates. But does it reflect how these individuals see themselves?

The mixed-race choices complicate the issue of choosing a base on which to measure the progress of, or possible discrimination against, minorities, an important step in affirmative action programs. That is the reason some minority leaders opposed allowing the mixed-race option. If the base becomes smaller, the degree of discrimination that one may claim in noting how many members of the group have attained this or that position is reduced.

Now that the option exists, it is clear many are eager to choose two or even more races. Among blacks there seems to be less willingness to choose two races than among Asians and American Indians—perhaps because it may be seen as something like race betrayal. But it is noteworthy that younger persons more often choose two races than older ones. If one creates a combined black group by putting together blacks with those who choose black as one of the races they tick off, 2.3 percent of this combined group 50 years of age or older turn out to be multi-race choosers, but 8.1 percent of those 17 and younger choose more than one race. But those who choose the option of black-white are still quite few—fewer in number than those who choose white-other ("other" in the racial category means Hispanic), or white-Asian, or white-American Indian.

When the statistics of intermarriage are analyzed, one can be sure there will be a considerable rise in white-black marriages since 1990, even if the percentage of such intermarriages is considerably less than white-Asian or Hispanic-non-Hispanic marriages. Blacks are still more segregated, more separated, in residence than other minority groups. They are more sharply defined in their consciousness as separate: History has made them so. But even among blacks, one sees the process of assimilation and integration, as measured by choice of race and by intermarriage, at work. By the census of 2010 or 2020, these processes will be further advanced. Indeed, one may perhaps look forward to a time when our complex system of racial and ethnic counting is made so confusing by the number of possible choices, singular and multiple, that the whole scheme is abandoned. Many Americans hope so.

Chapter 5

Civil Liberties

5-1

The Real World of Constitutional Rights

THE SUPREME COURT AND THE IMPLEMENTATION
OF THE ABORTION DECISIONS

Gerald N. Rosenberg

When one considers how exposed the Constitution's "religious establish-ment" clause is to continuous revision, it is not surprising to find other, less established rights deeply enmeshed in politics as well. The next essay exam-ines the right to an abortion, a controversial aspect of civil liberties policy that has been defended as an application of the "right to privacy."

The Supreme Court began asserting the right to privacy in earnest with Griswold v. Connecticut in 1965, when it ruled that a married couple's decision to use birth control lay beyond the purview of the government. The 1973 Roe v. Wade decision establishing a woman's right to an abortion—the best known and most controversial privacy right—has further established privacy as a class of rights implicit in the Bill of Rights. But, as Gerald Rosen-berg explains, Roe v. Wade left many aspects of abortion rights unresolved, and a lively public debate on the subject continues today.

Source: Gerald N. Rosenberg, "The Real World of Constitutional Rights: The Supreme Court and the Implementation of the Abortion Decisions," in *Contemplating Courts,* ed. Lee Epstein (Washington, D.C.: CQ Press, 1995), 390–419. Some notes and bibliographic references appearing in the original have been deleted.

IN *ROE V. WADE* and *Doe v. Bolton* (1973) the Supreme Court held unconstitutional Texas and Georgia laws prohibiting abortions except for "the purpose of saving the life of the mother" (Texas) and where "pregnancy would endanger the life of the pregnant mother or would seriously and permanently injure her health" (Georgia). The Court asserted that women had a fundamental right of privacy to decide whether or not to bear a child. Dividing pregnancy roughly into three trimesters, the Court held that in the first trimester the choice of abortion was a woman's alone, in consultation with a physician. During the second trimester, states could regulate abortion for the preservation and protection of women's health, and in approximately the third trimester, after fetal viability, could ban abortions outright, except where necessary to preserve a woman's life or health. Although responding specifically to the laws of Texas and Georgia, the broad scope of the Court's constitutional interpretation invalidated the abortion laws of almost every state and the District of Columbia.[1] According to one critic, *Roe* and *Doe* "may stand as the most radical decisions ever issued by the Supreme Court" (Noonan 1973, 261).

Roe and *Doe* are generally considered leading examples of judicial action in support of relatively powerless groups unable to win legislative victories. In these cases, women were that politically disadvantaged group; indeed, it has been claimed, "No victory for women's rights since enactment of the 19th Amendment has been greater than the one achieved" in *Roe* and *Doe* ("A Woman's Right" 1973, A4). But women are not the only disadvantaged interests who have attempted to use litigation to achieve policy ends. Starting with the famous cases brought by civil rights groups, and spreading to issues raised by environmental groups, consumer groups, and others, reformers have over the past decades looked to the courts as important producers of political and social change. Yet, during the same period, students of judicial politics have learned that court opinions are not always implemented with the speed and directness that rule by law assumes. This is particularly the case with decisions that touch on controversial, emotional issues or deeply held beliefs, such as abortion.

This chapter contains an exploration of the effect of the Court's abortion decisions, both *Roe* and *Doe,* and the key decisions based on them. How did the public, politicians, medical professionals, and interest groups react to them? Were the decisions implemented? Did they bring safe and legal abortions to all American women? To some American women? If the answer turns out to be only some, then I want to know why. What are the factors that have led a constitutional right to be unevenly available? More generally, are there conditions under which Court decisions on behalf of relatively powerless groups are more or less likely to be implemented?[2]

The analysis presented here shows that the effect and implementation of the Court's abortion decisions have been neither straightforward nor simple. Political response has varied and access to legal and safe abortion has increased, but in an uneven and nonuniform way. These findings are best explained by two related factors. First, at the time of the initial decisions there was widespread support for legal abortion from several sets of actors, including relevant political and professional elites on both the national and local level, the public at large, and activists. Second, the Court's decisions, by allowing clinics to perform abortions, made it possible for women to obtain abortions in some places where hospitals refused to provide them. Implementation by private clinics, however, has led to uneven availability of abortion services and has encouraged local political opposition.

The Abortion Cases

Roe and *Doe* were the Court's first major abortion decisions, but they were not its last.[3] In response to these decisions, many states rewrote their abortion laws, ostensibly to conform with the Court's constitutional mandate but actually with the goal of restricting the newly created right. Cases quickly arose, and continue to arise, challenging state laws as inconsistent with the Court's ruling, if not openly and clearly hostile to it. In general, the Court's response has been to preserve the core holding of *Roe* and *Doe* that a woman has a virtually unfettered constitutional right to an abortion before fetal viability, but to defer to legislation in areas not explicitly dealt with in those decisions. These cases require brief mention.

Areas of Litigation

Since *Roe* and *Doe,* the Court has heard three kinds of cases on abortion. One type involves state and federal funding for abortion. Here, the Court has consistently upheld the right of government not to fund abortion services and to prohibit the provision of abortions in public hospitals, unless the abortion is medically necessary. In perhaps the most important case, *Harris v. McRae* (1980), the Court upheld the most restrictive version of the so-called Hyde Amendment, which barred the use of federal funds for even medically necessary abortions, including those involving pregnancies due to rape or incest.

A second area that has provoked a great deal of litigation is the degree of participation in the abortion decision constitutionally allowed to the spouse of a pregnant married woman or the parents of a pregnant single minor. The Court has consistently struck down laws requiring spousal involvement but has upheld laws requiring parental notification or consent, as long as there is a "judicial bypass" option allowing minors to bypass their parents and obtain permission from a court.

A third area generating litigation involves the procedural requirements that states can impose for abortions. Most of these cases have arisen from state attempts to make abortion as difficult as possible to obtain. Regulations include requiring all post–first trimester abortions to be performed in hospitals; the informed, written consent of a woman before an abortion can be performed; a twenty-four-hour waiting period before an abortion can be performed; a pathology report for each abortion and the presence of a second physician at abortions occurring after potential viability; the preservation by physicians of the life of viable fetuses; and restrictions on the disposal of fetal remains. The Court's most recent pronouncement on these issues, *Planned Parenthood of Southeastern Pennsylvania v. Casey* (1992), found informed consent, a twenty-four-hour waiting period, and certain reporting requirements constitutional.

Trends in Court Treatment of Abortion Cases

Since the late 1980s, as *Casey* suggests, the Court has upheld more restrictions on the abortion right. In *Webster v. Reproductive Health Services* (1989), the Court upheld a 1986 restrictive Missouri law, and in 1991, in *Rust v. Sullivan,* it upheld government regulations prohibiting family-planning organizations that receive federal funds from counseling patients about abortion or providing abortion referrals. Most important, in *Casey* the Court abandoned the trimester framework of *Roe.* Although the justices did not agree on the proper constitutional standard for assessing state restrictions on abortion, Justices Sandra Day O'Connor, Anthony M. Kennedy, and David H. Souter adopted an "undue burden" standard. Under this standard, states may regulate abortion but may not place an undue burden on women seeking an abortion of a nonviable fetus.

Many commentators expected *Casey* to generate an avalanche of litigation centering directly on the abortion rights. Given the ambiguity of the undue burden standard, they expected expanded state activity to limit abortion. These expectations may yet be fulfilled, but, interestingly, Court cases since *Casey* have not specifically focused on the abortion right per se. Rather, in recent litigation the Court has been asked to resolve questions concerning access to abortion; namely, what steps can courts take to prevent antiabortion advocates from interfering with public access to family-planning and abortion clinics? The reason these kinds of questions arose is not difficult to discern; the 1990s has seen the rise of militant tactics—ranging from boisterous protests to harassment of clinic workers and even to the murder of physicians performing abortions—by certain segments of the antiabortion movement.

These "access" cases have generated mixed Court rulings. In *Bray v. Alexandria Women's Health Clinic* (1993), the Court rejected an attempt by pro-choice groups to use the 1871 Ku Klux Klan Act as a way to bring federal courts into this area. But, in *Madsen v. Women's Health Center* (1994), the Court upheld parts of a Florida trial court injunction permanently enjoining antiabortion protesters from blocking access to an abortion clinic and from physically harassing persons leaving or entering it. With the enactment by Congress of the Freedom of Access to Clinic Entrances Act in 1994, and the immediate filing of a legal challenge, it is likely that the Court will have another opportunity to address this issue.

Implementing Constitutional Rights

How have the public, politicians, medical professionals, and interest groups reacted to the Court decisions since *Roe* and *Doe*? How has access to legal and safe abortion changed in the wake of these decisions? In other words, when the Supreme Court announces a new constitutional right, what happens?

Legal Abortions: The Numbers

An obvious way to consider this question, at least in the abortion realm, is to look at the number of legal abortions performed before and after the 1973 decisions. For, if the Court has had an important effect on society in this area, we might expect to find dramatic increases in the number of legal abortions obtained after 1973. Collecting statistics on legal abortion, however, is not an easy task. Record keeping is not as precise and complete as one would hope. Two organizations, the public Centers for Disease Control and Prevention in Atlanta and the private Alan Guttmacher Institute in New York, are the most thorough and reliable collectors of the information. The data they have collected on the number of legal abortions performed between 1966 and 1992 and the yearly percentage change are shown in Figure 1.

Interestingly, these data present a mixed picture of the effect of the abortion decisions. On the one hand, they suggest that after *Roe* the number of legal abortions increased at a strong pace throughout the 1970s (the solid line in Figure 1). On the other hand, they reveal that the changes after 1973 were part of a trend that started in 1970, three years before the Court acted. Strikingly, the largest increase in the number of legal abortions occurs between 1970 and 1971, two years before *Roe*! In raw numerical terms, the increase between 1972 and 1973 is 157,800, a full 134,500 fewer than the pre-*Roe* increase in 1970–1971. It is possible, of course, that the effect of *Roe* was not felt in 1973. Even though the decision

Figure 1. Legal Abortions, 1966–1992

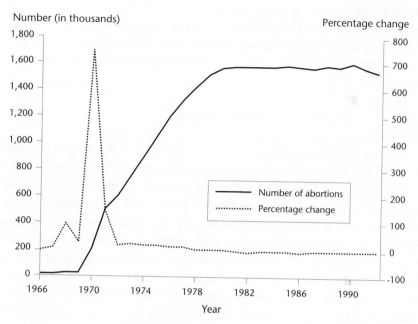

Sources: Estimates by the Alan Guttmacher Institute and the Centers for Disease Control and Prevention in Henshaw and Van Vort 1994, 100–106, 112; Lader 1973, 209; U.S. Congress 1974, 1976; Weinstock et al. 1975, 23. When sources differed, I have relied on data from the Alan Guttmacher Institute since its estimates are based on surveys of all known abortion providers and are generally more complete. Data points for 1983, 1986, and 1990 are estimates based on interpolations made by the Alan Guttmacher Institute.

was handed down in January, perhaps the 1973–1974 comparison gives a more accurate picture. If this is the case, the increase, 154,000, is still substantially smaller than the change during 1970–1971. And while the number of legal abortions continued to increase in the years immediately after 1974, that rate eventually stabilized and by the 1990s had actually declined. The dotted line in Figure 1 (representing the percentage change in the number of legal abortions performed from one year to the next) shows, too, that the largest increases in the number of legal abortions occurred in the years prior to *Roe*. ...

The data presented above show that the largest numerical increases in legal abortions occurred in the years prior to initial Supreme Court action. . . . There was no steep or unusual increase in the number of legal abortions following *Roe*. To be sure, it is possible that without constitutional protection for abortion no more states would have liberalized or repealed their laws and those that had done so might have overturned their previous efforts. And the fact that the number of

legal abortions continued to increase after 1973 suggests that the Court was effective in easing access to safe and legal abortion. But those increases, while large,
were smaller than those of previous years. Hence, the growth in the number of
legal abortions can be only partially attributed to the Court; it might even be the
case that the increases would have continued without the Court's 1973 decisions.

What Happened?

Particularly interesting about the data presented above is that they suggest that
Roe itself failed to generate major changes in the number of legal abortions. This
finding is compatible with political science literature, in which it is argued that
Supreme Court decisions, particularly ones dealing with emotional and controversial issues, are not automatically and completely implemented. It also appears
to fit nicely with an argument I have made elsewhere (Rosenberg 1991), which
suggests that several factors must be present for new constitutional rights to be
implemented. These include widespread support from political and professional
elites on both the national and local level, from the public at large, and from
activists and a willingness on the part of those called on to implement the decision to act accordingly. This is true, as Alexander Hamilton pointed out two centuries ago, because courts lack the power of "either the sword or the purse." To
a greater extent than other government institutions, courts are dependent on
both elite and popular support for their decisions to be implemented.

To fill out my argument in greater detail, I examine both pre- and post-1973
actions as they relate to the implementation of the abortion right. In so doing, I
reach two important conclusions. First, by the time the Court reached its decisions in 1973, little political opposition to abortion existed on the federal level,
relevant professional elites and social activists gave it widespread support, it was
practiced on a large scale (see Figure 1), and public support for it was growing.
These positions placed abortion reform in the American mainstream. Second, in
the years after 1973, opposition to abortion strengthened and grew.

Pre-*Roe* Support

In the decade or so prior to *Roe*, there was a sea change in the public position of
abortion in American life. At the start of the 1960s, abortion was not a political
issue. Abortions, illegal as they were, were performed clandestinely, and women
who underwent the procedure did not talk about it.[4] By 1972, however, abortion
had become a public and political issue. While little legislative or administrative

action was taken on the federal level, a social movement, organized in the mid- and late 1960s, to reform and repeal prohibitions on abortion met with some success at the state level, and public opinion swung dramatically from opposition to abortion in most cases to substantial support.

Elites and Social Activists

Although abortions have always been performed, public discussion did not surface until the 1950s. In 1962 the American Law Institute (ALI) published its Model Penal Code on abortion, permitting abortion if continuing the pregnancy would adversely affect the physical or mental health of the woman, if there was risk of birth defects, or if the pregnancy resulted from rape or incest. Publicity about birth defects caused by Thalidomide, a drug prescribed in the 1960s to cure infertility, and a German measles epidemic in the years 1962–1965 kept the issue prominent. By November 1965 the American Medical Association Board of Trustees approved a report urging adoption of the ALI law.

In 1966, reform activists began making numerous radio and television appearances.[5] By then there were several pro-choice groups, including the Society for Humane Abortion in California; the Association for the Study of Abortion in New York, a prestigious board of doctors and lawyers; and the Illinois Committee for Medical Control of Abortion, which advocated repeal of all abortion laws. Abortion referral services were also started. Previously, pro-choice activists had made private referrals to competent doctors in the United States and Mexico, who performed illegal but safe abortions. But by the late 1960s, abortion referral groups operated publicly. In New York City, in 1967, twenty-two clergy announced the formation of their group, gaining front-page coverage in the *New York Times* (Fiske 1967). The Chicago referral service took out a full page ad in the *Sun-Times* announcing its services. In Los Angeles, the referral service was serving more than a thousand women per month. By the late 1960s pro-choice organizations, including abortion-referral services, were operating in many major U.S. cities. And by 1971, the clergy referral service operated publicly in eighteen states with a staff of about 700 clergy and lay people (Hole and Levine 1971, 299).

In order to tap this emerging support, the National Association for the Repeal of Abortion Laws (NARAL) was founded.[6] Protesting in the streets, lecturing, and organizing "days of anger" began to have an effect. Women who had undergone illegal abortions wrote and spoke openly about them. Seventy-five leading national groups endorsed the repeal of all abortion laws between 1967 and the end of 1972, including twenty-eight religious and twenty-one medical groups. Among the religious groups, support ranged from the American Jewish Congress to the American Baptist Convention. Medical groups included the American Public Health Association, the American Psychiatric Association, the American Medical Association, the National Council of Obstetrics-Gynecology, and the American College of Obstetricians and Gynecologists. Among other groups, support included the American Bar Association and a host of liberal organizations. Even the YWCA supported repeal (U.S. Congress 1976, 4:53–91).

The Federal Government

In the late 1960s, while the abortion law reform battle was being fought in the states, the federal arena was quiet. For example, although states with less restrictive laws received Medicaid funds that paid for some abortions, for "six years after 1967, not a single bill was introduced, much less considered, in Congress to curtail the use of federal funds for abortion" (Rosoff 1975, 13). The pace momentarily quickened in 1968 when the Presidential Advisory Council on the Status of Women, appointed by President Lyndon Johnson, recommended the repeal of all abortion laws (Lader 1973, 81–82).

Still, abortion was not a major issue in the 1968 presidential campaign. Despite his personal beliefs, the newly elected president, Richard M. Nixon, did not take active steps to limit abortion, and the U.S. government did not enter *Roe* nor, after the decision, did it give support to congressional efforts to limit abortion.[7] Although it is true that in 1973 and 1974 President Nixon was occupied with other matters, his administration essentially avoided the abortion issue.

In Congress there was virtually no abortion activity prior to 1973. In April 1970, Sen. Bob Packwood (R-Ore.) introduced a National Abortion Act designed to "guarantee and protect" the "fundamental constitutional right" of a woman "to control her own fertility" (U.S. Congress 1970a). He also introduced a bill to liberalize the District of Columbia's abortion law (U.S. Congress 1970b). Otherwise, Congress remained essentially inactive on the abortion issue.

The States

It is not at all surprising that the president and Congress did not involve themselves in the abortion reform movement of the 1960s. Laws banning abortion were state laws, so most of the early abortion law reform activity was directed at state governments. In the early and middle parts of the decade there was some legislative discussion in California, New Hampshire, and New York. By 1967, reform bills were introduced in twenty-eight states, including California, Colorado, Delaware, Florida, Georgia, Maryland, Oklahoma, New Jersey, New York, North Carolina, and Pennsylvania (Rubin 1982). The first successful liberalization drive was in Colorado, which adopted a reform bill, modeled on the ALI's Model Penal Code. Interestingly, another early reform state was California, where Gov. Ronald Reagan, despite intense opposition, signed a reform bill.

These victories further propelled the reform movement, and in 1968, abortion legislation was pending in some thirty states. During 1968–1969 seven states— Arkansas, Delaware, Georgia, Kansas, Maryland, New Mexico, and Oregon— enacted reform laws based on or similar to the ALI model (Lader 1973, 84). In 1970, four states went even further. In chronological order, Hawaii, New York, Alaska, and Washington essentially repealed prohibitions on abortions in the first two trimesters.

To sum up, in the five or so years prior to the Supreme Court's decisions, reform and repeal bills had been debated in most states, and seventeen plus the District of Columbia acted to liberalize their laws (Craig and O'Brien 1993, 75). State action had removed some obstacles to abortion, and safe and legal abortions were thus available in scattered states. And, as indicated in Figure 1, in 1972, nearly 600,000 legal abortions were performed. Activity was widespread, vocal, and effective.

Public Opinion

Another important element in the effectiveness of the Court is the amount of support from the population at large. By the eve of the Court's decision in 1973, public opinion had dramatically shifted from opposition to abortion in most cases to substantial, if not majority, support. Indeed, in the decades that have followed, opinion on abortion has remained remarkably stable.[8]

Looking at the 1960s as a whole, Blake (1971, 543, 544) found that opinions on discretionary abortion were "changing rapidly over time" and polls were recording "rapidly growing support." For example, relying on data from Gallup polls, Blake (1977b, 49) found that support for elective abortion increased approximately two and one-half times from 1968 to 1972. One set of Gallup polls recorded a fifteen-point drop in the percentage of respondents disapproving of abortions for financial reasons in the eight months between October 1969 and June 1970 (Blake 1977a, 58). . . . In 1971, a national poll taken for the Commission on Population Growth and the American Future found 50 percent of its respondents agreeing with the statement that the abortion "decision should be left up to persons involved and their doctor" (Rosenthal 1971, 22). Thus, in the words of one study, "[b]y the time the Supreme Court made its ruling, there was strong public support behind the legalization of abortion" (Ebaugh and Haney 1980, 493).

Much of the reason for the growth in support for the repeal of the laws on abortion, both from the public and from organizations, may have come from changes in opinion by the professional elite. Polls throughout the late 1960s reported that important subgroups of the American population were increasingly supportive of abortion law reform and repeal. Several nonscientific polls of doctors, for example, suggested a great deal of support for abortion reform. A scientific poll of nearly thirteen thousand respondents in nursing, medical, and social work schools in the autumn and winter of 1971 showed strong support for repeal. The poll found split opinions among nursing students and faculty but found that 69 percent of medical students, 71 percent of medical faculty, 76 percent of social work students, and 75 percent of social work faculty supported "freely accessible abortion" (Rosen et al. 1974, 165). And a poll by the American Council of Education of 180,000 college freshmen in 1970 found that 83 percent favored the legalization of abortion (Currivan 1970). It is clear that in the late 1960s and early 1970s, the public was becoming increasingly supportive of legal abortion.

Post-*Roe* Activity

The relative quiet of the early 1960s has yet to return to the abortion arena. Rather than settling the issue, the Court's decisions added even more controversy. On the federal level, legislative and administrative action dealing with abortion has swung back and forth, from more or less benign neglect prior to 1973 to open antipathy to modest support. State action has followed a different course. Legislative efforts in the 1960s and early 1970s to reform and repeal abortion laws gave way to efforts to limit access to abortions. Public opinion remained stable until the *Webster* decision, after which there was a noticeable shift toward the pro-choice position. Finally, the antiabortion movement grew both more vocal and more violent.

The Federal Government: The President

On the presidential level, little changed in the years immediately after *Roe*. Nixon, as noted, took no action, and Gerald R. Ford, during his short term, said little about abortion until the presidential campaign in 1976, when he took a middle-of-the-road, antiabortion position, supporting local option, the law before *Roe*, and opposing federal funding of abortion (Craig and O'Brien 1993, 160–161). His Justice Department, however, did not enter the case of *Planned Parenthood of Central Missouri v. Danforth*, in which numerous state restrictions on the provision of abortion were challenged, and the Ford administration took no major steps to help the antiabortion forces.[9]

The Carter administration, unlike its Republican predecessors, did act to limit access to abortion. As a presidential candidate Carter opposed federal spending for abortion, and as president, during a press conference in June 1977, he stated his support for the Supreme Court's decisions allowing states to refuse Medicaid funding for abortions (Rubin 1982, 107). The Carter administration also sent its solicitor general into the Supreme Court to defend the Hyde Amendment.

Ronald Reagan was publicly committed to ending legal abortion. Opposition to *Roe* was said to be a litmus test for federal judicial appointments, and Reagan repeatedly used his formidable rhetorical skills in support of antiabortion activists. Under his presidency, antiabortion laws enacted included prohibiting fetal tissue research by federal scientists, banning most abortions at military hospitals, and denying funding to organizations that counseled or provided abortion services abroad. His administration submitted amicus curiae cases in all the Court's abortion cases, and in two (*Thornburgh v. American College of Obstetricians and Gynecologists*, 1986, and *Webster*) urged that *Roe* be overturned. Yet, despite the rhetoric and the symbolism, these actions had little effect on the abortion rate. As Craig and O'Brien (1993, 190) put it, "in spite of almost eight years of antiabortion rhetoric, Reagan had accomplished little in curbing abortion."

The administration of George Bush was as, if not more, hostile to the constitutional right to abortion as its predecessor. It filed antiabortion briefs in several abortion cases and urged that *Roe* be overturned. During Bush's presidency, the Food and Drug Administration placed RU-486, a French abortion drug, on the list of unapproved drugs, making it ineligible to be imported for personal use. And, in the administration's most celebrated antiabortion action, the secretary of the Health and Human Services Department, Louis W. Sullivan, issued regulations prohibiting family-planning organizations that received federal funds from counseling patients about abortion or providing referrals (the "gag rule" upheld in *Rust*).

President Bill Clinton brought a sea change to the abortion issue. As the first pro-choice president since *Roe,* he acted quickly to reverse decisions of his predecessors. In particular, on the third day of his administration, and the twentieth anniversary of *Roe,* Clinton issued five abortion-related memos.

1. He rescinded the ban on abortion counseling at federally financed clinics (negating *Rust*).
2. He rescinded restrictions on federal financing of fetal tissue research.
3. He eased U.S. policy on abortions in military hospitals.
4. He reversed Reagan policy on aid to international family planning programs involved in abortion-related activities.
5. He called for review of the ban on RU-486, the French abortion pill (Toner 1993).

In addition, in late May 1994, he signed the Freedom of Access to Clinic Entrances Act, giving federal protection to facilities and personnel providing abortion services. And, in early August 1994, the U.S. Justice Department sent U.S. marshals to help guard abortion clinics in at least twelve communities around the country (Thomas 1994). Furthermore, his two Supreme Court appointees as of 1994, Ruth Bader Ginsburg and Stephen Breyer, are apparently both pro-choice.

The Federal Government: Congress

In contrast to the executive branch, Congress engaged in a great deal of antiabortion activity after 1973, although almost none of it was successful, and some supportive activity actually occurred in the late 1980s and early 1990s. By means of legislation designed to overturn Roe, riders to various spending bills, and constitutional amendments, many members of Congress made their opposition to abortion clear. Perhaps the most important congressional action was the passage of the Hyde Amendment, which restricted federal funding of abortion: First passed in 1976, and then in subsequent years, the amendment prohibited the use of federal funds for abortion except in extremely limited circumstances. Although the wording varied in some years, the least limited version allowed funding only to save the life of the woman, when rape or incest had occurred, or when some long-lasting health damage, certified by two physicians, would result from the pregnancy. The amendment has been effective and the number of federally funded abortions fell from 294,600 in 1977 to 267 in 1992 (Daley and Gold 1994, 250).

Despite the amount of congressional activity, the Hyde Amendment was the only serious piece of antiabortion legislation enacted.[10] And, in 1994, Congress actually enacted legislation granting federal protection to abortion clinics. Thus, Congress was hostile in words but cautious in action with abortion. While not supporting the Court and the right to abortion, congressional action did not bar legal abortion.[11]

The States

Prior to 1973 the states had been the main arena for the abortion battle, and Court action did not do much to change that. In the wake of the Court decisions, all but a few states had to rewrite their abortion laws to conform to the Court's constitutional mandate. Their reactions, like those on the federal level, varied enormously. Some states acted to bring their laws into conformity with the Court's ruling, while others reenacted their former restrictive laws or enacted regulations designed to impede access to abortion. Since abortion is a state matter, the potential for state action affecting the availability of legal abortion was high.

At the outset, a national survey reported that state governments "moved with extreme caution in implementing the Supreme Court's ruling" (Brody 1973, A1). By the end of 1973, Blake (1977b, 46) reports, 260 abortion-related bills had been introduced in state legislatures and 39 enacted. In 1974, 189 bills were introduced and 19 enacted. In total, in the two years immediately following the Court decisions, 62 laws relating to abortion were enacted by 32 states. And state activity continued, with more abortion laws enacted in 1977 than in any year since 1973 (Rubin 1982, 126, 136).

Many of these laws were hostile to abortion. "Perhaps the major share," Blake (1977b, 61 n. 2) believes, was "obstructive and unconstitutional." They included spousal and parental consent requirements, tedious written-consent forms describing the "horrors" of abortion, funding limitations, waiting periods, hospitalization requirements, elaborate statistical reporting requirements, and burdensome medical procedures. Other action undertaken by states was simple and directly to the point. North Dakota and Rhode Island, for example, responded to the Court's decisions by enacting laws allowing abortion only to preserve the life of the woman (Weinstock et al. 1975, 28; "Rhode Island" 1973). Virginia rejected a bill bringing its statutes into conformity with the Court's order (Brody 1973, 46). Arkansas enforced a state law allowing abortion only if the pregnancy threatened the life or health of the woman ("Abortions Legal for Year" 1973, A14). In Louisiana, the attorney general threatened to take away the license of any physician performing an abortion, and the state medical society declared that any physician who performed an abortion, except to save the woman's life, violated the ethical principles of medicine (Weinstock et al. 1975, 28). The Louisiana State Board of Medical Examiners also pledged to prevent physicians from performing abortions (Brody 1973). In Pennsylvania, the state medical society announced that it did "not condone abortion on demand" and retained its strict standards (King 1973, 35). And in Saint Louis, the city attorney threatened to arrest any physician who performed an abortion (King 1973). Given this kind of activity, it can be concluded that in many states the Court's intent was "widely and purposively frustrated" (Blake 1977b, 60–61).

Variation in state response to the constitutional right to an abortion continues to this day. Although legal abortions are performed in all states, the availability of abortion services varies enormously. As noted, a variety of restrictions on abortion have been enacted across the country. In the wake of the Court's decision in *Webster* (1989), which upheld a restrictive Missouri law, a new round of state restrictions on abortion was generally expected. Indeed, within two years of the decision nine states and Guam enacted restrictions. Nevertheless, four states enacted legislation protecting a woman's right to abortion (Craig and O'Brien 1993, 280). The Pennsylvania enactments were challenged in *Casey* (1992), in

Figure 2. Public Opinion and Abortion, Selected Years, 1975–1992

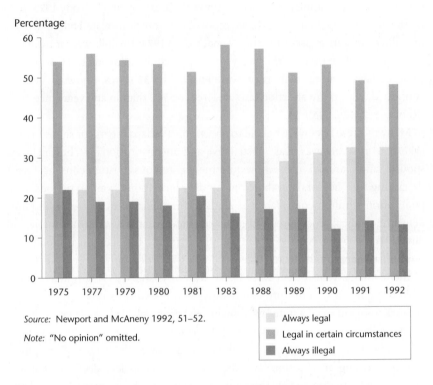

Percentage

Source: Newport and McAneny 1992, 51–52.

Note: "No opinion" omitted.

- Always legal
- Legal in certain circumstances
- Always illegal

which the "undue burden" standard was announced. The lack of clarity in this standard virtually ensures that restrictions will continue to be enacted.

Public Opinion

As shown in Figure 2, public opinion changed little from the early 1970s (pre-*Roe*) until the *Webster* decision in 1989, after which a small but important growth in pro-choice support occurred. Although differently worded questions produce different results, it is clear that the American public remains strongly supportive of abortion when the woman's health is endangered by continuing the pregnancy, when there is a strong chance of a serious fetal defect, and when the pregnancy is the result of rape or incest. The public is more divided when abortion is sought for economic reasons, by single unmarried women unwilling to marry, and by married women who do not want more children. "The overall picture that emerges is that a majority supports leaving abortion legal and available to women unfortunate enough to need it, though many in the majority remain concerned about the moral implications" (Craig and O'Brien 1993, 269). . . .

Anti-Abortion Activity

Organized opposition to abortion increased dramatically in the years following the Court's initial decisions. National groups such as the American Life Lobby, Americans United for Life, the National Right to Life Committee, the Pro-Life Action League, and Operation Rescue and numerous local groups have adopted some of the tactics of the reformers. They have marched, lobbied, and protested, urging that abortion be made illegal in most or all circumstances. In addition, in the 1980s, groups like Operation Rescue began to adopt more violent tactics. And, since 1982, the U.S. Bureau of Alcohol, Tobacco and Firearms has reported 146 incidents of bombing, arson, or attempts against clinics and related sites in thirty states, causing more than $12 million in damages (Thomas 1994). The high level of harassment of abortion clinics is shown in Table 1.

The level of harassment appears to have increased over time. In just 1992 and 1993 the U.S. Bureau of Alcohol, Tobacco and Firearms recorded thirty-six incidents, which resulted in an estimated $3.8 million in damages (Thomas 1994). The National Abortion Federation, representing roughly half of the nation's clinics, noted that incidents of reported vandalism at its clinics more than doubled from 1991 to 1992 (Barringer 1993). From May 1992 to August 1993 the U.S. Bureau of Alcohol, Tobacco and Firearms reported that 123 family-planning clinics were bombed or burned (Baum 1993). In 1992 more than forty clinics were attacked with butyric acid (a chemical injected through key holes, under doors, or into ventilation shafts) forcing clinic closures and requiring costly repairs (Anderson and Binstein 1993, C27). One of the aims of this violence appears to be to raise the cost of operating abortion clinics to such an extent as to force their closure. In 1992 and 1993, for example, arson destroyed clinics in Missoula and Helena, Montana, and in Boise, Idaho. The clinics have either been unable to reopen or have had great difficulty in doing so because of the difficulty of finding owners willing to rent to them and obtaining insurance coverage. In 1990, in the wake of such violence, one major insurer, Traveler's Insurance Company, decided not to insure any abortion-related concerns (Baum 1993).

Another tactic aimed at shutting down abortion clinics is to conduct large, sustained protests. During the summer of 1991, for example, Operation Rescue staged forty-six days of protest in Wichita, Kansas, resulting in the arrest of approximately 2,700 people. During the summer of 1993, Operation Rescue launched a seven-city campaign with similar aims. In addition, there have been individual acts of violence against abortion providers. Dr. David Gunn was murdered in March 1993 outside an abortion clinic in Pensacola, Florida; Dr. George Tiller was shot in August 1993 in Wichita, Kansas; and Dr. John Britton and his escort, James Barrett, a retired air force lieutenant colonel, were murdered in late July 1994, also in Pensacola. Commenting on the murders of Dr. Britton and James

Table 1. Abortion Clinics Reporting Harassment,
1985 and 1988 (in percentage)

Activity	1985	1988
Picketing	80	81
Picketing with physical contact or blocking	47	46
Demonstrations resulting in arrests	—	38
Bomb threats	48	36
Vandalism	28	34
Picketing homes of staff members	16	17

Note: Dash = question not asked.

Source: Surveys of all abortion providers taken by the Alan Guttmacher Institute in Henshaw (1991, 246–252, 263).

Barrett, Don Treshman, director of the antiabortion group Rescue America, issued an ominous warning: "Up to now, the killings have been on one side, with 30 million dead babies and hundreds of dead and maimed mothers. On the other side, there are two dead doctors. Maybe the balance is going to shift" (quoted in Lewin 1994, A7).[12] In sum, as Forrest and Henshaw (1987, 13) concluded, "antiabortion harassment in the United States is widespread and frequent."

Two important facts can be gleaned from the foregoing discussion. First, at the time of the 1973 abortion decisions, large segments of the political and professional elite were either indifferent to or supported abortion reform. Second, after the decisions, many political leaders vociferously opposed abortion. Congress enacted antiabortion legislation as did some of the states. In addition, activist opposition was growing. How this opposition affected the implementation of the decisions is the focus of the next section.

The Effect of Opposition on the
Implementation of Abortion Rights

On the eve of the abortion decisions, there was widespread support from critical professional elites, growing public support, successful reform in many states, and indifference from most national politicians. Is this sufficient for the implementation of constitutional rights?

Constitutional rights are not self-implementing. That is, to make a right a reality, the behavior of individuals and the policies of the institutions in which they work must change. Because abortion is a medical procedure, and because safe

Table 2. Hospitals Providing Abortions, Selected Years,
1973–1992 (percentage)

Year	Private, short-term non-Catholic, general	Public
1973	24	—
1974	27	17
1975	30	—
1976	31	20
1977	31	21
1978	29	—
1979	28	—
1980	27	17
1982	26	16
1985	23	17
1988	21	15
1992	18	13

Note: Dash = unavailable.

Sources: Forrest, Sullivan, and Tietze 1978, table 5; Henshaw 1986, 253; Henshaw et al. 1982, table 7; Henshaw, Forrest, and Van Vort 1987, 68; Henshaw and Van Vort 1990, 102–108, 142; Henshaw and Van Vort 1994, 100–106, 122; Rubin 1982, 154; Sullivan, Tietze, and Dryfoos, 1977, figure 10; Weinstock et al. 1975, 32.

abortion requires trained personnel, the implementation of abortion rights depends on the medical profession to provide abortion services. When done properly, first-term and most second-term abortions can be performed on an outpatient basis, and there is less risk of death in the procedure than there is in childbirth or in such routine operations as tonsillectomies. Thus, no medical or technical reasons stand in the way of the provision of abortion services. Following Supreme Court action, however, the medical profession moved with "extreme caution" in making abortion available (Brody 1973, 1). Coupled with the hostility of some state legislatures, barriers to legal abortion remained.

These barriers have proved to be strong. Perhaps the strongest barrier has been opposition from hospitals. In Table 2, I track the response of hospitals to the Court's decisions. The results are staggering. Despite the relative ease and safety of the abortion procedure, and the unambiguous holding of the Court, both public and private hospitals throughout America have refused to perform abortions. *The vast majority of public and private hospitals have never performed an abortion!* In 1973 and the first quarter of 1974, for example, slightly more than three-quarters of public and private non-Catholic general care short-term hospitals did not perform a single abortion (Weinstock et al. 1975, 31). As illustrated in the table, the passage of time has not improved the situation. By 1976, three years after the decision, at least 70 percent of hospitals provided no abortion services. By 1992 the situation had further deteriorated: only 18 percent of private non-Catholic general care short-term hospitals and only 13 percent of public hospitals provided abortions. As Stanley Henshaw (1986, 253, emphasis added) concluded, reviewing the data in 1986, "most hospitals have *never* performed abortions."

These figures mask the fact that even the limited availability of hospital abortions detailed here varies widely across states. In 1973, for example, only 4 percent of all abortions were performed in the eight states that make up the East South Central and West South Central census divisions (Weinstock et al. 1975, 25).[13] Two states, on the other hand, New York and California (which are home to about 20 percent of all U.S. women), accounted for 37 percent of all abortions in 1974 (Alan Guttmacher Institute 1976). In eleven states, "not a single public hospital reported performance of a single abortion for any purpose whatsoever in all of 1973" (Weinstock et al. 1975, 31). By 1976, three years after Court action, no hospitals, public or private, in Louisiana, North Dakota, and South Dakota performed abortions. The Dakotas alone had thirty public and sixty-two private hospitals. In five other states, which had a total of eighty-two public hospitals, not one performed an abortion. In thirteen additional states, less than 10 percent of each state's public hospitals reported performing any abortions (Forrest, Sullivan, and Tietze 1979, 46). Only in the states of California, Hawaii, New York, and North Carolina and in the District of Columbia did more than half the public hospitals perform any abortions during 1974–1975 (Alan Guttmacher Institute 1976, 30). By 1992, the situation was little better, with five states (California, New York, Texas, Florida, and Illinois) accounting for 49 percent of all legal abortions (Henshaw and Van Vort 1994, 102).

This refusal of hospitals to perform abortions means that women seeking them, particularly from rural areas, have to travel, often a great distance, to exercise their constitutional rights. In 1973, for example, 150,000 women traveled out of their state of residence to obtain abortions. By 1982 the numbers had dropped, but more than 100,000 women were still forced to travel to another state for abortion services. . . .

Even when women can obtain abortions within their states of residence, they may still have to travel a great distance to do so. In 1974, the year after *Roe*, the Guttmacher Institute found that between 300,000 and 400,000 women left their home communities to obtain abortions (Alan Guttmacher Institute 1976). In 1980, across the United States, more than one-quarter (27 percent) of all women who had abortions had them outside of their home counties (Henshaw and O'Reilly 1983, 5). And in 1988, fifteen years after *Roe*, an estimated 430,000

(27 percent) women who had abortions in nonhospital settings traveled more than fifty miles from their home to reach their abortion provider. This includes over 140,000 women who traveled more than 100 miles to obtain a legal abortion (Henshaw 1991, 248).[14]

The general problem that faces women who seek to exercise their constitutional right to abortion is the paucity of abortion providers. From the legalization of abortion in 1973 to the present, at least 77 percent of all U.S. counties have been without abortion providers. And the problem is not merely rural. In 1980, seven years after Court action, there were still fifty-nine metropolitan areas in which no facilities could be identified that provided abortions (Henshaw et al. 1982, 5). The most recent data suggest that the problem is worsening. In 1992, 84 percent of all U.S. counties, home to 30 percent of all women of reproductive age, had no abortion providers. Ninety-one of the country's 320 metropolitan (28 percent) areas have no identified abortion provider, and an additional 14 (4 percent) have providers who perform fewer than fifty abortions per year. . . .

Even when abortion service is available, providers have tended to ignore the time periods set out in the Court's opinions. In 1988, fifteen years after the decisions, only 43 percent of all providers perform abortions after the first trimester. More than half (55 percent) of the hospitals that perform abortions have refused to perform second-trimester procedures, a time in pregnancy at which hospital services may be medically necessary. Only at abortion clinics have a majority of providers been willing to perform abortions after the first trimester. Indeed, in 1988 a startling 22 percent of all providers refused to perform abortions past the tenth week of pregnancy, several weeks within the first trimester, during which, according to the Court, a woman's constitutional right is virtually all-encompassing (Henshaw 1991, 251).

Finally, although abortion is "the most common surgical procedure that women undergo" (Darney et al. 1987, 161) and is reportedly the most common surgical procedure performed in the United States, an *increasing* percentage of residency programs in obstetrics and gynecology do not provide training for it. A survey taken in 1985 of all such residency programs found that 28 percent of them offered no training at all, a nearly fourfold increase since 1976. According to the results of the survey, approximately one-half of the programs made training available as an option, while only 23 percent included it routinely (Darney et al. 1987, 160). By 1992 the percentage of programs requiring abortion training had dropped nearly to half, to 12 percent (Baum 1993). In a study done in 1992 of 216 of 271 residency programs, it was found that almost half (47 percent) of graduating residents had never performed a first-trimester abortion, and only 7 percent had ever performed one in the second trimester (Cooper 1993). At least part of the reason for the increasing lack of training is harassment by antiabortion activists. "Anti-abortion groups say these numbers prove that harassment of doctors, and in turn, medical schools which train residents in abortion procedures, is an effective tactic," Cooper reported. "'You humiliate the school. . . . We hope that in 10 years, there'll be none' that train residents how to perform abortions" (Randall Terry, founder of Operation Rescue, quoted in Cooper 1993, B3). . . .

It is clear that hospital administrators, both public and private, refused to change their abortion policies in reaction to the Court decisions. In the years since the Court's decisions, abortion services have remained centered in metropolitan areas and in those states that reformed their abortion laws and regulations prior to the Court's decisions. In 1976 the Alan Guttmacher Institute (1976, 13) concluded that "[t]he response of hospitals to the legalization of abortion continues to be so limited . . . as to be tantamount to no response." Jaffe, Lindheim, and Lee (1981, 15) concluded that "the delivery pattern for abortion services that has emerged since 1973 is distorted beyond precedent." Reviewing the data in the mid-1980s, Henshaw, Forrest, and Blaine (1984, 122) summed up the situation this way: "There is abundant evidence that many women still find it difficult or impossible to obtain abortion services because of the distance of their home to the nearest provider, the cost, a lack of information on where to go, and limitations on the circumstances under which a provider will make abortions available." Most recently, Henshaw (1991, 253) concluded that "an American woman seeking abortion services will find it increasingly difficult to find a provider who will serve her in an accessible location and at an affordable cost."

Implementing Constitutional Rights: The Market

The foregoing discussion presents a seeming dilemma. There has been hostility to abortion from some politicians, most hospital administrators, many doctors, and parts of the public. On the whole, in response to the Court, hospitals did not change their policies to permit abortions. Yet, as demonstrated in Figure 1, the number of legal abortions performed in the United States continued to grow. How is it, for example, that congressional and state hostility seemed effectively to prevent progress in civil rights in the 1950s and early 1960s but did not prevent abortion in the 1970s? The answer to this question not only removes the dilemma but also illustrates why the Court's abortion decisions were effective in making legal abortion more easily available. The answer, in a word, is *clinics*.

The Court's decisions prohibited the states from interfering with a woman's right to choose an abortion, at least in the first trimester. They did not uphold hospitalization requirements, and later cases explicitly rejected hospitalization requirements for second-trimester abortions.[15] Room was left for abortion reformers, population control groups, women's groups, and individual physicians to set up clinics to perform abortions. The refusal of many hospitals, then, to perform abortions could be countered by the creation of clinics willing to do the job. And that's exactly what happened.

In the wake of the Court's decisions the number of abortion providers sharply increased. In the first year after the decisions, the number of providers grew by nearly 25 percent. Over the first three years the percentage increase was almost 58 percent. The number of providers reached a peak in 1982 and has declined more than 18 percent since then. These raw data, however, do not indicate who these providers were.

. . . [T]he number of abortion providers increased because of the increase in the number of clinics. To fill the void that hospitals had left, clinics opened in large numbers. Between 1973 and 1974, for example, the number of nonhospital abortion providers grew 61 percent. Overall, between 1973 and 1976 the number of nonhospital providers grew 152 percent, nearly five times the rate of growth of hospital providers. In metropolitan areas . . . the growth rate was 140 percent between 1973 and 1976, five times the rate for hospital providers; in nonmetropolitan areas it was a staggering 304 percent, also about five times the growth rate for nonmetropolitan hospitals.

The growth in the number of abortion clinics was matched by the increase in the number of abortions performed by them. By 1974, nonhospital clinics were performing approximately 51 percent of all abortions, and nearly an additional 3 percent were being performed in physicians' offices. Between 1973 and 1974, the number of abortions performed in hospitals rose 5 percent, while the number performed in clinics rose 39 percent. By 1976, clinics accounted for 62 percent of all reported abortions, despite the fact that they were only 17 percent of all providers (Forrest, Sullivan, and Tietze 1979). From 1973 to 1976, the years immediately following Court action, the number of abortions performed in hospitals increased by only 8 percent, whereas the number performed in clinics and physicians' offices increased by a whopping 113 percent (Forrest et al. 1979).[16] The percentages continued to rise, and by 1992, 93 percent of all abortions were performed in nonhospital settings. Clinics satisfied the need that hospitals, despite the Court's actions, refused to meet.

In permitting abortions to be performed in clinics as well as hospitals, the Court's decisions granted a way around the intransigence of hospitals. The decisions allowed individuals committed to safe and legal abortion to make use of the market and create their own structures to meet the demand. They also provided a financial incentive for services to be provided. At least some clinics were formed solely as money-making ventures. As the legal activist Janice Goodman put it, "Some doctors are going to see a very substantial amount of money to be made on this" (quoted in Goodman, Schoenbrod, and Stearns 1973, 31). Nancy Stearns, who filed a pro-choice amicus brief in *Roe,* agreed: "[In the abortion cases] the people that are necessary to effect the decision are doctors, most of whom are not opposed, probably don't give a damn, and in fact have a whole lot to gain . . . because of the amount of money they can make" (quoted in Goodman et al. 1973, 29). Even the glacial growth of hospital abortion providers in the early and mid-1970s may be due, in part, to financial considerations. In a study of thirty-six general hospitals in Harris County (Houston), Texas, the need for increased income was found to be an important determinant of whether hospitals performed abortions. Hospitals with low occupancy rates, and therefore low income, the study reported, "saw changing abortion policy as a way to fill beds and raise income" (Kemp, Carp, and Brady 1978, 27).

Although the law of the land was that the choice of an abortion was not to be denied a woman in the first trimester, and regulated only to the extent necessary to preserve a woman's health in the second trimester, American hospitals, on the whole, do not honor the law. By allowing the market to meet the need, however, the Court's decisions resulted in at least a continuation of some availability of safe and legal abortion. Although no one can be sure what might have happened if clinics had not been allowed, if the sole burden for implementing the decisions had been on hospitals, hospital practice suggests that resistance would have been strong. After all, the Court did find abortion constitutionally protected, and most hospitals simply refused to accept that decision.

The implementation of constitutional rights, then, may depend a great deal on the beliefs of those necessary to implement them. The data suggest that without clinics the Court's decisions, constitutional rights notwithstanding, would have been frustrated.

Court Decisions and Political Action

It is generally believed that winning a major Supreme Court case is an invaluable political resource. The victorious side can use the decision to dramatize the issue, encourage political mobilization, and ignite a political movement. In an older view, however, this connection is dubious. Writing at the beginning of the twentieth century, Thayer (1901) suggested that reliance on litigation weakens political organizing. Because there have been more than twenty years of litigation in regard to abortion, the issue provides a good test of these competing views.

The evidence suggests that *Roe* and *Doe* may have seriously weakened the political effectiveness of the winners—pro-choice forces—and inspired the losers. After the 1973 decisions, many pro-choice activists simply assumed they had won and stopped their activity. According to J. Hugh Anwyl, then the executive director of Planned Parenthood of Los Angeles, pro-choice activists went "on a long siesta" after the abortion decisions (quoted in Johnston 1977, 1). Alfred F. Moran, an executive vice president at Planned Parenthood of New York, put it this way: "Most of us really believed that was the end of the controversy. The Supreme Court had spoken, and while some disagreement would remain, the issue had been tried, tested and laid to rest" (Brozan 1983, A17). These views were joined by a NARAL activist, Janet Beals: "Everyone assumed that when the Supreme Court made its decision in 1973 that we'd got what we wanted and the battle was over. The movement afterwards lost steam" (quoted in Phillips 1980, 3). By 1977 a survey of pro-choice and antiabortion activity in thirteen states nationwide revealed that abortion rights advocates had failed to match the activity of their opponents (Johnston 1977).[17] The political organization and momentum that had changed laws nationwide dissipated in reaction to Court victory. This may help explain why abortion services remain so unevenly available.

Reliance on Court action seems to have harmed the pro-choice movement in a second way. The most restrictive version of the Hyde Amendment, banning federal funding of abortions even where abortion is necessary to save the life of the woman, was passed with the help of a parliamentary maneuver by pro-choice legislators. Their strategy, as reported the following day on the front pages of the *New York Times* and the *Washington Post,* was to pass such a conservative bill that the Court would have no choice but to overturn it (Russell 1977; Tolchin 1977). This reliance on the Court was totally unfounded. With hindsight, Karen Mulhauser, a former director of NARAL, suggested that "had we made more gains through the legislative and referendum processes, and taken a little longer at it, the public would have moved with us" (quoted in Williams 1979, 12). By winning a Court case "without the organization needed to cope with a powerful opposition" (Rubin 1982, 169), pro-choice forces vastly overestimated the power and influence of the Court.

By the time of *Webster* (1989), however, pro-choice forces seemed to have learned from their mistakes, while right-to-life activists miscalculated. In early August 1989, just after *Webster,* a spokesperson for the National Right to Life Committee proclaimed: "[F]or the first time since 1973, we are clearly in a position of strength" (Shribman 1989, A8). Pro-choice forces, however, went on the offensive by generating a massive political response. Commenting on *Webster,* Nancy Broff, NARAL's legislative and political director, noted, "It finally gave us the smoking gun we needed to mobilize people" (quoted in Kornhauser 1989, 11). Membership and financial support grew rapidly. "In the year after *Webster,* membership in the National Abortion Rights Action League jumped from 150,000 to 400,000; in the National Organization for Women [NOW], from 170,000 to 250,000" (Craig and O'Brien 1993, 296). Furthermore, NARAL "nearly tripled" its income in 1989, and NOW "nearly doubled" its income, as did the Planned Parenthood Federation of America (Shribman 1989, A8). In May 1989 alone, NARAL raised $1 million (Kornhauser 1989).

This newfound energy was turned toward political action. In gubernatorial elections in Virginia and New Jersey in the fall of 1989, pro-choice forces played an important role in electing the pro-choice candidates L. Douglas Wilder and James J. Florio over antiabortion opponents. Antiabortion legislation was defeated in Florida, where Gov. Bob Martinez, an opponent of abortion, called a special session of the legislature to enact it. Congress passed legislation that allowed the District of Columbia to use its own tax revenues to pay for abortions and that essentially repealed the so-called gag rule, but President Bush vetoed both bills, and the House of Representatives failed to override the vetoes. As Paige Cunningham, of the antiabortion group Americans United for Life, put it: "The pro-life movement has been organized and active for twenty years, and some of us are tired. The pro-choice movement is fresh so they're operating with a much greater energy reserve. They've really rallied in light of *Webster*" (quoted in Berke 1989, 1).

This new understanding was also seen in *Casey*. Although pro-choice forces had seen antiabortion restrictions upheld in *Webster* and *Rust,* and the sure antiabortion vote of Justice Clarence Thomas had replaced the pro-choice vote of Justice Thurgood Marshall on the Supreme Court in the interim, pro-choice forces appealed the lower-court decision to the Supreme Court. As the *New York Times* reported, this was "a calculated move to intensify the political debate on abortion before the 1992 election" (Berke 1989, 1). Further increasing the stakes, they asked the Court either to reaffirm women's fundamental right to abortion or to overturn *Roe*. Berke (1991, B8) declared that "[t]he action marked an adjustment in strategy by the abortion rights groups, who seem now to be looking to the Court as a political foil rather than a source of redress."

All this suggests that Thayer may have the stronger case. That is, Court decisions do seem to have a mobilizing potential, but for the losers![18] Both winners and losers appear to assume that Court decisions announcing or upholding constitutional rights will be implemented, but they behave in different ways. Winners celebrate and relax, whereas losers redouble their efforts. Note, too, that in the wake of *Webster*, public opinion moved in a pro-choice direction, counter to the tenor of the opinion. Court decisions do matter, but in complicated ways.

Conclusion

"It does no good to have the [abortion] procedure be legal if women can't get it," stated Gwenyth Mapes, the executive director of the Missoula (Montana) Blue Mountain Clinic destroyed by arson in March 1993 (quoted in Baum 1993, A1).

Courts do not exist in a vacuum. Supreme Court decisions, even those finding constitutional rights, are not implemented automatically or in any straightforward or simple way. They are merely one part of the broader political picture. At best, they can contribute to the process of change. In and of themselves, they accomplish little.

The implementation of the Court's abortion decisions, partial though it has been, owes its success to the fact that the decisions have been made in a time when the role of women in American life is changing dramatically. Out of the social turmoil of the 1960s grew a women's movement that continues to press politically, socially, and culturally for ending restrictions on women's opportunities. Access to safe and legal abortion is part of this movement. In 1973 the Supreme Court lent its support by finding a constitutional right to abortion. And in the years since, it has maintained its support for that core constitutional right. Yet, I have argued that far more important in making safe and legal abortion available are the beliefs of politicians, relevant professionals, and the public. When these groups are supportive of abortion choice, that choice is available. Where they have opposed abortion, they have fought against the Court's decisions, successfully minimizing access to abortion. Lack of support from hospital administrators and some politicians and intense opposition from a small group of politicians and activists have limited the availability of abortion services. On the whole, in states that were supportive of abortion choice before Court action, access remains good. In the states that had the most restrictive abortion laws before *Roe,* abortion services are available but remain difficult to obtain. As Gwenyth Mapes put it, "It does no good to have the [abortion] procedure be legal if women can't get it."

This analysis suggests that in general, constitutional rights have a greater likelihood of being implemented when they reflect the preexisting beliefs of politicians, relevant professionals, and the public. When at least some of these groups are opposed, locally or nationally, implementation is less likely. The assumption that the implementation of Court decisions and constitutional rights is unproblematic both reifies and removes courts from the political, social, cultural, and economic systems in which they operate. Courts are political institutions, and their role must be understood accordingly. Examining their decisions without making the political world central to that examination may make for fine reading in constitutional-law textbooks, but it tells the reader very little about the lives people lead.

NOTES

1. Alaska, Hawaii, New York, and Washington had previously liberalized their laws. The constitutional requirements set forth in *Roe* and *Doe* were basically, although not completely, met by these state laws.

2. For a fuller examination, see Rosenberg 1991.

3. In 1971, before *Roe* and *Doe*, the Court heard an abortion case (*United States v. Vuitch*) from Washington, D.C. The decision, however, did not settle the constitutional issues involved in the abortion controversy.

4. Estimates of the number of legal abortions performed each year prior to *Roe* vary enormously, ranging from 50,000 to nearly 2 million. See Rosenberg 1991, 353–355.

5. The following discussion, except where noted, is based on Lader 1973.

6. After the 1973 decisions, NARAL kept its acronym but changed its name to the National Abortion Rights Action League.

7. Nixon's "own personal views" were that "unrestricted abortion policies, or abortion on demand" could not be squared with his "personal belief in the sanctity of human life" (quoted in Lader 1973, 176–177).

8. Franklin and Kosaki (1989, 762) argue that in the wake of *Roe* opinions hardened. That is, those who were pro-choice before the decision became even more so after; the same held true for those opposed to abortion. Court action did not change opinions; abortion opponents did not become abortion supporters (and vice versa). See Epstein and Kobylka 1992, 203.

9. Ford did veto the 1977 appropriations bill containing the Hyde Amendment. He stated that he did so for budgetary reasons (the bill was $4 billion over his budget request) and reasserted his support for "restrictions on the use of federal funds for abortion" (quoted in Craig and O'Brien 1993, 161).

10. The Congressional Research Service reports that Congress enacted thirty restrictive abortion statutes during 1973–1982 (Davidson 1983).

11. The growth in violent attacks on abortion clinics, and illegal, harassing demonstrations in front of them, may demonstrate a growing awareness of this point by the foes of abortion.

12. Treshman is not the only antiabortion activist to express such views. Goodstein (1994, A1) writes that "there is a sizable faction among the antiabortion movement's activists . . . who have applauded Hill [the convicted killer of Dr. Britton and Mr. Barrett] as a righteous defender of babies."

13. The East South Central states are Kentucky, Tennessee, Alabama, and Mississippi. The West South Central states are Arkansas, Louisiana, Oklahoma, and Texas. Together, these eight states contained 16 percent of the U.S. population in 1973.

14. It is possible, of course, that some women had personal reasons for not obtaining an abortion in their home town. Still, that seems an unlikely explanation as to why 100,000 women each year would leave their home states to obtain abortions.

15. *Akron v. Akron Center for Reproductive Health* (1983); *Planned Parenthood v. Ashcroft* (1983). The vast majority of abortions in the United States are performed in the first trimester. As early as 1976, the figure was 90 percent. See Forrest et al. 1979, 32.

16. The percentage for clinics is not artificially high because there were only a small number of clinic abortions in the years preceding Court action. In 1973, clinics performed more than 330,000 abortions, or about 45 percent of all abortions (see Alan Guttmacher Institute 1976, 27).

17. Others in agreement with this analysis include Tatalovich and Daynes (1981, 101, 164), participants in a symposium at the Brookings Institution (in Steiner 1983), and Jackson and Vinovskis (1983, 73), who found that after the decisions "state-level pro-choice grounds disbanded, victory seemingly achieved."

18. This also appears to have been the case in 1954 with the Court's school desegregation decision, *Brown v. Board of Education*. After that decision, the Ku Klux Klan was reinvigorated and the White Citizen's Councils were formed, with the aim of preserving racial segregation through violence and intimidation.

REFERENCES

"Abortions Legal for Year, Performed for Thousands." 1973. *New York Times,* December 31, sec. A.

Alan Guttmacher Institute. 1976. *Abortion 1974–1975: Need and Services in the United States, Each State and Metropolitan Area.* New York: Planned Parenthood Federation of America.

Anderson, Jack, and Michael Binstein. 1993. "Violent Shift in Abortion Battle." *Washington Post,* March 18, sec. C.

Barringer, Felicity. 1993. "Abortion Clinics Said to Be in Peril." *New York Times,* March 6, Sec. A.

Baum, Dan. 1993. "Violence Is Driving Away Rural Abortion Clinics." *Chicago Tribune,* August 21, Sec. A.

Berke, Richard L. 1989. "The Abortion Rights Movement Has Its Day." *New York Times,* October 15, Sec. 4.

_____.1991. "Groups Backing Abortion Rights Ask Court to Act." *New York Times,* November 8, Sec. A.

Blake, Judith. 1971. "Abortion and Public Opinion: The 1960–1970 Decade." *Science,* February 12.

_____.1977a. "The Abortion Decisions: Judicial Review and Public Opinion." In *Abortion: New Directions for Policy Studies,* edited by Edward Manier, William Liu, and David Solomon. Notre Dame, Ind.: University of Notre Dame Press.

_____.1977b. "The Supreme Court's Abortion Decisions and Public Opinion in the United States." *Population and Development Review* 3:45–62.

Brody, Jane E. 1973. "States and Doctors Wary on Eased Abortion Ruling." *New York Times,* February 16, Sec. A.

Brozan, Nadine. 1983. "Abortion Ruling: 10 Years of Bitter Conflict." *New York Times,* January 15, Sec. A.

Cooper, Helene. 1993. "Medical Schools, Students Shun Abortion Study." *Wall Street Journal,* Midwest edition, March 12, Sec. B.

Craig, Barbara Hinkson, and David M. O'Brien. 1993. *Abortion and American Politics.* Chatham, N.J.: Chatham House.

Currivan, Gene. 1970. "Poll Finds Shift to Left among College Freshmen." *New York Times,* December 20, Sec. 1.

Daley, Daniel, and Rachel Benson Gold. 1994. "Public Funding for Contraceptive, Sterilization, and Abortion Services, Fiscal Year 1992." *Family Planning Perspectives* 25:244–251.

Darney, Philip D., Uta Landy, Sara MacPherson, and Richard L. Sweet. 1987. "Abortion Training in U.S. Obstetrics and Gynecology Residency Programs." *Family Planning Perspectives* 19:158–162.

Davidson, Roger H. 1983. "Procedures and Politics in Congress." In *The Abortion Dispute and the American System,* edited by Gilbert Y. Steiner. Washington, D.C.: Brookings Institution.

Ebaugh, Helen Rose Fuchs, and C. Allen Haney. 1980. "Shifts in Abortion Attitudes: 1972–1978." *Journal of Marriage and the Family* 42:491–499.

Epstein, Lee, and Joseph F. Kobylka. 1992. *The Supreme Court and Legal Change.* Chapel Hill: University of North Carolina Press.

Fiske, Edward B. 1967. "Clergymen Offer Abortion Advice." *New York Times,* May 22, Sec. A.

Forrest, Jacqueline Darroch, and Stanley K. Henshaw. 1987. "The Harassment of U.S. Abortion Providers." *Family Planning Perspectives* 19:9–13.

Forrest, Jacqueline Darroch, Ellen Sullivan, and Christopher Tietze. 1978. "Abortion in the United States, 1976–1977." *Family Planning Perspectives* 10:271–279.

_____. 1979. *Abortion 1976–1977: Need and Services in the United States, Each State and Metropolitan Area.* New York: Alan Guttmacher Institute.

Franklin, Charles H., and Liane C. Kosaki. 1989. "Republican Schoolmaster: The U.S. Supreme Court, Public Opinion, and Abortion." *American Political Science Review* 83:751–771.

Goodman, Janice, Rhonda Copelon Schoenbrod, and Nancy Stearns. 1973. "Doe and Roe." *Women's Rights Law Reporter* 1:20–38.

Goodstein, Laurie. 1994. "Life and Death Choices: Antiabortion Faction Tries to Justify Homicide." *Washington Post,* August 13, Sec. A.

Henshaw, Stanley K. 1986. "Induced Abortion: A Worldwide Perspective." *Family Planning Perspectives* 18:250–254.

_____. 1991. "The Accessibility of Abortion Services in the United States." *Family Planning Perspectives* 23:246–252, 263.

Henshaw, Stanley K., and Kevin O'Reilly. 1983. "Characteristics of Abortion Patients in the United States, 1979 and 1980." *Family Planning Perspectives* 15:5.

Henshaw, Stanley K., and Jennifer Van Vort. 1990. "Abortion Services in the United States, 1987 and 1988." *Family Planning Perspectives* 22:102–108, 142.

_____. 1994. "Abortion Services in the United States, 1991 and 1992." *Family Planning Perspectives* 26:100–106, 122.

Henshaw, Stanley K., Jacqueline Darroch Forrest, and Ellen Blaine. 1984. "Abortion Services in the United States, 1981 and 1982." *Family Planning Perspectives* 16:119–127.

Henshaw, Stanley K., Jacqueline Darroch Forrest, and Jennifer Van Vort. 1987. "Abortion Services in the United States, 1984 and 1985." *Family Planning Perspectives* 19:63–70.

Henshaw, Stanley K., Jacqueline Darroch Forrest, Ellen Sullivan, and Christopher Tietze. 1982. "Abortion Services in the United States, 1979 and 1980." *Family Planning Perspectives* 14:5–15.

Henshaw, Stanley K., Lisa M. Koonin, and Jack C. Smith. 1991. "Characteristics of U.S. Women Having Abortions, 1987." *Family Planning Perspectives* 23:75–81.

Hole, Judith, and Ellen Levine. 1971. *Rebirth of Feminism.* New York: Quadrangle.

Jackson, John E., and Maris A. Vinovskis. 1983. "Public Opinion, Elections, and the 'Single-Issue' Issue." In *The Abortion Dispute and the American System,* edited by Gilbert Y. Steiner. Washington, D.C.: Brookings Institution.

Jaffe, Frederick S., Barbara L. Lindheim, and Phillip R. Lee. 1981. *Abortion Politics.* New York: McGraw-Hill.

Johnston, Laurie. 1977. "Abortion Foes Gain Support as They Intensify Campaign." *New York Times,* October 23, Sec. 1.

Kemp, Kathleen A., Robert A. Carp, and David W. Brady. 1978. "The Supreme Court and Social Change: The Case of Abortion." *Western Political Quarterly* 31:19–31.

King, Wayne. 1973. "Despite Court Ruling, Problems Persist in Gaining Abortions." *New York Times,* May 20, Sec. 1.

Kornhauser, Anne. 1989. "Abortion Case Has Been Boon to Both Sides." *Legal Times,* July 3.

Lader, Lawrence. 1973. *Abortion II: Making the Revolution.* Boston: Beacon Press.

Lewin, Tamar. 1994. "A Cause Worth Killing For? Debate Splits Abortion Foes." *New York Times,* July 30, Sec. A.

Newport, Frank, and Leslie McAneny. 1992. "Whose Court Is It Anyhow? O'Connor, Kennedy, Souter Position Reflects Abortion Views of Most Americans." *Gallup Poll Monthly* 322 (July): 51–53.

Noonan, John T., Jr. 1973. "Raw Judicial Power." *National Review,* March 2.

Phillips, Richard. 1980. "The Shooting War over 'Choice' or 'Life' Is Beginning Again." *Chicago Tribune,* April 20, Sec. 12.

"Rhode Island Abortion Law Is Declared Unconstitutional." 1973. *New York Times,* May 17, Sec. A.

Rosen, R. A. Hudson, H. W. Werley Jr., J. W. Ager, and F. P. Shea. 1974. "Health Professionals' Attitudes toward Abortion." *Public Opinion Quarterly* 38:159–173.

Rosenberg, Gerald N. 1991. *The Hollow Hope: Can Courts Bring About Social Change?* Chicago: University of Chicago Press.

Rosenthal, Jack. 1971. "Survey Finds 50% Back Liberalization of Abortion Policy." *New York Times,* October 28, Sec. A.

Rosoff, Jeannie I. 1975. "Is Support for Abortion Political Suicide?" *Family Planning Perspectives* 7:13–22.

Rubin, Eva R. 1982. *Abortion, Politics, and the Courts.* Westport, Conn.: Greenwood Press.

Russell, Mary. 1977. "House Bars Use of U.S. Funds in Abortion Cases." *Washington Post,* June 18, Sec. A.

Shribman, David. 1989. "Abortion-Issue Foes, Preaching to the Converted in No Uncertain Terms, Step Up Funding Pleas." *Wall Street Journal,* December 26, Sec. A.

Steiner, Gilbert Y., ed. 1983. *The Abortion Dispute and the American System.* Washington, D.C.: Brookings Institution.

Sullivan, Ellen, Christopher Tietze, and Joy G. Dryfoos. 1977. "Legal Abortion in the United States, 1975–1976." *Family Planning Perspectives* 9:116.

Tatalovich, Raymond, and Byron W. Daynes. 1981. *The Politics of Abortion.* New York: Praeger.

Thayer, James Bradley. 1901. *John Marshall.* Boston: Houghton, Mifflin.

Thomas, Pierre. 1994. "U.S. Marshals Dispatched to Guard Abortion Clinics." *Washington Post,* August 2, Sec. A.

Tolchin, Martin. 1977. "House Bars Medicaid Abortions and Funds for Enforcing Quotas." *New York Times,* June 18, Sec. A.

Toner, Robin. 1993. "Clinton Orders Reversal of Abortion Restrictions Left by Reagan and Bush." *New York Times,* January 23, Sec. A.

United States. Congress. Senate. 1970a. *Congressional Record.* Daily ed. 91st Cong., 2d sess. April 23, S3746.

_____. 1970b. *Congressional Record.* Daily ed. 91st Cong., 2d sess. February 24, S3501.

_____. 1974. Committee on the Judiciary. *Hearings before the Subcommittee on Constitutional Amendments.* Vol. 2. 93d Cong., 2d sess.

_____. 1976. Committee on the Judiciary. *Hearings before the Subcommittee on Constitutional Amendments.* Vol. 4. 94d Cong., 1st sess.

Weinstock, Edward, Christopher Tietze, Frederick S. Jaffe, and Joy G. Dryfoos. 1975. "Legal Abortions in the United States since the 1973 Supreme Court Decisions." *Family Planning Perspectives* 7:23–31.

Williams, Roger M. 1979. "The Power of Fetal Politics." *Saturday Review,* June 9.

"A Woman's Right." 1973. *Evening Star* (Washington, D.C.), January 27, Sec. A.

5-2

The Effect of War on the Supreme Court

Lee Epstein, Daniel E. Ho, Gary King, and Jeffrey A. Segal

Inter arma silent leges ("During war the laws are silent").
—A Roman legal maxim

During wartime, do Americans generally experience a loss of personal liberties? This is an age-old question on which judicial scholars disagree. Certainly some Americans suddenly find their life circumstances altered in ways they would never have expected, the most egregious such case being the sudden relocation, and financial ruin, of Japanese immigrants and citizens living on the West Coast after Pearl Harbor. With the current war on terrorism unlikely to end anytime soon, the question can commonly be heard in Congress and the federal courts by critics of the Bush administration's domestic surveillance and detention practices. Lee Epstein, Daniel E. Ho, Gary King, and Jeffrey A. Segal seek to answer the question systematically by examining sixty-two wartime Supreme Court decisions since 1941 in which constitutionally protected liberties were at issue.

> The Constitution of the United States is a law for rulers and people, equally in war and in peace, and covers with the shield of its protection all classes of men, at all times, and under all circumstances. . . . When peace prevails, and the authority of the government is undisputed, there is no difficulty of preserving the safeguards of liberty . . . but if society is disturbed by civil commotion . . . these safeguards need, and should receive, the watchful care of those entrusted with the guardianship of the Constitution and laws.

—*Ex parte Milligan* (1866), in which the Supreme Court held that a civilian accused of disloyalty to the Union could not be tried in a military court in areas where the regular courts remained open.

Source: Summary of Lee Epstein, Daniel E. Ho, Gary King, and Jeffrey A. Segal, "The Supreme Court During Crisis: How War Affects Only Non-War Cases," *New York University Law Review* 80, no. 1 (April 2005): 1–116. A copy of the article, along with a replication data file and the statistical software used, is available at http://gking.harvard.edu/files/abs/crisis-abs.shtml.

> We uphold the exclusion order. . . . In doing so, we are not unmindful of
> the hardships imposed by it upon a large group of American citizens. But
> hardships are part of war, and war is an aggregation of hardships. All cit-
> izens alike, both in and out of uniform, feel the impact of war in greater
> or lesser measure. Citizenship has its responsibilities as well as its privi-
> leges, and in time of war the burden is always heavier. Compulsory exclu-
> sion of large groups of citizens from their homes, except under circum-
> stances of direst emergency and peril, is inconsistent with our basic
> governmental institutions. But when under conditions of modern war-
> fare our shores are threatened by hostile forces, the power to protect
> must be commensurate with the threatened danger.

—*Korematsu v. United States* (1944), in which the Court upheld an executive order authorizing the exclusion of Japanese
Americans from areas of the Pacific Coast.

Running through these quotations from landmark Supreme Court decisions is a
common strand: The justices seem to suggest that their institution ought to play
a different role in times of "emergency and peril" than when "peace prevails."
But the cases cited above stand for fundamentally different propositions about
that role. *Milligan* implies that the justices must become especially vigilant in protecting rights and liberties during "commotions." *Korematsu* commends quite the
opposite: that the justices ought to be especially willing to subordinate rights and
liberties when America is threatened. If *Korematsu* is testimony to the continued
viability of Cicero's maxim "Inter arma silent leges" ("During war law is silent"),
as many suggest that it is, then *Milligan* provides a counterpunch: During war the
law speaks loudly.

The Supreme Court has not expressly overruled either decision. Both appear
to remain valid law, but not so in the eyes of many members of the legal community, an overwhelming majority of whom believe that the Court's jurisprudence in times of crisis is far more in line with the dictates of *Korematsu* than with
the language of *Milligan*. Indeed, the belief that the Court acts to suppress rights
and liberties under conditions of threat is so widely accepted in post-9/11 America, and has been so widely accepted since the World War I period, that most
observers no longer debate whether the Court, in fact, behaves in this way.
Instead, the discussions are over how it came about or whether the Court should
embrace a "crisis jurisprudence." As the legal scholar Norman Dorsen puts it:

> [N]ational security . . . has been a graveyard for civil liberties for much of
> our recent history. The questions to be answered are not whether this is
> true—it demonstrably is—but why we have come to this pass and how we
> might begin to relieve the Bill of Rights of at least some of the burden thus
> imposed on it.[1]

On this logic we might expect to see the Court upholding many of the steps that the George W. Bush administration has taken in the name of protecting America's security, including its warrantless wiretapping program and its use of military commissions to try suspected terrorists. These are policies that the justices might otherwise deem unconstitutional but for the threat posed to the United States. Or so the argument goes.

It is a strong argument and one strongly endorsed by a large fraction of the analysts who have examined the relationship between Supreme Court decisions and threats to national security. But does this claim, sometimes called the "crisis thesis," accurately capture jurisprudence during threats to the nation's security? Do the justices, in fact, rally round the flag, supporting curtailments of rights and liberties in wartime that they would not support during periods of peace?

We raise these questions because—despite the crisis thesis's resilience—virtually all evidence for it comes from isolated anecdotes or descriptions of a few highly selected Court decisions rather than from systematic analyses of a broad class of cases. Determining whether a piece of conventional wisdom can withstand rigorous scrutiny is almost always a worthwhile undertaking, but it is made even more so here because the crisis thesis continues to be the subject of debate. A number of judges, along with a handful of commentators, challenge the idea in its entirety and suggest that, in line with *Milligan*, the Court acts as a guardian, not a suppressor, of rights during times of war.

Debate continues for good reason: No one has yet attempted a large-scale, systematic study addressing the factual underpinnings of the crisis thesis. Only in the last decade or so have scholars developed the high-quality data and statistical tools required to conduct such a study. With those data and tools now in place, we examine the validity of the crisis thesis. Using the best data available on the causes and outcomes of every civil rights and liberties case decided by the Supreme Court from 1941 to 2001, and employing methods chosen and tuned especially for this problem, we explore systematically the Court's decisions during periods when the country is in "emergency and peril" and when it is in relative peace. Our findings provide the first systematic support for the existence of a crisis jurisprudence: The justices are, in fact, significantly more likely to curtail rights and liberties during times of war and other international threat. On the other hand, contrary to what every proponent of the crisis thesis has so far suggested, whereas the presence of war does affect cases unrelated to the war, there is no evidence that the presence of war affects cases directly related to the war.

We demonstrate and explain this apparently contradictory result in three steps. We begin with the crisis thesis and examine its supporting literature, why the Court might respond to threats to national security by suppressing rights, and what kind of evidence exists for such an outcome. Although less consensus exists in the literature about what types of cases are likely to be affected by war, virtually all supporters of the crisis thesis suggest that the effect is strongest for cases most directly related to war. The second part of the chapter explains the basic approach we bring to the debate, defining the concepts of a "crisis" and war-related cases, describing the set of civil rights and liberties cases we analyze, and explaining our methods. We then detail our results, which both support and challenge conventional views about the effect of war on the Court.

Political and Judicial Responses to War

Proponents of the crisis thesis argue that the Supreme Court assumes "a highly deferential attitude when called upon to review governmental actions and decisions" during times of threat to the nation's security, supporting curtailments of civil liberties and rights it otherwise would not.[2] On this account, then, there are two relevant sets of responses to crises: the government's and the Court's. The former takes steps to curtail rights and liberties during wartime, and the justices—to a greater extent than they would in times of peace—uphold those measures, along with others that may infringe on rights and liberties.

We detail these responses, beginning with the political branches of government and then turning to the primary focus of our inquiry, the Court.

Political Responses to War

When societies confront crises, they respond in different ways. Sometimes they use military force to attack their aggressors; sometimes they do not. Sometimes they impose economic sanctions; sometimes they do not. Sometimes they undertake diplomatic efforts; sometimes they do not. But, as many studies reveal, one response appears essentially universal: In times of emergency— whether arising from wars, internal rebellions, or terrorist attacks—governments tend to suppress the rights and liberties of persons living within their borders. They may respond in this way out of a desire to present a unified front to outsiders, perceiving that cleavages are dangerous, or, of course, out of a belief that national security and military necessity must outweigh liberty interests if government is to be protected and preserved.

Whatever the reason, the United States is no exception to this rule. Indeed, America's history is replete with executive and legislative attempts, during times of urgency, to restrict the people's ability to speak, publish, and organize; to erode guarantees usually afforded to the criminally accused; or to tighten restrictions on

Figure 1. Percentage of Americans Approving of George W. Bush's Handling of His Job: The "Rally Effect" Generated by September 11, 2001

Date of Poll

Note: Between February 1, 2001, and February 2, 2003, the Gallup Organization fielded eighty-three polls on the public's approval of President George W. Bush. The question asked in all instances was: "Do you approve or disapprove of the way George W. Bush is handling his job as president?" We depict the percentages of respondents approving his performance. September 14, 2001, is the date of the first Gallup poll after September 11, 2001. The data may be found in David W. Moore, Bush Approval Rating Remains at 70% Level, *(May 1, 2003), www.gallup.com/poll/content/degault.aspx?ci=8308 (retrieved Nov. 13, 2004).*

foreigners or perceived enemies. The "ink had barely dried on the First Amendment,"[3] as Justice William Brennan once observed, when Congress passed two restrictive laws: the Sedition Act, which prohibited speech critical of the United States, and the Enemy Alien Act, which empowered the president to detain or deport alien enemies and which the government has used during declared wars to stamp out political opposition. During the Civil War, President Abraham Lincoln took steps to suppress "treacherous" behavior out of the belief "that the nation must be able to protect itself in war against utterances which actually cause insubordination."[4] Prior to America's entry into World War I, President Woodrow Wilson "predicted a dire fate for civil liberties should we become involved." With passage of the Espionage Act of 1917 and the Sedition Act of 1918, Wilson's prediction was realized—with Wilson as a prime accomplice. World War II brought yet more repressive measures, most notably executive orders limiting the movements and providing for the internment of Japanese Americans. The Korean War and the supposed "communist menace" resulted in an "epidemic of witch-hunting, paranoia, and political grandstanding" directed against "reds" across the country. And Vietnam was accompanied by governmental efforts to silence war protests. In the United States, then, "[t]he struggle between the needs of national security and political or civil liberties has been a continual one."[5]

Of course, politicians would have a difficult time enacting and implementing curtailments of rights and liberties if those measures lacked public support. But that has not been the case during the crises for which we have survey data. In a general sense, the data reveal that public confidence in the president, who is often the catalyst for repressive legislation, soars in international crises. This "rally effect" gave Franklin Roosevelt a twelve-point increase after the Japanese attacked Pearl Harbor, John Kennedy a thirteen-point lift during the Cuban Missile Crisis, and George H. W. Bush a fourteen-point boost when Iraq invaded Kuwait. As Figure 1 shows, after September 11, 2001, George W. Bush's approval rating jumped a record-setting thirty-five points, from 51 percent on September 7 to 86 percent on September 14.

Survey data also reveal a public supportive of specific efforts on the part of political actors to curtail rights and liberties. Consider Americans' response after the attacks of September 11. As Table 1 shows, all but one of a list of restrictions on rights designed to furnish the government with greater authority to combat terrorism attained the support of a substantial majority of respondents—the indefinite detainment of terrorist suspects without charging them being the sole exception.[6]

The Court's Response to War

In light of the public opinion data, it should not be a surprise that the U.S. Justice Department undertook many of the activities listed in Table 1 or that Congress passed and the president signed the USA PATRIOT Act of 2001, which also contains some of these measures. Nor should we be surprised that legislators, with the backing of the president, proposed the Patriot Act in the first instance. Such a response by elected officials to an "emergency" is not an anomaly.

In contrast to the president and Congress, the Supreme Court lacks an electoral connection and is ostensibly insulated from public pressure by life tenure and salary protection under Article III of the Constitution. Although it can take years for lawsuits connected to conflicts to make their way to the nation's highest tribunal, does the Supreme Court nevertheless respond contemporaneously to crises? The answer to this question falls generally under one of two rubrics: (a) the *Milligan* thesis of the Court as a guardian of civil rights and liberties, leading the Court to depart dramatically from the preferences of the public and elected officials; and (b) the crisis thesis, reflecting *Korematsu*, that the Court's response mirrors those of the citizenry and its leaders.

Table 1. Percentages of Americans Supporting and Opposing
Antiterrorist Measures after September 11, 2001

Measure	Support	Oppose	Don't know
Wiretap telephone	69	29	2
Intercept e-mail	72	23	5
Intercept ordinary mail	57	39	4
Examine Internet activity	82	15	3
Detain suspects for a week without charging them	58	38	3
Detain terrorists indefinitely without charging them	48	48	4
Examine students' education records	76	22	2
Examine telephone records	82	17	1
Examine bank records	79	20	1
Track credit card purchases	75	21	4
Examine tax records	75	24	1

Proponents of the *Milligan* thesis stress difference: Whereas the balance of American society rallies round the flag in times of crisis, the Court takes a more deliberate approach, electing to protect rather than curtail rights and liberties. The justifications for this claim are many, but each begins with the design of the federal judiciary as juxtaposed against the political branches of government. Because the justices hold life-tenured positions, they are freer than elected officials to ignore public opinion. In fact, by removing the Court from the whims of the electorate and elected officials, the Framers explicitly sought to create an institution of government that would stand above the fray and enforce the law free from overt political influences. The Court would be a force for legal stability. It would decide cases not on the basis of politics but according to the law and would "guard the constitution and the rights of individuals from the effects of those ill humours which the arts of designing men, or the influence of particular conjunctures, sometimes disseminate among the people themselves." [7]

Many prominent legal scholars and jurists have subscribed to the *Milligan* thesis of the Court as a guardian of rights in times of war, not a suppressor of those rights. But far more commentators and a number of federal judges have advanced the crisis thesis. Whether writing in the early 1900s, the early 2000s, or eras in between, they argue that when the nation's security is under threat, the Court adopts a jurisprudential stance that leads it to curtail rights and liberties it otherwise would not, an effect that is widely perceived to be stronger for cases directly related to the war. The Court's response to wars is the same as that of the rest of American society: It, too, endorses the efforts of elected officials to suppress rights and does not "guard" the Constitution.

Why would the Court act in this way? Proponents of the crisis thesis offer a number of answers. One is that the Constitution demands judicial deference to the executive and the legislature during times of international crisis. Such a reading might follow from the Constitution's grant of emergency powers to the executive and the legislature and its silence with regard to the judiciary. It also follows, supporters of the crisis thesis assert, from the fact that the elected branches, not the courts, are best equipped to cope with the emergency at hand. If the Court failed to recognize this fact, if it failed to treat the Constitution as accommodating necessary trade-offs between security and liberty, the Court would be "convert[ing] the Bill of Rights into a suicide pact." [8]

A second answer stresses the behavioral response of justices to wars and other national emergencies. To supporters of the crisis thesis, that response takes the form of a patriotic fervor on the part of justices, rather than an impulse to act as guardians, and manifests itself in actions to repress rights. As political scientist Joel Grossman writes, "When World War II broke out, feelings of patriotism and concern about the success of the war effort affected Americans nearly universally, including the Justices of the Supreme Court." [9] Other scholars have variously described this behavioral phenomenon as one in which "domestic judicial institutions tend to 'go to war'" or "rally round the flag." Whatever they deem it, the overall message is the same: In times of war, a justice's underlying preferences toward rights and liberties grow more conservative, resulting in behavior that falls in line with the crisis thesis.

An Empirical Examination

The crisis thesis, as we have explained, is sufficiently convincing to the vast majority of the legal community that one version or another has made its way into judicial opinions and off-the-bench writings of Supreme Court justices. And yet, empirical support for it is rather flimsy. It consists not of systematically derived data and carefully designed and executed analyses, but rather of anecdotal evidence. So, for example, in efforts to show that the Court tends to be swept up in the patriotic fervor surrounding it, scholars tell stories of justices who, at the request of presidents, spoke to lay audiences on the importance of supporting military efforts; of some who were "active proponents of [governmental] war policies"; [10] and of others who chastised colleagues inclined to support individual liberties, rights, or justice claims. Capturing the flavor of this form of evidence is the often-told story of Chief Justice Edward D. White's response to an attorney who, during oral argument, claimed that the military draft lacked public support: "I don't think your statement has a thing to do with legal arguments and should not have been said in this Court. It is a very unpatriotic statement to make."

Ultimately, then, the crisis thesis falls short of being a well-supported theory about the Court's role in wartime. It is rather a hypothesis necessitating systematic evaluation. Undertaking that systematic evaluation could take us in several directions. However, because our interest lies in determining the extent to which the thesis accurately captures Court responses to national security threats across a range of disputes and litigants, we focus on cases (a) in which parties claimed a deprivation of their rights or liberties, and (b) that the Supreme Court resolved on the merits, whether in times of war or not, and whether directly related to the international crisis or not, over the last six decades (1941–2001 terms).

Such a focus enables us to scrutinize the key observable implication of the crisis thesis: When the nation's security or its soldiers are at risk, the justices should be less likely to rule in favor of criminal defendants, war protesters, and other litigants who allege violations of their rights.

Research Tasks

Assessing that implication required undertaking four research tasks: First, using Harold J. Spaeth's U.S. Supreme Court Database, which contains detailed information on Court decisions, we identified all cases involving rights, liberties, and justice issues decided since 1941.[11] We also gathered information about whether the Court ruled in favor of or against the individual who claimed a deprivation of rights.

Second, we determined whether the Court heard arguments in the cases during a time of war. For purposes of this study, we defined "wars" as World War II; the Korean, Vietnam, and Gulf Wars; and the recent war in Afghanistan.[12] Third, and relatedly, we sought to assess whether each case in our dataset was connected to one of the wars. Although less consensus exists in the literature about the extent to which a case must be related to the war for decisions to become more conservative, all supporters of the crisis thesis seem to believe that the effect is stronger for cases more related to the war, compared with "ordinary" (non-war-related) cases. For our purposes, a case was related to the war if (a) the controversy began during the war and (b) the genesis of the case was the war itself. War-related cases thus include wartime draft cases; war protest cases; military takings; and deportation, citizenship, and relocation cases resulting from the war.

In all, we gathered information on 3,344 cases, of which 23 percent were decided while a war was going on. Only 2 percent, or sixty-two cases, a very small percentage, resulted directly from the war itself.

Analysis

The final task involved estimating the degree to which wars cause the Court to suppress rights and liberties in ways that it would not during times of peace. Estimating this causal effect involves *counterfactual* inference; that is, we care about what the outcomes of the cases would have been had they not arisen during a war.

In a research environment without any constraints, generating an estimate would be simple enough: We would create a world without a war and ask the U.S. Supreme Court to decide a case; then we would rerun history, holding everything constant other than the absence of a war, and (without its knowing about the first part of our experiment) ask the Court to decide the same case. If in the version of our history without a war we observed support for civil liberties, but in the version with a war we observed a lack of support, then we might conclude that that the war had an effect on the Court with respect to that case in the direction anticipated by the crisis thesis.

This kind of counterfactual inference in examining crisis jurisprudence was evident to Justice Jackson in *Korematsu*. In a dissenting opinion, he observed, "If Congress in peace-time legislation should enact such a criminal law, I should suppose this Court would refuse to enforce it." In other words, in the counterfactual world, in which President Roosevelt's order interning Japanese Americans came before the Supreme Court during a time of peace, the Court would not have upheld the order.

Of course it is impossible to rerun history to estimate the counterfactual and obtain the causal effect for each particular case. This impossibility is known as the "fundamental problem of causal inference," which in concrete terms means that we cannot observe the counterfactual, such as the *Korematsu* decision during peacetime.

To estimate the causal effect of war we employ a technique called "matching," the intuition of which is quite simple. Although we may not be able to rerun history to see if the Court would decide the same case differently in times of war versus peace, we can match cases that are as similar as possible in all observable respects that affect how the court decides, except whether the Court decided them during a war. Consider the study by Epstein and Rowland that sought to investigate whether the participation of interest groups (such as the ACLU and NAACP) increases the odds of victory in court.[13] To conduct their analysis, Epstein and Rowland paired similar cases, decided by the same judge, in which the only relevant point of distinction was whether an interest group participated or not. Similarly, Walker and Barrow matched male and female judges of similar backgrounds to try to determine whether women speak "in a different voice." [14] In both of those studies, the researchers attempted to control for relevant differences (judges or backgrounds) so that they could examine the effect of a causal factor (interest group participation or the sex of the judge).

Our objective is similar. We seek to match cases that are analogous on all pertinent dimensions except the key causal variable war, so that we can assess the effect of that key variable on Court outcomes. The intuition is that once we have matched on all relevant factors, we can infer that the remaining difference in the proportions of cases decided in favor of the party alleging an abridgment of rights and against that party is due to war.

After identifying those other relevant factors (including how liberal or conservative the court was, whether the case was of national importance, how the lower court ruled on the case, and the year in which the justices resolved the dispute), all that remained was to match the cases using automated computer software.[15]

Results

What did we learn from comparing pairs of cases that were similar except for being decided during a war or not? Chiefly we found that for cases unrelated to any ongoing war, the probability of the Supreme Court's deciding a case in favor of a litigant claiming an infringement of his or her rights decreases by about ten percentage points when a war is in progress.

How substantial is 10 percent? In some sense, that depends on the Court itself. We illustrate this point in Figure 2, which shows the actual proportion of U.S. Supreme Court decisions supporting a rights, liberties, or justice claim. The proportion varies a great deal—note, for example, the unparalleled levels of liberalism in the 1960s (in the .80 range, or eighty of 100 cases in support of the rights claimant). But never has the Court been so dominated by conservatives that the proportion dipped below .30 (or thirty of 100 cases decided in favor of the party alleging a rights infringement). On average the figure has hovered around a moderate .49 since the 1953 term.

It is in light of the rather temperate contemporary patterns in decision making depicted in Figure 2 that the importance of our findings moves into relief: Assuming that the past is the best indicator of the future, the causal effect of war on nonwar cases of 10 percent is substantial. The finding is hardly shocking; actually it sits quite comfortably with the crisis thesis.

But other results from our study do come as something of a surprise. Consider first the influence of the presence of war on cases that directly derive from war. We can examine this by taking advantage of the fact that of all the cases that derive from a war, some will reach the Court during wartime, while others will not arrive on the Court's docket until after the conflict has ended. This allows us to test whether the presence of a war—as compared with the subsequent peace—

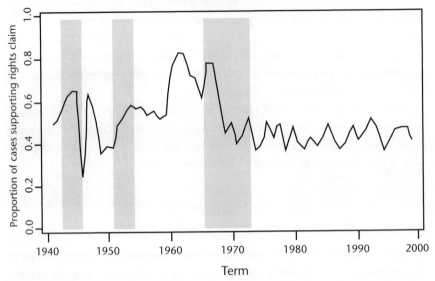

Figure 2. Percentage of U.S. Supreme Court Decisions
Supporting Rights, Liberties, or Justice Claims,
1953–2001 terms.

Note: The line depicts the proportion of support. The gray shading depicts wartime terms during which the Supreme Court heard a civil liberties case. Proportions of support derived by the authors from the U.S Supreme Court Database.

influences cases that derive from war. Given our previous finding that the presence of war substantially influences ordinary rights and liberties cases, it is paradoxical that for cases that derived from a war, we found that whether that war was ongoing or had ended had no detectable effect on Supreme Court decision making. In these cases, the Supreme Court was no more likely to support an infringement of an individual's civil liberties when a war was ongoing than when the country was at peace. The solution to this paradox, we believe, is that when cases are directly related to the war, the traditional liberal-conservative dimension, inherent in the crisis and *Milligan* theses and operative in most of American politics, becomes less meaningful. For cases that are directly related to the war or conflict, the Court seeks to shift responsibility toward Congress and the executive. Politically, this may be desirable for the justices, precisely because war-related cases present potentially severe threats to the judiciary's legitimacy. Focusing on congressional authorization ensures the political legitimacy of a ruling.

Second, when we examined particular areas of the law, we found that war decreased the probability of a liberal decision not only in First Amendment cases (those involving free speech and press, for example) but also in cases of gender

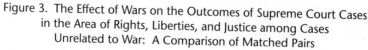

Figure 3. The Effect of Wars on the Outcomes of Supreme Court Cases in the Area of Rights, Liberties, and Justice among Cases Unrelated to War: A Comparison of Matched Pairs

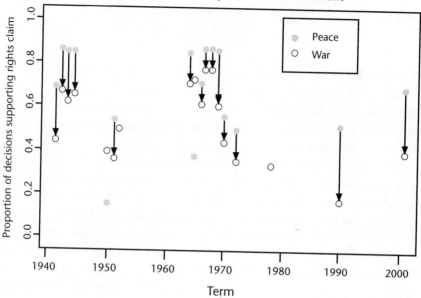

and race discrimination. This calls into question the assertions of some scholars that international crises lead to enhanced protection for minorities.

Third, the effect of war on ordinary cases is not uniform. Figure 3 plots all cases matched to terms in which there was a war on the horizontal axis and the proportion of cases decided liberally on the vertical axis. The grey and black circles indicate the proportions of cases decided liberally during peace and war, respectively, and the arrows indicate the estimated causal effect of war. As one can see, we estimate relatively small effects from the Vietnam War (in the 1960s). Taking the nine Vietnam War terms collectively, the justices became neither distinctly more nor less likely to support rights. In stark contrast is the consistent impact of World War II. In each of the four terms encompassed by the war, the (relatively left-of-center) Court supported curtailments of rights and liberties that it otherwise would not have tolerated—with, of course, the internment at issue in *Korematsu* among them. Likewise, the justices who sat during the Gulf War appear to have become more willing to rule against litigants claiming a deprivation of their rights, though that may stem from the small number of cases available. Indeed, however conservative the majorities on those Courts toward individual rights and liberties in the absence of conflict, the presence of war intensified those ideological predilections. For the majority of matched pairs, war reduced the probability of a liberal decision in wartime.

Conclusion

Our work is the only large-scale, systematic, quantitative test of the crisis thesis to date. The large volume of prior literature devoted to the subject is entirely qualitative, and although it contains much useful description and considerable analytic wisdom, our evidence indicates that most of the causal inferences drawn about the crisis thesis are incorrect or, at best, incomplete.

Our evidence, which spans all civil liberties decisions over six decades, strongly suggests that the decisions made by the Supreme Court during wartime would have been systematically different if the same cases had been decided during peacetime. We have shown that war causes the Court to decide cases unrelated to the war in a markedly more conservative direction than it otherwise would.

However, war appears to have no effect on the conservatism of the Court's decisions in cases closely related to an ongoing military conflict. In those cases the Court retreats from its usual security-versus-liberty focus of decision making to a focus on institutional process.[16] What this means, to put it in contemporary terms, is that the justices may be willing to support the Bush administration's measures to combat terrorism if those measures have the backing of Congress. Indeed, they already have upheld the administration's power to detain alleged terrorists (even if they are American citizens) because Congress had authorized such action.[17]

Seen in this way, resort to the judiciary is no cure for wartime curtailments of civil rights. Contrary to the rhetoric of *Ex parte Milligan*, the justices of the U.S. Supreme Court seem to feel little responsibility to "rebuke the legislative and executive authorities when, under the stress of war [those authorities] have sought to suppress the rights of dissenters."[18] On the other hand, the justices have not acted entirely in accordance with Cicero's maxim, either. During times of war, the Court does indeed speak, but in a paradoxical manner, curtailing civil rights and liberties with more frequency in times of war than in peacetime, but only in cases unrelated to war. In fact, ordinary civil rights and liberties cases are precisely the ones on which war has the most detectable impact.

NOTES

1. Norman Dorsen, "Foreign Affairs and Civil Liberties," *American Journal of International Law* 83 (1989): 840–879 (quote 840).

2. Oren Gross, " 'Once More unto the Breach': The Systemic Failure of Applying the European Convention on Human Rights to Entrenched Emergencies" *Yale Journal of International Law* 23 (1998): 437–502 (quote 491).

3. Justice William J. Brennan Jr., "The Quest to Develop a Jurisprudence of Civil Liberties in Times of Security Crises," address at the Law School of Hebrew University, December 22, 1987, available at www.brennancenter.org/resources/downloads/nation_security_brennan.pdf.

4. Zechariah Chafee Jr., *Free Speech in the United States* (Cambridge: Harvard University Press, 1941), 266.

5. Note, "Developments in the Law—The National Security Interest and Civil Liberties," *Harvard Law Review* 85 (1972): 1130–1326 (quote 1133).

6. The 603 survey respondents were asked the question: "In order to reduce the threat of terrorism in the U.S., would you support or oppose giving law enforcement broader authority to do the following things? Would you support or oppose giving them broader authority to . . . ?" (see Table 1 for list). The data are from a National Public Radio/Kaiser Family Foundation/Kennedy School of Government survey conducted from October 31, 2001, to November 12, 2001. The results are available at www.npr.org/programs/specials/poll/civil_liberties/civil_liberties_static_results_4.html (retrieved October 30, 2004).

7. Alexander Hamilton, *The Federalist,* No. 78. Ed. Terence Ball (New York: Cambridge University Press, 2003), 381.

8. *Terminiello v. Chicago,* 337 U.S. 1, 37 (1949) (Jackson, J., dissenting).

9. Joel B. Grossman, "The Japanese American Cases and the Vagaries of Constitutional Adjudication in Wartime: An Institutional Perspective," *University of Hawaii Law Review* 19 (1997): 649–696 (quote 672–673).

10. David M. Rabban, "The Emergence of Modern First Amendment Doctrine," *University of Chicago Law Review* 50 (1983): 1205–1355 (quote 1331).

11. Spaeth's database actually dates back only to 1953. Following Spaeth's coding rules and with his guidance, we backdated the dataset to include the 1941–1952 terms.

12. In a larger study, we expanded this definition to include major international conflicts (the Berlin blockade, the Cuban Missile and Iran Hostage crises, and September 11).

13. Lee Epstein and C. K. Rowland, "Debunking the Myth of Interest Group Invincibility in the Courts," *American Political Science Review* 85 (1991): 205–217.

14. Thomas G. Walker and Deborah J. Barrow, "The Diversification of the Federal Bench: Policy and Process Ramifications," *Journal of Politics* 47 (1985): 596–617 (quote 601–603 (1985).

15. See Daniel E. Ho, Kosuke Imai, Gary King, and Elizabeth Stuart, "MatchIt: Nonparametric Preprocessing for Parametric Causal Inference" (2004), available at http://gking.harvard.edu/matchit/, which implements the matching methods proposed in Daniel E. Ho, Kosuke Imai, Gary King, and Elizabeth Stuart, "Matching as Nonparametric Preprocessing for Improving Parametric Causal Inference," available at http://gking.harvard.edu/files/abs/matchp-abs.shtml.

16. See Samuel Issacharoff and Richard H. Pildes, "Between Civil Libertarianism and Executive Unilateralism: An Institutional Process Approach to Rights during Wartime," *Theoretical Inquiries in Law* 5 (2004): 1–45. (2004).

17. *Hamdi v. Rumsfeld,* 542 U.S. 507 (2004). On the other hand, the justices were nearly unanimous in their belief that "a state of war is not a blank check for the President when it comes to the rights of the Nation's citizens." As a result, they held that "enemy combatants" are entitled to challenge that classification and to be afforded "a fair opportunity to rebut the Government's factual assertions before a neutral decision maker."

18. Abe Fortas, *Concerning Dissent and Civil Disobedience* (New York: New American Library, 1968), 38 (1968).

5-3

Miranda v. Arizona

Supreme Court of the United States

In their efforts to protect rights guaranteed by the Constitution, courts some-times establish rules of behavior for government officials. In 1966 the Supreme Court considered a number of instances in which police officers or prosecutors failed to give arrested individuals notice of their rights at the outset of the interrogations. The Court held that prosecutors could not use statements stem-ming from custodial interrogation unless they demonstrated the use of proce-dural safeguards "effective to secure the privilege again self-incrimination" as provided by the Fifth Amendment. To ensure that Fifth Amendment rights were protected, the Court outlined the specific warnings interrogators must give to suspects, including notice of the right to remain silent and the right to have counsel present during questioning.

MIRANDA v. ARIZONA

384 U.S. 436 (1966)

CERTIORARI TO THE SUPREME COURT OF ARIZONA.

Decided June 13, 1966.

MR. CHIEF JUSTICE WARREN delivered the opinion of the Court.

The cases before us raise questions which go to the roots of our concepts of American criminal jurisprudence: the restraints society must observe consistent with the Federal Constitution in prosecuting individuals for crime. More specifi-cally, we deal with the admissibility of statements obtained from an individual who is subjected to custodial police interrogation and the necessity for proce-dures which assure that the individual is accorded his privilege under the Fifth Amendment to the Constitution not to be compelled to incriminate himself. . . .

We dealt with certain phases of this problem recently in *Escobedo v. Illi-nois* . . . (1964). There, as in the four cases before us, law enforcement officials took the defendant into custody and interrogated him in a police station for the purpose of obtaining a confession. The police did not effectively advise him of his right to remain silent or of his right to consult with his attorney. Rather, they confronted him with an alleged accomplice who accused him of having perpetrated a murder. When the defendant denied the accusation and said "I didn't shoot Manuel, you did it," they handcuffed him and took him to an interrogation room. There, while handcuffed and standing, he was questioned for four hours until he confessed. During this interrogation, the police denied his request to speak to his attorney, and they prevented his retained attorney, who had come to the police station, from consulting with him. At his trial, the State, over his objection, introduced the confession against him. We held that the statements thus made were constitutionally inadmissible.

This case has been the subject of judicial interpretation and spirited legal debate since it was decided two years ago. Both state and federal courts, in assessing its implications, have arrived at varying conclusions. A wealth of scholarly material has been written tracing its ramifications and underpinnings. Police and prosecutor have speculated on its range and desirability. We granted certiorari in these cases . . . in order further to explore some facets of the problems, thus exposed, of applying the privilege against self-incrimination to in-custody interrogation, and to give concrete constitutional guidelines for law enforcement agencies and courts to follow.

We start here, as we did in Escobedo, with the premise that our holding is not an innovation in our jurisprudence, but is an application of principles long recognized and applied in other settings. We have undertaken a thorough re-examination of the Escobedo decision and the principles it announced, and we reaffirm it. That case was but an explication of basic rights that are enshrined in our Constitution—that "No person . . . shall be compelled in any criminal case to be a witness against himself," and that "the accused shall . . . have the Assistance of Counsel"—rights which were put in jeopardy in that case through official overbearing. These precious rights were fixed in our Constitution only after centuries of persecution and struggle. And in the words of Chief Justice Marshall, they were secured "for ages to come, and . . . designed to approach immortality as nearly as human institutions can approach it," *Cohens v. Virginia,* 6 Wheat. 264, 387 (1821).

Over 70 years ago, our predecessors on this Court eloquently stated:

> The maxim *nemo tenetur seipsum accusare* had its origin in a protest against the inquisitorial and manifestly unjust methods of interrogating accused persons, which [have] long obtained in the continental system, and, until the expulsion of the Stuarts from the British throne in 1688, and the erection of additional barriers for the protection of the people against the exercise of arbitrary power, [were] not uncommon even in England. While the admissions or confessions of the prisoner, when voluntarily and freely made, have always ranked high in the scale of incriminating evidence, if an accused person be

asked to explain his apparent connection with a crime under investigation, the ease with which the questions put to him may assume an inquisitorial character, the temptation to press the witness unduly, to browbeat him if he be timid or reluctant, to push him into a corner, and to entrap him into fatal contradictions, which is so painfully evident in many of the earlier state trials, notably in those of Sir Nicholas Throckmorton, and Udal, the Puritan minister, made the system so odious as to give rise to a demand for its total abolition. The change in the English criminal procedure in that particular seems to be founded upon no statute and no judicial opinion, but upon a general and silent acquiescence of the courts in a popular demand. But, however adopted, it has become firmly embedded in English, as well as in American jurisprudence. So deeply did the iniquities of the ancient system impress themselves upon the minds of the American colonists that the States, with one accord, made a denial of the right to question an accused person a part of their fundamental law, so that a maxim, which in England was a mere rule of evidence, became clothed in this country with the impregnability of a constitutional enactment. *Brown v. Walker*, 161 U.S. 591, 596–597 (1896).

In stating the obligation of the judiciary to apply these constitutional rights, this Court declared in *Weems v. United States* . . . (1910):

> . . . our contemplation cannot be only of what has been but of what may be. Under any other rule a constitution would indeed be as easy of application as it would be deficient in efficacy and power. Its general principles would have little value and be converted by precedent into impotent and lifeless formulas. Rights declared in words might be lost in reality. And this has been recognized. The meaning and vitality of the Constitution have developed against narrow and restrictive construction.

This was the spirit in which we delineated, in meaningful language, the manner in which the constitutional rights of the individual could be enforced against overzealous police practices. . . .

Our holding will be spelled out with some specificity in the pages which follow but briefly stated it is this: the prosecution may not use statements, whether exculpatory or inculpatory, stemming from custodial interrogation of the defendant unless it demonstrates the use of procedural safeguards effective to secure the privilege against self-incrimination. By custodial interrogation, we mean questioning initiated by law enforcement officers after a person has been taken into custody or otherwise deprived of his freedom of action in any significant way. As for the procedural safeguards to be employed, unless other fully effective means are devised to inform accused persons of their right of silence and to assure a continuous opportunity to exercise it, the following measures are required. Prior to any questioning, the person must be warned that he has a right to remain silent, that any statement he does make may be used as evidence against him, and that he has a right to the presence of an attorney, either retained or appointed. The defendant may waive effectuation of these rights, provided the waiver is made voluntarily, knowingly and intelligently. If, however, he indicates in any manner and at any stage of the process that he wishes to consult with an attorney before speaking there can be no questioning. Likewise, if the individual is alone and indicates in any manner that he does not wish to be interrogated, the police may not question him. The mere fact that he may have answered some questions or volunteered some statements on his own does not deprive him of the right to refrain from answering any further inquiries until he has consulted with an attorney and thereafter consents to be questioned. . . .

The constitutional issue we decide in each of these cases is the admissibility of statements obtained from a defendant questioned while in custody or otherwise deprived of his freedom of action in any significant way. In each, the defendant was questioned by police officers, detectives, or a prosecuting attorney in a room in which he was cut off from the outside world. In none of these cases was the defendant given a full and effective warning of his rights at the outset of the interrogation process. In all the cases, the questioning elicited oral admissions, and in three of them, signed statements as well which were admitted at their trials. They all thus share salient features—incommunicado interrogation of individuals in a police-dominated atmosphere, resulting in self-incriminating statements without full warnings of constitutional rights.

An understanding of the nature and setting of this in-custody interrogation is essential to our decisions today. The difficulty in depicting what transpires at such interrogations stems from the fact that in this country they have largely taken place incommunicado. From extensive factual studies undertaken in the early 1930's, including the famous Wickersham Report to Congress by a Presidential Commission, it is clear that police violence and the "third degree" flourished at that time. In a series of cases decided by this Court long after these studies, the police resorted to physical brutality—beating, hanging, whipping—and to sustained and protracted questioning incommunicado in order to extort confessions. The Commission on Civil Rights in 1961 found much evidence to indicate that "some policemen still resort to physical force to obtain confessions," 1961 Comm'n on Civil Rights Rep., Justice, pt. 5, 17. The use of physical brutality and violence is not, unfortunately, relegated to the past or to any part of the country. Only recently in Kings County, New York, the police brutally beat, kicked and placed lighted cigarette butts on the back of a potential witness under interrogation for the purpose of securing a statement incriminating a third party. . . .

The examples given above are undoubtedly the exception now, but they are sufficiently widespread to be the object of concern. Unless a proper limitation upon custodial interrogation is achieved—such as these decisions will advance—

there can be no assurance that practices of this nature will be eradicated in the foreseeable future. . . .

Again we stress that the modern practice of in-custody interrogation is psychologically rather than physically oriented. As we have stated before, "Since *Chambers v. Florida,* 309 U.S. 227, this Court has recognized that coercion can be mental as well as physical, and that the blood of the accused is not the only hallmark of an unconstitutional inquisition." *Blackburn v. Alabama,* 361 U.S. 199, 206 (1960). Interrogation still takes place in privacy. Privacy results in secrecy and this in turn results in a gap in our knowledge as to what in fact goes on in the interrogation rooms. A valuable source of information about present police practices, however, may be found in various police manuals and texts which document procedures employed with success in the past, and which recommend various other effective tactics. These texts are used by law enforcement agencies themselves as guides. . . .

. . . the setting prescribed by the manuals and observed in practice becomes clear. In essence, it is this: To be alone with the subject is essential to prevent distraction and to deprive him of any outside support. The aura of confidence in his guilt undermines his will to resist. He merely confirms the preconceived story the police seek to have him describe. Patience and persistence, at times relentless questioning, are employed. To obtain a confession, the interrogator must "patiently maneuver himself or his quarry into a position from which the desired objective may be attained." When normal procedures fail to produce the needed result, the police may resort to deceptive stratagems such as giving false legal advice. It is important to keep the subject off balance, for example, by trading on his insecurity about himself or his surroundings. The police then persuade, trick, or cajole him out of exercising his constitutional rights. . . .

In the cases before us today, given this background, we concern ourselves primarily with this interrogation atmosphere and the evils it can bring. In No. 759, *Miranda v. Arizona,* the police arrested the defendant and took him to a special interrogation room where they secured a confession. In No. 760, *Vignera v. New York,* the defendant made oral admissions to the police after interrogation in the afternoon, and then signed an inculpatory statement upon being questioned by an assistant district attorney later the same evening. In No. 761, *Westover v. United States,* the defendant was handed over to the Federal Bureau of Investigation by local authorities after they had detained and interrogated him for a lengthy period, both at night and the following morning. After some two hours of questioning, the federal officers had obtained signed statements from the defendant. Lastly, in No. 584, *California v. Stewart,* the local police held the defendant five days in the station and interrogated him on nine separate occasions before they secured his inculpatory statement. . . .

It is obvious that such an interrogation environment is created for no purpose other than to subjugate the individual to the will of his examiner. This atmosphere carries its own badge of intimidation. To be sure, this is not physical intimidation, but it is equally destructive of human dignity. The current practice of incommunicado interrogation is at odds with one of our Nation's most cherished principles—that the individual may not be compelled to incriminate himself. Unless adequate protective devices are employed to dispel the compulsion inherent in custodial surroundings, no statement obtained from the defendant can truly be the product of his free choice. . . .

. . . unless we are shown other procedures which are at least as effective in apprising accused persons of their right of silence and in assuring a continuous opportunity to exercise it, the following safeguards must be observed.

At the outset, if a person in custody is to be subjected to interrogation, he must first be informed in clear and unequivocal terms that he has the right to remain silent. For those unaware of the privilege, the warning is needed simply to make them aware of it—the threshold requirement for an intelligent decision as to its exercise. More important, such a warning is an absolute prerequisite in overcoming the inherent pressures of the interrogation atmosphere. It is not just the subnormal or woefully ignorant who succumb to an interrogator's imprecations, whether implied or expressly stated, that the interrogation will continue until a confession is obtained or that silence in the face of accusation is itself damning and will bode ill when presented to a jury. Further, the warning will show the individual that his interrogators are prepared to recognize his privilege should he choose to exercise it.

The Fifth Amendment privilege is so fundamental to our system of constitutional rule and the expedient of giving an adequate warning as to the availability of the privilege so simple, we will not pause to inquire in individual cases whether the defendant was aware of his rights without a warning being given. Assessments of the knowledge the defendant possessed, based on information as to his age, education, intelligence, or prior contact with authorities, can never be more than speculation; a warning is a clearcut fact. More important, whatever the background of the person interrogated, a warning at the time of the interrogation is indispensable to overcome its pressures and to insure that the individual knows he is free to exercise the privilege at that point in time.

The warning of the right to remain silent must be accompanied by the explanation that anything said can and will be used against the individual in court. This warning is needed in order to make him aware not only of the privilege, but also of the consequences of forgoing it. It is only through an awareness of these consequences that there can be any assurance of real understanding and intelligent exercise of the privilege. Moreover, this warning may serve to make the individual more acutely aware that he is faced with a phase of the adversary system—that he is not in the presence of persons acting solely in his interest.

The circumstances surrounding in-custody interrogation can operate very quickly to overbear the will of one merely made aware of his privilege by his interrogators. Therefore, the right to have counsel present at the interrogation is indispensable to the protection of the Fifth Amendment privilege under the system we delineate today. Our aim is to assure that the individual's right to choose between silence and speech remains unfettered throughout the interrogation process. . . .

The presence of counsel at the interrogation may serve several significant subsidiary functions as well. If the accused decides to talk to his interrogators, the assistance of counsel can mitigate the dangers of untrustworthiness. With a lawyer present the likelihood that the police will practice coercion is reduced, and if coercion is nevertheless exercised the lawyer can testify to it in court. The presence of a lawyer can also help to guarantee that the accused gives a fully accurate statement to the police and that the statement is rightly reported by the prosecution at trial. . . .

An individual need not make a pre-interrogation request for a lawyer. While such request affirmatively secures his right to have one, his failure to ask for a lawyer does not constitute a waiver. No effective waiver of the right to counsel during interrogation can be recognized unless specifically made after the warnings we here delineate have been given. The accused who does not know his rights and therefore does not make a request may be the person who most needs counsel. . . .

If an individual indicates that he wishes the assistance of counsel before any interrogation occurs, the authorities cannot rationally ignore or deny his request on the basis that the individual does not have or cannot afford a retained attorney. The financial ability of the individual has no relationship to the scope of the rights involved here. The privilege against self-incrimination secured by the Constitution applies to all individuals. The need for counsel in order to protect the privilege exists for the indigent as well as the affluent. In fact, were we to limit these constitutional rights to those who can retain an attorney, our decisions today would be of little significance. . . .

In order fully to apprise a person interrogated of the extent of his rights under this system then, it is necessary to warn him not only that he has the right to consult with an attorney, but also that if he is indigent a lawyer will be appointed to represent him. Without this additional warning, the admonition of the right to consult with counsel would often be understood as meaning only that he can consult with a lawyer if he has one or has the funds to obtain one. . . .

Once warnings have been given, the subsequent procedure is clear. If the individual indicates in any manner, at any time prior to or during questioning, that he wishes to remain silent, the interrogation must cease. At this point he has shown that he intends to exercise his Fifth Amendment privilege; any statement taken after the person invokes his privilege cannot be other than the product of compulsion, subtle or otherwise. Without the right to cut off questioning, the setting of in-custody interrogation operates on the individual to overcome free choice in producing a statement after the privilege has been once invoked. If the individual states that he wants an attorney, the interrogation must cease until an attorney is present. At that time, the individual must have an opportunity to confer with the attorney and to have him present during any subsequent questioning. If the individual cannot obtain an attorney and he indicates that he wants one before speaking to police, they must respect his decision to remain silent. . . .

If the interrogation continues without the presence of an attorney and a statement is taken, a heavy burden rests on the government to demonstrate that the defendant knowingly and intelligently waived his privilege against self-incrimination and his right to retained or appointed counsel. *Escobedo v. Illinois,* 378 U.S. 478, 490, n. 14. . . .

An express statement that the individual is willing to make a statement and does not want an attorney followed closely by a statement could constitute a waiver. But a valid waiver will not be presumed simply from the silence of the accused after warnings are given or simply from the fact that a confession was in fact eventually obtained. . . .

The principles announced today deal with the protection which must be given to the privilege against self-incrimination when the individual is first subjected to police interrogation while in custody at the station or otherwise deprived of his freedom of action in any significant way. It is at this point that our adversary system of criminal proceedings commences, distinguishing itself at the outset from the inquisitorial system recognized in some countries. Under the system of warnings we delineate today or under any other system which may be devised and found effective, the safeguards to be erected about the privilege must come into play at this point. . . .

To summarize, we hold that when an individual is taken into custody or otherwise deprived of his freedom by the authorities in any significant way and is subjected to questioning, the privilege against self-incrimination is jeopardized. Procedural safeguards must be employed to protect the privilege, and unless other fully effective means are adopted to notify the person of his right of silence and to assure that the exercise of the right will be scrupulously honored, the following measures are required. He must be warned prior to any questioning that he has the right to remain silent, that anything he says can be used against him in a court of law, that he has the right to the presence of an attorney, and that if he cannot afford an attorney one will be appointed for him prior to any questioning if he so desires. Opportunity to exercise these rights must be afforded to him throughout the interrogation. After such warnings have been given, and such opportunity afforded him, the individual may knowingly and intelligently waive these rights and agree to answer questions or make a statement. But unless and until such warnings and waiver are demonstrated by the prosecution at trial, no evidence obtained as a result of interrogation can be used against him. . . .

5-4

Roe v. Wade

Supreme Court of the United States

To what extent can rights perceived by the people, but not explicitly protected by the Constitution, be recognized as constitutional principles by the courts? Judges often disagree on where the lines should be drawn. This question arose in Roe v. Wade, *the Supreme Court's 1973 decision on abortion. The specific issue was, Does the Constitution embrace a woman's right to terminate her pregnancy by abortion? A 5–4 majority on the Supreme Court held that a woman's right to an abortion fell within the right to privacy protected by the Fourteenth Amendment. The decision gave a woman autonomy over the pregnancy during the first trimester and defined different levels of state interest for the second and third trimesters. The Court's ruling affected the laws of forty-six states. Justice Harry Blackmun, arguing for the majority, insisted that the Court had recognized such a right in a long series of cases and that it was appropriate to extend the right to a woman's decision to terminate a pregnancy. In a dissenting opinion, Justice William Rehnquist, who later became chief justice, argued that because abortion was not considered an implicit right at the time the Fourteenth Amendment, states must be allowed to regulate it.*

ROE ET AL. v. WADE, DISTRICT ATTORNEY OF DALLAS COUNTY

410 U.S. 113

APPEAL FROM THE UNITED STATES DISTRICT COURT FOR THE NORTHERN DISTRICT OF TEXAS.

Decided January 22, 1973.

MR. JUSTICE BLACKMUN delivered the opinion of the Court.

This Texas federal appeal and its Georgia companion, *Doe v. Bolton, post,* . . . present constitutional challenges to state criminal abortion legislation. The Texas statutes under attack here are typical of those that have been in effect in many States for approximately a century. . . .

We forthwith acknowledge our awareness of the sensitive and emotional nature of the abortion controversy, of the vigorous opposing views, even among physicians, and of the deep and seemingly absolute convictions that the subject inspires. One's philosophy, one's experiences, one's exposure to the raw edges of human existence, one's religious training, one's attitudes toward life and family and their values, and the moral standards one establishes and seeks to observe, are all likely to influence and to color one's thinking and conclusions about abortion. . . .

Our task, of course, is to resolve the issue by constitutional measurement, free of emotion and of predilection. We seek earnestly to do this, and, because we do, we have inquired into, and in this opinion place some emphasis upon, medical and medical-legal history and what that history reveals about man's attitudes toward the abortion procedure over the centuries. We bear in mind, too, Mr. Justice Holmes' admonition in his now-vindicated dissent in *Lochner v. New York*, 198 U. S. 45, 76 (1905):

> [The Constitution] is made for people of fundamentally differing views, and the accident of our finding certain opinions natural and familiar or novel and even shocking ought not to conclude our judgment upon the question whether statutes embodying them conflict with the Constitution of the United States.

. . . Jane Roe [a pseudonym used to protect the identity of the woman], a single woman who was residing in Dallas County, Texas, instituted this federal action in March 1970 against the District Attorney of the county. She sought a declaratory judgment that the Texas criminal abortion statutes were unconstitutional on their face, and an injunction restraining the defendant from enforcing the statutes.

Roe alleged that she was unmarried and pregnant; that she wished to terminate her pregnancy by an abortion "performed by a competent, licensed physician, under safe clinical conditions"; that she was unable to get a "legal" abortion in Texas because her life did not appear to be threatened by the continuation of her pregnancy; and that she could not afford to travel to another jurisdiction in order to secure a legal abortion under safe conditions. She claimed that the Texas statutes were unconstitutionally vague and that they abridged her right of personal privacy, protected by the First, Fourth, Fifth, Ninth, and Fourteenth Amendments. By an amendment to her complaint Roe purported to sue "on behalf of herself and all other women" similarly situated. . . .

The principal thrust of appellant's attack on the Texas statutes is that they improperly invade a right, said to be possessed by the pregnant woman, to choose to terminate her pregnancy. Appellant would discover this right in the concept of personal "liberty" embodied in the Fourteenth Amendment's Due Process Clause; or in personal, marital, familial, and sexual privacy said to be protected by the Bill of Rights or its penumbras, . . . or among those rights reserved to the people by the Ninth Amendment. . . .

It perhaps is not generally appreciated that the restrictive criminal abortion laws in effect in a majority of States today are of relatively recent vintage. Those laws, generally proscribing abortion or its attempt at any time during pregnancy except when necessary to preserve the pregnant woman's life, are not of ancient or even of common-law origin. Instead, they derive from statutory changes effected, for the most part, in the latter half of the 19th century. . . .

It is thus apparent that at common law, at the time of the adoption of our Constitution, and throughout the major portion of the 19th century, abortion was viewed with less disfavor than under most American statutes currently in effect. Phrasing it another way, a woman enjoyed a substantially broader right to terminate a pregnancy than she does in most States today. At least with respect to the early stage of pregnancy, and very possibly without such a limitation, the opportunity to make this choice was present in this country well into the 19th century. Even later, the law continued for some time to treat less punitively an abortion procured in early pregnancy. . . .

The Constitution does not explicitly mention any right of privacy. In a line of decisions, however, going back perhaps as far as *Union Pacific R. Co. v. Botsford* . . . (1891), the Court has recognized that a right of personal privacy, or a guarantee of certain areas or zones of privacy, does exist under the Constitution. In varying contexts, the Court or individual Justices have, indeed, found at least the roots of that right in the First Amendment . . . ; in the Fourth and Fifth Amendments . . . ; in the penumbras of the Bill of Rights . . . ; in the Ninth Amendment . . . ; or in the concept of liberty guaranteed by the first section of the Fourteenth Amendment. . . . These decisions make it clear that only personal rights that can be deemed "fundamental" or "implicit in the concept of ordered liberty," . . . are included in this guarantee of personal privacy. They also make it clear that the right has some extension to activities relating to marriage . . . ; procreation . . . ; contraception . . . ; family relationships . . . ; and child rearing and education. . . .

This right of privacy, whether it be founded in the Fourteenth Amendment's concept of personal liberty and restrictions upon state action, as we feel it is, or, as the District Court determined, in the Ninth Amendment's reservation of rights to the people, is broad enough to encompass a woman's decision whether or not to terminate her pregnancy. The detriment that the State would impose upon the pregnant woman by denying this choice altogether is apparent. Specific and direct harm medically diagnosable even in early pregnancy may be involved.

Maternity, or additional offspring, may force upon the woman a distressful life and future. Psychological harm may be imminent. Mental and physical health may be taxed by child care. There is also the distress, for all concerned, associated with the unwanted child, and there is the problem of bringing a child into a family already unable, psychologically and otherwise, to care for it. In other cases, as in this one, the additional difficulties and continuing stigma of unwed motherhood may be involved. All these are factors the woman and her responsible physician necessarily will consider in consultation.

On the basis of elements such as these, appellant and some *amici* argue that the woman's right is absolute and that she is entitled to terminate her pregnancy at whatever time, in whatever way, and for whatever reason she alone chooses. With this we do not agree. Appellant's arguments that Texas either has no valid interest at all in regulating the abortion decision, or no interest strong enough to support any limitation upon the woman's sole determination, are unpersuasive. The Court's decisions recognizing a right of privacy also acknowledge that some state regulation in areas protected by that right is appropriate. As noted above, a State may properly assert important interests in safeguarding health, in maintaining medical standards, and in protecting potential life. At some point in pregnancy, these respective interests become sufficiently compelling to sustain regulation of the factors that govern the abortion decision. The privacy right involved, therefore, cannot be said to be absolute. . . .

We, therefore, conclude that the right of personal privacy includes the abortion decision, but that this right is not unqualified and must be considered against important state interests in regulation. . . .

Where certain "fundamental rights" are involved, the Court has held that regulation limiting these rights may be justified only by a "compelling state interest," . . . and that legislative enactments must be narrowly drawn to express only the legitimate state interests at stake. . . .

In the recent abortion cases . . . courts have recognized these principles. Those striking down state laws have generally scrutinized the State's interests in protecting health and potential life, and have concluded that neither interest justified broad limitations on the reasons for which a physician and his pregnant patient might decide that she should have an abortion in the early stages of pregnancy. Courts sustaining state laws have held that the State's determinations to protect health or prenatal life are dominant and constitutionally justifiable. . . .

The District Court held that the appellee [the district attorney, defending the Texas law] failed to meet his burden of demonstrating that the Texas statute's infringement upon Roe's rights was necessary to support a compelling state interest, and that, although the appellee presented "several compelling justifications for state presence in the area of abortions," the statutes outstripped these justifications and swept "far beyond any areas of compelling state interest." 314 F. Supp., at 1222–1223. Appellant and appellee both contest that holding. Appellant, as has been indicated, claims an absolute right that bars any state imposition of criminal penalties in the area. Appellee argues that the State's determination to recognize and protect prenatal life from and after conception constitutes a compelling state interest. As noted above, we do not agree fully with either formulation.

A. The appellee and certain *amici* argue that the fetus is a "person" within the language and meaning of the Fourteenth Amendment. In support of this, they outline at length and in detail the well-known facts of fetal development. If this suggestion of personhood is established, the appellant's case, of course, collapses, for the fetus' right to life would then be guaranteed specifically by the Amendment. The appellant conceded as much on reargument. On the other hand, the appellee conceded on reargument that no case could be cited that holds that a fetus is a person within the meaning of the Fourteenth Amendment.

The Constitution does not define "person" in so many words. Section 1 of the Fourteenth Amendment contains three references to "person." The first, in defining "citizens," speaks of "persons born or naturalized in the United States." The word also appears both in the Due Process Clause and in the Equal Protection Clause. "Person" is used in other places in the Constitution: in the listing of qualifications for Representatives and Senators, Art. I, § 2, cl. 2, and § 3, cl. 3; in the Apportionment Clause, Art. I, § 2, cl. 3; in the Migration and Importation provision, Art. I, § 9, cl. 1; in the Emolument Clause, Art. I, § 9, cl. 8; in the Electors provisions, Art. II, § 1, cl. 2, and the superseded cl. 3; in the provision outlining qualifications for the office of President, Art. II, § 1, cl. 5; in the Extradition provisions, Art. IV, § 2, cl. 2, and the superseded Fugitive Slave Clause 3; and in the Fifth, Twelfth, and Twenty-second Amendments, as well as in §§ 2 and 3 of the Fourteenth Amendment. But in nearly all these instances, the use of the word is such that it has application only postnatally. None indicates, with any assurance, that it has any possible pre-natal application.

All this, together with our observation, *supra,* that throughout the major portion of the 19th century prevailing legal abortion practices were far freer than they are today, persuades us that the word "person," as used in the Fourteenth Amendment, does not include the unborn. This is in accord with the results reached in those few cases where the issue has been squarely presented. . . . Indeed, our decision in *United States v. Vuitch,* 402 U. S. 62 (1971), inferentially is to the same effect, for we there would not have indulged in statutory interpretation favorable to abortion in specified circumstances if the necessary consequence was the termination of life entitled to Fourteenth Amendment protection.

This conclusion, however, does not of itself fully answer the contentions raised by Texas, and we pass on to other considerations.

B. The pregnant woman cannot be isolated in her privacy. She carries an embryo and, later, a fetus, if one accepts the medical definitions of the developing young in the human uterus. See Dorland's *Illustrated Medical Dictionary* 478–479, 547 (24th ed. 1965). The situation therefore is inherently different from marital intimacy, or bedroom possession of obscene material, or marriage, or procreation, or education, with which *Eisenstadt* and *Griswold, Stanley, Loving, Skinner,* and *Pierce* and *Meyer* were respectively concerned. As we have intimated above, it is reasonable and appropriate for a State to decide that at some point in time another interest, that of health of the mother or that of potential human life, becomes significantly involved. The woman's privacy is no longer sole and any right of privacy she possesses must be measured accordingly.

Texas urges that, apart from the Fourteenth Amendment, life begins at conception and is present throughout pregnancy, and that, therefore, the State has a compelling interest in protecting that life from and after conception. We need not resolve the difficult question of when life begins. When those trained in the respective disciplines of medicine, philosophy, and theology are unable to arrive at any consensus, the judiciary, at this point in the development of man's knowledge, is not in a position to speculate as to the answer.

It should be sufficient to note briefly the wide divergence of thinking on this most sensitive and difficult question. There has always been strong support for the view that life does not begin until live birth. This was the belief of the Stoics. It appears to be the predominant, though not the unanimous, attitude of the Jewish faith. It may be taken to represent also the position of a large segment of the Protestant community, insofar as that can be ascertained; organized groups that have taken a formal position on the abortion issue have generally regarded abortion as a matter for the conscience of the individual and her family. As we have noted, the common law found greater significance in quickening. Physicians and their scientific colleagues have regarded that event with less interest and have tended to focus either upon conception, upon live birth, or upon the interim point at which the fetus becomes "viable," that is, potentially able to live outside the mother's womb, albeit with artificial aid. Viability is usually placed at about seven months (28 weeks) but may occur earlier, even at 24 weeks. The Aristotelian theory of "mediate animation," that held sway throughout the Middle Ages and the Renaissance in Europe, continued to be official Roman Catholic dogma until the 19th century, despite opposition to this "ensoulment" theory from those in the Church who would recognize the existence of life from the moment of conception. The latter is now, of course, the official belief of the

Catholic Church. As one brief *amicus* discloses, this is a view strongly held by many non-Catholics as well, and by many physicians. Substantial problems for precise definition of this view are posed, however, by new embryological data that purport to indicate that conception is a "process" over time, rather than an event, and by new medical techniques such as menstrual extraction, the "morning-after" pill, implantation of embryos, artificial insemination, and even artificial wombs. . . .

In view of all this, we do not agree that, by adopting one theory of life, Texas may override the rights of the pregnant woman that are at stake. We repeat, however, that the State does have an important and legitimate interest in preserving and protecting the health of the pregnant woman, whether she be a resident of the State or a nonresident who seeks medical consultation and treatment there, and that it has still *another* important and legitimate interest in protecting the potentiality of human life. These interests are separate and distinct. Each grows in substantiality as the woman approaches term and, at a point during pregnancy, each becomes "compelling." . . .

The judgment of the District Court as to intervenor Hallford is reversed, and Dr. Hallford's complaint in intervention is dismissed. In all other respects, the judgment of the District Court is affirmed. Costs are allowed to the appellee.

It is so ordered.

MR. JUSTICE REHNQUIST, dissenting.

The Court's opinion brings to the decision of this troubling question both extensive historical fact and a wealth of legal scholarship. While the opinion thus commands my respect, I find myself nonetheless in fundamental disagreement with those parts of it that invalidate the Texas statute in question, and therefore dissent. . . .

. . . I have difficulty in concluding, as the Court does, that the right of "privacy" is involved in this case. Texas, by the statute here challenged, bars the performance of a medical abortion by a licensed physician on a plaintiff such as Roe. A transaction resulting in an operation such as this is not "private" in the ordinary usage of that word. Nor is the "privacy" that the Court finds here even a distant relative of the freedom from searches and seizures protected by the Fourth Amendment to the Constitution, which the Court has referred to as embodying a right to privacy. *Katz v. United States,* 389 U. S. 347 (1967).

If the Court means by the term "privacy" no more than that the claim of a person to be free from unwanted state regulation of consensual transactions may be a form of "liberty" protected by the Fourteenth Amendment, there is no doubt that similar claims have been upheld in our earlier decisions on the basis of that liberty. I agree with the statement of MR. JUSTICE STEWART in his concurring opinion that the "liberty," against deprivation of which without due process the Fourteenth Amendment protects, embraces more than the rights found in the Bill of Rights. But that liberty is not guaranteed absolutely against deprivation, only against deprivation without due process of law. The test traditionally applied in the area of social and economic legislation is whether or not a law such as that challenged has a rational relation to a valid state objective. . . . The Due Process Clause of the Fourteenth Amendment undoubtedly does place a limit, albeit a broad one, on legislative power to enact laws such as this. If the Texas statute were to prohibit an abortion even where the mother's life is in jeopardy, I have little doubt that such a statute would lack a rational relation to a valid state objective under the test stated in *Williamson, supra*. But the Court's sweeping invalidation of any restrictions on abortion during the first trimester is impossible to justify under that standard, and the conscious weighing of competing factors that the Court's opinion apparently substitutes for the established test is far more appropriate to a legislative judgment than to a judicial one.

The Court eschews the history of the Fourteenth Amendment in its reliance on the "compelling state interest" test. . . . But the Court adds a new wrinkle to this test by transposing it from the legal considerations associated with the Equal Protection Clause of the Fourteenth Amendment to this case arising under the Due Process Clause of the Fourteenth Amendment. Unless I misapprehend the consequences of this transplanting of the "compelling state interest test," the Court's opinion will accomplish the seemingly impossible feat of leaving this area of the law more confused than it found it.

While the Court's opinion quotes from the dissent of Mr. Justice Holmes in *Lochner v. New York* . . . (1905), the result it reaches is more closely attuned to the majority opinion of Mr. Justice Peckham in that case. As in *Lochner* and similar cases applying substantive due process standards to economic and social welfare legislation, the adoption of the compelling state interest standard will inevitably require this Court to examine the legislative policies and pass on the wisdom of these policies in the very process of deciding whether a particular state interest put forward may or may not be "compelling." The decision here to break pregnancy into three distinct terms and to outline the permissible restrictions the State may impose in each one, for example, partakes more of judicial legislation than it does of a determination of the intent of the drafters of the Fourteenth Amendment.

The fact that a majority of the States reflecting, after all, the majority sentiment in those States, have had restrictions on abortions for at least a century is a strong indication, it seems to me, that the asserted right to an abortion is not "so rooted in the traditions and conscience of our people as to be ranked as fundamental,"

Snyder v. Massachusetts . . . (1934). Even today, when society's views on abortion are changing, the very existence of the debate is evidence that the "right" to an abortion is not so universally accepted as the appellant would have us believe.

To reach its result the Court necessarily has had to find within the scope of the Fourteenth Amendment a right that was apparently completely unknown to the drafters of the Amendment. As early as 1821, the first state law dealing directly with abortion was enacted by the Connecticut Legislature. . . . By the time of the adoption of the Fourteenth Amendment in 1868, there were at least 36 laws enacted by state or territorial legislatures limiting abortion. While many States have amended or updated their laws, 21 of the laws on the books in 1868 remain in effect today. Indeed, the Texas statute struck down today was, as the majority notes, first enacted in 1857 and "has remained substantially unchanged to the present time." . . .

There apparently was no question concerning the validity of this provision or of any of the other state statutes when the Fourteenth Amendment was adopted. The only conclusion possible from this history is that the drafters did not intend to have the Fourteenth Amendment withdraw from the States the power to legislate with respect to this matter. . . .

For all of the foregoing reasons, I respectfully dissent.

5-5

Planned Parenthood of Southeastern Pennsylvania v. Casey

Supreme Court of the United States

Roe v. Wade *hardly resolved the abortion rights issue. In fact, during the intervening decades it has never receded far from the national political stage. Every presidential election campaign has found candidates debating the fundamental right to abortion and various regulations circumscribing access to abortion. State legislatures have enacted dozens of regulatory laws setting up procedures for obtaining (and in the view of abortion rights supporters, discouraging) abortions. With the appointment of Bush nominees John Roberts in 2005 and Samuel Alito in 2006, the prospect that* Roe v. Wade *might be overturned as a constitutional right has resurfaced.*

In light of recent changes in the Court's membership, it is useful to reexamine the 1992 decision Planned Parenthood v. Casey, *which produced a reconfirmation of the Constitutional basis of abortion rights but also recognized an appropriate role for state regulation. The Court overturned one provision of state law that required that a woman seeking an abortion notify the father. Samuel Alito, who at the time served on the appeals court with jurisdiction over the case, had ruled that such a requirement did not place an undue burden on access to abortions. Clearly, during the next few years* Roe *will be challenged and* Casey *will be consulted as a new Court reassesses once more the state's role in regulating abortion. [Only three justices wholly agreed with the "Court's opinion." All of the others either agreed with the decision for different reasons, objected to some parts and agreed with other parts of the decision or dissented. The absence of consensus on both sides of the decision made for a lengthy opinion (hence an edited version is reprinted here) and one bound to be challenged and revisited by the Roberts' Court.]*

Source: Lee Epstein and Thomas G. Walker, *Constitutional Law for a Changing America: Rights, Liberties, and Justice,* 5th ed. (Washington, D.C.: CQ Press, 2004), 458–469.

PLANNED PARENTHOOD OF SOUTHEASTERN PENNSYLVANIA v. CASEY

505 u.s. 833 (1992)

Opinion announcing the judgment of the Court and delivering the opinion of the Court: KENNEDY, O'CONNOR, SOUTER

Concurring in part: BLACKMUN, REHNQUIST, SCALIA, STEVENS, THOMAS, WHITE

Dissenting in part: BLACKMUN, REHNQUIST, SCALIA, STEVENS, THOMAS, WHITE

Opinions concurring in part and dissenting in part: BLACKMUN, REHNQUIST, SCALIA, STEVENS

JUSTICE O'CONNOR, JUSTICE KENNEDY, and JUSTICE SOUTER announced the judgment of the Court and delivered the opinion of the Court with respect to Parts I, II, III, V-A, V-C, and VI, an opinion with respect to Part V-E, in which JUSTICE STEVENS joins, and an opinion with respect to Parts IV, V-B, and V-D.

Liberty finds no refuge in a jurisprudence of doubt. Yet 19 years after our holding that the Constitution protects a woman's right to terminate her pregnancy in its early stages, *Roe v. Wade* (1973), that definition of liberty is still questioned. Joining the respondents as amicus curiae, the United States, as it has done in five other cases in the last decade, again asks us to overrule *Roe.*

. . . And at oral argument in this Court, the attorney for the parties challenging the statute took the position that none of the enactments can be upheld without overruling *Roe v. Wade.* We disagree with that analysis; but we acknowledge that our decisions after *Roe* cast doubt upon the meaning and reach of its holding. Further, the chief justice admits that he would overrule the central holding of *Roe* and adopt the rational relationship test as the sole criterion of constitutionality. State and federal courts as well as legislatures throughout the Union must have guidance as they seek to address this subject in conformance with the Constitution. Given these premises, we find it imperative to review once more the principles that define the rights of the woman and the legitimate authority of the State respecting the termination of pregnancies by abortion procedures.

After considering the fundamental constitutional questions resolved by *Roe,* principles of institutional integrity, and the rule of *stare decisis,* we are led to conclude this: the essential holding of *Roe v. Wade* should be retained and once again reaffirmed.

It must be stated at the outset and with clarity that *Roe*'s essential holding, the holding we reaffirm, has three parts. First is a recognition of the right of the woman to choose to have an abortion before viability and to obtain it without undue interference from the State. Before viability, the State's interests are not strong enough to support a prohibition of abortion or the imposition of a substantial obstacle to the woman's effective right to elect the procedure. Second is a confirmation of the State's power to restrict abortions after fetal viability, if the law contains exceptions for pregnancies which endanger a woman's life or health. And third is the principle that the State has legitimate interests from the outset of the pregnancy in protecting the health of the woman and the life of the fetus that may become a child. These principles do not contradict one another; and we adhere to each.

II

... These considerations begin our analysis of the woman's interest in terminating her pregnancy but cannot end it, for this reason: though the abortion decision may originate within the zone of conscience and belief, it is more than a philosophic exercise. Abortion is a unique act. It is an act fraught with consequences for others: for the woman who must live with the implications of her decision; for the persons who perform and assist in the procedure; for the spouse, family, and society which must confront the knowledge that these procedures exist, procedures some deem nothing short of an act of violence against innocent human life; and, depending on one's beliefs, for the life or potential life that is aborted. Though abortion is conduct, it does not follow that the State is entitled to proscribe it in all instances. That is because the liberty of the woman is at stake in a sense unique to the human condition and so unique to the law. The mother who carries a child to full term is subject to anxieties, to physical constraints, to pain that only she must bear. That these sacrifices have from the beginning of the human race been endured by woman with a pride that ennobles her in the eyes of others and gives to the infant a bond of love cannot alone be grounds for the State to insist she make the sacrifice. Her suffering is too intimate and personal for the State to insist, without more, upon its own vision of the woman's role, however dominant that vision has been in the course of our history and our culture. The destiny of the woman must be shaped to a large extent on her own conception of her spiritual imperatives and her place in society. . . .

While we appreciate the weight of the arguments made on behalf of the State in the case before us, arguments which in their ultimate formulation conclude that *Roe* should be overruled, the reservations any of us may have in reaffirming the central holding of *Roe* are outweighed by the explication of individual liberty we have given combined with the force of stare decisis. We turn now to that doctrine.

III

A

. . . The sum of . . . precedential inquiry . . . shows *Roe*'s underpinnings unweakened in any way affecting its central holding. While it has engendered disapproval, it has not been unworkable. An entire generation has come of age free to assume *Roe*'s concept of liberty in defining the capacity of women to act in society, and to make reproductive decisions; no erosion of principle going to liberty or personal autonomy has left *Roe*'s central holding a doctrinal remnant; *Roe* portends no developments at odds with other precedent for the analysis of personal liberty; and no changes of fact have rendered viability more or less appropriate as the point at which the balance of interests tips. Within the bounds of normal *stare decisis* analysis, then, and subject to the considerations on which it customarily turns, the stronger argument is for affirming *Roe*'s central holding, with whatever degree of personal reluctance any of us may have, not for overruling it.

B

In a less significant case, *stare decisis* analysis could, and would, stop at the point we have reached. . . .

C

. . . Our analysis would not be complete, however, without explaining why overruling *Roe*'s central holding would not only reach an unjustifiable result under principles of *stare decisis,* but would seriously weaken the Court's capacity to exercise the judicial power and to function as the Supreme Court of a Nation dedicated to the rule of law. To understand why this would be so it is necessary to understand the source of this Court's authority, the conditions necessary for its preservation, and its relationship to the country's understanding of itself as a constitutional Republic.

The root of American governmental power is revealed most clearly in the instance of the power conferred by the Constitution upon the Judiciary of the United States and specifically upon this Court. As Americans of each succeeding generation are rightly told, the Court cannot buy support for its decisions by spending money and, except to a minor degree, it cannot independently coerce obedience to its decrees. The Court's power lies, rather, in its legitimacy, a product of substance and perception that shows itself in the people's acceptance of the Judiciary as fit to determine what the Nation's law means and to declare what it demands.

The underlying substance of this legitimacy is of course the warrant for the Court's decisions in the Constitution and the lesser sources of legal principle on which the Court draws. That substance is expressed in the Court's opinions, and our contemporary understanding is such that a decision without principled justification would be no judicial act at all. But even when justification is furnished by apposite legal principle, something more is required. Because not every conscientious claim of principled justification will be accepted as such, the justification claimed must be beyond dispute. The Court must take care to speak and act in ways that allow people to accept its decisions on the terms the Court claims for them, as grounded truly in principle, not as compromises with social and political pressures having, as such, no bearing on the principled choices that the Court is obliged to make. Thus, the Court's legitimacy depends on making legally principled decisions under circumstances in which their principled character is sufficiently plausible to be accepted by the Nation.

The need for principled action to be perceived as such is implicated to some degree whenever this, or any other appellate court, overrules a prior case. This is not to say, of course, that this Court cannot give a perfectly satisfactory explanation in most cases. People understand that some of the Constitution's language is hard to fathom and that the Court's Justices are sometimes able to perceive significant facts or to understand principles of law that eluded their predecessors and that justify departures from existing decisions. However upsetting it may be to those most directly affected when one judicially derived rule replaces another, the country can accept some correction of error without necessarily questioning the legitimacy of the Court.

In two circumstances, however, the Court would almost certainly fail to receive the benefit of the doubt in overruling prior cases. There is, first, a point beyond which frequent overruling would overtax the country's belief in the Court's good faith. Despite the variety of reasons that may inform and justify a decision to overrule, we cannot forget that such a decision is usually perceived (and perceived correctly) as, at the least, a statement that a prior decision was wrong. There is a limit to the amount of error that can plausibly be imputed to prior courts. If that limit should be exceeded, disturbance of prior rulings would be taken as evidence that justifiable reexamination of principle had given way to drives for particular results in the short term. The legitimacy of the Court would fade with the frequency of its vacillation.

That first circumstance can be described as hypothetical; the second is to the point here and now. Where, in the performance of its judicial duties, the Court decides a case in such a way as to resolve the sort of intensely divisive controversy reflected in *Roe* and those rare, comparable cases, its decision has a dimension that the resolution of the normal case does not carry. It is the dimension present whenever the Court's interpretation of the Constitution calls the contending sides of a national controversy to end their national division by accepting a common mandate rooted in the Constitution.

The Court is not asked to do this very often, having thus addressed the Nation only twice in our lifetime, in the decisions of *Brown* [*v. Board of Education*] and *Roe*. But when the Court does act in this way, its decision requires an equally rare precedential force to counter the inevitable efforts to overturn it and to thwart its implementation. Some of those efforts may be mere unprincipled emotional reactions; others may proceed from principles worthy of profound respect. But whatever the premises of opposition may be, only the most convincing justification under accepted standards of precedent could suffice to demonstrate that a later decision overruling the first was anything but a surrender to political pressure, and an unjustified repudiation of the principle on which the Court staked its authority in the first instance. So to overrule under fire in the absence of the most compelling reason to reexamine a watershed decision would subvert the Court's legitimacy beyond any serious question. . . .

The Court's duty in the present case is clear. In 1973, it confronted the already-divisive issue of governmental power to limit personal choice to undergo abortion, for which it provided a new resolution based on the due process guaranteed by the Fourteenth Amendment. Whether or not a new social consensus is developing on that issue, its divisiveness is no less today than in 1973, and pressure to overrule the decision, like pressure to retain it, has grown only more intense. A decision to overrule *Roe*'s essential holding under the existing circumstances would address error, if error there was, at the cost of both profound and unnecessary damage to the Court's legitimacy, and to the Nation's commitment to the rule of law. It is therefore imperative to adhere to the essence of *Roe*'s original decision, and we do so today.

IV

. . . The woman's right to terminate her pregnancy before viability is the most central principle of *Roe v. Wade*. It is a rule of law and a component of liberty we cannot renounce. . . .

Yet it must be remembered that *Roe v. Wade* speaks with clarity in establishing not only the woman's liberty but also the State's "important and legitimate interest in potential life." That portion of the decision in *Roe* has been given too little acknowledgment and implementation by the Court in its subsequent cases.

Those cases decided that any regulation touching upon the abortion decision must survive strict scrutiny, to be sustained only if drawn in narrow terms to further a compelling state interest. Not all of the cases decided under that formulation can be reconciled with the holding in *Roe* itself that the State has legitimate interests in the health of the woman and in protecting the potential life within her. In resolving this tension, we choose to rely upon *Roe*, as against the later cases.

Roe established a trimester framework to govern abortion regulations. Under this elaborate but rigid construct, almost no regulation at all is permitted during the first trimester of pregnancy; regulations designed to protect the woman's health, but not to further the State's interest in potential life, are permitted during the second trimester; and during the third trimester, when the fetus is viable, prohibitions are permitted provided the life or health of the mother is not at stake. Most of our cases since *Roe* have involved the application of rules derived from the trimester framework. See, *e.g., Thornburgh v. American College of Obstetricians and Gynecologists; Akron [v. Akron Center]*. . . .

We reject the trimester framework, which we do not consider to be part of the essential holding of *Roe*. . . . Measures aimed at ensuring that a woman's choice contemplates the consequences for the fetus do not necessarily interfere with the right recognized in *Roe*, although those measures have been found to be inconsistent with the rigid trimester framework announced in that case. A logical reading of the central holding in *Roe* itself, and a necessary reconciliation of the liberty of the woman and the interest of the State in promoting prenatal life, require, in our view, that we abandon the trimester framework as a rigid prohibition on all previability regulation aimed at the protection of fetal life. The trimester framework suffers from these basic flaws: in its formulation it misconceives the nature of the pregnant woman's interest; and in practice it undervalues the State's interest in potential life, as recognized in *Roe*.

As our jurisprudence relating to all liberties save perhaps abortion has recognized, not every law which makes a right more difficult to exercise is, *ipso facto*, an infringement of that right. An example clarifies the point. We have held that not every ballot access limitation amounts to an infringement of the right to vote. Rather, the States are granted substantial flexibility in establishing the framework within which voters choose the candidates for whom they wish to vote.

The abortion right is similar. Numerous forms of state regulation might have the incidental effect of increasing the cost or decreasing the availability of medical care, whether for abortion or any other medical procedure. The fact that a law which serves a valid purpose, one not designed to strike at the right itself, has the incidental effect of making it more difficult or more expensive to procure an abortion cannot be enough to invalidate it. Only where state regulation imposes an undue burden on a woman's ability to make this decision does the power of the State reach into the heart of the liberty protected by the Due Process Clause. . . .

The concept of an undue burden has been utilized by the Court as well as individual members of the Court, including two of us, in ways that could be considered inconsistent. . . . Because we set forth a standard of general application to which we intend to adhere, it is important to clarify what is meant by an undue burden.

A finding of an undue burden is a shorthand for the conclusion that a state regulation has the purpose or effect of placing a substantial obstacle in the path of a woman seeking an abortion of a nonviable fetus. A statute with this purpose is invalid because the means chosen by the State to further the interest in potential life must be calculated to inform the woman's free choice, not hinder it. And a statute which, while furthering the interest in potential life or some other valid state interest, has the effect of placing a substantial obstacle in the path of a woman's choice cannot be considered a permissible means of serving its legitimate ends. To the extent that the opinions of the Court or of individual Justices use the undue burden standard in a manner that is inconsistent with this analysis, we set out what in our view should be the controlling standard. . . . Understood another way, we answer the question, left open in previous opinions discussing the undue burden formulation, whether a law designed to further the State's interest in fetal life which imposes an undue burden on the woman's decision before fetal viability could be constitutional. See, *e.g., Akron I* (O'CONNOR, J., dissenting). The answer is no.

Some guiding principles should emerge. What is at stake is the woman's right to make the ultimate decision, not a right to be insulated from all others in doing so. Regulations which do no more than create a structural mechanism by which the State, or the parent or guardian of a minor, may express profound respect for the life of the unborn are permitted, if they are not a substantial obstacle to the woman's exercise of the right to choose. Unless it has that effect on her right of choice, a state measure designed to persuade her to choose childbirth over abortion will be upheld if reasonably related to that goal. Regulations designed to foster the health of a woman seeking an abortion are valid if they do not constitute an undue burden.

Even when jurists reason from shared premises, some disagreement is inevitable. That is to be expected in the application of any legal standard which must accommodate life's complexity. We do not expect it to be otherwise with respect to the undue burden standard. We give this summary:

(a) To protect the central right recognized by *Roe v. Wade* while at the same time accommodating the State's profound interest in potential life, we will employ the undue burden analysis as explained in this opinion. An undue burden exists, and therefore a provision of law is invalid, if its purpose or effect is to place a substantial obstacle in the path of a woman seeking an abortion before the fetus attains viability.

(b) We reject the rigid trimester framework of *Roe v. Wade.* To promote the State's profound interest in potential life, throughout pregnancy the State may take measures to ensure that the woman's choice is informed, and measures designed to advance this interest will not be invalidated as long as their purpose is to persuade the woman to choose childbirth over abortion. These measures must not be an undue burden on the right.

(c) As with any medical procedure, the State may enact regulations to further the health or safety of a woman seeking an abortion. Unnecessary health regulations that have the purpose or effect of presenting a substantial obstacle to a woman seeking an abortion impose an undue burden on the right.

(d) Our adoption of the undue burden analysis does not disturb the central holding of *Roe v. Wade,* and we reaffirm that holding. Regardless of whether exceptions are made for particular circumstances, a State may not prohibit any woman from making the ultimate decision to terminate her pregnancy before viability.

(e) We also reaffirm *Roe's* holding that "subsequent to viability, the State in promoting its interest in the potentiality of human life may, if it chooses, regulate, and even proscribe, abortion except where it is necessary, in appropriate medical judgment, for the preservation of the life or health of the mother." *Roe v. Wade.*

These principles control our assessment of the Pennsylvania statute, and we now turn to the issue of the validity of its challenged provisions.

V

The Court of Appeals applied what it believed to be the undue burden standard and upheld each of the provisions except for the husband notification requirement. We agree generally with this conclusion, but refine the undue burden analysis in accordance with the principles articulated above. We now consider the separate statutory sections at issue.
[A omitted]

B [Informed Consent]

. . . Our prior decisions establish that as with any medical procedure, the State may require a woman to give her written informed consent to an abortion. . . .

In this respect, the statute is unexceptional. Petitioners challenge the statute's definition of informed consent because it includes the provision of specific information by the doctors and the mandatory 24-hour waiting period. The conclusions reached by a majority of the Justices in separate opinions filed today and the undue burden standard adopted in this opinion require us to overrule in part some of the Court's past decisions, decisions driven by the trimester framework's prohibition of all previability regulation designed to further the State's interest in fetal life.

In *Akron I* (1983), we invalidated an ordinance which required that a woman seeking an abortion be provided by her physician with specific information "designed to influence the woman's informed choice between abortion or childbirth." As we later described the *Akron I* holding in *Thornburgh v. American College of Obstetricians and Gynecologists,* there were two purported flaws in the Akron ordinance: the information was designed to dissuade the woman from having an abortion and the ordinance imposed "a rigid requirement that a specific body of information be given in all cases, irrespective of the particular needs of the patient. . . ."

To the extent *Akron I* and *Thornburgh* find a constitutional violation when the government requires, as it does here, the giving of truthful, nonmisleading information about the nature of the procedure, the attendant health risks and those of childbirth, and the "probable gestational age" of the fetus, those cases go too far, are inconsistent with *Roe*'s acknowledgment of an important interest in potential life, and are overruled. . . .

. . . Even the broadest reading of *Roe* . . . has not suggested that there is a constitutional right to abortion on demand. . . . Rather, the right protected by *Roe* is a right to decide to terminate a pregnancy free of undue interference by the State. Because the informed consent requirement facilitates the wise exercise of that right it cannot be classified as an interference with the right *Roe* protects. The informed consent requirement is not an undue burden on that right.

C [Spousal Notification]

. . . The limited research that has been conducted with respect to notifying one's husband about an abortion, although involving samples too small to be representative . . . [suggests that] [t]he vast majority of women notify their male partners of their decision to obtain an abortion. In many cases in which married women do not notify their husbands, the pregnancy is the result of an extramarital affair. Where the husband is the father, the primary reason women do not notify their husbands is that the husband and wife are experiencing marital difficulties, often accompanied by incidents of violence.

This information . . . reinforce[s] what common sense would suggest. In well-functioning marriages, spouses discuss important intimate decisions such as whether to bear a child. But there are millions of women in this country who are the victims of regular physical and psychological abuse at the hands of their husbands. Should these women become pregnant, they may have very good reasons for not wishing to inform their husbands of their decision to obtain an abortion. Many may have justifiable fears of physical abuse, but may be no less fearful of the consequences of reporting prior abuse to the Commonwealth of Pennsylvania. Many may have a reasonable fear that notifying their husbands will provoke further instances of child abuse. . . .

The spousal notification requirement is thus likely to prevent a significant number of women from obtaining an abortion. It does not merely make abortions a little more difficult or expensive to obtain; for many women, it will impose a substantial obstacle. We must not blind ourselves to the fact that the significant number of women who fear for their safety and the safety of their children are likely to be deterred from procuring an abortion as surely as if the Commonwealth had outlawed abortion in all cases. . . .

Section 3209 embodies a view of marriage consonant with the common-law status of married women but repugnant to our present understanding of marriage and of the nature of the rights secured by the Constitution. Women do not lose their constitutionally protected liberty when they marry. The Constitution protects all individuals, male or female, married or unmarried, from the abuse of governmental power, even where that power is employed for the supposed benefit of a member of the individual's family. These considerations confirm our conclusion that §3209 is invalid.

D [Parental Consent]

We next consider the parental consent provision. . . .

We have been over most of this ground before. Our cases establish, and we reaffirm today, that a State may require a minor seeking an abortion to obtain the consent of a parent or guardian, provided that there is an adequate judicial bypass procedure. . . .

E [Recordkeeping and Reporting]

. . . In [*Planned Parenthood v.*] *Danforth*, we held that recordkeeping and reporting provisions "that are reasonably directed to the preservation of maternal health and that properly respect a patient's confidentiality and privacy are permissible." We think that under this standard, all the provisions at issue here except that relating to spousal notice are constitutional. Although they do not relate to the State's interest in informing the woman's choice, they do relate to health. The collection of information with respect to actual patients is a vital element of medical research, and so it cannot be said that the requirements serve no purpose other than to make abortions more difficult. Nor do we find that the requirements impose a substantial obstacle to a woman's choice. At most they might increase the cost of some abortions by a slight amount. While at some point increased cost could become a substantial obstacle, there is no such showing on the record before us.

Subsection (12) of the reporting provision requires the reporting of, among other things, a married woman's "reason for failure to provide notice" to her husband. This provision in effect requires women, as a condition of obtaining an abortion, to provide the Commonwealth with the precise information we have already recognized that many women have pressing reasons not to reveal. Like the spousal notice requirement itself, this provision places an undue burden on a woman's choice, and must be invalidated for that reason.

VI

Our Constitution is a covenant running from the first generation of Americans to us and then to future generations. It is a coherent succession. Each generation must learn anew that the Constitution's written terms embody ideas and aspirations that must survive more ages than one. We accept our responsibility not to retreat from interpreting the full meaning of the covenant in light of all of our precedents. We invoke it once again to define the freedom guaranteed by the Constitution's own promise, the promise of liberty.

Affirmed in part, reversed in part, and remanded.

JUSTICE STEVENS, concurring in part and dissenting in part.

[I omitted]

II

My disagreement with the joint opinion begins with its understanding of the trimester framework established in *Roe*. Contrary to the suggestion of the joint opinion, it is not a "contradiction" to recognize that the State may have a legitimate interest in potential human life and, at the same time, to conclude that interest does not justify the regulation of abortion before viability (although other interests, such as maternal health, may). The fact that the State's interest is legitimate does not tell us when, if ever, that interest outweighs the pregnant woman's interest in personal liberty. . . .

In my opinion, the principles established in this long line of cases and the wisdom reflected in Justice Powell's opinion for the Court in *Akron* (and followed by the Court just six years ago in *Thornburgh*) should govern our decision today. Under these principles, §§3205(a)(2)(i)-(iii) of the Pennsylvania statute are unconstitutional. Those sections require a physician or counselor to provide the woman with a range of materials clearly designed to persuade her to choose not to undergo the abortion. While the State is free . . . to produce and disseminate such material, the State may not inject such information into the woman's deliberations just as she is weighing such an important choice.

Under this same analysis, §§3205(a)(1)(i) and (iii) of the Pennsylvania statute are constitutional. Those sections, which require the physician to inform a woman of the nature and risks of the abortion procedure and the medical risks of carrying to term, are neutral requirements comparable to those imposed in other medical procedures. Those sections indicate no effort by the State to influence the woman's choice in any way. If anything, such requirements enhance, rather than skew, the woman's decision-making.

III

The 24-hour waiting period . . . raises even more serious concerns. Such a requirement arguably furthers the State's interests in two ways, neither of which is constitutionally permissible.

First, it may be argued that the 24-hour delay is justified by the mere fact that it is likely to reduce the number of abortions, thus furthering the State's interest in potential life. But such an argument would justify any form of coercion that placed an obstacle in the woman's path. The State cannot further its interests by simply wearing down the ability of the pregnant woman to exercise her constitutional right.

Second, it can more reasonably be argued that the 24-hour delay furthers the State's interest in ensuring that the woman's decision is informed and thoughtful. But there is no evidence that the mandated delay benefits women or that it is necessary to enable the physician to convey any relevant information to the patient. The mandatory delay thus appears to rest on outmoded and unacceptable assumptions about the decision-making capacity of women. While there are well-established and consistently maintained reasons for the State to view with skepticism the ability of minors to make decisions, none of those reasons applies to an adult woman's decision-making ability. Just as we have left behind the belief that a woman must consult her husband before undertaking serious matters, so we must reject the notion that a woman is less capable of deciding matters of gravity. . . .

IV

In my opinion, a correct application of the "undue burden" standard leads to the same conclusion concerning the constitutionality of these requirements. A state-imposed burden on the exercise of a constitutional right is measured both by its effects and by its character: A burden may be "undue" either because the burden is too severe or because it lacks a legitimate, rational justification.

The 24-hour delay requirement fails both parts of this test. The findings of the District Court establish the severity of the burden that the 24-hour delay imposes on many pregnant women. Yet even in those cases in which the delay is not especially onerous, it is, in my opinion, "undue" because there is no evidence that such a delay serves a useful and legitimate purpose. As indicated above, there is no legitimate reason to require a woman who has agonized over her decision to leave the clinic or hospital and return again another day. While a general requirement that a physician notify her patients about the risks of a proposed medical procedure is appropriate, a rigid requirement that all patients wait 24 hours or (what is true in practice) much longer to evaluate the significance of information that is either common knowledge or irrelevant is an irrational and, therefore, "undue" burden. . . .

Accordingly, while I disagree with Parts IV, V-B, and V-D of the joint opinion, I join the remainder of the Court's opinion.

JUSTICE BLACKMUN, concurring in part, concurring in the judgment in part, and dissenting in part.

I join parts I, II, III, V-A, V-C, and VI of the joint opinion of JUSTICES O'CONNOR, KENNEDY, and SOUTER.

Three years ago [1989], in *Webster v. Reproductive Health Serv.*, four Members of this Court appeared poised to "cas[t] into darkness the hopes and visions of every woman in this country" who had come to believe that the Constitution guaranteed her the right to reproductive choice. All that remained between the promise of *Roe* and the darkness of the plurality was a single, flickering flame. . . . But now, just when so many expected the darkness to fall, the flame has grown bright.

I do not underestimate the significance of today's joint opinion. Yet I remain steadfast in my belief that the right to reproductive choice is entitled to the full protection afforded by this Court before *Webster*. And I fear for the darkness as four Justices anxiously await the single vote necessary to extinguish the light.

I

Make no mistake, the joint opinion of JUSTICES O'CONNOR, KENNEDY, and SOUTER is an act of personal courage and constitutional principle. In contrast to previous decisions in which JUSTICES O'CONNOR and KENNEDY postponed reconsideration of *Roe v. Wade* (1973), the authors of the joint opinion today join JUSTICE STEVENS and me in concluding that "the essential holding of *Roe* should be retained and once again reaffirmed." In brief, five Members of this Court today recognize that "the Constitution protects a woman's right to terminate her pregnancy in its early stages." . . .

In striking down the Pennsylvania statute's spousal notification requirement, the Court has established a framework for evaluating abortion regulations that responds to the social context of women facing issues of reproductive choice. In determining the burden imposed by the challenged regulation, the Court inquires whether the regulation's "*purpose* or *effect* is to place a substantial obstacle in the path of a woman seeking an abortion before the fetus attains viability." . . .

. . . [W]hile I believe that the joint opinion errs in failing to invalidate the other regulations, I am pleased that the joint opinion has not ruled out the possibility that these regulations may be shown to impose an unconstitutional burden. The joint opinion makes clear that its specific holdings are based on the insufficiency of the record before it. I am confident that in the future evidence will be produced to show that "in a large fraction of the cases in which [these regulations are] relevant, [they] will operate as a substantial obstacle to a woman's choice to undergo an abortion." . . .

II

. . . *Roe*'s requirement of strict scrutiny as implemented through a trimester framework should not be disturbed. No other approach has gained a majority, and no other is more protective of the woman's fundamental right. Lastly, no other approach properly accommodates the woman's constitutional right with the State's legitimate interests. . . .

Application of the strict scrutiny standard results in the invalidation of all the challenged provisions. Indeed, as this Court has invalidated virtually identical provisions in prior cases, *stare decisis* requires that we again strike them down. . . .

III

At long last, THE CHIEF JUSTICE admits it. Gone are the contentions that the issue need not be (or has not been) considered. There, on the first page, for all to see, is what was expected: "We believe that *Roe* was wrongly decided, and that it can and should be overruled consistently with our traditional approach to *stare decisis* in constitutional cases." If there is much reason to applaud the advances made by the joint opinion today, there is far more to fear from the chief justice's opinion. . . .

IV

In one sense, the Court's approach is worlds apart from that of THE CHIEF JUSTICE and JUSTICE SCALIA. And yet, in another sense, the distance between the two approaches is short—the distance is but a single vote.

I am 83 years old. I cannot remain on this Court forever, and when I do step down, the confirmation process for my successor well may focus on the issue before us today. That, I regret, may be exactly where the choice between the two worlds will be made.

CHIEF JUSTICE REHNQUIST, with whom JUSTICE WHITE, JUSTICE SCALIA, and JUSTICE THOMAS join, concurring in the judgment in part and dissenting in part.

The joint opinion, following its newly-minted variation on *stare decisis,* retains the outer shell of *Roe v. Wade* (1973), but beats a wholesale retreat from the substance of that case. We believe that *Roe* was wrongly decided, and that it can and should be overruled consistently with our traditional approach to *stare decisis* in constitutional cases. We would adopt the approach of the plurality in *Webster v. Reproductive Health Services* (1989), and uphold the challenged provisions of the Pennsylvania statute in their entirety.

I

. . . We think . . . both in view of this history and of our decided cases dealing with substantive liberty under the Due Process Clause, that the Court was mistaken in *Roe* when it classified a woman's decision to terminate her pregnancy as a "fundamental right" that could be abridged only in a manner which withstood "strict scrutiny." . . .

We believe that the sort of constitutionally imposed abortion code of the type illustrated by our decisions following *Roe* is inconsistent "with the notion of a Constitution cast in general terms, as ours is, and usually speaking in general principles, as ours does." *Webster v. Reproductive Health Services* (plurality opinion). The Court in *Roe* reached too far when it analogized the right to abort a fetus to the right . . . involved in . . . *Griswold,* and thereby deemed the right to abortion fundamental. . . .

II

. . . [T]he joint opinion . . . state[s] that when the Court "resolve[s] the sort of intensely divisive controversy reflected in *Roe* and those rare, comparable cases," its decision is exempt from reconsideration under established principles of *stare decisis* in constitutional cases. This is so, the joint opinion contends, because in those "intensely divisive" cases the Court has "call[ed] the contending sides of a national controversy to end their national division by accepting a common mandate rooted in the Constitution," and must therefore take special care not to be perceived as "surrender[ing] to political pressure" and continued opposition. This is a truly novel principle, one which is contrary to both the Court's historical practice and to the Court's traditional willingness to tolerate criticism of its opinions. Under this principle, when the Court has ruled on a divisive issue, it is apparently prevented from overruling that decision for the sole reason that it was incorrect, *unless opposition to the original decision has died away.*

The . . . difficulty with this principle lies in its assumption that cases which are "intensely divisive" can be readily distinguished from those that are not. The question of whether a particular issue is "intensely divisive" enough to qualify for special protection is entirely subjective and dependent on the individual assumptions of the members of this Court. In addition, because the Court's duty is to ignore public opinion and criticism on issues that come before it, its members are in perhaps the worst position to judge whether a decision divides the Nation deeply enough to justify such uncommon protection. Although many of the Court's decisions divide the populace to a large degree, we have not previously on that account shied away from applying normal rules of *stare decisis* when urged to reconsider earlier decisions. Over the past 21 years, for example, the Court has overruled in whole or in part 34 of its previous constitutional decisions. . . .

The end result of the joint opinion's paeans of praise for legitimacy is the enunciation of a brand new standard for evaluating state regulation of a woman's right to abortion—the "undue burden" standard. As indicated above, *Roe v. Wade* adopted a "fundamental right" standard under which state regulations could survive only if they met the requirement of "strict scrutiny." While we disagree with that standard, it at least had a recognized basis in constitutional law at the time *Roe* was decided. The same cannot be said for the "undue burden" standard, which is created largely out of whole cloth by the authors of the joint opinion. It is a standard which even today does not command the support of a majority of this Court. And it will not, we believe, result in the sort of "simple limitation," easily applied, which the joint opinion anticipates. In sum, it is a standard which is not built to last.

. . . Accordingly, we think that the correct analysis is that set forth by the plurality opinion in *Webster.* A woman's interest in having an abortion is a form of liberty protected by the Due Process Clause, but States may regulate abortion procedures in ways rationally related to a legitimate state interest. . . .

[III omitted]

IV

[Using this standard] we . . . would hold that each of the challenged provisions of the Pennsylvania statute is consistent with the Constitution. It bears emphasis that our conclusion in this regard does not carry with it any necessary approval of these regulations. Our task is, as always, to decide only whether the challenged provisions of a law comport with the United States Constitution. If, as we believe, these do, their wisdom as a matter of public policy is for the people of Pennsylvania to decide.

JUSTICE SCALIA, with whom THE CHIEF JUSTICE, JUSTICE WHITE, and JUSTICE THOMAS join, concurring in the judgment in part and dissenting in part.

My views on this matter are unchanged from those I set forth in my separate opinion . . . in *Webster v. Reproductive Health Services* (1989) (SCALIA, J., concurring in part and concurring in judgment). . . . The States may, if they wish, permit abortion-on-demand, but the Constitution does not *require* them to do so. The permissibility of abortion, and the limitations upon it, are to be resolved like most important questions in our democracy: by citizens trying to persuade one another and then voting. . . .

Beyond that brief summary of the essence of my position, I will not swell the United States Reports with repetition of what I have said before; and applying the rational basis test, I would uphold the Pennsylvania statute in its entirety. I must, however, respond to a few of the more outrageous arguments in today's opinion, which it is beyond human nature to leave unanswered. I shall discuss each of them under a quotation from the Court's opinion to which they pertain. . . .

"Liberty finds no refuge in a jurisprudence of doubt."

One might have feared to encounter this august and sonorous phrase in an opinion defending the real *Roe v. Wade,* rather than the revised version fabricated today by the authors of the joint opinion. The shortcomings of *Roe* did not include lack of clarity: Virtually all regulation of abortion before the third trimester was invalid. But to come across this phrase in the joint opinion—which calls upon federal district judges to apply an "undue burden" standard as doubtful in application as it is unprincipled in origin—is really more than one should have to bear.

The joint opinion frankly concedes that the amorphous concept of "undue burden" has been inconsistently applied by the Members of this Court in the few brief years since that "test" was first explicitly propounded by JUSTICE O'CONNOR in her dissent in *Akron I.* Because the three Justices now wish to "set forth a standard of general application," the joint opinion announces that "it is important to clarify what is meant by an undue burden." I certainly agree with that, but I do not agree that the joint opinion succeeds in the announced endeavor. To the contrary, its efforts at clarification make clear only that the standard is inherently manipulable and will prove hopelessly unworkable in practice.

The joint opinion explains that a state regulation imposes an "undue burden" if it "has the purpose or effect of placing a substantial obstacle in the path of a woman seeking an abortion of a nonviable fetus." An obstacle is "substantial," we are told, if it is "calculated, [not] to inform the woman's free choice, [but to] hinder it." This latter statement cannot possibly mean what it says. *Any* regulation of abortion that is intended to advance what the joint opinion concedes is the State's "substantial" interest in protecting unborn life will be "calculated [to] hinder" a decision to have an abortion. It thus seems more accurate to say that the joint opinion would uphold abortion regulations only if they do not *unduly* hinder the woman's decision. That, of course, brings us right back to square one: Defining an "undue burden" as an "undue hindrance" (or a "substantial obstacle") hardly "clarifies" the test. Consciously or not, the joint opinion's verbal shell game will conceal raw judicial policy choices concerning what is "appropriate" abortion legislation. . . .

> "While we appreciate the weight of the arguments . . . that *Roe* should be overruled, the reservations any of us may have in reaffirming the central holding of *Roe* are outweighed by the explication of individual liberty we have given combined with the force of *stare decisis*."

The Court's reliance upon *stare decisis* can best be described as contrived. It insists upon the necessity of adhering not to all of *Roe*, but only to what it calls the "central holding." . . .

I am certainly not in a good position to dispute that the Court *has saved* the "central holding" of *Roe*, since to do that effectively I would have to know what the Court has saved, which in turn would require me to understand (as I do not) what the "undue burden" test means. I must confess, however, that I have always thought, and I think a lot of other people have always thought, that the arbitrary trimester framework, which the Court today discards, was quite as central to *Roe* as the arbitrary viability test, which the Court today retains. It seems particularly ungrateful to carve the trimester framework out of the core of *Roe*, since its very rigidity (in sharp contrast to the utter indeterminability of the "undue burden" test) is probably the only reason the Court is able to say, in urging *stare decisis*, that *Roe* "has in no sense proven 'unworkable.'" I suppose the Court is entitled to call a "central holding" whatever it wants to call a "central holding"—which is, come to think of it, perhaps one of the difficulties with this modified version of *stare decisis*. I thought I might note, however, that the following portions of *Roe* have not been saved:

- Under *Roe*, requiring that a woman seeking an abortion be provided truthful information about abortion before giving informed written consent is unconstitutional, if the information is designed to influence her choice, *Thornburgh; Akron I*. Under the joint opinion's "undue burden" regime (as applied today, at least) such a requirement is constitutional.

- Under *Roe*, requiring that information be provided by a doctor, rather than by nonphysician counselors, is unconstitutional, *Akron I*. Under the "undue burden" regime (as applied today, at least) it is not.

- Under *Roe*, requiring a 24-hour waiting period between the time the woman gives her informed consent and the time of the abortion is unconstitutional, *Akron I*. Under the "undue burden" regime (as applied today, at least) it is not.

- Under *Roe,* requiring detailed reports that include demographic data about each woman who seeks an abortion and various information about each abortion is unconstitutional, *Thornburgh.* Under the "undue burden" regime (as applied today, at least) it generally is not. . . .

The Imperial Judiciary lives. . . .

We should get out of this area, where we have no right to be, and where we do neither ourselves nor the country any good by remaining.

Chapter 6

Congress

———❧———

6-1

The Senate in Bicameral Perspective

Richard F. Fenno Jr.

Rules matter, and constitutional rules often matter most. The Framers of the Constitution created a bicameral national legislature and made the two houses of Congress different in their constituencies, size, and length of terms, with the expectation that they were shaping the way in which the House and Senate would behave. In the following essay, Richard Fenno introduces the differences between the House and the Senate that originated in the Constitution. He then traces the influence of the differences between the two chambers on the way representatives and senators campaign and govern.

BICAMERALISM WAS A bedrock element of the constitutional arrangement of 1787. A resolution "that the national legislature ought to consist of two branches" was the second one passed—"without debate or dissent"—at the federal convention.[1] When, later in the proceedings, several delegates defended the adequacy of the one-chamber Congress then existing under the Articles of Confederation, they did so as part of a strategic effort to secure the equal representation of states in the new system. The principle of bicameralism was never challenged. Twelve of the thirteen states already had bicameral legislatures. George Mason took this fact as evidence that "an attachment to more than one branch in the legislature"

Source: Richard F. Fenno Jr., *The United States Senate: A Bicameral Perspective* (Washington, D.C.: American Enterprise Institute, 1982), 1–6, 26–46.

was—along with "an attachment to republican government"—one of the two points on which "the mind of the people of America . . . was well settled."[2] When James Madison introduced the subject of a second chamber in *The Federalist*, he declared it to be "founded on such clear principles, and now so well understood in the United States that it would be more than superfluous to enlarge on it."[3] He and his colleagues did, of course, "enlarge" upon these "clear principles" in their debates and writings. And I shall do so briefly, to explicate the bicameral perspective.

The framers wanted to create a government, but at the same time they distrusted the power of government. To protect individual liberty, they believed, it was necessary to control the power of government, first through the electoral process and second by dividing authority among and within political institutions. Madison described the "principles" this way:

> In framing a government which is to be administered by men over men, the great difficulty lies in this: you must first enable the government to control the governed; and in the next place oblige it to control itself. A dependence on the people is, no doubt, the primary control on the government; but experience has taught mankind the necessity of auxiliary precautions.[4]

Bicameralism should be viewed most broadly as one of those "auxiliary precautions." Indeed, it is the first one mentioned by Madison after the paragraph quoted above. It came first because the framers believed that the most powerful institution of government and the one most likely to run out of control was the legislature. And they believed that "in order to control the legislative authority, you must divide it."[5]

"Is there no danger of legislative despotism?" James Wilson asked his convention colleagues rhetorically:

> Theory and practice both proclaim it. If the legislative authority be not restrained, there can be neither liberty nor stability; and it can only be restrained by dividing it within itself into distinct and independent branches.[6]

Madison elaborated in *The Federalist*:

> In republican government, the legislative authority necessarily predominates. The remedy for this inconveniency is to divide the legislature into different branches; and to render them, by different modes of election and different principles of action, as little connected with each other as the nature of their common functions and their common dependence on the society will admit.[7]

(Here we have enunciated the basic ideas of bicameralism: that the legislature consist of two "distinct and independent" bodies and that these bodies be "different" from one another.)

The framers, of course, had ideas about just what differences should exist between the Senate and the House. For one thing, they believed that the differences ought to be substantial. In Madison's words:

> As the improbability of sinister combinations will be in proportion to the dissimilarity in the genius of the two bodies, it must be politic to distinguish them from each other by every circumstance which will consist with a due harmony in all proper measures, and with the genuine principles of republican government.[8]

In pursuit of this goal, they determined that the Senate and the House should be structurally dissimilar with respect to their constituencies, their size, and the length of their terms. They also gave each chamber some distinctive policy prerogatives. The controversy over Senate and House constituencies very nearly broke up the entire enterprise. Once that was settled, however, the decisions of 1787 fixed the enduring agenda for discussions of bicameralism. For a long time the decision to establish different modes of election was also part of that agenda, but the Seventeenth Amendment, providing for the popular election of senators, removed it in 1913.

There is more, however, to the framers' conception of bicameralism than two legislative institutions differently constituted. They also believed that the two institutions should and would behave differently. The basic notion was simply that they would behave so as to check one another. In the very act of dividing power, the framers believed they had created two "different bodies of men who might watch and check each other."[9] Their favorite idea, that institutions should and would check one another, was a particularly strong element in their thinking about the Senate.

The House of Representatives was acknowledged to be "the grand repository of the democratic principle of the government."[10] That is why it was given the prerogative of initiating all legislation on taxes, where sensitivity to popular sentiment was deemed especially important. But the House was also thought likely to possess certain infirmities endemic to large, popularly elected legislatures—tendencies to instability in action, to impulsive, unpredictable, changeable decisions, and to a short-run view of good public policy. The Senate was thought of as providing a restraining, stabilizing counterweight, as being the source of a more deliberate, more knowledgeable, longer-run view of good public policy. Said Madison: "As a numerous body of Representatives was liable to err, also, from fickleness and passion, [a] necessary fence against this danger would be to select a portion of enlightened citizens, whose limited number, and firmness might reasonably interpose against impetuous councils." Madison also said: "The use of the Senate is to consist in its proceeding with more coolness, with more system and with more wisdom, than the popular branch."[11] On the basis of such a prediction, the Senate was granted prerogatives in foreign policy, where a steady view of the national interest and the respect of other nations was deemed especially important.

The framers based their predictions of House and Senate behavior on a set of assumptions about the importance of the structural differences they had pre-scribed. The superior "coolness," "system," and "wisdom" of the Senate, for example, were assumed to flow from its smaller size, the longer term of its mem-bers, and their election by state legislatures. If we ask whether the various pre-dictions or their underlying assumptions have worked out as planned, the answer would be: not now—if ever. Some of the predicted differences—that the Senate would be "a more capable set of men" and would act with more "firmness"—seem almost quaint.[12] Research on the contemporary Congress has argued either that observable Senate-House differences do not follow the lines set forth by the framers or that those differences may be less important than the ever-growing similarities.[13] So there is evidence that the particular predictions and the particular linking assumptions of the framers do not hold true today.

Still, that is not a sufficient reason to abandon their original proposition: that structural differences would affect behavioral ones. The structural change to the popular election of senators, for instance, undoubtedly gave a major push to today's behavioral similarities. Other scholars, too, suggest that performance dif-ferences are related to structural differences.[14] So let us continue to assume that the enduring Senate-House differences—in constituency, size, and term—can have consequences for behavior, and let us consider such matters reasonable sub-jects for empirical investigation.

If encouragement be needed, it is provided by the existence of at least one cru-cial Senate-House difference in which the framers' assumptions about the effect of structures on behavior have been correct. By setting up two distinct and different bodies, they made it necessary that the Senate and the House take separate action. They wanted to make certain that the "concurrence of separate and dissimilar bodies is required in every public act."[15] Separate action means, at a minimum, sequential action, and sequential action very likely means different actions. That is because sequential action implies the passage of time and with it the changing of relevant contexts. Different contexts very likely lead to different behavior.

Not surprisingly, the exemplary anecdote about the Senate is an anecdote about sequence. It is the conversation between George Washington and Thomas Jefferson in which Jefferson, in France during the convention, asked Washington why he had consented to a second chamber. "Why," asked Washington, "did you pour that coffee into your saucer?" "To cool it," said Jefferson. "Even so," said Washington, "we pour legislation into the senatorial saucer to cool it." It was the Senate, of course, that was designed to contribute "coolness." But in the execu-tion, it has been the existence of two separate legislative stages that has brought coolness to the legislative process. The anecdote is an exemplary one not just for the Senate, but for the Congress as a whole, for what it illustrates is the importance of separate, sequential action by the two chambers. The Senate is as likely to initiate heatedly as the House; the House is as likely to be the cooling saucer as the Senate.

If this is so, then the analysis of sequence becomes basic to an understanding of bicameral behavior—more basic than an analysis of whether the Senate is more liberal or more conservative than the House. The framers did not so much create one precipitate chamber and one stabilizing chamber as they did force decision making to move across two separate chambers, however those chambers might be constituted. The strategic maneuverings necessitated by such a process become a subject for empirical investigation—as in the analysis of conference committee behavior by Gerald Strom and Barry Rundquist.[16] For reasons of strategy, it would be important for members of the two chambers to assess each other's relative liberalism or conservatism. But analysts of sequencing strategies must recognize the more general proposition that the actions and reactions, the expectations and anticipations, of the two-stage process are as likely to flow one way across the two chambers as the other. The idea of two legislative institutions acting separately and sequentially and thereby having an effect on each other is another ingredient of a bicameral perspective. Although it is not pursued in this essay, it gives additional purpose to what is pursued here.

In sum, the framers of the constitution consciously created a bicameral legislature. They tried to create two different institutions, to construct them so that they would behave differently, and to provide for legislative action at two separate stages. Their legacy leaves us with two questions. What, if any, are the differences between the Senate and House? What, if any, difference do the differences make? To research these questions is a tall order. It calls for observation and description of both houses of Congress and of legislators both individually and collectively, both in and outside Washington. This essay attempts a beginning. Because its ultimate interest is in the Senate, it treats the Senate more than the House. Further, it treats senators more individually than collectively, and it treats them more outside than inside Washington. But it tries to do what it does comparatively—in accordance with a bicameral perspective. . . .

A Bicameral Perspective: Campaigning and Governing

The Six-Year Term

. . . House members campaign continuously. Although an analytical distinction can be drawn between the campaign and the rest of their term, the activity of campaigning never stops. The typical House member's attitude was expressed by one who said, "If an incumbent doesn't have the election won before the campaign begins, he's in trouble. It's hard for me to step up my campaign. I've never been home less than forty times a year since I've been in Congress." When I traveled during the campaign with House members, I rarely had the sense that they were doing anything extraordinary. Their schedules might be a bit more crowded and might include a larger number of partisan events than during an off-year visit, but I felt that they were engaging in their familiar, year-round routines. Two weeks before election one of them remarked, typically, "We are doing now just about the same thing—I'll say the very same thing—I do when I come home weekends." My visits to their districts in nonelection years confirmed this view.

But a researcher does not get the same feeling during incumbent senators' campaigns. There one senses that they have geared up for a qualitatively different effort from anything they have engaged in recently. House members talk a lot about "last time." They campaign "the way we did it last time." Memories of "last time," that is, the last election, are vivid. In a senator's campaign, however, there is noticeably less talk about "last time." The campaign workers tend not to have been involved "last time." Last time is much less of a benchmark for this time; to the degree that it is, recollections of it are vague. In other words, although House members never stop campaigning, senators do. That is why it is impossible to make the easy inferences from campaign styles to home styles for senators that can be made for House members. For senators, campaign styles are not necessarily home styles. There is undoubtedly a relation between them, stronger in some instances than in others. I shall have something to say about this later. Now I propose to examine the underlying structural feature that gives rise to this observed House-Senate difference: the six-year term. It is another legacy of the decisions of 1787.

Traveling the two campaign trails sensitizes the researcher to the difference between the two-year term and the six-year term. It is a big difference. This statement may come as no surprise, but it is not self-evident. The most widely read and reprinted political science treatment of Senate-House differences, by Lewis Froman, contains not one word about the difference in the length of terms. In his chapter "Differences between the House and the Senate," Froman writes:

> Probably the two most important differences between the House and the Senate, and the two from which most of the others are derived, are that the House is more than four times as large as the Senate and that Senators represent sovereign states in a federal system, whereas most congressmen represent smaller and sometimes shifting parts of states.[17]

And in the chart that follows, entitled "Major Differences between the House and the Senate," Froman lists eleven major differences, not one of which has anything to do with the difference between the two-year term and the six-year term. It is largely a matter of research perspective. Froman studied the House and Senate from the inside, in Washington, and he saw only internal, organizational differences. One who begins research in the constituencies at campaign time sees other differences and carries other perspectives to Capitol Hill.

From the perspective of a Senate campaign, six years seems like a long time. Incumbent candidates talk less about last time precisely because it was so long ago—long enough to render the last campaign irrelevant, even if it could be remembered. A defeated senator discussed the six-year change in his state's policy climate:

> When I went in, the war was still on—Vietnam. The fellow I ran against was very closely associated with that. That was of interest to people. There was not building up, then, that avalanche of antigovernment feeling, in the sense that the government could not solve problems. There was a suspicion of people in government, the sense that government was remote. That feeling was there. But the lack of faith in government has grown enormously in six years. [Six years ago] there was a lot more support for farm price supports. There was more support for government programs to help *me*. . . . Now there's the Goldwater spirit, that government never has done anything right and never will. . . . So the mood changed in six years. There's no doubt about that. The impact was very great, I think. People said about me, "He is not a bad guy. He works hard at it. He's honest. He comes back. But he's just too liberal. He hasn't kept up with this change and is holding out for old ideas. There's nothing wrong with him but his views."

This comment about change is not meant to explain an electoral outcome, although perhaps it does. Nor is it meant to explain why campaigning senators have difficulty delineating their supportive constituencies, although perhaps it may. It is meant, rather, to convey some sense of just how long a six-year term can be. Six years, especially six years without any electoral feedback, is plenty of time to get out of touch with one's constituency. Six years, in short, can be a political lifetime.

We cannot understand the Senate without examining the effects of this lengthy term. Six years between elections is long enough to encourage a senator to stop campaigning for a while and do something else with his or her time. House members, too, have this option, but they are constrained by the two-year term to a degree that senators are not—constrained to devote their time and energies fairly continuously and fairly heavily to campaigning for reelection. It is not happenstance that the hardest Senate campaigner I have traveled with was one who was serving a two-year term—a senator with a House member's term of office. "We started running four years ago and we have been running ever since," he said. "I have visited 165 cities and towns, places where no sitting senator has ever been." He came home every weekend for a year and a half. And he was introduced, everywhere, as "a man who is accessible." "Our campaign organization never shut down," said his campaign manager. He campaigned, in other words, like a House member; he did so because of the constraints of the two-year term. Like a House member, he had no choice. Even more, he had to cultivate a constituency much larger than that of a House member.

All senators, I assume, worry a lot about reelection, too. I also assume, however, that their reelection concerns are less immediate, less central, and less overwhelming than they are for House members, at least for some of the time. The amplitude of the six-year cycle gives senators more of a choice. To the degree that they choose to campaign less than continuously, it should be easier for outsiders to disentangle their campaign activities from their noncampaign activities. It gives us an incentive to analyze the effect of one kind of activity on the other and to examine the choices senators make about their noncampaign activity. That is what I propose to do. As I proceed, the focus of description will shift gradually from the constituencies to Washington, from outside the Senate into the Senate, and from the processes of campaigning to the processes of governing.

The Electoral Cycle

A two-year term compresses campaign activity and noncampaign activity so that they appear, to the observer, to proceed simultaneously. A six-year term makes it easier to separate the two kinds of activities and view them sequentially. It invites a view in which the mixture of campaign and noncampaign activity changes over the course of the six years, campaign activity visibly increasing as election time approaches and visibly decreasing afterward. Senators themselves speak in the language of cycles. "Your life has a six-year cycle to it," said one eighteen-year veteran:

> We say in the Senate that we spend four years as a statesman and two years as a politician. You should get cracking as soon as the last two years open up. You should take a poll on the issues, identify people to run your campaign in different parts of the states, raise money, start your PR, and so forth.

A five-term senator, Russell Long, said, "My usual pattern in the first three years of a term is to stick close to the job here and in the last three years to step up the pace in Louisiana."[18] Some evidence, both cross-sectional and longitudinal, exists in support of this cyclical view of senatorial behavior.

The presence of three distinct classes of senators, each with a different reelection date, makes possible some cross-sectional analysis. At the constitutional convention James Wilson noted, "As one-third would go out triennially, there would always be divisions holding their places for unequal terms and consequently acting under the influence of different views and different impulses."[19] Among

Table 1. Average Amount Raised per Senator, 1977 and 1979 (in dollars)

| | *Reelection Date* | | |
	One year away	Three years away	Five years away
1977	250,000 (22)	5,000 (34)	32,000 (30)
1979	391,000 (29)	64,000 (29)	112,000 (33)

Source: Federal Election Commission.

Note: Senators who did not file reports have been omitted. Numbers of senators in each group in parentheses.

those "different views and different impulses" is the impulse to campaign for reelection. In a cyclical view of the matter, the impulse would be strongest in that class for which election day was closest at hand.

I have examined the campaign contributions of all senators for the years 1977 and 1979, the years before the 1978 and 1980 Senate elections. The amount of money raised by each senator is taken to be a measure of that senator's campaign activity in that year. The results, reported in Table 1, do indeed indicate that the senators one year away from reelection campaign harder, that is, raise more money, than the senators for whom election day is either three years or five years away. The average amounts raised by the three classes (one year, three years, and five years away from reelection) were $250,000, $5,000, and $32,000 for 1978 and $391,000, $64,000, and $112,000 for 1980. In each year senators whose next election was furthest away ranked second in average amount collected. The pattern, then, is curvilinear. Those whose reelection was five years away "campaigned harder" than those whose reelection was only three years away. But they did so presumably because they were paying off the debts of a campaign just concluded. They were looking backward to the previous election, not forward to the next one.

Two changes between 1978 and 1980 are worth noting. Senators in all classes raised more money in 1979 than they did in 1977; campaigning is getting more expensive for everyone. The largest proportionate increase in fund raising occurred in the middle group, the class whose reelection was three years away. The average amount collected in this middle group jumped from $5,000 in 1977 to $64,000 in [1979], and the total amount collected by that one-third of the Senate jumped from $170,000 in 1977 to $1.9 million in 1979. This may indicate that senators are beginning their fund raising earlier than previously. As Robert Peabody has recently written:

> Few Senators can afford the proverbial luxury of serving as statesmen for four years, then reverting to the political role for the remaining two years of the

term. Many of the younger group of Senators appear to be following the practice of running hard through most of the six-year term, not unlike the experience of House incumbents.[20]

Table 1 contains some evidence of this change and at the same time demonstrates that some behavior still follows the electoral cycle.

The table indicates that there is a perceptible quickening of fund raising around the fifth year. Students of campaign finance have noted the same phenomenon. Herbert Alexander has observed, "It's becoming almost imperative for senators to spend the fifth year of their term to sew up the following year's elections."[21] Gary Jacobson has shown, for House races, that once a challenger starts spending large amounts of money, the incumbent cannot win simply by raising more money than the challenger.[22] It may be necessary, of course, for the incumbent to raise money in the sixth year to combat a strong challenger. But it can be even more important for an incumbent to use his or her fund-raising ability earlier, so as to keep a strong challenger from emerging. The appearance of electoral vulnerability can be disastrous for an incumbent, since potential challengers and the elites who fund them base their decisions partly on the perceived vulnerability of an incumbent.[23] Moreover, they will be making their calculations in the fifth year. One way to appear invulnerable is to raise a lot of money early. Such is the logic of fifth-year fund raising: at least, be prepared; at most, ward off a strong challenge. The logic of the preemptive strike may be even more important in the Senate than in the House, given the greater ability of Senate challengers to get media attention and to raise money once they have become committed to the race.

Two weeks before election, one incumbent senator talked about his fifth-year campaigning activity:

> Eighteen months ago, we started thinking about the strategy of the campaign. Our first strategy was to scare off other people from running by showing strength. And we did many interesting things to show our strength. . . . It worked in scaring off the governor and a congressman. It didn't work on my opponent. Whether or not we scared off the right people, we'll know on election day.

One of the "interesting things" this senator had done in the year before the election was to raise over $300,000. His press secretary talked about some of the others:

> In June of last year, we made a major strategic decision—to put an aura of invincibility around the senator. We collected money from all segments of the population of the state. We brought him and his family back home to the state. We ran a spring primary campaign as if we had an opponent—a heavy-schedule television campaign. In June of this year, we took a poll. He was ahead of his opponent by over twenty points.

This fifth-year activity may well have been the key to what turned out to be a narrow victory. Back in Washington after his reelection, the senator commented:

> Here's something that would interest you from your professional standpoint. All the political leaders in the state, on both sides, thought my opponent was in a hopeless race. They believed the polls. The other party's leaders believed it so much that they gave up on him. They didn't dig down and help him. That may have hurt him more than anything else.

He believes the strategy worked. Although it is not my purpose to explain election outcomes, this case illustrates the rationale behind one cyclical pattern of campaign activity.

A second, less direct indicator of cyclical campaign activity might be the frequency with which the different classes of senators return to their home states. We would expect that those senators whose reelection was less than two years away would return home to campaign more often than those whose reelection was more than two years away. We have already noted that senators as a group return to their electoral constituencies a good deal less frequently than House members do. Among senators, however, do those up for reelection behave differently from those who are not? In general, there is some evidence that they do. Such patterns as there are run in the expected direction: more attentiveness to their constituencies by senators in the reelection class than by those in the other two classes. The differences are not overwhelming, however, and the small numbers in many categories argue against strong assertions. Still, the evidence is weakly supportive.

In 1977 the twenty-two incumbents facing reelection in 1978 averaged twenty-three trips to their home states, those whose reelection was three years away averaged sixteen trips, and those whose reelection was five years away averaged eighteen trips. Senators who retired in 1978, a group totally lacking in electoral incentives, averaged twelve trips home in 1977 (see Table 2). The difference between this group and their colleagues running for reelection is substantial. It surely testifies to a relationship between the proximity of reelection and trips home, if not to any great strength in its cyclical nature.

Among the three nonretiring groups, the findings resemble those for campaign finance activity. Senators up for reelection are most active, and recently elected senators seem to engage in more electorally related activity than senators in the middle of their term. In the area of campaign finance, the newly elected senators are still paying off their debts. In the matter of trips home, they are probably slow to throttle down from their recent campaigns. This might be particularly true of senators elected for the first time, whose sense of electoral insecurity might remain with them. In any case, it is the first-term senators whose performance accounts for the slightly higher average among the newly elected

Table 2. Trips Home by Senate Class, 1977

Number of trips home	Reelection 1978		Reelection 1980		Reelection 1982		Retiring 1978	
	Number	Percent	Number	Percent	Number	Percent	Number	Percent
31+	5	23	3	9	5	18	0	0
21–30	7	32	6	19	4	14	2	29
11–20	9	41	13	41	12	43	1	14
0–10	1	5	10	31	7	25	4	57
Total	22	100	32	100	28	100	7	100
Average	23		16		18		12	

Source: Travel vouchers submitted to the secretary of the Senate.

Note: Excludes senators from Delaware, Maryland, and Virginia; senators who had served less than a full year; and senators whose records were obviously incomplete.

class. Veteran senators in that class, that is, those elected in 1976, did not go home any more frequently in 1977 than those senators who had been elected in 1974. There is thus some evidence, although it is not overwhelming, for a cyclical explanation of senatorial attentiveness to home.

Table 2 presents further evidence for an electoral cycle. The distribution of trips home within the reelection class differs from that of the other two classes and the retiring senators. Senators running for reelection are clustered more heavily in the top two categories than are senators in the other two classes or those who are retiring. The differences are greatest in the category of ten or fewer trips home; only one reelection-bound senator dared risk such infrequent visits. The retiring senators, of course, look very different from all other senators, but there is no clear pattern differentiating between the two classes of senators not running for reelection. Although reelection concerns have some effect on one class of senators, then, Table 2 conveys no information about other phases of a more defined electoral cycle.

A confounding circumstance affecting the distribution of trips home is the simple matter of distance from Washington, D.C. Among House members, it was found that distance, that is, the expenditure of time, money, and energy, was strongly related to trips home.[24] There is no reason to believe that this would not be true of the Senate, and it is. Table 3 presents a distribution of trips home by senators according to the region from which they come, region being employed as a surrogate for distance, as it was with House members. The farther senators live from Washington, the more difficult it is for them to get home. Senators from the East go home more often than any other group; those from the Far West go home less often than any other group. No senator from the Far West is

Table 3. Trips Home by Senators, by Region, 1977

Number of trips home	East	South	Border	Midwest	Far West
31+	8	3	0	2	0
21–30	5	7	5	2	0
11–20	3	5	1	12	14
0–10	1	3	2	5	11
Total	17	18	8	21	25
Average	27	21	19	16	11

Source: Travel vouchers submitted to the secretary of the Senate.

Note: Excludes senators from Delaware, Maryland, and Virginia; senators who had served less than a full year; and senators whose records were obviously incomplete.

to be found in the highest two categories of trips home. Senators from the Midwest also go home markedly less often than those from the East and South. So striking are these patterns that the question arises whether or not they overwhelm such evidence as supports the notion of a reelection effect. Perhaps region explains all the differences observed in Table 2. Senate classes may be skewed toward one region or another; thus an apparent reelection effect may mask what really is a distance effect.

The 1980 and 1982 Senate classes, for example, are more skewed toward the Far West, 31 percent and 32 percent respectively, than is the class of 1978, only 21 percent of whose members are from the Far West. These regional differences could account for the higher average number of trips among the group of senators running for reelection. One way to check for independent reelection effects would be to see whether, within each region, senators running for reelection were more attentive than senators in the two other classes to their home states. When this calculation is made, the effect of the electoral cycle remains. Of the twenty-two senators running for reelection, sixteen exceeded the average of all senators from their region, and six averaged fewer trips than their regional colleagues. Thus, although distance has an important effect on the frequency of senators' visits home, the proximity to reelection has an independent effect.

Other factors that might be thought to affect a cyclical-reelection explanation for trips home but do not do so—at least in terms of a bivariate relationship—include election margin, seniority, size of state, and previous service in the House. A more idiosyncratic factor, home style, probably does take an additional toll on the cyclical rationale of trips home. Consider, for example, the twenty cases where a senator faced reelection and his or her colleague from the same state did not. With distance thus held constant, we would expect, according to a cyclical rationale, that the campaigning senator would return home more often than his noncampaigning colleague. In ten cases he clearly did; but in six cases he clearly did not, and four cases were virtual ties. It seems likely, therefore, that some senators adopt and maintain a home style calling for frequent personal appearances back home and much personal attentiveness to the electorate. It is a decision having nothing to do with the amplitude of the electoral cycle or the proximity of reelection. Such a style may be adopted to make a deliberate contrast with the senator's same-state colleague. It is worth noting that in all six cases in the noncyclical pattern, it was the junior senator (five of whom were in their first term) who went home most often, even though the senior senator was the one running for reelection. Support for a cyclical-reelection explanation of behavior is weakened a bit more by this finding, and the importance of decisions about home style, taken independent of reelection proximity, is reasserted.

A final strand of research gives some support to a cyclical view of senatorial behavior. It is the body of work that demonstrates that the roll-call or other policy-related behavior of senators changes in the direction of the policy sentiments of their constituents as their reelection approaches. Since these changes are calculated to improve a senator's electoral prospects, we can think of this as another form of campaign activity. The prototype for this research is not about the U.S. Senate at all; it is James Kuklinski's study of California legislators. He found that the voting of state senators, who serve four-year terms, moved toward the policy preferences of their constituents as reelection time approached and moved away from those preferences after their reelection, while the voting of assemblymen, who serve two-year terms, showed no such cyclical change. Ryan Amacher and William Boyes argue a similar conclusion for the Senate. "Long terms, such as the U.S. Senate, seem to produce cycles in which the representative is able to behave independently when first elected and then becomes more representative as reelection approaches." [25] Their conclusion, unfortunately, rests on a methodology far less convincing than Kuklinski's.

John Jackson found that among senators whose 1963 constituency-related voting behavior was not consistent with their previously observed constituency-related voting behavior, the change could be explained by increased attention to the constituency among those whose reelection was closest at hand and decreased attention among those just reelected. Keith Poole has shown that senators' roll-call behavior, as measured by interest group ratings, becomes more ambiguous, or less consistent ideologically, the closer they get to reelection. Finally, Warren Kostroski and Richard Fleisher found that the voting behavior of senators up for reelection was more responsive to the policy wishes of their supportive constituencies than the voting behaviors of senators not up for reelection. [26]

In all these studies there is evidence, produced cross-sectionally, in support of a cyclical effect on campaign activity. Still, the evidence is not strong. The first study was not about the Senate at all. The second study, where the finding is the most applicable, used very questionable methods. The presence of cyclical effects was not the major finding of the last three studies but a subsidiary result. Their major findings emphasized behavioral consistency. Thus the body of evidence leaves us just about where we were at the conclusion of the discussion of trips home. There is weakly supportive evidence for the operation of an electoral cycle and for its systematic effect on campaign activity.

Evidence that constituency-related voting increases at the end of the cycle is buttressed a bit, however, by evidence that such voting can be diluted at the beginning of the electoral cycle. Evidence for the proposition—the "states-man" proposition—is fragmentary, but several senators talked about it. Said one in his first year, "I wouldn't have voted against food stamps as I did last Saturday if I had to run in a year. The six-year term gives you insurance. Well, not exactly—it gives you a cushion. It gives you some squirming room." Said another newcomer:

> It [the six-year term] helps you to take politically unpopular positions. Right now I'm trying to think of a way to change cost-of-living indexing. I'm convinced we've got to find a way of turning that process around. I don't know whether I'll get anywhere. Indexing is very popular. None of the people running for reelection next year will tackle it. I wouldn't either if I had to get reelected next year.

The idea is, of course, that such political actions would not be possible if the senator were near the end of his term. House members, by contrast, are always near the end of their term. As a House member put it, "You are tied down a lot closer to your constituency here than in the Senate. . . . Over there at least one-third of the senators can afford to be statesmen. Here you have to be a politician all the time because you have to run every two years." A third senator reflected, similarly, on the Senate's passage of the Panama Canal treaty:

> Two years is a much shorter leash. I think it makes a real difference. I don't think you would ever have gotten the Panama Canal treaty through the House. Not with the election coming up and the mail coming in so heavily against it. The sentiment in the House might not have been any different from what it was in the Senate. But you could never have passed it.

The implication is that some portion of the Senate was freed from the intense reelection pressure by the insulating effect of the length of term. Patterned action taken near the beginning of the cycle thus testifies to its existence as much as patterned action taken at the end of the cycle.

All this puts us a little bit in mind of an observation by H. Douglas Price: "Cycles have a deservedly bad reputation in most of the social sciences, but they seem to exercise an irresistible pull on explorers of poorly understood subjects." [27] Perhaps when we understand more about the Senate, the appeal of the electoral cycle will vanish. But until such time, it will continue to seem a useful way of exploring the consequences of the six-year term.

The Adjustment from Campaigning to Governing

There is a cycle-related admonition that senators repeat to one another: "Your most important years here are your first and your fifth." They sometimes argue over which is the more important. We know why the fifth year is important. It is the reelection year. We can guess why the first year is important. It is the adjustment year. Political scientists have devoted a great deal of attention to the adjustment period in the Senate, much more than they have paid to the reelection period. In the 1960s the writing about adjustment was dominated by the idea that newly elected senators had to attune themselves to the informal "folkways" of the institution. Especially prominent among those folkways was the notion that first-term senators should observe an apprenticeship. Donald Matthews, in his classic 1960 study, called it "the first rule of Senate behavior" that a newcomer "is expected to keep his mouth shut, not to take the lead in floor fights, to listen and to learn." [28] Recent writings on the Senate, however, have demonstrated beyond any doubt that this "norm of apprenticeship" is dead.[29] That does not mean, however, that the period of adjustment is any the less crucial for a newly elected senator—either in his eyes or in the eyes of those who make judgments about him. Political scientists, therefore, face the problem of confronting a crucial period in the life of a senator at the same time that they have undermined their favorite intellectual framework for studying it.

The suggestion offered here is to view the adjustment period from the perspective of the campaign and the electoral cycle. Newly elected senators can be seen as making a transition from campaign activity, during which time their noncampaign activity will be affected to varying degrees by their campaign activity. The adjustment they make is not so much something that takes place in Washington as it is an adjustment that takes place between constituency behavior and Washington behavior. The relationship, from this perspective, between campaign activity and noncampaign activity has long been deemed important by students of Congress. "It is difficult, really, to understand the Senators, how they act and why," asserted Matthews, "without considering what happens to them while they are running for office." [30] John Bibby and Roger Davidson have written, "The relationship of the campaign to the legislator's total world is of special fascination to students of the legislative process." [31] Yet both works make partic- ular mention of the need for scholarly research into the relationship. Matthews, indeed, admits that his book has little to say on the subject.[32]

Senate newcomers are emerging from their campaigns and are positioned at the beginning of a six-year electoral cycle. From a cyclical view, they should be gearing down their campaign activity and stepping up their noncampaign activ- ity. The six-year senatorial term relaxes their electoral constraints sufficiently so that they can, at some point, stop their campaigning and devote their time and energy to something else. Or, at least, they can alter the mixture of their activi- ties. Indeed, it could be argued that all senators must make some such adjust- ment. If the amplitude of the electoral cycle is not a sufficient inducement, outsiders—particularly the media—will doubtless fix a set of noncampaign expectations for them. Just what is meant by "noncampaign activity" remains purposely vague, but it has something to do with the conduct of the legislature's business, with governing the country. Senators will make the adjustment from campaigning to governing at different rates of speed, in different ways, and with different consequences.

A senator's early days in office provide the observer with a natural setting in which to explore the variety of ways in which the campaign just concluded can impinge on the legislative behavior just taking shape. On the first visit to a newly elected senator's office, for example, an observer is struck by the number of familiar faces there, by the presence of acquaintances from the campaign trail. Whatever their ultimate adjustment to life in the Senate may be, newly elected senators want some people from the campaign with them in Washington.

I followed six neophyte senators from their campaigns into the Senate. On the average, one-third of their Senate staffs—in Washington and back home—were people who had worked in their campaigns. All six campaign managers became members of the Washington staffs, three as chief administrative assistants, two as chief legislative assistants. All six campaign press secretaries became senatorial press secretaries, five in Washington and one in the home state. This direct exchange of jobs, greater than for any other staff position, testifies to the con- tinuing importance of the media for senators as well as for Senate candidates. One method, therefore, of coping with the adjustment period is to maintain some continuity in personnel, some "binding ties." [33]

The presence of people from the campaign ensures the continuance of some campaign activity throughout the six-year term—or if not campaign activity, at least what might be called a campaign metabolism. Senators want some people around who have the requisite metabolic makeup. They want people who have a first-hand sensitivity to electoral forces and electoral problems in the state. They want people who have proven political skill, proven political loyalty, and proven ability to function under pressure. They want people who can understand the senator's political obligations and assess his political risks. All these qualities are best discovered, developed, and tested in the crucible of a campaign. All will be needed to conduct whatever campaign activity is conducted over the next six years, and all will affect noncampaign activity as well. If we, on the outside, are to understand a senator's noncampaign activity, we shall have to know that some members of his staff possess this campaign metabolism. They will automatically factor into all their judgments perceptions of the last campaign and considerations of the next campaign, even as they go about their noncampaign activity. Looking back over six years, an administrative assistant to a first-term senator, the man who also managed the first campaign, provided an example:

> I started worrying the day after his election. He was the first member of the party elected from our state in many years. His reelection was never out of my mind. I thought everything we did here meant something could be done about our political situation or our political base. The senator may not have seen it that way. He's not a political guy. He's the least political senator around.

Staffers with a campaign metabolism will join the senator in making decisions about what is politically wise or politically feasible. Indeed, it may not even be possible to understand certain decisions made by senators unless we know that they have been made by people who had been campaigners.

Another set of continuing influences flows from the events and the rhetoric (I hesitate to say dialogue) of the campaign. At the most obvious level, there are the policy positions taken during the campaign that must now be addressed in office. "The problems I talked about in the campaign are the problems I'm still interested in—the auto industry," said one senator two months into his first term. "It's a continuum," said another, at the same stage:

> There are a lot of campaign promises to be fulfilled. We have to look after the export of coal, coal regulation, steel, pollution issues, Japanese imports, textiles. The NEA [National Education Association], which was a big help to me in the campaign, want more recognition on education matters. There are Jewish issues. There are the problems of [particular cities]. . . . I'm interested in a full plate of things.

John Bibby and Roger Davidson wrote of Senator Abraham Ribicoff that "the Senate campaign provided an important testing ground for the issues and themes that were to mark his early Senate career."[34] During their campaigns Senate candidates emphasize certain public policy concerns, and they carry the emphasis with them into the Senate.

How long the policy emphases of the campaign remain on the senator's "plate of things" is a matter of conjecture. Donald Matthews suggests that "the Senator's initial mandate—partly self-defined, partly reflecting popular sentiment . . . may be a major influence on his voting record many years after it was received."[35] One implication is that policy positions taken in the campaign may persist for so long that eventually the senator can get badly out of touch with his constituency—and, of course, lose. Another implication is that the duration of the campaign emphasis will depend on just how strong the senator believes the initial mandate to be. The finding of Alan Abramowitz that some Senate campaigns are more ideological than others and that voters respond ideologically to the more ideological campaigns may help to sort out the kinds of campaigns that have the most lasting effects on victorious senators.[36] I have already noted that Senate campaigns tend to be more policy oriented than House campaigns, but Senate campaigns can vary widely in the amount of policy controversy they contain.

One way to maintain a campaign policy interest is to institutionalize it by obtaining membership on the committee that deals with it. In an after-dinner campaign speech at a rural high school, I heard one Senate candidate say to the growers of a particular farm product, "I hope I become a member of the Agriculture Committee. I want to become a member of that committee. If I get to the Senate, I'm going to make the point loud and clear that in all the Department of Agriculture there's not one advocate of your industry." It was a campaign promise made to a group of his very strongest supporters. In Washington, in January, he was somewhat less enthusiastic. "The Agriculture Committee is a shambles. . . . When I told other senators I wanted it, they said 'too bad' or 'maybe we can reduce the size of the committee so you won't have to go on.'" But he felt constrained to do so. As his administrative assistant put it, "He's going to go on Agriculture whether he wants to or not." The first legislative staff person he hired was an agricultural expert. The first bill he introduced was an agricultural bill. Altogether it was a very direct, specific, and continuing influence of the campaign on this senator's subsequent legislative work.

To the degree that the adjustment period follows the presumed pattern of the electoral cycle, newly elected senators should gradually subordinate campaign-related behavior to behavior related to legislative work. But they will not all act to do so with the same speed or produce the same degree of subordination. We now know, for example, that some senators must remain active for a while in fund raising to pay off campaign debts. Moreover, some senators enjoy campaigning and are therefore less likely to ease up on it.

Candidate A—now Senator A—is such a person. He likes to campaign. During the campaign he had exclaimed at one point, "I like what we are doing here better than what I do in Washington. The House is a zoo. People say the Senate is much better. . . . [They say] 'you'll even enjoy it.'" Whereas a number of his former House colleagues saw in the six-year term a welcome opportunity to stop their incessant campaigning, he saw nothing attractive in that particular feature of Senate life. Three months into his term, he commented:

> I never gave the six-year term one minute's thought. People say to me, "Aren't you glad you're in for six years?" I say, "No." I always liked campaigning. I always won big in elections. I'll campaign just as often as a senator as I did in the House and in exactly the same way. I was back there over the recess, traveled over the state and made fifteen speeches in five days. Campaigning is the best part of the job. It's the most fun. The six-year term makes absolutely no difference to me.

It will be interesting to see whether, in spite of himself, the six-year term has some effect on his campaign rhythms. Certainly the mixture of activities will be far different for him than for some others, and the play of cyclical effects will be diminished. It seems very likely that, just as his established campaign style did not change when he ran for the Senate, his established home style will not change much while he is in the Senate.

Candidate B—now Senator B—experienced a different adjustment period. When I talked with him three months into his first term, he said, "Nobody talks about their campaigns. It's over. You start fresh. It's the same as your being in the House. That doesn't matter over here either. It's a clean slate." And that was the way he wanted it. Unlike Senator A, he was trying to establish a clean slate with his constituents. "I set a certain standard of expectation when I was in the House, going home every weekend, but I'm not going to do that now. One of the reasons I ran for the Senate was so I wouldn't have to go home every weekend." His determination to disengage quickly from campaign activities was not just a matter of personal preference. It was a decision that emerged out of the dynamics of the campaign itself. His election opponents had called him a "show horse" and had described the contest as "a show horse against a work horse." He was sufficiently affected by this campaign rhetoric that he worked hard to negate it during his early days in office. Two and a half months into his term, he commented:

> Yesterday I got a call from the editor of the state's largest paper asking me why I was keeping such a low profile back in the state. They are going to write a criticism of me for not appearing at every bean supper back home. I've been studying hard, doing my homework, showing up on time. During the campaign, I had to confront the show horse–work horse argument. I've been trying to be a work horse. I've been down here for a month and a half without going home.

Senator B was moving along the cycle in the direction we would normally expect, but his movement was accelerated by his experience in the campaign. It seems likely that Senator B's campaign may have an effect on his home style, changing it from what it was in the House; but we shall have to wait and see.

In general, when the campaign rhetoric emphasizes policy matters, policy concerns can be expected to have an important effect on the adjustment period. When the rhetoric of the campaign emphasizes stylistic matters, however, stylistic concerns can be expected to have an important effect on the adjustment period. Whether the effect is to speed up or retard the movement toward non-campaign activity by the newly elected senator depends entirely on the substantive content of the campaign rhetoric.

The case of candidate C—now Senator C—is instructive. Senator C was a person who wanted to gear down his campaigning during the adjustment period but found it nearly impossible to do so. When I originally asked candidate C why he wanted to leave the House, he answered, "You run for election all the time. You win one month, and a month later you find out who your opponent will be. You go to bean suppers eight days in a row." One month after his election, I asked him what he would miss least about the House. He answered quickly and with a smile. "The two-year term. Now I can do what I want to do well." He is a highly issue-oriented person, and he was impatient to begin some sustained legislative work. Yet, in the first four months of his tenure, he made thirteen trips home and spent thirty-one days there. Senator B, in that same period, went home five times and spent nine days there. Why the contrast?

Once again, we must look to the dynamics of the campaign itself. Candidate C's main line of attack against the incumbent senator had been a stylistic one—his lack of accessibility. "When was the last time you saw your senator?" he would ask. "He hasn't been in my district more than twice in six years. . . . He's very much of a Washingtonian and all that implies. He's on the Washington-overseas shuttle." The implied campaign promise was, of course, to be accessible—as accessible, he sometimes said, as he had been when he was in the House. "I will hold town meetings like I did as a congressman—twenty a year," he told a reporter in January. "I'll also do 'work days': spend a day doing what people do for a living. My wife will go back once a month and go around meeting people and giving speeches." It seemed easy to contemplate. "I was more involved in my congressional district than any congressman ever; so it's nothing more than an extension of what I'm into already. I'm comfortable with it, and I think it will work." In his early days, he tried to make it work. Indeed, he did not stop campaigning.

In May, he exclaimed:

> In the House, I tried to do everything I was asked to do, go everywhere I was invited. The problem is: How do you learn to say no? I'm doing fourteen

commencements this spring. Can you believe it? Part of it is my own doing. After the campaign, I never stopped. I went around thanking everybody. So I never recouped from the campaign. And I haven't stopped since. The result is I'm tired all the time.

As we drove around the state one day in June, he revealed another reason for his continuing campaign activity—a degree of electoral insecurity evidenced by neither Senator A nor Senator B. They, however, represented states the same size and twice the size of their House districts whereas Senator C was trying to digest a vastly larger statewide constituency. "There are so many places I haven't been where I want to get established," he said that day. Passing through one small town, he said, "This could be a good place for a town meeting. They would appreciate it. I haven't been here before." In the car, he leafed through a pile of "thank you" letters. "When you accept appearances like these and do them well, the recognition is tremendous. So the temptation is to keep it up. . . . Politically it's fantastic; but personally it's devastating." He added, "I can't keep up the pace." A couple of years later he looked back on his adjustment period:

> There was a definite period of confusion and wandering. It lasted for about a year. We didn't know what we were doing. We didn't know what issues to work on. I was running around the state like a madman. The problem was that I still thought of myself as a congressman; but I wasn't a congressman, and I had ten times the territory to cover. You need to make judgments about what you want to do here, and we began to do that.

Finally he had begun to enjoy the fruits of the six-year term he had so coveted in the beginning. In the Senate Office Building he told a group of college students that same day, "This is the best job there is. The six-year term gives you time to think. In the House, you just finish packing away the decorations from the victory celebration when someone announces against you, and you have to start campaigning all over again." By that time he had subordinated his campaign activity to his noncampaign activity. But as one of his chief campaigners and chief Senate staffers said, "It took us a long time to get over the campaign."

There is a lot more to any senator's adjustment period than the campaign effects I have discussed. There are a whole series of adjustments to be made to one's fellow senators, to the internal routines of legislative work, and to the other actors in the Washington political community. All adjustment problems, however, can be seen as matters of choice. Senators will choose—in accordance with their personal goals, their perception of their political world, and the objective constraints within which they operate—their modes of adjustment. They will decide what kind of senators they want to be and how they will spend their resources of time, intelligence, energy, and support. I have discussed a few such senatorial adjustment choices, concerning staff, policy, committee, style, as they are affected by the campaign. I have suggested that the campaign perspective will help us understand the adjustment period, but I suggest no more than that. Just as the senators themselves gradually subordinate campaign activity to noncampaign activity, so must the observer subordinate the campaign perspective to other perspectives in order to comprehend a fuller range of Senate activities. For us as for them, there is a transition from the matter of campaigning to the matter of governing. But that is for another essay.

NOTES

1. James Madison, *Notes of Debates in the Federal Convention of 1787* (New York: W. W. Norton, 1969), pp. 38–39.

2. Ibid., p. 158.

3. *The Federalist Papers* (New York: New American Library, 1969), no. 62, p. 379.

4. Ibid., no. 51, p. 322

5. Madison, *Notes,* p. 127.

6. Ibid., pp. 126–27.

7. *Federalist,* no. 51, p. 322.

8. Ibid., no. 62, p. 379.

9. Madison, *Notes,* p. 193.

10. Ibid., p. 39.

11. Ibid., pp. 194, 83.

12. Ibid., pp. 113, 194.

13. Gary E. Gammon, "The Role of the United States: Its Conception and Its Performance" (Ph.D. diss., Claremont Graduate School, 1978); and Norman J. Ornstein, "The House and the Senate in a New Congress," in Thomas E. Mann and Norman J. Ornstein, eds., *The New Congress* (Washington, D.C.: American Enterprise Institute, 1981).

14. Joseph M. Bessette, "Deliberative Democracy: The Majority Principle in Republican Government," in Robert A. Goldwin and William A. Schambra, eds., *How Democratic Is the Constitution?* (Washington, D.C.: American Enterprise Institute, 1980); and Nelson W. Polsby, "Strengthening Congress in National Policymaking," *Yale Review* (Summer 1970), pp. 481–97.

15. *Federalist,* no. 63, p. 386.

16. Gerald S. Strom and Barry S. Rundquist, "A Revised Theory of Winning in House-Senate Conferences," *American Political Science Review* (June 1997).

17. Lewis A. Froman Jr., *The Congressional Process: Strategies, Rules, and Procedures* (Boston: Little, Brown, 1967), pp. 7–8.

18. *New York Times,* April 15, 1979.

19. James Madison, *Notes of Debates in the Federal Convention of 1787* (New York: W. W. Norton, 1969), p. 198.

20. Robert Peabody, "Senate Party Leadership: From the 1950s to the 1980s" (unpublished manuscript, Baltimore, 1980), p. 27; see also, Norman J. Ornstein, "The House and the Senate in a New Congress," in Thomas E. Mann and Norman J. Ornstein, eds., *The New Congress* (Washington, D.C.: American Enterprise Institute, 1981).

21. *Congressional Quarterly Weekly Report,* July 28, 1979, p. 1539.

22. Gary Jacobson, *Money in Congressional Elections* (New Haven, Conn.: Yale University Press, 1980).

23. Gary Jacobson and Samuel Kernell, *Strategy and Choice in Congressional Elections* (New Haven, Conn.: Yale University Press, 1982).

24. Richard F. Fenno Jr., *Home Style: House Members in Their Districts* (Boston: Little, Brown, 1978).

25. James H. Kuklinski, "Representativeness and Elections: A Political Analysis," *American Political Science Review* (March 1978), pp. 165–77; and Ryan C. Amacher and William J. Boyes, "Cycles in Senatorial Voting Behavior: Implications for the Optimal Frequency of Elections," *Public Choice* (1978), pp. 5–13.

26. John Jackson, *Constituencies and Leaders in Congress* (Cambridge, Mass.: Harvard University Press, 1974), chap. 5; Keith T. Poole, "Dimensions of Interest Group Evaluation of the U.S. Senate, 1969–1978," *American Journal of Political Science* (February 1981), pp. 49–67; and Warren Kostroski and Richard Fleisher, "Competing Models of Electoral Linkage: Senatorial Voting Behavior, 1963–1964" (unpublished manuscript, 1977?).

27. H. Douglas Price, "'Critical Elections' and Party History: A Critical Review," *Polity* (1971), pp. 236–42, at p. 239.

28. Donald R. Matthews, *U.S. Senators and Their World* (Chapel Hill: University of North Carolina Press, 1960), pp. 92–99.

29. David Rohde, Norman Ornstein, and Robert Peabody, "Political Change and Legislative Norms in the U.S. Senate" (paper delivered at the annual meeting of the American Political Science Association, Chicago, 1974); Ross Baker, *Friend and Foe in the U.S. Senate* (New York: Free Press, 1980); and Michael Foley, *The New Senate* (New Haven, Conn.: Yale University Press, 1980).

30. Matthews, *U.S. Senators*, p. 68.

31. John Bibby and Roger Davidson, *On Capitol Hill* (New York: Holt, Rinehart, 1967), p. 51.

32. Matthews, *U.S. Senators*, p. 50; see also Bibby and Davidson, *On Capitol Hill*, p. 52.

33. Robert Salisbury and Kenneth Shepsle, "Congressional Staff Turnover and the Ties-That-Bind," *American Political Science Review* (June 1981), pp. 381–96.

34. Bibby and Davidson, *On Capitol Hill*, p. 52.

35. Matthews, *U.S. Senators*, pp. 234–35.

36. Alan Abramowitz, "Choices and Echoes in the 1978 U.S. Senate Elections: A Research Note," *American Journal of Political Science* (February 1981), pp. 112–118.

6-2

from *Congress: The Electoral Connection*

David R. Mayhew

Many unflattering stereotypes permeate public thinking about members of Congress. Legislators are sometimes viewed as partisans who are preoccupied with scoring political points against the opposition party. At other times, they are treated as ideologues pursuing their personal policy interests at the expense of the nation's collective interest. Sometimes they are even considered to be a special psychological type—power-hungry politicians. In the following essay, David Mayhew explores the implications of a more realistic assumption—that legislators seek reelection. He argues that legislators' efforts to gain reelection produce predictable behavior while in office. In particular, legislators seek to claim credit for legislation that sends money for projects in their constituencies back home, they find taking positions on issues more important than passing bills, and, of course, they advertise themselves.

THE DISCUSSION TO COME will hinge on the assumption that United States congressmen are interested in getting reelected—indeed, in their role here as abstractions, interested in nothing else. Any such assumption necessarily does some violence to the facts, so it is important at the outset to root this one as firmly as possible in reality. A number of questions about that reality immediately arise.

First, is it true that the United States Congress is a place where members wish to stay once they get there? . . .

In the modern Congress the "congressional career" is unmistakably upon us. Turnover figures show that over the past century increasing proportions of members in any given Congress have been holdovers from previous Congresses—members who have both sought reelection and won it. Membership turnover noticeably declined among southern senators as early as the 1850s, among senators generally just after the Civil War. The House followed close behind, with turnover dipping in the late nineteenth century and continuing to decline throughout the twentieth. Average number of terms served has gone up

Source: David R. Mayhew, *Congress: The Electoral Connection* (New Haven: Yale University Press, 1974), 13–27, 49–77. Notes appearing in the original have been deleted.

and up, with the House in 1971 registering an all-time high of 20 percent of its members who had served at least ten terms. It seems fair to characterize the modern Congress as an assembly of professional politicians spinning out political careers. The jobs offer good pay and high prestige. There is no want of applicants for them. Successful pursuit of a career requires continual reelection.

A second question is this: even if congressmen seek reelection, does it make sense to attribute that goal to them to the exclusion of all other goals? Of course the answer is that a complete explanation (if one were possible) of a congressman's or any one else's behavior would require attention to more than just one goal. There are even occasional congressmen who intentionally do things that make their own electoral survival difficult or impossible. . . . The electoral goal has an attractive universality to it. It has to be the *proximate* goal of everyone, the goal that must be achieved over and over if other ends are to be entertained. One former congressman writes, "All members of Congress have a primary interest in getting re-elected. Some members have no other interest." Reelection underlies everything else, as indeed it should if we are to expect that the relation between politicians and public will be one of accountability. What justifies a focus on the reelection goal is the juxtaposition of these two aspects of it—its putative empirical primacy and its importance as an accountability link. . . .

. . . Congressmen must constantly engage in activities related to reelection. There will be differences in emphasis, but all members share the root need to do things—indeed, to do things day in and day out during their terms. The next step here is to present a typology, a short list of the *kinds* of activities congressmen find it electorally useful to engage in. The case will be that there are three basic kinds of activities. . . .

One activity is *advertising,* defined here as any effort to disseminate one's name among constituents in such a fashion as to create a favorable image but in messages having little or no issue content. A successful congressman builds what amounts to a brand name, which may have a generalized electoral value for other politicians in the same family. The personal qualities to emphasize are experience, knowledge, responsiveness, concern, sincerity, independence, and the like. Just getting one's name across is difficult enough; only about half the electorate, if asked, can supply their House members' names. It helps a congressman to be known. . . . A vital advantage enjoyed by House incumbents is that they are much better known among voters than their November challengers. They are better known because they spend a great deal of time, energy, and money trying to make themselves better known. There are standard routines—frequent visits to the constituency, nonpolitical speeches to home audiences, the sending out of infant care booklets and letters of condolence and congratulation. . . . Anniversaries and other events aside, congressional advertising is done largely at public expense. Use of the franking privilege has mushroomed in recent years; in early 1973 one estimate predicted that House and Senate members would send out about 476 million pieces of mail in the year 1974, at a public cost of $38.1 million—or about 900,000 pieces per member with a subsidy of $70,000 per member. By far the heaviest mailroom traffic comes in Octobers of even-numbered years. There are some differences between House and Senate members in the ways they go about getting their names across. House members are free to blanket their constituencies with mailings for all boxholders; senators are not. But senators find it easier to appear on national television—for example, in short reaction statements on the nightly news shows. Advertising is a staple congressional activity, and there is no end to it. For each member there are always new voters to be apprised of his worthiness and old voters to be reminded of it.

A second activity may be called *credit claiming,* defined here as acting so as to generate a belief in a relevant political actor (or actors) that one is personally responsible for causing the government, or some unit thereof, to do something that the actor (or actors) considers desirable. The political logic of this, from the congressman's point of view, is that an actor who believes that a member can make pleasing things happen will no doubt wish to keep him in office so that he can make pleasing things happen in the future. The emphasis here is on individual accomplishment (rather than, say, party or governmental accomplishment) and on the congressman as doer (rather than as, say, expounder of constituency views). Credit claiming is highly important to congressmen, with the consequence that much of congressional life is a relentless search for opportunities to engage in it.

Where can credit be found? If there were only one congressman rather than 535, the answer would in principle be simple enough. Credit (or blame) would attach in Downsian fashion to the doings of the government as a whole. But there are 535. Hence it becomes necessary for each congressman to try to peel off pieces of governmental accomplishment for which he can believably generate a sense of responsibility. For the average congressman the staple way of doing this is to traffic in what may be called "particularized benefits." Particularized governmental benefits, as the term will be used here, have two properties: (1) Each benefit is given out to a specific individual, group, or geographical constituency, the recipient unit being of a scale that allows a single congressman to be recognized (by relevant political actors and other congressmen) as the claimant for the benefit (other congressmen being perceived as indifferent or hostile). (2) Each benefit is given out in apparently ad hoc fashion (unlike, say, social security checks) with a congressman apparently having a hand in the allocation. A particularized benefit can normally be regarded as a member of a class.

That is, a benefit given out to an individual, group, or constituency can normally be looked upon by congressmen as one of a class of similar benefits given out to sizable numbers of individuals, groups, or constituencies. Hence the impression can arise that a congressman is getting "his share" of whatever it is the government is offering. (The classes may be vaguely defined. Some state legislatures deal in what their members call "local legislation.")

In sheer volume the bulk of particularized benefits come under the heading of "casework"—the thousands of favors congressional offices perform for supplicants in ways that normally do not require legislative action. High school students ask for essay materials, soldiers for emergency leaves, pensioners for location of missing checks, local governments for grant information, and on and on. Each office has skilled professionals who can play the bureaucracy like an organ—pushing the right pedals to produce the desired effects. But many benefits require new legislation, or at least they require important allocative decisions on matters covered by existent legislation. Here the congressman fills the traditional role of supplier of goods to the home district. It is a believable role; when a member claims credit for a benefit on the order of a dam, he may well receive it. Shiny construction projects seem especially useful. In the decades before 1934, tariff duties for local industries were a major commodity. In recent years awards given under grant-in-aid programs have become more useful as they have become more numerous. Some quests for credit are ingenious; in 1971 the story broke that congressmen had been earmarking foreign aid money for specific projects in Israel in order to win favor with home constituents. It should be said of constituency benefits that congressmen are quite capable of taking the initiative in drumming them up; that is, there can be no automatic assumption that a congressman's activity is the result of pressures brought to bear by organized interests. Fenno shows the importance of member initiative in his discussion of the House Interior Committee.

A final point here has to do with geography. The examples given so far are all of benefits conferred upon home constituencies or recipients therein (the latter including the home residents who applauded the Israeli projects). But the properties of particularized benefits were carefully specified so as not to exclude the possibility that some benefits may be given to recipients outside the home constituencies. Some probably are. Narrowly drawn tax loopholes qualify as particularized benefits, and some of them are probably conferred upon recipients outside the home districts. (It is difficult to find solid evidence on the point.) Campaign contributions flow into districts from the outside, so it would not be surprising to find that benefits go where the resources are.

How much particularized benefits count for at the polls is extraordinarily difficult to say. But it would be hard to find a congressman who thinks he can afford to wait around until precise information is available. The lore is that they count—furthermore, given home expectations, that they must be supplied in regular quantities for a member to stay electorally even with the board. Awareness of favors may spread beyond their recipients, building for a member a general reputation as a good provider. "Rivers Delivers." "He Can Do More For Massachusetts." . . .

. . . Is credit available elsewhere for governmental accomplishments beyond the scale of those already discussed? The general answer is that the prime mover role is a hard one to play on larger matters—at least before broad electorates. A claim, after all, has to be credible. If a congressman goes before an audience and says, "I am responsible for passing a bill to curb inflation," or "I am responsible for the highway program," hardly anyone will believe him. There are two reasons why people may be skeptical of such claims. First, there is a numbers problem. On an accomplishment of a sort that probably engaged the supportive interest of more than one member it is reasonable to suppose that credit should be apportioned among them. But second, there is an overwhelming problem of information costs. For typical voters Capitol Hill is a distant and mysterious place; few have anything like a working knowledge of its maneuverings. Hence there is no easy way of knowing whether a congressman is staking a valid claim or not. The odds are that the information problem cuts in different ways on different kinds of issues. On particularized benefits it may work in a congressman's favor; he may get credit for the dam he had nothing to do with building. Sprinkling a district with dams, after all, is something a congressman is supposed to be able to do. But on larger matters it may work against him. For a voter lacking an easy way to sort out valid from invalid claims the sensible recourse is skepticism. Hence it is unlikely that congressmen get much mileage out of credit claiming on larger matters before broad electorates.

Yet there is an obvious and important qualification here. For many congressmen credit claiming on nonparticularized matters is possible in specialized subject areas because of the congressional division of labor. The term "governmental unit" in the original definition of credit claiming is broad enough to include committees, subcommittees, and the two houses of Congress itself. Thus many congressmen can believably claim credit for blocking bills in subcommittee, adding on amendments in committee, and so on. The audience for transactions of this sort is usually small. But it may include important political actors (e.g., an interest group, the president, the *New York Times*, Ralph Nader) who are capable of both paying Capitol Hill information costs and deploying electoral resources. There is a well-documented example of this in Fenno's treatment of post office politics in the 1960s. The postal employee unions used to watch very closely the activities of the House and Senate Post Office Committees and supply valuable electoral resources (money, volunteer work) to members who did their bidding on salary bills. . . .

The third activity congressmen engage in may be called *position taking*, defined here as the public enunciation of a judgmental statement on anything likely to be of interest to political actors. The statement may take the form of a roll call vote. The most important classes of judgmental statements are those prescribing American governmental ends (a vote cast against the war; a statement that "the war should be ended immediately") or governmental means (a statement that "the way to end the war is to take it to the United Nations"). The judgments may be implicit rather than explicit, as in: "I will support the president on this matter." But judgments may range far beyond these classes to take in implicit or explicit statements on what almost anybody should do or how he should do it: "The great Polish scientist Copernicus has been unjustly neglected"; "The way for Israel to achieve peace is to give up the Sinai." The congressman as position taker is a speaker rather than a doer. The electoral requirement is not that he make pleasing things happen but that he make pleasing judgmental statements. The position itself is the political commodity. Especially on matters where governmental responsibility is widely diffused it is not surprising that political actors should fall back on positions as tests of incumbent virtue. For voters ignorant of congressional processes the recourse is an easy one. . . .

The ways in which positions can be registered are numerous and often imaginative. There are floor addresses ranging from weighty orations to mass-produced "nationality day statements." There are speeches before home groups, television appearances, letters, newsletters, press releases, ghostwritten books, . . . articles, even interviews with political scientists. On occasion congressmen generate what amount to petitions; whether or not to sign the 1956 Southern Manifesto defying school desegregation rulings was an important decision for southern members. Outside the roll call process the congressman is usually able to tailor his positions to suit his audiences. A solid consensus in the constituency calls for ringing declarations; for years the late Senator James K. Vardaman (D., Miss.) campaigned on a proposal to repeal the Fifteenth Amendment. Division or uncertainty in the constituency calls for waffling; in the late 1960s a congressman had to be a poor politician indeed not to be able to come up with an inoffensive statement on Vietnam ("We must have peace with honor at the earliest possible moment consistent with the national interest"). On a controversial issue a Capitol Hill office normally prepares two form letters to send out to constituent letter writers—one for the pros and one (not directly contradictory) for the antis. . . .

. . . Versatility of this sort is occasionally possible in roll call voting. For example a congressman may vote one way on recommittal and the other on final passage, leaving it unclear just how he stands on a bill. Members who cast identical votes on a measure may give different reasons for having done so. Yet it is on roll calls that the crunch comes; there is no way for a member to avoid making a record on hundreds of issues, some of which are controversial in the home constituencies. Of course, most roll call positions considered in isolation are not likely to cause much of a ripple at home. But broad voting patterns can and do; member "ratings" calculated by the Americans for Democratic Action, Americans for Constitutional Action, and other outfits are used as guidelines in the deploying of electoral resources. And particular issues often have their alert publics. Some national interest groups watch the votes of all congressmen on single issues and ostentatiously try to reward or punish members for their positions; over the years some notable examples of such interest groups have been the Anti-Saloon League, the early Farm Bureau, the American Legion, the American Medical Association, and the National Rifle Association. On rare occasions single roll calls achieve a rather high salience among the public generally. This seems especially true of the Senate, which every now and then winds up for what might be called a "showdown vote," with pressures on all sides, presidential involvement, media attention given to individual senators' positions, and suspense about the outcome. Examples are the votes on the nuclear test-ban treaty in 1963, civil rights cloture in 1964, civil rights cloture again in 1965, the Haynsworth appointment in 1969, the Carswell appointment in 1970, and the ABM in 1970. Controversies on roll calls like these are often relived in subsequent campaigns, the southern Senate elections of 1970 with their Haynsworth and Carswell issues being cases in point.

Probably the best position-taking strategy for most congressmen at most times is to be conservative—to cling to their own positions of the past where possible and to reach for new ones with great caution where necessary. Yet in an earlier discussion of strategy the suggestion was made that it might be rational for members in electoral danger to resort to innovation. The form of innovation available is entrepreneurial position taking, its logic being that for a member facing defeat with his old array of positions it makes good sense to gamble on some new ones. It may be that congressional marginals fulfill an important function here as issue pioneers—experimenters who test out new issues and thereby show other politicians which ones are usable. An example of such a pioneer is Senator Warren Magnuson (D., Wash.), who responded to a surprisingly narrow victory in 1962 by reaching for a reputation in the area of consumer affairs. Another example is Senator Ernest Hollings (D., S.C.), a servant of a shaky and racially heterogeneous southern constituency who launched "hunger" as an issue in 1969—at once pointing to a problem and giving it a useful nonracial definition. One of the most successful issue entrepreneurs of recent decades was the late

Senator Joseph McCarthy (R., Wis.); it was all there—the close primary in 1946, the fear of defeat in 1952, the desperate casting about for an issue, the famous 1950 dinner at the Colony Restaurant where suggestions were tendered, the decision that "Communism" might just do the trick.

The effect of position taking on electoral behavior is about as hard to measure as the effect of credit claiming. Once again there is a variance problem; congressmen do not differ very much among themselves in the methods they use or the skills they display in attuning themselves to their diverse constituencies. All of them, after all, are professional politicians. . . .

There can be no doubt that congressmen believe positions make a difference. An important consequence of this belief is their custom of watching each other's elections to try to figure out what positions are salable. Nothing is more important in Capitol Hill politics than the shared conviction that election returns have proven a point. . . .

These, then, are the three kinds of electorally oriented activities congressmen engage in—advertising, credit claiming, and position taking. It remains only to offer some brief comments on the emphases different members give to the different activities. No deterministic statements can be made; within limits each member has freedom to build his own electoral coalition and hence freedom to choose the means of doing it. Yet there are broad patterns. For one thing senators, with their access to the media, seem to put more emphasis on position taking than House members; probably House members rely more heavily on particularized benefits. But there are important differences among House members. Congressmen from the traditional parts of old machine cities rarely advertise and seldom take positions on anything (except on roll calls), but devote a great deal of time and energy to the distribution of benefits. In fact they use their office resources to plug themselves into their local party organizations. . . .

. . . [A] difference appears if the initial assumption of a reelection quest is relaxed to take into account the "progressive" ambitions of some members—the aspirations of some to move up to higher electoral offices rather than keep the ones they have. There are two important subsets of climbers in the Congress—House members who would like to be senators (over the years about a quarter of the senators have come up directly from the House), and senators who would like to be presidents or vice presidents (in the Ninety-third Congress about a quarter of the senators had at one time or another run for these offices or been seriously "mentioned" for them). In both cases higher aspirations seem to produce the same distinctive mix of activities. For one thing credit claiming is all but useless. It does little good to talk about the bacon you have brought back to a district you are trying to abandon. And, as Lyndon Johnson found in 1960, claiming credit on legislative maneuvers is no way to reach a new mass audience;

it baffles rather than persuades. Office advancement seems to require a judicious mixture of advertising and position taking. Thus a House member aiming for the Senate heralds his quest with press releases; there must be a new "image," sometimes an ideological overhaul to make ready for the new constituency. Senators aiming for the White House do more or less the same thing—advertising to get the name across, position taking ("We can do better"). In recent years presidential aspirants have sought Foreign Relations Committee membership as a platform for making statements on foreign policy.

There are these distinctions, but it would be a mistake to elevate them over the commonalities. For most congressmen most of the time all three activities are essential. . . .

6-3

Congressional Trends

Steven S. Smith

Congress is the world's most powerful national legislature, in large part because of the formal powers granted to it by the U.S. Constitution more than two centuries ago. Yet as political scientist Steven Smith explains in this essay, Congress still is a rapidly changing institution. New-style politics, the new media, an evolving membership, new policy demands, election outcomes, and most recently the war against terrorism have changed virtually every aspect of congressional politics—the setting, the players, institutional advantages, and the issue arenas. Smith argues that members of Congress suffer from their inability to act efficiently, to prevent occasional scandals, to resist the pressures of constituency demands and campaigns, to avoid intense partisanship, and to compete effectively with the president, particularly in the area of national security.

THE UNITED STATES Congress is the world's most powerful national legislature. It serves as an important check on one-man rule by the president. Many dedicated individuals, both elected and unelected, work in Congress. To be sure, there is much about congressional politics that is distasteful—partisanship and political intrigue infuse it, large egos roam the halls of Capitol Hill, and the formalities often seem stuffy and antiquated. Still, the ability of 535 elected representatives to peacefully resolve the conflicts that arise in a society approaching 300 million people remains an amazing feat.

Congress is always changing. New problems—war, hurricanes, international health threats, scientific breakthroughs, and more—invariably create new interests and conflicts in society that generate demands on legislators to act. Elections bring new members, who often alter the balance of opinion in the House and the Senate. And each new president asks for support for a new policy program. Members of Congress usually respond to those demands by passing new legislation. But as they compete with one another for control over policy and react to pressure from presidents, lobbyists, and the public, lawmakers often seek to gain advantage by altering the procedures and organization of Congress itself. This is made possible by the fact that the Constitution outlines only a few key features of congressional decision-making processes: Both houses must agree to legislation before it is sent to the president for signature or veto; one-fifth of each house may demand the yeas and nays (a recorded vote); an elected Speaker presides over the House of Representatives; the vice president serves as the president of the Senate.

The purpose of this essay is to highlight modern trends in congressional politics and explore the reasons behind them. Overall, Congress has become a more representative institution, but a number of recent developments in American politics have challenged its members' ability to exercise independent judgment in policymaking. Open government, sharp partisanship, new technologies, and new issues make the lawmakers' tasks more challenging. In spite of their great collective power, members of Congress suffer from their inability to act efficiently, to prevent occasional scandals, to resist the pressures of constituency demands and campaigns, to avoid intense partisanship, and to compete effectively with the president, particularly in the area of national security.

Self-Inflicted Wounds

For James Madison, representative government served two purposes—to make the law responsive to the values and interests of the people and to allow representatives to make law. The second purpose was, and is, controversial. Madison explained in *Federalist* No. 10 (see chapter 2) that he hoped representatives would rise above the inevitable influence of public opinion to make policy for the public "good." Arguing in favor of representative government for a large country, Madison insisted that America would be best served by "representatives whose enlightened views and virtuous sentiments" would "render them superior to local prejudices and schemes of injustice." Representatives were more likely than the people themselves to be good policymakers.

Modern Americans do not seem to share Madison's view. A poll conducted in 2001 by Princeton Survey Research Associates for the Kaiser Foundation showed that only a minority of Americans would agree with Madison that legislators should be *trustees*—representing their constituents by exercising independent judgment about the interests of the nation. Most Americans seem to expect elected representatives to faithfully present their constituents' views—that is, to be *delegates* for their constituents.

Moreover, political scientists John R. Hibbing and Elizabeth Theiss-Morse have discovered that although Americans appreciate the role of Congress as an institution, they have little confidence in its members collectively.[1] The general public seldom gives the performance of Congress high marks; in fact, its ratings

Figure 1. Percentages of Respondents Saying That They Have a "Great Deal" of Confidence in National Political Institutions (Gallup Poll)

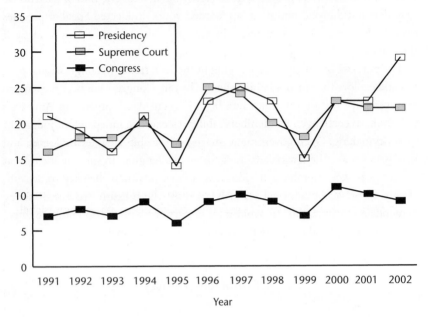

Source: http://roperweb.ropercenter.uconn.edu/cgi-bin/hsrun.exe/roperweb/pom/pom.htx;start=HS _special_topics?Topic=congress.

are often very, very low. For many years, the Gallup organization has asked a sample of respondents how much confidence they have in Congress, the president, and the Supreme Court. As Figure 1 shows, Americans always report less confidence in Congress than in the other institutions. Congress's openness to the news media and the public, in contrast to the closed decision-making meetings of the White House and Supreme Court, may make it especially vulnerable to unfavorable comparisons. The legislative process is easy to dislike—it often generates political posturing and grandstanding, it necessarily involves compromise and deal making, and it frequently leaves broken campaign promises in its trail.

Still, members of Congress themselves often are responsible for the disparagement and ridicule directed at their institution. Scandals, which involve only a tiny fraction of the membership, add to the public's frustration with Congress and seem to regularly contribute to the institution's low ratings in opinion polls. The flow of congressional scandals is remarkably constant (see Box 1).

Political scientist Norman J. Ornstein worries that the news media have placed increasing emphasis on the negative and sensational side of Congress, which he labels the "tabloidization" of media coverage. "The drive to emulate the *National*

Box 1: Congressional Scandals since 1980

- In 1980 five House members were convicted of accepting bribes from undercover FBI agents in return for favors.
- In 1984 Rep. George Hanson, R-Idaho, was convicted of failing to report loans and income as required under the Ethics in Government Act.
- In 1986 Rep. Dan Daniel, D-Va., was found to have violated House rules by accepting free flights from the Beech Aircraft Co.
- In 1987 Rep. Mario Biaggi was convicted of receiving illegal gratuities and other crimes in efforts to help the Coastal Drydock Co.
- In 1987 Rep. Austin Murphy, D-Pa., was reprimanded for allowing another member to cast votes for him on the House floor, for having a no-show employee, and for allowing his former law firm to use his congressional office resources.
- In 1988 Delegate Fofo Sunia, D-American Samoa, pleaded guilty to creating a "ghost" employee in order to defraud the government.
- In 1988 Rep. Patrick Swindall, R-Ga., was convicted of perjury in connection with an investigation of his acceptance of a loan from a drug-money launderer and an undercover law enforcement agent.
- In 1989 House Speaker James Wright, D-Texas, resigned after Republicans charged him with ethics violations in connection with his royalties on a book.
- In 1991 Sen. David Durenburger, R-Minn., in a unanimously approved Senate resolution, was condemned for a book deal and for seeking reimbursement for expenses of staying in a condo that he owned.
- The Senate's handling of Anita Hill's charges of sexual harassment against Supreme Court nominee Clarence Thomas raised questions about fairness and sensitivity in the Senate.
- The disclosure that many House members had repeatedly overdrawn their accounts at the House bank led people to believe that members enjoyed special privileges, and it led to news stories about cheap haircuts, special parking privileges, and other perks for lawmakers.
- Questions about the propriety of campaign contributions were raised in the "Keating Five" affair, which concerned the relationship between five senators and a prominent savings and loan owner seeking to block an investigation of his financial dealings.
- Two top House employees pleaded guilty to charges of taking money from operations they had supervised.
- In 1995 a long investigation of sexual harassment charges against Sen. Robert Packwood, R-Ore., led to his forced resignation from office.

continues

Box 1 continued

- In 1995 Rep. Dan Rostenkowski, D-Ill., former chairman of the Ways and Means Committee, was found guilty of illegally receiving cash for personal use from the House post office. He later served a prison term.
- In 1995 Rep. Enid Waldholtze, R-Utah, retired after her husband was charged with felonies in conjunction with raising funds for her campaign.
- In 1997 Speaker Newt Gingrich, R-Ga., agreed to pay $300,000 in fines based on charges that he used nonprofit organizations for political purposes and misled the House Committee on Standards of Official Conduct.
- In 1998 Rep. Jay Kim, R-Calif., pleaded guilty to charges involving more than $250,000 in illegal campaign contributions.
- In 2001 Rep. Gary Condit, D-Calif., was embarrassed by disclosure of an affair with an office intern who later disappeared and was found murdered (authorities did not associate Condit with the murder).
- In 2002 Rep. James A. Traficant Jr., D-Ohio, was found guilty of receiving bribes in exchange for helping businesses get government contracts and of engaging in a pattern of racketeering since taking office in 1985.
- In 2002 Sen. Robert Torricelli, D-N.J., dropped out of a bid for reelection after it became clear that he would be defeated because of Senate ethics committee condemnation for accepting money and gifts from a donor.
- In 2002 the bankruptcy of the energy market giant Enron brought attention to the fact that the company had donated about $1.1 million to congressional candidates in the previous eleven years, including donations to 188 representatives and 71 senators of that Congress.
- In 2004 Rep. Tom DeLay, R-Texas, was admonished for improperly promising to endorse a colleague's son's candidacy for Congress in exchange for the colleague's vote on the floor, for creating the appearance that energy company donors were receiving special access when the Congress was considering energy legislation, and for asking a federal agency to intervene in Texas politics by finding a plane carrying Democratic members of the state legislature who were avoiding a quorum vote related to a Republican redistricting plan.
- In 2005 Rep. Tom DeLay, R-Texas, was indicted for funneling corporate money to Texas state legislative candidates by laundering it through a national party committee.

Enquirer and the *Star* has spread to the most respectable newspapers and magazines," Ornstein argues, "while network news divisions have begun to compete with tabloids like 'Inside Edition' and 'Hard Copy' with their own tabloid shows like 'Prime Time Live' and 'Dateline: NBC,' and with changed coverage on the nightly news." Stories or rumors of scandal—both individual and institutional—

have dominated news coverage of politics and politicians in recent decades more than at any other time in modern history, and not just in terms of column inches or broadcast minutes but in emphasis as well. Ornstein explains that "the expansion of radio and cable television talk shows also seems to have increased the speed with which bad news about Congress is disseminated and the frequency with which bad news is repeated. On many of these programs, there is a premium on a quick wit and a good one-liner and little time for sober, balanced commentary." [2]

Candidates for Congress quickly exploit themes that resonate with the public. As a result, running *for* Congress by running *against* Congress, an old art form in congressional campaigns, has gained an even more prominent place in recent decades. Indeed, many recent arrivals on Capitol Hill have promised to end "business as usual" in Washington and to push through reforms to "fix" Congress—to end the system of congressional perks, to stop the influence of special interests, and so on. Among each new cohort of legislators are members who complained about the "inside-the-beltway" (referring to the freeway that encircles the District of Columbia) mentality of their predecessors. The repetition of anti-Congress themes by its own members has contributed, no doubt, to the declining ratings for Congress and its lawmakers in public opinion polls.

The Plebiscitary Syndrome

Congress suffers from the increasingly plebiscitary nature of American politics, according to political scientist Robert Dahl. By "a movement toward plebiscitary politics," Dahl means more direct communication between the public and elected officials and the demise of intermediaries—such as parties and civic groups—that once served to represent public opinion to elected officials.[3] New technologies facilitate communication and feedback. For example, legislators get more frequent measures of public opinion through polls that have become more affordable with advances in telephone and computer technology. Radio and television call-in shows enable nearly every constituent to talk directly to a member of Congress from time to time. "Town meetings" broadcast on radio and television serve the same function. Computerized mass mailings flow into and out of Washington every day. Satellite technology allows members to communicate easily and inexpensively with groups in their districts or home states. Constituents can reach most members by electronic mail. And advances in air travel allow a large number of representatives and senators to be back in their districts and states for most weekends. For elected officials, the urge to exploit the new technologies is irresistible.

Plebiscitary politics may appear to be an encouraging development. It seems better to have public opinion influencing members' decisions than to have highly paid lobbyists who represent organized interests swaying congressional votes. But as Dahl notes, the effects of direct communication between the people and their representatives on Capitol Hill may not be so desirable for several reasons. First, elected officials and special interests could manipulate direct communication to their advantage. If the politicians are the ones who choose the time and place for direct communication, the process could create nothing more than a deceiving appearance of responsiveness. Second, the members of the public likely to communicate directly with members may not be representative of the members' larger constituencies. They would probably be people intensely interested in either politics in general or a single issue, who can afford, and know how to use, new information technologies. If so, then members' impressions of public opinion could be distorted by such communication. And third, as Madison might have argued, direct communication with more constituents could lead members to make premature public commitments on more issues, diminish the importance of their own experience and expertise, and reduce their flexibility in negotiating compromises in the legislative arena. The likely result would be that demagoguery and grandstanding would take precedence over resolving conflicts and solving problems. Public opinion could win out over the public interest.

If Dahl is right, then new information technologies could further intensify public frustration with Congress and encourage even more catering to public opinion by members. The emergence of a plebiscitary syndrome in Congress-marked by hypersensitivity to public opinion, grandstanding, rigidity, and paralysis, with new policy enacted only when the risk of inaction becomes too severe-could be the result. The natural response of elected officials and their challengers to such circumstances could be to encourage even more plebiscitary democracy and make matters worse.

The Perpetual Campaign

A close cousin to the plebiscitary syndrome is the perpetual campaign—the merging of campaigning and governing. Of course, we hope for a strong linkage between governing and campaigning as a basis for holding policymakers accountable. Yet in recent decades campaigning has become more fully integrated with governing. No longer is governing done in Washington and campaigning done at home. Members and top leaders now gear their daily routines to the demands of campaigning, and decisions by policymakers appear to be an extension of campaigns.

The costs of modern campaigns are staggering. Today a victor in a Senate race in an average-sized state can spend nearly $10 million; the number of House victors spending more than a million dollars is high and rising. (Many races in recent years actually have been far more expensive when one includes money spent by parties and outside groups.) For an incumbent seeking reelection, that is an average of more than $32,000 for each week served during a six-year Senate term and about $10,000 for each week served during a two-year House term. These figures reflect a rapid rise in campaign expenditures since the early 1990s. Competitive pressures, between incumbents and challengers and between the two parties, have produced a perpetual search for cash. The need for money reduces time for other activities, including time for the give-and-take of legislating.

The unending campaign extends beyond the rank-and-file members to congressional leaders. Party leaders spend many evenings and weekends at fund-raising events. Nearly all leaders have created their own political action committees ("leadership PACs," they have been called) to raise and distribute money to colleagues. Leaders have formed public relations task forces within their parties, and the campaign committees of the congressional parties have greatly expanded their activities. Perhaps most important, congressional leaders now often use political and information technology developed for campaigning in legislative battles. Professional consultants and pollsters help fashion legislative priorities and tactics. Parties conduct local polls to determine which local politicians might be the best candidates for Congress. Opposition research—digging up dirt on your election opponent—is conducted against congressional colleagues of the opposite party. Media campaigns are planned for major legislative proposals, with the assistance of television advertising specialists. Money, media, and partisanship feed on one another.

The Lobbying Cauldron

In recent decades the number of interest groups in Washington and the rest of the country has multiplied many times over. By one count, the number of groups increased from about one thousand in the late 1940s to more than seven thousand in the early 1980s. This is primarily a byproduct of the expanding scope of the federal government's activities—as federal programs affected more interests, more interests sought representation in Washington. Technological developments in transportation, information management, and communications have enabled scattered people, corporations, and even state and local governments to easily organize, raise money, and set up offices and staff in Washington. The process feeds on itself, with new groups forming to counter the influence of other groups. As a result, there has been a tremendous increase in the demands placed on members of Congress by lobbyists from organized groups.

Interest groups have not only multiplied but also become more diverse. In addition to groups associated with economic interests, many representing new industries, "citizens'" groups sprouted in the 1960s and 1970s and continue to grow in number. These are often outgrowths of national movements—such as those for civil rights, women's rights, children's rights, the elimination of hunger, consumers' rights, welfare rights, gay rights, environmental protection, and helping the homeless. Many of the groups attract funding from foundations and philanthropists, and some enjoy memberships numbering in the hundreds of thousands.

In recent years groups also have become more skilled in camouflaging their true identities—and thereby the nature of their interests. For most major legislative battles, coalitions of groups and corporations form under appealing, all-American names and pool their resources to fund mass media campaigns to generate support for their position. They often dissolve as quickly as they were created. Many coalitions are the handiwork of entrepreneurs in law firms, consulting outfits, and public relations shops, who are paid to coordinate the activity of the coalitions they spearhead.

Campaign finance reforms in the early 1970s enabled all interest groups, both for profit and nonprofit, to create political action committees and become active contributors to legislators' election campaigns. Campaign contributors have an edge over others in gaining the attention of legislators—and legislators often are quite open about it. More than that, the availability of money from political action committees has greatly reduced candidates' reliance on parties for the resources critical to winning elections. In the past decade unregulated contributions—called "soft money"—to parties and other political entities have exceeded direct, regulated contributions to candidates.

The roots have been taken out of grassroots lobbying. New technologies provide the ability to make highly targeted, highly efficient appeals to stimulate constituency demands on Washington. By the late 1980s computerized telephone messages allowed groups to communicate with many thousands of people within a few hours. Technology now allows a group to telephone its own members, a targeted group (such as one House member's constituency), or the general public and briefly interview the respondents about their views on a subject. For respondents who favor the group's position, it can provide a few more facts to reinforce their views, urge them to write letters to members of Congress, or quickly transfer the calls to the appropriate Capitol Hill offices before the respondents hang up. Several groups have developed television programs—some shown on the many cable television channels available in most communities—as a way of reaching specific audiences. Lobbyists are already take advantage of electronic mail and interactive video technologies to flood Congress with constituent messages. As a result, for a group with money, the absence of a large membership is not much of an obstacle to generating public pressure on members of Congress.

It would be a mistake, however, to conclude that all the pressuring in Washington comes from lobbyists. Members of Congress, particularly the most powerful, put the squeeze on lobbyists for campaign contributions. Furthermore, powerful members often call on the lobbyists to employ their resources to fund ad campaigns and engage in person-to-person lobbying to support the lawmakers in their legislative battles. In the cauldron of political relationships between legislators and organized interests, influence runs in many directions.

The Unexpected and the Complex

New issues—such as the war against terrorism—always present some difficulty for Congress. They often create problems for congressional committees, whose official jurisdictions were defined years earlier when no one anticipated those issues. Committees scramble to assert jurisdiction, and committee leaders or the parent chambers are asked to referee. After a certain amount of infighting and delay, committees eventually manage to adjust. In the view of some observers, however, new issues are surfacing at an increasing rate, and Congress's ability to adjust in a timely manner is becoming more and more strained.

The issues facing Congress are also becoming more technical and complex. Increasingly, expertise in science, engineering, information technology, economics, or other specialized fields is required to understand policy problems and alternatives. Congress often solves this problem, political scientist Theodore J. Lowi emphasizes, by setting broad policy goals and delegating the power to make the necessary technical decisions to experts in the executive branch.[4] In this way, Congress is able to respond to demands for action—but it does so at the cost of enhancing the executive branch's power over the details of public policy. Scientific and medical research, defense programs, environmental protection, the regulation of financial institutions, international trade, and many other fields of public policy are no longer within the common experiences of elected officials. Thus most members must look to competing interpretations of proposed legislation offered by executive agency officials, staff specialists, lobbyists, and outside experts.

The increasing complexity of the issues facing Congress is a result of the increasing complexity of American society, of technological and organizational innovation, and of the integration of the international and domestic economies. Fewer major policies can be debated in isolation from other major policies. For

Figure 2. Numbers of Bills Enacted and Pages Enacted

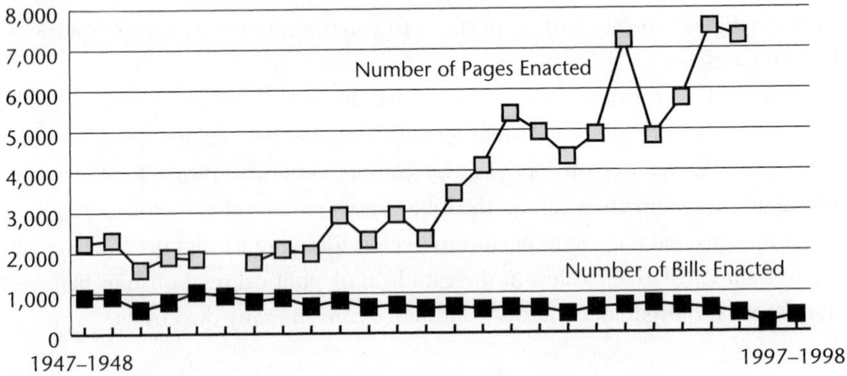

Source: *United States Statutes at Large* (Washington, D.C.: Government Printing Office, 1937–)

example, health care reform concerns issues such as employer-employee relations, economic growth, welfare reform, and tax policy. This complexity leads Congress to craft unwieldy bills, often written by multiple committees, laden with technical language, and comprising several hundred pages. Other factors, such as the desire to consolidate legislation into omnibus bills, have contributed to bill size as well. Figure 2 shows the increasing length of the average bill enacted in recent decades. The length of bills presents a serious challenge to legislators who want to understand the legislation on which they are asked to cast votes.

Political scientist Lawrence L. Dodd believes that Congress, at least as it now operates, cannot cope with the important issues of our time. In his view, the problem lies in the relationship between members and their constituents:

The voters may see the decay of urban infrastructure, sense the declining educational and job opportunities of their children, acknowledge the ecological damage of industrial pollution, and worry about the long-term effects of a mounting deficit. But as they consider their vote for senator and representative, the citizens override any broad concerns they may have with collective issues and vote in accord with ensuring immediate benefits; they do so by voting for the powerful local incumbent who can assist with a desired local defense contract or who can help them with their veterans claim or Medicare benefits. They do so because of the immediate influence that a powerful incumbent legislator can have on their particularized interests. Likewise, the legislators may share a growing concern with collective societal and economic reversals. But their efforts to maintain electoral

Table 1. Changes in the Apportionment of House Seats,
by Region, 1960–2000

Region	Post-1960 seats	Post-2000 seats	Difference
East	108	83	−25
Midwest	125	100	−25
South	133	154	+21
West	69	98	+29
Total	435	435	

Source: U.S. Census Bureau, www.census.gov/population/www/censusdata/apportionment.html.

security and exercise personal influence in Congress are best served by focusing on those particularized programs that mobilize group support, that help them build a solid reputation as effective legislators, and that ensure election. The emerging collective problems of the new era thus go unacknowledged and tear away at the fabric of society.[5]

If Dodd is right, then the public's ratings of congressional performance will be low for many years to come.

Congress's tendency is to allow the president to define solutions to the nation's problems and then to criticize those solutions from narrow, often parochial, perspectives. Unfortunately, plebiscitary politics, the proliferation of interest groups, and the new ways technology has provided for influencing members of Congress reinforce this tendency. Modern politics puts more pressure than ever on members to explain themselves in terms readily understood by the folks back home. Political scientist and congressman David E. Price, D-N.C., observes, "Members must constantly explain themselves and their actions in terms of ordinary knowledge. A decision that does not lend itself to such an explanation often has a heavy burden of proof against it. In the era of television journalism, of thirty-second ads and negative advertising, a defensive deference to ordinary knowledge has probably become more important in congressional behavior than it was before."[6] The gap between what legislators do and what they can explain seems to be widening.

The Power Shift

In recent decades demographic and social changes in American society have altered the composition of Congress in important ways. One significant change

Table 2. Numbers of Women and Minorities in the House
and Senate, 1971–2005

Congress (First year)	Women		African Americans		Hispanic Americans	
	House	Senate	House	Senate	House	Senate
92nd (1971)	12	1	12	1	5	1
93nd (1973)	14	0	15	1	5	1
94th (1975)	18	0	16	1	5	1
95th (1977)	18	0	16	1	5	0
96th (1979)	16	1	16	0	6	0
97th (1981)	19	2	16	0	6	0
98th (1983)	21	2	20	0	10	0
99th (1985)	22	2	19	0	11	0
100th (1987)	23	2	22	0	11	0
101st (1989)	25	2	23	0	11	0
102rd (1991)	29	2	25	0	10	0
103rd (1993)	48	6	38	1	17	0
104th (1995)	49	8	39	1	18	0
105th (1997)	51	9	37	1	18	0
106th (1999)	58	9	39	0	19	0
107th (2001)	49	13	36	0	19	0
108th (2003)	60	14	37	0	22	0
109th (2005)	70	14	40	1	22	2

Sources: *Vital Statistics on American Politics* (Washington, D.C.: CQ Press, 2000), 201; 107th–109th Congresses data collected by the author.

has occurred in the allocation of House seats among the states. The 435 seats of the House are reapportioned every ten years to reflect changes in the distribution of the nation's population across the states. A formula in law guides the Census Bureau, which calculates the number of districts for each state every ten years after the decennial census. Population shifts have allowed certain states in the South and West to gain seats in the House of Representatives at the expense of several eastern and midwestern states. The regional shifts are visible in Table 1.

The redistribution of seats away from the northern industrial states has reduced their political clout at a time when they could use it. The need for infrastructure repairs, worker retraining, low-income housing, and other government services is more severe in the old industrial states than in other regions of the country. Yet these states' declining influence in the House is reducing their ability to acquire financial assistance from the federal government. Indeed, the shift of power to the more conservative regions of the country has undercut congressional support for a major federal role in the rehabilitation of the industrial cities of the northern-tier states.

Economic growth, an influx of workers from the older industrial states, and the expansion of the middle class in the South and West have all spurred the population growth there. The most obvious consequence of these developments is that the South is no longer a one-party region, as it was just three decades ago. Republicans are now competitive in Senate races throughout the South and hold many House seats as well. As recently as 1960 Republicans held no Senate seats and only 6 of 104 House seats in the states of the old Confederacy. After the 1992 elections Republicans held 13 of the 22 Senate seats and 48 of the 125 House seats in the region, with their largest numbers in Florida and Texas. The southern Senate seats were critical to Republicans between 1981 and 1986, when they controlled the Senate, and again after 1994.

The houses of Congress have also acquired sizable contingents of women and minorities. The growing strength of women's and minority groups, the acquisition of political experience by women and minority politicians in state and local government, and new voting laws have contributed to the recent improvement in congressional representation. In 1993 the Senate gained its first black woman, Carol Moseley-Braun, D-Ill., and its first Native American, Ben Nighthorse Campbell, D-Colo. (who later switched parties). Table 2 shows the gains that women, African Americans, and Hispanics have made in Congress in recent years. Even more—many more—women and minorities have been running for Congress. More than one hundred women have been major party candidates for Congress in each election since 1992.

Though women and minorities remain greatly underrepresented in Congress, most observers agree that female and minority lawmakers have already had a substantial impact. Most obviously, the Congressional Caucus for Women's Issues (fifty-six members in 2001), the Congressional Black Caucus (thirty-seven members in 2001), and, to a lesser extent, the Congressional Hispanic Caucus (twenty-one members in 2001) have become important factions within the House Democratic Party, although all three have Republican members. More generally, party leaders have given higher priority to issues important to these groups, and the interests of women and minorities have had greater prominence in debates on many pieces of legislation. Indeed, social and economic problems seem to be more frequently discussed in the first person today—that is, more members refer to their personal experiences when addressing their colleagues and constituents. Two women have held first-tier positions (Rep. Nancy Pelosi of California was elected House Democratic whip in 2001 and then minority leader in 2002; Rep. Deborah Pryce of Ohio was elected House Republican Conference chair in 2002), others have held second-tier party positions, and even more have gained sufficient seniority to chair important committees and subcommittees. Only one African American, J. C. Watts of Oklahoma, who served as House Republican Conference chair in 1998–2002, has held a first-tier position. When Rep. Robert Menendez of New Jersey became the House Democratic Caucus chair in 2002, he became the highest-ranking Hispanic legislator in the history of Congress.

Notable changes have occurred as well in members' occupational profiles. Though lawyers and business executives still predominate (with nearly 250 lawyers and 150 executives) and the number of farmers has declined (down from about seventy-five in the 1950s to about twenty-five in 1994), the occupational backgrounds of members overall are now somewhat more diverse than three or four decades ago. Educators, for instance, have become more numerous.

These trends in the membership of Congress—the shift to the Sunbelt, the growing numbers of women and minority members, and the greater diversity in members' previous experience—are likely to continue well into this century. They will probably continue to be sources of change in the way Congress conducts its business and in the policy choices Congress makes.

Oscillating Party Control

Shifting majority control has been perhaps the most conspicuous change in Congress in recent years—the advent of Republican control of both houses after the 1994 elections, the switch back to Democratic control in the Senate in 2001, after Sen. James Jeffords of Vermont gave up his Republican affiliation, and the Republicans' victories in 2002 that allowed them to regain a Senate majority. With an evenly divided electorate, we have experienced a prolonged period of narrow majorities in both houses in the last decade.

Political scientist Richard F. Fenno Jr. argues that frequent changes in party control keep the arrogance of the majority party in check.[7] They may also reduce the temptation for a new majority to overreach itself once in office. For instance, according to Fenno, because in 1994 it had been forty years since the Republicans had controlled the House, when they took over they were both inexperienced and impatient. That led them to overstate their mandate from the 1994 elections and to translate that inflated mandate into rigid and ultimately unsuccessful legislative strategies; it may have contributed to the reelection of Democrat Bill Clinton to the presidency in 1996.

Fenno also observes that the long era of Democratic rule led the Republicans, prior to their 1994 takeover, to adopt radical measures to end it. The Republicans assumed an uncompromising stance in Congress, making legislating more difficult and heightening partisanship. Then after the Republicans gained control, Speaker Newt Gingrich, R-Ga., led a rhetorical assault on the very institution his party had fought to control, contributing to a further loss of public support for Congress.

If Fenno is correct, frequently alternating control of Congress will produce greater flexibility in Democratic and Republican policy positions, more pragmatic party strategies, greater civility in political discourse, and perhaps greater public support for the institution. A political "uncertainty principle"—that an uncertain electoral future breeds political moderation—may be at work.

Evidence that electoral uncertainty produces civility in politics seems hard to find. A reasonable argument can be made that split party control, even with occasional change in party control, has contributed to intensified partisanship and a politics of blame. The last decade has hardly yielded more moderation and civility.

The Geopolitical Partisan Bias

Since the 1970s Republicans have come to enjoy a considerable advantage over Democrats in electing legislators, for reasons that have to do with the states and districts in which elections are conducted. In the Senate, small states enjoy representation equal to that of large states, and yet small and large states currently differ greatly in the political composition of their electorates. Because the small states are disproportionately conservative and Republican, Democrats can gain votes in Senate elections nationwide and still be unable to dislodge enough Republicans to gain a Senate majority. Journalist Hendrick Hertzberg observes that in the 2000, 2002, and 2004 elections, Democrats received 2.4 million more votes than Republicans yet won eleven fewer Senate seats than the Republicans. "If each of every state's two senators is taken to represent half that state's population," Hertzberg notes, "then the Senate's fifty-five Republicans represent 131 million people, while its forty-four Democrats represent 161 million." [8]

The source of bias in House districts is different, but the effect is the same. Due to districting plans put in place by Republican legislatures, Democratic voters are packed in fewer districts than are Republican voters. Political scientists Jacob Hacker and Paul Pierson report that in 2004 President Bush won just less than 51 percent of the nationwide popular vote, but he came out ahead in 59 percent of the House districts. Republicans have more districts leaning their way even when nationwide partisan preferences are nearly evenly divided between the parties. [9]

These geopolitical advantages for the Republicans in the first decade of the twenty-first century have created an obstacle to alternation in party control of the houses of Congress. In the absence of a significant change in the electorate's partisan preferences, the Republican advantages in the Senate will last for many years. The Republican advantage in House districting will continue until a new round of redistricting occurs after the 2010 census. It may extend through the next decade if the Republicans maintain their edge in key state legislatures.

Revived Centralization

During most of the twentieth century, the standard assessment of Congress was that most policy decisions were really made by committees and ratified by the parent house. Analysts described reliance on committees as "decentralized" decision making, which contrasted with a hypothetical "centralized" pattern in which leaders of the majority party orchestrated policymaking. The decentralized pattern seemed appropriate—legislators who specialized in the subject matter of their committees would guide policymaking. In fact, the decentralized-centralized continuum always fit the larger House of Representatives better than the Senate. In the Senate, with the possibility of floor filibusters and the ability of senators to offer amendments on nearly any subject to most bills, more decisions were effectively made on the floor. Decision making in the Senate might better have been called "collegial" rather than either "centralized" or "decentralized."

The House and Senate went through a period of reform in the early 1970s that led observers of the day to warn about the dangers of fragmentation in congressional policymaking. In the House, majority-party Democrats guaranteed that most legislation would originate in well-staffed subcommittees, under the guidance of chairs who operated independently of full committee chairs. The coordinating and integrating influence of the central leaders and committee chairs appeared to be waning, and Congress seemed to be losing whatever ability it had to enact coherent policy. All of this happened at a time when pressures from new interest groups, new lobbying strategies, and new issues were mounting. Although Congress had become a more open and democratic institution, its capacity to manage the nation's affairs seemed diminished.

By the mid-1980s, however, Congress—again, particularly the House—had not turned out as many observers expected. The congressional agenda had become more focused, the parties more polarized, and central party leaders more assertive, and the decentralization of power to the subcommittees had been tempered. Although Congress did not revert to its old ways, it acquired a new mix of characteristics that justified a new label—"the postreform Congress." The root causes seemed to be changes in the parties' electoral coalitions, the dominance of budget politics, divided party control of the houses of Congress and the presidency, and the associated intensification of partisanship.

Perhaps the most important electoral trend of the late twentieth century was the replacement of some conservative southern Democrats with conservative Republicans. The partisan replacement made the Democrats in Congress more liberal, on balance, and reinforced the conservatism of congressional Republicans. This polarization of congressional parties led members to turn to party leaders for more central coordination of legislative and electoral strategies and contributed to sharpened partisanship in Washington.

The large federal budget deficit was a dominant force in legislative politics from 1980 to 1995. Few new federal programs were initiated, and much, if not most, of the period's important legislation consisted of large budget bills, particularly budget reconciliation bills, which are the handiwork of many congressional committees and affect the full range of federal programs over multiple years. This emphasis on large, all-encompassing budget bills further reduced the ability of committees and individual members to pursue policy initiatives. The great electoral importance of such comprehensive bills required that top leaders—the president and congressional party leaders—be intimately involved in the negotiations. With the advent of the war against terrorism, renewed large deficits guarantee that centralized strategizing and negotiations will continue.

Divided party control of the House, Senate, and the presidency has appeared to further intensify partisanship since the 1970s, as each institution and party has tried to avoid blame for ballooning deficits, unmet demands for action on social problems, and economic hard times. In the past three decades, top party leaders have begun to speak more authoritatively for their parties, and party regulars have looked to those leaders to define a legislative program and more aggressively promote party views in the news media. For at least a year or so after the Republicans gained a majority of House seats in 1994, Speaker Gingrich came to be recognized as the most powerful Speaker since Joseph Cannon, R-Ill., in the first decade of the twentieth century. Gingrich's successor, Speaker Dennis Hastert, R-Ill., remains remarkably active in all major policy decisions. Even Senate party leaders—Republican Bill Frist and Democrat Harry Reid—are deeply involved in defining and promoting legislative programs originating in party, rather than committee, deliberations.

Secret Government and Transparent Policymaking

Perhaps the most serious challenge to Congress's role in the American constitutional system is secret government necessitated by national security. The war against terrorism has revived fears that secrecy in the national security agencies will undermine Congress's ability to influence the direction of policy, to oversee the expenditure of public funds, and to hold executive officials accountable. Executive branch officials are hesitant to reveal certain information to members of Congress because they do not trust the legislators to keep it secret. For their part, legislators cannot know what information is being withheld from Congress, so secret government tends to breed distrust on Capitol Hill.

In the 1970s, in the aftermath of the Vietnam War and disclosures of misdeeds by intelligence agencies, Congress enacted various laws that required notification of Congress before the commitment of armed forces abroad, arms sales, and covert operations. Congress also granted itself the power to approve or dis-approve such actions in certain cases. In addition, Congress created intelligence committees and established other mechanisms for handling classified informa-tion. Yet since then, many members of Congress have been unwilling to assume some responsibility for national security policy by exploiting the new laws or insisting on presidential cooperation. Presidents of both parties have disliked being constrained by these laws, arguing at times that they unconstitutionally impinge on presidential powers. The result is continuing uncertainty about when congressional approval is required. Congressional participation in national secu-rity policymaking varies from case to case, driven as much by political consider-ations as by legal ones.

The fight against terrorism poses special challenges for members of Congress. More classified activity, more covert action, and a bewildering array of tech-nologies are involved. More domestic police activity is conducted under the umbrella of national security. The need for quick, coordinated, multiagency action has intensified. Congress is not well suited to effectively checking such executive action. It is open and slow, its division of labor among committees not well matched to the executive agencies involved, and its members are hesitant to challenge the executive branch on high-risk policies and in areas where the pub-lic is likely to defer to the president.

In President George W. Bush's second term, public support for the president's conduct of the war in Iraq eroded. Predictably, congressional opposition to the war increased, and the president had to fight off legislative efforts to constrain him. And yet the president's ability to deploy troops was not seriously chal-lenged.

A Resilient Institution

The ways in which representation and lawmaking are pursued in Congress have evolved in important ways in recent decades. As this essay has implied, not all of the developments have improved representation or lawmaking. Plebiscitary politics, interest group pressure, media coverage, and secret government present new challenges to members of Congress. They risk being so politically con-strained in their decision making that their potential for creative, independent policymaking will be undermined.

Still, however serious we judge the problems of today's Congress to be, we should remember that it is a remarkably resilient institution. Its place in the polit-ical process is not threatened. It is rich in resources; critics even charge that it is too strong. The legitimacy of its decisions is not seriously questioned by the chief executive, the courts, the states, or the American people, and Congress remains a vital check on the exercise of power by other institutions of government.

NOTES

1. John R. Hibbing and Elizabeth Theiss-Morse, *Congress as Public Enemy: Public Attitudes toward American Political Institutions* (New York: Cambridge University Press, 1995).

2. Norman J. Ornstein, "Congress Inside Out: Here's Why Life on the Hill Is Meaner Than Ever," *Roll Call,* September 20, 1993, 27.

3. Robert A. Dahl, "Americans Struggle to Cope with a New Political Order That Works in Opaque and Mysterious Ways," *Public Affairs Report* (Institute of Governmental Studies, University of California, Berkeley, September 1993) 1: 4–6.

4. See Theodore J. Lowi, "Toward a Legislature of the First Kind," in *Knowledge, Power, and the Congress,* ed. William H. Robinson and Clay H. Wellborn (Washington, D.C.: Congressional Quarterly, 1991), 9–36.

5. Lawrence C. Dodd, "Congress and the Politics of Renewal: Redressing the Crisis of Legitimation," in *Congress Reconsidered,* 5th ed., ed. Lawrence C. Dodd and Bruce I. Oppenheimer (Washington, D.C.: CQ Press, 1993), 426.

6. David E. Price, "Comment," in *Knowledge, Power, and the Congress,* ed. William H. Robinson and Clay H. Wellborn (Washington, D.C.: Congressional Quarterly, 1991), 128.

7. Richard F. Fenno Jr., *Learning to Govern: An Institutional View of the 104th Congress* (Washington, D.C.: Brookings Institution Press, 1997).

8. Hendrick Hertzberg, "Time to Filibuster?" *The New Yorker,* March 14, 2005, 55.

9. Jacob Hacker and Paul Pierson, "The Center No Longer Holds," *New York Times Magazine,* December 4, 2005, 32.

Chapter 7

The Presidency

7-1

from *Presidential Power*

Richard E. Neustadt

In his classic treatise Presidential Power, *Richard E. Neustadt presents a problem that confronts every occupant of the White House: His authority does not match the expectations for his performance. We expect our presidents to be leaders, Neustadt tells us, but the office guarantees no more than that they will be clerks. In the following excerpt, Neustadt explains that the key to presidential success lies in persuasion and shows how the ability to persuade depends on bargaining.*

THE LIMITS ON COMMAND suggest the structure of our government. The Constitutional Convention of 1787 is supposed to have created a government of "separated powers." It did nothing of the sort. Rather, it created a government of separated institutions *sharing* powers.[1] "I am part of the legislative process," Eisenhower often said in 1959 as a reminder of his veto.[2] Congress, the dispenser of authority and funds, is no less part of the administrative process. Federalism adds another set of separated institutions. The Bill of Rights adds others. Many public purposes can only be achieved by voluntary acts of private institutions; the press, for one, in Douglass Cater's phrase, is a "fourth branch of government." [3]

Source: Richard Neustadt, *Presidential Power and the Modern Presidents: The Politics of Leadership from Roosevelt to Reagan* (1960; New York: Simon & Schuster, 1990), 29–49.

And with the coming of alliances abroad, the separate institutions of a London, or a Bonn, share in the making of American public policy.

What the Constitution separates our political parties do not combine. The parties are themselves composed of separated organizations sharing public authority. The authority consists of nominating powers. Our national parties are confederations of state and local party institutions, with a headquarters that represents the White House, more or less, if the party has a President in office. These confederacies manage presidential nominations. All other public offices depend upon electorates confined within the states.[4] All other nominations are controlled within the states. The President and congressmen who bear one party's label are divided by dependence upon different sets of voters. The differences are sharpest at the stage of nomination. The White House has too small a share in nominating congressmen, and Congress has too little weight in nominating presidents for party to erase their constitutional separation. Party links are stronger than is frequently supposed, but nominating processes assure the separation.[5]

The separateness of institutions and the sharing of authority prescribe the terms on which a President persuades. When one man shares authority with another, but does not gain or lose his job upon the other's whim, his willingness to act upon the urging of the other turns on whether he conceives the action right for him. The essence of a President's persuasive task is to convince such men that what the White House wants of them is what they ought to do for their sake and on their authority. (Sex matters not at all; for *man* read *woman*.)

Persuasive power, thus defined, amounts to more than charm or reasoned argument. These have their uses for a President, but these are not the whole of his resources. For the individuals he would induce to do what he wants done on their own responsibility will need or fear some acts by him on his responsibility. If they share his authority, he has some share in theirs. Presidential "powers" may be inconclusive when a President commands, but always remain relevant as he persuades. The status and authority inherent in his office reinforce his logic and his charm.

Status adds something to persuasiveness; authority adds still more. When Truman urged wage changes on his secretary of commerce [Charles Sawyer] while the latter was administering the [recently seized] steel mills, he and Secretary Sawyer were not just two men reasoning with one another. Had they been so, Sawyer probably would never have agreed to act. Truman's status gave him special claims to Sawyer's loyalty or at least attention. In Walter Bagehot's charming phrase, "no man can *argue* on his knees." Although there is no kneeling in this country, few men—and exceedingly few cabinet officers—are immune to the impulse to say "yes" to the President of the United States. It grows harder to say "no" when they are seated in his Oval Office at the White House, or in his study on the second floor, where almost tangibly he partakes of the aura of his physical surroundings. In Sawyer's case, moreover, the President possessed formal authority to intervene in many matters of concern to the secretary of commerce. These matters ranged from jurisdictional disputes among the defense agencies to legislation pending before Congress and, ultimately, to the tenure of the secretary, himself. There is nothing in the record to suggest that Truman voiced specific threats when they negotiated over wage increases. But given his formal powers and their relevance to Sawyer's other interests, it is safe to assume that Truman's very advocacy of wage action conveyed an implicit threat.

A President's authority and status give him great advantages in dealing with the men he would persuade. Each "power" is a vantage point for him in the degree that other men have use for his authority. From the veto to appointments, from publicity to budgeting, and so down a long list, the White House now controls the most encompassing array of vantage points in the American political system. With hardly an exception, those who share in governing this country are aware that at some time, in some degree, the doing of *their* jobs, the furthering of *their* ambitions, may depend upon the President of the United States. Their need for presidential action, or their fear of it, is bound to be recurrent if not actually continuous. Their need or fear is his advantage.

A President's advantages are greater than mere listing of his "powers" might suggest. Those with whom he deals must deal with him until the last day of his term. Because they have continuing relationships with him, his future, while it lasts, supports his present influence. Even though there is no need or fear of him today, what he could do tomorrow may supply today's advantage. Continuing relationships may convert any "power," any aspect of his status, into vantage points in almost any case. When he induces other people to do what he wants done, a President can trade on their dependence now and later.

The President's advantages are checked by the advantages of others. Continuing relationships will pull in both directions. These are relationships of mutual dependence. A President depends upon the persons whom he would persuade; he has to reckon with his need or fear of them. They too will possess status or authority, or both, else they would be of little use to him. Their vantage points confront his own; their power tempers his.

Persuasion is a two-way street. Sawyer, it will be recalled, did not respond at once to Truman's plan for wage increases at the steel mills. On the contrary, the secretary hesitated and delayed and only acquiesced when he was satisfied that publicly he would not bear the onus of decision. Sawyer had some points of vantage all his own from which to resist presidential pressure. If he had to reckon with coercive implications in the President's "situations of strength," so had Truman to be mindful of the implications underlying Sawyer's place as a department head, as steel administrator, and as a cabinet spokesman for business. Loyalty is reciprocal. Having taken on a dirty job in the steel crisis, Sawyer had strong claims to loyal support. Besides, he had authority to do some things that the White House could ill afford. . . . [H]e might have resigned in a huff (the removal power also works two ways). Or . . . he might have declined to sign necessary orders. Or he might have let it be known publicly that he deplored what he was told to do and protested its doing. By following any of these courses Sawyer almost surely would have strengthened the position of management, weakened the position of the White House, and embittered the union. But the whole purpose of a wage increase was to enhance White House persuasiveness in urging settlement upon union and companies alike. Although Sawyer's status and authority did not give him the power to prevent an increase outright, they gave him capability to undermine its purpose. If his authority over wage rates had been vested by a statute, not by revocable presidential order, his power of prevention might have been complete. So Harold Ickes [Sr.] demonstrated in the famous case of helium sales to Germany before the Second World War.[6]

The power to persuade is the power to bargain. Status and authority yield bargaining advantages. But in a government of "separated institutions sharing power," they yield them to all sides. With the array of vantage points at his disposal, a President may be far more persuasive than his logic or his charm could make him. But outcomes are not guaranteed by his advantages. There remain the counter pressures those whom he would influence can bring to bear on him from vantage points at their disposal. Command has limited utility; persuasion becomes give-and-take. It is well that the White House holds the vantage points it does. In such a business any President may need them all—and more.

THIS VIEW OF POWER as akin to bargaining is one we commonly accept in the sphere of congressional relations. Every textbook states and every legislative session demonstrates that save in times like the extraordinary Hundred Days of 1933—times virtually ruled out by definition at mid-century—a President will often be unable to obtain congressional action on his terms or even to halt action he opposes. The reverse is equally accepted: Congress often is frustrated by the President. Their formal powers are so intertwined that neither will accomplish very much, for very long, without the acquiescence of the other. By the same token, though, what one demands the other can resist. The stage is set for that great game, much like collective bargaining, in which each seeks to profit from the other's needs and fears. It is a game played catch-as-catch-can, case by case. And everybody knows the game, observers and participants alike.

The concept of real power as a give-and-take is equally familiar when applied to presidential influence outside the formal structure of the federal government. . . . When he deals with [governors, union officials, company executives and even citizens or workers] a President draws bargaining advantage from his status or authority. By virtue of their public places or their private rights they have some capability to reply in kind.

In spheres of party politics the same thing follows, necessarily, from the confederal nature of our party organizations. Even in the case of national nominations a President's advantages are checked by those of others. In 1944 it is by no means clear that Roosevelt got his first choice as his running mate. In 1948 Truman, then the President, faced serious revolts against his nomination. In 1952 his intervention from the White House helped assure the choice of Adlai Stevenson, but it is far from clear that Truman could have done as much for any other candidate acceptable to him.[7] In 1956 when Eisenhower was President, the record leaves obscure just who backed Harold Stassen's efforts to block Richard Nixon from renomination as vice president. But evidently everything did not go quite as Eisenhower wanted, whatever his intentions may have been.[8] The outcomes in these instances bear all the marks of limits on command and of power checked by power that characterize congressional relations. Both in and out of politics these checks and limits seem to be quite widely understood.

Influence becomes still more a matter of give-and-take when Presidents attempt to deal with allied governments. A classic illustration is the long unhappy wrangle over Suez policy in 1956. In dealing with the British and the French before their military intervention, Eisenhower had his share of bargaining advantages but no effective power of command. His allies had their share of counterpressures, and they finally tried the most extreme of all: action despite him. His pressure then was instrumental in reversing them. But had the British government been on safe ground at home, Eisenhower's wishes might have made as little difference after intervention as before. Behind the decorum of diplomacy—which was not very decorous in the Suez affair—relationships among allies are not unlike relationships among state delegations at a national convention. Power is persuasion, and persuasion becomes bargaining. The concept is familiar to everyone who watches foreign policy.

In only one sphere is the concept unfamiliar: the sphere of executive relations. Perhaps because of civics textbooks and teaching in our schools, Americans instinctively resist the view that power in this sphere resembles power in all others. Even Washington reporters, White House aides, and congressmen are not immune to the illusion that administrative agencies comprise a single structure, "the" executive branch, where presidential word is law, or ought to be. Yet . . . when a President seeks something from executive officials his persuasiveness is subject to the same sorts of limitations as in the case of congressmen, or governors, or national committeemen, or private citizens, or foreign governments. There are no generic differences, no differences in kind and only sometimes in degree. The incidents preceding the dismissal of [General Douglas] MacArthur and the incidents surrounding seizure of the steel mills make it plain that here as elsewhere influence derives from bargaining advantages; power is a give-and-take.

Like our governmental structure as a whole, the executive establishment consists of separated institutions sharing powers. The President heads one of these; cabinet officers, agency administrators, and military commanders head others. Below the departmental level, virtually independent bureau chiefs head many more. Under mid-century conditions, federal operations spill across dividing lines on organization charts; almost every policy entangles many agencies; almost every program calls for interagency collaboration. Everything somehow involves the President. But operating agencies owe their existence least of all to one another—and only in some part to him. Each has a separate statutory base; each has its statutes to administer; each deals with a different set of subcommittees at the Capitol. Each has its own peculiar set of clients, friends, and enemies outside the formal government. Each has a different set of specialized careerists inside its own bailiwick. Our Constitution gives the President the "take-care" clause and the appointive power. Our statutes give him central budgeting and a degree of personnel control. All agency administrators are responsible to him. But they also are responsible to Congress, to their clients, to their staffs, and to themselves. In short, they have five masters. Only after all of those do they owe any loyalty to each other.

"The members of the cabinet," Charles G. Dawes used to remark, "are a president's natural enemies." Dawes had been Harding's budget director, Coolidge's vice president, and Hoover's ambassador to London; he also had been General Pershing's chief assistant for supply in World War I. The words are highly colored, but Dawes knew whereof he spoke. The men who have to serve so many masters cannot help but be somewhat the "enemy" of any one of them. By the same token, any master wanting service is in some degree the "enemy" of such a servant. A President is likely to want loyal support but not to relish trouble on his doorstep. Yet the more his cabinet members cleave to him, the more they may need help from him in fending off the wrath of rival masters. Help, though, is synonymous with trouble. Many a cabinet officer, with loyalty ill rewarded by his lights and help withheld, has come to view the White House as innately hostile to department heads. Dawes's dictum can be turned around.

A senior presidential aide remarked to me in Eisenhower's time: "If some of these cabinet members would just take time out to stop and ask themselves, 'What would I want if I were President?' they wouldn't give him all the trouble he's been having." But even if they asked themselves the question, such officials often could not act upon the answer. Their personal attachment to the President is all too often overwhelmed by duty to their other masters.

Executive officials are not equally advantaged in their dealings with a President. Nor are the same officials equally advantaged all the time. Not every officeholder can resist like a MacArthur or Sawyer. . . . The vantage points conferred upon officials by their own authority and status vary enormously. The variance is heightened by particulars of time and circumstance. In mid-October 1950, Truman, at a press conference, remarked of the man he had considered firing in August and would fire the next April for intolerable insubordination:

> Let me tell you something that will be good for your souls. It's a pity that you . . . can't understand the ideas of two intellectually honest men when they meet. General MacArthur . . . is a member of the Government of the United States. He is loyal to that Government. He is loyal to the President. He is loyal to the President in his foreign policy. . . . There is no disagreement between General MacArthur and myself.[9]

MacArthur's status in and out of government was never higher than when Truman spoke those words. The words, once spoken, added to the general's credibility thereafter when he sought to use the press in his campaign against the President. And what had happened between August and October? Near victory had happened, together with that premature conference on postwar plans, the meeting at Wake Island.

If the bargaining advantages of a MacArthur fluctuate with changing circumstances, this is bound to be so with subordinates who have at their disposal fewer powers, lesser status, to fall back on. And when officials have no powers in their own right, or depend upon the President for status, their counterpressure may be limited indeed. White House aides, who fit both categories, are among the most responsive men of all, and for good reason. As a director of the budget once remarked to me, "Thank God I'm here and not across the street. If the President doesn't call me, I've got plenty I can do right here and plenty coming up to me, by rights, to justify my calling him. But those poor fellows over there, if the boss doesn't call them, doesn't ask them to do something, what *can* they do but sit?" Authority and status so conditional are frail reliances in resisting a President's own wants. Within the White House precincts, lifted eyebrows may suffice to set an aide in motion; command, coercion, even charm aside. But even in the White House a President does not monopolize effective power. Even there persuasion is akin to bargaining. A former Roosevelt aide once wrote of cabinet officers:

> Half of a President's suggestions, which theoretically carry the weight of orders, can be safely forgotten by a Cabinet member. And if the President asks about a suggestion a second time, he can be told that it is being investigated. If he asks a third time, a wise Cabinet officer will give him at least part of what he suggests. But only occasionally, except about the most important matters, do Presidents ever get around to asking three times.[10]

The rule applies to staff as well as to the cabinet, and certainly has been applied *by* staff in Truman's time and Eisenhower's.

Some aides will have more vantage points than a selective memory. Sherman Adams, for example, as the assistant to the President under Eisenhower, scarcely deserved the appellation "White House aide" in the meaning of the term before his time or as applied to other members of the Eisenhower entourage. Although Adams was by no means "chief of staff" in any sense so sweeping—or so simple— as press commentaries often took for granted, he apparently became no more dependent on the President than Eisenhower on him. "I need him," said the President when Adams turned out to have been remarkably imprudent in the Goldfine case, and delegated to him, at least nominally, the decision on his own departure.[11] This instance is extreme, but the tendency it illustrates is common enough. Any aide who demonstrates to others that he has the President's consistent confidence and a consistent part in presidential business will acquire so much business on his own account that he becomes in some sense independent of his chief. Nothing in the Constitution keeps a well-placed aide from converting status into power of his own, usable in some degree even against the President—an outcome not unknown in Truman's regime or, by all accounts, in Eisenhower's.

The more an officeholder's status and his powers stem from sources independent of the President, the stronger will be his potential pressure on the President. Department heads in general have more bargaining power than do most members of the White House staff; but bureau chiefs may have still more, and specialists at upper levels of established career services may have almost unlimited reserves of the enormous power which consists of sitting still. As Franklin Roosevelt once remarked:

> The Treasury is so large and far-flung and ingrained in its practices that I find it almost impossible to get the action and results I want—even with Henry [Morgenthau] there. But the Treasury is not to be compared with the State Department. You should go through the experience of trying to get any changes in the thinking, policy, and action of the career diplomats and then you'd know what a real problem was. But the Treasury and the State Department put together are nothing compared with the Na-a-vy. The admirals are really something to cope with—and I should know. To change anything in the Na-a-vy is like punching a feather bed. You punch it with your right and you punch it with your left until you are finally exhausted, and then you find the damn bed just as it was before you started punching.[12]

In the right circumstances, of course, a President can have his way with any of these people. . . . [But] as between a President and his "subordinates," no less than others on whom he depends, real power is reciprocal and varies markedly with organization, subject matter, personality and situation. The mere fact that persuasion is directed at executive officials signifies no necessary easing of his way. Any new congressman of the Administration's party, especially if narrowly elected, may turn out more amenable (though less useful) to the President than any seasoned bureau chief "downtown." *The probabilities of power do not derive from the literary theory of the Constitution.*

THERE IS a widely held belief in the United States that were it not for folly or for knavery, a reasonable President would need no power other than the logic of his argument. No less a personage than Eisenhower has subscribed to that belief in many a campaign speech and press-conference remark. But faulty reasoning and bad intentions do not cause all quarrels with Presidents. The best of reasoning and of intent cannot compose them all. For in the first place, what the President wants will rarely seem a trifle to the people he wants it from. And in the second place, they will be bound to judge it by the standard of their own responsibilities, not his. However logical his argument according to his lights, their judgment may not bring them to his view.

Those who share in governing this country frequently appear to act as though they were in business for themselves. So, in a real though not entire sense, they are and have to be. When Truman and MacArthur fell to quarreling, for example, the stakes were no less than the substance of American foreign policy, the risks of greater war or military stalemate, the prerogatives of Presidents and field commanders, the pride of a proconsul and his place in history. Intertwined, inevitably, were other stakes as well: political stakes for men and factions of both parties; power stakes for interest groups with which they were or wished to be affiliated. And every stake was raised by the apparent discontent in the American public mood. There is no reason to suppose that in such circumstances men of large but differing responsibilities will see all things through the same glasses. On the contrary, it is to be expected that their views of what ought to be done and what they then should do will vary with the differing perspectives their particular responsibilities evoke. Since their duties are not vested in a "team" or a "collegium" but in themselves, as individuals, one must expect that they will see things for themselves. Moreover, when they are responsible to many masters and when an event or policy turns loyalty against loyalty—a day-by-day occurrence in the nature of the case—one must assume that those who have the duties to perform will choose the terms of reconciliation. This is the essence of their personal responsibility. When their own duties pull in opposite directions, who else but they can choose what they will do?

When Truman dismissed MacArthur, the latter lost three posts: the American command in the Far East, the Allied command for the occupation of Japan, and the United Nations command in Korea. He also lost his status as the senior officer on active duty in the United States armed forces. So long as he held those positions and that status, though, he had a duty to his troops, to his profession, to himself (the last is hard for any man to disentangle from the rest). As a public figure and a focus for men's hopes he had a duty to constituents at home, and in Korea and Japan. He owed a duty also to those other constituents, the UN governments contributing to his field forces. As a patriot he had a duty to his country. As an accountable official and an expert guide he stood at the call of Congress. As a military officer he had, besides, a duty to the President, his constitutional commander. Some of these duties may have manifested themselves in terms more tangible or more direct than others. But it would be nonsense to argue that the last negated all the rest, however much it might be claimed to override them. And it makes no more sense to think that anybody but MacArthur was effectively empowered to decide how he himself would reconcile the competing demands his duties made upon him.

. . . Reasonable men, it is so often said, *ought* to be able to agree on the requirements of given situations. But when the outlook varies with the placement of each man, and the response required in his place is for each to decide, their reasoning may lead to disagreement quite as well—and quite as reasonably. Vanity, or vice, may weaken reason, to be sure, but it is idle to assign these as the cause of . . . MacArthur's defiance. Secretary Sawyer's hesitations, cited earlier, are in the same category. One need not denigrate such men to explain their conduct. For the responsibilities they felt, the "facts" they saw, simply were not the same as those of their superiors; yet they, not the superiors, had to decide what they would do.

Outside the executive branch the situation is the same, except that loyalty to the President may often matter *less*. There is no need to spell out the comparison with governors of Arkansas, steel company executives, trade union leaders, and the like. And when one comes to congressmen who can do nothing for themselves (or their constituents) save as they are elected, term by term, in districts and through party structures differing from those on which a President depends, the case is very clear. An able Eisenhower aide with long congressional experience remarked to me in 1958: "The people on the Hill don't do what they might *like* to do, they do what they think they *have* to do in their own interest as *they* see it." This states the case precisely.

The essence of a President's persuasive task, with congressmen and everybody else, is to induce them to believe that what he wants of them is what their own appraisal of their own responsibilities requires them to do in their interest, not his. Because men may differ in their views on public policy, because differences in outlook stem from differences in duty—duty to one's office, one's constituents, oneself—that task is bound to be more like collective bargaining than like a reasoned argument among philosopher kings. Overtly or implicitly, hard bargaining has characterized all illustrations offered up to now. This is the reason why: Persuasion deals in the coin of self-interest with men who have some freedom to reject what they find counterfeit.

A PRESIDENT DRAWS influence from bargaining advantages. But does he always need them? . . . [S]uppose most players of the governmental game see policy objectives much alike, then can he not rely on logic (or on charm) to get him what he wants? The answer is that even then most outcomes turn on bargaining. The reason for this answer is a simple one: Most who share in governing have interests of their own beyond the realm of policy objectives. The sponsorship of policy, the form it takes, the conduct of it, and the credit for it separate their interest from the President's despite agreement on the end in view. In political government the means can matter quite as much as ends; they often matter more. And there are always differences of interest in the means.

Let me introduce a case externally the opposite of my previous examples: the European Recovery Program of 1948, the so-called Marshall Plan. This is perhaps the greatest exercise in policy agreement since the Cold War began. When the then secretary of state, George Catlett Marshall, spoke at the Harvard commencement in June 1947, he launched one of the most creative, most imaginative ventures in the history of American foreign relations. What makes this policy most notable for present purposes, however, is that it became effective upon action by the Eightieth Congress, at the behest of Harry Truman, in the election year 1948.[13]

Eight months before Marshall spoke at Harvard, the Democrats had lost control of both houses of Congress for the first time in fourteen years. Truman, whom the secretary represented, had just finished his second troubled year as President-by-succession. Truman was regarded with so little warmth in his own party that in 1946 he had been urged not to participate in the congressional campaign. At the opening of Congress in January 1947, Senator Robert A. Taft, "Mr. Republican," had somewhat the attitude of a President-elect. This was a vision widely shared in Washington, with Truman relegated thereby to the role of caretaker-on-term. Moreover, within just two weeks of Marshall's commencement address, Truman was to veto two prized accomplishments of Taft's congressional majority: the Taft-Hartley Act and tax reduction.[14] Yet scarcely ten months later the Marshall Plan was under way on terms to satisfy its sponsors, its authorization completed, its first-year funds in sight, its administering agency in being: all managed by as thorough a display of executive-congressional cooperation as any we have seen since the Second World War. For any President at any time this would have been a great accomplishment. In years before mid-century it would have been enough to make the future reputation of his term. And for a Truman, at this time, enactment of the Marshall Plan appears almost miraculous.

How was the miracle accomplished? How did a President so situated bring it off? In answer, the first thing to note is that he did not do it by himself. Truman had help of a sort no less extraordinary than the outcome. Although each stands for something more complex, the names of Marshall, Vandenberg, Patterson, Bevin, Stalin tell the story of that help.

In 1947, two years after V-J Day, General Marshall was something more than secretary of state. He was a man venerated by the President as "the greatest living American," literally an embodiment of Truman's ideals. He was honored at the Pentagon as an architect of victory. He was thoroughly respected by the secretary of the Navy, James V. Forrestal, who that year became the first secretary of defense. On Capitol Hill, Marshall had an enormous fund of respect stemming from his war record as Army chief of staff, and in the country generally no officer had come out of the war with a higher reputation for judgment, intellect, and probity. Besides, as secretary of state, he had behind him the first generation of matured foreign service officers produced by the reforms of the 1920s, and mingled with them, in the departmental service, were some of the ablest of the men drawn by the war from private life to Washington. In terms both of staff talent and staff use, Marshall's years began a State Department "golden age" that lasted until the era of McCarthy. Moreover, as his under secretary, Marshall had, successively, Dean Acheson and Robert Lovett, men who commanded the respect of the professionals and the regard of congressmen. (Acheson had been brilliantly successful at congressional relations as assistant secretary in the war and postwar years.) Finally, as a special undersecretary Marshall had Will Clayton, a man highly regarded, for good reason, at both ends of Pennsylvania Avenue.

Taken together, these are exceptional resources for a secretary of state. In the circumstances, they were quite as necessary as they obviously are relevant. The Marshall Plan was launched by a lame-duck Administration "scheduled" to leave office in eighteen months. Marshall's program faced a congressional leadership traditionally isolationist and currently intent upon economy. European aid was viewed with envy by a Pentagon distressed and virtually disarmed through budget cuts, and by domestic agencies intent on enlarged welfare programs. It was not viewed with liking by a Treasury intent on budget surpluses. The plan had need of every asset that could be extracted from the personal position of its nominal author and from the skills of his assistants.

Without the equally remarkable position of the senior senator from Michigan, Arthur H. Vandenberg, it is hard to see how Marshall's assets could have been enough. Vandenberg was chairman of the Senate Foreign Relations Committee. Actually, he was much more than that. Twenty years a senator, he was the senior member of his party in the chamber. Assiduously cultivated by FDR and Truman, he was a chief Republican proponent of bipartisanship in foreign policy and consciously conceived himself its living symbol to his party, to the country, and abroad. Moreover, by informal but entirely operative agreement with his colleague Taft, Vandenberg held the acknowledged lead among Senate Republicans in the whole field of international affairs. This acknowledgment meant more in 1947 than it might have meant at any other time. With confidence in the advent of a Republican administration two years hence, most of the gentlemen were in a mood to be responsive and responsible. The war was over, Roosevelt dead, Truman a caretaker, theirs the trust. That the senator from Michigan saw matters in this light his diaries make clear.[15] And this was not the outlook from the Senate side alone; the attitudes of House Republicans associated with the Herter Committee and its tours abroad suggest the same mood of responsibility. Vandenberg was not the only source of help on Capitol Hill. But relatively speaking his position there was as exceptional as Marshall's was downtown.

Help of another sort was furnished by a group of dedicated private citizens who organized one of the most effective instruments for public information seen since the Second World War: the Committee for the Marshall Plan, headed by the eminent Republicans whom FDR in 1940 had brought to the Department of War: Henry L. Stimson as honorary chairman and Robert P. Patterson as active spokesman. The remarkable array of bankers, lawyers, trade unionists, and editors, who had drawn together in defense of "internationalism" before Pearl Harbor and had joined their talents in the war itself, combined again to spark the work of this committee. Their efforts generated a great deal of vocal public support to buttress Marshall's arguments, and Vandenberg's, in Congress.

But before public support could be rallied, there had to be a purpose tangible enough, concrete enough, to provide a rallying ground. At Harvard, Marshall had voiced an idea in general terms. That this was turned into a hard program susceptible of presentation and support is due, in major part, to Ernest Bevin, the British foreign secretary. He well deserves the credit he has sometimes been assigned as, in effect, coauthor of the Marshall Plan. For Bevin seized on Marshall's Harvard speech and organized a European response with promptness and concreteness beyond the State Department's expectations. What had been virtually a trial balloon to test reactions on both sides of the Atlantic was hailed in London as an invitation to the Europeans to send Washington a bill of particulars. This they promptly organized to do, and the American Administration then organized in turn for its reception without further argument internally about the pros and cons of issuing the "invitation" in the first place. But for Bevin there might have been trouble from the secretary of the treasury and others besides.[16]

If Bevin's help was useful at that early stage, Stalin's was vital from first to last. In a mood of self-deprecation Truman once remarked that without Moscow's "crazy" moves "we would never have had our foreign policy . . . we never could have got a thing from Congress." [17] George Kennan, among others, had deplored the anti-Soviet overtone of the case made for the Marshall Plan in Congress and the country, but there is no doubt that this clinched the argument for many segments of American opinion. There also is no doubt that Moscow made the crucial contributions to the case.

By 1947 events, far more than governmental prescience or open action, had given a variety of publics an impression of inimical Soviet intentions (and of Europe's weakness) and a growing urge to "do something about it." Three months before Marshall spoke at Harvard, Greek-Turkish aid and promulgation of the Truman Doctrine had seemed rather to crystallize than to create a public mood and a congressional response. The Marshall planners, be it said, were poorly placed to capitalize on that mood, nor had the secretary wished to do so. Their object, indeed, was to cut across it, striking at the cause of European weakness rather than at Soviet aggressiveness, per se. A strong economy in Western Europe called, ideally, for restorative measures of continental scope. American assistance proffered in an anti-Soviet context would have been contradictory in theory and unacceptable in fact to several of the governments that Washington was anxious to assist. As Marshall, himself, saw it, the logic of his purpose forbade him to play his strongest congressional card. The Russians then proceeded to play it for him. When the Europeans met in Paris, Molotov walked out. After the Czechs had shown continued interest in American aid, a Communist coup overthrew their government while Soviet forces stood along their borders within easy reach of Prague. Molotov transformed the Marshall Plan's initial presentation; Czechoslovakia assured its final passage, which followed by a month the takeover in Prague.

Such was the help accorded Truman in obtaining action on the Marshall Plan. Considering his politically straitened circumstances he scarcely could have done with less. Conceivably some part of Moscow's contribution might have been dispensable, but not Marshall's or Vandenberg's or Bevin's or Patterson's or that of the great many other men whose work is represented by their names in my account. Their aid was not extended to the President for his own sake. He was not favored in this fashion just because they liked him personally or were spellbound by his intellect or charm. They might have been as helpful had all held him in disdain, which some of them certainly did. The Londoners who seized the ball, Vandenberg and Taft and the congressional majority, Marshall and his planners, the officials of other agencies who actively supported them or "went along," the host of influential private citizens who rallied to the cause—all these played the parts they did because they thought they had to, in their interest, given their responsibilities, not Truman's. Yet they hardly would have found it in their interest to collaborate with one another or with him had he not furnished them precisely what they needed from the White House. Truman could not do without their help, but he could not have had it without unremitting effort on his part.

The crucial thing to note about this case is that despite compatibility of views on public policy, Truman got no help he did not pay for (except Stalin's). Bevin scarcely could have seized on Marshall's words had Marshall not been plainly backed by Truman. Marshall's interest would not have comported with the exploitation of his prestige by a president who undercut him openly or subtly or even inadvertently at any point. Vandenberg, presumably, could not have backed proposals by a White House that begrudged him deference and access gratifying to his fellow partisans (and satisfying to himself). Prominent Republicans in private life would not have found it easy to promote a cause identified with Truman's claims on 1948—and neither would the prominent New Dealers then engaged in searching for a substitute.

Truman paid the price required for their services. So far as the record shows, the White House did not falter once in firm support for Marshall and the Marshall Plan. Truman backed his secretary's gamble on an invitation to all Europe. He made the plan his own in a well-timed address to the Canadians. He lost no opportunity to widen the involvements of his own official family in the cause. Averell Harriman, the secretary of commerce; Julius Krug, the secretary of the interior; Edwin Nourse, the Economic Council chairman; James Webb, the director of the budget—all were made responsible for studies and reports contributing directly to the legislative presentation. Thus these men were committed in advance. Besides, the President continually emphasized to everyone in reach that he did not have doubts, did not desire complications and would foreclose all he could. Reportedly his emphasis was felt at the Treasury, with good effect. And Truman was at special pains to smooth the way for Vandenberg. The senator insisted on "no politics" from the Administration side; there was none. He thought a survey of American resources and capacity essential; he got it in the Krug and Harriman reports. Vandenberg expected advance consultation; he received it, step by step, in frequent meetings with the President and weekly conferences with Marshall. He asked for an effective liaison between Congress and agencies concerned; Lovett and others gave him what he wanted. When the senator decided on the need to change financing and administrative features of the legislation, Truman disregarded Budget Bureau grumbling and acquiesced with grace. When, finally, Vandenberg desired a Republican to head the new administering agency, his candidate, Paul Hoffman, was appointed despite the President's own preference for another. In all these ways Truman employed the sparse advantages his "powers" and his status then accorded him to gain the sort of help he had to have.

Truman helped himself in still another way. Traditionally and practically, no one was placed as well as he to call public attention to the task of Congress (and its Republican leadership). Throughout the fall and winter of 1947 and on into the spring of 1948, he made repeated use of presidential "powers" to remind the country that congressional action was required. Messages, speeches, and an extra session were employed to make the point. Here, too, he drew advantage from his place. However, in his circumstances, Truman's public advocacy might have hurt, not helped, had his words seemed directed toward the forthcoming election. Truman gained advantage for his program only as his own endorsement of it stayed on the right side of that fine line between the "caretaker" in office and the would-be candidate. In public statements dealing with the Marshall Plan he seems to have risked blurring this distinction only once, when he called Congress into session in November 1947 asking both for interim aid to Europe and for peacetime price controls. The second request linked the then inflation with the current Congress (and with Taft), becoming a first step toward one of Truman's major themes in 1948. By calling for both measures at the extra session he could have been accused—and was—of mixing home-front politics with foreign aid. In the event no harm was done the European program (or his politics). But in advance a number of his own advisers feared that such a double call would jeopardize the Marshall Plan. Their fears are testimony to the narrowness of his advantage in employing his own "powers" for its benefit.[18]

It is symptomatic of Truman's situation that bipartisan accommodation by the White House then was thought to mean congressional consultation and conciliation on a scale unmatched in Eisenhower's time. Yet Eisenhower did about as well with opposition congresses as Truman did, in terms of requests granted for defense and foreign aid. It may be said that Truman asked for more extraordinary measures. But it also may be said that Eisenhower never lacked for the prestige his predecessor had to borrow. It often was remarked, in Truman's time, that he seemed a split personality, so sharply did his conduct differentiate domestic politics from national security. But personality aside, how else could he, in his first term, gain ground for an evolving foreign policy? The plain fact is that Truman had to play bipartisanship as he did or lose the game.

HAD TRUMAN LACKED the personal advantages his "powers" and his status gave him, or if he had been maladroit in using them, there probably would not have been a massive European aid program in 1948. Something of the sort, perhaps quite different in its emphasis, would almost certainly have come to pass before the end of 1949. Some American response to European weakness and to Soviet expansion was as certain as such things can be. But in 1948 temptations to await a Taft plan or a Dewey plan might well have caused at least a year's postponement of response had the outgoing Administration bungled its congressional or public or allied or executive relations. Quite aside from the specific virtues of their plan, Truman and his helpers gained that year, at least, in timing the American response. As European time was measured then, this was a precious gain. The President's own share in this accomplishment was vital. He made his contribution by exploiting his advantages. Truman, in effect, lent Marshall and the rest the perquisites and status of his office. In return they lent him their prestige and their own influence. The transfer multiplied his influence despite his limited authority in form and lack of strength politically. Without the wherewithal to make this bargain, Truman could not have contributed to European aid.

Bargaining advantages convey no guarantees. Influence remains a two-way street. In the fortunate instance of the Marshall Plan, what Truman needed was actually in the hands of men who were prepared to "trade" with him. He personally could deliver what they wanted in return. Marshall, Vandenberg, Harriman, et al., possessed the prestige, energy, associations, staffs essential to the legislative effort. Truman himself had a sufficient hold on presidential messages and speeches, on budget policy, on high-level appointments, and on his own time and temper to carry through all aspects of his necessary part. But it takes two to make a bargain. It takes those who have prestige to lend it on whatever terms. Suppose that Marshall had declined the secretaryship of state in January 1947; Truman might not have found a substitute so well equipped to furnish what he needed in the months ahead. Or suppose that Vandenberg had fallen victim to a cancer two years before he actually did; Senator Wiley of Wisconsin would not have seemed to Taft a man with whom the world need be divided. Or suppose that the secretary of the treasury had been possessed of stature, force, and charm commensurate with that of his successor in Eisenhower's time, the redoubtable George M. Humphrey. And what if Truman then had seemed to the Republicans what he turned out to be in 1948, a formidable candidate for President? It is unlikely that a single one of these "supposes" would have changed the final outcome; two or three, however, might have altered it entirely. Truman was not guaranteed more power than his "powers" just because he had continuing relationships with cabinet secretaries and with senior senators. Here, as everywhere, the outcome was conditional on who they were and what he was and how each viewed events, and on their actual performance in response.

Granting that persuasion has no guarantee attached, how can a President reduce the risks of failing to persuade? How can he maximize his prospects for effectiveness by minimizing chances that his power will elude him? The Marshall Plan suggests an answer: He guards his power prospects in the course of making choices. Marshall himself, and Forrestal and Harriman, and others of the sort held office on the President's appointment. Vandenberg had vast symbolic value partly because FDR and Truman had done everything they could, since 1944, to build him up. The Treasury Department and the Budget Bureau—which together might have jeopardized the plans these others made—were headed by officials whose prestige depended wholly on their jobs. What Truman needed from those "givers" he received, in part, because of his past choice of men and measures. What they received in turn were actions taken or withheld by him, himself. The things they needed from him mostly involved his own conduct where his current choices ruled. The President's own actions in the past had cleared the way for current bargaining. His actions in the present were his trading stock. Behind each action lay a personal choice, and these together comprised his control over the give-and-take that gained him what he wanted. In the degree that Truman, personally, affected the advantages he drew from his relationships with other men in government, his power was protected by his choices.

By "choice" I mean no more than what is commonly referred to as "decision": a President's own act of doing or not doing. Decision is so often indecisive, and indecision is so frequently conclusive, that *choice* becomes the preferable term. "Choice" has its share of undesired connotations. In common usage it implies a black-and-white alternative. Presidential choices are rarely of that character. It also may imply that the alternatives are set before the choice maker by someone else. A President is often left to figure out his options for himself. . . .

If Presidents could count upon past choices to enhance their current influence, as Truman's choice of men had done for him, persuasion would pose fewer difficulties than it does. But Presidents can count on no such thing. Depending on the circumstances, prior choices can be as embarrassing as they were helpful in the instance of the Marshall Plan. . . . Truman's hold upon MacArthur was weakened by his deference toward him in the past.

Assuming that past choices have protected influence, not harmed it, present choices still may be inadequate. If Presidents could count on their own conduct to provide them enough bargaining advantages, as Truman's conduct did where Vandenberg and Marshall were concerned, effective bargaining might be much easier to manage than it often is. In the steel crisis, for instance, Truman's own persuasiveness with companies and union, both, was burdened by the conduct of an independent wage board and of government attorneys in the courts, to say nothing of Wilson, Arnall, Sawyer, and the like. Yet in practice, if not theory, many of *their* crucial choices never were the President's to make. Decisions that are legally in others' hands, or delegated past recall, have an unhappy way of proving just the trading stock most needed when the White House wants to trade. One reason why Truman was consistently more influential in the instance of the Marshall Plan than in the steel case or the MacArthur case is that the Marshall Plan directly involved Congress. In congressional relations there are some things that no one but the President can do. His chance to choose is higher when a message must be sent, or a nomination submitted, or a bill signed into law, than when the sphere of action is confined to the executive, where all decisive tasks may have been delegated past recall.

But adequate or not, a President's choices are the only means in his own hands of guarding his own prospects for effective influence. He can draw power from continuing relationships in the degree that he can capitalize upon the needs of others for the Presidency's status and authority. He helps himself to do so, though, by nothing save ability to recognize the preconditions and the chance advantages and to proceed accordingly in the course of the choice making that comes his way. To ask how he can guard prospective influence is thus to raise a further question: What helps him guard his power stakes in his own acts of choice?

NOTES

1. The reader will want to keep in mind the distinction between two senses in which the word *power* is employed. When I have used the word (or its plural) to refer to formal constitutional, statutory, or customary authority, it is either qualified by the adjective "formal" or placed in quotation marks as "power(s)." Where I have used it in the sense of effective influence on the conduct of others, it appears without quotation marks (and always in the singular). Where clarity and convenience permit, *authority* is substituted for "power" in the first sense and *influence* for power in the second.

2. See, for example, his press conference of July 22, 1959, as reported in the New York Times, July 23, 1959.

3. See Douglass Cater, *The Fourth Branch of Government* (Boston: Houghton Mifflin, 1959).

4. With the exception of the vice presidency, of course.

5. See David B. Truman's illuminating study of party relationships in the Eighty-first Congress, *The Congressional Party* (New York: Wiley, 1959), especially chaps. 4, 6, 8.

6. As secretary of the interior in 1939, Harold Ickes refused to approve the sale of helium to Germany despite the insistence of the State Department and the urging of President Roosevelt. Without the secretary's approval, such sales were forbidden by statute. See *The Secret Diaries of Harold L. Ickes* (New York: Simon & Schuster, 1954), vol. 2, especially pp. 391–93, 396–99.

In this instance the statutory authority ran to the secretary as a matter of his discretion. A President is unlikely to fire cabinet officers for the conscientious exercise of such authority. If the President did so, their successors might well be embarrassed both publicly and at the Capitol were they to reverse decisions previously taken. As for a President's authority to set aside discretionary determinations of this sort, it rests, if it exists at all, on shaky legal ground not likely to be trod save in the gravest of situations.

7. Truman's *Memoirs* indicate that having tried and failed to make Stevenson an avowed candidate in the spring of 1952, the President decided to support the candidacy of Vice

President Barkley. But Barkley withdrew early in the convention for lack of key northern support. Though Truman is silent on the matter, Barkley's active candidacy nearly was revived during the balloting, but the forces then aligning to revive it were led by opponents of Truman's Fair Deal, principally Southerners. As a practical matter, the President could not have lent his weight to their endeavors and could back no one but Stevenson to counter them. The latter's strength could not be shifted, then, to Harriman or Kefauver. Instead the other Northerners had to be withdrawn. Truman helped withdraw them. But he had no other option. See Harry S Truman, *Memoirs*, vol. 2, *Years of Trial and Hope* (Garden City, N.Y.: Doubleday, Time Inc., 1956), pp. 495–96.

8. The reference is to Stassen's public statement of July 23, 1956, calling for Nixon's replacement on the Republican ticket by Governor Herter of Massachusetts, the later secretary of state. Stassen's statement was issued after a conference with the President. Eisenhower's public statements on the vice-presidential nomination, both before and after Stassen's call, permit of alternative inferences: either that the President would have preferred another candidate, provided this could be arranged without a showing of White House dictation, or that he wanted Nixon on condition that the latter could show popular appeal. In the event, neither result was achieved. Eisenhower's own remarks lent strength to rapid party moves that smothered Stassen's effort. Nixon's nomination thus was guaranteed too quickly to appear the consequence of popular demand. For the public record on this matter see reported statements by Eisenhower, Nixon, Stassen, Herter, and Leonard Hall (the National Republican Chairman) in the *New York Times* for March 1, 8, 15, 16; April 27; July 15, 16, 25–31; August 3, 4, 17, 23, 1956. See also the account from private sources by Earl Mazo in *Richard Nixon: A Personal and Political Portrait* (New York: Harper, 1959), pp. 158–87

9. Stenographic transcript of presidential press conference, October 19, 1950, on file in the Truman Library at Independence, Missouri.

10. Jonathan Daniels, *Frontier on the Potomac* (New York: Macmillan, 1946), pp. 31–32.

11. Transcript of presidential press conference, June 18, 1958, in *Public Papers of the Presidents Dwight D. Eisenhower, 1958* (Washington, D.C.: National Archives, 1959), p. 479. In the summer of 1958, a congressional investigation into the affairs of a New England textile manufacturer, Bernard Goldfine, revealed that Sherman Adams had accepted various gifts and favors from him (the most notoriety attached to a vicuna coat). Adams also had made inquiries about the status of a Federal Communications Commission proceeding in which Goldfine was involved. In September 1958 Adams was allowed to resign. The episode was highly publicized and much discussed in that year's congressional campaigns.

12. As reported in Marriner S. Eccles (*Beckoning Frontiers*, New York: Knopf, 1951), p. 336.

13. In drawing together these observations on the Marshall Plan, I have relied on the record of personal participation by Joseph M. Jones, *The Fifteen Weeks* (New York: Viking, 1955), especially pp. 89–256; on the recent study by Harry Bayard Price, *The Marshall Plan and Its Meaning* (Ithaca: Cornell University Press, 1955), especially pp. 1–86; on the Truman *Memoirs*, vol. 2, chaps. 7–9; on Arthur H. Vandenberg, Jr., ed., *The Private Papers of Senator Vandenberg* (Boston: Houghton Mifflin, 1952), especially pp. 373 ff.; and on notes of my own made at the time. This is an instance of policy development not covered, to my knowledge, by any of the university programs engaged in the production of case studies.

14. Secretary Marshall's speech, formally suggesting what became known as the Marshall Plan, was made at Harvard on June 5, 1947. On June 20 the President vetoed the Taft-Hartley

Act; his veto was overridden three days later. On June 16 he vetoed the first of two tax reduction bills (HR 1) passed at the first session of the Eightieth Congress; the second of these (HR 3950), a replacement for the other, he also disapproved on July 18. In both instances his veto was narrowly sustained.

15. *Private Papers of Senator Vandenberg*, pp. 378–79, 446.

16. The initial reluctance of the Secretary of the Treasury, John Snyder, to support large-scale spending overseas became a matter of public knowledge on June 25, 1947. At a press conference on that day he interpreted Marshall's Harvard speech as a call on Europeans to help themselves, by themselves. At another press conference the same day, Marshall for his own part had indicated that the United States would consider helping programs on which Europeans agreed. The next day Truman held a press conference and was asked the inevitable question. He replied, "General Marshall and I are in complete agreement." When pressed further, Truman remarked sharply, "The secretary of the treasury and the secretary of state and the President are in complete agreement." Thus the President cut Snyder off, but had programming gathered less momentum overseas, no doubt he would have been heard from again as time passed and opportunity offered.

The foregoing quotations are from the stenographic transcript of the presidential press conference June 26, 1947, on file in the Truman Library at Independence, Missouri.

17. A remark made in December 1955, three years after he left office, but not unrepresentative of views he expressed, on occasion, while he was President.

18. This might also be taken as testimony to the political timidity of officials in the State Department and the Budget Bureau where that fear seems to have been strongest. However, conversations at the time with White House aides incline me to believe that there, too, interjection of the price issue was thought a gamble and a risk. For further comment see my "Congress and the Fair Deal: A Legislative Balance Sheet," *Public Policy*, vol. 5 (Cambridge: Harvard University Press, 1954), pp. 362–64.

7-2

from *Going Public*

Samuel Kernell

Richard Neustadt, writing in 1960, judged that the president's ability to lead depended on skill at the bargaining table in cutting deals with other politicians. In the following essay Samuel Kernell examines how the leadership strategy of modern presidents has evolved. He finds that, rather than limiting their leadership to quiet diplomacy with fellow Washingtonians, modern presidents often "go public," a set of activities borrowed from presidential election campaigns and directed toward persuading other politicians to adopt their policy preferences. Some examples of going public are a televised press conference, a special prime-time address to the nation, traveling outside Washington to deliver a speech to a business or professional convention, and a visit to a day care center with network cameras trailing behind.

Introduction: Going Public in Theory and Practice

WHEN PRESIDENT BUSH delivered his State of the Union address to the joint assembly of the mostly Democratic Congress in January 1992, he assumed what has become a familiar stance with Congress:

> I pride myself that I am a prudent man, and I believe that patience is a virtue. But I understand that politics is for some a game. . . . I submit my plan tomorrow. And I am asking you to pass it by March 20. And I ask the American people to let you know they want this action by March 20.
>
> From the day after that, if it must be: The battle is joined.
>
> And you know when principle is at stake, I relish a good fair fight.

Once upon a time, these might have been fighting words, but in this era of divided government, with the legislative and executive branches controlled by different parties, and presidents who therefore routinely enlist public support in their dealings with other Washington politicians, such rhetoric caused hardly a ripple in Congress.

Source: Samuel Kernell, *Going Public: New Strategies of Presidential Leadership,* 3d ed. (Washington, D.C.: CQ Press, 1997), 1–12, 17–26, 34–38, 57–64.

By 1992, presidential appeals for public support had, in fact, become commonplace. Jimmy Carter delivered four major television addresses on the energy crisis alone and was about to give a fifth when his pollster convinced him that he would be wasting his time. Richard Nixon employed prime-time television so extensively to promote his policies on Vietnam that the Federal Communications Commission (FCC) took an unprecedented step when it applied the "fairness doctrine" to a presidential appeal and granted critics of the war response time on the networks.[1] (In the past, the FCC had occasionally invoked the "equal time" rule during presidential campaigns.) More than any other of Bush's predecessors, Ronald Reagan excelled in rallying public opinion behind presidential policies, but by the end of his second term, he had worn out his welcome with the networks, who stood to lose at least $200,000 in advertising each time he delivered one of his prime-time addresses. They instituted an independent assessment of the likely newsworthiness of the president's address, thereby managing to pare down the frequency of Reagan's televised speeches.[2]

I call the approach to presidential leadership that has come into vogue at the White House "going public." It is a strategy whereby a president promotes himself and his policies in Washington by appealing to the American public for support. Forcing compliance from fellow Washingtonians by going over their heads to appeal to their constituents is a tactic not unknown during the first half of the century, but it was seldom attempted. Theodore Roosevelt probably first enunciated the strategic principle of going public when he described the presidency as the "bully pulpit." Moreover, he occasionally put theory into practice with public appeals for his Progressive reforms. During the next thirty years, other presidents also periodically summoned public support to help them in their dealings with Congress. Perhaps the most famous such instance is Woodrow Wilson's ill-fated whistle-stop tour of the country on behalf of his League of Nations treaty. Another historic example is Franklin D. Roosevelt's series of radio "fireside chats," which were designed less to subdue congressional opposition than to remind politicians throughout Washington of his continuing national mandate for the New Deal.

These historical instances are significant in large part because they were rare. Unlike President Nixon, who thought it important "to spread the White House around" by traveling and speaking extensively,[3] these earlier presidents were largely confined to Washington and obliged to speak to the country through the nation's newspapers. The concept and legitimizing precedents of going public may have been established during these years, but the emergence of presidents who *routinely* do so to promote their policies in Washington awaited the development of modern systems of transportation and mass communications. Going public should be appreciated as a strategic adaptation to the information age.

The regularity with which recent presidents have sought public backing for their Washington dealings has altered the way politicians both inside and outside the White House regard the office. The following [excerpts] of this book present numerous instances of presidents preoccupied with public relations, as if these activities chiefly determined their success. Cases are recounted of other Washington politicians intently monitoring the president's popularity ratings and his addresses on television, as if his performance in these realms governed their own behavior. Also examined are testimonials of central institutional figures, such as those from various Speakers of the House of Representatives, citing the president's prestige and rhetoric as they explain Congress's actions. If the public ruminations of politicians are to be believed, the president's effectiveness in rallying public support has become a primary consideration for those who do business with him.

Presidential Theory

Going public merits study because presidents now appeal to the public routinely. But there is another reason as well. Compared with many other aspects of the modern presidency, scholarship has only recently directed its attention toward this feature of the president's repertoire. Although going public had not become a keystone of presidential leadership in the 1950s and 1960s when much of the influential scholarship on the subject was written, sufficient precedents were available for scholars to consider its potential for presidential leadership in the future.

Probably the main reason presidential scholarship has shortchanged going public is its fundamental incompatibility with bargaining. Presidential power is the "power to bargain," as Richard E. Neustadt taught a generation of students of the presidency.[4] When Neustadt gave this theme its most evocative expression in 1960, the "bargaining president" had already become a centerpiece of pluralist theories of American politics. Nearly a decade earlier, Robert A. Dahl and Charles E. Lindblom had described the politician in America generically as "the human embodiment of a bargaining society." They made a special point to include the president in writing that despite his possessing "more hierarchical controls than any other single figure in the government . . . like everyone else . . . the President must bargain constantly." [5] Since Neustadt's landmark study, other major works in the field have reinforced and elaborated on the concept of the bargaining president.[6]

Going public violates bargaining in several ways. First, it rarely includes the kinds of exchanges necessary, in pluralist theory, for the American political system to function properly. At times, going public will be merely superfluous—

fluff compared with the substance of traditional political exchange. Practiced in a dedicated way, however, it can threaten to displace bargaining.

Second, going public fails to extend benefits for compliance, but freely imposes costs for noncompliance. In appealing to the public to "tell your senators and representatives by phone, wire, and Mailgram that the future hangs in balance," the president seeks the aid of a third party—the public—to force other politicians to accept his preferences.[7] If targeted representatives are lucky, the president's success may cost them no more than an opportunity at the bargaining table to shape policy or to extract compensation. If unlucky, they may find themselves both capitulating to the president's wishes and suffering the reproach of constituents for having resisted him in the first place. By imposing costs and failing to offer benefits, going public is more akin to force than to bargaining. Nelson W. Polsby makes this point when he says that members of Congress may "find themselves ill disposed toward a president who prefers to deal indirectly with them [by going public] through what they may interpret as coercion rather than face-to-face in the spirit of mutual accommodation."[8] The following comment of one senator may well sum up commonly felt sentiments, if not the actions, of those on Capitol Hill who find themselves repeatedly pressured by the president's public appeals: "A lot of Democrats, even if they like the President's proposal, will vote against him because of his radio address on Saturday."[9]

Third, going public entails public posturing. To the extent that it fixes the president's bargaining position, posturing makes subsequent compromise with other politicians more difficult. Because negotiators must be prepared to yield some of their clients' preferences to make a deal, bargaining proverbially proceeds best behind closed doors. Consider the difficulty Ronald Reagan's widely publicized challenge "My tax proposal is a line drawn in dirt" posed for subsequent budget negotiations in Washington.[10] Similarly, during his nationally televised State of the Union address in 1994, President Bill Clinton sought to repair his reputation as someone too willing to compromise away his principles by declaring to the assembled joint session of Congress, "If you send me [health care] legislation that does not guarantee every American private health insurance that can never be taken away, you will force me to take this pen, veto the legislation, and we'll come right back here and start all over again."[11] Not only did these declarations threaten to cut away any middle ground on which a compromise might be constructed, they probably stiffened the resolve of the president's adversaries, some of whom would later be needed to pass the administration's legislative program.

Finally, and possibly most injurious to bargaining, going public undermines the legitimacy of other politicians. It usurps their prerogatives of office, denies their role as representatives, and questions their claim to reflect the interests of their constituents. For a traditional bargaining stance with the president to be restored, these politicians would first have to reestablish parity, probably at a cost of conflict with the White House.[12]

Given these fundamental incompatibilities, one may further speculate that by spoiling the bargaining environment, going public renders the president's future influence ever more dependent upon his ability to generate popular support for himself and his policies. The degree to which a president draws upon public opinion determines the kind of leader he will be.

Presidential Practice

Bargaining and going public have never been, in principle, particularly congenial styles of leadership. One can imagine, however, that in an earlier era, when technology limited the capacity and tendency of presidents to engage in public relations, these two strategies of leadership might have coexisted in quiet tension. In modern times, though, when going public is likely to take the form of a political campaign which engages the energies of numerous presidential aides and the president's attention, the choice has become clear: to choose one strategy of leadership makes it increasingly difficult to undertake the other. And since they cannot be naively combined, the decision to go public at one juncture may preclude and undermine the opportunity to bargain at another, and vice versa. All this means that the decision to bargain or to go public must be carefully weighed.

The two case studies below reveal that modern presidents and their advisers carefully attend to this strategic issue. As we shall do throughout this book, we compare instances of presidential success and failure in order to understand the potential gains and losses embedded in presidents' choices.

Ronald Reagan Enlists Public Opinion as a Lever

No president has enlisted public strategies to better advantage than did Ronald Reagan. Throughout his tenure, he exhibited a full appreciation of bargaining and going public as the modern office's principal strategic alternatives. The following examples from a six-month survey of White House news coverage show how entrenched this bifurcated view of presidential strategy has become. The survey begins in late November 1984, when some members of the administration were pondering how the president might exploit his landslide victory and others were preparing a new round of budget cuts and a tax reform bill for the next Congress.

November 29, 1984. Washington Post columnist Lou Cannon reported the following prediction from a White House official: "We're going to have confrontation on spending and consultation on tax reform." The aide explained, "We have somebody to negotiate with us on tax reform, but may not on budget cuts." [13] By "confrontation" he was referring to the president's success in appealing to the public on national television, that is, in going public. By "consultation" he meant bargaining.

January 25, 1985. The above prediction proved accurate two months later when another staffer offered as pristine an evocation of going public as one is likely to find: "We have to look at it, in many ways, like a campaign. He [Reagan] wants to take his case to the people. You have a constituency of 535 legislators as opposed to 100 million voters. But the goal is the same—to get the majority of voters to support your position." [14]

February 10, 1985. In a nationally broadcast radio address, President Reagan extended an olive branch inviting members of Congress to "work with us in the spirit of cooperation and compromise" on the budget. This public statement probably did little to allay the frequently voiced suspicion of House Democratic leaders that such overtures were mainly intended for public consumption. One Reagan aide insisted, however, that the president simply sought to reassure legislators that "he would not 'go over their heads' and campaign across the country for his budget without trying first to reach a compromise." [15] In this statement the aide implicitly concedes the harm public pressure can create for bargaining but seeks to incorporate it advantageously into the strategic thinking of the politicians with whom the administration must deal by not forswearing its use.

March 9, 1985. After some public sparring, the administration eventually settled down to intensive budget negotiations with the Republican-led Senate Finance Committee. Failing to do as well as he would like, however, Reagan sent a message to his party's senators through repeated unattributed statements to the press that, if necessary, he would "go to the people to carry our message forward." [16] Again, public appeals, though held in reserve, were threatened.

March 11, 1985. In an interview with a *New York Times* correspondent, a senior Reagan aide sized up his president: "He's liberated, he wants to get into a fight, he feels strongly and wants to push his program through himself. . . . Reagan never quite believed his popularity before the election, never believed the polls. Now he has it, and he's going to push . . . ahead with our agenda." [17]

May 16, 1985. To avoid entangling tax reform with budget deliberations in Congress, Reagan, at the request of Republican leaders, delayed unveiling his tax reform proposal until late May. A couple of weeks before Reagan's national television address on the subject, White House aides began priming the press with leaks on the proposal's content and promises that the president would follow it with a public relations blitz. In the words of one White House official, the plan was to force Congress to make a "binary choice between tax reform or no tax reform." [18] The administration rejected bargaining, as predicted nearly six months earlier by a White House aide, apparently for two strategic reasons.

First, Reagan feared that in a quietly negotiated process, the tax reform package would unravel under the concerted pressure of the special interests. Second, by taking the high profile approach of "standing up for the people against the special interests," in the words of one adviser, tax reform might do for Republicans what social security did for Democrats—make them the majority party.[19]

During these six months when bargaining held out promise—as it had during negotiations with the Senate Finance Committee—public appeals were held in reserve. The White House occasionally, however, threatened an appeal in trying to gain more favorable consideration. On other occasions, when opponents of the president's policies appeared capable of extracting major concessions—House Democrats on the budget and interest groups on tax reform, for example—the White House disengaged from negotiation and tried through public relations to force Congress to accept his policies. Although by 1985 news items such as the preceding excerpts seemed unexceptional as daily news, they are a recent phenomenon. One does not routinely find such stories in White House reporting twenty years earlier when, for example, John Kennedy's legislative agenda was stalled in Congress.

President Clinton Snares Himself by Bargaining

Shortly after assuming office, President Clinton received some bad news. The Bush administration had underestimated the size of the next year's deficit by $50 billion. The president's campaign promises of new domestic programs and a middle-class tax cut would have to be put on hold in favor of fulfilling his third, now urgent pledge to trim $500 billion from the deficit over the next five years. On February 17, 1993, President Clinton appeared before a joint session of Congress and a national television audience to unveil his deficit reduction package. The president's deficit-cutting options were constrained by two considerations: he wanted to include minimal stimulus spending to honor his campaign promise, and he faced a Congress controlled by fellow Democrats who were committed to many of the programs under the budget ax. Even with proposed cuts in defense spending, the only way the budget could accommodate these constraints was through a tax increase. The package raised taxes on the highest income groups and introduced a broad energy consumption tax. During the following weeks, the president and his congressional liaison team quietly lobbied Congress. He would not again issue a public appeal until the eve of the final vote in August.

The president soon learned that Republicans in both chambers had united in opposition to the administration proposal. Led by Newt Gingrich in the House of Representatives and Bob Dole in the Senate, Republicans retreated to the sidelines and assumed the role of Greek chorus, ominously chanting "tax and spend liberals." This meant that the administration needed virtually every Democratic vote to win. Democratic members appreciated this, and many began exploiting the rising value of their votes to extract concessions that would make the legislation more favorable to their constituents.

By June the president's bargaining efforts had won him a watered down bill that even he had difficulty being enthusiastic about. Meanwhile, the Republicans' public relations campaign had met with success. The American public had come to regard President Clinton as a "tax and spend liberal." Whereas shortly after the speech, the *Los Angeles Times* had found half of their polling respondents willing to describe the president's initiative as "bold and innovative" and only 35 percent of them willing to describe it as "tax and spend," by June these numbers had reversed. Now, 53 percent labeled it "tax and spend" and only 28 percent still regarded it as "bold and innovative." [20] Given this turnaround in the public's assessment of the initiative, it was not surprising that the public also downgraded its evaluation of the initiative's sponsor. During the previous five months, President Clinton's approval rating had plunged from 58 to 41 percent.

This was the situation when several of Clinton's senior campaign consultants sounded the alarm in a memo: in only six months the president had virtually exhausted his capacity for leadership. If he did not turn back the current tide of public opinion, he would be weakened beyond repair. In response, the president assembled his senior advisers to evaluate current strategy. This set the stage for a confrontation between those advisers who represented the president in bargaining with other Washingtonians and those staffers who manned the White House public relations machinery. The argument that erupted between these advisers should disabuse anyone of the notion that bargaining and cultivating public support are separate, self-contained spheres of action that do not encroach on one another.[21]

The president's chief pollster, Stanley Greenberg, opened the discussion by stating his and his fellow consultants' position: "We do not exaggerate when we say that our current course, advanced by our economic team and Congressional leaders, threatens to sink your popularity further and weaken your presidency." "The immediate problem," Greenberg explained, "is that thanks to the Republican effort no one views your economic package as anything other than a tax scheme. You must exercise a 'bold zero option,' which is consultant talk for 'rid your policy of any taxes that affect the middle class.'" (In fact, the only tax still in the bill was a 4.3-cent-per-gallon gasoline tax that would raise a modest $20 billion.) Greenberg then unveiled polling data that found broad public support for such a move. He closed by warning everyone in the room, "We have a very short period of time. And if we don't communicate something serious and focused in the period, we're going to be left with what our detractors used to characterize our plan. . . . Don't assume we can fix it in August." This concluded the case for going public. And in order to use this strategy, Clinton had to change course on taxes.

According to those present, the economic and congressional advisers had listened to this argument "with a slow burn." Finally, the president's chief lobbyist, Howard Paster, blurted out, "This isn't an election! The Senate breaks its ass to get a 4.3-cent-a-gallon tax passed, and we can't just abandon it." Besides, they needed the $20 billion provided by the tax to offset other concessions that would be necessary to get the bill passed. "I need all the chips that are available," Paster pleaded. "Don't bargain them away here. Let me have maximum latitude."

From here, the discussion deteriorated into name calling and assignment of blame. It stopped when Clinton started screaming at everyone—"a purple fit" is the way one participant described it. In the end the president decided that he had to stay the course but that he would begin traveling around the country to explain to the public that his economic package was the "best" one that could be enacted. In mid-August, after a concerted public relations campaign that concluded with a nationally televised address, the legislation barely passed. (In the Senate, Vice President Al Gore cast the tie-breaking vote.) The new administration's first legislative initiative had drained its resources both in Congress and across the nation. From here, the Clinton administration limped toward even more difficult initiatives represented by the North American Free Trade Agreement (NAFTA) and health care reform.

Clearly, as both case studies show, going public appears to foster political relations that are quite at odds with those traditionally cultivated through bargaining. One may begin to examine this phenomenon by asking, what is it about modern politics that would inspire presidents to go public in the first place?

How Washington and Presidents Have Changed

The incompatibility of bargaining and going public presents a pressing theoretical question. Why should presidents come to favor a strategy of leadership that appears so incompatible with the principles of pluralist theory? Why, if other Washington elites legitimately and correctly represent the interests of their clients and constituents, would anything be gained by going over their heads? The answers to these questions are several and complex, having to do with the ways Washington and presidents have changed. All in all, bargaining has shown declining efficiency, and opportunities to go public have increased. . . .

There is another, more fundamental reason for the discrepancy between theory and current practice. Presidents have preferred to go public in recent years perhaps because the strategy offers a better prospect of success than it did in the past. Politicians in Washington may no longer be as tractable to bargaining as they once were. We are in an era of divided government, with one party controlling

Congress and the other holding the presidency. Each side frequently finds political advantage in frustrating the other. On such occasions, posturing in preparation for the next election takes precedence over bargaining.

The decoupling of voters from political parties across the nation, which makes possible the occurrence of divided government, has also had more pervasive consequences for political relations among politicians in Washington. Weaker leaders, looser coalitions, more individualistic politicians, and stronger public pressure are among the developments reworking political relations in Washington that may inspire presidents to embrace a strategy of leadership antithetical to that prescribed by theory....

The President's Place in Institutionalized Pluralism

Constructing coalitions across the broad institutional landscape of Congress, the bureaucracy, interest groups, courts, and state governments requires a politician who possesses a panoramic view and commands the resources necessary to engage the disparate parochial interests of Washington's political elites. Only the president enjoys such vantage and resources. Traditional presidential scholarship leaves little doubt as to how they should be employed....

> Status and authority yield bargaining advantages. But in a government of "separated institutions sharing powers," they yield them to all sides. With the array of vantage points at his disposal, a President may be far more persuasive than his logic or his charm could make him. But outcomes are not guaranteed by his advantages. There remain the counter pressures those whom he would influence can bring to bear on him from vantage points at their disposal. Command has limited utility; persuasion becomes give-and-take....[22]

Bargaining is thus the essence of presidential leadership, and pluralist theory explicitly rejects unilateral forms of influence as usually insufficient and ultimately costly. The ideal president is one who seizes the center of the Washington bazaar and actively barters with fellow politicians to build winning coalitions. He must do so, according to this theory, or he will forfeit any claim to leadership....

The President's Calculus

...No politician within Washington is better positioned than the president to go outside of the community and draw popular support. With protocoalitions in disarray and members more sensitive to influences from beyond Washington, the president's hand in mobilizing public opinion has been strengthened. For the new Congress—indeed, for the new Washington generally—going public may at times be the most effective course available.

Under these circumstances, the president's prestige assumes the currency of power. It is something to be spent when the coffers are full, to be conserved when low, and to be replenished when empty. As David Gergen remarked when he was President Reagan's communications director, "Everything here is built on the idea that the President's success depends on grassroots support." [23]

Sixteen years later White House officials continue to adhere to this view. Early in 1997, when asked by campaign-weary news reporters why President Clinton maintained such a heavy travel schedule after the election victory, press secretary Michael D. McCurry lectured them on modern political science: "Campaigns are about framing a choice for the American people. . . . When you are responsible for governing you have to use the same tools of public persuasion to advance your program, to build public support for the direction you are attempting to lead." [24]

Modern presidents must be attentive to the polls, but they need not crave the affection of the public. Their relationship with it may be purely instrumental. However gratifying public approval may be, popular support is a resource the expenditure of which must be coolly calculated. As another Clinton aide explained, "Clinton has come to believe that if he keeps his approval ratings up and sells his message as he did during the campaign, there will be greater acceptability for his program. . . . The idea is that you have to sell it as if in a campaign." [25]

Bargaining presidents require the sage advice of politicians familiar with the bargaining game; presidents who go public need pollsters. Compare the relish with which President Nixon was reported by one of his consultants to have approached the polls with the disdain Truman expressed. "Nixon had all kinds of polls all the time; he sometimes had a couple of pollsters doing the same kind of survey at the same time. He really studied them. He wanted to find the thing that would give him an advantage." [26] The confidant went on to observe that the president wanted poll data "on just about anything and everything" throughout his administration.

Indicative of current fashion, presidents from Carter through Clinton have all had in-house pollsters taking continuous—weekly, even daily—readings of public opinion. [27] When George Bush reportedly spent $216,000 of Republican National Committee money on in-house polling in one year, many Washington politicians probably viewed the president's use of this resource as excessive. But this figure looked modest after Bill Clinton spent nearly ten times that amount in 1993. That year he averaged three or four polls and an equal number of focus groups each month. [28]

Pollsters vigilantly monitor the pulse of opinion to warn of slippage and to identify opportunities for gain. Before recommending a policy course, they assess its costs in public support. Sometimes, as with Clinton's pollsters, they go so far as to ask the public whether the president should bargain with Congress's leaders or challenge them by mobilizing public opinion.[29] These advisers' regular and frequently unsolicited denials that they affected policy belie their self-effacement.

To see how the strategic prescriptions of going public differ from those of bargaining, consider the hypothetical case of a president requiring additional votes if he is to prevail in Congress. If a large number of votes is needed, the most obvious and direct course is to go on prime-time television to solicit the public's active support. Employed at the right moment by a popular president, the effect may be dramatic. This tactic, however, has considerable costs and risks. A real debit of lost public support may occur when a president takes a forthright position. There is also the possibility that the public will not respond, which damages the president's future credibility. Given this, a president understandably finds the *threat* to go public frequently more attractive than the *act*. To the degree such a threat is credible, the anticipated responses of some representatives and senators may suffice to achieve victory.

A more focused application of popular pressure becomes available as an election nears. Fence-sitting representatives and senators may be plied with promises of reelection support or threats of presidential opposition. This may be done privately and selectively, or it may be tendered openly to all who may vote on the president's program. Then there is the election itself. By campaigning, the president who goes public can seek to alter the partisan composition of Congress and thereby gain influence over that institution's decisions in the future.

All of these methods for generating publicity notwithstanding, going public offers fewer and simpler stratagems than does its pluralist alternative. At the heart of the latter lies bargaining, which above all else involves choice: choice among alternative coalitions, choice of specific partners, and choice of the goods and services to be bartered. The number and variety of choices place great demands upon strategic calculation, so much so that pluralist leadership must be understood as an art. In Neustadt's schema, the president's success ultimately reduces to intuition, an ability to sense "right choices." [30]

Going public also requires choice, and it leaves ample room for the play of talent. (One need only compare the television performance of Carter and Reagan.) Nonetheless, public relations appears to be a less obscure matter. Going public promises a straightforward presidency—its options fewer, its strategy simpler, and consequently, its practitioner's behavior more predictable.

Thus there is a rationale for modern presidents to go public in the emerging character of Washington politics. As Washington comes to depend on looser, more individualistic political relations, presidents searching for strategies that work will increasingly go public.

So far, I have said little about the individual in the White House or the personal character of leadership. To consider these ingredients important does not violate any of the assumptions made here. Rationality does not leave choice to be determined strictly by the environment. To the degree occupants of the Oval Office differ in their skills and conceptions of leadership, one may expect that similar circumstances will sometimes result in different presidential behavior.

Perhaps, as has frequently been suggested, presidents go public more today because of who they are. What did Jimmy Carter and Ronald Reagan have in common? The answer is their lack of interest in active negotiation with fellow politicians and their confidence in speaking directly to the voters.

The Calculus of Those Who Deal with the President

Those Washingtonians who conduct business with the president observe his behavior carefully. Their judgment about his leadership guides them in their dealings with him. Traditionally, the professional president watchers have asked themselves the following questions: What are his priorities? How much does he care whether he wins or loses on a particular issue? How will he weigh his options? Is he capable of winning?

Each person will answer these questions about the president's will and skill somewhat differently, of course, depending upon his or her institutional vantage. The chief lobbyist for the United Auto Workers, a network White House correspondent, and the mayor of New York City may size up the president differently depending upon what they need from him. Nonetheless, they arrive at their judgments about the president in similar ways. Each observes the same behavior, inspects the same personal qualities, evaluates the views of the same recognized opinion leaders—columnists and commentators, among others—and tests his or her own tentative opinions with those of fellow community members. Local opinion leaders promote a general agreement among Washingtonians in their assessments of the president. Their agreement is his reputation.[31]

A president with a strong reputation does better in his dealings largely because others expect fewer concessions from him. Accordingly, he finds them more compliant; an orderly marketplace prevails. Saddled with a weak reputation, conversely, a president must work harder. Because others expect him to be less effective, they press him harder in expectation of greater gain. Comity at the bargaining table may give way to contention as other politicians form unreasonable expectations of gain. Through such expectations, the president's reputation regulates community relations in ways that either facilitate or impede his success. In a world of institutionalized pluralism, bargaining presidents seldom actively traded upon their prestige, leaving it to influence Washington political elites only through their anticipation of the electorate's behavior. As a consequence, prestige remained largely irrelevant to other politicians' assessments of the president.[32] Once presidents began going public and interjecting prestige directly into their relations with fellow politicians, and once these politicians found their resistance to this pressure diminished because of their own altered circumstances, the president's ability to marshal public opinion soon became an important ingredient of his reputation. New questions were added to traditional ones. Does the president feel strongly enough about an issue to go public? Will he follow through on his threats to do so? Does his standing in the country run so deep that it will likely be converted into mail to members of Congress, or is it so shallow that it will expire as he attempts to use it?

In today's Washington, the answers to these questions contribute to the president's reputation. As a consequence, his prestige and reputation have lost much of their separateness. The community's estimates of Carter and Reagan rose and fell with the polls. Through reputation, prestige has begun to play a larger role in regulating the president's day-to-day transactions with other community members. Grappling with the unclear causes of Carter's failure in Washington, Neustadt arrived at the same conclusion:

> A President's capacity to draw and stir a television audience seems every bit as interesting to current Washingtonians as his ability to wield his formal powers. This interest is his opportunity. While national party organizations fall away, while congressional party discipline relaxes, while interest groups proliferate and issue networks rise, a President who wishes to compete for leadership in framing policy and shaping coalitions has to make the most he can out of his popular connection. Anticipating home reactions, Washingtonians . . . are vulnerable to any breeze from home that presidential words and sights can stir. If he is deemed effective on the tube they will anticipate. That is the essence of professional reputation.[33]

The record supports Neustadt's speculation. In late 1978 and early 1979, with his monthly approval rating dropping to less than 50 percent, President Carter complained that it was difficult to gain Congress's attention for his legislative proposals. As one congressional liaison official stated, "When you go up to the Hill and the latest polls show Carter isn't doing well, then there isn't much reason for a member to go along with him." [34] A member of Congress concurred: "The relationship between the President and Congress is partly the result of how well the President is doing politically. Congress is better behaved when he does well. . . . Right now, it's almost as if Congress is paying no attention to him." [35]

NOTES

1. Newton N. Minow, John Bartlow Martin, and Lee M. Mitchell, *Presidential Television* (New York: Basic Books, 1973), 84–87.

2. Peter J. Boyer, "Networks Refuse to Broadcast Reagan's Plea," *New York Times*, February 3, 1988.

3. Robert B. Semple Jr., "Nixon Eludes Newsmen on Coast Trip," *New York Times,* August 3, 1970, 16.

4. Richard E. Neustadt, *Presidential Power* (New York: John Wiley and Sons, 1980).

5. Robert A. Dahl and Charles E. Lindblom, *Politics, Economics, and Welfare* (New York: Harper and Row, 1953), 333.

6. Among them are Aaron Wildavsky, *The Politics of the Budgetary Process* (Boston: Little, Brown, 1964); Graham T. Allison, *The Essence of Decision: Explaining the Cuban Missile Crisis* (New York: HarperCollins, 1987); Hugh Heclo, *The Government of Strangers* (Washington, D.C.: Brookings Institution, 1977); and Nelson W. Polsby, *Consequences of Party Reform* (New York: Oxford University Press, 1983).

7. From Ronald Reagan's address to the nation on his 1986 budget. Jack Nelson, "Reagan Calls for Public Support of Deficit Cuts," *Los Angeles Times,* April 25, 1985, 1.

8. Nelson W. Polsby, "Interest Groups and the Presidency: Trends in Political Intermediation in America," in *American Politics and Public Policy,* ed. Walter Dean Burnham and Martha Wagner Weinbey (Cambridge: MIT Press, 1978), 52.

9. Hedrick Smith, "Bitterness on Capitol Hill," *New York Times,* April 24, 1985, 14.

10. Ed Magnuson, "A Line Drawn in Dirt," *Time,* February 22, 1982, 12–13.

11. William J. Clinton, *Public Papers of the Presidents of the United States: William J. Clinton, 1994,* vol. 1 (Washington, D.C.: Government Printing Office, 1995), 126–135.

12. See David S. Broder, "Diary of a Mad Majority Leader," *Washington Post,* December 13, 1981, C1, C5; David S. Broder, "Rostenkowski Knows It's His Turn," *Washington Post National Weekly Edition,* June 10, 1985, 13.

13. Lou Cannon, "Big Spending-Cut Bill Studied," *Washington Post,* November 29, 1984, A8.

14. Bernard Weinraub, "Reagan Sets Tour of Nation to Seek Economic Victory," *New York Times,* January 25, 1985, 43.

15. Bernard Weinraub, "Reagan Calls for 'Spirit of Cooperation' on Budget and Taxes," *New York Times,* February 10, 1985, 32. On Democratic suspicions of Reagan's motives see Hedrick Smith, "O'Neill Reflects Democratic Strategy on Budget Cuts and Tax Revisions," *New York Times,* December 6, 1984, B20; and Margaret Shapiro, "O'Neill's New Honeymoon with Reagan," *Washington Post National Weekly Edition,* February 11, 1985, 12.

16. Jonathan Fuerbringer, "Reagan Critical of Budget View of Senate Panel," *New York Times,* March 9, 1985, 1. Senate Majority Leader Bob Dole told reporters that if the president liked the Senate's final budget package he would campaign for it "very vigorously . . . going to television, whatever he needs to reduce federal spending." Karen Tumulty, "Reagan May Get Draft of Budget Accord Today," *Los Angeles Times,* April 4, 1985, 1.

17. Bernard Weinraub, "In His 2nd Term, He Is Reagan the Liberated," *New York Times,* March 11, 1985, 10.

18. David E. Rosenbaum, "Reagan Approves Primary Elements of Tax Overhaul," *New York Times,* May 16, 1985, 1.

19. Robert W. Merry and David Shribman, "G.O.P. Hopes Tax Bill Will Help It Become Majority Party Again," *Wall Street Journal,* May 23, 1985, 1. See also Rosenbaum, "Reagan Approves Primary Elements of Tax Overhaul," 14. Instances such as those reported here continued into summer. See, for example, Jonathan Fuerbringer, "Key Issues Impede Compromise on Cutting Deficit," *New York Times,* June 23, 1985, 22.

20. These figures are reported in Richard E. Cohen, *Changing Course in Washington* (New York: Macmillan, 1994), 180.

21. The account of this meeting comes from Bob Woodward, *The Agenda* (New York: Simon and Schuster, 1994).

22. Richard E. Neustadt, *Presidential Power*, 28–29. Compare with Dahl and Lindblom's earlier observation: "The President possesses more hierarchical controls than any other single figure in the government; indeed, he is often described somewhat romantically and certainly ambiguously as the most powerful democratic executive in the world. Yet like everyone else in the American policy process, the President must bargain constantly—with Congressional leaders, individual Congressmen, his department heads, bureau chiefs, and leaders of nongovernmental organizations" (Dahl and Lindblom, *Politics, Economics, and Welfare*, 333).

23. Sidney Blumenthal, "Marketing the President," *New York Times Magazine*, September 13, 1981, 110.

24. Alison Mitchell, "Clinton Seems to Keep Running Though the Race Is Run and Won," *New York Times*, February 12, 1997, A1, A12.

25. Ibid., A12.

26. Cited in George C. Edwards III, *The Public Presidency* (New York: St. Martin's Press, 1983), 14.

27. B. Drummond Ayres Jr., "G.O.P. Keeps Tabs on Nation's Mood," *New York Times*, November 16, 1981, 20.

28. These figures are cited in George C. Edwards III, "Frustration and Folly: Bill Clinton and the Public Presidency," in *The Clinton Presidency: First Appraisals*, ed. Colin Campbell and Bert A. Rockman (Chatham, N.J.: Chatham House, 1996), 234.

29. In 1993 Clinton's chief pollster, Stanley Greenberg, added such a question to one of his national surveys. Unsurprisingly, a sizable majority favored cooperation with Congress. Bob Woodward, *The Agenda* (New York: Simon and Schuster, 1994), 268–269.

30. Neustadt, *Presidential Power*, especially chap. 8; and Peter Sperlich, "Bargaining and Overload: An Essay on Presidential Power," in *Perspectives on the Presidency*, ed. Aaron Wildavsky (Boston: Little, Brown, 1975).

31. This discussion of reputation follows closely that of Neustadt in *Presidential Power* (New York: John Wiley and Sons, 1980), chap. 4.

32. Neustadt observed that President Truman's television appeal for tighter price controls in 1951 had little visible effect on how Washington politicians viewed the issue. This is the only mention of a president going public in the original eight chapters of the book. Neustadt, *Presidential Power*, 45.

33. Neustadt, *Presidential Power*, 238.

34. Cited in Gary C. Jacobson, *The Politics of Congressional Elections*, 4th ed. (New York: Longman, 1997), 193–194.

35. Statement by Rep. Richard B. Cheney cited in Charles O. Jones, "Congress and the Presidency," in *The New Congress*, eds. Thomas E. Mann and Norman J. Ornstein (Washington, D.C.: American Enterprise Institute, 1981), 241.

How Cable Ended the Golden Age
of Presidential Television: From 1969 to 2006

Matthew A. Baum and Samuel Kernell

Numerous technological advances in communications and transportation during the twentieth century steadily expanded opportunities for presidents to go public. None was more important than television. From the late 1950s on, virtually every home had at least one television set. President John Kennedy grasped the opportunity television afforded presidents when he conducted the first live televised press conference in 1961. From then until the rise of cable television, presidents pretty much enjoyed the prerogative to enter America's homes whenever they "asked" the networks for airtime. More recently, however, technology has turned against presidents' easy access to the public. In this article Matthew Baum and Samuel Kernell trace the growth of cable and satellite subscription services and show that this trend is closely associated with the sharply declining audiences for presidents' national television addresses.

"THE PRESIDENT IS not irrelevant here." Bill Clinton's response to a reporter's pointed question during a nationally televised, prime-time news conference on April 18, 1995, came across as little more than a desperate denial of the truth. Having seized firm control of Congress in the previous fall's midterm elections and now marching in step toward enacting their legislative program, the "Contract with America," congressional Republicans had given the nation ample reason to suspect that perhaps this Democratic president had indeed become irrelevant.

Many Americans had apparently already answered the question for themselves. Nielsen Media Research reported that only 6.5 percent of households with televisions watched the president assert his relevance. In March 1969, in contrast, when President Richard Nixon conducted one of his routine prime-time press conferences, all three networks broadcast it, and according to Nielsen, 59 percent of America's television households tuned in.[1] Figure 1 shows more systematic evidence of this trend. The average audience ratings depicted in the

Source: This essay summarizes, partially excerpts, and updates research originally reported in Baum and Kernell, "Has Cable Ended the Golden Age of Presidential Television?" *American Political Science Review* 55 (March 1999): 99–114.

Figure 1. Average Percentage of Households with Televisions Watching
Prime-Time Presidential TV Appearances, 1969–2006

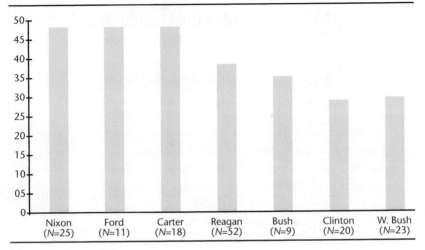

Source: Nielsen Media Research
Note: "Rating" is a commonly reported variable that Nielsen Media Research defines as the percentage of
households owning televisions that are tuned in to an average minute of a given program.

figure, based on 158 televised, prime-time addresses and news conferences, show
a steady downward trend, beginning with the Reagan presidency.[2]

Presidents appear to be losing their television audience at precisely the time
when they most need it. Increasingly they have staked their leadership in Washington on their ability to attract the public's support for themselves and their
policies (Kernell 1997). Whether measured by public appearances, number of
speeches, or days of travel, each recent president has in some way matched or
eclipsed his predecessors' efforts to communicate directly with the American
people. Substantial research has also demonstrated "going public" to be a viable
leadership strategy. Through speeches, popular presidents can influence public
preferences on policy (Mondak 1993; Page, Shapiro, and Dempsey 1987) and elevate the salience of some national issues over others (Bartels 1993; Cohen 1995).
As Bill Clinton conclusively demonstrated with his 1998 State of the Union
address, a president's public appeals can also boost his standing in the polls (Brace
and Hinckley 1993; Simon and Ostrom 1989; Ragsdale 1984).[3] More than ever,
presidents act on Neustadt's (1960) early insight that good things happen to popular presidents. Given these benefits, it comes as no surprise to find that about a
third of the White House staff is engaged in some aspect of public relations to
promote the president and his policies with the American public.

If modern presidents lose their prime-time audience, they will have surrendered a political asset that will be difficult to replace by other means. The alter-

native of speaking to the American public through the news media is being closed off by increasingly unobliging journalistic practices. Presidents complain, with some justification, that the news media prefer to report unfavorable news about them (Groeling and Kernell 1998; Patterson 1996, Baum and Groeling 2004). More importantly, however, network television news no longer allows presidents to speak for themselves. The average presidential sound bite on the network evening news has shrunk from forty seconds in 1968 to less than seven seconds in 1996 (Center for Media and Public Affairs 1996; Hallin 1994). With reporters and anchors on camera more, and presidents less, how reporters and their editors decide to frame a story can greatly influence how the audience will consume it (Miller and Krosnik 1996). The finding that news coverage of a president's policy preferences generally fails to influence public opinion is therefore unsurprising (Page, Shapiro, and Dempsey 1987; Edwards 2003). Modern news practices offer presidents a poor substitute for direct appeals on television.

Why are modern presidents losing their television audience? This is the central question we seek to answer in this study. Past research has largely ignored audience ratings, and so the scholarly literature offers few answers. We investigate the question in two distinct ways: In the next section we examine survey responses to questions measuring individuals' consumption of presidential messages. The statistical relationships reported below offer suggestive evidence of the underlying opinion dynamics that account for the trend in Figure 1. The cumulative evidence indicates that cable (and, more recently, satellite) technology has allowed the public to become strategically discriminating in its viewing decisions. So, too, our evidence suggests, have presidents and network executives, as they appraise this increasingly fickle audience in deciding, respectively, whether to deliver and broadcast a prime-time press conference or address to the nation.

The Utility of Watching the President

Twenty-five years ago, CBS, NBC and ABC enjoyed an oligopoly. As one network executive reminisced, "When viewers turned on the TV set, they had five choices, and the networks were three of them . . . [They] collectively accounted for about 90% of the television audience" (Lowry 1997). Between 1969 and 2005, the number of households subscribing to cable rose sharply from 6 percent to 83 percent.[4] Moreover, in 1983 cable subscribers received, on average, less than fifteen channels; today the average exceeds one hundred (*IT Facts*; Webster and Lichty 1991). As Figure 2 shows, both trends in cable subscriptions and programming choices have taken a heavy toll on the audience shares of the major networks.[5]

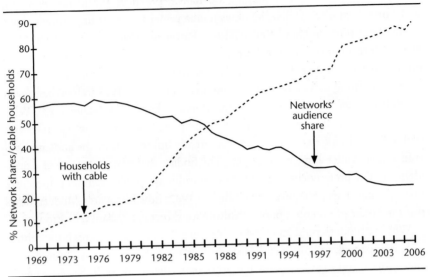

Figure 2. Network Audience Share and Households
with Cable, 1969–2006

Sources: (1) Cable households data - *Statistical Abstract of the United States* (Washington, D.C.: U.S. Government Printing Office, various years); (2) Networks' audience shares supplied by A.C, Nielsen.
Note: "% Network shares" refers to the combined prime-time Nielsen ratings of the three major broadcast networks (each rating point is equivalent to 1% of U.S. households); "Cable households" refers to the percentage of U.S. households subscribing to cable.

To appreciate how cable and other potential factors might erode the president's audience, we begin by stating the viewing decision using the standard utility model, $PB - C$. The "expected benefit" of consuming a president's message is made up of two terms: B, representing the potential benefit or value to the viewer of information that the president might provide, discounted by P, which is the probability that the president will actually offer credible information on a subject. When the viewing decision is stated in these terms, we can see that citizens who think politicians are crooks and liars will expect to derive little benefit from watching the president, regardless of what he has to say.

Against this expected benefit the viewer must weigh various costs, or C, and here is where cable programming enters the equation. Aside from the direct effort, or "transaction cost," of tuning in to the president's address, the viewer considers the "opportunity costs" entailed in watching the president rather than watching some other program or undertaking some other pleasurable activity. Back in the days when the several broadcast networks dominated the airwaves, they could manipulate viewers' opportunity costs by agreeing to suspend commercial programming and jointly broadcast the president's address. (They even used the same cameras.) This practice left voters with few programming alternatives. That, in turn, served the networks' purposes, in preventing serious audience erosion when commercial programming resumed, and the president's goal, by guaranteeing the largest possible audience.

The success of this practice depended, of course, on viewers' staying tuned throughout the president's appearance. Networks had little cause to worry. One study (Foote 1988) found sixteen of President Gerald Ford's nineteen television appearances commanding market shares as high as, or higher than, the regularly scheduled commercial programming the president's appearance had preempted. That even President Ford's notably uncharismatic appearances did not prompt viewers to turn off their televisions (or tune over to public or local independent programming) offers compelling evidence that during the pre-cable era, watching the president imposed minimal opportunity costs. Even those viewers who might have anticipated negligible benefit from watching President Ford nonetheless did so. Viewers behaved as if media critics were right in calling them "captives" of network television. Throughout our discussion we will enlist this term to characterize the predicament of this once-dominant class of broadcast viewers. As it concerns presidential television, a viewer's "captive" status results from the combination of limited channels, an unwillingness to turn off the television, and the networks' joint suspension of commercial programming during a presidential appearance.

Cable gives viewers choices, and for this reason, it makes watching the president costly. As the number of alternative programs increases, so too does the likelihood that one of them will prove more attractive than the president's message, prompting the viewer to change channels.[6] So, cable subscribers will be less likely to watch a presidential appearance than will those viewers who remain captive to the broadcast signal.

Although it is substantively important, this prediction is intuitive and does not need to be depicted formally to be appreciated. There is, however, a second, less-obvious hypothesis embedded in the utility calculus of watching the president, particularly when one of the prominent possible states is that of captive viewer. In Figure 3 we graph the probability of watching the president as a function of these cost-benefit comparisons. Because captive viewers will experience negligible opportunity costs in watching the president, they will tend to do so even when they anticipate minimal benefit. Cable subscribers, on the other hand, are free to move along Figure 3's curve, and so their assessment of benefit will heavily influence their viewing decision. The qualitative difference between captive, antenna-tethered viewers and cable viewers in the choice to watch the president should show up statistically in an interaction between cable access and those variables that reflect the attractiveness of a presidential appearance. Below we test this utility hypothesis in two ways: on individuals' self-reported viewing habits and on aggregate trends of audience shares. Although they similarly confirm the model, each level of analysis offers distinct insights into the president's declining audience.

Watching the 1996 Presidential Debates

For the vast majority of the American people television has emerged over the past few decades as the primary source of information about politics. For some it represents their sole means of becoming informed about the issues of the day. Newspaper readership, conversely, has declined steadily since the 1960s and in a way that suggests a massive substitution of television for newspapers as a source for civic information (Briller 1990; Lichty and Gomery 1992; Moisy 1997; Stanley and Niemi 1998).[7]

Reflecting the rise of alternative information technologies, recent American National Election Study (NES) surveys, which are the chief source of scholarly research on voting behavior in national elections, have queried respondents about their preferred sources of information about politics. The 1996 NES survey asked respondents if they subscribed to cable or satellite television service, giving us an opportunity to examine systematically its effect on political communication. The survey also asked respondents whether they watched the first and second presidential debates between President Bill Clinton and his Republican opponent, Bob Dole. Although debates represent a different kind of presidential appearance, we have little reason to suspect that they differ materially from the addresses to the nation and press conferences tallied in Figure 1. In recent years the American public has shown just as great an inclination to abandon presidential debates as other forms of televised presidential communication. More people typically watch the debates, but Nielsen (2006) reports erosion in the share of television viewers who tune in to them from more than half of those watching television to roughly a third in recent elections.[8]

We have hypothesized that respondents with cable will approach their viewing choices differently, since they enjoy numerous programming options unavailable to the broadcast audience and hence are more likely to engage in a cost-benefit calculation with respect to watching the president. In an extensive analysis of the covariates of debate watching reported elsewhere (Baum and Kernell 1999), we found a much stronger propensity to watch the debates among those cable subscribers who are highly informed about politics than among their poorly informed counterparts. Among broadcast viewers, this difference did not emerge.[9] The relationships displayed in Figure 4 closely follow the utility logic of viewing decisions depicted in Figure 3.[10] Among cable subscribers, reported

Figure 3. The Probability of Viewing the President
as a Function of Expected Utility

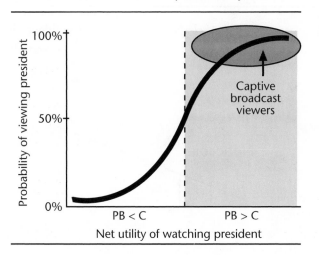

debate watching is strongly related to the respondent's level of political information. The differences between these low- and high-information respondents
are eighteen and twenty-seven percentage points ($p < .05$) for the first and second
debates, respectively, and highly informed cable subscribers actually eclipsed
their captive counterparts in tuning in to these events. Additionally, the differences between cable subscribers and nonsubscribers are greatest among the
least-well-informed respondents. Poorly informed cable subscribers dropped out
of the debate audience in droves, presumably because they changed channels in
favor of entertainment programming.

Also as predicted, noncable respondents confirm their captive status by reporting watching the debates at about the same rate regardless of how politically
informed they are. In neither debate did the percentage point differences of -.12
and -.07 between low- and high-information nonsubscribers reach the .05 significance level. Nonetheless, the fact that subscribers and nonsubscribers trend in
opposite directions across levels of political awareness presents an intriguing possibility: Why would the least politically informed broadcast viewers be the most
likely to watch the presidential debates? Perhaps the answer lies in their greater
overall exposure to television programming. If these poorly informed captive
viewers watch more television, then more of them than their better informed
counterparts might well have been tuned in when the networks (including Fox)
preempted evening commercial programming to present the debates.

Unfortunately, the NES survey does not ask about overall viewing habits, and
so we cannot directly control for the effects of overall exposure to television

Figure 4. Probability of Watching the 1996 Presidential Debates:
Cable Subscribers versus Nonsubscribers

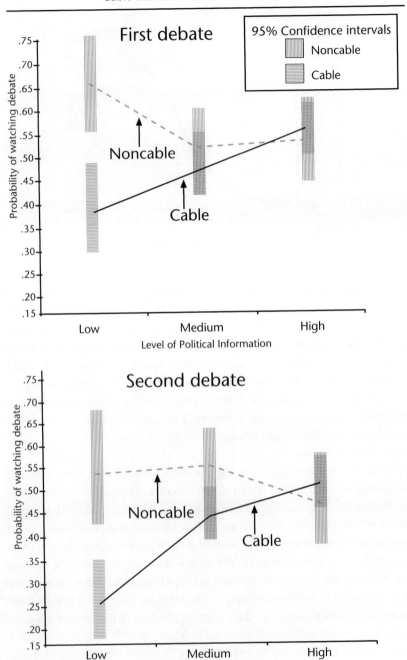

Source: Baum and Kernell (1999): Probabilities represent percentages derived from transformed logit coefficients.

programming on these relationships. Yet suggestive circumstantial evidence is available in the 1996 General Social Survey (GSS), which did include respondents' viewing habits and found the amount of time logged in front of the television to be inversely associated with education (Davis 1996).[11] Political information is highly correlated with education in the NES survey ($r = .49$). Hence, more of our low-information respondents in Figure 4 might have watched the debates simply because more of them were watching TV when the debates aired.

Assigning the GSS respondents' television-viewing levels for the different educational categories to our low- and high-political-information, noncable NES respondents allows us to estimate these groups' different levels of exposure to television. By this estimate, our low-information respondents averaged almost an hour more of daily television viewing than high-information respondents—3.4 compared to 2.6 hours per day. Perhaps, then, the inverse relationship of political information and debate watching for noncable respondents is not so paradoxical. Tuning in to the debates might impose comparatively low opportunity costs for the captive viewers who, despite their typically poorer understanding of politics, are nonetheless drawn to it merely by virtue of their relatively heavy diet of television.

If, as these relationships suggest, the changing media marketplace frees uninterested viewers to abandon political programming, the effects should manifest over time in a steady decline of the president's audience ratings, as cable and satellite services offer more programming alternatives to more citizens.

The President's Audience Ratings

As suggestive as the survey differences between cable and broadcast viewers may be, we need information over time to confirm that they are at the root of recent presidents' audience losses. The presidents' average audience ratings in Figure 1 are based on the 158 prime-time presidential addresses and press conferences for which we have Nielsen ratings data. These ratings reflect the percentage of households with television that are viewing the appearance.

Our key treatment variable is cable's share of the household audience. We could measure this in various ways, including, obviously, the percentage of households subscribing to cable, as shown in Figure 2. Instead, however, we have adopted a closely correlated indicator, Network Share, or the average share of the audience watching one of the three broadcast networks during prime time. This measure performs slightly better, we suspect because it takes into account not only the fast-growing share of homes wired to cable or sporting a satellite dish but also the increasing number of viewing options available to subscribers. We also test a number of other situational variables that might contribute to the utility of viewing the president. Others have found the public's receptivity to the president's messages closely associated with its assessment of his job perform- ance (Page, Shapiro, and Dempsey 1987; Zaller 1997). Hence we have added "Approve," the Gallup poll's familiar share of the public approving the president's job performance at the time of the television appearance. We take into account the effect of the economy on the public's receptivity to presidential appear- ances.[12] The variable "Bad Economy" is based on the percentage of respondents who answered "bad" when asked to forecast the next year's business conditions in the University of Michigan's monthly Survey of Consumer Sentiment.

This group of variables may reflect the viewer's assessment of the value or benefit of watching the president's address. On the cost side of the ledger, we have identified several variables that might influence these time-series relation- ships. During the Clinton administration, the networks began rotating coverage of some presidential appearances. Of the twenty Clinton prime-time addresses and press conferences for which we have audience data, only fourteen were broadcast by all three major networks. President George W. Bush has fared somewhat better, perhaps reflecting the crisis content of many of his addresses during his first term. During the first five years of his presidency only seven of his twenty-three appearances failed to receive full network coverage. Selective network broadcasts are a modern development that rarely occurred in past administrations. We suspect the change reflects the growing costliness to the net- works of interrupting their commercial programming and finding large shares of their audience subsequently changing to a cable channel and not returning to the networks for the remainder of the prime-time evening. When a network opts out of covering a presidential event, it adds a major programming alternative to the menus of *both* broadcast and cable viewers. This sharply increases the oppor- tunity costs associated with watching the president and should, according to our model, reduce his audience share commensurately. In a preliminary analysis we found the largest audience losses occurring when only one network carried an event, such as President Clinton's ill-starred press conference, with which we opened our discussion. Accordingly we shall represent these instances with a dummy variable, "One Network."

Media research (Webster and Lichty 1991, 154–157) identifies two other vari- ables—represented in our analysis by "Summer" and "9 p.m."—relating to costs that systematically limit the size of the prime-time audience. For television pro- ducers, July and August are indeed "the dog days of summer." Longer days and vacations conspire to reduce the numbers of people watching television, and hence reruns become the staple. Similarly, whatever the season or day of the week, the 9:00 p.m.-to-10:00 p.m. time slot normally finds a television turned on in more households than at any other time of the day. If a president runs afoul of these preferred viewing times and seasons, fewer viewers will be watching TV when he appears.

In the first equation of Table 1 (whose results appear in the first two columns) we have regressed the 158 presidential audience ratings summarized in Figure 1 on these benefit and costs variables. For the most part, the relationships closely follow our expectations and parallel the survey results. The presence of viewing options is, again, a powerful predictor of the president's audience share. Presidential approval displays the correct sign and is significant; concern with the economy significantly increases the audience. International crises attract audiences; apparently, crises give viewers a special reason to learn what the president has to say. Two days after the attack of 9/11, a record 88 percent of America's households tuned in to see how President Bush planned to respond. The several schedule variables reflecting time of address, season, and number of networks showing the president are all significantly related to watching the president. The same structural features of the market mediate the president's audience rating as do so for commercial programming.[13] The one variable that fails to produce a statistically significant relationship for the full 1969 to 2006 series is the president's approval rating; more on this below.

Earlier we argued that variations in an address's expected benefit will have less effect on the viewing choices of those who remain dependent on the broadcast signal, for the simple reason that they have nowhere else to go. The ideal way of testing this hypothesis on marginal changes in the president's audience shares over time entails analyzing the relationships separately for cable and broadcast viewers. Unfortunately, Nielsen Media Research does not provide such partially disaggregated data for scholarly research. There is, however, another, indirect approach available. Note that Figure 2 shows neither cable penetration of households nor network audience shares changing greatly until the early 1980s. During the Nixon-to-Carter era, for example, the big three networks' share of the market declined only about one percentage point (from 56 percent to 55 percent), compared to a thirty-four percentage point decline (from 55 percent to 21 percent) for the 1981–2006 period. Consequently, presidents' audience ratings (see Figure 1) were both higher and more stable during the Nixon, Ford, and Carter presidencies than for more recent presidents. By estimating the equations separately for these two time periods, we obtain series with distinct mixes of cable and broadcast audiences. According to our model, stronger time-series relationships should occur for the second period, when far more members of the television audience possessed many more viewing options and consequently a meaningful choice whenever the president appeared on the screen.

Table 1. The Presidents' Audience Rating as a Function
of Network Share, Political Setting, and Schedule

Independent Variable	Equation 1 Full Series (N = 158)		Equation 2 Nixon–Carter (N = 54)		Equation 3 Reagan–W. Bush (N = 104)	
	Coef.	Std. Error	Coef.	Std. Error	Coef.	Std. Error
Network share	.51***	.05	-.57	1.25	.34***	.07
Approve	.00	.00	.19*	.10	.00	.00
Bad economy	.08	.04	.11	.08	.12*	.05
Crisis	.06**	.02	.06	.03	.06**	.02
Summer	-.06***	.02	-.11**	.03	-.05**	.02
9:00 p.m.	.05***	.01	.06***	.02	.03*	.01
One network	-.08**	.03			-.10***	.03
Constant	.02	.04	.63	.73	.05	.04
Adjusted R^2	.05		.27		.43	

$^*p < .05, ^{**}p < .01, ^{***}p < .001$

Source: Baum and Kernell (1999), updated through 2006 by authors. The above equations report OLS regression estimates of the full and partial time series of presidents' national audience ratings.

This is precisely what we find in the second and third equations of Table 1. Only the scheduling variables are statistically significant for both the first and second periods. This is perfectly consistent with our model, since these variables capture *whether* people are watching television, rather than their particular choice of programming. Moreover, "Network Share" is appropriately weak and insignificant during the early period, reflecting cable's limited penetration into American households. By comparison, the president's audience ratings during the Reagan-to-G. W. Bush era tracked all of the independent variables except, again, presidential approval ("Approve"). At first glance, this null finding is surprising. Elsewhere, however, we offer evidence suggesting that because it is important, other actors incorporate the president's public prestige into their strategic decisions of whether ("One Network") and when ("9:00 p.m.") to broadcast the event (Baum and Kernell, 1999).

Conclusion

The textbook assessment that "television has brought about . . . the greater ease with which American presidents can communicate directly with the American people" (Erikson and Tedin 1995, 235) increasingly represents the reality of a bygone "golden age" of presidential television. In the 1960s and 1970s, when more homes in America had televisions than had indoor plumbing and virtually all viewers (including early cable subscribers) depended on the networks for their programming, presidents possessed an enviable tool of persuasion. President Kennedy introduced the live, prime-time press conference in 1961 so that he could, as he explained to a reporter at the inaugural session, "speak directly to the American people." Over the next several decades, direct appeals to the captive American audience became commonplace. In 1970 President Nixon delivered nine prime-time addresses to the nation. He and other presidents did not hesitate to take to the airwaves to exhort the public to write, call, and send mailgrams to their members of Congress in support of their policies. The urge to go public with a prime-time address was tempered only by the consideration that the president might wear out his welcome (Kernell 1997, 107).

What broadcast technology gave the president, cable technology appears to be taking away. In recent years, as the number of television households receiving cable has swelled, along with the programming alternatives it offers, the number of viewers who reach for their remote at the first sight of the president has grown steadily. That in turn has prompted the broadcast networks to reassess their willingness to surrender prime-time slots to the president. Rotating coverage is increasingly favored, and some presidential coverage requests have been rejected outright. Gone are the days when a president could "appear simultaneously on all national radio and television networks at prime, large-audience evening hours, virtually whenever and however the president wishes" (Minow et al. 1973).

The recent origin of this phenomenon necessarily renders speculative any assessment of its implications. We can reasonably conclude, nonetheless, that presidents' diminished access to the national television audience will present future presidents with a serious strategic dilemma: How will they promote their policies to a citizenry that depends almost entirely on television for its news and information yet is increasingly unwilling to allow the president into their homes?

NOTES

1. Over the years, A. C. Nielsen Company has established itself as the authoritative source and arbiter of television viewing habits. Two of Nielsen's better known audience rating indexes gauge audience size as a percentage of households using television (HUT) and as a percentage of households owning televisions, which it calls "Average Audience Household" (AAH). The former is best suited for assessing a program's performance in a given time slot and consequently is favored by network producers. The latter better measures a program's overall audience penetration and allows program comparisons across time slots. AAH is the Nielsen rating for an average minute of programming. For our study, we use AAH, which rep-

resents the percentage of those U.S. households possessing television that tuned into the president's address during an average minute of that program.

2. At least one of the four major networks (including Fox) broadcast each of these addresses and press conferences. Only since 1993 has a presidential address or press conference received less than full coverage.

3. Shortly after the Monica Lewinsky sex scandal broke into the news, President Clinton's political standing became so unstable that several newspaper and network surveys launched daily tracking surveys to monitor the president's pulse in public opinion. But then the president delivered a well-received State of the Union address, his polling numbers shot up to their highest levels ever, and the polling subsided. The results of the CBS/New York Times Survey are typical (Berke 1998).

4. The 2005 figure include satellite subscriptions. Henceforth we shall drop references to these subscriptions, which are functionally equivalent to cable and have been added to subsequent figures as "cable" subscribers.

5. Recently even the broadcast market has started to expand and offer viewers more choices. A fourth broadcast network, Fox, started up in 1991, and in 1994 UPN and WB entered the market.

6. During President Clinton's much-anticipated 1998 State of the Union speech, during the first days of the Lewinsky scandal, the fledgling WB network enjoyed its highest-rated program ever, when almost eight million viewers tuned in to a new series (Snow 1998).

7. Over the past decade, the Internet has begun to emerge as an important alternative to television as a source of political information. However, survey evidence (e.g., Pew Center 2002, 2004) suggests that for a vast majority Americans, television remains the overwhelmingly predominant source of news about politics.

8. Fifty-one percent of NES respondents claimed to have watched the first debate when it was broadcast on all four network channels, PBS, and CNN on October 6, 1996, and 47 percent reported watching the second debate ten days later. The Nielsen ratings, comparable to those in Figure 1, record much more modest audiences of 32 percent and 26 percent of households with television, respectively, for the two debates.

9. This variable represents the NES interviewer's estimate of the respondent's level of political information. Despite problems of reliability that would appear inherent in such a subjective measure, Zaller (1992) found that this variable, measured in the preelection interview, performs as well as or better than any other NES-based indicator of political awareness, including education, political participation, media exposure, interest in politics, and various informational indices he constructed (which we replicated).

10. Following a simulation procedure for generating significance levels developed by King, Tomz, and Wittenberg (2000), we have also plotted the 95 percent confidence intervals for each expected probability.

11. The 1996 General Social Survey asked respondents how many hours per day they watched television. Responses were coded 0 through 24 hours per day. Separating respondents by education level, those with less than a ninth grade education averaged fully two more hours per day of television viewing than their college educated counterparts—4.2 versus 2.2 hours per day.

12. We also tested the effects of various presidential scandals during this era. These events drive down a president's approval rating, which apparently accounts for their failure to yield significant statistical relationships in the multivariate analysis.

13. Although the scheduling of presidential addresses is constrained by events (e.g., a sudden international crisis) or obligations (e.g., the State of the Union address), they are not randomly distributed with respect to time and season. Instead, the address schedule represents a negotiated agreement between network executives and White House advisers and consequently may be partly endogenous to the equation.

REFERENCES

Bartels, Larry M. 1993. "Messages Received: The Political Impact of Media Exposure." *American Political Science Review* 87 (June): 267–285.

Baum, Matthew A., and Tim Groeling. 2004. "Crossing the Water's Edge: Elite Rhetoric, Media Coverage and the Rally-Round-the-Flag Phenomenon, 1979–2003." Paper presented to the annual meeting of the American Political Science Association, Chicago, Ill., Sept.

Baum, Matthew A., and Samuel Kernell. 1999. "Has Cable Ended the Golden Age of Presidential Television?" *American Political Science Review* 93 (March): 99–114.

Berke, Richard L. 1998. "A Wild Ride, with No End Now in Sight." *New York Times,* January 30, A14.

Brace, Paul, and Barbara Hinckley. 1993. "Presidential Activities from Truman through Reagan: Timing and Impact." *Journal of Politics* 55 (May): 382–398.

Briller, Bert R. 1990. "Zooming in Closer on the News Audience." *Television Quarterly* 25 (Winter): 107–116.

Center for Media and Public Affairs (CMPA). 1996. "Markle Presidential Election Watch: Report Card." www.cmpa.com/politics/Elections/ewarchiv.htm.

Cohen, Jeffrey, E. 1995. "Presidential Rhetoric and the Public Agenda." *American Journal of Political Science* 39 (February): 7–107.

Davis, James Allen. 1996. "General Social Surveys, 1972–1999." [computer file]: Principal investigator, James A. Davis; director and co-principal investigator, Tom W. Smith. Chicago: National Opinion Research Center [producer]; Storrs, [Conn.]: Roper Public Opinion Research Center [distributor, 1996]. NORC edition.

Edwards, George C. 2003. *On Deaf Ears.* New Haven: Yale University Press.

Erikson, Robert S., and Kent L. Tedin. 1995. *American Public Opinion: Its Origins, Content, and Impact.* 5th edition. Boston: Allyn and Bacon.

Foote, Joe S. 1988. "Ratings Decline of Presidential Television." *Journal of Broadcasting and Electronic Media* 32 (Spring): 225–230.

Groeling, Tim, and Samuel Kernell. 1998. "Is Network News Coverage of the President Biased?" *Journal of Politics* 60 (November): 1064–1086.

Hallin, Daniel C. 1994. *We Keep America on Top of the World: Television Journalism and the Public Sphere.* London and New York: TJ Press (Padstow) Ltd.

IT Facts. 2004. www.itfacts.biz/index.php?id=P1654 (original source: A. C. Nielsen).

Kernell, Samuel. 1997. *Going Public.* 3rd edition. Washington, D.C.: CQ Press.

King, Gary, Michael Tomz, and Jason Wittenberg. 2000. "Making the Most of Statistical Analyses: Improving Interpretation and Presentation." *American Journal of Political Science* 44 (April): 347–361.

Lichty, Lawrence W., and Douglas Gomery. 1992. "More Is Less." In *The Future of News: Television, Newspapers, Wire Services, News Magazines.* Washington, D.C.: Woodrow Wilson Center Press.

Lowry, Brian. 1997. "Cable Stations Gather Strength." *Los Angeles Times,* September 2, F1.

Media Monitor. 1991. Newsletter of the Center for Media and Public Affairs, Washington, D.C. Spring, 4.

Miller, Joanne, and Jon Krosnick. 1996. "News Media Impact on the Ingredients of Presidential Evaluations: A Program of Research on the Priming Hypothesis." In *Presidential Persuasion and Attitudinal Change,* ed. Diana C. Mutz and Paul M. Sniderman. Ann Arbor: University of Michigan Press.

Minow, Newton N., John Bartlow Martin, and Lee M. Mitchell. 1973. *Presidential Television.* New York: Basic Books.

Moisy, Claude. 1997. "Myths of the Global Information Village." *Foreign Policy* 107 (Summer): 78–87.

Mondak, Jeffrey J. 1993. "Source Cues and Policy Approval: The Cognitive Dynamics of Public Support for the Reagan Agenda." *American Journal of Political Science* 37 (February): 186–212.

Neustadt, Richard E. 1960. *Presidential Power and the Modern Presidents.* New York: John Wiley.

Nielsen Media Research. 2006. *Nielsen Tunes in to Politics.* New York: Nielsen Media Research.

Page, Benjamin, Robert Shapiro, and G. Dempsey. 1987. "What Moves Public Opinion." *American Political Science Review* 81 (September): 815–831.

Patterson, Thomas. 1996. "Bad News, Period." *PS: Political Science and Politics* 29 (March): 17–20.

Pew Research Center for the People and the Press. 2002. *Biennial Media Consumption Survey.* Princeton Survey Research Associates (April).

——. 2004. *Biennial Media Consumption Survey.* Princeton Survey Research Associates (April).

Ragsdale, Lyn. 1984. "The Politics of Presidential Speechmaking, 1949–1980." *American Political Science Review* 78 (December): 971–984.

Rosenstone, Steven J., Donald R. Kinder, Warren E. Miller, and the National Election Studies. 1997. *American National Election Study, 1996: Pre- and Post-Election Survey* [Computer file]. 2nd release. Ann Arbor, Mich.: University of Michigan, Center for Political Studies[producer], 1997. Ann Arbor, Mich.: Inter-university Consortium for Political and Social Research [distributor], 1997.

Simon, Dennis M., and Charles W. Ostrom Jr. 1989. "The Impact of Televised Speeches and Foreign Travel on Presidential Approval." *Public Opinion Quarterly* 53 (Spring): 58–82.

Snow, Shauna. 1998. "Morning Report: Arts and Entertainment Reports from the Times, National and International News Services and the Nation's Press." *Los Angeles Times,* January 22, F50.

Stanley, Harold W., and Richard G. Niemi. 1998. *Vital Statistics on American Politics, 1997–1998.* Washington D.C.: Congressional Quarterly Press.

Webster, James G., and Lawrence W. Lichty. 1991. *Ratings Analysis: Theory and Practice.* New Jersey and London: Lawrence Erlbaum Associates.

Zaller, John, R. 1992. *The Nature and Origins of Mass Opinion.* New York: Cambridge University Press.

——. 1997. "A Model of Communication Effects at the Outbreak of the Gulf War." In *Do the Media Govern? Politicians, Voters, and Reporters in America.* Ed. Shanto Iyengar and Richard Reeves. Thousand Oaks: Sage. 296–311

Chapter 8

The Bureaucracy

8-1

from *Bureaucracy*

James Q. Wilson

When Congress and the president create new programs and assign responsibility for implementing them to executive agencies, they are delegating power that might be used arbitrarily by unelected bureaucrats. To avoid the arbitrary use of power—one of the prime objectives of democracy—they impose rules on agencies. These rules, which serve as beneficial constraints, may limit bureaucrats' options and create inefficiencies in the implementation of policy. In the following essay James Q. Wilson examines the causes and consequences of discretion and arbitrariness and of rules and inefficiencies.

ON THE MORNING of May 22, 1986, Donald Trump, the New York real estate developer, called one of his executives, Anthony Gliedman, into his office. They discussed the inability of the City of New York, despite six years of effort and the expenditure of nearly $13 million, to rebuild the ice-skating rink in Central Park. On May 28 Trump offered to take over the rink reconstruction, promising to do the job in less than six months. A week later Mayor Edward Koch accepted the offer and shortly thereafter the city appropriated $3 million on the understanding that Trump would have to pay for any cost overruns out of his own pocket.

Source: James Q. Wilson, *Bureaucracy: What Government Agencies Do and Why They Do It* (New York: Basic Books, 2000), 315–345. Notes appearing in the original have been deleted.

On October 28, the renovation was complete, over a month ahead of schedule and about $750,000 under budget. Two weeks later, skaters were using it.

For many readers it is obvious that private enterprise is more efficient than are public bureaucracies, and so they would file this story away as simply another illustration of what everyone already knows. But for other readers it is not so obvious what this story means; to them, business is greedy and unless watched like a hawk will fob off shoddy or overprices goods on the American public, as when it sells the government $435 hammers and $3,000 coffeepots. Trump may have done a good job in this instance, but perhaps there is something about skating rinks or New York City government that gave him a comparative advantage; in any event, no larger lessons should be drawn from it.

Some lessons can be drawn, however, if one looks closely at the incentives and constraints facing Trump and the department of Parks and Recreation. It becomes apparent that there is not one "bureaucracy problem" but several, and the solution to each in some degree is incompatible with the solution to every other. First there is the problem of accountability—getting agencies to serve agreed-upon goals. Second there is the problem of equity—treating all citizens fairly, which usually means treating them alike on the basis of clear rules known in advance. Third there is the problem of responsiveness—reacting reasonably to the special needs and circumstances of particular people. Fourth there is the problem of efficiency—obtaining the greatest output for a given level of resources. Finally there is the problem of fiscal integrity—assuring that public funds are spent prudently for public purposes. Donald Trump and Mayor Koch were situated differently with respect to most of these matters.

Accountability. The Mayor wanted the old skating rink refurbished, but he also wanted to minimize the cost of the fuel needed to operate the rink (the first effort to rebuild it occurred right after the Arab oil embargo and the attendant increase in energy prices). Trying to achieve both goals led city hall to select a new refrigeration system that as it turned out would not work properly. Trump came on the scene when only one goal dominated: get the rink rebuilt. He felt free to select the most reliable refrigeration system without worrying too much about energy costs.

Equity. The Parks and Recreation Department was required by law to give every contractor an equal chance to do the job. This meant it had to put every part of the job out to bid and to accept the lowest without much regard to the reputation or prior performance of the lowest bidder. Moreover, state law forbade city agencies from hiring a general contractor and letting him select the subcontractors; in fact, the law forbade the city from even discussing the project in advance with a general contractor who might later bid on it—that would have been collusion. Trump, by contrast, was free to locate the rink builder with the best reputation and give him the job.

Fiscal Integrity. To reduce the chance of corruption or sweetheart deals the law required Parks and Recreation to furnish complete, detailed plans to every contractor bidding on the job; any changes after that would require renegotiating the contract. No such law constrained Trump; he was free to give incomplete plans to his chosen contractor, hold him accountable for building a satisfactory rink, but allow him to work out the details as he went along.

Efficiency. When the Parks and Recreation Department spent over six years and $13 million and still could not reopen the rink, there was public criticism but no city official lost money. When Trump accepted a contract to do it, any cost overruns or delays would have come out of his pocket and any savings could have gone into his pocket (in this case, Trump agreed not to take a profit on the job).

Gliedman summarized the differences neatly: "The problem with government is that government can't say, 'yes' . . . there is nobody in government that can do that. There are fifteen or twenty people who have to agree. Government has to be slower. It has to safeguard the process."

Inefficiency

The government can't say "yes." In other words, the government is constrained. Where do the constraints come from? From us.

Herbert Kaufman has explained red tape as being of our own making: "Every restraint and requirement originates in somebody's demand for it." Applied to the Central Park skating rink Kaufman's insight reminds us that civil-service reformers demanded that no city official benefit personally from building a project; that contractors demanded that all be given an equal chance to bid on every job; and that fiscal watchdogs demanded that all contract specifications be as detailed as possible. For each demand a procedure was established; viewed from the outside, those procedures are called red tape. To enforce each procedure a manager was appointed; those managers are called bureaucrats. No organized group demanded that all skating rinks be rebuilt as quickly as possible, no procedure existed to enforce that demand, and no manager was appointed to enforce it. The political process can more easily enforce compliance with constraints than the attainment of goals.

When we denounce bureaucracy for being inefficient we are saying something that is half true. Efficiency is a ratio of valued resources used to valued outputs produced. The smaller that ratio the more efficient the production. If the valued output is a rebuilt skating rink, then whatever process uses the fewest dollars or the least time to produce a satisfactory rink is the most efficient process. By this test Trump was more efficient than the Parks and Recreation Department.

But that is too narrow a view of the matter. The economic definition of efficiency (efficiency in the small, so to speak) assumes that there is only one valued output, the new rink. But government has many valued outputs, including a reputation for integrity, the confidence of the people, and the support of important interest groups. When we complain about skating rinks not being built on time we speak as if all we cared about were skating rinks. But when we complain that contracts were awarded without competitive bidding or in a way that allowed bureaucrats to line their pockets we acknowledge that we care about many things besides skating rinks; we care about the contextual goals—the constraints—that we want government to observe. A government that is slow to build rinks but is honest and accountable in its actions and properly responsive to worthy constituencies may be a very efficient government, *if* we measure efficiency in the large by taking into account *all* of the valued outputs.

Calling a government agency efficient when it is slow, cumbersome, and costly may seem perverse. But that is only because we lack any objective way for deciding how much money or time should be devoted to maintaining honest behavior, producing a fair allocation of benefits, and generating popular support as well as to achieving the main goal of the project. If we could measure these things, and if we agreed as to their value, then we would be in a position to judge the true efficiency of a government agency and decide when it is taking too much time or spending too much money achieving all that we expect of it. But we cannot measure these things nor do we agree about their relative importance, and so government always will appear to be inefficient compared to organizations that have fewer goals.

Put simply, the only way to decide whether an agency is truly inefficient is to decide which of the constraints affecting its action ought to be ignored or discounted. In fact that is what most debates about agency behavior are all about. In fighting crime are the police handcuffed? In educating children are teachers tied down by rules? In launching a space shuttle are we too concerned with safety? In building a dam do we worry excessively about endangered species? In running the Postal Service is it important to have many post offices close to where people live? In the case of the skating rink, was the requirement of competitive bidding for each contract on the basis of detailed specifications a reasonable one? Probably not. But if it were abandoned, the gain (the swifter completion of the rink) would have to be balanced against the costs (complaints from contractors who might lose business and the chance of collusion and corruption in some future projects).

Even allowing for all of these constraints, government agencies may still be inefficient. Indeed, given the fact that bureaucrats cannot (for the most part) benefit monetarily from their agencies' achievements, it would be surprising if they were not inefficient. Efficiency, in the large or the small, doesn't pay. . . .

Military procurement, of course, is the biggest source of stories about waste, fraud, and mismanagement. There cannot be a reader of this book who has not heard about the navy paying $435 for a hammer or the air force paying $3,000 for a coffeepot, and nobody, I suspect, believes Defense Department estimates of the cost of a new airplane or missile. If ever one needed evidence that bureaucracy is inefficient, the Pentagon supplies it.

Well, yes. But what kind of inefficiency? And why does it occur? To answer these questions one must approach the problem just as we approached the problem of fixing up a skating rink in New York City: We want to understand why the bureaucrats, all of whom are rational and most of whom want to do a good job, behave as they do.

To begin, let us forget about $435 hammers. They never existed. A member of Congress who did not understand (or did not want to understand) government accounting rules created a public stir. The $3,000 coffeepot existed, but it is not clear that it was overpriced. But that does not mean there are no problems; in fact, the real problems are far more costly and intractable than inflated price tags on hammers and coffeemakers. They include sticking too long with new weapons of dubious value, taking forever to acquire even good weapons, and not inducing contractors to increase their efficiency. What follows is not a complete explanation of military procurement problems; it is only an analysis of the contribution bureaucratic systems make to those problems.

When the military buys a new weapons system—a bomber, submarine, or tank—it sets in motion a procurement bureaucracy comprised of two key actors, the military program manager and the civilian contract officer, who must cope with the contractor, the Pentagon hierarchy, and Congress. To understand how they behave we must understand how their tasks get defined, what incentives they have, and what constraints they face.

Tasks

The person nominally in charge of buying a major new weapon is the program manager, typically an army or air force colonel or a navy captain. Officially, his job is to design and oversee the acquisition strategy by establishing specifications and schedules and identifying problems and tradeoffs. Unofficially, his task is somewhat different. For one thing he does not have the authority to make many important decisions; those are referred upward to his military superiors, to Defense Department civilians, and to Congress. For another, the program he oversees must constantly be sold and resold to the people who control the resources (mostly, the key congressional committees). And finally, he is surrounded by inspectors and auditors looking for any evidence of waste, fraud, or abuse and by the advocates of all manner of special interests (contractors' representatives, proponents of small and minority business utilization, and so on). As the Packard Commission observed, the program manager, "far from being the manager of the program . . . is merely one of the participants who can influence it."

Under these circumstances the actual task of the program manager tends to be defined as selling the program and staying out of trouble. Harvard Business School professor J. Ronald Fox, who has devoted much of his life to studying and participating in weapons procurement, found that a program manager must spend 30 to 50 percent of his time defending his program inside DOD and to Congress. It is entirely rational for him to do this, for a study by the General Accounting Office showed that weapons programs with effective advocates survived (including some that should have been terminated) and systems without such advocates were more likely to be ended (even some that should have been completed). Just as with the New York City skating rink, in the Pentagon there is no one who can say "yes" and make it stick. The only way to keep winning the support of the countless people who must say "yes" over and over again is to forge ahead at full speed, spending money at a rate high enough to prevent it from being taken away.

The program manager's own background and experience reinforce this definition of his task. He is a military officer, which means he cares deeply about having the best possible airplane, tank, or submarine. In recommending any tradeoffs between cost and performance, his natural inclination is to favor performance over savings. After all, someday he may have to fly in that airplane or sail on that ship. This often leads to what is commonly called "goldplating": seeking the best possible, most sophisticated weapon and making frequent changes in the contract specifications in order to incorporate new features. The program manager, of course, does not make these decisions, but he is an integral part of a user-dominated process that does make them.

The civilian counterpart to the program manager is the contracting officer. What is clear is that he or she, and not the program manager, is the only person legally authorized to sign the contract. In addition, the contracting officer administers the contract and prepares a report on contractor performance. Everything else is unclear. In principle, contracting officers are supposed to be involved in every step of the acquisition process, from issuing an invitation to bid on the contract through the completion of the project. In practice, as Ronald Fox observes, contracting officers often play only a small role in designing the acquisition strategy or in altering the contracts (this tends to be dominated by the program manager) and must share their authority over enforcing the terms of the contract with a small army of auditors and advocates.

What dominates the task of the contract officer are the rules, the more than 1,200 pages of the Federal Acquisition Regulation and Defense Acquisition Regulation in addition to the countless other pages in DOD directives and congressional authorization legislation and the unwritten "guidance" that arrives with every visit to a defense plant where a contracting officer works. Contract officers are there to enforce constraints, and those constraints have grown exponentially in recent years.

Incentives

In theory, military program managers are supposed to win promotions if they have done a good job supervising weapons procurement. In fact, promotions to the rank of general or admiral usually have been made on the basis of their reputation as combat officers and experience as military leaders. . . . The perceived message is clear: Traditional military specialties are a surer route to the top than experience as a program manager.

Reinforcing this bias against acquisition experience is the generalist ethos of the armed services—good officers can do any job; well-rounded officers have done many jobs. As a result, the typical program manager has a brief tenure in a procurement job. In 1986, the GAO found that the average program manager spent twenty-seven months on the job, and many spent less than two years. By contrast, it takes between eleven and twenty years to procure a major new weapons system, from concept to deployment. This means that during the acquisition of a new aircraft or missile, the identity of the program will change five or ten times.

In 1987, the services, under congressional prodding, established career paths for acquisition officers so that they could rise in rank while continuing to develop experience in procurement tasks. It is not yet clear how significant this change will be. If it encourages talented officers to invest ten or twenty years in mastering procurement policies it will be a major gain, one that will enable program managers from DOD to deal more effectively with experienced industry executives and encourage officers to make tough decisions rather than just keeping the program alive.

Civilian contract officers do have a distinct career path, but as yet not one that produces in them much sense of professional pride or organizational mission. Of the more than twenty thousand civilian contract administrators less than half have a college degree and the great majority are in the lower civil-service grades (GS-5 to GS-12). Even the most senior contract officers rarely earn (in 1988) more than $50,000 a year, less than half or even one-third of what their industry counterparts earn. Moreover, all are aware that they work in offices where the top posts usually are held by military officers; in civil-service jargon, the "head room" available for promotions is quite limited. . . .

The best evidence of the weakness of civilian incentives is the high turnover rate. Fox quotes a former commander of the military acquisition program as saying that "good people are leaving in droves" because "there is much less psychic income today" that would make up for the relatively low monetary income. The Packard Commission surveyed civilian procurement personnel and found that over half would leave their jobs if offered comparable jobs elsewhere in the federal government or in private industry.

In short, the incentives facing procurement officials do not reward people for maximizing efficiency. Military officers are rewarded for keeping programs alive and are encouraged to move on to other assignments, civilian personnel have weak inducements to apply a complex array of inconsistent constraints to contract administration.

Constraints

These constraints are not designed to produce efficiency but to reduce costs, avoid waste, fraud, and abuse, achieve a variety of social goals, and maintain the productive capacity of key contractors.

Reducing costs is not the same thing as increasing efficiency. If too little money is spent, the rate of production may be inefficient and the managerial flexibility necessary to cope with unforeseen circumstances may be absent. Congress typically appropriates money one year at a time. If Congress wishes to cut its spending or if DOD is ordered to slash its budget requests, the easiest thing to do is to reduce the number of aircraft, ships, or missiles being purchased in a given year without reducing the total amount purchased. This stretch-out has the effect of increasing the cost of each individual weapon as manufacturers forgo the economies that come from large-scale production. As Fox observes (but as many critics fail to understand), the typical weapons program in any given year is not overfunded, it is *under*funded. Recognizing that, the Packard Commission called for adopting a two-year budget cycle.

Reducing costs and eliminating fraud are not the same as increasing efficiency. There no doubt are excessive costs and there may be fraud in military procurement, but eliminating them makes procurement more efficient only if the costs of eliminating the waste and fraud exceed the savings thereby realized. To my knowledge no one has systematically compared the cost of all the inspectors, rules, and auditors with the savings they have achieved to see if all the checking and reviewing is worth it. Some anecdotal evidence suggests that the checking does not always pay for itself. In one case the army was required to spend $5,400 to obtain fully competitive bids for spare parts that cost $11,000. In exchange for the $5,400 and the 160 days it took to get the bids, the army saved $100. In short, there is an optimal level of "waste" in any organization, public or private: It is that level below which further savings are worth less than the cost of producing them.

The weapons procurement system must serve a number of "social" goals mandated by Congress. It must support small business, provide opportunities for minority-owned businesses, buy American-made products whenever possible, rehabilitate prisoners, provide employment for the handicapped, protect the environment, and maintain "prevailing" wage rates. One could lower the cost of procurement by eliminating some or all of the social goals the process is obliged to honor; that would produce increases in efficiency, narrowly defined. But what interest group is ready to sacrifice its most cherished goal in the name of efficiency? And if none will volunteer, how does one create a congressional majority to compel the sacrifice?

Weapons procurement also is designed to maintain the productive capacity of the major weapons builders. There is no true market in the manufacture of missiles, military aircraft, and naval vessels because typically there is only one buyer (the government) and no alternative uses for the production lines established to supply this buyer. Northrop, Lockheed, Grumman, McDonnell Douglas, the Bath Iron Works, Martin Marietta—these firms and others like them would not exist, or would exist in very different form, if they did not have a continuous flow of military contracts. As a result, each new weapons system becomes a do-or-die proposition for the executives of these firms. Even if the Pentagon cared nothing about their economic well-being it would have to care about the productive capacity that they represent, for if it were ever lost or much diminished the armed services would have nowhere else to turn when the need arose for a new airplane or ship. And if by chance the Pentagon did not care, Congress would; no member believes he or she was elected to preside over the demise of a major employer.

This constraint produces what some scholars have called the "follow-on imperative": the need to give a new contract to each major supplier as work on an old contract winds down. If one understands this it is not necessary to imagine some sinister "military-industrial complex" conspiring to keep new weapons flowing. The armed services want them because they believe, rightly, that their task is to defend the nation against real though hard to define threats; the contractors want them because they believe, rightly, that the nation cannot afford to dismantle its productive capacity; Congress wants them because its members believe, rightly, that they are elected to maintain the prosperity of their states and districts.

When these beliefs encounter the reality of limited resources and the need to make budget choices, almost everyone has an incentive to overstate the benefits and understate the costs of a new weapons system. To do otherwise—to give a cautious estimate of what the weapon will achieve and a candid view of what it will cost—is to invite rejection. And none of the key actors in the process believe they can afford rejection.

The Bottom Line

The incentives and constraints that confront the military procurement bureaucracy push its members to overstate benefits, understate costs, make frequent and detailed changes in specifications, and enforce a bewildering array of rules designed to minimize criticism and stay out of trouble. There are hardly any incentives pushing officials to leave details to manufacturers or delegate authority to strong program managers whose career prospects will depend on their ability to produce good weapons at a reasonable cost.

In view of all this, what is surprising is that the system works as well as it does. In fact, it works better than most people suppose. The Rand Corporation has been studying military procurement for over thirty years. A summary of its findings suggests some encouraging news, most of it ignored amidst the headlines about hammers and coffeepots. There has been steady improvement in the performance of the system. Between the early 1960s and the mid-1980s, cost overruns, schedule slippages, and performance shortfalls have all decreased. Cost overruns of military programs on the average are now no greater than they are for the civil programs of the government such as highway and water projects and public buildings. Moreover, there is evidence that for all its faults the American system seems to work as well or better than that in many European nations. . . .

Arbitrary Rule

Inefficiency is not the only bureaucratic problem nor is it even the most important. A perfectly efficient agency could be a monstrous one, swiftly denying us our liberties, economically inflicting injustices, and competently expropriating our wealth. People complain about bureaucracy as often because it is unfair or unreasonable as because it is slow or cumbersome.

Arbitrary rule refers to officials acting without legal authority, or with that authority in a way that offends our sense of justice. Justice means, first, that we require the government to treat people equally on the basis of clear rules known in advance: If Becky and Bob both are driving sixty miles per hour in a thirty-mile-per hour zone and the police give a ticket to Bob, we believe they also should give a ticket to Becky. Second, we believe that justice obliges the government to take into account the special needs and circumstances of individuals: If Becky is speeding because she is on her way to the hospital to give birth to a child and Bob is speeding for the fun of it, we may feel that the police should ticket Bob but not Becky. Justice in the first sense means fairness, in the second it means responsiveness. Obviously, fairness and responsiveness often are in conflict.

The checks and balances of the American constitutional system reflect our desire to reduce the arbitrariness of official rule. That desire is based squarely on the premise that inefficiency is a small price to pay for freedom and responsiveness. Congressional oversight, judicial review, interest-group participation, media investigations, and formalized procedures all are intended to check administrative discretion. It is not hyperbole to say that the constitutional order is animated by the desire to make the government "inefficient."

This creates two great tradeoffs. First, adding constraints reduces the efficiency with which the main goal of an agency can be attained but increases the chances that the agency will act in a nonarbitrary manner. Efficient police departments would seek out criminals without reading them their rights, allowing them to call their attorneys, or releasing them in response to a writ of habeas corpus. An efficient building department would issue construction permits on demand without insisting that the applicant first show that the proposed building meets fire, safety, sanitation, geological, and earthquake standards.

The second great tradeoff is between nonarbitrary governance defined as treating people equally and such governance defined as treating each case on its merits. We want the government to be both fair and responsive, but the more rules we impose to insure fairness (that is, to treat all people alike) the harder we make it for the government to be responsive (that is, to take into account the special needs and circumstances of a particular case).

The way our government manages these tradeoffs reflects both our political culture as well as the rivalries of our governing institutions. Both tend toward the same end: We define claims as rights, impose general rules to insure equal treatment, lament (but do nothing about) the resulting inefficiencies, and respond to revelations about unresponsiveness by adopting new rules intended to guarantee that special circumstances will be handled with special care (rarely bothering to reconcile the rules that require responsiveness with those that require equality). And we do all this out of the best of motives: a desire to be both just and benevolent. Justice inclines us to treat people equally, benevolence to treat them differently; both inclinations are expressed in rules, though in fact only justice can be. It is this futile desire to have a rule for every circumstance that led Herbert Kaufman to explain "how compassion spawns red tape."

Discretion at the Street Level

We worry most about arbitrary rule at the hands of those street-level bureaucracies that deal with us as individuals rather than as organized groups and that touch the more intimate aspects of our lives: police, schools, prisons, housing inspectors, mental hospitals, welfare offices, and the like. That worry is natural; in these settings we feel helpless and The State seems omnipotent. We want these bureaucracies to treat us fairly but we also want them to be responsible to our particular needs. The proper reconciliation of these competing desires requires a careful understanding of the tasks of these organizations.

There are at least two questions that must be answered: What constitutes in any specific organization the exercise of arbitrary or unjust power? Under what circumstances will the elaboration of rules reduce at an acceptable cost the unjust use of power? Police officers act unjustly when they arrest people without cause. "Equality before the law" is the bedrock principle of our criminal justice system, however imperfectly it may be realized. And so we create rules defining when people can be arrested. . . .

Discretion at the Headquarters Level

Interest groups also complain about arbitrariness, especially when they deal with regulatory agencies that have either no clear rules (and so the groups do not know whether policies in effect today will be in effect tomorrow) or rules so clear and demanding that there is no freedom to adjust their activities to conform to economic or technological imperatives.

The exercise of discretion by regulatory agencies does not occur because their activities are invisible or their clients are powerless but because these agencies and their legislative supporters have certain beliefs about what constitutes good policy. For many decades after the invention of the regulatory agency, Progressives believed that good decisions were the result of empowering neutral experts to decide cases on the basis of scientifically determined facts and widely shared principles. No one took it amiss that these "principles" often were so vague as to lack any meaning at all. The Federal Communications Commission (FCC) was directed to issue broadcast licenses as the "public interest, convenience, and necessity" shall require. A similar "standard" was to govern the awarding of licenses to airline companies by the now-defunct Civil Aeronautics Board (CAB). The Antitrust Division of the Justice Department was charged with enforcing the Sherman Act that made "combinations in restraint of trade" illegal.

What the statute left vague "experts" were to imbue with meaning. But expert opinion changes and some experts in fact are politicians who bow to the influence of organized interests or ideologues who embrace the enthusiasms of zealous factions. The result was an invitation for interests to seek particular results in the absence of universal standards.

One might suppose that the agencies, noticing the turmoil caused by having to decide hard cases on the basis of vacuous standards, would try to formulate and state clear policies that would supply to their clients the guidance that the legislature was unwilling to provide; but no. For the most part regulatory agencies with ambiguous statutes did not clarify their policies. I conjecture that this is because the agencies realized what Michel Crozier has stated: Uncertainty is power. If one party needs something from another and cannot predict how that second party will behave, the second party has power over the first. In the extreme case we will do almost anything to please a madman with life-or-death power over us because we cannot predict which behavior will produce what reaction. . . .

Conclusions

Neither inefficiency nor arbitrariness is easily defined and measured. Inefficiency in the small, that is, the excessive use of resources to achieve the main goal of an agency, is probably commonplace; but inefficiency in the large—the excessive use of resources to achieve all the goals, including the constraints—may not be so common. To evaluate the efficiency of a government agency one first must judge the value of the constraints under which it operates; to improve its efficiency one must decide which constraints one is willing to sacrifice. The best way to think about this is to ask whether we would be willing to have the same product or service delivered by a private firm.

If we decide that the constraints are important then we should be clear-eyed about the costs of retaining them. Those costs arise chiefly from the fact that most bureaucrats will be more strongly influenced by constraints than by goals. Constraints apply early in the process: You know from day one what will get you into trouble. Goals apply late in the process (if then): You must wait to see if the goal is achieved, assuming (a big assumption) that you can state the goal or confirm its achievement. Constraints are strongly enforced by attentive interest groups and their allies in Congress, the White House, the courts, and the media; goal attainment is weakly enforced because an agency head can always point to factors beyond one's control that prevented success. Constraints dissipate managerial authority; every constraint is represented in the organization by someone who can say no. Goals, if they exist and can be attained, are the basis for increasing managerial authority; a clear and attainable goal provides an opportunity for one person to say yes.

Bureaucracies will differ in their vulnerability to the tradeoff between goal attainment and constraint observance. Production organizations, having clear and attainable goals, are more easily evaluated from the standpoint of economic efficiency and thus the cost of any given constraint is more easily assessed. Coping and procedural organizations are impossible to evaluate in terms of economic efficiency and so the cost of a constraint is hard to assess. Craft organizations are a mixed case; because their outputs are observable, we know if they are attaining their goal, but because their work is hard to observe we may think mistakenly that we can alter those work procedures without paying a cost in goal attainment.

The Social Security Administration and the Postal Service are not hard to judge in efficiency terms, though the latter presents a more difficult case than the former because we want the USPS to serve a number of partially inconsistent purposes. The State Department and public schools are impossible to evaluate in efficiency terms, and so we regularly pile on more constraints without any sense that we are paying a price. Police detectives or the Army Corps of Engineers can be evaluated, but only after the fact—the crook is caught, the bridge completed—but we are at somewhat of a loss to know what alteration in procedures would have what effect on these outcomes. Prisons can be evaluated in terms of the resources they consume and the complaints they engender, but ordinarily we have little information as to whether changes in resources or complaints have any effect on such objectives as security, rehabilitation, or deterrence.

Arbitrariness means acting without legal authority, or with such authority in ways that treat like cases in an unlike manner or unlike cases in a similar manner. Deciding what constitutes a "like case" is the heart of the problem. Prisons require rules, but what ends should the rules serve—custody? Security? Self-governance? Rehabilitation? Regulatory agencies formulate rules, but under what circumstances can those rules be clear and comprehensive as opposed to vague and partial? The next [section] will not answer all these questions, but it will suggest how Americans have tried to use rules, as well as the problems with rule-oriented bureaucracy.

Rules

On February 8, 1967, Robert H. Weaver, the secretary of the Department of Housing and Urban Development, announced that henceforth persons applying for apartments in federally financed public housing projects would be given such apartments on a first-come, first-served basis. Weaver, who is black, issued the new rule in response to the criticism of civil-rights organizations (including a group he once headed) that the local managers of these projects practiced or condoned segregation.

Under the old rules the city agencies that ran these projects gave to individual project managers great discretion to pick their tenants. The effect of that discretion, combined with the preferences of the tenants, was that projects tended to be all-white or all-black. In Boston, for example, there were twenty-five public housing projects built for low-income tenants. Thirteen of these were more than 96 percent white, two were entirely black, and the rest were predominately of one race or the other. These differences could not be explained entirely by neighborhood considerations. The Mission Hill project was 100 percent white; across the street from it, the Mission Hill Extension project was 80 percent black.

Weaver's order became known as the "1-2-3 Rule." It worked this way: All housing applicants would be ranked in numerical order based on the date they applied for housing, their need for housing, and the size of their families. When a vacancy became available it would be offered to the family at the top of the list. If there were more than one vacancy the one offered first would be drawn from the project with the most vacancies. If the family turned it down it would be offered another, and then a third. If all three vacancies were rejected the family would go to the bottom of the list and the next family in line would receive the offer. The Weaver order was an effort, typical of many in government, to prevent the arbitrary use of discretion by replacing discretion with a rule.

Eight years later a group of tenants sued the Boston Housing Authority (BHA). In his findings, the Housing Court judge determined that public housing in Boston still was being allocated in a way that perpetuated racial segregation, a view confirmed by a 1976 report of the Department of Housing and Urban Development. What had gone wrong? How could a discriminatory pattern of tenant assignment persist for so long after the BHA had implemented, albeit reluctantly, a clear federal rule that on its face did not allow race to be taken into account in choosing tenants?

The answer, supplied by the research of Jon Pynoos and Jeffrey M. Prottas, suggests the limit to rules as a means for controlling the discretion of bureaucrats. First, the 1-2-3 Rule combined three criteria: date, need, and family size. To rank applicants by these criteria someone had to decide how to measure "need" and then how much weight to give to need as opposed to family size or date of application. The evaluation of need inevitably was subjective. Moreover, the neediest families almost by definition were those who had been on the waiting list for the least time. For example, a family living on the street because its home had burned down the night before clearly is going to be regarded as needier than one whose home is livable but who may have been on the waiting list for many months. Second, the rules were inconsistent with the incentives facing the applicants. Applicants wanted to live in the "nicest" projects, but these usually had few vacancies. The worst projects, those with the most crime, litter, and graffiti, had the most vacancies. Applicants would rather turn down a bad project, even if it meant going to the bottom of the list. Since the bad projects often were all-black, this meant that hardly any families, especially any white families, were willing to move in, and so they tended to remain all-black. Third, the rules were inconsistent with the incentives facing the project managers. Managers were exposed to pressure from the tenants in the buildings they operated to keep out the "bad element"—drug users, prostitutes, families with noisy children—and to attract the "good element," such as retired couples and the elderly. The managers bent to these pressures by various stratagems such as concealing the existence of vacancies from the central office or finding ways to veto the applications of certain tenants.

Rules and Discretion

Max Weber said that the great virtue of bureaucracy—indeed, perhaps its defining characteristic—was that it was an institutional method for applying general rules to specific cases, thereby making the actions of government fair and predictable. Weber's belief in the superiority of rule-based governance has been echoed by Theodore J. Lowi, who has criticized the exercise of administrative discretion in the modern American state on the grounds that it leads to the domination of the state by interest groups, thereby weakening popular control and creating new structures of privilege. To restore democratic accountability he called for replacing discretionary authority with what he termed "juridical democracy": governance based on clear legislative standards for bureaucratic action or, failing that, on clear rules formulated by the bureaucracies themselves. When rules are clear, governance is better. Lawrence Friedman has argued that welfare and public housing programs are especially suitable for governance by rule because they involve the simple allocation of resources on an equitable basis. . . .

On occasion, Americans have temporarily abandoned their fear of discretion and their insistence on rules. During the New Deal a number of regulatory agencies—the Securities and Exchange Commission, the National Labor Relations Board, the Federal Communications Commission—were endowed with great powers and vague standards. But in time we have returned to our natural posture, insisting that the powers of any new agencies carefully be circumscribed by law (as they were with the Environmental Protection Agency) and that the powers of existing agencies be if not precisely defined then at least judicially reviewable. But the love of rules has obscured the question of the circumstances under which rules will work. Clearly, an apparently simple rule did not solve the problems of the Boston Housing Authority.

As we saw, the first-come, first-served rule had several defects. Those defects suggest some of the properties a workable and fair rule should have. First, a good rule should treat equals equally. The BHA rule attempted to allocate dissimilar things among dissimilar claimants. Not all apartments were the same: They varied in size, amenity, and, above all, location. Not all clients were the same: Some were law-abiding, some lawless; some were orderly, some disorderly. Second, an effective rule will specify the tradeoffs to be made among the criteria governing the application of the rule. The BHA rule did not do this and in fact could not have done it. Need and time on the waiting list often were in conflict and there was no nonarbitrary way to resolve the conflict. Third, a workable rule will be consistent with the incentives operating on the administrators and on at least some of the clients. Neither the BHA clients nor its managers had many incentives to conform to the rules. The clients wanted to move into "nice" housing; very few wanted to integrate housing, whatever the cost in amenity. The managers wanted to get "nice" clients; very few wanted problem families. We want rules to be clear, but the BHA rule only seemed to be clear.

Rules and Tasks

When the work and the outcomes of a government agency are observable and unambiguous some but not all of the conditions for management by rule are present. I have called such bureaus production agencies. . . . Processing claims for old-age and survivors' insurance in the Social Security Administration (SSA) is subject to very detailed rules. These rules seem to work well. This happens not only because the work (processing claims) and the outcomes (who gets how much money) are easily observed, but also because the rules meet or come very close to meeting the tests described in the preceding section: They refer to comparable cases (people of a defined age and marital status), they do not involve difficult tradeoffs (unless the Social Security Trust Fund runs out of money, everybody who meets certain tests gets money), and they conform to the natural incentives of the agency members (the service ethos of the SSA leads its employees to want to give money to every eligible person).

SSA also manages the disability insurance program. This makes the use of rules a bit more complicated because the definition of a disabled person is much more ambiguous than that of an elderly or retired one. In his excellent book on SSA management of the disability program [*Bureaucratic Justice: Managing Social Security Claims* (1983)], Jerry Mashaw concluded that despite the ambiguity the program works reasonably well. One reason is that every disabled person is entitled to benefits whatever his or her financial need; thus the definition of "disabled," although vague, does not have to be traded off against an even vaguer definition of need. Moreover, the lack of clarity in the rules defining disability is made up for by the working environment of the operators. The examiners who review claims for disability payments work elbow-to-elbow with their peers and supervisors. The claims are all in writing, there is no need to make snap judgments, and the decisions are reviewable by quality assurance inspectors. Dissatisfied claimants can appeal the decisions to administrative law judges. Out of this deliberate process there has emerged a kind of common law of disability, a set of precedents that reflects pooled experience and shared judgments.

The use of rules becomes more difficult in local welfare offices. These agencies administer the federal Aid to Families with Dependent Children program that, until it was changed in 1988, authorized the states to pay money to needy women who had children but no husbands and were otherwise fit but unemployable parents. It is very hard to make clear rules on these matters. What is a "fit" or an "employable" parent? How much does a given woman "need"? Some countries such as Great Britain do not try to solve these problems by rule; instead they empower welfare workers to make a judgment about each case and to use their discretion in approving payments.

In the United States, we use rules—up to a point. Since many of the rules are inevitably vague, the welfare workers who administer them have a significant amount of discretion. An intake worker could use that discretion to deny benefits to women on grounds of fitness or employability. But in fact they rarely do. Joel Handler, who studied welfare administration in Wisconsin in the 1960s, described how welfare workers used the rules they were given: In essence they focused on what was measurable. In each of the six counties investigated by Handler, the questions asked of applicants chiefly involved assessing the women's financial resources. The rule that was enforced was the means test: "Are your resources sufficiently inadequate as to justify your participation in this program?" If the applicant passed the means test the rest of the interview was about her budget—how much money she needed and for what. In only a minority of the cases were any questions asked about employability, marriage plans, or child-care practices. Though the federal government once tried by a law passed in 1962 to get welfare workers to deliver "social services" to their clients, the workers did not deliver them.

Welfare workers could get in trouble for allowing ineligible clients to get on the welfare rolls. But only *financial* ineligibility was easily determined, and so the rules governing money were the rules that were enforced. The workers had little incentive to find out how the clients led their lives and even less to tell them how they ought to lead those lives.

If rules are such an imperfect guide to action even in welfare and housing agencies (where according to Friedman their application was supposed to be straightforward), it is not hard to imagine how much more imperfect their use will be in coping, procedural, or craft agencies. Consider police patrol officers. We expect them to prevent disorderly conduct, but it is virtually impossible to define disorderly (or orderly) conduct. Behavior that is frightening to an old woman or nerve-wracking to a diamond-cutter is fun to a teenager or necessary to a garbage collector. Because we cannot produce a clear rule by which to guide the police control of disorderly conduct does not mean that the police should do nothing about disorder. But what they will do always will be a matter of dispute.

Or consider the "rules" contained in the Education for All Handicapped Children Act passed by Congress in 1975. It required each state to guarantee by a certain date a free and appropriate education for all handicapped children between the ages of three and twenty-one. That goal, however laudable, strained the capacity of every state's educational system. But if tight timetables and scarce resources were the only problems the law would not have raised any fundamental administrative problems. What made matters worse was that the law did not leave the selection of means to local authorities; instead it required the schools to develop for each eligible child an Individualized Education Program, or IEP, that specified short-term and annual instructional goals as well as the services that were to be supplied to attain those goals. Each IEP was to be developed jointly by a team comprised of the child's teacher and parents together with specialists in education for the handicapped and others "as necessary." If a parent disagreed with the IEP, he or she was afforded a due-process hearing. Here, a bureaucracy—the public school—the work and outputs of which can barely be observed (much less measured) was obliged to follow a rule that called for the education of every handicapped child (but not every "normal" one) on the basis of an individual plan that could be shaped and enforced by going to court.

Rules, like ideas, have consequences. When there is a mismatch between legal rules and bureaucratic realities, the rules get subverted. The subversion in this case took two forms. First, teachers struggling to find the time and energy for their daily tasks would not refer potentially eligible children to the special-education program. And when they did refer them they often made the decision on the basis not of which child most needed special education but of which child was giving the teacher the most trouble in the classroom. Second, some parents but not others took advantage of their due-process rights. Most observers agree that competent, middle-class parents were more effective at using the legal system than less competent, lower-class parents.

Because of the law, more is being done today for handicapped children than was once the case, but how it is being done cannot readily be inferred from the IEP rules. If some critics are right the insistence on defining education by means of formal, legally enforceable rules has led to substituting paperwork and procedure for services and results. This should not be surprising. A rule is a general statement prescribing how a class of behaviors should be conducted. Using a general statement to produce an individualized result is almost a contradiction in terms. We tailor behavior in accordance with individual circumstances precisely in those cases when the circumstances defy classification by rule.

The bureaucratic behaviors that most easily can be defined by rule tend to be those that are frequent, similar, and patterned—those that are routine. SSA easily applied rules in advance to its retirement benefits; with somewhat more difficulty it began to develop rules for disability claims. By contrast, the National Labor Relations Board (NLRB) has few rules. "Neither the fulminations of commentators nor the prodding of courts," Mashaw writes, "has convinced it that any of its vague adjudicatory doctrines can bear particularization or objectification in regulatory form." The Federal Communications Commission (FCC) for a long time resisted demands that it formulate into clear rules the standards it would use for awarding broadcast licenses. The NLRB and the FCC saw themselves as quasi-judicial bodies that decided each unique case on its individual merits. In fact, many NLRB and FCC policies probably could have been reduced to rule. The FCC did this when it finally announced what it had long practiced: that broadcast licenses routinely would be renewed absent some showing that they should not be. Commissions, like courts, resist routinization, perhaps because they delve so deeply into the matters before them that they see differences where others see similarities.

Rules and Impermissible Outcomes

Even where bureaucratic behavior is not so routinized that it can be conveniently prescribed by rule, we insist on rules when there is a significant risk of an impermissible outcome. There is no reason in principle why we could not repeal the laws against homicide and create in their stead a Commission on Life Enhancement and Preservation (CLEP) that would hear complaints about persons who had killed other persons. It would consider evidence about the character of the deceased: Was he lazy or dutiful, decent or disorderly, likable or hateful? On the basis of this evaluation of the lost life and relying on the professional judgment of its staff, the CLEP would decide whether the life lost was worth losing and, if not, whether the person who took it was justified in doing so. By thus decriminalizing homicide, we surely would experience a reduction in the number of events officially labeled murders since the CLEP would undoubtedly conclude that many who had been killed richly deserved their fate.

Most of us would not vote for such a proposal because we attach so high a value to human life that we are unwilling to trust anyone, especially any bureaucrat employed by CLEP, to decide who should die and who should live. We hold this view despite our belief that there are probably some (perhaps many) that the world would be better off without. In short, the risk of error—in this case, wrongly deciding that a worthy life had been a worthless one—is so great that we allow no discretion to the government. If a person who kills another is to escape punishment, it must be for particular excusing conditions (for example, self-defense) and not because of a government-assessed valuation of the lost life.

The laws of this country have multiplied beyond measure the number of outcomes that are deemed impermissible. From 1938 to 1958, the Food and Drug Administration (FDA) had the authority to prevent the sale or distribution of any drug unless it was shown by "adequate tests" to be safe. In 1958 new legislation was passed that directed it to bar from sale or distribution any food additive, food color, or drug administered to food animals if "it is found to induce cancer when ingested by man or animal." This was the so-called Delaney Amendment, named after the New York congressman who sponsored it.

Ignoring for the moment certain exceptions, the Delaney Amendment implied that we should swallow nothing that might cause cancer in the kinds of laboratory animals on which scientists test foods. In principle, this meant that the FDA was hostage to progress in analytical chemistry: As scientists improved their ability to detect cancer-causing chemicals, the FDA would be obliged to ban those chemicals (and the foods they contained) from the supermarket shelves. Cancer was a risk, the FDA was told, that it was impermissible to run, whatever the costs. Thus it was to enforce the rule, "no cancer."

But when the FDA in 1979 used this rule to ban saccharin, the artificial sweetener used in such products as "Sweet 'n Low," it suddenly discovered that Congress did not mean what it had said—at least in this case. "All hell broke loose," recalled one representative. Consumers wanted to use saccharin in order to lose weight, even if scientists had discovered that in very high dosages it induced bladder cancer in laboratory animals. Faced with this popular revolt, Congress swiftly passed a law delaying (and ultimately prohibiting) the FDA ban on saccharin. But Congress did not review the Delaney Amendment: It stood as a rule that could not (with certain minor exceptions) be traded off against any other rule. . . .

The United States relies on rules to control the exercise of official judgment to a greater extent than any other industrialized democracy. The reason, I think, has little to do with the kinds of bureaucrats we have and everything to do with the political environment in which those bureaucrats must work. If we wish to complain about how rule-ridden our government agencies seem to be, we should direct those complaints not to the agencies but to the Congress, the courts, and the organized interests that make effective use of Congress and the courts.

Rules: Gains and Losses

The difficulty of striking a reasonable balance between rules and discretion is an age-old problem for which there is no "objective" solution any more than there is to the tension between other competing human values such as freedom and order, love and discipline, or change and stability. At best we can sensitize ourselves to the gains and losses associated with governance by rule rather than by discretion.

Rules, if they are clear, induce agencies to produce certain observable outcomes: nursing homes must have fire sprinklers, hotels must have smoke alarms, dairy products may not contain polychorinated biphenyls (PCBs), automobiles must be equipped with crashworthy bumpers and steering wheels. But rules often cannot induce organizations to improve hard-to-observe processes. A nursing home may be safer because it has certain equipment installed, but it will not be well run unless it has competent head nurses. Eugene Bardach and Robert Kagan make this point by comparing public and private factory inspections. An inspector from OSHA charged with enforcing rules will evaluate the physical aspects of a factory: the ventilation, guardrails, and safety devices. By contrast, an inspector from an insurance company charged with assessing the insurability of the firm will evaluate the attitude and policies of management: its safety consciousness. The difference in approaches is important because, if John Mendeloff is correct, "most workplace injuries are not caused by violations of standards [i.e., rules], and even fewer are caused by violations that inspectors can detect."

Rules create offices, procedures, and claims inside an organization that can protect precarious values. An automobile company is required to comply with OSHA rules. If the only effect of the rules were the company's fear of inspectors, not much would happen. But to cope with the inspectors the company will hire its own industrial safety experts, and these in turn will establish procedures and generate pressures that alter the company's behavior even when it is not being inspected. At the same time, rules generate paperwork and alter human relationships in ways that can reduce the ability of the organization to achieve its goals and its incentives to cooperate with those who enforce the rules. To verify that military aircraft are built according to government specifications, hundreds of pounds of forms must be filled out that document each operation on each aircraft; these forms, one set for every individual airplane, must be stored for twenty years. Nurses must record every step in medical treatments. Personnel officers must document the grounds for every hiring and promotional decision. Teachers must fill out sign-in sheets, absence slips, attendance records, textbook requests, lesson plans, student evaluations, questionnaires, ethnic and language surveys, free-lunch applications, time cards, field-trip requests, special-needs assessments, and parental conference reports. Rarely does anybody read these forms. They are, after all, what Bardach and Kagan call a "declaration of innocence"; no aircraft company, charge nurse, personnel officer, or schoolteacher will use these forms to admit their wrongdoing, and so no government inspector will read them. The rules and the forms contribute to the adversarial relationship that so often characterizes the relationship between regulator and regulatee.

Rules specify minimum standards that must be met. This is a clear gain when an organization, public or private, is performing below the minimum. But minimum standards often become maximum standards. Alvin Gouldner first noticed this in his study of a private firm, the General Gypsum Company (a pseudonym). Suppose workers were expected to "get the day's job done." Some would work less than eight hours, some much longer. Now suppose that a rule is announced—"everybody will work eight hours"—and a device (the time clock) is installed to enforce it. Laggards would now work eight hours but zealots would stop working more than eight. Bardach and Kagan observed this in the case of OSHA rules: At one time, a company would improve ventilating or lighting systems when workers or union leaders complained about these matters; later, the company would make no changes unless required by OSHA rules.

To decide whether the gains from imposing a rule outweigh the costs you must carefully judge the particular circumstances of a given organization. In other words, no rule can be promulgated that tells you when promulgating rules is a good idea. But at least the tensions highlighted in this section should make you aware that rules have risks and teach you to be sensitive to the fact that the American political system is biased toward solving bureaucratic problems by issuing rules. Given that bias, people who worry about the costs of rules usually will not be heard very clearly in the hubbub of concern about an unmet need or a bureaucratic failure.

Talented, strongly motivated people usually will find ways of making even rule-ridden systems work. This is especially the case when complying with the rules is seen as a mere formality; a form to be filled out, a box to be checked, a file to be kept. Teachers, nurses, police officers, and housing project managers can find ways of getting the job done—if they want to.

The managerial problem arises from two facts: First, talented, strongly motivated workers are a minority in any organization. People who can cope with rules will be outnumbered by people who hide behind them. . . .

Second, whatever behavior will get an agency executive in trouble will get a manager in trouble; whatever gets a manager in trouble will get an operator in trouble. Or put another way: Agency executives have a strong incentive to enforce on their subordinates those rules the violation of which create external political difficulties for the executive. This means that even talented and motivated operators will not be free to violate rules that threaten their agency, even if the rule itself is silly. Many agency executives do not understand this. They are eager to deflect or mollify critics of their agencies. In their eagerness they suppose that announcing a rule designed to forbid whatever behavior led to the criticism actually will work. Their immediate subordinates, remote from field pressures (and perhaps eager to ingratiate themselves with the executive) will assure their bosses that the new rule will solve the problem. But unless the rule actually redefines the core tasks of the operators in a meaningful and feasible way, or significantly alters the incentives those operators value, the rule will be seen as just one more constraint on getting the job done (or, more graphically, as "just another piece of chicken——t").

8-2

The Politics of Bureaucratic Structure

Terry M. Moe

Legislators, presidents, and other political players care about the content and implementation of policy. They also care about the way executive agencies are structured: Where in the executive branch are new agencies placed? What kind of bureaucrat will be motivated to aggressively pursue, or to resist the pursuit of, certain policy goals? Who should report to whom? What rules should govern bureaucrats' behavior? In the following essay, Terry M. Moe observes that these questions are anticipated and answered by politicians as they set policy. They are the subjects of "structural" politics. The federal bureaucracy is not structured on the basis of a theory of public administration, Moe argues, but should instead be viewed as the product of politics.

AMERICAN PUBLIC BUREAUCRACY is not designed to be effective. The bureaucracy arises out of politics, and its design reflects the interests, strategies, and compromises of those who exercise political power.

This politicized notion of bureaucracy has never appealed to most academics or reformers. They accept it—indeed, they adamantly argue its truth—and the social science of public bureaucracy is a decidedly political body of work as a result. Yet, for the most part, those who study and practice public administration have a thinly veiled disdain for politics, and they want it kept out of bureaucracy as much as possible. They want presidents to stop politicizing the departments and bureaus. They want Congress to stop its incessant meddling in bureaucratic affairs. They want all politicians to respect bureaucratic autonomy, expertise, and professionalism.[1]

The bureaucracy's defenders are not apologists. Problems of capture, inertia, parochialism, fragmentation, and imperialism are familiar grounds for criticism. And there is lots of criticism. But once the subversive influence of politics is mentally factored out, these bureaucratic problems are understood to have bureaucratic solutions—new mandates, new rules and procedures, new personnel systems, better training and management, better people. These are the quintessential reforms that politicians are urged to adopt to bring about effective bureau-

Source: John E. Chubb and Paul E. Peterson, eds., *Can the Government Govern?* (Washington, D.C.: Brookings Institution Press, 1989), 267–285. Some notes appearing in the original have been deleted.

cracy. The goal at all times is the greater good: "In designing any political structure, whether it be the Congress, the executive branch, or the judiciary, it is important to build arrangements that weigh the scale in favor of those advocating the national interest." [2]

The hitch is that those in positions of power are not necessarily motivated by the national interest. They have their own interests to pursue in politics—the interests of southwest Pennsylvania or cotton farmers or the maritime industry—and they exercise their power in ways conducive to those interests. Moreover, choices about bureaucratic structure are not matters that can be separated off from all this, to be guided by technical criteria of efficiency and effectiveness. Structural choices have important consequences for the content and direction of policy, and political actors know it. When they make choices about structure, they are implicitly making choices about policy. And precisely because this is so, issues of structure are inevitably caught up in the larger political struggle. Any notion that political actors might confine their attention to policymaking and turn organizational design over to neutral criteria or efficiency experts denies the realities of politics.

This essay is an effort to understand bureaucracy by understanding its foundation in political choice and self-interest. The central question boils down to this: what sorts of structures do the various political actors—interest groups, presidents, members of Congress, bureaucrats—find conducive to their own interests, and what kind of bureaucracy is therefore likely to emerge from their efforts to exercise political power? In other words, why do they build the bureaucracy they do? ...

A Perspective on Structural Politics

Most citizens do not get terribly excited about the arcane details of public administration. When they choose among candidates in elections, they pay attention to such things as party or image or stands on policy. If pressed, the candidates would probably have views or even voting records on structural issues—for example, whether the Occupational Safety and Health Administration should be required to carry out cost-benefit analysis before proposing a formal rule or whether the Consumer Product Safety Commission should be moved into the Commerce Department—but this is hardly the stuff that political campaigns are made of. People just do not know or care much about these sorts of things.

Organized interest groups are another matter. They are active, informed participants in their specialized issue areas, and they know that their policy goals are crucially dependent on precisely those fine details of administrative structure that cause voters' eyes to glaze over. Structure is valuable to them, and they have every incentive to mobilize their political resources to get what they want. As a result, they are normally the only source of political pressure when structural issues are at stake. Structural politics is interest group politics.

Interest Groups: The Technical Problem of Structural Choice

Most accounts of structural politics pay attention to interest groups, but their analytical focus is on the politicians who exercise public authority and make the final choices. This tends to be misleading. It is well known that politicians, even legislators from safe districts, are extraordinarily concerned about their electoral popularity and, for that reason, are highly responsive to their constituencies. To the extent this holds true, their positions on issues are not really their own, but are induced by the positions of others. If one seeks to understand why structural choices turn out as they do, then, it does not make much sense to start with politicians. The more fundamental questions have to do with how interest groups decide what kinds of structures they want politicians to provide. This is the place to start.

In approaching these questions about interest groups, it is useful to begin with an extreme case. Suppose that, in a given issue area, there is a single dominant group (or coalition) with a reasonably complex problem—pollution, poverty, job safety, health—it seeks to address through governmental action, and that the group is so powerful that politicians will enact virtually any proposal the group offers, subject to reasonable budget constraints. In effect, the group is able to exercise public authority on its own by writing legislation that is binding on everyone and enforceable in the courts.

The dominant group is an instructive case because, as it makes choices about structure, it faces no political problems. It need not worry about losing its grip on public authority or about the influence of its political opponents—considerations which would otherwise weigh heavily in its calculations. Without the usual uncertainties and constraints of politics, the group has the luxury of concerning itself entirely with the technical requirements of effective organization. Its job is to identify those structural arrangements that best realize its policy goals.

It is perhaps natural to think that, since a dominant group can have anything it wants, it would proceed by figuring out what types of behaviors are called for by what types of people under what types of conditions and by writing legislation spelling all this out in the minutest detail. If an administrative agency were necessary to perform services, process applications, or inspect business operations, the jobs of bureaucrats could be specified with such precision that they would have little choice but to do the group's bidding.

For simple policy goals—requiring, say, little more than transfer payments—these strategies would be attractive. But they are quite unsuited to policy problems of any complexity. The reason is that, although the group has the political power to impose its will on everyone, it almost surely lacks the knowledge to do it well. It does not know what to tell people to do.

In part, this is an expertise problem. Society as a whole simply has not developed sufficient knowledge to determine the causes of or solutions for most social problems; and the group typically knows much less than society does, even when it hires experts of its own. These knowledge problems are compounded by uncertainty about the future. The world is subject to unpredictable changes over time, and some will call on specific policy adjustments if the group's interests are to be pursued effectively. The group could attempt to specify all future contingencies in the current legislation and, through continuous monitoring and intervention, update it over time. But the knowledge requirements of a halfway decent job would prove enormously costly, cumbersome, and time-consuming.

A group with the political power to tell everyone what to do, then, will typically not find it worthwhile to try. A more attractive option is to write legislation in general terms, put experts on the public payroll, and grant them the authority to "fill in the details" and make whatever adjustments are necessary over time. This compensates nicely for the group's formidable knowledge problems, allowing it to pursue its own interests without knowing exactly how to implement its policies and without having to grapple with future contingencies. The experts do what the group is unable to do for itself. And because they are public officials on the public payroll, the arrangement economizes greatly on the group's resources and time.

It does, however, raise a new worry: there is no guarantee the experts will always act in the group's best interests. Experts have their own interests—in career, in autonomy—that may conflict with those of the group. And, due largely to experts' specialized knowledge and the often intangible nature of their outputs, the group cannot know exactly what its expert agents are doing or why. These are problems of conflict of interest and asymmetric information, and they are unavoidable. Because of them, control will be imperfect.

When the group's political power is assured, as we assume it is here, these control problems are at the heart of structural choice. The most direct approach is for the group to impose a set of rules to constrain bureaucratic behavior. Among other things, these rules might specify the criteria and procedures bureaucrats are to use in making decisions; shape incentives by specifying how bureaucrats are to be evaluated, rewarded, and sanctioned; require them to collect and report certain kinds of information on their internal operations, and set up oversight procedures by which their activities can be monitored. These are basic components of bureaucratic structure.

But some slippage will remain. The group's knowledge problems, combined with the experts' will and capacity to resist (at least at the margins), make perfect control impossible. Fortunately, though, the group can do more than impose a set of rules on its agents. It also has the power to choose who its agents will be—and wise use of this power could make the extensive use of rules unnecessary.

The key here is reputation. Most individuals in the expert market come with reputations that speak to their job-relevant traits: expertise, intelligence, honesty, loyalty, policy preferences, ideology. "Good" reputations provide reliable information. The reason is that individuals value good reputations, they invest in them—by behaving honestly, for instance, even when they could realize short-term gains through cheating—and, having built up reputations, they have strong incentives to maintain them through consistent behavior. To the group, therefore, reputation is of enormous value because it allows predictability in an uncertain world. And predictability facilitates control.

To see more concretely how this works, consider an important reputational syndrome: professionalism. If individuals are known to be accountants or securities lawyers or highway engineers, the group will immediately know a great deal about their "type." They will be experts in certain issues. They will have specialized educations and occupational experiences. They will analyze issues, collect data, and propose solutions in characteristic ways. They will hew to the norms of their professional communities. Particularly when professionalism is combined with reputational information of a more personal nature, the behavior of these experts will be highly predictable.

The link between predictability and control would seem especially troublesome in this case, since professionals are widely known to demand autonomy in their work. And, as far as restrictive rules and hierarchical directives are concerned, their demand for autonomy does indeed pose problems. But the group is forced to grant experts discretion anyway, owing to its knowledge problems. What professionalism does—via reputation—is allow the group to anticipate how expert discretion will be exercised under various conditions; it can then plan accordingly as it designs a structure that takes best advantage of their expertise. In the extreme, one might think of professionals as automatons, programmed to behave in specific ways. Knowing how they are programmed, the group can select those with the desired programs, place them in a structure designed to accommodate them, and turn them loose to exercise free choice. The professionals would see themselves as independent decision makers. The group would see them as under control. And both would be right.

The purpose of this illustration is not to emphasize professionalism per se, but to clarify a general point about the technical requirements of organizational design. A politically powerful group, acting under uncertainty and concerned with solving a complex policy problem, is normally best off if it resists using its power to tell bureaucrats exactly what to do. It can use its power more productively by selecting the right types of bureaucrats and designing a structure that affords them reasonable autonomy. Through the judicious allocation of bureaucratic roles and responsibilities, incentive systems, and structural checks on bureaucratic choice, a select set of bureaucrats can be unleashed to follow their expert judgment, free from detailed formal instructions.

Interest Groups: The Political Problem of Structural Choice

Political dominance is an extreme case for purposes of illustration. In the real world of democratic politics, interest groups cannot lay claim to unchallenged legal authority. Because this is so, they face two fundamental problems that a dominant group does not. The first I will call political uncertainty, the second political compromise. Both have enormous consequences for the strategic design of public bureaucracy—consequences that entail substantial departures from effective organization.

Political uncertainty is inherent in democratic government. No one has a perpetual hold on public authority nor, therefore, a perpetual right to control public agencies. An interest group may be powerful enough to exercise public authority today, but tomorrow its power may ebb, and its right to exercise public authority may then be usurped by its political opponents. Should this occur, they would become the new "owners" of whatever the group had created, and they could use their authority to destroy—quite legitimately—everything the group had worked so hard to achieve.

A group that is currently advantaged, then, must anticipate all this. Precisely because its own authority is not guaranteed, it cannot afford to focus entirely on technical issues of effective organization. It must also design its creations so that they have the capacity to pursue its policy goals in a world in which its enemies may achieve the right to govern. The group's task in the current period, then, is to build agencies that are difficult for its opponents to gain control over later. Given the way authority is allocated and exercised in a democracy, this will often mean building agencies that are insulated from public authority in general—and thus insulated from formal control by the group itself.

There are various structural means by which the group can try to protect and nurture its bureaucratic agents. They include the following:

- It can write detailed legislation that imposes rigid constraints on the agency's mandate and decision procedures. While these constraints will tend to be flawed, cumbersome, and costly, they serve to remove important types of decisions from future political control. The reason they are so attractive is rooted in the American separation-of-powers system, which sets up obstacles that make formal legislation extremely difficult to achieve—and, if achieved, extremely difficult to overturn. Should the group's opponents gain in political power, there is a good chance they would still not be able to pass corrective legislation of their own.

- It can place even greater emphasis on professionalism than is technically justified, since professionals will generally act to protect their own autonomy and resist political interference. For similar reasons, the group can be a strong supporter of the career civil service and other personnel systems that insulate bureaucratic jobs, promotion, and pay from political intervention. And it can try to minimize the power and number of political appointees, since these too are routes by which opponents may exercise influence.

- It can oppose formal provisions that enhance political oversight and involvement. The legislative veto, for example, is bad because it gives opponents a direct mechanism for reversing agency decisions. Sunset provisions, which require reauthorization of the agency after some period of time, are also dangerous because they give opponents opportunities to overturn the group's legislative achievements.

- It can see that the agency is given a safe location in the scheme of government. Most obviously, it might try to place the agency in a friendly executive department, where it can be sheltered by the group's allies. Or it may favor formal independence, which provides special protection from presidential removal and managerial powers.

- It can favor judicialization of agency decision making as a way of insulating policy choices from outside interference. It can also favor making various types of agency actions—or inactions—appealable to the courts. It must take care to design these procedures and checks, however, so that they disproportionately favor the group over its opponents.

The driving force of political uncertainty, then, causes the winning group to favor structural designs it would never favor on technical grounds alone: designs that place detailed formal restrictions on bureaucratic discretion, impose complex procedures for agency decision making, minimize opportunities for oversight, and otherwise insulate the agency from politics. The group has to protect itself and its agency from the dangers of democracy, and it does so by imposing structures that appear strange and incongruous indeed when judged by almost any reasonable standards of what an effective organization ought to look like.

But this is only part of the story. The departure from technical rationality is still greater because of a second basic feature of American democratic politics: legislative victory of any consequence almost always requires compromise. This means that opposing groups will have a direct say in how the agency and its mandate are constructed. One form that this can take, of course, is the classic compromise over policy that is written about endlessly in textbooks and newspapers. But there is no real disjunction between policy and structure, and many of the opponents' interests will also be pursued through demands for structural concessions. What sorts of arrangements should they tend to favor?

- Opponents want structures that work against effective performance. They fear strong, coherent, centralized organization. They like fragmented authority, decentralization, federalism, checks and balances, and other structural means of promoting weakness, confusion, and delay.
- They want structures that allow politicians to get at the agency. They do not want to see the agency placed within a friendly department, nor do they favor formal independence. They are enthusiastic supporters of legislative veto and reauthorization provisions. They favor onerous requirements for the collection and reporting of information, the monitoring of agency operations, and the review of agency decisions—thus laying the basis for active, interventionist oversight by politicians.
- They want appointment and personnel arrangements that allow for political direction of the agency. They also want more active and influential roles for political appointees and less extensive reliance on professionalism and the civil service.
- They favor agency decision making procedures that allow them to participate, to present evidence and arguments, to appeal adverse agency decisions, to delay, and, in general, to protect their own interests and inhibit effective agency action through formal, legally sanctioned rules. This means that they will tend to push for cumbersome, heavily judicialized decision processes, and that they will favor an active, easily triggered role for the courts in reviewing agency decisions.
- They want agency decisions to be accompanied by, and partially justified in terms of, "objective" assessments of their consequences: environmental impact statements, inflation impact statements, cost-benefit analysis. These are costly, time-consuming, and disruptive. Even better, their methods and conclusions can be challenged in the courts, providing new opportunities for delaying or quashing agency decisions.

Political compromise ushers the fox into the chicken coop. Opposing groups are dedicated to crippling the bureaucracy and gaining control over its decisions, and they will pressure for fragmented authority, labyrinthine procedures, mechanisms of political intervention, and other structures that subvert the bureaucracy's performance and open it up to attack. In the politics of structural choice, the inevitability of compromise means that agencies will be burdened with structures fully intended to cause their failure.

In short, democratic government gives rise to two major forces that cause the structure of public bureaucracy to depart from technical rationality. First, those currently in a position to exercise public authority will often face uncertainty about their own grip on political power in the years ahead, and this will prompt them to favor structures that insulate their achievements from politics. Second, opponents will also tend to have a say in structural design, and, to the degree they do, they will impose structures that subvert effective performance and politicize agency decisions.

Legislators and Structural Choice

If politicians were nothing more than conduits for political pressures, structural choice could be understood without paying much attention to them. But politicians, especially presidents, do sometimes have preferences about the structure of government that are not simple reflections of what the groups want. And when this is so, they can use their control of public authority to make their preferences felt in structural outcomes.

The conduit notion is not so wide of the mark for legislators, owing to their almost paranoid concern for reelection. In structural politics, well informed interest groups make demands, observe legislators' responses, and accurately assign credit and blame as decisions are made and consequences realized. Legislators therefore have strong incentives to do what groups want—and, even in the absence of explicit demands, to take entrepreneurial action in actively representing group interests. They cannot satisfy groups with empty position taking. Nor can they costlessly "shift the responsibility" by delegating tough decisions to the bureaucracy. Interest groups, unlike voters, are not easily fooled.

This does not mean that legislators always do what groups demand of them. Autonomous behavior can arise even among legislators who are motivated by nothing other than reelection. This happens because politicians, like groups, recognize that their current choices are not just means of responding to current pressures, but are also means of imposing structure on their political lives. This will sometimes lead them to make unpopular choices today in order to reap political rewards later on.

It is not quite right, moreover, to suggest that legislators have no interest of their own in controlling the bureaucracy. The more control legislators are able to exercise, the more groups will depend on them to get what they want; and this, in itself, makes control electorally attractive. But the attractiveness of control is diluted by other factors. First, the winning group—the more powerful side—will pressure to have its victories removed from political influence. Second, the capacity for control can be a curse for legislators in later conflict, since both sides will descend on them repeatedly. Third, oversight for purposes of serious policy control is time-consuming, costly, and difficult to do well; legislators typically have much more productive ways to spend their scarce resources.

The result is that legislators tend not to invest in general policy control. Instead, they value "particularized" control: they want to be able to intervene quickly, inexpensively, and in ad hoc ways to protect or advance the interests of particular clients in particular matters. This sort of control can be managed by an individual legislator without collective action; it has direct payoffs; it will generally be carried out behind the scenes; and it does not involve or provoke conflict. It generates political benefits without political costs. Moreover, it fits in quite nicely with a bureaucratic structure designed for conflict avoidance: an agency that is highly autonomous in the realm of policy yet highly constrained by complex procedural requirements will offer all sorts of opportunities for particularistic interventions.

The more general point is that legislators, by and large, can be expected either to respond to group demands in structural politics or to take entrepreneurial action in trying to please them. They will not be given to flights of autonomous action or statesmanship.

Presidents and Structural Choice

Presidents are motivated differently. Governance is the driving force behind the modern presidency. All presidents, regardless of party, are expected to govern effectively and are held responsible for taking action on virtually the full range of problems facing society. To be judged successful in the eyes of history—arguably the single most important motivator for presidents—they must appear to be strong leaders. They need to achieve their policy initiatives, their initiatives must be regarded as socially valuable, and the structures for attaining them must appear to work.

This raises two basic problems for interest groups. The first is that presidents are not very susceptible to the appeals of special interests. They want to make groups happy, to be sure, and sometimes responding to group demands will contribute nicely to governance. But this is often not so. In general, presidents have incentives to think in grander terms about what is best for society as a whole, or at least broad chunks of it, and they have their own agendas that may depart substantially from what even their more prominent group supporters might want. Even when they are simply responding to group pressures—which is more likely, of course, during their first term—the size and heterogeneity of their support coalitions tend to promote moderation, compromise, opposition to capture, and concern for social efficiency.

The second problem is that presidents want to control the bureaucracy. While legislators eagerly delegate their powers to administrative agencies, presidents are driven to take charge. They do not care about all agencies equally, of course. Some agencies are especially important because their programs are priority items on the presidential agenda. Others are important because they deal with sensitive issues that can become political bombshells if something goes wrong. But most all agencies impinge in one way or another on larger presidential responsibilities—for the budget, for the economy, for national defense—and presidents must have the capacity to direct and constrain agency behavior in basic respects if these larger responsibilities are to be handled successfully. They may often choose not to use their capacity for administrative control; they may even let favored groups use it when it suits their purposes. But the capacity must be there when they need it.

Presidents therefore have a unique role to play in the politics of structural choice. They are the only participants who are directly concerned with how the bureaucracy as a whole should be organized. And they are the only ones who actually want to run it through hands-on management and control. Their ideal is a rational, coherent, centrally directed bureaucracy that strongly resembles popular textbook notions of what an effective bureaucracy, public or private, ought to look like.

In general, presidents favor placing agencies within executive departments and subordinating them to hierarchical authority. They want to see important oversight, budget, and policy coordination functions given to department superiors—and, above them, to the Office of Management and Budget and other presidential management agencies—so that the bureaucracy can be brought under unified direction. While they value professionalism and civil service for their contributions to expertise, continuity, and impartiality, they want authority in the hands of their own political appointees—and they want to choose appointees whose types appear most conducive to presidential leadership.

This is just what the winning group and its legislative allies do not want. They want to protect their agencies and policy achievements by insulating them from politics, and presidents threaten to ruin everything by trying to control these agencies from above. The opposing groups are delighted with this, but they cannot always take comfort in the presidential approach to bureaucracy either. For presidents will tend to resist complex procedural protections, excessive judicial review, legislative veto provisions, and many other means by which the losers try to protect themselves and cripple bureaucratic performance. Presidents want agencies to have discretion, flexibility, and the capacity to take direction. They do not want agencies to be hamstrung by rules and regulations—unless, of course, they are presidential rules and regulations designed to enhance presidential control.

Legislators, Presidents, and Interest Groups

Obviously, presidents and legislators have very different orientations to the politics of structural choice. Interest groups can be expected to anticipate these differences from the outset and devise their own strategies accordingly.

Generally speaking, groups on both sides will find Congress a comfortable place in which to do business. Legislators are not bound by any overarching notion of what the bureaucracy as a whole ought to look like. They are not intrinsically motivated by effectiveness or efficiency or coordination or management or any other design criteria that might limit the kind of bureaucracy they are willing to create. They do not even want to retain political control for themselves.

The key thing about Congress is that it is open and responsive to what the groups want. It willingly builds, piece by piece—however grotesque the pieces, however inconsistent with one another—the kind of bureaucracy interest groups incrementally demand in their structural battles over time. This "congressional bureaucracy" is not supposed to function as a coherent whole, nor even to constitute one. Only the pieces are important. That is the way groups want it.

Presidents, of course, do not want it that way. Interest groups may find them attractive allies on occasion, especially when their interests and the presidential agenda coincide. But, in general, presidents are a fearsome presence on the political scene. Their broad support coalitions, their grand perspective on public policy, and their fundamental concern for a coherent, centrally controlled bureaucracy combine to make them maverick players in the game of structural politics. They want a "presidential bureaucracy" that is fundamentally at odds with the congressional bureaucracy everyone else is busily trying to create.

To the winning group, presidents are a major source of political uncertainty over and above the risks associated with the future power of the group's opponents. This gives it even greater incentives to pressure for structures that are insulated from politics—and, when possible, disproportionately insulated from presidential politics. Because of the seriousness of the presidency's threat, the winning group will place special emphasis on limiting the powers and numbers of political appointees, locating effective authority in the agency and its career personnel, and opposing new hierarchical powers—of review, coordination, veto—for units in the Executive Office or even the departments.

The losing side is much more pragmatic. Presidents offer important opportunities for expanding the scope of conflict, imposing new procedural constraints on agency action, and appealing unfavorable decisions. Especially if presidents are not entirely sympathetic to the agency and its mission, the losing side may actively support all the trappings of presidential bureaucracy—but only, of course, for the particular case at hand. Thus, while presidents may oppose group efforts to cripple the agency through congressional bureaucracy, groups may be able to achieve much the same end through presidential bureaucracy. The risk, however, is that the next president could turn out to be an avid supporter of the agency, in which case presidential bureaucracy might be targeted to quite different ends indeed. If there is a choice, sinking formal restrictions into legislative concrete offers a much more secure and permanent fix.

Bureaucracy

Bureaucratic structure emerges as a jerry-built fusion of congressional and presidential forms, their relative roles and particular features determined by the powers, priorities, and strategies of the various designers. The result is that each agency cannot help but begin life as a unique structural reflection of its own politics.

Once an agency is created, the political world becomes a different place. Agency bureaucrats are now political actors in their own right. They have career and institutional interests that may not be entirely congruent with their formal missions, and they have powerful resources—expertise and delegated authority—that might be employed toward these selfish ends. They are new players whose interests and resources alter the political game.

It is useful to think in terms of two basic types of bureaucratic players: political appointees and careerists. Careerists are the pure bureaucrats. As they carry out their jobs, they will be concerned with the technical requirements of effective organization, but they will also face the same problem that all other political actors face: political uncertainty. Changes in group power, committee composition, and presidential administration represent serious threats to things that bureaucrats hold dear. Their mandates could be restricted, their budgets cut, their discretion curtailed, their reputations blemished. Like groups and politicians, bureaucrats cannot afford to concern themselves solely with technical matters. They must take action to reduce their political uncertainty.

One attractive strategy is to nurture mutually beneficial relationships with groups and politicians whose political support the agency needs. If these are to provide real security, they must be more than isolated quid pro quos; they must be part of an ongoing stream of exchanges that give all participants expectations of future gain and thus incentives to resist short-term opportunities to profit at one another's expense. This is most easily done with the agency's initial supporters. Over time, however, the agency will be driven to broaden its support base, and it may move away from some of its creators—as regulatory agencies sometimes have, for example, in currying favor with the business interests they are supposed to be regulating. All agencies will have a tendency to move away from presidents, who, as temporary players, are inherently unsuited to participation in stable, long-term relationships.

Political appointees are also unattractive allies. They are not long-term participants, and no one will treat them as though they are. They have no concrete basis for participating in the exchange relationships of benefit to careerists. Indeed, they may not want to, for they have incentives to pay special attention to White House policy, and they will try to forge alliances that further those ends. Their focus is on short-term presidential victories, and relationships that stabilize politics for the agency may get in the way and have to be challenged.

As this begins to suggest, the strategy of building supportive relationships is inherently limited. In the end, much of the environment remains out of control. This prompts careerists to rely on a second, complementary strategy of uncertainty avoidance: insulation. If they cannot control the environment, they can try to shut themselves off from it in various ways. They can promote further professionalization and more extensive reliance on civil service. They can formalize and judicialize their decision procedures. They can base decisions on technical expertise, operational experience, and precedent, thus making them "objective" and agency-centered. They can try to monopolize the information necessary for effective political oversight. These insulating strategies are designed, moreover, not simply to shield the agency from its political environment, but also to shield it from the very appointees who are formally in charge.

All of this raises an obvious question: why can't groups and politicians anticipate the agency's alliance and insulationist strategies and design a structure ex ante that adjusts for them? The answer, of course, is that they can. Presidents may push for stronger hierarchical controls and greater formal power for appointees than they otherwise would. Group opponents may place even greater emphasis on opening the agency up to political oversight. And so on. The agency's design, therefore, should from the beginning incorporate everyone's anticipations about its incentives to form alliances and promote its own autonomy.

Thus, however active the agency is in forming alliances, insulating itself from politics, and otherwise shaping political outcomes, it would be a mistake to regard the agency as a truly independent force. It is literally manufactured by the other players as a vehicle for advancing and protecting their own interests, and their structural designs are premised on anticipations about the roles the agency and its bureaucrats will play in future politics. The whole point of structural choice is to anticipate, program, and engineer bureaucratic behavior. Although groups and politicians cannot do this perfectly, the agency is fundamentally a product of their designs, and so is the way it plays the political game. That is why, in our attempt to understand the structure and politics of bureaucracy, we turn to bureaucrats last rather than first.

Structural Choice as a Perpetual Process

The game of structural politics never ends. An agency is created and given a mandate, but, in principle at least, all of the choices that have been made in the formative round of decision making can be reversed or modified later.

As the politics of structural choice unfolds over time, three basic forces supply its dynamics. First, group opponents will constantly be on the lookout for opportunities to impose structures of their own that will inhibit the agency's performance and open it up to external control. Second, the winning group must constantly be ready to defend its agency from attack—but it may also have attacks of its own to launch. The prime reason is poor performance: because the agency is burdened from the beginning with a structure unsuited to the lofty goals it is supposed to achieve, the supporting group is likely to be dissatisfied and to push for more productive structural arrangements. Third, the president will try to ensure that agency behavior is consistent with broader presidential priorities, and he will take action to impose his own structures on top of those already put in place by Congress. He may also act to impose structures on purely political grounds in response to the interests of either the winning or opposing group.

All of this is going on all the time, generating pressures for structural change that find expression in both the legislative and executive processes. These are potentially of great importance for bureaucracy and policy, and all the relevant participants are intensely aware of it. However, the choices about structure that are made in the first period, when the agency is designed and empowered with a mandate, are normally far more enduring and consequential than those that will be made later. They constitute an institutional base that is protected by all the impediments to new legislation inherent in separation of powers, as well as by the political clout of the agency's supporters. Most of the pushing and hauling in subsequent years is likely to produce only incremental change. This, obviously, is very much on everyone's minds in the first period.

NOTES

1. Harold Seidman and Robert Gilmour, *Politics, Position, and Power: From the Positive to the Regulatory State*, 4th ed. (Oxford University Press, 1986); and Frederick C. Mosher, *Democracy and the Public Service*, 2d ed. (Oxford University Press, 1982).

2. Seidman and Gilmour, *Politics, Position, and Power*, p. 330.

8-3

By the Horns

Paul Singer

When presidents enter office, a large executive branch bureaucracy is already in place. Because the numerous departments and agencies set regulations and implement policies, managing them effectively becomes a major challenge for presidents. In this essay, Paul Singer reports on the extensive efforts of the administration of George W. Bush, first elected in 2000 and reelected in 2004, to control departments and agencies. Administration strategies affected nearly every facet of executive agency operations. Singer describes the major controversies and the partisan implications of presidential management strategies.

Two weeks before George W. Bush's 2001 inauguration, the Heritage Foundation issued a paper offering the new president advice on "taking charge of federal personnel."

The authors—two former officials at the Office of Personnel Management and a former congressional staffer who is now at OPM—laid out an ambitious agenda to overhaul civil service rules and "reassert managerial control of government." The paper emphasized the importance of appointing strong leaders to key government positions and holding bureaucrats "personally accountable for achievement of the president's election-endorsed and value-defined program."

Reminded of this paper recently, co-author Robert Moffit, who has moved on to other issues at Heritage, dusted off a copy and called a reporter back with a hint of rejoicing in his voice. "They apparently are really doing this stuff," he said.

To Moffit and other proponents of strong management, the Bush White House has indeed initiated a dramatic transformation of the federal bureaucracy, trying to create a leaner, more results-oriented government that can better account for taxpayer dollars. Reshaping the agenda of government to match the president's priorities is the purpose of democratic elections, Moffit said.

But critics charge that the White House is embarking on a crusade to replace expert judgment in federal agencies with political calculation, to marginalize or eliminate longtime civil servants, to change laws without going through

Source: Paul Singer, "By the Horns," *National Journal,* March 26, 2005.

Congress, to silence dissenting views within the government, and to centralize decision-making in the White House.

"A president cannot wave a wand and wipe prior policy, as implemented by duly enacted statutes, off the books," said Rena Steinzor, a founder and board member of the Center for Progressive Regulation, a think tank of liberal academics. "We have made a judgment as a nation, for decades, that an independent bureaucracy is very important." The Bush administration, she said, is "politicizing and terrorizing the bureaucracy, and turning it 180 degrees."

Critics point to a long list of manifestations of greater White House control. Among them:

- Reorganizations in various federal agencies, such as major staff cuts anticipated at NASA, that eliminate career civil service staff, or replace managers with political appointees;
- New management systems to grade federal agencies on the results they achieve, with the White House in charge of defining "success";
- Increased White House oversight of regulations issued by the Environmental Protection Agency, the Department of Labor, and other departments and agencies;
- The president's proposal to replace the civil service employment system with new, government-wide "pay-for-performance" rules that make it easier for managers to promote, reward, or fire employees;
- "Competitive sourcing" requirements that force thousands of federal workers to compete against private contractors to keep their jobs;
- A series of steps that may weaken traditional watchdogs and the office that protects whistle-blowers;
- New restrictions on the public release of government information, including a huge jump in the number of documents labeled "classified";
- A growing cadre of government employees who are going public with charges that their recommendations were ignored, their reports edited, or their conclusions reversed by their political-appointee managers, at the behest of the White House.

Many presidents have tried to reshape the federal bureaucracy to their liking. President Nixon had his "Management by Objective" program that attempted to rein in anti-poverty programs; President Clinton had his "Reinventing Government" initiative that aimed to improve government services and streamline rules. But under Bush, White House control of the federal agencies is "more coordinated and centralized than it has ever been," said New York University professor of public service Paul Light, who is also a senior fellow at the Brookings Institution. "It is a sea change from what it was under the Clinton administration."

Clay Johnson, who as deputy director for management at the Office of Management and Budget is the point man for Bush's "management agenda," denied any "Republican conspiracy" to control the bureaucracy or silence civil servants. "It's about things working better; it's not about controlling," Johnson said. "The thing that we can impose more of than anything else is clarity—clarity of purpose. We want to have a real clear definition of what success is," he said.

"The overall goal of all that we are doing," Johnson added, "is, we want to get to the point in three or four years where we can say to the American taxpayer that every program is getting better every year."

The federal bureaucracy is a notoriously unwieldy beast. It includes about 1.9 million civilian employees, many of whom have agendas that differ from the president's. Each administration, Republican or Democratic, struggles with its relationship with an army of workers who were on the job before the new political team arrived, and who expect to be there after the team leaves.

"You have this bizarre cycle, where the leader comes into the room and says, 'We are going to march north,' and the bureaucracy all applaud," said former House Speaker Newt Gingrich, R-Ga. "Then the leader leaves the room, and the bureaucracy says, 'Yeah, well, this "march north" thing is terrific, but this year, to be practical, we have to keep marching south. But what we'll do is, we'll hire a consultant to study marching north, so that next year we can begin to think about whether or not we can do it.' "

The White House is proud of its management initiatives and Bush's reputation as "the M.B.A. president." The administration regularly issues press releases to announce progress on the President's Management Agenda—a list of priorities that includes competitive sourcing and development of "e-government." And Bush's fiscal 2006 budget includes cuts based on performance assessments for hundreds of individual federal programs. But critics fear that the management agenda, combined with an array of other administration initiatives, has established a framework that makes it easier for political appointees to overrule, marginalize, or even fire career employees who question the president's agenda.

For example, the Environmental Protection Agency issued a rule earlier this month to regulate emissions of mercury from power plants. In unveiling the rule, the EPA asserted that it represents the most stringent controls on mercury ever issued. According to the agency, the requirements are cost-effective, will achieve significant health benefits, and will create an economic incentive for companies to continually improve their environmental performance.

But the rule is driven by the Bush administration's novel—some say, illegal—interpretation of the Clean Air Act that allows the EPA to avoid imposing mandatory emissions controls on each facility. Environmentalists, and some EPA staff, contend that the mercury rule is far weaker than one the Clinton administration proposed, and that political appointees at the agency ignored the scientific and legal judgment of career staff to push the rule through the regulatory process.

The battle over the mercury rule has been bitter and public. Many other efforts to tighten central control are buried deep within the bowels of the bureaucracy.

Structures

The Natural Resources Conservation Service [NRCS] is not generally a political hotbed. A division of the Agriculture Department, the NRCS—working through "conservationist" offices in each state—is responsible for helping farmers implement soil and water conservation measures, such as restoring wetlands, building dams, and designing systems to prevent animal waste from running off into waterways.

In a major reorganization over the past two years, NRCS chief Bruce Knight eliminated the service's six regional offices, which were headed by career managers and oversaw the state offices. He replaced the six regional managers with three political appointees in Washington and shuffled 200 career staffers from the regional offices into other offices throughout the agency.

Knight said the reorganization is "really just a strong business case." It created a "flatter, leaner structure" that relies much more heavily on the expertise of the state conservationists and makes better use of employees, he said. "I had about 200 highly valuable [employees] scattered around the country, and I needed to put them at the mission of the agency."

But in so doing, Knight has also raised concerns about the independence of the technical staffers who oversee conservation measures across the country.

Under the new structure, career NRCS scientists might worry that their technical decisions about where to spend money and how to implement programs will be overruled for political purposes, said Rich Duesterhaus, a former NRCS staffer and now director of government affairs for the National Association of Conservation Districts.

"They clearly now have a direct line from the politically appointed chief, through these three politically appointed regional assistant chiefs, to the line officers who supervise and carry out these programs," Duesterhaus said. And why should political control over a soil and water conservation agency matter? Because the 2002 farm bill doubled the NRCS's budget for assistance to farmers, from about $1.5 billion in 2001 to $2.8 billion in 2006, with a total increase of $18 billion slated through 2012.

"In the old days, the money wasn't big enough to matter," Duesterhaus said, but the influx of cash in 2002 has made the NRCS "a contender in terms of spoils, and where those spoils go becomes an issue." With direct political oversight of the state conservationists, Duesterhaus said, "it becomes a little easier to say, 'Well, we need Ohio, so make sure we put a little extra money in Ohio.'"

Earlier this month, Charles Adams, one of the six career regional conservationists who were unseated in the reorganization, filed a discrimination complaint against Knight and other agency officials, arguing that the reorganization derailed his 37-year career in favor of three political appointees with far less expertise. "I allege that . . . a calculated, arbitrary, and capricious decision was made to preclude me from the line and leadership of this agency," Adams wrote in his complaint to the Agriculture Department's Office of Civil Rights.

Knight rejects any suggestion that he has politicized the work of a technical agency. "The real power is in the state conservationist, the career individual in the state who manages the budget and the people," he said. "Most people will agree that we are more scientifically and technologically based now" than before the reorganization. The agency has about 12,500 staff members and only a dozen political appointees, Knight said.

But employees in other federal agencies have also asserted that reorganization plans have bumped career managers from senior positions, or diluted their authority.

The Centers for Disease Control and Prevention is instituting a major overhaul that will create a new layer of "coordinating centers"—including a strategic center responsible for developing long-term goals for the agency—between CDC Director Julie Gerberding and the health and science centers that formerly reported directly to her. Gerberding said, "I don't think our goal is to have control over the organization—our goal is to have an impact on health."

But some career staffers say they are being pushed aside and losing the ability to manage their programs. *The Washington Post* earlier this month reported a memo from a top CDC official warning that CDC employees are suffering a "crisis of confidence" and that they feel "cowed into silence." CDC aides—who are unwilling to have their names published for fear of reprisals—say they are losing the ability to make independent professional judgments on topics ranging from sexual abstinence, to drug use, to influenza. Gerberding replied, "I think that is a very inaccurate assessment of what is going on at CDC."

Nevertheless, throughout the federal government, complaints can be heard from disgruntled civil servants who feel they are being elbowed aside by the political leadership—though it is hard to assess whether the invariably anonymous sources have been targeted for elimination or are simply frightened of the change.

Some of the administration's efforts have attracted congressional scrutiny. On March 16, the House Science panel's Space and Aeronautics Subcommittee held a hearing on the administration's plan to slash funding for aeronautics research at NASA and to eliminate 2,000 jobs in order to focus the agency on the president's "Vision for Space Exploration," which includes the goal of manned missions to Mars.

But the administration is not backing down. In fact, it wants more authority to carry out these reorganizations. The White House has said it is drafting legislative proposals to create a "sunset" process requiring federal programs to rejustify their existence every 10 years and to set up "reform" commissions giving the president authority to initiate major restructuring of programs. House Government Reform Committee Chairman Tom Davis, R-Va., said in an interview this month that he believes that Congress should restore the president's unilateral authority to reorganize executive branch agencies—authority that presidents held from the late 1930s until 1984, and that Nixon used when he created the Environmental Protection Agency in 1970.

Procedures

Beyond its tinkering with organizational structures, the White House is pursuing a sweeping overhaul of personnel rules that is aimed at giving managers across the federal government more flexibility to promote, punish, or fire hundreds of thousands of civil servants. While a proposed transformation of the pay systems at the Defense and Homeland Security departments has spurred vigorous debate—fueled by the administration's announcement in January that it wants to extend these systems to the rest of the federal government—less fanfare attended last year's rollout of a new pay-for-performance plan for the roughly 6,000 veteran federal government managers who constitute the Senior Executive Service.

Together, the two new approaches give political appointees in federal agencies greater authority to reward or discipline senior career managers, and give managers the same authority over the civil servants below them. The White House calls this a "modern" personnel system, where everyone is judged on results. Critics call it a process for weeding out recalcitrant civil servants or political opponents.

The new pay-for-performance plan for the Senior Executive Service eliminates annual raises for top career managers and replaces them with a system of merit ratings. Some career executives fear that the system will allow the White House to simply push aside managers who are unenthusiastic about the president's agenda.

"We all know that performance is in the eyes of the beholder, no matter what you say about wanting to have many numerical indicators and so forth," said Carol Bonosaro, president of the Senior Executives Association, which represents members of the SES. "The concern is that if you know that your boss has the total authority to not give you a pay raise, are you going to be more inclined to skirt an ethics requirement for them? Are you going to be more inclined to do what is perhaps not really right?"

And the layers of performance ratings based on the president's goals serve to reinforce the agenda throughout the bureaucracy, Bonosaro said. "You kick the general, and the general comes back and kicks the soldiers, and it goes down the line."

In another move, which could affect thousands of civil servants, Bush has made "competitive sourcing" one of his primary management goals for federal agencies, requiring government workers to compete for their jobs against private contractors.

In January, OMB [Office of Management and Budget] reported that government employees had won about 90 percent of the 30,000 jobs awarded in 2003 and 2004, with decisions still to be made on about 15,000 jobs offered for competition in those years. But in February, the Federal Aviation Administration announced that Lockheed Martin had won the government's largest-ever job competition, covering about 2,300 flight-service jobs. FAA workers slated to be displaced under the contract filed an appeal this month, complaining that the agency's bidding process was flawed.

"Everything they do is sending the signal [to employees] that they can be replaced easily by contractors, if the work they do isn't done by whatever standards the president is going to put out in his new measurement system," said Colleen Kelley, president of the National Treasury Employees Union.

"It's all about putting more power in the hands of the appointees and making it easier to downgrade, get rid of, use the rules as a weapon against employees who are not in lockstep with you," said Mark Roth, general counsel of the American Federation of Government Employees.

OMB's Johnson denies any intent to enforce political orthodoxy on the civil service. "Rewarding people for their political views is against the law. It's like incest: verboten. Not allowed. Doesn't happen," Johnson said.

"You are being encouraged, and evaluated, and mentored, and managed, and held accountable for doing things that the administration considers to be important," he said. "That does not mean vote Republican versus Democrat; that doesn't mean be pro-life or pro-choice, or be for strict-constructionist judges, or be against strict-constructionist judges," Johnson contended.

"We are controlling what the definition of success is, but shame on us if that's a bad idea. I think it's a really good idea," Johnson said. "It is a mind-set and an approach, and it is a focus on results that [the president] is imposing. It's not 'I want everyone to be like me and have the same political beliefs as me.'"

Checks and Balances

But what if "incest" does happen? Where would a civil servant go to report "verboten" behavior?

Critics of the administration charge that the White House is tampering with the independent structures that protect against waste, fraud, abuse, and political retribution—the federal inspectors general and the Office of General Counsel. The White House vehemently denies the charge.

Rep. Henry Waxman, D-Calif., the top Democrat on the House Government Reform Committee, issued a report last October—and updated it in January—declaring that the Bush administration was appointing inspectors general [IGs] with political connections to the White House much more frequently than the Clinton administration did. Working with a very small sample—11 IGs appointed by Bush, 32 appointed by Clinton—Waxman's report concludes that 64 percent of the Bush appointees had political experience on their resumes, and only 18 percent had audit experience. For the Clinton appointees, the ratios were reversed: 22 percent had political backgrounds, 66 percent had audit experience.

Gaston Gianni, who until his retirement in December was the Clinton-appointed inspector general at the Federal Deposit Insurance Corporation and vice chairman of the President's Council on Integrity and Efficiency—an IG professional group—said, "I've read the Waxman report. Factually, it's correct. The conclusions, I don't think flow from the facts."

Gianni said it is true that the Bush administration is favoring political background rather than investigative experience in appointing IGs, but he said there is no evidence that the people Bush has appointed have any less independence or zeal for their work.

Nevertheless, Gianni said, the practice worries him. "The environment is such, as we go forward, that the perception will be that, rather than 'small-p' political appointees, they are going to become 'capital-P' Political appointees. Even though nothing else has changed, that is what the perception will be."

Steinzor and NYU's Light agree that the White House has generally sent the message to inspectors that an excess of independence may be bad for their careers.

Last July, Johnson and Gianni signed a memo to inspectors general and agency heads, spelling out the "working relationship principles" for both positions and emphasizing the need for mutual respect, objectivity, and communication between an IG and his or her agency head. Johnson serves as the chairman of the president's council on integrity, and the memo was his idea. Some critics read it as a warning to IGs not to be too aggressive, but Johnson denies any such message.

"The IGs should not be, by definition, adversarial agents," Johnson said. "They are there to prevent waste, fraud, and abuse. The heads of agency are there to prevent waste, fraud, and abuse. The IGs, by definition, are for positive change . . . . Where you get into disagreements is when somebody tries to constantly play 'gotcha,' or where the IG gets a little too enamored of their independent status and tries to do things in a negative fashion, tries to uproot things, or identify things that will hurt the agency," he said. "The IG is there to help the agency."

Johnson said that he had recommended the "relationship principles" to the professional group, but that IGs and agency officials drafted the principles.

Light said there is nothing untoward about principles extolling the virtues of communication and common decency, but he argued that the memo—together with the pattern noted in the Waxman report and some high-profile firings of IGs early in the Bush administration—sets a tone that may have a chilling effect on inspectors.

Johnson dismisses this concern. "I don't think there is any information that suggests that the IGs are less critical than they have been. I don't think there is anything that says they are finding less waste, fraud, and abuse, that they are being less effective IGs as a result of this 'Republican conspiracy.'"

The Office of Special Counsel is a bigger concern for administration critics. Established as an independent agency charged with protecting whistle-blowers and civil servants who are mistreated for political or other reasons unconnected with their performance, the office is in a bitter feud with several of its employees who argue that they are being punished for resisting attempts by Bush's appointee to dismantle the operation.

Among other things, current and former employees charge that Special Counsel Scott Bloch has summarily dismissed hundreds of whistle-blower complaints, instigated a reorganization of the office that will significantly increase political control of investigations, and forced senior staff members critical of his work to choose between relocating to regional offices or being fired. Several anonymous employees, joined by four public-interest groups, filed formal charges against Bloch on March 3, and at least half a dozen staff members have resigned or been fired for refusing to relocate.

Bloch characterizes the complaints against his office as the work of a few disgruntled employees, reinforced by groups that are on a mission to embarrass the White House. Together, these critics are "going out and making reckless allegations that have no truth. They don't like the success Bush officials are having in dealing with the bureaucracy," Bloch said. "They don't want a Bush appointee like myself to get credit" for reducing a large backlog of old cases that were languishing when Bloch took office in 2004. "We have doubled our enforcement over prior years in all areas," Bloch said. His critics "hurl accusations at the office and basically say insulting things about their fellow employees, and they are false."

Levers of Government

An Interior Department official who has worked in the federal government for 30 years denied that the White House is trying to marginalize the civil service, arguing that what people are seeing is simply better executive management from the White House.

"This administration runs a more effective management of the government than did the previous administration, which was a lot more loosey-goosey," this person said, requesting anonymity to speak freely about his bosses. "They bring more of a business mind-set, but I don't think that's a particularly bad thing. They are more organized, and they are smart about it."

The sharper management focus extends into the minutiae of government, giving the White House oversight and control of the executive branch at several levels. In some cases, the Bush administration is creating new approaches, but in most cases, officials are simply using authorities created under prior administrations and applying them more aggressively.

For example, Clinton issued a regulatory-review executive order in 1993, charging OMB's Office of Information and Regulatory Affairs [OIRA] with ensuring that regulations "are consistent with applicable law [and] the president's priorities." The order emphasized use of the best available science and the most cost-effective approach to regulations.

The Bush administration has built on this executive order, setting new requirements for reviewing the costs and benefits of regulatory proposals, establishing a higher threshold for reaching scientific certainty in regulatory decisions, and creating new opportunities for outside experts to challenge the government's conclusions about the dangers that a rule is designed to mitigate.

A regulatory agency career official who demanded anonymity said that OIRA, under the Bush administration, is "much more active" in the regulatory process. "They get involved much earlier in the process on large rules," the official said. "They are reviewing drafts of preambles as they are being written for some rules, or sections of rules."

The executive order gives OMB 90 days to review agency rules, but OIRA Administrator John Graham said in an e-mail response to a reporter's query: "During an important rule-making, OIRA may work informally with agencies at the early stages of the rule-making. This early OIRA participation is designed to make sure that our benefit-cost perspective receives a fair hearing, before key decisions are made and final documents are drafted."

Graham added, "A key benefit of early OIRA involvement is that the pace of rule-making is accelerated by building consensus early in the process and avoiding contentious delays beyond the 90-day review period." He said that the majority of OMB staffers are career civil servants with significant expertise in their issue areas and that, contrary to the assumptions of many critics, OMB involvement does not always result in an outcome that is more favorable to industry. For example, he said, OMB initiated a Food and Drug Administration rule-making to require that producers add the trans-fat content of foods to nutritional labels.

Sally Katzen, who held both John Graham's job and Clay Johnson's job during her years in the Clinton administration, said, "There is nothing wrong with more-centralized review, guidance, and oversight. It is, after all, a president—singular—who is the head of the executive branch." But, she cautioned, "the problems we face are often highly technical or otherwise highly complicated, and those who serve in the White House or OMB do not have all the answers. And they certainly don't have the manpower, the expertise, or the intimate familiarity with the underlying detail. They cannot—and, in my mind, should not—replace the agency expertise, the agency knowledge, and the agency experience."

While OIRA serves as the central regulatory-review office for the White House, OMB has also positioned itself as the central performance-accountability office, with the establishment of the "President's Management Agenda" and the Program Assessment Rating Tool, or PART, under which the White House grades every agency and program on the basis of its management activities and real-world results. After several years of conducting the assessments without imposing any real consequences for failure, the administration, in the first budget proposal of Bush's second term, used the results assessments to justify eliminating or significantly reducing funding for about 150 federal programs.

John Kamensky, who was deputy director of the National Performance Review (the "reinventing government" initiative) in the Clinton administration, said that Bush's White House is, in many ways, simply expanding on efforts begun in the previous administration.

"We had proposed, in the Clinton administration, tying performance to budget, but there wasn't enough performance information to do that. The Bush administration has that information, finally, so it's sort of a natural progression," Kamensky said.

But critics worry that the review process gives the administration the opportunity to establish its own measures of success for programs, without taking into account the requirements established by Congress.

For example, OMB's review declared the Housing and Urban Development Department's Community Development Block Grant [CDBG] program "ineffective," charging that its mission is unclear, it has few measures of success, and it "does not effectively target funds to the most-needy communities."

But a study by a National Academy of Public Administration panel in February disputed OMB's assessment. The program's "statutory mission or purpose seems clear," the panel said. As a block grant, CDBG is able to fund a broad range of community-development functions, and "if the CDBG program lacks clarity, it is likely because the statute intended it so," according to the report. The breadth of the program's activities makes it difficult to provide specific measures of success, the panel concluded, and the White House suggestion that funding be geographically targeted "seems to contradict the statute's intent."

Donald Plusquellic, mayor of Akron, Ohio, and president of the U.S. Conference of Mayors, defends the CDBG program. "I can evaluate anything as a failure if I get to set up the standards," he said.

Johnson acknowledges that CDBG fails the test in part because the administration is applying a new definition of success. "We believe the goal of housing programs is not just to build houses, but the economic development that comes with them. So those are the results we want to focus on," Johnson said. "You can say we are imposing our political views on people, or our favored views of the housing world or the CDBG world on people. Well, guilty as charged. It's important to focus on outcomes, not outputs."

The president has proposed to eliminate the $4 billion block-grant program and shift its functions into a new community and economic development initiative in the Commerce Department. The Senate voted 66–32 last week for a budget amendment designed to block the administration plan.

NYU's Light says the administration has instituted a host of other procedures that centralize power in the White House, ranging from a vetting process for political appointees that allows little independent decision-making for Cabinet officials, to regular conference calls between the White House and the agency chiefs of staff that help to "focus [the staffers'] attention up Pennsylvania Avenue to the White House, and away from down in your department."

But is that a bad thing? The Heritage Foundation's Moffit doesn't think so. "Why would that be anything other than 100 percent American?" Moffit asks. "I elected a president, and I expect the president to run the executive branch of the government. And there is an issue about whether he is? That's absurd."

The role of the civil service is "to make the car run," Moffit said. "And if they have been driving the car east for the past 25 years of their professional life, but the president says, 'Fine, I know you've been going east, but now we're going to go west; you're going to do a 180-degree turn and go in exactly the opposite direction,' their job is to make sure the car goes exactly in the opposite direction. Nobody elected them to do anything else."

Roth of the American Federation of Government Employees disagrees. "You do not entirely change your entire focus every time a president is elected, because it is not the job of the president to pass the laws. It is the job of the president to execute the laws," Roth said. "These laws are on the books, these programs are in regulations." An administration "can't just say, 'We don't like it, so don't do it.'"

Chapter 9

The Judiciary

9-1

from *A Matter of Interpretation: Federal Courts and the Law*

Antonin Scalia

Supreme Court judges and indeed—as we learn in the essay by Carp, Manning, and Stidham, later in this section—judges at every level of the federal judiciary decide cases in close accord with the political views of those who appointed them. Years of Democratic control of the White House and Congress created the activist federal judiciary of the 1960s and 1970s that advanced federal protections of civil rights and civil liberties. With the resurgence of the Republican Party in national politics, the federal judiciary has gradually, with turnover in members, become more conservative. Some observers note these trends and conclude that judges are little more than partisan politicians disguised in robes. Unsurprisingly, judges do not view themselves this way. Instead, they account for their sometimes sharply differing opinions on criteria that do not fit neatly on the familiar partisan or ideological dimensions that are used to classify elected officeholders. In the next two essays, two current Supreme Court justices—one conservative and appointed

Source: Antonin Scalia, "Common-Law Courts in a Civil-Law System: The Role of United States Federal Courts in Interpreting the Constitution and Laws," from *A Matter of Interpretation: Federal Courts and the Law,* (Princeton University Press: 1997), 3–47. Some notes appearing in the original have been deleted.

*by a Republican president, the other a moderate, appointed by a Democrat—
explain how they approach decisions, decisions on which they frequently
disagree. As you read and weigh these alternative views, note that both
judges begin with the same assumption—that as the unelected branch the
judiciary should, when possible, defer to the decisions of democratically
elected officeholders.*

*In the following essay, excerpted from his highly regarded series of lectures to
Princeton law students, Justice Antonin Scalia explains how he approaches
decisions. Some call this style "literalist" or "originalist," in that Scalia
weighs decisions against a close reading of the texts of laws and the Constitution. He reminds us that in a constitutional democracy judges are not
charged with deciding what fair and just policy should be. This responsibility
belongs with elected officials, who better reflect their citizenry's views on such
matters. Nor should judges try to read the minds of those who make the law.
A judge's role begins and ends with applying the law (including the Constitution) to the particular circumstances of a legal disagreement. Scalia's critics
have complained that the application of law is frequently not so simple.
Laws conflict or fail to consider the many contingencies that reach the
Supreme Court.*

THE FOLLOWING ESSAY attempts to explain the current neglected state of the science of construing legal texts, and offers a few suggestions for improvement. It
is addressed not just to lawyers but to all thoughtful Americans who share our
national obsession with the law.

The Common Law

The first year of law school makes an enormous impact upon the mind. Many
students remark upon the phenomenon. They experience a sort of intellectual
rebirth, the acquisition of a whole new mode of perceiving and thinking. Thereafter, even if they do not yet know much law, they do—as the expression goes—
"think like a lawyer."

The overwhelming majority of the courses taught in that first year, and surely
the ones that have the most profound effect, teach the substance, and the
methodology, of the common law—torts, for example; contracts; property;
criminal law. American lawyers cut their teeth upon the common law. To understand what an effect that must have, you must appreciate that the common law
is not really common law, except insofar as judges can be regarded as common.

That is to say, it is not "customary law," or a reflection of the people's practices, but is rather law developed by the judges. Perhaps in the very infancy of Anglo-Saxon law it could have been thought that the courts were mere expositors of generally accepted social practices; and certainly, even in the full maturity of the common law, a well-established commercial or social practice could form the basis for a court's decision. But from an early time—as early as the Year Books, which record English judicial decisions from the end of the thirteenth century to the beginning of the sixteenth—any equivalence between custom and common law had ceased to exist, except in the sense that the doctrine of *stare decisis* rendered prior judicial decisions "custom." The issues coming before the courts involved, more and more, refined questions to which customary practice provided no answer.

Oliver Wendell Holmes's influential book *The Common Law*[1]—which is still suggested reading for entering law students—talks a little bit about Germanic and early English custom. . . . This is the image of the law—the common law—to which an aspiring American lawyer is first exposed, even if he has not read Holmes over the previous summer as he was supposed to. He learns the law, not by reading statutes that promulgate it or treatises that summarize it, but rather by studying the judicial opinions that invented it. This is the famous case-law method, pioneered by Harvard Law School in the last century, and brought to movies and TV by the redoubtable Professor Kingsfield of *Love Story* and *The Paper Chase*. The student is directed to read a series of cases, set forth in a text called a "casebook," designed to show how the law developed. . . . Famous old cases are famous, you see, not because they came out right, but because the rule of law they announced was the intelligent one. Common-law courts performed two functions: One was to apply the law to the facts. All adjudicators—French judges, arbitrators, even baseball umpires and football referees—do that. But the second function, and the more important one, was to *make* the law.

If you were sitting in on Professor Kingsfield's class when *Hadley* v. *Baxendale* was the assigned reading, you would find that the class discussion would not end with the mere description and dissection of the opinion. [This case, a familiar example of 19th century English common law, involves liability in failing to perform a contracted obligation.-Ed.] Various "hypotheticals" would be proposed by the crusty (yet, under it all, good-hearted) old professor, testing the validity and the sufficiency of the "foreseeability" rule. What if, for example, you are a black-smith, and a young knight rides up on a horse that has thrown a shoe. He tells you he is returning to his ancestral estate, Blackacre, which he must reach that very evening to claim his inheritance, or else it will go to his wicked, no-good cousin, the sheriff of Nottingham. You contract to put on a new shoe, for the going rate of three farthings. The shoe is defective, or is badly shod, the horse goes lame, and the knight reaches Blackacre too late. Are you really liable for the full amount of his inheritance? Is it reasonable to impose that degree of liability for three far-things? Would not the parties have set a different price if liability of that amount had been contemplated? Ought there not to be, in other words, some limiting principle to damages beyond mere foreseeability? Indeed, might not that princi-ple—call it presumed assumption of risk—explain why *Hadley* v. *Baxendale* reached the right result after all, though not for the precise reason it assigned?

What intellectual fun all of this is! It explains why first-year law school is so exhilarating: because it consists of playing common-law judge, which in turn consists of playing king—devising, out of the brilliance of one's own mind, those laws that ought to govern mankind. How exciting! And no wonder so many law students, having drunk at this intoxicating well, aspire for the rest of their lives to be judges!

Besides the ability to think about, and devise, the "best" legal rule, there is another skill imparted in the first year of law school that is essential to the mak-ing of a good common-law judge. It is the technique of what is called "distin-guishing" cases. That is a necessary skill, because an absolute prerequisite to common-law lawmaking is the doctrine of *stare decisis*—that is, the principle that a decision made in one case will be followed in the next. Quite obviously, with-out such a principle common-law courts would not be making any "law"; they would just be resolving the particular dispute before them. It is the requirement that future courts adhere to the principle underlying a judicial decision which causes that decision to be a legal rule. (There is no such requirement in the civil-law system, where it is the text of the law rather than any prior judicial interpre-tation of that text which is authoritative. Prior judicial opinions are consulted for their persuasive effect, much as academic commentary would be; but they are not *binding*.)

Within such a precedent-bound common-law system, it is critical for the lawyer, or the judge, to establish whether the case at hand falls within a principle that has already been decided. Hence the technique—or the art, or the game— of "distinguishing" earlier cases. It is an art or a game, rather than a science, because what constitutes the "holding" of an earlier case is not well defined and can be adjusted to suit the occasion. . . .

It should be apparent that by reason of the doctrine of *stare decisis*, as limited by the principle I have just described, the common law grew in a peculiar fash-ion—rather like a Scrabble board. No rule of decision previously announced could be *erased*, but qualifications could be *added* to it. The first case lays on the board: "No liability for breach of contractual duty without privity"; the next player adds "unless injured party is member of household." And the game con-tinues.

As I have described, this system of making law by judicial opinion, and making law by distinguishing earlier cases, is what every American law student, every newborn American lawyer, first sees when he opens his eyes. And the impression remains for life. His image of the great judge—the Holmes, the Cardozo—is the man (or woman) who has the intelligence to discern the best rule of law for the case at hand and then the skill to perform the broken-field running through earlier cases that leaves him free to impose that rule: distinguishing one prior case on the left, straight-arming another one on the right, high-stepping away from another precedent about to tackle him from the rear, until (bravo!) he reaches the goal—good law. That image of the great judge remains with the former law student when he himself becomes a judge, and thus the common-law tradition is passed on.

Democratic Legislation

All of this would be an unqualified good, were it not for a trend in government that has developed in recent centuries, called democracy. In most countries, judges are no longer agents of the king, for there are no kings. . . . [O]nce we have taken this realistic view of what common-law courts do, the uncomfortable relationship of common-law lawmaking to democracy (if not to the technical doctrine of the separation of powers) becomes apparent. Indeed, that was evident to many even before legal realism carried the day. It was one of the principal motivations behind the law-codification movement of the nineteenth century. . . .

The nineteenth-century codification movement . . . was generally opposed by the bar, and hence did not achieve substantial success, except in one field: civil procedure, the law governing the trial of civil cases.[2] (I have always found it curious, by the way, that the only field in which lawyers and judges were willing to abandon judicial lawmaking was a field important to nobody except litigants, lawyers, and judges. Civil procedure used to be the *only* statutory course taught in first-year law school.) Today, generally speaking, the old private-law fields— contracts, torts, property, trusts and estates, family law—remain firmly within the control of state common-law courts.[3] Indeed, it is probably true that in these fields judicial lawmaking can be more freewheeling than ever, since the doctrine of *stare decisis* has appreciably eroded. Prior decisions that even the cleverest mind cannot distinguish can nowadays simply be overruled.

My point in all of this is not that the common law should be scraped away as a barnacle on the hull of democracy. I am content to leave the common law, and the process of developing the common law, where it is. It has proven to be a good method of developing the law in many fields—and perhaps the very best method. An argument can be made that development of the bulk of private law by judges (a natural aristocracy, as Madison accurately portrayed them)[4] is a desirable limitation upon popular democracy. . . .

But though I have no quarrel with the common law and its process, I do question whether the *attitude* of the common-law judge—the mind-set that asks, "What is the most desirable resolution of this case, and how can any impediments to the achievement of that result be evaded?"—is appropriate for most of the work that I do, and much of the work that state judges do. We live in an age of legislation, and most new law is statutory law. . . . Every issue of law resolved by a federal judge involves interpretation of text—the text of a regulation, or of a statute, or of the Constitution. Let me put the Constitution to one side for the time being, since many believe that that document is in effect a charter for judges to develop an evolving common law of freedom of speech, of privacy rights, and the like. I think that is wrong—indeed, as I shall discuss below, I think it frustrates the whole purpose of a written constitution. But we need not pause to debate that point now, since a very small proportion of judges' work is constitutional interpretation in any event. (Even in the Supreme Court, I would estimate that well less than a fifth of the issues we confront are constitutional issues—and probably less than a twentieth if you exclude criminal-law cases.) By far the greatest part of what I and all federal judges do is to interpret the meaning of federal statutes and federal agency regulations. Thus the subject of statutory interpretation deserves study and attention in its own right, as the principal business of judges and (hence) lawyers. It will not do to treat the enterprise as simply an inconvenient modern add-on to the judge's primary role of common-law lawmaker. Indeed, attacking the enterprise with the Mr. Fix-it mentality of the common-law judge is a sure recipe for incompetence and usurpation.

The Science of Statutory Interpretation

The state of the science of statutory interpretation in American law is accurately described by a prominent treatise on the legal process as follows:

> Do not expect anybody's theory of statutory interpretation, whether it is your own or somebody else's, to be an accurate statement of what courts actually do with statutes. The hard truth of the matter is that American courts have no intelligible, generally accepted, and consistently applied theory of statutory interpretation.[5]

Surely this is a sad commentary: We American judges have no intelligible theory of what we do most.

Even sadder, however, is the fact that the American bar and American legal education, by and large, are unconcerned with the fact that we have no intelligible theory. Whereas legal scholarship has been at pains to rationalize the common law—to devise the *best* rules governing contracts, torts, and so forth—it has been seemingly agnostic as to whether there is even any such thing as good or bad rules of statutory interpretation. There are few law-school courses on the subject, and certainly no required ones; the science of interpretation (if it is a science) is left to be picked up piecemeal, through the reading of cases (good and bad) in substantive fields of law that happen to involve statutes, such as securities law, natural resources law, and employment law. . . .

"Intent of the Legislature"

Statutory interpretation is such a broad subject that the substance of it cannot be discussed comprehensively here. It is worth examining a few aspects, however, if only to demonstrate the great degree of confusion that prevails. We can begin at the most fundamental possible level. So utterly unformed is the American law of statutory interpretation that not only is its methodology unclear, but even its very *objective* is. Consider the basic question: What are we looking for when we construe a statute?

You will find it frequently said in judicial opinions of my court and others that the judge's objective in interpreting a statute is to give effect to "the intent of the legislature." This principle, in one form or another, goes back at least as far as Blackstone.[6] Unfortunately, it does not square with some of the (few) generally accepted concrete rules of statutory construction. One is the rule that when the text of a statute is clear, that is the end of the matter. Why should that be so, if what the legislature *intended*, rather than what it *said*, is the object of our inquiry? In selecting the words of the statute, the legislature might have misspoken. Why not permit that to be demonstrated from the floor debates? Or indeed, why not accept, as proper material for the court to consider, later explanations by the legislators—a sworn affidavit signed by the majority of each house, for example, as to what they *really* meant?

Another accepted rule of construction is that ambiguities in a newly enacted statute are to be resolved in such fashion as to make the statute, not only internally consistent, but also compatible with previously enacted laws. We simply assume, for purposes of our search for "intent," that the enacting legislature was aware of all those other laws. Well of course that is a fiction, and if we were really looking for the subjective intent of the enacting legislature we would more likely find it by paying attention to the text (and legislative history) of the new statute in isolation.

The evidence suggests that, despite frequent statements to the contrary, we do not really look for subjective legislative intent. We look for a sort of "objectified" intent—the intent that a reasonable person would gather from the text of the law, placed alongside the remainder of the *corpus juris*. As Bishop's old treatise nicely put it, elaborating upon the usual formulation: "[T]he primary object of all rules for interpreting statutes is to ascertain the legislative intent; *or, exactly, the meaning which the subject is authorized to understand the legislature intended.*" [7] And the reason we adopt this objectified version is, I think, that it is simply incompatible with democratic government, or indeed, even with fair government, to have the meaning of a law determined by what the lawgiver meant, rather than by what the lawgiver promulgated. That seems to me one step worse than the trick the emperor Nero was said to engage in: posting edicts high up on the pillars, so that they could not easily be read. Government by unexpressed intent is similarly tyrannical. It is the *law* that governs, not the intent of the law-giver. That seems to me the essence of the famous American ideal set forth in the Massachusetts constitution: A government of laws, not of men. Men may intend what they will; but it is only the laws that they enact which bind us.

In reality, however, if one accepts the principle that the object of judicial inter-pretation is to determine the intent of the legislature, being bound by genuine but unexpressed legislative intent rather than the law is only the *theoretical* threat. The *practical* threat is that, under the guise or even the self-delusion of pursuing unexpressed legislative intents, common-law judges will in fact pursue their own objectives and desires, extending their lawmaking proclivities from the common law to the statutory field. When you are told to decide, not on the basis of what the legislature said, but on the basis of what it *meant*, and are assured that there is no necessary connection between the two, your best shot at figuring out what the legislature meant is to ask yourself what a wise and intelligent person *should* have meant; and that will surely bring you to the conclusion that the law means what you think it *ought* to mean—which is precisely how judges decide things under the common law. As Dean Landis of Harvard Law School (a believer in the search for legislative intent) put it in a 1930 article:

> [T]he gravest sins are perpetrated in the name of the intent of the legisla-
> ture. Judges are rarely willing to admit their role as actual lawgivers, and
> such admissions as are wrung from their unwilling lips lie in the field of
> common and not statute law. To condone in these instances the practice of
> talking in terms of the intent of the legislature, as if the legislature had
> attributed a particular meaning to certain words, when it is apparent that
> the intent is that of the judge, is to condone atavistic practices too reminis-
> cent of the medicine man.[8] . . .

The text is the law, and it is the text that must be observed. I agree with Justice Holmes's remark, quoted approvingly by Justice Frankfurter in his article on the construction of statutes: "Only a day or two ago—when counsel talked of the intention of a legislature, I was indiscreet enough to say I don't care what their intention was. I only want to know what the words mean." [9] And I agree with Holmes's other remark, quoted approvingly by Justice Jackson: "We do not inquire what the legislature meant; we ask only what the statute means." [10]

Textualism

The philosophy of interpretation I have described above is known as textualism. In some sophisticated circles, it is considered simpleminded—"wooden," "unimaginative," "pedestrian." It is none of that. To be a textualist in good standing, one need not be too dull to perceive the broader social purposes that a statute is designed, or could be designed, to serve; or too hidebound to realize that new times require new laws. One need only hold the belief that judges have no authority to pursue those broader purposes or write those new laws.

Textualism should not be confused with so-called strict constructionism, a degraded form of textualism that brings the whole philosophy into disrepute. I am not a strict constructionist, and no one ought to be—though better that, I suppose, than a nontextualist. A text should not be construed strictly, and it should not be construed leniently; it should be construed reasonably, to contain all that it fairly means. The difference between textualism and strict constructionism can be seen in a case my Court decided four terms ago.[11] The statute at issue provided for an increased jail term if, "during and in relation to . . . [a] drug trafficking crime," the defendant "uses . . . a firearm." The defendant in this case had sought to purchase a quantity of cocaine; and what he had offered to give in exchange for the cocaine was an unloaded firearm, which he showed to the drug-seller. The Court held, I regret to say, that the defendant was subject to the increased penalty, because he had "used a firearm during and in relation to a drug trafficking crime." The vote was not even close (6–3). I dissented. Now I cannot say whether my colleagues in the majority voted the way they did because they are strict-construction textualists, or because they are not textualists at all. But a proper textualist, which is to say my kind of textualist, would surely have voted to acquit. The phrase "uses a gun" fairly connoted use of a gun for what guns are normally used for, that is, as a weapon. As I put the point in my dissent, when you ask someone, "Do you use a cane?" you are not inquiring whether he has hung his grandfather's antique cane as a decoration in the hallway.

But while the good textualist is not a literalist, neither is he a nihilist. Words do have a limited range of meaning, and no interpretation that goes beyond that range is permissible. My favorite example of a departure from text—and certainly the departure that has enabled judges to do more freewheeling law-making than any other—pertains to the Due Process Clause found in the Fifth and Fourteenth Amendments of the United States Constitution, which says that no person shall "be deprived of life, liberty, or property without due process of law." It has been interpreted to prevent the government from taking away certain liberties *beyond* those, such as freedom of speech and of religion, that are specifically named in the Constitution. (The first Supreme Court case to use the Due Process Clause in this fashion was, by the way, *Dred Scott*[12]-not a desirable parentage.) Well, it may or may not be a good thing to guarantee additional liberties, but the Due Process Clause quite obviously does not bear that interpretation. By its inescapable terms, it guarantees only process. Property can be taken by the state; liberty can be taken; even life can be taken; but not without the *process* that our traditions require—notably, a validly enacted law and a fair trial. To say otherwise is to abandon textualism, and to render democratically adopted texts mere springboards for judicial lawmaking.

Of all the criticisms leveled against textualism, the most mindless is that it is "formalistic." The answer to that is, *of course it's formalistic!* The rule of law is *about* form. If, for example, a citizen performs an act—let us say the sale of certain technology to a foreign country—which is prohibited by a widely publicized bill proposed by the administration and passed by both houses of Congress, *but not yet signed by the President*, that sale is lawful. It is of no consequence that everyone knows both houses of Congress and the President wish to prevent that sale. Before the wish becomes a binding law, it must be embodied in a bill that passes both houses and is signed by the President. Is that not formalism? A murderer has been caught with blood on his hands, bending over the body of his victim; a neighbor with a video camera has filmed the crime; and the murderer has confessed in writing and on videotape. We nonetheless insist that before the state can punish this miscreant, it must conduct a full-dress criminal trial that results in a verdict of guilty. Is that not formalism? Long live formalism. It is what makes a government a government of laws and not of men. . . .

Legislative History

Let me turn now . . . to an interpretive device whose widespread use is relatively new: legislative history, by which I mean the statements made in the floor debates, committee reports, and even committee testimony, leading up to the enactment of the legislation. My view that the objective indication of the words, rather than the intent of the legislature, is what constitutes the law leads me, of course, to the conclusion that legislative history should not be used as an authoritative indication of a statute's meaning. This was the traditional English, and the traditional American, practice. Chief Justice Taney wrote:

> In expounding this law, the judgment of the court cannot, in any degree, be influenced by the construction placed upon it by individual members of Congress in the debate which took place on its passage, nor by the motives or reasons assigned by them for supporting or opposing amendments that were offered. The law as it passed is the will of the majority of both houses, *and the only mode in which that will is spoken is in the act itself;* and we must gather their intention from the language there used, comparing it, when any ambiguity exists, with the laws upon the same subject, and looking, if necessary, to the public history of the times in which it was passed.[13]

That uncompromising view generally prevailed in this country until the present century. The movement to change it gained momentum in the late 1920s and 1930s, driven, believe it or not, by frustration with common-law judges' use of "legislative intent" and phonied-up canons to impose their own views—in those days views opposed to progressive social legislation. I quoted earlier an article by Dean Landis inveighing against such judicial usurpation. The solution he proposed was not the banishment of legislative intent as an interpretive criterion, but rather the use of legislative history to place that intent beyond manipulation.[14]

Extensive use of legislative history in this country dates only from about the 1940s. . . . In the past few decades, however, we have developed a legal culture in which lawyers routinely—and I do mean routinely—make no distinction between words in the text of a statute and words in its legislative history. My Court is frequently told, in briefs and in oral argument, that "Congress said thus-and-so"—when in fact what is being quoted is not the law promulgated by Congress, nor even any text endorsed by a single house of Congress, but rather the statement of a single committee of a single house, set forth in a committee report. Resort to legislative history has become so common that lawyerly wags have popularized a humorous quip inverting the oft-recited (and oft-ignored) rule as to when its use is appropriate: "One should consult the text of the statute," the joke goes, "only when the legislative history is ambiguous." Alas, that is no longer funny. Reality has overtaken parody. A few terms ago, I read a brief that *began* the legal argument with a discussion of legislative history and then continued (I am quoting it verbatim): "Unfortunately, the legislative debates are not helpful. Thus, we turn to the other guidepost in this difficult area, statutory language." [15]

As I have said, I object to the use of legislative history on principle, since I reject intent of the legislature as the proper criterion of the law. What is most exasperating about the use of legislative history, however, is that it does not even make sense for those who *accept* legislative intent as the criterion. It is much more likely to produce a false or contrived legislative intent than a genuine one. . . .

Ironically, but quite understandably, the more courts have relied upon legislative history, the less worthy of reliance it has become. In earlier days, it was at least genuine and not contrived—a real part of the legislation's *history*, in the sense that it was part of the *development* of the bill, part of the attempt to inform and persuade those who voted. Nowadays, however, when it is universally known and expected that judges will resort to floor debates and (especially) committee reports as authoritative expressions of "legislative intent," affecting the courts rather than informing the Congress has become the primary purpose of the exercise. It is less that the courts refer to legislative history because it exists than that legislative history exists because the courts refer to it. One of the routine tasks of the Washington lawyer-lobbyist is to draft language that sympathetic legislators can recite in a prewritten "floor debate"—or, even better, insert into a committee report. . . .

I think that Dean Landis, and those who joined him in the prescription of legislative history as a cure for what he called "willful judges," would be aghast at the results a half century later. On balance, it has facilitated rather than deterred decisions that are based upon the courts' policy preferences, rather than neutral principles of law. Since there are no rules as to how much weight an element of legislative history is entitled to, it can usually be either relied upon or dismissed with equal plausibility. If the willful judge does not like the committee report, he will not follow it; he will call the statute not ambiguous enough, the committee report too ambiguous, or the legislative history (this is a favorite phrase) "as a whole, inconclusive." . . .

Interpreting Constitutional Texts

Without pretending to have exhausted the vast topic of textual interpretation, I wish to address a final subject: the distinctive problem of constitutional interpretation. The problem is distinctive, not because special principles of interpretation apply, but because the usual principles are being applied to an unusual text. Chief Justice Marshall put the point as well as it can be put in *McCulloch v. Maryland*:

> A constitution, to contain an accurate detail of all the subdivisions of which its great powers will admit, and of all the means by which they may be carried into execution, would partake of the prolixity of a legal code, and could

scarcely be embraced by the human mind. It would probably never be understood by the public. Its nature, therefore, requires, that only its great outlines should be marked, its important objects designated, and the minor ingredients which compose those objects be deduced from the nature of the objects themselves.[16]

In textual interpretation, context is everything, and the context of the Constitution tells us not to expect nit-picking detail, and to give words and phrases an expansive rather than narrow interpretation—though not an interpretation that the language will not bear.

Take, for example, the provision of the First Amendment that forbids abridgment of "the freedom of speech, or of the press." That phrase does not list the full range of communicative expression. Handwritten letters, for example, are neither speech nor press. Yet surely there is no doubt they cannot be censored. In this constitutional context, speech and press, the two most common forms of communication, stand as a sort of synecdoche for the whole. That is not strict construction, but it is reasonable construction.

It is curious that most of those who insist that the drafter's intent gives meaning to a statute reject the drafter's intent as the criterion for interpretation of the Constitution. I reject it for both. . . . [T]he Great Divide with regard to constitutional interpretation is not that between Framers' intent and objective meaning, but rather that between *original* meaning (whether derived from Framers' intent or not) and *current* meaning. The ascendant school of constitutional interpretation affirms the existence of what is called The Living Constitution, a body of law that (unlike normal statutes) grows and changes from age to age, in order to meet the needs of a changing society. And it is the judges who determine those needs and "find" that changing law. Seems familiar, doesn't it? Yes, it is the common law returned, but infinitely more powerful than what the old common law ever pretended to be, for now it trumps even the statutes of democratic legislatures. . . .

If you go into a constitutional law class, or study a constitutional law casebook, or read a brief filed in a constitutional law case, you will rarely find the discussion addressed to the text of the constitutional provision that is at issue, or to the question of what was the originally understood or even the originally intended meaning of that text. The starting point of the analysis will be Supreme Court cases, and the new issue will presumptively be decided according to the logic that those cases expressed, with no regard for how far that logic, thus extended, has distanced us from the original text and understanding. Worse still, however, it is known and understood that if that logic fails to produce what in the view of the current Supreme Court is the *desirable* result for the case at hand, then, like good common-law judges, the Court will distinguish its precedents, or narrow them, or if all else fails overrule them, in order that the Constitution might mean what it *ought* to mean. Should there be—to take one of the less controversial examples—a constitutional right to die? If so, there is.[17] Should there be a constitutional right to reclaim a biological child put out for adoption by the other parent? Again, if so, there is.[18] If it is good, it is so. Never mind the text that we are supposedly construing; we will smuggle these new rights in, if all else fails, under the Due Process Clause (which, as I have described, is textually incapable of containing them). Moreover, what the Constitution meant yesterday it does not necessarily mean today. As our opinions say in the context of our Eighth Amendment jurisprudence (the Cruel and Unusual Punishments Clause), its meaning changes to reflect "the evolving standards of decency that mark the progress of a maturing society." [19]

This is preeminently a common-law way of making law, and not the way of construing a democratically adopted text. . . . Proposals for "dynamic statutory construction," such as those of Judge Calabresi . . . are concededly avant-garde. The Constitution, however, even though a democratically adopted text, we formally treat like the common law. What, it is fair to ask, is the justification for doing so?

One would suppose that the rule that a text does not change would apply *a fortiori* to a constitution. If courts felt too much bound by the democratic process to tinker with statutes, when their tinkering could be adjusted by the legislature, how much more should they feel bound not to tinker with a constitution, when their tinkering is virtually irreparable. It certainly cannot be said that a constitution naturally suggests changeability; to the contrary, its whole purpose is to prevent change—to embed certain rights in such a manner that future generations cannot readily take them away. A society that adopts a bill of rights is skeptical that "evolving standards of decency" always "mark progress," and that societies always "mature," as opposed to rot. Neither the text of such a document nor the intent of its framers (whichever you choose) can possibly lead to the conclusion that its only effect is to take the power of changing rights away from the legislature and give it to the courts.

Flexibility and Liberality of the Living Constitution

The argument most frequently made in favor of the Living Constitution is a pragmatic one: Such an evolutionary approach is necessary in order to provide the "flexibility" that a changing society requires; the Constitution would have snapped if it had not been permitted to bend and grow. This might be a persuasive argument if most of the "growing" that the proponents of this approach have brought upon us in the past, and are determined to bring upon us in the future, were the *elimination* of restrictions upon democratic government. But just the opposite is true. Historically, and particularly in the past thirty-five years, the "evolving" Constitution has imposed a vast array of new constraints—new inflexibilities—upon administrative, judicial, and legislative action. To mention only a few things that formerly could be done or not done, as the society desired, but now cannot be done:

- admitting in a state criminal trial evidence of guilt that was obtained by an unlawful search;[20]
- permitting invocation of God at public-school graduations;[21]
- electing one of the two houses of a state legislature the way the United States Senate is elected, i.e., on a basis that does not give all voters numerically equal representation;[22]
- terminating welfare payments as soon as evidence of fraud is received, subject to restoration after hearing if the evidence is satisfactorily refuted;[23]
- imposing property requirements as a condition of voting;[24]
- prohibiting anonymous campaign literature;[25]
- prohibiting pornography.[26]

And the future agenda of constitutional evolutionists is mostly more of the same—the creation of *new* restrictions upon democratic government, rather than the elimination of old ones. *Less* flexibility in government, not *more*. As things now stand, the state and federal governments may either apply capital punishment or abolish it, permit suicide or forbid it—all as the changing times and the changing sentiments of society may demand. But when capital punishment is held to violate the Eighth Amendment, and suicide is held to be protected by the Fourteenth Amendment, all flexibility with regard to those matters will be gone. No, the reality of the matter is that, generally speaking, devotees of The Living Constitution do not seek to facilitate social change but to prevent it.

There are, I must admit, a few exceptions to that—a few instances in which, historically, greater flexibility has been the result of the process. But those exceptions serve only to refute another argument of the proponents of an evolving Constitution, that evolution will always be in the direction of greater personal liberty. (They consider that a great advantage, for reasons that I do not entirely understand. All government represents a balance between individual freedom and social order, and it is not true that every alteration of that balance in the direction of greater individual freedom is necessarily good.) But in any case, the record of history refutes the proposition that the evolving Constitution will invariably enlarge individual rights. The most obvious refutation is the modern Court's limitation of the constitutional protections afforded to property. The provision prohibiting impairment of the obligation of contracts, for example, has been gutted.[27] I am sure that We the People agree with that development; we value property rights less than the Founders did. So also, we value the right to bear arms less than did the Founders (who thought the right of self-defense to be absolutely fundamental), and there will be few tears shed if and when the Second Amendment is held to guarantee nothing more than the state National Guard. But this just shows that the Founders were right when they feared that some (in their view misguided) future generation might wish to abandon liberties that they considered essential, and so sought to protect those liberties in a Bill of Rights. We may *like* the abridgment of property rights and *like* the elimination of the right to bear arms; but let us not pretend that these are not *reductions* of *rights*.

Or if property rights are too cold to arouse enthusiasm, and the right to bear arms too dangerous, let me give another example: Several terms ago a case came before the Supreme Court involving a prosecution for sexual abuse of a young child. The trial court found that the child would be too frightened to testify in the presence of the (presumed) abuser, and so, pursuant to state law, she was permitted to testify with only the prosecutor and defense counsel present, with the defendant, the judge, and the jury watching over closed-circuit television. A reasonable enough procedure, and it was held to be constitutional by my Court.[28] I dissented, because the Sixth Amendment provides that "[i]n *all* criminal prosecutions the accused shall enjoy the right . . . to be confronted with the witnesses against him" (emphasis added). There is no doubt what confrontation meant— or indeed means today. It means face-to-face, not watching from another room. And there is no doubt what one of the major purposes of that provision was: to induce *precisely* that pressure upon the witness which the little girl found it difficult to endure. It is difficult to accuse someone to his face, particularly when you are lying. Now no extrinsic factors have changed since that provision was adopted in 1791. Sexual abuse existed then, as it does now; little children were more easily upset than adults, then as now; a means of placing the defendant out of sight of the witness existed then as now (a screen could easily have been erected that would enable the defendant to see the witness, but not the witness the defendant). But the Sixth Amendment nonetheless gave *all* criminal defendants the right to *confront* the witnesses against them, because that was thought to be an important protection. The only significant things that *have* changed, I think, are the society's sensitivity to so-called psychic trauma (which is what we are told the child witness in such a situation suffers) and the society's assessment of where the proper balance ought to be struck between the two extremes of a procedure that assures convicting 100 percent of all child abusers, and a procedure that assures acquitting 100 percent of those falsely accused of child abuse. I have no doubt that the society is, as a whole, happy and pleased with what my Court decided. But we should not pretend that the decision did not *eliminate* a liberty that previously existed. . . .

It seems to me that that is where we are heading, or perhaps even where we have arrived. Seventy-five years ago, we believed firmly enough in a rock-solid, unchanging Constitution that we felt it necessary to adopt the Nineteenth Amendment to give women the vote. The battle was not fought in the courts, and few thought that it could be, despite the constitutional guarantee of Equal Protection of the Laws; that provision did not, when it was adopted, and hence did not in 1920, guarantee equal access to the ballot but permitted distinctions on the basis not only of age but of property and of sex. Who can doubt that if the issue had been deferred until today, the Constitution would be (formally) unamended, and the courts would be the chosen instrumentality of change? The American people have been converted to belief in The Living Constitution, a "morphing" document that means, from age to age, what it ought to mean. And with that conversion has inevitably come the new phenomenon of selecting and confirming federal judges, at all levels, on the basis of their views regarding a whole series of proposals for constitutional evolution. If the courts are free to write the Constitution anew, they will, by God, write it the way the majority wants; the appointment and confirmation process will see to that. This, of course, is the end of the Bill of Rights, whose meaning will be committed to the very body it was meant to protect against: the majority. By trying to make the Constitution do everything that needs doing from age to age, we shall have caused it to do nothing at all.

NOTES

I am grateful for technical and research assistance by Matthew P. Previn, and for substantive suggestions by Eugene Scalia.

1. Oliver Wendell Holmes, Jr., *The Common Law* (1881).

2. The country's first major code of civil procedure, known as the Field Code (after David Dudley Field, who played a major role in its enactment), was passed in New York in 1848. By the end of the nineteenth century, similar codes had been adopted in many states. *See* Lawrence M. Friedman, *A History of American Law* 340–47 (1973).

3. The principal exception to this statement consists of so-called Uniform Laws, statutes enacted in virtually identical form by all or a large majority of state legislatures, in an effort to achieve nationwide uniformity with respect to certain aspects of some common-law fields. *See, e.g.*, Uniform Commercial Code, 1 U.L.A. 5 (1989); Uniform Marriage and Divorce Act 9A U.L.A. 156 (1987); Uniform Consumer Credit Code, 7A U.L.A. 17 (1985).

4. "The [members of the judiciary department], by the mode of their appointment, as well as by the nature and permanency of it, are too far removed from the people to share much in their prepossessions." *The Federalist* No. 49, at 341 (Jacob E. Cooke ed., 1961).

5. Henry M. Hart, Jr. & Albert M. Sacks, *The Legal Process* 1169 (William N. Eskridge, Jr. & Philip P. Frickey eds., 1994).

6. *See* 1 William Blackstone, *Commentaries on the Laws of England* 59–62, 91 (photo reprint 1979) (1765).

7. Joel Prentiss Bishop, *Commentaries on the Written Laws and Their Interpretation* 57–58 (Boston: Little, Brown, & Co. 1882) (emphasis added) (citation omitted).

8. James M. Landis, *A Note on "Statutory Interpretation,"* 43 Harv. L. Rev. 886, 891 (1930).

9. Felix Frankfurter, *Some Reflections on the Reading of Statutes*, 47 Colum. L. Rev. 527, 538 (1947).

10. Oliver Wendell Holmes, *Collected Legal Papers* 207 (1920), *quoted in* Schwegmann Bros. v. Calvert Distillers Corp., 341 U.S. 384, 397 (1951) (Jackson, J., concurring).

11. Smith v. United States, 508 U.S. 223 (1993).

12. Dred Scott v. Sandford, 60 U.S. (19 How.) 393, 450 (1857).

13. Aldridge v. Williams, 44 U.S. (3 How.) 9, 24 (1845) (emphasis added).

14. *See* Landis, *supra* note 17, at 891–92.

15. Brief for Petitioner at 21, Jett v. Dallas Indep. Sch. Dist., 491 U.S. 701 (1989), *quoted in* Green v. Bock Laundry Machine Co., 490 U.S. 504, 530 (1989) (Scalia, J., concurring).

16. McCulloch v. Maryland, 17 U.S. (4 Wheat.) 316, 407 (1819).

17. *See* Cruzan v. Director, Mo. Dep't of Health, 497 U.S. 261, 279 (1990).

18. *See In re* Kirchner, 649 N.E.2d 324, 333 (Ill.), *cert. denied*, 115 S. Ct. 2599 (1995).

19. Rhodes v. Chapman, 452 U.S. 337, 346 (1981), quoting from Trop v. Dulles, 356 U.S. 86, 101 (1958) (plurality opinion).

20. *See* Mapp v. Ohio, 367 U.S. 643 (1961).

21. *See* Lee v. Weisman, 505 U.S. 577 (1992).

22. *See* Reynolds v. Sims, 377 U.S. 533 (1964).

23. *See* Goldberg v. Kelly, 397 U.S. 254 (1970).

24. *See* Kramer v. Union Free Sch. Dist., 395 U.S. 621 (1969).

25. *See* McIntyre v. Ohio Elections Comm'n, 115 S. Ct. 1511 (1995).

26. Under current doctrine, pornography may be banned only if it is "obscene," *see* Miller v. California, 413 U.S. 15 (1973), a judicially crafted term of art that does not embrace material that excites "normal, healthy sexual desires," Brocket v. Spokane Arcades, Inc., 472 U.S. 491, 498 (1985).

27. *See* Home Building & Loan Ass'n v. Blaisdell, 290 U.S. 398 (1934).

28. *See* Maryland v. Craig, 497 U.S. 836 (1990).

9-2

from *Active Liberty*

Stephen Breyer

Justice Stephen Breyer's book Active Liberty, *from which this essay is excerpted, has been widely viewed as an activist judge's response to Justice Scalia's paean to judicial restraint. Yet Breyer does not envision a broadly activist role for judges in shaping social policy. For one thing, he agrees fundamentally with Scalia that unelected, life-tenured judges should subordinate their personal views on policy to those who are elected to make these decisions. Reflecting this, Breyer's decisions show his reluctance to overrule acts of Congress and executive decisions. For Breyer, the primacy of democracy requires that judges play a special role as guardians of citizens' rights and opportunities to influence government. On a variety of issues, this hierarchy of values leads Breyer to decide cases in ways that Scalia believes overstep judges' mandate. Breyer accepts broad regulation of campaign finance as advancing the performance of democracy, whereas Scalia argues that such laws affront First Amendment protections of free speech.*

THE THEME AS I here consider it falls within an interpretive tradition. . . . That tradition sees texts as driven by *purposes*. The judge should try to find and "honestly . . . say what was the underlying purpose expressed" in a statute. The judge should read constitutional language "as the revelation of the great purposes which were intended to be achieved by the Constitution" itself, a "framework for" and a "continuing instrument of government." The judge should recognize that the Constitution will apply to "new subject matter . . . with which the framers were not familiar." Thus, the judge, whether applying statute or Constitution, should "reconstruct the past solution imaginatively in its setting and project the purposes which inspired it upon the concrete occasions which arise for their decision." Since law is connected to life, judges, in applying a text in light of its purpose, should look to *consequences*, including "contemporary conditions, social, industrial, and political, of the community to be affected." And since "the

Source: Stephen Breyer, from *Active Liberty: Interpreting Our Democratic Constitution,* (Alfred A. Knopf: 2005), 17–34, 85–101. Some notes appearing in the original have been deleted.

purpose of construction is the ascertainment of meaning, nothing that is logically relevant should be excluded." [1]

That tradition does not expect highly general instructions themselves to determine the outcome of difficult concrete cases where language is open-ended and precisely defined purpose is difficult to ascertain. Certain constitutional language, for example, reflects "fundamental aspirations and . . . 'moods,' embodied in provisions like the due process and equal protection clauses, which were designed not to be precise and positive directions for rules of action." A judge, when interpreting such open-ended provisions, must avoid being "willful, in the sense of enforcing individual views." A judge cannot "enforce whatever he thinks best." "In the exercise of" the "high power" of judicial review, says Justice Louis Brandeis, "we must be ever on our guard, lest we erect our prejudices into legal principles." At the same time, a judge must avoid being "wooden, in uncritically resting on formulas, in assuming the familiar to be the necessary, in not realizing that any problem can be solved if only one principle is involved but that unfortunately all controversies of importance involve if not a conflict at least an interplay of principles." [2]

How, then, is the judge to act between the bounds of the "willful" and the "wooden"? The tradition answers with an *attitude*, an attitude that hesitates to rely upon any single theory or grand view of law, of interpretation, or of the Constitution. It champions the need to search for purposes; it calls for restraint, asking judges to "speak . . . humbly as the voice of the law." And it finds in the democratic nature of our system more than simply a justification for judicial restraint. Holmes reminds the judge as a general matter to allow "[c]onsiderable latitude . . . for differences of view." . . .

[O]ne can reasonably view the Constitution as focusing upon active liberty, both as important in itself and as a partial means to help secure individual (modern) freedom. The Framers included elements designed to "control and mitigate" the ill effects of more direct forms of democratic government, but in doing so, the Framers "did not see themselves as repudiating either the Revolution or popular government." Rather, they were "saving both from their excesses." The act of ratifying the Constitution, by means of special state elections with broad voter eligibility rules, signaled the democratic character of the document itself.[3]

As history has made clear, the original Constitution was insufficient. It did not include a majority of the nation within its "democratic community." It took a civil war and eighty years of racial segregation before the slaves and their descendants could begin to think of the Constitution as theirs. Nor did women receive the right to vote until 1920. The "people" had to amend the Constitution, not only to extend its democratic base but also to expand and more fully to secure basic individual (negative) liberty.

But the original document sowed the democratic seed. Madison described something fundamental about American government, then and now, when he said the Constitution is a "charter . . . of power . . . granted by liberty," not (as in Europe) a "charter of liberty . . . granted by power." [4] . . .

In sum, our constitutional history has been a quest for workable government, workable democratic government, workable democratic government protective of individual personal liberty. Our central commitment has been to "government of the people, by the people, for the people." And the applications following illustrate how this constitutional understanding helps interpret the Constitution—in a way that helps to resolve problems related to *modern* government. . . .

Statutory Interpretation

The [first] example concerns statutory interpretation. It contrasts a literal text-based approach with an approach that places more emphasis on statutory purpose and congressional intent. It illustrates why judges should pay primary attention to a statute's purpose in difficult cases of interpretation in which language is not clear. It shows how overemphasis on text can lead courts astray, divorcing law from life-indeed, creating law that harms those whom Congress meant to help. And it explains why a purposive approach is more consistent with the framework for a "delegated democracy" that the Constitution creates.[5]

The interpretive problem arises when statutory language does not clearly answer the question of what the statute means or how it applies. Why does a statute contain such language? Perhaps Congress used inappropriate language. Perhaps it failed to use its own drafting expertise or failed to have committee hearings, writing legislation on the floor instead. Perhaps it chose politically symbolic language or ambiguous language over more precise language—possibilities that modern, highly partisan, interest-group-based politics (responding to overly simplified media accounts) make realistic. Perhaps no one in Congress thought about how the statute would apply in certain circumstances. Perhaps it is impossible to use language that foresees how a statute should apply in all relevant circumstances.

The founding generation of Americans understood these or similar possibilities. They realized that judges, though mere "fallible men," would have to exercise judgment and discretion in applying newly codified law. But they expected that judges, when doing so, would remain faithful to the legislators' will. The problem of statutory interpretation is how to meet that expectation.

Most judges start in the same way. They look first to the statute's language, its structure, and its history in an effort to determine the statute's purpose. They then use that purpose (along with the language, structure, and history) to determine the proper interpretation. Thus far, there is agreement. But when the problem is truly difficult, these factors without more may simply limit the universe of possible answers without clearly identifying a final choice. What then?

At this point judges tend to divide in their approach. Some look primarily to text, i.e., to language and text-related circumstances, for further enlightenment. They may try to tease further meaning from the language and structure of the statute itself. They may look to language-based canons of interpretation in the search for an "objective" key to the statute's proper interpretation, say a canon like *noscitur a sociis*, which tells a judge to interpret a word so that it has the same kind of meaning as its neighbors. Textualism, it has been argued, searches for "meaning . . . in structure." It means "preferring the language and structure of the law whenever possible over its legislative history and imputed values." It asks judges to avoid invocation of vague or broad statutory purposes and instead to consider such purposes at "lower levels of generality." It hopes thereby to reduce the risk that judges will interpret statutes subjectively, substituting their own ideas of what is good for those of Congress.[6]

Other judges look primarily to the statute's purposes for enlightenment. They avoid the use of interpretive canons. They allow context to determine the level of generality at which they will describe a statute's purpose—in the way that context tells us not to answer the lost driver's request for directions, "Where am I?" with the words "In a car." They speak in terms of congressional "intent," while understanding that legal conventions govern the use of that term to describe, not the intent of any, or every, individual legislator, but the intent of the group—in the way that linguistic conventions allow us to speak of the intentions of an army or a team, even when they differ from those of any, or every, soldier or member. And they examine legislative history, often closely, in the hope that the history will help them better understand the context, the enacting legislators' objectives, and ultimately the statute's purposes. At the heart of a purpose-based approach stands the "reasonable member of Congress"—a legal fiction that applies, for example, even when Congress did not in fact consider a particular problem. The judge will ask how this person (real or fictional), aware of the statute's language, structure, and general objectives (actually or hypothetically), *would have wanted* a court to interpret the statute in light of present circumstances in the particular case.

[A] recent case illustrate[s] the difference between the two approaches. In [it] the majority followed a more textual approach; the dissent, a more purposive approach. . . . The federal habeas corpus statute is ambiguous in respect to the time limits that apply when a state prisoner seeks access to federal habeas corpus. It says that a state prisoner (ordinarily) must file a federal petition within one year after his state court conviction becomes final. But the statute tolls that one-year period during the time that "a properly filed application for State post-conviction *or other collateral review*" is pending. Do the words "other collateral review" include an earlier application for a federal habeas corpus petition? Should the one-year period be tolled, for example, when a state prisoner mistakenly files a habeas petition in federal court before he exhausts all his state collateral remedies?"

It is unlikely that anyone in Congress thought about this question, for it is highly technical. Yet it is important. More than half of all federal habeas corpus petitions fall into the relevant category—i.e., state prisoners file them prematurely before the prisoner has tried to take advantage of available state remedies. In those cases, the federal court often dismisses the petition and the state prisoner must return to state court to exhaust available state remedies before he can once again file his federal habeas petition in federal court. If the one-year statute of limitations is not tolled while the first federal habeas petition was pending, that state prisoner will likely find that the one year has run—and his federal petition is time-barred—before he can return to federal court.[7]

A literal reading of the statute suggests that this is just what Congress had in mind. It suggests that the one-year time limit is tolled only during the time that *state* collateral review (or similar) proceedings are in process. And that reading is supported by various linguistic canons of construction.[8]

Nonetheless, the language does not foreclose an alternative interpretation—an interpretation under which such petitions would fall within the scope of the phrase "other collateral review." The word "State" could be read to modify the phrase "post-conviction . . . review," permitting "*other* collateral review" to refer to federal proceedings. The phrase "properly filed" could be interpreted to refer to purely formal filing requirements rather than calling into play more important remedial questions such as the presence or absence of "exhaustion." A purposive approach favors this latter linguistic interpretation.[9]

Why? [Consider] our hypothetical legislator, the reasonable member of Congress. Which interpretation would that member favor (if he had thought of the problem, which he likely had not)? Consider the consequences of the more literal interpretation. That interpretation would close the doors of federal habeas courts to many or most state prisoners who mistakenly filed a federal habeas petition too soon, but not to all such prisoners. Whether the one-year window was still open would depend in large part on how long the federal court considering the premature federal petition took to dismiss it. In cases in which the court ruled quickly, the short time the federal petition was (wrongly) present in the federal court might not matter. But if a premature federal petition languishes on the federal court's docket while the one year runs, the petitioner would likely lose his one meaningful chance to seek federal habeas relief. By way of contrast, state court delay in considering a prisoner petition in state court would not matter. Whenever *state* proceedings are at issue, the statute tolls the one-year limitations period.

Now ask *why* our reasonable legislator would want to bring about these consequences. He might believe that state prisoners have too often abused the federal writ by filing too many petitions. But the distinction that a literal interpretation would make between those allowed to file and those not allowed to file—a distinction that in essence rests upon federal court processing delay—is a *random* distinction, bearing no logical relation to any abuse-related purpose. Would our reasonable legislator, even if concerned about abuse of the writ, choose to deny access to the Great Writ on a *random* basis? Given our traditions, including those the Constitution grants through its habeas corpus guarantees, the answer to this question is likely no. Would those using a more literal text-based approach answer this question differently? I do not think so. But my real objection to the text-based approach is that it would prevent them from posing the question at all.[10]

[This] example suggest[s] the danger that lurks where judges rely too heavily upon just text and textual aids when interpreting a statute. . . . [W]hen difficult statutory questions are at issue, courts do better to focus foremost upon statutory purpose, ruling out neither legislative history nor any other form of help in order to locate the role that Congress intended the statutory words in question to play.

For one thing, near-exclusive reliance upon canons and other linguistic interpretive aids in close cases can undermine the Constitution's democratic objective. Legislation in a delegated democracy is meant to embody the people's will, either directly (insofar as legislators see themselves as translating how their constituents feel about each proposed law) or indirectly (insofar as legislators see themselves as exercising delegated authority to vote in accordance with what they see as the public interest). Either way, an interpretation of a statute that tends to implement the legislator's will helps to implement the public's will and is therefore consistent with the Constitution's democratic purpose. For similar reasons an interpretation that undercuts the statute's objectives tends to undercut that constitutional objective. . . .

Use of a "reasonable legislator" fiction also facilitates legislative accountability. Ordinary citizens think in terms of general purposes. They readily understand their elected legislators' thinking similarly. It is not impossible to ask an ordinary citizen to determine whether a particular law is consistent with a general purpose the ordinary citizen might support. It is not impossible to ask an ordinary citizen to determine what general purpose a legislator sought to achieve in enacting a particular statute. And it is not impossible for the ordinary citizen to judge the legislator accordingly. But it *is* impossible to ask an ordinary citizen (or an ordinary legislator) to understand the operation of linguistic canons of interpretation. And it *is* impossible to ask an ordinary citizen to draw any relevant electoral conclusion from consequences that might flow when courts reach a purpose-thwarting interpretation of the statute based upon their near-exclusive use of interpretive canons. Were a segment of the public unhappy about application of the Arbitration Act to ordinary employment contracts, whom should it blame?

For another thing, that approach means that laws will work better for the people they are presently meant to affect. Law is tied to life, and a failure to understand how a statute is so tied can undermine the very human activity that the law seeks to benefit. The more literal text-based, canon-based interpretation of the Foreign Sovereign Immunities jurisdictional statute, for example, means that foreign nations, those using tiered corporate ownership, will find their access to federal courts cut off, undermining the statute's basic jurisdictional objectives. The textual approach to the habeas corpus statute randomly closes courthouse doors in a way that runs contrary to our commitment to basic individual liberty. And it does so because it tends to stop judges from asking a relevant purpose-based question: Why would Congress have wanted a statute that produces those consequences?[11]

In sum, a "reasonable legislator" approach is a workable method of implementing the Constitution's democratic objective. It permits ready translation of the general desire of the public for certain ends, through the legislator's efforts to embody those ends in legislation, into a set of statutory words that will carry out those general objectives. I have argued that the Framers created the Constitution's complex governmental mechanism in order better to translate public will, determined through collective deliberation, into sound public policy. The courts constitute part of that mechanism. And judicial use of the "will of the reasonable legislator"—even if at times it is a fiction—helps statutes match their means to their overall public policy objectives, a match that helps translate the popular will into sound policy. An overly literal reading of a text can too often stand in the way.

Constitutional Interpretation: Speech

The [next] example focuses on the First Amendment and how it . . . show[s] the importance of reading the First Amendment not in isolation but as seeking to maintain a system of free expression designed to further a basic constitutional purpose: creating and maintaining democratic decision-making institutions.

The example begins where courts normally begin in First Amendment cases. They try to classify the speech at issue, distinguishing among different speech-related activities for the purpose of applying a strict, moderately strict, or totally relaxed presumption of unconstitutionality. Is the speech "political speech," calling for a strong pro-speech presumption, "commercial speech," calling for a midrange presumption, or simply a form of economic regulation presumed constitutional?

Should courts begin in this way? Some argue that making these kinds of categorical distinctions is a misplaced enterprise. The Constitution's language makes no such distinction. It simply protects "the freedom of speech" from government restriction. "Speech is speech and that is the end of the matter." But to limit distinctions to the point at which First Amendment law embodies the slogan "speech is speech" cannot work. And the fact that the First Amendment seeks to protect active liberty as well as modern liberty helps to explain why.[12]

The democratic government that the Constitution creates now regulates a host of activities that inevitably take place through the medium of speech. Today's workers manipulate information, not wood or metal. And the modern information-based workplace, no less than its more materially based predecessors, requires the application of community standards seeking to assure, for example, the absence of anti-competitive restraints; the accuracy of information; the absence of discrimination; the protection of health, safety, the environment, the consumer; and so forth.

Laws that embody these standards obviously affect speech. Warranty laws require private firms to include on labels statements of a specified content. Securities laws and consumer protection laws insist upon the disclosure of information that businesses might prefer to keep private. Health laws forbid tobacco advertising, say, to children. Anti-discrimination laws insist that employers prevent employees from making certain kinds of statements. Communications laws require cable broadcasters to provide network access. Campaign finance laws restrict citizen contributions to candidates.

To treat all these instances alike, to scrutinize them all as if they all represented a similar kind of legislative effort to restrain a citizen's "modern liberty" to speak, would lump together too many different kinds of activities under the aegis of a single standard, thereby creating a dilemma. On the one hand, if strong First Amendment standards were to apply across the board, they would prevent a democratically elected government from creating necessary regulation. The strong free speech guarantees needed to protect the structural democratic governing process, if applied without distinction to all governmental efforts to control speech, would unreasonably limit the public's substantive economic (or social) regulatory choices. The limits on substantive choice would likely exceed what any liberty-protecting framework for democratic government could require, depriving the people of the democratically necessary room to make decisions, including the leeway to make regulatory mistakes. . . . Most scholars, including "speech is speech" advocates, consequently see a need for distinctions. The question is, Which ones? Applied where?

At this point, reference to the Constitution's more general objectives helps. First, active liberty is particularly at risk when law restricts speech directly related to the shaping of public opinion, for example, speech that takes place in areas related to politics and policy-making by elected officials. That special risk justifies especially strong pro-speech judicial presumptions. It also justifies careful review whenever the speech in question seeks to shape public opinion, particularly if that opinion in turn will affect the political process and the kind of society in which we live.

Second, whenever ordinary commercial or economic regulation is at issue, this special risk normally is absent. Moreover, strong pro-speech presumptions risk imposing what is, from the perspective of active liberty, too severe a restriction upon the legislature—a restriction that would dramatically limit the size of the legislative arena that the Constitution opens for public deliberation and action. The presence of this second risk warns against use of special, strong pro-speech judicial presumptions or special regulation-skeptical judicial review.

The upshot is that reference to constitutional purposes in general and active liberty in particular helps to justify the category of review that the Court applies to a given type of law. But those same considerations argue, among other things, against category boundaries that are too rigid or fixed and against too mechanical an application of those categories. Rather, reference to active liberty will help courts define and apply the categories case by case.

Consider campaign finance reform. The campaign finance problem arises out of the explosion of campaign costs, particularly those related to television advertising, together with the vast disparity in ability to make a campaign contribution. In the year 2000, for example, election expenditures amounted to $1.4 billion, and the two presidential candidates spent about $310 million. In 2002, an off-year without a presidential contest, campaign expenditures still amounted to more than $1 billion. A typical House election cost $900,000, with an open seat costing $1.2 million; a typical Senate seat cost about $4.8 million, with an open contested seat costing about $7.1 million.[13] . . .

A small number of individuals and groups underwrite a very large share of these costs. In 2000, about half the money the parties spent, roughly $500 million, was soft money, i.e., money not subject to regulation under the then current campaign finance laws. Two-thirds of that money—almost $300 million—came from just 800 donors, each contributing a minimum of $120,000. Of these donors, 435 were corporations or unions (whose *direct* contributions the law forbids). The rest, 365, were individual citizens. At the same time, 99 percent of the

200 million or so citizens eligible to vote gave less than $200. Ninety-six percent gave nothing at all.[14]

The upshot is a concern, reflected in campaign finance laws, that the few who give in large amounts may have special access to, and therefore influence over, their elected representatives or, at least, create the appearance of undue influence. (One study found, for example, that 55 percent of Americans believe that large contributions have a "great deal" of impact on how decisions are made in Washington; fewer than 1 percent believed they had no impact.) These contributions (particularly if applied to television) may eliminate the need for, and in that sense crowd out, smaller individual contributions. In either case, the public may lose confidence in the political system and become less willing to participate in the political process. That, in important part, is why legislatures have tried to regulate the size of campaign contributions.[15]

Our Court in 1976 considered the constitutionality of the congressional legislation that initially regulated campaign contributions, and in 2003 we considered more recent legislation that tried to close what Congress considered a loophole— the ability to make contributions in the form of unregulated soft money. The basic constitutional question does not concern the desirability or wisdom of the legislation but whether, how, and the extent to which the First Amendment permits the legislature to impose limits on the amounts that individuals or organizations or parties can contribute to a campaign. Here it is possible to sketch an approach to decision-making that draws upon the Constitution's democratic objective.[16]

It is difficult to find an easy answer to this basic constitutional question in language, in history, or in tradition. The First Amendment's language says that Congress shall not abridge "the freedom of speech." But it does not define "the freedom of speech" in any detail. The nation's Founders did not speak directly about campaign contributions. . .

Neither can we find the answer through the use of purely conceptual arguments. Some claim, for example, that "money is speech." Others say, "money is not speech." But neither contention helps. Money is not speech, it is money. But the expenditure of money enables speech, and that expenditure is often necessary to communicate a message, particularly in a political context. A law that forbade the expenditure of money to communicate could effectively suppress the message.

Nor does it resolve the problem simply to point out that campaign contribution limits inhibit the political "speech opportunities" of those who wish to contribute more. Indeed, that is so. But the question is whether, in context, such a limitation is prohibited as an abridgment of "the freedom of speech." To announce that the harm imposed by a contribution limit is under no circumstances justified is simply to state an ultimate constitutional conclusion; it is not to explain the underlying reasons.[17]

Once we remove our blinders, however, paying increased attention to the Constitution's general democratic objective, it becomes easier to reach a solution. To understand the First Amendment as seeking in significant part to protect active liberty, "participatory self-government," is to understand it as protecting more than the individual's modern freedom. It is to understand the amendment as seeking to facilitate a conversation among ordinary citizens that will encourage their informed participation in the electoral process. It is to suggest a constitutional purpose that goes beyond protecting the individual from government restriction of information about matters that the Constitution commits to individual, not collective, decision-making. It is to understand the First Amendment as seeking primarily to encourage the exchange of information and ideas necessary for citizens themselves to shape that "public opinion which is the final source of government in a democratic state." In these ways the Amendment helps to maintain a form of government open to participation (in Constant's words) by "all the citizens, without exception." [18]

To focus upon the First Amendment's relation to the Constitution's democratic objective is helpful because the campaign laws seek to further a similar objective. They seek to democratize the influence that money can bring to bear upon the electoral process, thereby building public confidence in that process, broadening the base of a candidate's meaningful financial support, and encouraging greater public participation. Ultimately, they seek thereby to maintain the integrity of the political process—a process that itself translates political speech into governmental action. Insofar as they achieve these objectives, those laws, despite the limits they impose, will help to further the kind of open public political discussion that the First Amendment seeks to sustain, both as an end and as a means of achieving a workable democracy.

To emphasize the First Amendment's protection of active liberty is not to find the campaign finance laws automatically constitutional. Rather, it is to recognize that basic democratic objectives, including some of a kind that the First Amendment seeks to further, lie on both sides of the constitutional equation. Seen in terms of modern liberty, they include protection of the citizen's speech from government interference; seen in terms of active liberty, they include promotion of a democratic conversation. That, I believe, is why our Court has refused to apply a strong First Amendment presumption that would almost automatically find the laws unconstitutional. Rather the Court has consistently rejected "strict scrutiny" as the proper test, instead examining a campaign finance law "close[ly]" while applying what it calls "heightened scrutiny. In doing so, the Court has emphasized the power of large campaign contributions to "erod[e] public confidence in the electoral process." It has noted that contribution limits are "aimed at protecting the integrity of the process"; pointed out that in doing so they "tangibly benefit public participation in political debate"; and concluded that that is why "there is no place for the strong presumption against constitutionality, of the sort often thought to accompany the words 'strict scrutiny.'" In this statement it recognizes the possibility that, just as a restraint of trade is sometimes lawful because it furthers, rather than restricts, competition, so a restriction on speech, even when political speech is at issue, will sometimes prove reasonable, hence lawful. Consequently the Court has tried to look realistically both at a campaign finance law's *negative* impact upon those primarily wealthier citizens who wish to engage in more electoral communication and its *positive* impact upon the public's confidence in, and ability to communicate through, the electoral process. And it has applied a constitutional test that I would describe as one of proportionality. Does the statute strike a reasonable balance between electoral speech-restricting and speech-enhancing consequences? Or does it instead impose restrictions on speech that are disproportionate when measured against their electoral and speech-related benefits, talking into account the kind, the importance, and the extent of those benefits, as well as the need for the restriction in order to secure them?[19]

In trying to answer these questions, courts need not totally abandon what I have referred to as judicial modesty. Courts can defer to the legislature's own judgment insofar as that judgment concerns matters (particularly empirical matters) about which the legislature is comparatively expert, such as the extent of the campaign finance problem, a matter that directly concerns the realities of political life. But courts should not defer when they evaluate the risk that reform legislation will defeat the participatory self-government objective itself. That risk is present, for example, when laws set contribution limits so low that they elevate the reputation-related or media-related advantages of incumbency to the point of insulating incumbent officeholders from effective challenge.[20]

A focus upon the Constitution's democratic objective does not offer easy answers to the difficult questions that campaign finance laws pose. But it does clarify the First Amendment's role in promoting active liberty and suggests an approach for addressing those and other vexing questions. In turn, such a focus can help the Court arrive at answers faithful to the Constitution, its language, and its parts, read together as a consistent whole. Modesty suggests when, and how, courts should defer to the legislature in doing so. . . .

My argument is that, in applying First Amendment presumptions, we must distinguish among areas, contexts, and forms of speech. Reference . . . back to at least one general purpose, active liberty, helps both to generate proper distinctions and also properly to apply the distinctions generated. The active liberty reference helps us to preserve speech that is essential to our democratic form of government, while simultaneously permitting the law to deal effectively with such modern regulatory problems as campaign finance. . . .

NOTES

1. Hand, *supra* note I, at 109; *United States v. Classic*, 313 U.S. 299, 316 (1941) (Stone, J.); Hand, *id.*, at 157; Aharon Barak, *A Judge on Judging: The Role of a Supreme Court in a Democracy*, 116 Harv. L. Rev. 16, 28 (2002) ("The law regulates relationships between people. It prescribes patterns of behavior. It reflects the values of society. The role of the judge is to understand the purpose of law in society and to help the law achieve its purpose."); Goldman, *supra* note I, at 115; Felix Frankfurter, *Some Reflections on the Reading of Statutes*, 47 Colum. L. Rev. 527, 541 (1947).

2. Felix Frankfurter, *The Supreme Court in the Mirror of Justices*, in *Of Law and Life & Other Things That Matter* 94 (Philip B. Kurland ed., 1965); *id.* at 95; Hand, *supra* note I, at 109; *New State Ice Co. v. Liebmann*, 285 U.S. 262, 311 (1932) (Brandeis, J., dissenting); Frankfurter, *supra* note 3, at 95.

3. *Id.* at 517.

4. Bailyn, *supra* note I, at 55 (quoting James Madison).

5. Aharon Barak, *A Judge on Judging: The Role of a Supreme Court in a Democracy*, 116 Harv. L. Rev. 28-29 (2002).

6. See, e.g., Antonin Scalia, *Common-Law Courts in a Civil-Law System: The Role of United States Federal Courts in Interpreting the Constitution and Laws*, in *A Matter of Interpretation: Federal Courts and the Law* 26–27 (Amy Gutmann ed., 1997); see William N. Eskridge Jr., Philip P. Frickey, & Elizabeth Garrett, *Cases and Materials on Legislation-Statutes and the Creation of Public Policy* 822 (3d ed. 2001); Frank H. Easterbrook, *Text, History, and Structure in Statutory Interpretation*, 17 Harv. J. L. & Pub. Pol'y 61, 64 (1994).

7. *Duncan*, 533 U.S. 167 at 185 (Breyer, J. dissenting) (citing U.S. Dept. of Justice, Office of Justice Programs, Bureau of Justice Statistics, *Federal Habeas Corpus Review: Challenging State Court Criminal Convictions* 17 [1995]).

8. See *id.* at 172–75.

9. *Id.* at 190–93 (Breyer, J., dissenting).

10. *Id.* at 190 (Breyer, J., dissenting).

11. Barak, *supra* note I, at 28–29.

12. See, e.g., Alex Kozinski & Stuart Banner, *Who's Afraid of Commercial Speech?* 76 Va. L. Rev. 627, 631 (1990); Martin H. Redish, *The First Amendment in the Marketplace: Commercial Speech and the Values of Free Expression*, 39 Geo. Wash. L. Rev. 429, 452–48 (1971); cf. *44 Liquormart, Inc. v. Rhode Island*, 517 U.S. 484, 522 (1996) (Thomas, J., concurring in part and concurring in the judgment); U.S. Const. art. I.

13. Ctr. for Responsive Politics, *Election Overview, 2000 Cycle: Stats at a Glance*, at http://www.opensecrets.org/overview/index.asp?Cycle=2000 accessed Mar. 8, 2002 (aggregating totals using Federal Election Commission data); Ctr. for Responsive Politics, *Election*

Overview, at http://www.opensecrets.org/overview/stats.asp accessed Nov. 21, 2003 (based on FEC data).

14. Taken from the record developed in *McConnell v. Federal Election Comm'n,* No. 02-1674 et al., Joint Appendix 1558. In the 2002 midterm election, less than one-tenth of one percent of the population gave 83 percent of all (hard and soft) itemized campaign contributions. Ctr. for Responsive Politics, see *supra* note 2.

15. Taken from the record developed in *McConnell,* No. 02-1674 et al., Joint Appendix 1564.

16. *Buckley v. Valeo,* 424 U.S. I (1976); *McConnell v. FEC,* 540 U.S. 93 (2003).

17. U.S. Const. amend. I.

18. *Masses Publishing Co. v. Patten,* 244 F.535, 540 (S.D.N.Y. 1917 [(Hand, J.)]; Benjamin Constant, *The Liberty of the Ancients Compared with That of the Moderns* (1819), in *Political Writings,* at 327 (Biancamaria Fontana trans. & ed., 1988).

19. *McConnell,* 540 U.S. at 136, 231; see also *Nixon v. Shrink Mo. Gov't PAC,* 528 U.S. 377, 399–402 (2000) (Breyer, J., concurring); *id.* at 136 (internal quotation marks omitted); *id.* at 137 (internal quotation marks omitted); see *Board of Trade of Chicago v. United States,* 246 U.S. 231 (1918); see *McConnell,* 540 U.S. at 134–42.

20. *McConnell,* 540 U.S. at 137.

9-3

Federalist No. 78

Alexander Hamilton
May 28, 1788

Of the several branches laid out in the Constitution, the judiciary is the least democratic—that is, the least responsive to the expressed preferences of the citizenry. Indeed, it is hard to imagine an institution designed to be less responsive to the public than the Supreme Court, whose unelected judges enjoy lifetime appointments. During the Constitution's ratification, this fact exposed the judiciary to all sorts of wild speculation from opponents about the dire consequences the judiciary would have for the new republic. In one of the most famous passages of The Federalist, *Alexander Hamilton seeks to calm fears by declaring the judiciary to be "the least dangerous branch." Unlike the president, the Court does not control a military force, and unlike Congress, it cannot confiscate citizens' property through taxation. At the same time, Hamilton does not shrink from assigning the judiciary a critical role in safeguarding the Constitution against congressional and presidential encroachments he sees as bound to occur from time to time. By assigning it this role, he assumed that the Supreme Court has the authority of "judicial review" even though there was no provision for it in the Constitution.*

WE PROCEED now to an examination of the judiciary department of the proposed government. In unfolding the defects of the existing Confederation, the utility and necessity of a federal judicature have been clearly pointed out. It is the less necessary to recapitulate the considerations there urged, as the propriety of the institution in the abstract is not disputed; the only questions which have been raised being relative to the manner of constituting it, and to its extent. To these points, therefore, our observations shall be confined.

The manner of constituting it seems to embrace these several objects: 1st. The mode of appointing the judges. 2d. The tenure by which they are to hold their places. 3d. The partition of the judiciary authority between different courts, and their relations to each other.

First.

As to the mode of appointing the judges; this is the same with that of appointing the officers of the Union in general, and has been so fully discussed . . . that nothing can be said here which would not be useless repetition.

Second.

As to the tenure by which the judges are to hold their places; this chiefly concerns their duration in office; the provisions for their support; the precautions for their responsibility.

According to the plan of the convention, all judges who may be appointed by the United States are to hold their offices during good behavior. . . . The standard of good behavior for the continuance in office of the judicial magistracy, is certainly one of the most valuable of the modern improvements in the practice of government. In a monarchy it is an excellent barrier to the despotism of the prince; in a republic it is a no less excellent barrier to the encroachments and oppressions of the representative body. And it is the best expedient which can be devised in any government, to secure a steady, upright, and impartial administration of the laws.

Whoever attentively considers the different departments of power must perceive, that, in a government in which they are separated from each other, the judiciary, from the nature of its functions, will always be the least dangerous to the political rights of the Constitution; because it will be least in a capacity to annoy or injure them. The Executive not only dispenses the honors, but holds the sword of the community. The legislature not only commands the purse, but prescribes the rules by which the duties and rights of every citizen are to be regulated. The judiciary, on the contrary, has no influence over either the sword or the purse; no direction either of the strength or of the wealth of the society; and can take no active resolution whatever. It may truly be said to have neither FORCE nor WILL, but merely judgment; and must ultimately depend upon the aid of the executive arm even for the efficacy of its judgments.

This simple view of the matter suggests several important consequences. It proves incontestably, that the judiciary is beyond comparison the weakest of the three departments of power[1]; that it can never attack with success either of the other two; and that all possible care is requisite to enable it to defend itself against their attacks. It equally proves, that though individual oppression may now and then proceed from the courts of justice, the general liberty of the people can never be endangered from that quarter; I mean so long as the judiciary remains truly distinct from both the legislature and the Executive. For I agree, that "there is no liberty, if the power of judging be not separated from the legislative and executive powers."[2] And it proves, in the last place, that as liberty can have nothing to fear from the judiciary alone, but would have every thing to fear from its union with either of the other departments; that as all the effects of such a union must ensue from a dependence of the former on the latter, notwithstanding a nominal and apparent separation; that as, from the natural feebleness of the judiciary, it is in continual jeopardy of being overpowered, awed, or influenced by its co-ordinate branches; and that as nothing can contribute so much to its firmness and independence as permanency in office, this quality may therefore be justly regarded as an indispensable ingredient in its constitution, and, in a great measure, as the citadel of the public justice and the public security.

The complete independence of the courts of justice is peculiarly essential in a limited Constitution. By a limited Constitution, I understand one which contains certain specified exceptions to the legislative authority; such, for instance, as that it shall pass no bills of attainder, no ex post facto laws, and the like. Limitations of this kind can be preserved in practice no other way than through the medium of courts of justice, whose duty it must be to declare all acts contrary to the manifest tenor of the Constitution void. Without this, all the reservations of particular rights or privileges would amount to nothing.

Some perplexity respecting the rights of the courts to pronounce legislative acts void, because contrary to the Constitution, has arisen from an imagination that the doctrine would imply a superiority of the judiciary to the legislative power. It is urged that the authority which can declare the acts of another void, must necessarily be superior to the one whose acts may be declared void. As this doctrine is of great importance in all the American constitutions, a brief discussion of the ground on which it rests cannot be unacceptable.

There is no position which depends on clearer principles, than that every act of a delegated authority, contrary to the tenor of the commission under which it is exercised, is void. No legislative act, therefore, contrary to the Constitution, can be valid. To deny this, would be to affirm, that the deputy is greater than his principal; that the servant is above his master; that the representatives of the people are superior to the people themselves; that men acting by virtue of powers, may do not only what their powers do not authorize, but what they forbid.

If it be said that the legislative body are themselves the constitutional judges of their own powers, and that the construction they put upon them is conclusive upon the other departments, it may be answered, that this cannot be the natural presumption, where it is not to be collected from any particular provisions in the Constitution. It is not otherwise to be supposed, that the Constitution could intend to enable the representatives of the people to substitute their will to that of their constituents. It is far more rational to suppose, that the courts were designed to be an intermediate body between the people and the legislature, in order, among other things, to keep the latter within the limits assigned to their authority. The interpretation of the laws is the proper and peculiar province of the courts. A constitution is, in fact, and must be regarded by the judges, as a fundamental law. It therefore belongs to them to ascertain its meaning, as well as the meaning of any particular act proceeding from the legislative body. If there should happen to be an irreconcilable variance between the two, that which has the superior obligation and validity ought, of course, to be preferred; or, in other words, the Constitution ought to be preferred to the statute, the intention of the people to the intention of their agents.

Nor does this conclusion by any means suppose a superiority of the judicial to the legislative power. It only supposes that the power of the people is superior to both; and that where the will of the legislature, declared in its statutes, stands in opposition to that of the people, declared in the Constitution, the judges ought to be governed by the latter rather than the former. They ought to regulate their decisions by the fundamental laws, rather than by those which are not fundamental.

This exercise of judicial discretion, in determining between two contradictory laws, is exemplified in a familiar instance. It not uncommonly happens, that there are two statutes existing at one time, clashing in whole or in part with each other, and neither of them containing any repealing clause or expression. In such a case, it is the province of the courts to liquidate and fix their meaning and operation. So far as they can, by any fair construction, be reconciled to each other, reason and law conspire to dictate that this should be done; where this is impracticable, it becomes a matter of necessity to give effect to one, in exclusion of the other. The rule which has obtained in the courts for determining their relative validity is, that the last in order of time shall be preferred to the first. But this is a mere rule of construction, not derived from any positive law, but from the nature and reason of the thing. It is a rule not enjoined upon the courts by legislative provision, but adopted by themselves, as consonant to truth and propriety, for the direction of their conduct as interpreters of the law. They thought it reasonable, that between the interfering acts of an EQUAL authority, that which was the last indication of its will should have the preference.

But in regard to the interfering acts of a superior and subordinate authority, of an original and derivative power, the nature and reason of the thing indicate the converse of that rule as proper to be followed. They teach us that the prior act of a superior ought to be preferred to the subsequent act of an inferior and subordinate authority; and that accordingly, whenever a particular statute contravenes the Constitution, it will be the duty of the judicial tribunals to adhere to the latter and disregard the former.

It can be of no weight to say that the courts, on the pretense of a repugnancy, may substitute their own pleasure to the constitutional intentions of the legislature. This might as well happen in the case of two contradictory statutes; or it might as well happen in every adjudication upon any single statute. The courts must declare the sense of the law; and if they should be disposed to exercise WILL instead of JUDGMENT, the consequence would equally be the substitution of their pleasure to that of the legislative body. The observation, if it prove any thing, would prove that there ought to be no judges distinct from that body.

If, then, the courts of justice are to be considered as the bulwarks of a limited Constitution against legislative encroachments, this consideration will afford a strong argument for the permanent tenure of judicial offices, since nothing will contribute so much as this to that independent spirit in the judges which must be essential to the faithful performance of so arduous a duty.

This independence of the judges is equally requisite to guard the Constitution and the rights of individuals from the effects of those ill humors, which the arts of designing men, or the influence of particular conjunctures, sometimes disseminate among the people themselves, and which, though they speedily give place to better information, and more deliberate reflection, have a tendency, in the meantime, to occasion dangerous innovations in the government, and serious oppressions of the minor party in the community. . . . Until the people have, by some solemn and authoritative act, annulled or changed the established form, it is binding upon themselves collectively, as well as individually; and no presumption, or even knowledge, of their sentiments, can warrant their representatives in a departure from it, prior to such an act. But it is easy to see, that it would require an uncommon portion of fortitude in the judges to do their duty as faithful guardians of the Constitution, where legislative invasions of it had been instigated by the major voice of the community.

But it is not with a view to infractions of the Constitution only, that the independence of the judges may be an essential safeguard against the effects of occasional ill humors in the society. These sometimes extend no farther than to the injury of the private rights of particular classes of citizens, by unjust and partial laws. Here also the firmness of the judicial magistracy is of vast importance in mitigating the severity and confining the operation of such laws. It not only serves to moderate the immediate mischiefs of those which may have been passed, but it operates as a check upon the legislative body in passing them; who, perceiving that obstacles to the success of iniquitous intention are to be expected from the scruples of the courts, are in a manner compelled, by the very motives of the injustice they meditate, to qualify their attempts. . . .

That inflexible and uniform adherence to the rights of the Constitution, and of individuals, which we perceive to be indispensable in the courts of justice, can certainly not be expected from judges who hold their offices by a temporary commission. Periodical appointments, however regulated, or by whomsoever made, would, in some way or other, be fatal to their necessary independence. If the power of making them was committed either to the Executive or legislature, there would be danger of an improper complaisance to the branch which possessed it; if to both, there would be an unwillingness to hazard the displeasure of either; if to the people, or to persons chosen by them for the special purpose, there would be too great a disposition to consult popularity, to justify a reliance that nothing would be consulted but the Constitution and the laws.

There is yet a further and a weightier reason for the permanency of the judicial offices, which is deducible from the nature of the qualifications they require. It has been frequently remarked, with great propriety, that a voluminous code of laws is one of the inconveniences necessarily connected with the advantages of a free government. To avoid an arbitrary discretion in the courts, it is indispensable that they should be bound down by strict rules and precedents, which serve to define and point out their duty in every particular case that comes before them; and it will readily be conceived from the variety of controversies which grow out of the folly and wickedness of mankind, that the records of those precedents must unavoidably swell to a very considerable bulk, and must demand long and laborious study to acquire a competent knowledge of them. Hence it is, that there can be but few men in the society who will have sufficient skill in the laws to qualify them for the stations of judges. And making the proper deductions for the ordinary depravity of human nature, the number must be still smaller of those who unite the requisite integrity with the requisite knowledge. . . .

NOTES

1. The celebrated Montesquieu, speaking of them, says: "Of the three powers above mentioned, the judiciary is next to nothing." "Spirit of Laws." vol. i., page 186. [See Charles de Secondat, Baron de Montesquieu, *The Spirit of Laws,* trans. Thomas Nugent, rev. J. V. Pritchard (London: G. Bell & Sons Ltd., 1914]

2. Idem, page 181.

9-4

Congress and the Politics of Judicial Appointments

Sarah A. Binder and Forrest Maltzman

In distributing power across the separate branches of government, the Constitution's Framers followed the blueprint of "checks and balances" wherever possible. Clearly, requiring Senate confirmation ("advice and consent") of presidential nominations to the Supreme Court and secondary federal courts was intended to put in place justices who enjoyed broad support. Whenever opposing political parties controlled the executive and the legislature, judicial appointments have been susceptible to conflict, in part because, unlike budgets, a single appointment is difficult to compromise. Historically, presidential nomination and judicial confirmation decisions were generally transacted in a bipartisan fashion. Quiet diplomacy in identifying acceptable nominees and informal rules of "senatorial courtesy" guided the delicate business of recruiting federal judges. Over the past several decades, however, Supreme Court appointments have emerged as among the most contentious issues to confront politicians in Washington. In this essay, Sarah Binder and Forrest Maltzman test various possible explanations for this development. In the course of their investigation they account for the numerous ways in which national politics has changed in recent years.

HALF A DOZEN computers and network servers seized, a renowned counterespionage and antiterrorism forensic expert hired, Secret Service investigators brought in, and scores of Senate staff interviewed by the Senate's sergeant-at-arms. Murder in the Capitol? Terrorist plot? No, it was just another skirmish in the battle over confirming federal judges. This time, in fall 2003, Republican staff pilfered computer files from Democrats, revealing the Democrats' collusion with organized interests to block controversial judicial nominees. Although Republicans cried foul, the stolen memos confirmed what seasoned observers of the Senate had come to expect: Selecting and confirming federal judges has become

Source: Sarah A. Binder and Forrest Maltzman, "Congress and the Politics of Judicial Appointments," in *Congress Reconsidered*, by Lawrence C. Dodd and Bruce I. Oppenheimer (CQ Press: 2005), 13:1–13:21. Some notes appearing in the original have been deleted.

a no-holds-barred game among senators, presidents, and organized interests, each seeking to influence the ideological tenor of the federal bench.

In this chapter we explore the politics of judicial selection, focusing on partisan, institutional, and temporal forces that shape the fate of presidential appointments to the lower federal courts. Assessing patterns over the past fifty years, we depict broad trends in the process of judicial selection and pinpoint recent developments that have fueled conflict over the makeup of the federal bench. Although today's tactics in the battles over federal judges—from stolen memos to successful filibusters—are new, the underlying struggle to shape the federal bench is not. Both cooperation and competition are recurring themes in the politics of judicial selection, a politics strongly shaped not only by recent partisan pique but by enduring constitutional and institutional forces as well.

The Evolving Role of the Senate in Judicial Selection

Article II, Section 2 of the Constitution stipulates that presidential appointments must be made with the "Advice and Consent" of the Senate. Although Alexander Hamilton claimed in *Federalist No. 76* that the Senate's role would be limited, this means that the president and the Senate share the appointment power.[1] The Senate's constitutionally prescribed role clearly grants senators opportunities to influence the fate of presidential appointees and thus the chance to shape the makeup of the federal bench.

The geographic design of the federal courts strongly shapes the nature of Senate involvement in selecting federal judges. Because federal trial and appellate-level courts are territorially defined, each federal judgeship is associated with a home state, and new judges are typically drawn from that state. As a result, senators attempt to influence the president's choice of appointees to federal courts in their states. There is considerable variation across the states in how senators handle their role in the selection process. In some states, the more senior senator recommends candidates for White House consideration; in most states, only senators or other elected officials from the president's party participate—a practice stemming from the treatment of judgeships as party patronage starting in the nineteenth century.[2] And in just a few states today—including California and Wisconsin—bipartisan selection commissions generate judicial candidates for White House review. However designed, the selection process affords senators the opportunity to influence the selection of judicial nominees from their states.[3]

Presidents are not obliged to heed senators' views in selecting nominees. Although the Constitution prescribes Senate "advice" as well as "consent," nothing in the Constitution requires the president to respect the views of interested senators from the state. In practice, however, judicial nominees must pass muster with the entire chamber, and thus presidents have an incentive to anticipate objections from home state and other interested senators in making appointments. In the past, federal judgeships rarely elicited the interest of senators outside the nominee's home state, and so the views of the home state senators from the president's party were typically sufficient to determine whether or not nominees would be confirmed. Other senators would defer to the views of the home state senator from the president's party, thus establishing the norm of *senatorial courtesy*.[4] Moreover, the Senate Judiciary Committee in the early twentieth century established the "blue slip" to solicit the views of home state senators— regardless of whether they were of the president's party—once nominees were referred to the committee.[5] By institutionalizing home state senators' role in the confirmation process, senators also gained some leverage over the president at the nomination stage. Threats to block a nominee during confirmation could theoretically be used to encourage the president to consider senators' views before making an appointment.

By the early twentieth century, the modern process for judicial selection had been shaped. Because in the past judicial selection has rarely elicited national attention, and because Senate nominations have only occasionally triggered open conflict, the received wisdom emphasizes the cooperative relationship between presidents and senators in shaping the federal bench. Senate observers have often said that the president merely defers to the views of the home state senators from his party when selecting judges for the nation's trial courts, the U.S. District Courts. Senators themselves fuel such perceptions of the process. As Sen. Phil Gramm, R-Texas, once boasted, "I'm given the power to make the appointment. . . . The people elected me to do that." [6] Presidents are said to be less likely to defer to senators over the selection of appellate judges for the U.S. Circuit Courts of Appeals. Nevertheless, even here the process frequently reflects cooperation between home state senators and the White House.

Despite the conventional wisdom that cooperation is the rule, trends in the nomination and confirmation process suggest otherwise. Figure 1 shows the increasing length of time it takes a president to make a nomination for a vacant seat on the bench.[7] The amount of time it takes for the president to make a nomination surely reflects in large part the degree of disagreement over who should serve on the bench. The recent and marked increase in how long it takes to select nominees confirms recent charges that the process of advice and consent is newly politicized.

An examination of the confirmation process shows a similar pattern. The Senate took, on average, just one month to confirm judicial nominees during President Ronald Reagan's first term. By the end of President Bill Clinton's second

Figure 1. Length of Nomination Process for Judicial Nominees:
Mean Number of Days, by Congress, between
Vacancy and Nomination, 1947–1998

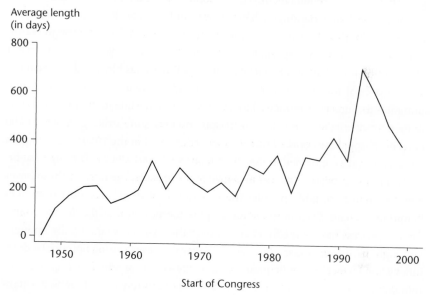

Source: Data compiled from Final Legislative and Executive Calendars, Senate Judiciary Committee, 80th–105th Congresses.

term, the wait had increased on average fivefold for district court nominees and sevenfold for appellate court nominees. At least a fourth of Clinton's judicial nominees in the 106th Congress (1999–2000) waited more than six months to be confirmed, including U.S. District Court Judge Richard Paez, who had waited nearly four years to be confirmed to the U.S. Court of Appeals for the Ninth Circuit. Confirmation delay continued to increase under President George W. Bush, reaching a record for appellate court nominees in the 107th Congress (2001–2002).

Still, delays weathered by recent presidents in securing confirmation of their nominees reflect more than Clinton's polarized relations with a Republican Senate or Bush's polarized relations with a Democratic Senate. Delays in the confirmation process were considerable in the mid-1980s, when Reagan saw Democratic Senates take, on average, nearly four months to confirm his judicial nominees. Even during a rare episode of unified Democratic control during 1993 and 1994, the Senate took an average of three months to confirm the majority party's nominees.

It would be a mistake to conclude that recent confirmation delays are entirely an aberration from the Senate's traditional mode of advice and consent. During

Eisenhower's last term, for example, the Democratic Senate averaged four months to confirm the president's judicial nominees. Parallel to the foot-dragging that has occurred in recent years, it sometimes took the Democratic Senate led by Lyndon Johnson longer than seven months to conclude action on nominees slated by Eisenhower for vacancies on the federal bench. Although confirmation delay may be especially pronounced in recent years, disagreement between the president and Senate over federal judges has historical precedent.

The roots of today's impasse over federal judges are also visible in confirmation rates for judicial nominees. In Figure 2, a sharp decline in the rate of confirmation for district and appellate court appointees is quite striking. A perfect 100 percent of appellate court nominees were confirmed in the 1950s, but less than 40 percent were confirmed in the 107th Congress (2001–2002). Although confirmation rates for trial court nominees are quite variable, the fates of these lower court nominees roughly parallel the experience of appellate court nominees before the Senate. Overall, the data support the notion that the Senate confirmation process has markedly changed over the past ten years. Oddly enough, although the White House now spends longer than ever vetting potential federal judges, the chance of confirmation is at a fifty-year low. Still, it is important to remember that polarization of the process is not entirely new. Troubled waters for judicial nominees were pronounced as early as the early 1970s, no doubt reflecting partisan and ideological disagreements between President Richard Nixon and a Democratic Senate.

The Politics of Advice and Consent

How do we account for the Senate's uneven performance in confirming federal judges? Why were nominees of the past decade particularly likely to be denied a seat on the federal bench, and why does it take so long for the Senate to render its decision? Five forces are at the root of the difficulties presidents face in securing confirmation of judicial nominees. First and foremost are ideological forces: the array of policy views across the three branches affects the probability of confirmation. Second, partisan forces matter: political contests between the president and the opposing Senate party help account for the Senate's treatment of judicial nominees. Third, institutional rules and practices in the Senate shape the likelihood of confirmation. Fourth, presidential capital and resources may matter. And finally, temporal forces shape the Senate's treatment of potential judges: the congressional calendar, electoral cycles, and historical changes in the importance of the federal bench combine to affect the fate of the president's nominees. We explore each of the forces in turn.

Figure 2. Confirmation Rates for Judicial Nominees, 1947–2002

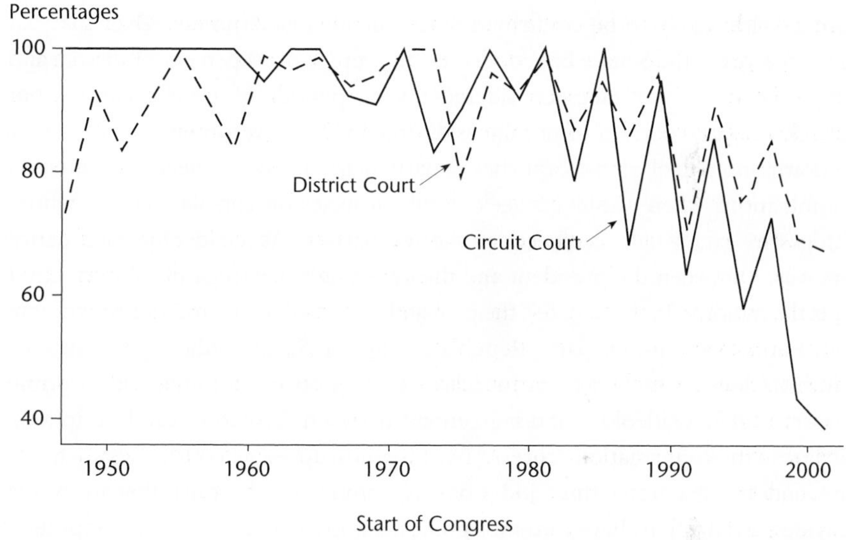

Sources: Data compiled from Final Legislative and Executive Calendars, Senate Judiciary Committee, 80th–105th Congresses. Data for 106th and 107th Congresses compiled from United States Senate Committee on the Judiciary Web site, http://judiciary.senate.gov.

Partisan and Ideological Forces

Partisan and ideological forces are of course inextricably linked in the contemporary Congress as the two legislative parties have diverged ideologically in recent decades. Not surprisingly then, pundits assessing the Senate's treatment of Clinton's nominees have typically pointed to poisoned relations between conservative Republicans and Clinton. It was often suggested that personal, partisan, and ideological antagonisms between Clinton and far-right conservatives led Republican senators to delay even the most highly qualified nominees. Democrats' obstruction of several of Bush's nominees in the 108th Congress (2003–2004) was similarly attributed to partisan pique, as liberal Democrats criticized Bush's tendency to nominate extremely conservative (and presumably Republican) judges.

Partisan politics may affect the process of advice and consent more broadly in the guise of divided party government. Because judges have lifetime tenure and the capacity to make lasting decisions on the shape of public law, senators have good cause to scrutinize the views of all potential federal judges. Because presidents overwhelmingly seek to appoint judges of the president's party, Senate scrutiny of judicial nominees should be particularly intense when different parties control the White House and the Senate. It is not a surprise, then, that nominees considered during a period of divided control take significantly longer to be confirmed than those nominated during unified control. Judicial nominees are also less likely to be confirmed during divided government: Over the past fifty-five years, the Senate has confirmed an average of 94 percent of district and appellate court nominees considered during periods of unified control but roughly only 80 percent of nominees during divided government.

Partisan control of the branches is particularly likely to affect the course of nominations when presidents seek to fill vacancies on appellate courts whose judges are evenly balanced between the two parties. [As the ideological distance increases between the president and the opposing party (regardless of whether it is the majority in the Senate), the probability of swift confirmation goes down. . . . Efforts by majority party Republicans on the Senate Judiciary Committee during Clinton's second term to delay hearings on his nominees are a prime example of how ideological disagreement between the parties can lead to long delays in the confirmation process.] Because most appellate court cases are heard by randomly generated three-judge panels, nominations to courts that are evenly divided are likely to have a more significant impact on the law's development, compared with appointments to courts that lean decidedly in one ideological direction. Senate majorities are especially reluctant to confirm nominees to such courts when the appointment would tip the court balance in the favor of a president from the opposing party. One of the hardest hit courts is the Sixth Circuit Court of Appeals, straddling populous Midwest states such as Michigan and Ohio. In recent years, a quarter of the bench has been vacant, including one seat declared a judicial emergency after sitting empty for five years. Moreover, the Sixth Circuit has been precariously balanced between the parties, with the bench roughly half-filled by judges appointed by Democrats. The Senate slowdown on appointments to that circuit during the Clinton administration was likely motivated by its strategic importance, since confirming Clinton's nominees would have eliminated the opportunity for a future Republican president to move a balanced court into the conservative camp. Similarly, once Bush took office, the two Michigan senators (both Democrats) went to great lengths to prevent the Senate from taking action on Bush's conservative nominees for that court. In short, partisan dynamics—fueled in part by ideological conflict—strongly shape the Senate's conduct of advice and consent, making it difficult for presidents to stack the federal courts as they would prefer.

Institutional Forces

Partisan and ideological forces do not, of course, operate in a vacuum. The process of advice and consent is equally shaped by an array of Senate rules that distribute power in a unique way across the institution. Thus, to explain the fate of the president's judicial nominees, we need to know something about not only the partisan and ideological context, but also the institutional arena in which senators dispense their advice and consent. Senators are wise to the ways in which Senate rules and practices may be exploited in the confirmation process. Understanding how senators motivated by policy and political interests exploit pivotal rules and practices is essential for explaining the outcomes of advice and consent.

A prime institutional step for any nominee is securing approval from the Senate Judiciary Committee. Two significant hurdles await judicial nominees in that committee. First, by tradition, senators from the home state of each judicial nominee cast the first judgment on him or her. As suggested above, the veto power of home state senators is institutionalized in Judiciary panel procedures. Both of the state's senators are asked their views about judicial nominees from their home state pending before the committee. Senators can return the "blue slip," demarking their support of or objection to the nominee, or they can refuse to return the blue slip altogether—an action signaling opposition. One negative blue slip from a home state senator traditionally was sufficient to block further action on a nominee. As the process has become more polarized in recent years, committee chairs have been tempted to ignore objections from minority party senators. At a minimum, blue slips today weigh heavily in the committee chair's assessment concerning whether, when, and how to proceed on a nominee, but senators' objections do not necessarily prevent the committee from proceeding.

Historically, large ideological differences between the president and the home state senator have led to longer confirmation proceedings than normal for appellate court nominees, suggesting the power of home state senators to affect panel proceedings. Conversely, the strong support of one's home state senator is essential in navigating the committee successfully. Given the often fractured attention of the Senate and the willingness of senators to heed the preferences of the home state senator, having a strong advocate in the Senate with an interest in seeing the nomination proceed is critical in smoothing the way for nominees.

Second, the experience of judicial nominees in committee drives home the importance of Senate rules that grant considerable procedural powers to committee chairs. Because of the generally low salience of most judicial nominations, the Senate largely defers to the Judiciary Committee's judgment on whether and when to proceed with a nomination. Discretion over the fate of each nominee is held by the committee chair, who holds the power to convene hearings and to schedule a committee vote to report a nomination to the chamber. Not surprisingly, then, ideological differences between the panel chair and the president show a discernible effect on the course of judicial nominations. The greater the ideological differences between the president and the chair of the Judiciary panel, the longer it takes for the committee to act.

Once approved by committee, a nomination has a second broad institutional hurdle to clear: making it onto the Senate's crowded agenda. By rule and precedent, both majority and minority party coalitions can delay nominations after they clear committee. Because the presiding officer of the chamber gives the majority leader priority in being recognized to speak on the Senate floor, the majority leader has the upper hand in setting the chamber's agenda. This is especially so given his control of the executive session agenda, the arena in which nominations are called up for confirmation. When the president's party controls the Senate, this means that nominations are usually confirmed more quickly; under divided control, nominations can be kept off the floor by the majority leader. Such procedural advantages clearly enhance the importance of support from the majority leader in shaping the fate of presidential appointees.

The majority leader's discretion over the executive session agenda is not wielded without challenge, however: nominations can be filibustered. The chance that a nomination might be filibustered usually motivates the majority leader to seek unanimous consent of the full chamber before bringing a nomination before the Senate. Such consultation between the two parties means that nominations are unlikely to clear the Senate without the endorsement of the minority party.

The de facto requirement of minority party assent suggests that the party opposing the president retains significant power to affect the fate of nominees, even when the opposing party does not control the Senate. As policy differences increase between the president and the opposing party, that party is more likely to exercise its power to delay nominees. Given the high degree of polarization between the two parties today, it is not surprising that judicial nominations have become such a flash point for the parties. As we discuss below, when Democrats lost control of the Senate after the 2002 elections, they turned to a new tactic to block objectionable nominees: the filibuster. Although in the past Senate majorities have periodically had to fight to close debate on judicial nominees via cloture, successful filibusters are without modern precedent for nominees to lower courts. Such extreme tactics clearly result from the increased polarization between the two parties and the rising salience of the federal courts across the interest group community. Much of the variation in the fates of judicial nominees before the Senate is thus seemingly driven by ideologically motivated players and parties in both the executive and legislative branches who exploit the rules of the game in an effort to shape the makeup of the federal bench.

Presidential Forces

Presidents are not powerless in trying to shape the outcome of advice and consent. Although the president lacks a formal means of pushing nominations through to confirmation, presidents have a few tools that may affect the fates of their appointees. . . . The president's ability to encourage confirmation may . . . be shaped by his popularity with the public. Presidents who are highly regarded tend to store up political capital that can be used to increase the chances of confirmation for judicial nominees. All told, presidents have some influence over the speed of advice and consent, but their influence likely is exercised only at the margins of the legislative arena.

Temporal Forces

Finally, it is important to consider how secular or cyclical elements of the political calendar may shape the fate of judicial nominees. It is often suggested, for example, that extreme delays encountered by judicial nominees in recent years may be a natural consequence of an approaching presidential election. For example, with control of both the Senate and the White House up for grabs in November 2000, it was expected that Republican senators would approach their duties of advice and consent with extreme caution. Rather than confirming an outgoing Democratic president's last judicial nominees, pragmatic politics would dictate, Republicans should save these lifetime appointments for a president of their own party. Not surprisingly, in the run-up to the 2000 election, forty judicial nominees remained in limbo. Most of them had not even received a hearing before the Senate Judiciary panel.

There is certainly some truth to the idea that an approaching presidential election affects the politics of advice and consent. Over the past fifty years, Senate treatment of judicial nominations submitted or pending during a presidential election year has been significantly different than its treatment of other judicial nominations. First, the Senate has historically taken longer to confirm nominees pending before a presidential election than those submitted earlier in a president's term. Second, and more notably, presidential-election-year nominees are significantly less likely to be confirmed. For all judicial nominations submitted between 1947 and 2002, appointments pending in the Senate before a presidential election were 25 percent less likely to be confirmed than ones submitted earlier in a president's term.

All the same, presidents can also benefit from the political calendar. Strategically timing referral of a nomination is essential, as nominations made earlier in a president's term tend to move more swiftly. Nominations also move more swiftly when the Senate's confirmation load is lighter. The fewer nominees pending, the quicker a nominee will sail to confirmation.

Finally, and perhaps most important, the broad belief that the confirmation process has become more protracted over time is confirmed by the evidence in

Figures 1 and 2, which shows the increasing amount of time it takes for presidents to select nominees and the declining rate of confirmation for both levels of the federal bench. As we explore below, such a secular increase in the length of the advice and consent process may result from the rising importance of the federal courts as policymaking players. Interest groups and politicians frequently and increasingly have used the federal courts as a means of resolving political disputes.[8] The result, we suspect, has been increased concern among political actors about the makeup of the federal bench and thus a heightened salience of the confirmation process beyond the affected court and state. . . .

The New Wars of Judicial Selection

Partisan conflict over advice and consent came to a head in March 2004 when the Senate Democratic Caucus vowed to block all executive and judicial nominations.[9] At issue were the president's decision to grant recess appointments to two of the judicial nominees filibustered by the Democrats and the White House's refusal to nominate Democratic choices for several bipartisan commissions. Such actions, Minority Leader Tom Daschle, D-S.D., charged on the Senate floor, "not only poison the nomination process, but they strike at the heart of the principle of checks and balances that is one of the pillars of the American democracy."[10] Democrats said they would lift the blockade after a couple of dozen Democrats had been appointed to bipartisan boards and commissions and after Bush had guaranteed that he would not make any more recess appointments.

Although that particular blockade was lifted two months later, the broader breakdown of the nomination process in 2004 suggests that the politics of judicial selection have changed markedly in recent years: the character of the process seems qualitatively different today than in the past. To be sure, not every nominee experiences intense opposition, as Democrats acquiesced to over a hundred of Bush's judicial appointees. But why has the process become so intensely polarized in recent years? The changing face of Senate obstruction in the battles over judges bears a deeper look.

Perhaps most striking about the new war over advice and consent is its visibility beyond the halls of the Senate. The rising salience of federal judgeships is visible on several fronts. First, intense interest in the selection of federal judges is no longer limited to the home state senators. Second, negative blue slips from home state senators no longer guarantee that a nomination will be killed, as recent Judiciary panel chairs have been hesitant to accord such influence to objections from the minority party. Third, recorded floor votes are now the norm for confirmation of appellate court judges, as nominations are of increased importance to groups outside the institution. And fourth, nominations now draw the attention of strategists within both political parties—as evidenced by the president's focus on judicial nominations in stumping for Republican Senate candidates in the 2002 midterm elections.

How do we account for the rising salience of federal judgeships to actors in and out of the Senate? It is tempting to claim that the activities of organized interests after the 1987 Supreme Court confirmation battle over Robert Bork are responsible. But interest groups have kept a close eye on judicial selection for quite some time. Both liberal and conservative groups were involved periodically from the late 1960s into the 1980s. And in 1984, liberal groups under the umbrella of the Alliance for Justice commenced systematic monitoring of judicial appointments, as had the conservative Judicial Reform Project of the Free Congress Foundation earlier in the decade. Although interest group tactics may have fanned the fires over judicial selection in recent years, the introduction of new blocking tactics in the Senate developed long after groups had become active in the process.[11] Outside groups may encourage senators to take more aggressive stands against judicial nominees, but by and large Senate opposition reflects senators' concerns about the policy impact of judges on the federal bench.

Rather than attribute the state of judicial selection to the lobbying of outside groups, we believe that the politics of judicial selection have been indelibly shaped by two concurrent trends. First, the two political parties are more ideologically opposed today than they have been for the past few decades. . . . Ideological differences between the parties encourage senators to exploit the rules of the game to their party's advantage.

Second, it is important to remember that if the courts were of little importance to the two parties, then polarized relations would matter little to senators and presidents in conducting advice and consent. However, the federal courts today are intricately involved in the interpretation and enforcement of federal law, particularly as the Supreme Court has limited its docket in recent years. . . . Intense ideological disagreement, coupled with the rising importance of a closely balanced federal bench, has brought combatants in the wars of advice and consent to new tactics and new crises, as the two parties struggle to shape the future of the federal courts. . . .

There are few signs that the wars of advice and consent will abate anytime soon. Reflecting on the Democrats' filibusters, Lindsay Graham, R-S.C., observed that "if you don't think down the road it will be answered in kind by the Republican Party, I think you are very naïve." [12] The new tactics, Graham warned, would become the norm. "Payback," Graham aptly summed up, "is hell." So long as ideological divisions lead senators to disagree over the makeup of the federal bench, and so long as the courts remain central in the interpretation of public law, battles over judicial selection are unlikely to go away. More likely, they will intensify—especially when the next vacancy on the Supreme Court occurs. Unless the president selects someone with moderate ideological stripes, past battles over confirming federal judges will pale in comparison. The stakes of who sits on the federal bench are simply too high for combatants in the battles of advice and consent to view the contest from the sidelines. Policy motivations and institutional opportunities will continue to shape the ideological character of the federal bench.

NOTES

1. For a discussion of the Framers' intentions regarding "advice and consent," see John Ferling, "The Senate and Federal Judges: The Intent of the Founding Fathers," *Capitol Studies* 2 (winter 1974): 57–70.

2. On the emergence of federal judgeships as patronage, see Kermit Hall, *The Politics of Justice* (Lincoln: University of Nebraska Press, 1979).

3. The influence of home state senators in the selection of nominees is probed in Sarah A. Binder and Forrest Maltzman, "The Limits of Senatorial Courtesy," *Legislative Studies Quarterly* 24 (February 2004): 5–22; and Donald Songer, Thomas Hansford, and Tajuana Massie, "The Timing of Presidential Nominations to the Lower Federal Courts," *Political Research Quarterly* (March 2004): 145–154.

4. The logic of senatorial courtesy is explored in Tonja Jacobi, "The Senatorial Courtesy Game: Explaining the Norm of Informal Vetoes in 'Advice and Consent' Nominations," *Legislative Studies Quarterly* (forthcoming).

5. See Sarah A. Binder, "Origins of the Senate 'Blue Slip': The Creation of Senate Norms" (paper presented at the annual meeting of the Midwest Political Science Association, Chicago, April 2004).

6. As cited in Robert A. Carp and Ronald Stidham, *Judicial Process in America*, 2nd ed. (Washington, D.C.: CQ Press, 1993), 232.

7. The data include all nominees for the federal District Courts and Circuit Courts of Appeal eventually confirmed by the Senate.

8. See Robert Kagan, *Adversarial Legalism* (Cambridge: Harvard University Press, 2001); Thomas F. Burke, *Lawyers, Lawsuits, and Legal Rights: The Battle over Litigation in American Society* (Berkeley: University of California Press, 2004); and Gordon Silverstein, *How Law Kills Politics* (New York: Norton, forthcoming).

9. See Paul Kane, "Nominations Put on Ice," *Roll Call*, March 29, 2004.

10. Sen. Tom Daschle, "Politicization of the Nomination Process," *Congressional Record*, March 26, 2004, S3200.

11. Recent tactics of two leading interest groups are detailed in Bob Davis and Robert S. Greenberger, "Two Old Foes Plot Tactics in Battle over Judgeships," *Wall Street Journal*, March 2, 2004.

12. As cited in Jennifer A. Dlouhy, "Judicial War far From Over," *CQ Weekly*, November 15, 2003, 2824.

The Voting Behavior of George W. Bush's Judges: How Sharp a Turn to the Right?

Robert A. Carp, Kenneth L. Manning, and Ronald Stidham

In recent years politics in Washington has become as intensely partisan and polarized ideologically as at any time in the past half-century. Partisanship periodically flares up in its most virulent form during divided government when the Senate deliberates confirmation of the president's judicial nominees. Democratic President Clinton complained continually that the Republican Senate was not giving his nominees a fair shake. Similarly, President Bush has blasted Democratic obstructionism. In this essay, the authors contribute a very important fact to our understanding of these political imbroglios: President Bush's appointments to the federal district courts appear in their decisions to be among the most ideologically homogeneous—in this instance, conservative—of any president's appointees.

WHAT IS THE ideological direction of the judges whom President George W. Bush has appointed during his first five years in office? Until now most of the information about this question has been anecdotal in nature or has come from quantitative studies with relatively small numbers.[1] Critics of the president, often liberal Democrats, have suggested that Bush's judicial appointees are ultraconservatives who are hostile to the interests of racial minorities, women, the environment, personal privacy, and so on. As vice president of the liberal People for the American Way, Elliot Mincberg sees Bush's judgeships

as a way that the White House can continue to appeal to and mobilize the far right base which sometimes may be disappointed with the president on taxes or on spending or on other kinds of issues. There are many disparate parts of the far right base. There's the more libertarian right, there's the religious right, there's others. All of them seem to be unified on the notion of, "We want judges and justices like Scalia and Thomas," which, of course, has been the President's slogan and mantra.[2]

Source: This piece is an original essay commissioned for this volume.

President Bush and his supporters clearly have a very different view of the men and women he is selecting for federal judicial posts. Former assistant attorney general Viet Dinh conceded that the administration was eschewing candidates who might appear to be "judicial activists," but he asserted,

> We are extremely clear in following the President's mandate that we should not, and do not employ any [political-ideological] litmus test on any one particular issue, because in doing so we would be guilty of politicizing the judiciary[,] and that is as detrimental as if we were unable to identify men and women who would follow the law rather than legislate from the bench.[3]

In this chapter we seek to shed some light on whether or not President Bush is making ideologically based appointments and whether his judicial cohort is deciding cases in the manner anticipated by most court observers. We have organized the chapter around two basic questions: What might we expect of the Bush administration's potential to have an ideological impact on the federal courts? and What do the empirical data tell us so far about the way that the Bush cohort has been deciding cases during the five years of his presidency?

Judicial scholars have identified four general factors that determine whether chief executives can obtain a judiciary that is sympathetic to their political values and attitudes: the degree of the president's commitment to making ideologically based appointments; the number of vacancies to be filled; the level of the chief executive's political clout; and the ideological climate that the new judicial appointees enter.[4]

Presidential Support for Ideologically Based Appointments

One key aspect of the success of chief executives in appointing a federal judiciary that mirrors their own political beliefs is the depth of their commitment to doing so. Some presidents may be content merely to fill the federal bench with party loyalists and pay little attention to their nominees' specific ideologies. Some may consider ideological factors when appointing Supreme Court justices but may not regard them as important for trial and appellate judges. Other presidents may discount ideologically grounded appointments because they themselves tend to be nonideological. Still others may place factors such as past political loyalty ahead of ideology in selecting judges.

For example, Harry Truman had strong political views, but when selecting judges he placed loyalty to himself ahead of the candidate's overall political orientation. On the other hand, Ronald Reagan and Lyndon Johnson are examples of presidents who had strong ideological beliefs on many issues and took great pains to select judges who shared those beliefs.

What do we know about whether President George W. Bush is committed to making ideologically based judicial appointments? The evidence suggests that the president is indeed using ideology as a basis for his nominations. Recall, for example that just prior to the election of 2000 George W. Bush publicly expressed admiration for Justice Antonin Scalia, who is one of the most conservative members of the Supreme Court.[5] Justice Scalia usually interprets the Constitution as restraining congressional power to regulate commerce and seeks to limit the expansion of many Bill of Rights freedoms (generally conservative positions).

In May 2001, after making his first batch of judicial nominations, President Bush made it clear that his judges will adhere to his conservative judicial philosophy: "Every judge I appoint will be a person who clearly understands the role of a judge is to interpret the law, not to legislate from the bench," he said.[6] And early in 2003, Bush's then assistant attorney general said in an interview, "We want to ensure that the president's mandate to us that the men and women who are nominated by him to be on the bench have his vision of the proper role of the judiciary. That is, a judiciary that will follow the law, not make the law. . . ."[7]

Surely there is no doubt that judicial appointments have commanded a key and central portion of President Bush's domestic agenda. As associate White House counsel Dabney Friedrich noted, "It is one of the president's most important domestic priorities. He has given a great deal of attention to judgeships over the past four years, and he will continue to do so."[8] Furthermore one Republican Senate aide observed that Bush's judicial policy agenda has been taken up by the Republican Senate leadership. The aide said that "it has been discussed at the vast majority of leadership meetings which are every week. It has come up at the vast majority of Policy Committee meetings over in the Capitol. And every week we are in session we go to lunch with all the Republican senators and it always comes up. It is always an issue, a constant issue."[9]

Still, as always, actions speak louder than words. So rather than quote the president and his spokesmen about what kind of judges they say they want to appoint, it is probably best to look at the backgrounds and records of the men and women they have already selected. In his thorough study of the lower court judges President Bush appointed during his first term in office, Sheldon Goldman and his fellow researchers found a group of individuals who are highly competent and comparatively diverse in their backgrounds. Still, the picture is of a cohort with highly conservative credentials and backgrounds, many of whom were selected from and vetted by the conservative Federalist Society.[10] As for the president's most visible judicial candidates, his nominees to the U.S. Supreme

Court, their conservative backgrounds and values are incontrovertible. Not counting Harriet Miers, who withdrew from the nomination process early in the game, both John Roberts and Samuel Alito have long and well-established voting records that strongly recommended them to their conservative supporters.[11]

In sum, the evidence is very compelling that President Bush does possess a strong desire to make ideologically based nominations to the federal judiciary and that he is prepared to spend considerable political capital to secure their confirmation.

The Number of Vacancies to be Filled

A second element affecting the capacity of chief executives to establish a policy link between themselves and the judiciary is the number of appointments available to them. The more judges a president can select, the greater his potential to put his stamp on the judicial branch. For example, George Washington's influence on the Supreme Court was significant because he was able to nominate ten individuals to the High Court. Jimmy Carter's was nil because no vacancies occurred during his term as president.

The number of appointment opportunities depends on several factors: how many judicial vacancies are inherited from the previous administration (Clinton, for example, was left with a whopping one hundred district and trial court vacancies—14 percent of the total—by his predecessor, George H. W. Bush), how many judges and justices die or resign during the president's term, how long the president serves, and whether Congress passes legislation that significantly increases the number of judgeships.

Historically, the last factor seems to have been the most important in influencing the number of judgeships available, and politics in its most basic form permeates that process. A study of proposals in thirteen Congresses to create new judgeships tested the following two hypotheses: (1) "Proposals to add new federal judges are more likely to pass if the same party controls the Presidency and Congress than if different parties are in power," and (2) "Proposals to add new federal judges are more likely to pass during the first two years of the president's term than during the second two years." The study author concluded that his "data support both hypotheses—proposals to add new judges are about five times more likely to pass if the same party controls the presidency and Congress than if different parties control, and about four times more likely to pass during the first two years of the president's term than during the second two years." He then noted that these findings serve "to remind us that not only is judicial selection a political process, but so is the creation of judicial posts."[12]

When George W. Bush assumed the presidency he inherited 82 vacancies, quite a sizable number by historical standards. The reason was largely the bitter partisan politics that had prevailed during the Clinton administration, which caused many of Clinton's judicial nominees to go without Senate confirmation. A second factor in the equation is that judges are dying or retiring from the bench at about the same rate during the Bush administration as during previous ones. By the end of 2005 President Bush had appointed 182 individuals to the federal district courts, or just over 27 percent of the total. (At the same time there were an additional 37 vacancies on the district courts and 14 nominations pending.) By January 1, 2006, the president had made 41 appointments to the courts of appeals, about 23 percent of the total. (There were also 14 vacancies and 5 pending nominations.) If the present trend continues, by the end of his two terms President Bush will have appointed about 40 percent of the total lower federal judiciary—a very substantial impact, although not an unprecedented one for a two-term president.

What about the possibility of Congress passing a new omnibus judges bill that would give the president the opportunity to pack the judiciary with men and women who share his values? Such an enactment greatly enhanced Presidents Kennedy and Carter's ideological impacts on the judiciary. Unfortunately for President Bush, he had had no such luck. It is true that in 2001 the Judicial Conference of the United States recommended to Congress that it create fifty-four new district and appellate judgeships. It also called for "permanent authorization" of seven previously established, temporary district judgeships. However, the politically divided Congress did not oblige. Congress refused to create any new appellate judgeships, established only eight new district court judgeships, and granted permanent authorization to only four temporary positions.[13] More recently, however, the president's prospects in this realm have started to look up. There is currently a bill pending in Congress, which experts believe has some real chance of success, that would create 9 permanent and 3 temporary circuit judgeships and 44 permanent and 12 temporary district judgeships. This measure also has the backing of the U.S. Judicial Conference.[14] If these legislative proposals are enacted into law, President Bush would appoint an additional 5 percent of the lower court judges in the United States.

So what is one to conclude about this second predictor of whether President Bush will potentially have a substantial impact on the ideological direction of the federal judiciary—the number of vacancies he can fill? The data suggest that in terms of pure numbers the president is having about an average set of opportunities to make an ideological impact on the federal bench. That means that after his second term almost half of the federal judges will likely bear the Bush stamp—a factor of no little consequence.

The President's Political Clout

Presidential skill in overcoming political obstacles is also a factor. The U.S. Senate can be a stumbling block. If the Senate is controlled by the president's party, the White House will find it much easier to secure confirmations. Sometimes, when the opposition is in power in the Senate, presidents are forced into political horse-trading to get their nominees approved. For example, in summer 1999 President Clinton was obliged to make a deal with the conservative chairman of the Senate Judiciary Committee, Orrin Hatch. To obtain smooth sailing for at least ten of Clinton's judicial nominations that were blocked in the Senate, the president agreed to nominate a Utah Republican, Ted Stewart, who was vigorously opposed by liberals and environmental groups.

The Senate Judiciary Committee can be another roadblock. Some presidents have been more adept than others at easing their candidates through the jagged rocks of the Judiciary Committee rapids. Both Presidents Kennedy and Johnson, for example, had to deal with the formidable James Eastland of Mississippi, then committee chairman, but only Johnson seems to have had the political adroitness to get most of his liberal nominees approved. Kennedy lacked that skill. Clinton, despite his considerable political acumen, was never able to parlay those skills into much clout with the conservative and often hostile Senate Judiciary Committee.

Finally, the president's personal popularity is another element in the political power formula. Chief executives who are well liked by the public and who command respect among opinion makers in the news media, the rank-and-file of their political party, and the leaders of the nation's major interest groups are much more likely to prevail over any forces that seek to thwart their judicial nominations.

How would we assess President Bush's capacity to make an ideological impact on the federal judiciary in light of this "political clout" variable? Immediately after the 2000 election, the Senate was evenly divided between the two political parties, but with Vice President Cheney available to break any tie vote, the Republicans were in control of the chamber. In principle, that should have enhanced President Bush's ability to obtain confirmation of judicial nominees of like-minded values. But soon after the election a series of events occurred that greatly clouded the scenario. First, the Democrats regained control of the Senate when Vermont senator Jim Jeffords unexpectedly left the Republican Party caucus. All legislative action came to a halt for several weeks as the struggle to reorganize the Senate became the major focus of attention. Equally important, after Jeffords's defection control of the Judiciary Committee went to the Democrats. The new committee chair, Sen. Patrick Leahy, was in no frame of mind to become a rubber stamp for President Bush's judicial nominees. Then came the terrorist attacks on September 11, 2001, and public and legislative attention became riveted on antiterrorism legislation and national security.

At the end of President Bush's first two years in office, his scorecard showed mixed results. On the downside, two of his nominees, Priscilla Owen and Charles Pickering, received negative votes from the Judiciary Committee, and the committee returned the names of twenty-eight other district and appellate court candidates to the president without taking any action. But the news was by no means all bad for the president. None of his judicial nominations was defeated on the floor of the Senate, and ninety-nine individuals, presumably all staunch conservatives, obtained approval by the Judiciary Committee and the full Senate.

Next, two series of events produced countervailing effects on the president's political clout in the Senate. On the positive side for President Bush, the Republicans regained control of the Senate, and thus control of the Judiciary Committee, in the midterm elections of 2002. The GOP retained control (and the president's reelection bid was successful) in 2004.

On the other hand, during the final year of his first term Senate Democrats were successful in blocking a number of the president's appellate court nominations by use of the filibuster. The Republicans, with a bare majority in the Senate, did not have the votes to cut off debate. President Bush retaliated by using recess appointments on two occasions, infuriating Democrats. In May 2004 a deal of sorts was cut between the White House and the Senate. Under it the president agreed to make no more recess appointments during the remainder of his first term, which ended January 20, 2005. "In return, Democrats, who had been holding up action on all of Bush's judicial choices since March to protest the recess appointments, agreed to allow votes on 25 mostly noncontroversial nominations to district and appeals posts over the next several weeks." [15] Then in spring 2005 there formed in the Senate what was dubbed the "Gang of Fourteen," a bipartisan group of moderates who (temporarily at least) ended the filibuster fight over the aforementioned appellate court nominations. They brought about an agreement that permitted some of the president's most controversial judges to take their seats on the appellate courts and denied Republicans the opportunity to exercise the so-called nuclear option of altering Senate rules to bar filibusters on judicial nominations. According to the agreement, the pivotal Gang of Fourteen would support a filibuster only in "extraordinary circumstances," a term left for the senators to define in their own way.

A second negative for the president was that after the elections of 2004 the chairmanship of the Senate Judiciary Committee went from the highly conservative Republican Orrin Hatch to middle-of-the-road Republican Arlen Specter of Pennsylvania. Coming from a state that voted for John Kerry in 2004, and with a sustained record as a moderate rather than a staunch conservative, Specter made it clear that as committee chair he did not intend to be a rubber stamp for the Bush administration. For example, immediately after President's Bush's reelection Specter said, "When you talk about judges who would change the right of a woman to choose, who'd overturn *Roe versus Wade,* I think that is unlikely. . . . . And I have said that bluntly during the course of the campaign, that *Roe versus Wade* was inviolate." That led the founder of the nonprofit Christian organization Focus on the Family, James Dobson, to comment that Senator Specter "is a big-time problem." [16] President Bush may well have similar thoughts about the chairman of the Judiciary Committee.

Yet a third negative for President Bush has been his declining popularity in the public opinion polls ever since his narrow reelection. The enduring war in Iraq has become more and more of a drag on the president's public support, and a variety of other factors have cost Bush support in the polls, as well (e.g., the apparent inaction and impotence of the government in the face of Hurricane Katrina, rising gasoline prices, charges of corruption and improprieties against various Republican members of Congress and the executive branch, and so on). By early 2006 some 54 percent of the American public disapproved of the way the president was handling his job.[17] Moderate members of the Senate and the Judiciary Committee are not oblivious to these polls; they can see that there might be little or no political cost to them from opposing the president's judicial nominees.

Perhaps the real test of the president's political clout in this area is his record in appointing members of the U.S. Supreme Court. When President Bush nominated the conservative but competent John Roberts to be chief justice of the United States, opposition was minimal and the president prevailed. Likewise, when the president nominated the equally conservative but somewhat more controversial Samuel Alito to the high Court, he prevailed. In the interim, however, when President Bush nominated White House counsel Harriet Miers to the Court, the result was quite different. Charged with being a mere political crony of the president and inexperienced in judicial matters, Miers wilted under a barrage of criticism from both liberals and conservatives. Not only did the president not possess the clout to push her nomination through, but Miers withdrew from the nomination process before she could even be considered by the Senate Judiciary Committee.

What, then, are we to conclude about this third determinant of whether a president will be successful in making ideologically based appointments—his political clout? Despite some notable setbacks, President Bush has enjoyed considerable success in securing the confirmation of most of his conservative judicial nominees. The only times when he has run into serious trouble have been when his nominees promised to be so extreme that they roused the opposition of Senate moderates (e.g., the Gang of Fourteen) or when they lacked the traditional measure of judicial competence.

The Judicial Climate the New Judges Enter

A final matter affects the capacity of chief executives to secure a federal judiciary that reflects their own political values: the philosophical orientations of the currently sitting district and appellate court judges, with whom the new appointees would interact. Because federal judges serve lifetime appointments during good behavior, presidents must accept the composition and value structure of the judiciary as it exists when they take office. If the existing judiciary already reflects the president's political and legal orientations, the impact of the new judicial appointees will be immediate and substantial. However, if the new chief executive faces a trial and appellate judiciary whose values are radically different from his own, the impact of that president's subsequent judicial appointments will be weaker and slower to materialize. New judges must respect the controlling legal precedents and the constitutional interpretations that prevail in the judiciary at the time they enter it, or they risk being overturned by a higher court. That reality may limit the capacity of a new set of judges to go their own way—at least in the short run.

President Reagan's impact on the judicial branch continues to be substantial. By the end of his second term he had appointed an unprecedented 368 federal judges, 50 percent of those on the bench. When he entered the White House, the Supreme Court was already teetering to the right because of Richard Nixon's and Gerald R. Ford's conservative appointments. Although Jimmy Carter's liberal appointees were still serving on trial and appellate benches, Reagan found a good many conservative Nixon and Ford judges on the bench when he took office. Thus he had a major role in shaping the entire federal judiciary in his own conservative image for some time to come. The George H. W. Bush judges had a much easier time making their impact felt because they entered a judicial realm wherein well over half of the judges already professed conservative Republican values.

President Clinton's impact on the judiciary was slower to manifest itself because his judicial nominees entered an arena in which more than 75 percent of the trial and appellate court judgeships were held by the appointees of GOP presidents with very conservative orientations. When George W. Bush entered the White House, 51 percent of the federal judges had been appointed by Democratic presidents.

How does this affect President Bush's potential to leave his ideological mark on the composition of the judiciary? When the president first took office, the partisan backgrounds of the judges were balanced with almost mathematical precision: 51 percent of those on the lower federal bench had been appointed by Republican presidents; 49 percent by Democrats. In such a situation, even a slight change in numbers can give one party a controlling edge in the judicial decision-making process and, perhaps more important, in the composition of the policy-making appeals court panels. Evidence that this is so was already compelling at the beginning of President Bush's sixth year in office. First of all, as we entered 2006, Republican control of the lower courts was roughly at the two-thirds level, and of course, seven of the nine members of the U.S. Supreme Court are Republican appointees.[18] Second, turning to the appellate courts, which make important policy decisions and which, at least in principle, oversee the decision making of the trial court judges, by January 2006, of the twelve U.S. circuits (including the District of Columbia Circuit but excluding what is known as the Federal Circuit), the appointees of Republican presidents now have a majority in ten. The Second Circuit is almost evenly split, and only in the Ninth Circuit do appointees of Democratic presidents make up a majority.[19]

In sum, the overall evidence suggests that President Bush should be able to continue to move the federal judiciary in a more conservative direction. He has indicated a clear desire to appoint more conservative jurists, and his Supreme Court appointments are vivid evidence of his commitment. He is filling an average number of new vacancies, although his declining popularity and the looming prospect of Republican losses in the 2006 elections may be clouds on the horizon. Finally, given the narrow balance of the judiciary between Republicans and Democrats at the beginning of his term, President Bush continues to be in a critical position to tilt the ideological balanced in a decidedly conservative direction.

Sources and Definitions

Before we examine the data we have collected, we need to say a word about the data's source, and offer working definitions of the terms "conservative" and "liberal." The data on trial court decisions were taken from a database consisting of more than 75,000 opinions, by almost 1,800 judges, published in the *Federal Supplement* from 1933 through fall 2005. Included in this overall data set were 795 decisions handed down by judges appointed by President George W. Bush.[20] Only those cases that fit easily into one of twenty-eight case types and that contained a clear, underlying liberal-conservative dimension were used. This included cases such as state and federal habeas corpus pleas, labor-management disputes, questions involving the right to privacy, and environmental protection cases. Excluded were cases involving patents, admiralty disputes, and land condemnation hearings. The number of cases not selected was about the same as the number included.

In the realm of civil rights and civil liberties, "liberal" judges would generally take a broadening position; that is, they would seek in their rulings to extend those freedoms. "Conservative" jurists, by contrast, would prefer to limit such rights. For example, in a case in which a government agency wanted to prevent a controversial person from speaking in a public park or at a state university, a liberal judge would be more inclined than a conservative to uphold the right of the would-be speech giver. Or, in a case concerning affirmative action in public higher education, a liberal judge would be more likely to take the side favoring special admissions for minority petitioners.

In the area of government regulation of the economy, liberal judges would probably uphold legislation that benefited working people or the economic underdog. Thus, if the secretary of labor sought an injunction against an employer for paying less than the minimum wage, a liberal judge would be more disposed to endorse the labor secretary's arguments, whereas a conservative judge would tend to side with business, especially big business.

Another broad category of cases often studied by judicial scholars is criminal justice. Liberal judges are, in general, more sympathetic to the motions made by criminal defendants. For instance, in a case in which the accused claimed to have been coerced by the government to make an illegal confession, liberal judges would be more likely than their conservative counterparts to agree that the government had acted improperly.

What the Data Reveal

In Figure 1 we compare the total "liberalism" scores of the judicial cohorts appointed by eight of the most recent chief executives, three Democrats and five Republicans.[21] The data indicate that only 33 percent of the decisions of the George W. Bush jurists have been decided in a liberal direction. This not only makes the Bush team the most conservative among those of the eight most recent presidents, but indeed it is the most conservative number that we have for all American presidents going back to Woodrow Wilson![22] The numbers are certainly more conservative than the scores of Presidents Johnson, Carter, and Clinton are liberal; their appointees' scores were respectively 52 percent, 52 percent, and 45 percent liberal. Bush appointees' decisions are also more right of center than those of his GOP predecessors Nixon, Ford, Reagan, and Bush Sr., which

Figure 1. Decisions Scored as Liberal by Judges Appointed
by the Eight Most Recent Presidents

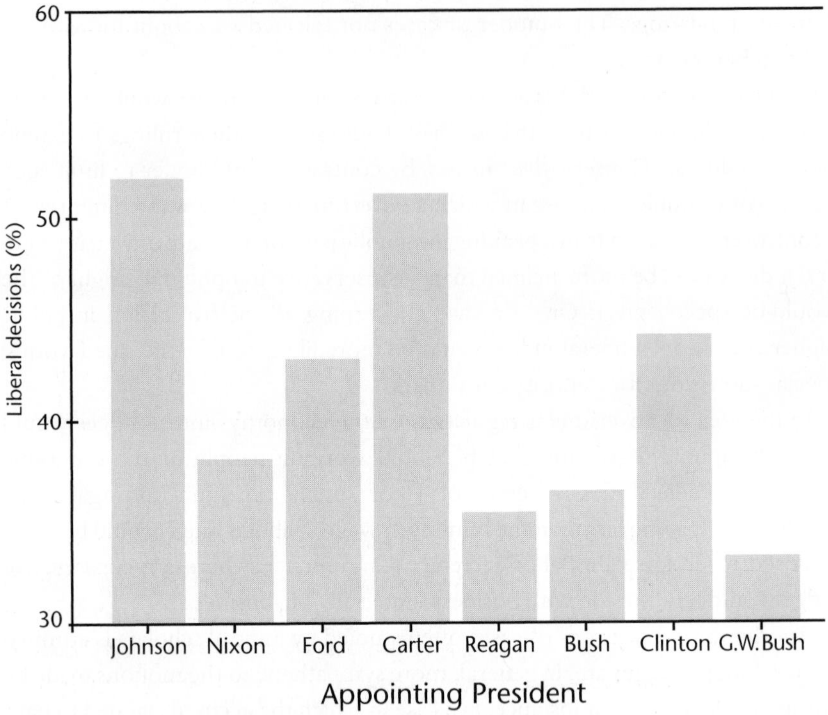

were respectively 38 percent, 43 percent, 36 percent, and 37 percent.[23] The differences between George W. Bush's judicial cohort and those of his three Republican predecessors are large enough that they are not likely to result from mere
chance.

Let us turn up our examining microscope a notch and compare the voting patterns of Bush jurists with the patterns of other modern presidents' appointees
on the three composite variables civil rights and liberties, criminal justice, and
labor and economic regulation. The first column in Table 1 focuses on civil rights
and liberties; that is, it examines judges' voting behavior on issues such as abortion, freedom of speech, the right to privacy, charges of racial minority discrimination, and so on. It is here that we find some of the best evidence for some
meaningful ideological screening by President's Bush judicial appointment staff.
Only 27 percent of the decisions of Bush cohort judges fell on the liberal side of
issues pertaining to Bill of Rights and civil rights matters, giving the president the
lowest score of any modern chief executive. Not only are Bush's trial judges
more conservative than the next-most-conservative cohort—Ronald Reagan's

Table 1. Percentages of Liberal Decisions in Three Case Types
by Judges Appointed by the Eight Most Recent Presidents

Appointing president	Civil liberties and rights	Criminal justice	Economic labor regulation	All cases
Johnson	57.9	36.6	62.9	51.9
Nixon	37.8	27.0	48.5	38.0
Ford	39.7	34.5	52.4	43.0
Carter	50.9	38.0	60.9	51.2
Reagan	32.0	25.3	48.6	35.5
Bush	32.1	29.0	49.8	36.5
Clinton	41.2	38.8	54.2	44.0
G.W. Bush	27.2	29.8	47.3	33.3

appointees—but the odds ratio score of .79 indicates that Bush judges are approximately 20 percent less likely than Reagan judges to hand down a liberal opinion in this issue area.[24] Such differences are statistically significant, meaning that they are very unlikely to have occurred by mere chance. Thus G. W. Bush judges are significantly more conservative in civil rights and liberties cases than judges selected by any other president.

This should come as little surprise, since the major controversies surrounding President Bush's judicial nominees have focused on their stances on issues such as affirmative action, gay rights, abortion, establishment of religion, and the right to privacy (all of which are included in our civil rights and liberties composite variable). Furthermore, the president's electoral base has clearly centered on these same issues, and there is considerable evidence to suggest that he has sought to please and strengthen that base through his judicial appointments.

The number of decisions we have in our database for the G. W. Bush judges is not large enough for us to examine all twenty-eight variables that go into our overall composite. However, the variable with the largest number of cases, Fourteenth Amendment and civil rights cases, contains some 170 decisions. Because of its comparatively large size and because it highlights a realm where the Bush jurists are singularly conservative, we will examine it here. In Table 2 we show the voting patterns of the Bush cohort compared with those of our seven other recent chief executives.

In the table we see that Bush appointees have decided only 19 percent of civil liberties cases in a liberal direction. Set against the background of the president's vigorous defense of the PATRIOT Act, indefinite detentions of "enemy

Table 2. Percentages of Liberal Decisions in Fourteenth Amendment Cases
by Judges Appointed by the Eight Most Recent Presidents

Appointing president	% Liberal decisions (N)	% Conservative decisions (N)
Johnson	53.9 (709)	46.1 (607)
Nixon	32.7 (585)	67.3 (1,204)
Ford	34.8 (144)	65.2 (270)
Carter	41.2 (868)	58.8 (1,241)
Reagan	26.8 (656)	73.2 (1,788)
Bush	27.5 (264)	72.5 (697)
Clinton	34.5 (404)	65.5 (766)
G.W. Bush	19.4 (33)	80.6 (137)

combatants" in the war on terrorism, and unauthorized domestic surveillance of American citizens, it is perhaps not surprising that the G. W. Bush judges have taken a more minimalist approach to the expansion and protection of individual liberties. That low number of 19 percent contrasts markedly with the liberal numbers of Presidents Johnson, Carter, and Clinton, which were respectively 54 percent, 41 percent, and 35 percent. But even compared with the numbers of Bush's GOP predecessors, Nixon, Ford, Reagan, and Bush Sr. (33 percent, 35 percent, 27 percent, and 28 percent, respectively) the G. W. Bush team is singularly right of center in this policymaking realm.

The battles over the nominations of John Roberts, Harriet Miers, and Samuel Alito to the Supreme Court focused primarily on the issues of abortion, right to life, gay rights, and so on—all components of our variable "Right to privacy." Unfortunately, the number of cases for this variable is too small for us justify in the production of a formal table. Still, the results we have are tantalizing and merit a brief reference: So far only 17 percent of the decisions that Bush judges have rendered in the realm of abortion, right to life, gay rights, and so on have been in a liberal direction. That compares with figures of 29 percent for Reagan's judges and 49 percent for the Bush Sr. cohort. As one might expect, Clinton's team is the most liberal in this key policy realm, with a liberalism score of 54 percent. Again, these conclusions are somewhat tentative until the numbers increase, but if additional data validate them, the G. W. Bush cohort is a clear and vivid reflection of the president's own values in this area.

Few observers, friend or foe, have commented on Bush's nominations in terms of their possible effect on judicial issues pertaining to labor-management disputes, the power of the bureaucracy, or major curtailments of the rights of routine criminal defendants. In previous presidential campaigns, Republican candidates have called for an end to "big government," for curtailment of the power of labor unions, for reversal of the key criminal justice decisions of the Warren Court, or for an end to deficit spending. But those issues carried little weight, if any, in the Bush campaign of 2004, which focused much more on issues of who could be better trusted to fight terrorism and which candidate was the better embodiment of moral values (often code words for issues pertaining to abortion, gay rights, and right to life issues). Thus one would not expect Bush's judicial candidates to be vetted for their stances on labor and economic questions or on (nonterrorist) criminal justice matters. One would therefore predict that G. W. Bush's judicial cohort in those two areas would be more moderate, and the data do not disappoint.

The second, "Criminal justice" column in Table 1 shows judges' voting on issues such as habeas corpus pleas, motions made before and during a criminal trial, and forfeiture of property in criminal cases. In this realm, the voting record of the Bush team is 30 percent liberal. It is certainly more conservative than the records of the cohorts appointed by Democratic presidents Johnson, Carter, and Clinton, which were respectively 37 percent, 38 percent, and 39 percent. But it is right in line with the scores of Reagan and Bush Sr., which were 25 percent and 29 percent. Again we would note that whereas President George W. Bush has been critical of the federal courts on issues such as abortion and the right to life, he has said little or nothing about routine issues of criminal justice. Thus, while G. W. Bush's jurists are distinctly conservative in this realm, they are well within the charts.

Table 1's third column shows judges' voting patterns in the realm of labor and economic regulation, in which a typical case might be that of a labor union versus a company, a worker alleging a violation of the Fair Labor Standards Act, or a petitioner challenging the right of a government regulator to circumscribe his activity. On this composite variable, 47 percent of the decisions of the Bush appointees have been on the liberal side. This puts his cohort several points to the right of center compared with those of Nixon, Reagan, and Bush Sr., which were respectively 49 percent, 49 percent, and 50 percent. The group is distinctly more conservative when contrasted with the liberal scores of the Johnson, Carter, and Clinton jurists—63 percent, 61 percent, and 54 percent. What are we to make of these findings?

First, there should be little surprise that the Bush cohort is not as dramatically conservative in the realm of labor and economic regulation as on civil rights and liberties. In his campaigns for the presidency, George W. Bush made no serious calls for cutting back the power of organized labor or for curtailing the power of federal government regulators. During his presidency there have been no major initiatives against organized labor; furthermore, the size of the federal government and the size of its deficits have soared. Thus there would be little reason to predict that the Bush administration has been screening its judicial nominees for particularly conservative values on labor and economic issues.

Second, what is notable about the labor and economic regulation scores of all appointees in the past quarter-century is how similar they are. This is part of a larger political-judicial phenomenon that we have discussed elsewhere: Since the end of the New Deal, and particularly since the 1950s, the major political battles between the presidential candidates, in Congress, and within the Supreme Court have been over Bill of Rights and Fourteenth Amendment issues, not over matters of labor and economic regulation.[25]

Moreover, in recent decades Congress has legislated, often with precision, in the areas of economic regulation and labor relations and thus has restricted the discretion of judges in these fields. In sum, the serious political and judicial battles of recent decades have not been fought in the labor and economic arenas, and relatively clear guidelines provided by Congress and the courts have reduced whatever wiggle room there might have been for Republicans to be inordinately conservative or Democrats to be correspondingly liberal. The moderate scores of Bush judges are a manifestation of this overall phenomenon.

Traditional versus Nontraditional Judges

One final subject of interest is the decision-making patterns of Bush's traditional (that is, white male) appointees compared with those of his nontraditional appointees (women and minorities). Such comparisons are increasingly meaningful because President Bush has appointed the largest number of women and minorities to the federal bench of any Republican president (of the Democrats, Clinton appointed the most).[26] Conventional wisdom often suggests that women and minorities might be somewhat more liberal in their voting patterns than their white male counterparts (although the evidence tends to be inconclusive).[27] The reason is that historically women and minorities have been subjected to racial and gender discrimination by law, as well as in the workplace in terms of equal pay for equal work and promotion to managerial positions.

Table 3 provides some modest evidence for that conventional wisdom: Overall, 32 percent of the decisions of Bush's traditional judges have been in a liberal

Table 3. Percentages of Liberal Decisions by Traditional and
Nontraditional Judges Appointed by George W. Bush[a]

	% Liberal decisions (N)	% Conservative decisions (N)
Traditional	32.1 (159)	67.9 (337)
Nontraditional	35.5 (106)	64.5 (193)

Notes: Odds ratio (a) = .859; chi square = .968 (p = .182).
[a] "Nontraditional" judges are women and/or members of an ethnic minority group. "Traditional" jurists are white males.

direction, whereas 36 percent of the rulings handed down by his female and minority jurists have been liberal. We are cautious in our conclusions here because the differences are substantively not very great, nor are they at levels of statistical significance that would allow us to have great confidence in the findings. We must await the accumulation of a larger number of decisions in our database before we can offer any final conclusions about this phenomenon.

Conclusion

We have explored the ideological impact that President George W. Bush has had so far on the decision-making patterns of the trial court judiciary. To perform this task, we sought to determine the degree to which Bush and his appointment team have possessed a strong commitment to make ideologically based appointments, the number of vacancies to be filled, the extent of the president's political clout, and the ideological climate that his judicial cohort is entering.

Our estimation is that President Bush is having a substantial impact on the ideological orientation of the federal judiciary, particularly in the realm of civil rights and liberties, since it is Bill of Rights and equality issues that have defined much of the president's domestic political and judicial agenda, and that is an area where judges still have maximum room for honest differences (as opposed to the more settled area of labor and economic regulation). The quantitative data from our investigation lend support to that estimation.

First, in their overall voting patterns President Bush's judges are not only the most conservative of the eight most recent administrations examined here, but indeed they are the most conservative for all presidential cohorts going back to Woodrow Wilson. The overall scores of the Bush judges are perhaps not "off the charts" in their level of conservatism, but they are sharply right of center. That is most evident in the realm of civil rights and liberties, where the Bush team is a full five percentage points more conservative than even the trial judges appointed by Presidents Reagan and Bush Sr. Our tentative look at the cases in the areas that make up the right to privacy variable suggests that the Bush cohort is highly reflective of the president's own social conservatism in this realm also. Finally, President Bush's nontraditional judges seem to be deciding cases in a somewhat more liberal manner than the white males who have been selected for judicial service.

NOTES

1. For example, see Robert A. Carp, Kenneth L. Manning, and Ronald Stidham, "The Decision-Making Behavior of George W. Bush's Judicial Appointees," *Judicature* 88, no. 1 (2004): 20–28.

2. Elliot Mincberg, quoted in Sheldon Goldman, Elliot Slotnick, Gerard Gryski, and Sara Schiavoni, "W. Bush's Judiciary: The First Term Record," *Judicature* 88, no. 6 (2005): 245–246.

3. Carp, Manning, and Stidham, "The Decision-Making Behavior," 20.

4. For a summary of this literature, see Robert A. Carp, Ronald Stidham, and Kenneth Manning, *Judicial Process in America*, 6th ed, chap. 7 (Washington, D.C.: CQ Press, 2004).

5. Stuart Taylor Jr., "The Supreme Question," *Newsweek*, July 10, 2000, 20.

6. Bennett Roth, "Bush Submits 11 names for Federal Bench," *Houston Chronicle*, May 10, 2001, A1.

7. Goldman et al., "W. Bush's Judiciary," 284.

8. Ibid., 245.

9. Ibid., 245–246.

10. Ibid., 244–275.

11. For example, see Evan Thomas and Stuart Taylor Jr., "Judging Roberts," *Newsweek*, August 1, 2005, 22–33; and Patty Reinert, "Battle Begins over Alito Record," *Houston Chronicle*, November 2, 2005, A1.

12. Jon R. Bond, "The Politics of Court Structure: The Addition of New Federal Judges," *Law and Policy Quarterly* 2 (1980): 182, 183, and 187.

13. Act of November 2, 2002; 116 Stat. 1786.

14. "Judiciary Gets Funding Increase, but Cuts May Still Come," *The Third Branch* 37 (2005): 4 and 6.

15. Helen Dewar, "President, Senate Reach Pact on Judicial Nominations," *Washington Post*, May 19, 2004, A21.

16. Retrieved from www.cnn.com/2004/ALLPOLITICS/11/07/specter.judiciary, November 9, 2004.

17. *Rasmussen Reports*, January 10, 2006, http://rasmussenreports.com/.

18. It should be remembered that not all of President Bush's judicial appointments are net gains for the Republicans, since many of the judges who are currently stepping aside are GOP jurists appointed by Ronald Reagan and Bush Sr. The really key gains will come when the Clinton judges begin to retire en masse in the coming years. In such situations a Democrat will be

replaced by a Republican, which will be a sort of two-for-one gain obviously not possible when a Reagan or Bush Sr. Republican is replaced by another GOP jurist.

19. The Ninth Circuit comprises Washington, Oregon, California, Alaska, Hawaii, Montana, Idaho, Nevada, and Arizona.

20. These rulings were handed down in three key issue areas: civil liberties and rights, $n = 394$; criminal justice, $n = 181$; and labor and economic regulation, $n = 220$. Though we coded only district court rulings, prior research suggests that the behavior of jurists at this level is comparable to that of judges appointed by the same president to the courts of appeals. See Ronald Stidham, Robert A. Carp, and Donald R. Songer, "The Voting Behavior of President Clinton's Judicial Appointees," *Judicature* 80 (1996): 16–20; and Robert A. Carp, Donald Songer, C. K. Rowland, and Lisa Richey-Tracy, "The Voting Behavior of Judges Appointed by President Bush," *Judicature* 76 (1993): 298–302.

21. The reader will note that we have made few references to President Gerald Ford in our generalizations about the voting behavior of recent Republican presidential cohorts. The reason is that President Ford was something of an outlier and an exception to the rule that the judges appointed by GOP chief executives are generally more conservative than those selected by Democratic presidents. (Ford's overall liberalism score of 44 percent makes him the most liberal of recent Republican presidents, although still more conservative than recent Democratic chief executives.) First, Ford was much less of a political ideologue than his predecessor in the White House, Richard Nixon, or his Republican successors, Reagan, Bush Sr., and George W. Bush. Also, because Ford's circuitous route to the presidency did not enhance his political effectiveness with the Senate, he would not have had the clout to force highly conservative Republican nominees through a liberal, Democratic Senate, even if he had wished to.

22. See Figure 7-1 in Carp, Stidham, and Manning, *Judicial Process in America,* 158.

23. It might be argued that the relationship between the appointing president and the voting patterns of his appointees would be comparatively weak for district judges because of the phenomenon of "senatorial courtesy," which in principle acts to restrict the president's appointing power. On the other hand, one might argue that the appointment effects would be greater for circuit court appointments, for which senatorial courtesy does not apply. In fact, however, studies over the years have demonstrated that presidential effects at the district court level have been quite robust. For example, see Carp, Stidham, and Manning, *Judicial Process in America,* 157–168 and 289–294.

24. For a brief explanation of the meaning of the odds ratio score, see Carp, Stidham, and Manning, *Judicial Process in America,* 292.

25. Ibid., 314–317.

26. Goldman et al., "W. Bush's Judiciary."

27. See Robert A. Carp, Kenneth L. Manning, and Ronald Stidham, "President Clinton's District Judges: 'Extreme Liberals' or Just Plain Moderates," *Judicature* 84 (2001): 284–288; and Carp, Stidham, and Manning, *Judicial Process in America,* 106–107.

Chapter 10

Public Opinion

10-1

Analyzing and Interpreting Polls

Herbert Asher

Public opinion polls have gained a prominent place in modern American politics. Polls themselves often are newsworthy, particularly during campaigns and times of political crisis. Unfortunately, as Herbert Asher shows in the following essay, polls are open to misinterpretation and misuse. The wording of questions, the construction of a sample, the choice of items to analyze and report, the use of surveys to measure trends, and the examination of subsets of respondents all pose problems of interpretation. Every consumer of polling information must understand these issues to properly use the information polls provide.

. . . INTERPRETING A POLL is more an art than a science, even though statistical analysis of poll data is central to the enterprise. An investigator examining poll results has tremendous leeway in deciding which items to analyze, which sample subsets or breakdowns to present, and how to interpret the statistical results. Take as an example a poll with three items that measure attitudes toward arms control negotiations. The investigator may construct an index from these three items. . . . Or the investigator may emphasize the results from one question, perhaps because of space and time constraints and the desire to keep matters simple, or because

Source: Herbert Asher, *Polling and the Public: What Every Citizen Should Know,* 4th ed. (Washington, D.C.: CQ Press, 1998), 141–169.

those particular results best support the analyst's own policy preferences. The investigator may examine results from the entire sample and ignore subgroups whose responses deviate from the overall pattern. Again time and space limitations or the investigator's own preferences may influence these choices. Finally, two investigators may interpret identical poll results in sharply different ways depending on the perspectives and values they bring to their data analysis; the glass may indeed be half full or half empty.

As the preceding example suggests, the analysis and interpretation of data entail a high degree of subjectivity and judgment. Subjectivity in this context does not mean deliberate bias or distortion, but simply professional judgments about the importance and relevance of information. Certainly, news organizations' interpretations of their polls are generally done in the least subjective and unbiased fashion. But biases can slip in—sometimes unintentionally, sometimes deliberately—when, for example, an organization has sponsored a poll to promote a particular position. Because this final phase of polling is likely to have the most direct influence on public opinion, this chapter includes several case studies to illustrate the judgmental aspects of analyzing and interpreting poll results.

Choosing Items to Analyze

Many public opinion surveys deal with multifaceted, complex issues. For example, a researcher querying Americans about their attitudes toward tax reform might find initially that they overwhelmingly favor a fairer tax system. But if respondents are asked about specific aspects of tax reform, their answers may reflect high levels of confusion, indifference, or opposition. And depending upon which items the researcher chooses to emphasize, the report might convey support, indifference, or opposition toward tax reform. American foreign policy in the Middle East is another highly complex subject that can elicit divergent reactions from Americans depending on which aspects of the policy they are questioned about.

Some surveys go into great depth on a topic through multiple items constructed to measure its various facets. The problem for an investigator in this case becomes one of deciding which results to report. Moreover, even though an extensive analysis is conducted, the media might publicize only an abbreviated version of it. In such a case the consumer of the poll results is at the mercy of the media to portray accurately the overall study. Groups or organizations that sponsor polls to demonstrate support for a particular position or policy option often disseminate results in a selective fashion which enables them to put the organization and its policies in a favorable light.

In contrast with in-depth surveys on a topic, *omnibus surveys* are superficial in their treatment of particular topics because of the need to cover many subjects in the same survey. Here the problem for an investigator becomes one of ensuring that the few questions employed to study a specific topic really do justice to the substance and complexity of that topic. It is left to the consumer of both kinds of polls to judge whether they receive the central information on a topic or whether other items might legitimately yield different substantive results.

The issue of prayer in public schools is a good example of how public opinion polling on a topic can be incomplete and potentially misleading. Typically, pollsters ask Americans whether they support a constitutional amendment that would permit voluntary prayer in public schools, and more than three-fourths of Americans respond that they would favor such an amendment. This question misses the mark. Voluntary prayer by individuals is in no way prohibited; the real issue is whether there will be *organized* voluntary prayer. But many pollsters do not include items that tap this aspect of the voluntary prayer issue. Will there be a common prayer? If so, who will compose it? Will someone lead the class in prayer? If so, who? Under what circumstances and when will the prayer be uttered? What about students who do not wish to participate or who prefer a different prayer?

The difficulty with both the in-depth poll and the omnibus survey is that the full set of items used to study a particular topic is usually not reported and thus the consumer cannot make informed judgments about whether the conclusions of the survey are valid. Recognizing this, individuals should take a skeptical view of claims by a corporate executive or an elected officeholder or even a friend that the polls demonstrate public support for or opposition to a particular position. The first question to ask is: What is the evidence cited to support the claim? From there one might examine the question wording, the response alternatives, the screening for nonattitudes, and the treatment of "don't know" responses. Then one might attempt the more difficult task of assessing whether the questions used to study the topic at hand were really optimal. Might other questions have been used? What aspects of the topic were not addressed? Finally, one might ponder whether different interpretations could be imposed on the data and whether alternative explanations could account for the reported patterns.

In evaluating poll results, there is always the temptation to seize upon those that support one's position and ignore those that do not. The problem is that one or two items cannot capture the full complexity of most issues. For example, a *Newsweek* poll conducted by the Gallup Organization in July 1986 asked a number of questions about sex laws and lifestyles. The poll included the following three items (Alpern 1986, 38):

Do you approve or disapprove of the Supreme Court decision upholding a state law against certain sexual practices engaged in privately by consenting adult homosexuals? [This question was asked of the 73 percent who knew about the Supreme Court decision.]

Disapprove	47%
Approve	41%

In general, do you think that states should have the right to prohibit particular sexual practices conducted in private between consenting adult homosexuals?

No	57%
Yes	34%

Do you think homosexuality has become an accepted alternative lifestyle or not?

Yes	32%
No	61%
Don't know	7%

Note that the first two items tap citizens' attitudes toward the legal treatment of homosexuals, while the third addresses citizens' views of homosexuality as a lifestyle. Although differently focused, all three questions deal with aspects of gay life. It would not be surprising to see gay rights advocates cite the results of the first two questions as indicating support for their position. Opponents of gay rights would emphasize the results of the third question.

An Eyewitness News/*Daily News* poll of New York City residents conducted in February 1986 further illustrates how the selective use and analysis of survey questions can generate very different impressions of popular opinion on an issue. This poll asked a number of gay rights questions:

On another matter, would you say that New York City needs a gay rights law or not?

Yes, need gay rights law	39%
No, do not need gay rights law	54%
Don't know/no opinion	8%

On another matter, do you think it should be against the law for landlords or private employers to deny housing or a job to someone because that person is homosexual or do you think landlords and employers should be allowed to do that if they want to?

Yes, should be against law	49%
No, should not be against law	47%
Volunteered responses	
Should be law only for landlord	1%
Should be law only for employers	8%
Don't know/no opinion	3%

Although a definite majority of the respondents oppose a gay rights law in response to the first question, a plurality also believe that it should be illegal for landlords and employers to deny housing and jobs to persons because they are homosexual. Here the two questions both address the legal status of homosexuals, and it is clear which question gay rights activists and gay rights opponents would cite in support of their respective policy positions. It is not clear, however, which question is the better measure of public opinion. The first question is unsatisfactory because one does not know how respondents interpreted the scope of a gay rights law. Did they think it referred only to housing and job discrimination, or did they think it would go substantially beyond that? The second question is inadequate if it is viewed as equivalent to a gay rights law. Lumping housing and jobs together constitutes another flaw since citizens might have divergent views on these two aspects of gay rights.

Additional examples of the importance of item selection are based on polls of Americans' attitudes about the Iraqi invasion of Kuwait in 1990. Early in the Persian Gulf crisis, various survey organizations asked Americans, using different questions, how they felt about taking military action against Iraq. Not surprisingly, the organizations obtained different results.

Do you favor or oppose direct U.S. military action against Iraq at this time? (Gallup, August 3–4, 1990)

Favor	23%
Oppose	68%
Don't know/refused	9%

Do you agree or disagree that the U.S. should take all actions necessary, including the use of military force, to make sure that Iraq withdraws its forces from Kuwait? (ABC News/*Washington Post*, August 8, 1990)

Agree	66%
Disagree	33%
Don't know	1%

Would you approve or disapprove of using U.S. troops to force the Iraqis to leave Kuwait? (Gallup, August 9–12, 1990, taken from *Public Perspective*, September/October 1990, 13)

Approve	64%
Disapprove	36%

(I'm going to mention some things that may or may not happen in the Middle East and for each one, please tell me whether the U.S. should or should not take military action in connection with it). . . . If Iraq refuses to withdraw from Kuwait? (NBC News/*Wall Street Journal*, August 18–19, 1990, taken from *Public Perspective*, September/October 1990, 13)

No military action	51%
Military action	49%

Note that the responses to these questions indicate varying levels of support for military action even though most of the questions were asked within two weeks of each other. The first question shows the most opposition to military action. This is easily explained: the question concerns military action *at this time,* an alternative that many Americans may have seen as premature until other means had been tried. The other three questions all indicate majority support for military action, although that support ranges from a bare majority to about two-thirds of all Americans. It is clear which question proponents and opponents of military action would cite to support their arguments.

Throughout the Persian Gulf crisis, public opinion was highly supportive of President Bush's policies; only in the period between October and December 1990 did support for the president's handling of the situation drop below 60 percent. For example, a November 1990 CBS News/*New York Times* poll showed the following patterns of response:

> Do you approve or disapprove of the way George Bush is handling Iraq's invasion of Kuwait?
>
> | | |
> |---|---|
> | Approve | 50% |
> | Disapprove | 41% |
> | Don't know/NA | 8% |

Likewise, an ABC News/*Washington Post* poll in mid-November reported:

> Do you approve or disapprove of the way George Bush is handling the situation caused by Iraq's invasion of Kuwait?
>
> | | |
> |---|---|
> | Approve | 59% |
> | Disapprove | 36% |
> | Don't know/NA | 5% |

Some opponents of the military buildup tried to use these and similar polls to demonstrate that support for the president's policies was decreasing, since earlier polls had indicated support levels in the 60–70 percent range. Fortunately, the *Washington Post* poll cited above asked respondents who disapproved of Bush's policy whether the president was moving too slowly or too quickly. It turned out that 44 percent of the disapprovers said "too slowly" and 37 percent "too quickly." Thus, a plurality of the disapprovers preferred more rapid action against Iraq—a result that provided little support for those critics of the president's policies who were arguing against a military solution.

Shortly before the outbreak of the war, the *Washington Post* conducted a survey of American attitudes about going to war with Iraq. To assess the effects of question wording, the *Post* split its sample in half and used two different versions of the same question followed by the identical follow-up question to each item.

Version 1

As you may know, the U.N. Security Council has authorized the use of force against Iraq if it doesn't withdraw from Kuwait by January 15. If Iraq does not withdraw from Kuwait, should the United States go to war against Iraq to force it out of Kuwait at some point after January 15 or not?

Go to war sometime after January 15	62%
No, do not go to war	32%

How long after January 15 should the United States wait for Iraq to withdraw from Kuwait before going to war to force it out?

Do not favor war at any point	32%
Immediately	18%
Less than one month	28%
1–3 months	8%
4 months or longer	2%

Version 2

The United Nations has passed a resolution authorizing the use of military force against Iraq if they do not withdraw their troops from Kuwait by January 15. If Iraq does not withdraw from Kuwait by then, do you think the United States should start military actions against Iraq, or should the United States wait longer to see if the trade embargo and economic sanctions work?

U.S. should start military actions	49%
U.S. should wait longer to see if sanctions work	47%

How long after January 15 should the United States wait for Iraq to withdraw from Kuwait before going to war to force it out?

U.S. should start military actions	49%

For those who would wait:

Less than a month	15%
1–3 months	17%
4 months or longer	9%

Morin (1991) points out how very different portraits of the American public can be painted by examining the two versions with and without the follow-up question. For example, version 1 shows 62 percent of Americans supporting war against Iraq, while version 2 shows only 49 percent. These different results stem from inclusion of the embargo and sanctions option in the second version. Thus it appears that version 2 gives a less militaristic depiction of the American public. Responses to the follow-up question, however, provide a different picture of the public. For example, the first version shows that 54 percent of Americans (18 + 28 + 8) favor going to war within three months. But the second version shows that 81 percent of Americans (49 + 15 + 17) favor war within three months. The point, of course, is that the availability of different items on a survey can generate differing descriptions of the public's preferences.

The importance of item selection is illustrated in a final example on the Gulf War from an April 3, 1991, ABC News/ *Washington Post* poll conducted just after the conflict. It included the following three questions:

> Do you approve or disapprove of the way that George Bush is handling the situation involving Iraqi rebels who are trying to overthrow Saddam Hussein?

Approve	69%
Disapprove	24%
Don't know	7%

> Please tell me if you agree or disagree with this statement: The United States should not have ended the war with Iraqi President Saddam Hussein still in power.

Agree	55%
Disagree	40%
Don't know	5%

> Do you think the United States should try to help rebels overthrow Hussein or not?

Yes	45%
No	51%
Don't know	4%

Note that the responses to the first item indicate overwhelming approval for the president. But if one analyzed the second question in isolation, one might conclude that a majority of Americans did not support the president and indeed wanted to restart the war against Saddam Hussein. But the third item shows that a majority of Americans oppose helping the rebels. The lesson of this and the previous examples is clear. Constructing an interpretation around any single survey item can generate a very inaccurate description of public opinion. Unfortunately, advocates of particular positions have many opportunities to use survey results selectively and misleadingly to advance their cause.

The health care debate in 1993 and 1994 also provides examples of how the selection of items for analysis can influence one's view of American public opinion. *Washington Post* polls asked Americans whether they thought the Clinton health plan was better or worse than the present system (Morin 1994). In one version of the question, the sample was given the response options "better" or "worse," while in the other version respondents could choose among "better," "worse," or "don't know enough about the plan to say." The following responses were obtained:

Version 1		*Version 2*	
better	52%	better	21%
worse	34%	worse	27%
don't know (volunteered)	14%	don't know enough	52%

Clearly, very different portrayals of American public opinion are presented by the two versions of the question. The first version suggests that a majority of Americans believed that the Clinton plan was better than the status quo, while the second version suggests that a plurality of citizens with opinions on the issue felt that the Clinton plan was worse. It is obvious which version of the question supporters and opponents of the Clinton health plan would be more likely to cite.

Another example from the health care reform area deals with Americans' feelings about the seriousness of the health care problem. Certainly, the more seriously the problem was viewed, the greater the impetus for changing the health care system. Different polling organizations asked a variety of questions designed to tap the importance of the health care issue (questions taken from the September/October 1994 issue of *Public Perspective*, 23, 26):

> Louis Harris and Associates (April 1994): Which of the following statements comes closest to expressing your overall view of the health care system in this country? . . . There are some good things in our health care system, but fundamental changes are needed to make it better. . . . Our health care system has so much wrong with it that we need to completely rebuild it. . . . On the whole, the health care system works pretty well and only minor changes are necessary to make it work.

Fundamental changes needed	54%
Completely rebuild it	31%
Only minor changes needed	14%

> NBC/*Wall Street Journal* (March 1994): Which of the following comes closest to your belief about the American health care system—the system is in crisis; the system has major problems, but is not in crisis; the system has problems, but they are not major; or the system has no problems?

Crisis	22%
Major problems	50%
Minor problems	26%

> Gallup (June 1994): Which of these statements do you agree with more: The country has health care problems, but no health care crisis, or, the country has a health care crisis?

Crisis	55%
Problems but no crisis	41%
Don't know	4%

> Gallup (June 1994): Which of these statements do you agree with more: The country has a health care crisis, or the country has health care problems, but no health care crisis?

Crisis	35%
Problems but no crisis	61%
Don't know	4%

Certainly if one were trying to make the case that health care reform was an absolute priority, one would cite the first version of the Gallup question in which

55 percent of the respondents labeled health care a crisis. But if one wanted to move more slowly and incrementally on the health care issue, one would likely cite the NBC News/*Wall Street Journal* poll in which only 22 percent of Americans said there was a crisis. Health care reform is the kind of controversial public policy issue that invites political leaders to seize upon those poll results to advance their positions. In such situations, citizens should be sensitive to how politicians are selectively using the polls.

Schneider (1996) has provided an excellent example of how examination of a single trial heat question may give a misleading impression of the electoral strength of presidential candidates. A better sense of the candidates' true electoral strength is achieved by adding to the analysis information about the incumbent's job approval rating. For example, in a trial heat question in May 1980 incumbent president Jimmy Carter led challenger Ronald Reagan by 40 to 32 percent, yet at the time Carter's job rating was quite negative: 38 percent approval and 51 percent disapproval. Thus Carter's lead in the trial heat item was much more fragile than it appeared; indeed, Reagan went on to win the election. Four years later, in May of 1984, President Reagan led challenger Walter Mondale by 10 percentage points in the trial heat question. But Reagan's job rating was very positive: 54 percent approval compared with 38 percent disapproval. Thus Reagan's 10-point lead looked quite solid in view of his strong job ratings, and he won overwhelmingly in November. Finally, in April 1992, incumbent president George Bush led challenger Bill Clinton by 50 to 34 percent in the trial heat question, a huge margin. But Bush's overall job rating was negative—42 percent approval versus 48 percent disapproval. Bush's lead over Clinton, then, was not as strong as it appeared, and Clinton ultimately won the election.

By collecting information on multiple aspects of a topic, pollsters are better able to understand citizens' attitudes (Morin and Berry 1996). One of the anomalies of 1996 was the substantial number of Americans who were worried about the health of the economy at a time when by most objective indicators the economy was performing very well. Part of the answer to this puzzle was Americans' ignorance and misinformation about the country's economic health. For example, even though unemployment was substantially lower in 1996 than in 1991, 33 percent of Americans said it was higher in 1996 and 28 percent said the same. The average estimate of the unemployment rate was 20.6 percent when in reality it was just over 5 percent. Americans' perceptions of inflation and the deficit were similar; in both cases Americans thought that the reality was much worse than it actually was. It is no wonder that many Americans expressed economic insecurity during good economic times; they were not aware of how strongly the economy was performing.

The final example in this section focuses on how the media selects what we learn about a poll even when the complete poll and analyses are available to the citizenry. The example concerns a book entitled *Sex in America: A Definitive Survey* by Robert T. Michael et al., published in 1994, along with a more specialized and comprehensive volume, *The Social Organization of Sexuality: Sexual Practices in the United States* by Edward O. Laumann et al. Both books are based on an extensive questionnaire administered by the National Opinion Research Center to 3,432 scientifically selected respondents. . . .

Because of the importance of the subject matter and because sex sells, media coverage of the survey was widespread. How various media reported the story indicates how much leeway the media have and how influential they are in determining what citizens learn about a given topic. For example, the *New York Times* ran a front-page story on October 7, 1994, entitled "Sex in America: Faithfulness in Marriage Thrives After All." Less prominent stories appeared in subsequent issues, including one on October 18, 1994, inaccurately entitled "Gay Survey Raises a New Question."

Two of the three major news magazines featured the sex survey on the covers of their October 17, 1994, issues. The *Time* cover simply read "Sex in America: Surprising News from the Most Important Survey since the Kinsey Report." The *U.S. News & World Report* cover was more risqué, showing a partially clad man and woman in bed; it read "Sex in America: A Massive New Survey, the Most Authoritative Ever, Reveals What We Do Behind the Bedroom Door." In contrast, *Newsweek* simply ran a two-page story with the lead "Not Frenzied, But Fulfilled. Sex: Relax. If you do it—with your mate—around twice a week, according to a major new study, you basically wrote the book of love."

Other magazines and newspapers also reported on the survey in ways geared to their readership. The November issue of *Glamour* featured the survey on its cover with the teaser "Who's doing it? And how? MAJOR U.S. SEX SURVEY." The story that followed was written by the authors of the book. While the cover of the November 15, 1994, *Advocate* read "What That Sex Survey Really Means," the story focused largely on what the survey had to say about the number of gays and lesbians in the population. The lead stated "10%: Reality or Myth? There's little authoritative information about gays and lesbians in the landmark study *Sex in America*—but what there is will cause big trouble." Finally, the *Chronicle of Higher Education,* a weekly newspaper geared to college and university personnel, in its October 17, 1994, issue headlined its story "The Sex Lives of Americans. Survey that had been target of conservative attacks produces few startling results."

Both books about the survey contain a vast amount of information and a large number of results and findings. But most of the media reported on such topics as marital fidelity, how often Americans have sex, how many sex partners people have, how often people experience orgasm, what percentages of the population are gay and lesbian, how long sex takes, and the time elapsed between a couple's first meeting and their first sexual involvement. Many of the reports also presented results for married vs. singles, men vs. women, and other analytical groupings. While most of the media coverage cited above was accurate in reporting the actual survey results, it also was selective in focusing on the more titillating parts of the survey, an unsurprising outcome given the need to satisfy their readerships.

Examining Trends with Polling Data

Researchers often use polling data to describe and analyze trends. To isolate trend data, a researcher must ensure that items relating to the topic under investigation are included in multiple surveys conducted at different points in time. Ideally, the items should be identically worded. But even when they are, serious problems of comparability can make trend analysis difficult. Identically worded items may not mean the same thing or provide the same stimulus to respondents over time because social and political changes in society have altered the meaning of the questions. For example, consider this question:

> Some say that the civil rights people have been trying to push too fast. Others feel they haven't pushed fast enough. How about you? Do you think that civil rights leaders are trying to push too fast, are going too slowly, or are they moving at about the right speed?

The responses to this item can be greatly influenced by the goals and agenda of the civil rights leadership at the time of the survey. A finding that more Americans think that the civil rights leaders are moving too fast or too slowly may reflect not a change in attitude from past views about civil rights activism but a change in the civil rights agenda itself. In this case, follow-up questions designed to measure specific components of the civil rights agenda are needed to help define the trend.

There are other difficulties in achieving comparability over time. For example, even if the wording of an item were to remain the same, its placement within the questionnaire could change, which in turn could alter the meaning of a question. Likewise, the definition of the sampling frame and the procedures used to achieve completed interviews could change. In short, comparability entails much more than simply wording questions identically. Unfortunately, consumers of poll results seldom receive the information that enables them to judge whether items are truly comparable over time.

Two studies demonstrate the advantages and disadvantages of using identical items over time. Abramson, Silver, and Anderson (1990) complained that the biennial National Election Studies (NES) conducted by the Survey Research Center at

the University of Michigan, Ann Arbor, were losing their longitudinal comparability as new questions were added to the surveys and old ones removed. Baumgartner and Walker (1988), in contrast, complained that the use of the same standard question over time to assess the level of group membership in the United
States had systematically underestimated the extent of such activity. They
argued that new measures of group membership should be employed, which, of
course, would make comparisons between past and present surveys more problematic. Although both the old and the new measures can be included in a survey, this becomes very costly if the survey must cover many other topics.

Two other studies show how variations in question wording can make the
assessment of attitude change over time difficult. Borrelli and colleagues (1987)
found that polls measuring Americans' political party loyalties in 1980 and in 1984
varied widely in their results. They attributed the different results in these polls to
three factors: whether the poll sampled voters only; whether the poll emphasized
"today" or the present in inquiring about citizens' partisanship; and whether the
poll was conducted close to election day, which would tend to give the advantage
to the party ahead in the presidential contest. The implications of this research for
assessing change in party identification over time are evident—that is, to conclude
that genuine partisan change occurred in either of the two polls, other possible
sources of observed differences, such as modifications in the wording of questions, must be ruled out. In a study of support for aid to the Nicaraguan contras
between 1983 and 1986, Lockerbie and Borrelli (1990) argue that much of the
observed change in American public opinion was not genuine. Instead, it was
attributable to changes in the wording of the questions used to measure support
for the contras. Again, the point is that one must be able to eliminate other potential explanations for observed change before one can conclude that observed
change is genuine change.

Smith's (1993) critique of three major national studies of anti-Semitism conducted in 1964, 1981, and 1992 is an informative case study of how longitudinal
comparisons may be undermined by methodological differences across surveys.
The 1981 and 1992 studies were ostensibly designed to build upon the 1964
effort, thereby facilitating an analysis of trends in anti-Semitism. But, as Smith
notes, longitudinal comparisons among the three studies were problematic
because of differences in sample definition and interview mode, changes in question order and question wording, and insufficient information to evaluate the
quality of the sample and the design execution. In examining an eleven-item anti-
Semitism scale, he did find six items highly comparable over time that indicated
a decline in anti-Semitic attitudes.

Despite the problems of sorting out true opinion change from change attributable to methodological factors, there are times when public opinion changes

markedly and suddenly in response to a dramatic occurrence and the observed change is indeed genuine. Two examples from CBS News/*New York Times* polls in 1991 about the Persian Gulf war illustrate dramatic and extensive attitude change. The first example concerns military action against Iraq. Just before the January 15 deadline imposed by the UN for the withdrawal of Iraq from Kuwait, a poll found that 47 percent of Americans favored beginning military action against Iraq if it did not withdraw; 46 percent were opposed. Two days after the deadline and after the beginning of the allied air campaign against Iraq, a poll found 79 percent of Americans saying the United States had done the right thing in beginning military action against Iraq. The second example focuses on people's attitudes toward a ground war in the Middle East. Before the allied ground offensive began, only 11 percent of Americans said the United States should begin fighting the ground war soon; 79 percent said bombing from the air should continue. But after the ground war began, the numbers shifted dramatically: 75 percent of Americans said the United States was right to begin the ground war, and only 19 percent said the nation should have waited longer. Clearly, the Persian Gulf crisis was a case in which American public opinion moved dramatically in the direction of supporting the president at each new stage.

Examining Subsets of Respondents

Although it is natural to want to know the results from an entire sample, often the most interesting information in a poll comes from examining the response patterns of subsets of respondents defined according to certain theoretically or substantively relevant characteristics. For example, a January 1986 CBS News/*New York Times* poll showed President Reagan enjoying unprecedented popularity for a six-year incumbent: 65 percent approved of the president's performance, and only 24 percent disapproved. But these overall figures mask some analytically interesting variations. For example, among blacks only 37 percent approved of the president's performance; 49 percent disapproved. The sexes also differed in their views of the president, with men expressing a 72 percent approval rate compared with 58 percent for women. (As expected among categories of party loyalists, 89 percent of the Republicans, 66 percent of the independents, and only 47 percent of the Democrats approved of the president's performance.) Why did blacks and whites—and men and women—differ in their views of the president?

There is no necessary reason for public opinion on an issue to be uniform across subgroups. Indeed, on many issues there are reasons to expect just the opposite. That is why a fuller understanding of American public opinion is gained by taking a closer look at the views of relevant subgroups of the sample. In doing so, however, one should note that dividing the sample into subsets increases the sampling error and lowers the reliability of the sample estimates. For example, a sample of 1,600 Americans might be queried about their attitudes on abortion. After the overall pattern is observed, the researcher might wish to break down the sample by religion—yielding 1,150 Protestant, 400 Catholic, and 50 Jewish respondents—to determine whether religious affiliation is associated with specific attitudes toward abortion. The analyst might observe that Catholics on the whole are the most opposed to abortion. To find out which Catholics are most likely to oppose abortion, she might further divide the 400 Catholics into young and old Catholics or regular church attenders and nonregular attenders, or into four categories of young Catholic churchgoers, old Catholic churchgoers, young Catholic nonattenders, and old Catholic nonattenders. The more breakdowns done at the same time, the quicker the sample size in any particular category plummets, perhaps leaving insufficient cases in some categories to make solid conclusions.

Innumerable examples can be cited to demonstrate the advantages of delving more deeply into poll data on subsets of respondents. An ABC News/*Washington Post* poll conducted in February 1986 showed major differences in the attitudes of men and women toward pornography; an examination of only the total sample would have missed these important divergences. For example, in response to the question "Do you think laws against pornography in this country are too strict, not strict enough, or just about right?" 10 percent of the men said the laws were too strict, 41 percent said not strict enough, and 47 percent said about right. Among women, only 2 percent said the laws were too strict, a sizable 72 percent said they were not strict enough, and 23 percent thought they were about right (Sussman 1986b, 37).

A CBS News/*New York Times* poll of Americans conducted in April 1986 found widespread approval of the American bombing of Libya; 77 percent of the sample approved of the action, and only 14 percent disapproved. Despite the overall approval, differences among various subgroups are noteworthy. For example, 83 percent of the men approved of the bombing compared with 71 percent of the women. Of the white respondents, 80 percent approved in contrast to only 53 percent of the blacks (Clymer 1986). Even though all of these demographically defined groups gave at least majority support to the bombing, the differences in levels of support are both statistically and substantively significant.

Polls showed dramatic differences by race in the O. J. Simpson case, with blacks more convinced of Simpson's innocence and more likely to believe that he could not get a fair trial. For example, a field poll of Californians (*U.S. News & World Report*, August 1, 1994) showed that only 35 percent of blacks believed that

Simpson could get a fair trial compared with 55 percent of whites. Also, 62 percent of whites thought Simpson was "very likely or somewhat likely" to be guilty of murder compared with only 38 percent for blacks. Comparable results were found in a national *Time*/CNN poll (*Time,* August 1, 1994): 66 percent of whites thought Simpson got a fair preliminary hearing compared with only 31 percent of black respondents, while 77 percent of the white respondents thought the case against Simpson was "very strong" or "fairly strong" compared with 45 percent for blacks. A *Newsweek* poll (August 1, 1994) revealed that 60 percent of blacks believed that Simpson was set up (20 percent attributing the setup to the police); only 23 percent of whites believed in a setup conspiracy. When asked whether Simpson had been treated better or worse than the average white murder suspect, whites said better by an overwhelming 52 to 5 percent margin, while blacks said worse by a 30 to 19 percent margin. These reactions to the Simpson case startled many Americans who could not understand how their compatriots of another race could see the situation so differently.

School busing to achieve racial integration has consistently been opposed by substantial majorities in national public opinion polls. A Harris poll commissioned by *Newsweek* in 1978 found that 85 percent of whites opposed busing (Williams 1979, 48). An ABC News/*Washington Post* poll conducted in February 1986 showed 60 percent of whites against busing (Sussman 1986a). The difference between the two polls might reflect genuine attitude change about busing in that eight-year period, or it might be a function of different question wording or different placement within the questionnaire. Whatever the reason, additional analysis of both these polls shows that whites are not monolithic in their opposition to busing. For example, the 1978 poll showed that 56 percent of white parents whose children had been bused viewed the experience as "very satisfactory." The 1986 poll revealed sharp differences in busing attitudes among younger and older whites. Among whites age thirty and under, 47 percent supported busing and 50 percent opposed it, while among whites over age thirty, 32 percent supported busing and 65 percent opposed it. Moreover, among younger whites whose families had experienced busing firsthand, 54 percent approved of busing and 46 percent opposed it. (Of course, staunch opponents of busing may have moved to escape busing, thereby guaranteeing that the remaining population would be relatively more supportive of busing.)

Another example of the usefulness of examining poll results within age categories is provided by an ABC News/*Washington Post* poll conducted in May 1985 on citizens' views of how the federal budget deficit might be cut. One item read, "Do you think the government should give people a smaller Social Security cost-of-living increase than they are now scheduled to get as a way of reducing the budget deficit, or not?" Among the overall sample, 19 percent favored granting a smaller cost-of-living increase and 78 percent opposed. To test the widespread view that young workers lack confidence in the Social Security system and doubt they will ever get out of the system what they paid in, Sussman (1985c) investigated how different age groups responded to the preceding question. Basically, he found that all age groups strongly opposed a reduction in cost-of-living increases. Unlike the busing issue, this question showed no difference among age groups— an important substantive finding, particularly in light of the expectation that there would be divergent views among the old and young. Too often people mistakenly dismiss null (no difference) results as uninteresting and unexciting; a finding of no difference can be just as substantively significant as a finding of a major difference.

An example where age does make a difference in people's opinions is the topic of physician-assisted suicide. A *Washington Post* poll conducted in 1996 asked a national sample of Americans, "Should it be legal or illegal for a doctor to help a terminally ill patient commit suicide?" (Rosenbaum 1997). The attitudes of older citizens and younger citizens were markedly different on this question—the older the age group, the greater the opposition to doctor-assisted suicide. For example, 52 percent of respondents between ages eighteen and twenty-nine thought doctor-assisted suicide should be legal; 41 percent said it should be illegal. But for citizens over age seventy, the comparable figures were 35 and 58 percent. Even more striking were some of the racial and income differences on this question. Whites thought physician involvement in suicide should be legal by a 55 to 35 percent margin; blacks opposed it 70 to 20 percent. At the lowest income levels, doctor-assisted suicide was opposed by a 54 to 37 percent margin; at the highest income level it was supported by a 58 to 30 percent margin.

In many instances the categories used for creating subgroups are already established or self-evident. For example, if one is interested in gender or racial differences, the categories of male and female or white and black are straightforward candidates for investigation. Other breakdowns require more thought. For example, what divisions might one use to examine the effects of age? Should they be young, middle-aged, and old? If so, what actual ages correspond to these categories? Is middle age thirty-five to sixty-five, forty to sixty, or what? Or should more than three categories of age be defined? In samples selected to study the effects of religion, the typical breakdown is Protestant, Catholic, and Jewish. But this simple threefold division might overlook some interesting variations; that is, some Protestants are evangelical, some are fundamentalist, and others are considered mainline denominations. Moreover, since most blacks are Protestants, comparisons of Catholics and Protestants that do not also control for race may be misleading.

Establishing categories is much more subjective and judgmental in other situations. For example, religious categories can be defined relatively easily by denominational affiliation, as mentioned earlier, but classifying respondents as evangelicals or fundamentalists is more complicated. Those who actually belong to denominations normally characterized as evangelical or fundamentalist could be so categorized. Or an investigator might identify some evangelical or fundamentalist beliefs, construct some polling questions around them, and then classify respondents according to their responses to the questions. Obviously, this would require some common core of agreement about the definition of an evangelical or fundamentalist. Wilcox (1984, 6) argues:

> Fundamentalists and evangelicals have a very similar set of religious beliefs, including the literal interpretation of the Bible, the need for a religious conversion known as being "born-again," and the need to convert sinners to the faith. The evangelicals, however, are less anti-intellectual and more involved in the secular world, while the fundamentalists criticize the evangelicals for failing to keep themselves "pure from the world."

Creating subsets by ideology is another common approach to analyzing public opinion. The most-often-used categories of ideology are liberal, moderate, and conservative, and the typical way of obtaining this information is to ask respondents a question in the following form: "Generally speaking, do you think of yourself as a liberal, moderate, or conservative?" However, one can raise many objections to this procedure, including whether people really assign common meanings to these terms. Indeed, the levels of ideological sophistication and awareness have been an ongoing topic of research in political science.

Journalist Kevin Phillips (1981) has cited the work of political scientists Stuart A. Lilie and William S. Maddox, who argue that the traditional liberal-moderate-conservative breakdown is inadequate for analytical purposes. Instead, they propose a fourfold classification of liberal, conservative, populist, and libertarian, based on two underlying dimensions: whether one supports or opposes governmental intervention in the economy and whether one supports or opposes expansion of individual behavioral liberties and sexual equality. They define liberals as those who support both governmental intervention in the economy and expansion of personal liberties, conservatives as those who oppose both, libertarians as citizens who favor expanding personal liberties but oppose governmental intervention in the economy, and populists as persons who favor governmental economic intervention but oppose the expansion of personal liberties. According to one poll, populists made up 24 percent of the electorate, conservatives 18 percent, liberals 16 percent, and libertarians 13 percent, with the rest of the electorate not readily classifiable or unfamiliar with ideological terminology.

This more elaborate breakdown of ideology may help us to better understand public opinion, but the traditional categories still dominate political discourse. Thus, when one encounters citizens who oppose government programs that affect the marketplace but support pro-choice court decisions on abortion, proposed gay rights statutes, and the Equal Rights Amendment, one feels uncomfortable calling them liberals or conservatives since they appear to be conservative on economic issues and liberal on lifestyle issues. One might feel more confident in classifying them as libertarians.

Additional examples of how an examination of subsets of respondents can provide useful insights into the public's attitudes are provided by two CBS News/*New York Times* surveys conducted in 1991, one dealing with the Persian Gulf crisis and the other with attitudes toward police. Although the rapid and successful conclusion of the ground war against Iraq resulted in widespread approval of the enterprise, before the land assault began there were differences of opinion among Americans about a ground war. For example, in the February 12–13 CBS News/*New York Times* poll, Americans were asked: "Suppose several thousand American troops would lose their lives in a ground war against Iraq. Do you think a ground war against Iraq would be worth the cost or not?" By examining the percentage saying it would be worth the cost, one finds the following results for different groups of Americans:

All respondents	45%	Independents	46%
Men	56%	Republicans	54%
Women	35%	Eighteen to twenty-nine year-olds	50%
Whites	47%	Thirty to forty-four year-olds	44%
Blacks	30%	Forty-five to sixty-four year-olds	51%
Democrats	36%	Sixty-five years and older	26%

Note that the youngest age group, the one most likely to suffer the casualties, is among the most supportive of a ground war. Note also the sizable differences between men and women, whites and blacks, and Democrats and Republicans.

Substantial racial differences in opinion also were expressed in an April 1–3, 1991, CBS News/*New York Times* poll on attitudes toward local police. Overall, 55 percent of the sample said they had substantial confidence in the local police, and 44 percent said little confidence. But among whites the comparable percentages were 59 percent and 39 percent, while for blacks only 30 percent had substantial confidence and fully 70 percent expressed little confidence in the police. Even on issues in which the direction of white and black opinion was the same, there were still substantial racial differences in the responses. For example, 69 percent of whites said that the police in their own community treat blacks and whites the same, and only 16 percent said the police were tougher on blacks than on whites. Although a plurality—45 percent—of blacks agreed that the police treat blacks and whites equally, fully 42 percent of black respondents felt that the police were tougher on blacks. Certainly if one were conducting a study to ascertain citizens' attitudes about police performance, it would be foolish not to examine the opinions of relevant subgroups.

Another example of the importance of examining subsets of respondents is provided by a January 1985 ABC News/*Washington Post* poll that queried Americans about their attitudes on a variety of issues and presented results not only for the entire sample but also for subsets of respondents defined by their attentiveness to public affairs (Sussman 1985b). Attentiveness to public affairs was measured by whether the respondents were aware of four news events: the subway shooting in New York City of four alleged assailants by their intended victim; the switch in jobs by two key Reagan administration officials, Donald Regan and James Baker; the Treasury Department's proposal to simplify the tax system; and protests against South African apartheid held in the United States. Respondents then were divided into four levels of awareness, with 27 percent in the highest category, 26 percent in the next highest, 25 percent in the next category, and 22 percent falling in the lowest. The next step in the analysis was to compare the policy preferences of the highest and lowest awareness subsets.

There were some marked differences between these two groups. For example, on the issue of support for the president's military buildup, 59 percent of the lowest awareness respondents opposed any major cuts in military spending to lessen the budget deficit. In contrast, 57 percent of the highest awareness group said that military spending should be limited to help with the budget deficit. On the issue of tax rates, a majority of both groups agreed with the president that taxes were too high, but there was a difference in the size of the majority. Among the lowest awareness respondents, 72 percent said taxes were too high and 24 percent said they were not, while among the highest awareness respondents, 52 percent said taxes were too high and 45 percent said they were not (Sussman 1985b).

Opinions about the future of Social Security and Medicare also are affected by citizens' knowledge about the two programs (Pianin and Brossard 1997). In one poll, the more people knew about Social Security and Medicare, the more likely they were to believe that these programs were in crisis and that major governmental action was needed. For example, among highly knowledgeable respondents, 88 percent believed that Social Security either was in crisis or had major problems; only 70 percent of respondents with little knowledge agreed. Likewise, 89 percent of the highly knowledgeable respondents believed Social Security would go bankrupt if Congress did nothing compared to only 61 percent for the less-informed respondents.

All these findings raise some interesting normative issues about public opinion polls. . . . [T]he methodology of public opinion polls is very democratic. All citizens have a nearly equal chance to be selected in a sample and have their views counted; all respondents are weighted equally (or nearly so) in the typical data analysis. Yet except at the polls all citizens do not have equal influence in shaping public policy. The distribution of political resources, whether financial or informational, is not uniform across the population. Polls themselves become a means to influence public policy, as various decision makers cite poll results to legitimize their policies. But should the views of all poll respondents be counted equally? An elitist critic would argue that the most informed segments of the population should be given the greatest weight. Therefore, in the preceding example of defense spending, more attention should be given to the views of the highest awareness subset (assuming the validity of the levels of awareness), which was more supportive of reducing military spending. An egalitarian argument would assert that all respondents should be counted equally. . . .

Interpreting Poll Results

An August 1986 Gallup poll on education showed that 67 percent of Americans would allow their children to attend class with a child suffering from AIDS, while 24 percent would not. What reaction might there be to this finding? Some people might be shocked and depressed to discover that almost one-fourth of Americans could be so mean-spirited toward AIDS victims when the scientific evidence shows that AIDS is not a disease transmitted by casual contact. Others might be reassured and relieved that two-thirds of Americans are sufficiently enlightened or tolerant to allow their children to attend school with children who have AIDS. Some people might feel dismay: How could 67 percent of Americans foolishly allow their children to go to school with a child who has AIDS when there is no absolute guarantee that AIDS cannot be transmitted casually?

Consider this example from a 1983 poll by the National Opinion Research Center (NORC): "If your party nominated a black for President, would you vote for him if he were qualified for the job?" Eighty-five percent of the white respondents said yes. How might this response be interpreted? One might feel positive about how much racial attitudes have changed in the United States. A different perspective would decry the fact that in this supposedly tolerant and enlightened era, 15 percent of white survey respondents could not bring themselves to say they would vote for a qualified black candidate.

In neither example can we assign a single correct meaning to the data. Instead, the interpretation one chooses will be a function of individual values and beliefs, and purposes in analyzing the survey. This is demonstrated in an analysis of two national surveys on gun control, one sponsored by the National Rifle Association (NRA) and conducted by Decision/Making/Information, Inc., and the other sponsored by the Center for the Study and Prevention of Handgun Violence and conducted by Cambridge Reports, Inc. (pollster Patrick Caddell's firm). Although the statistical results from both surveys were comparable, the two reports arrived at substantially different conclusions. The NRA's analysis concluded:

Majorities of American voters believe that we do *not* need more laws governing the possession and use of firearms and that more firearms laws would *not* result in a decrease in the crime rate. (Wright 1981, 25)

In contrast, the center's report stated:

It is clear that the vast majority of the public (both those who live with handguns and those who do not) want handgun licensing and registration. . . . The American public wants some form of handgun control legislation. (Wright 1981, 25)

Wright carefully analyzed the evidence cited in support of each conclusion and found that

the major difference between the two reports is not in the findings, but in what is said about or concluded about the findings: what aspects of the evidence are emphasized or de-emphasized, what interpretation is given to a finding, and what implications are drawn from the findings about the need, or lack thereof, for stricter weapons controls. (Wright 1981, 38)

In essence, it was the interpretation of the data that generated the difference in the recommendations.

Two polls on tax reform provide another example of how poll data can be selectively interpreted and reported (Sussman 1985a). The first poll, sponsored by the insurance industry, was conducted by pollster Burns Roper. Its main conclusion, reported in a press conference announcing the poll results, was that 77 percent of the American public "said that workers should not be taxed on employee benefits" and that only 15 percent supported such a tax, a conclusion very reassuring to the insurance industry. However, Roper included other items in the poll that the insurance industry chose not to emphasize. As Sussman points out, the 77 percent opposed to the taxing of fringe benefits were then asked, "Would you still oppose counting the value of employee benefits as taxable income for employees if the additional tax revenues went directly to the reduction of federal budget deficits and not into new spending?" Twenty-six percent were no longer opposed to taxing fringe benefits under this condition, bringing the overall opposition down to 51 percent of the sample.

A second follow-up question asked, "Would you still oppose counting the value of employee benefits as taxable income for employees if the additional tax revenues permitted an overall reduction of tax rates for individuals?" (a feature that was part of the Treasury Department's initial tax proposals). Now only 33 percent of the sample was opposed to taxing fringes, 50 percent supported it, and 17 percent were undecided. Thus, depending upon which results one used, one could show a majority of citizens supportive of or opposed to taxing fringe benefits.

The other poll that Sussman analyzed also tapped people's reactions to the Treasury Department's tax proposal. A number of questions in the survey demonstrated public hostility to the Treasury proposal. One item read:

> The Treasury Department has proposed changing the tax system. Three tax brackets would be created, but most current deductions from income would be eliminated. Non-federal income taxes and property taxes would not be deductible, and many deductions would be limited. Do you favor or oppose this proposal? (Sussman 1985a)

Not surprisingly, 57 percent opposed the Treasury plan, and only 27 percent supported it. But as Sussman points out, the question is highly selective and leading since it focuses on changes in the tax system that hurt the taxpayer. For example, nowhere does it inform the respondent that a key part of the Treasury plan was to reduce existing tax rates so that 80 percent of Americans would be paying either the same amount or less in taxes than they were paying before. Clearly, this survey was designed to obtain a set of results compatible with the sponsor's policy objectives.

Morin (1995) describes a situation in which polling data were misinterpreted and misreported in the *Washington Post* because of faulty communication between a *Post* reporter and a local polling firm that was conducting an omnibus survey in the Washington, D.C., area. Interested in how worried federal employees were about their jobs given the budgetary battles between the Clinton White House and the Republican Congress in 1995, the reporter commissioned the polling firm to include the following questions in its survey: "Do you think your agency or company will probably be affected by federal budget cutbacks? Do you think your own job will be affected?" The poll discovered that 40 percent of the federal workers interviewed believed their own jobs might be affected. Unfortunately, when the polling outfit prepared a report for its client, the reporter, the report concluded that these federal workers felt their jobs were jeopardized. And then the reporter's story stated, "Four out of every 10 federal employees fear losing their jobs because of budget reductions." As Morin points out, this conclusion does not follow from the polling questions asked. The belief that one's job will likely be affected is not equivalent to the fear of losing one's job. Instead, the effects might be lower salary increases, decreased job mobility, increased job responsibilities, and the like. A correction quickly appeared in the *Post* clarifying what the polling data actually had said. One lesson of this example is the responsibility that pollsters have to clients to communicate carefully and accurately what poll results mean. Another lesson is that one should not try to read too much into the responses to any single survey item. In this case, if the reporter wanted to know exactly how federal workers thought their jobs would be affected, a specific question eliciting this information should have been included in the survey.

Weighting the Sample

Samples are selected to be representative of the population from which they are drawn. Sometimes adjustments must be made to a sample before analyzing and reporting results. These adjustments may be made for substantive reasons or because of biases in the characteristics of the selected sample. An example of adjustments made for substantive reasons is pollsters' attempts to determine who the likely voters will be and to base their election predictions not on the entire sample but on a subset of likely voters.

To correct for biases, weights can be used so that the sample's demographic characteristics more accurately reflect the population's overall properties. Because sampling and interviewing involve statistics and probability theory as well as logistical problems of contacting respondents, the sample may contain too few blacks, or too few men, or too few people in the youngest age category. Assuming that one knows the true population proportions for sex, race, and age, one can adjust the sample by the use of weights to bring its numbers into line with the overall population values. For example, if females constitute 60 percent of the sample but 50 percent of the overall population, one might weight each female respondent by five-sixths, thereby reducing the percentage of females in the sample to 50 percent (five-sixths times 60 percent).

A 1986 *Columbus Dispatch* preelection poll on the gubernatorial preferences of Ohioans illustrates the consequences of weighting. In August 1986 the *Dispatch* sent a mail questionnaire to a sample of Ohioans selected from the statewide list of registered voters. The poll showed that incumbent Democratic governor Richard Celeste was leading former GOP governor James Rhodes, 48 percent to 43 percent, with Independent candidate and former Democratic mayor of Cleveland Dennis Kucinich receiving 9 percent; an undecided alternative was not provided to respondents (Curtin 1986a). Fortunately, the *Dispatch* report of its poll included the sample size for each category (unlike the practice of the national media). One table presented to the reader showed the following relationship between political party affiliation and gubernatorial vote preference (Curtin 1986b):

Gubernatorial preference	Democrat	Republican	Independent
Celeste	82%	14%	33%
Rhodes	9	81	50
Kucinich	9	5	17
Total %	100	100	100
(N)	(253)	(245)	(138)

Given the thrust of the news story that Celeste was ahead, 48 to 43 percent, the numbers in the table were surprising because Rhodes was running almost as well among Republicans as Celeste was among Democrats, and Rhodes had a substantial lead among Independents. Because the N's were provided, one could calculate the actual number of Celeste, Rhodes, and Kucinich votes in the sample as follows:

Celeste votes = .82(253) + .14(245) + .33(138) = 287

Rhodes votes = .09(253) + .81(245) + .50(138) = 291

Kucinich votes = .09(253) + .05(245) + .17(138) = 58

The percentages calculated from these totals show Rhodes slightly *ahead*, 46 to 45 percent, rather than trailing. At first I thought there was a mistake in the poll or in the party affiliation and gubernatorial vote preference. In rereading the news story, however, I learned that the sample had been weighted. The reporter wrote, "Results were adjusted, or weighted, slightly to compensate for demographic differences between poll respondents and the Ohio electorate as a whole" (Curtin 1986b). The reporter did inform the reader that the data were weighted, but nowhere did he say that the adjustment affected who was ahead in the poll.

The adjustment probably was statistically valid since the poll respondents did not seem to include sufficient numbers of women and blacks, two groups that were more supportive of the Democratic gubernatorial candidate. However, nowhere in the news story was any specific information provided on how the weighting was done. This example illustrates that weighting can be consequential, and it is probably typical in terms of the scant information provided to citizens about weighting procedures.

When Polls Conflict: A Concluding Example

A variety of factors can influence poll results and their subsequent interpretation. Useful vehicles for a review of these factors are the polls that led up to the 1980, 1984, 1988, 1992, and 1996 presidential elections—polls that were often highly inconsistent. For example, in the 1984 election, polls conducted at comparable times yielded highly dissimilar results. A Harris poll had Reagan leading Mondale by 9 percentage points, an ABC News/ *Washington Post* poll had Reagan ahead by 12 points, a CBS News/ *New York Times* survey had Reagan leading by 13 points, a *Los Angeles Times* poll gave Reagan a 17-point lead, and an NBC News poll had the president ahead by 25 points (Oreskes 1984). In September 1988 seven different polls on presidential preference were released within a three-day period with results ranging from Bush ahead by 8 points to a Dukakis lead of 6 points (Morin 1988). In 1992 ten national polls conducted in the latter part of August showed

Clinton with leads over Bush ranging from 5 to 19 percentage points (Elving 1992). And in 1996, the final preelection polls showed Clinton leading Dole by margins ranging from 7 to 18 percentage points. How can polls on an ostensibly straightforward topic such as presidential vote preference differ so widely? Many reasons can be cited, some obvious and others more subtle in their effects.

Among the more subtle reasons are the method of interviewing and the number of callbacks that a pollster uses to contact respondents who initially were unavailable. According to Lewis and Schneider (1982, 43), Patrick Caddell and George Gallup in their 1980 polls found that President Reagan received less support from respondents interviewed personally than from those queried over the telephone. Their speculation about this finding was that weak Democrats who were going to desert Carter found it easier to admit this in a telephone interview than in a face-to-face situation.

With respect to callbacks, Dolnick (1984) reports that one reason a Harris poll was closer than others in predicting Reagan's sizable victory in 1980 was that it made repeated callbacks, which at each stage "turned up increasing numbers of well-paid, well-educated Republican-leaning voters." A similar situation occurred in 1984. Traugott (1987) found that persistence in callbacks resulted in a more Republican sample, speculating that Republicans were less likely to have been at home or available initially.

Some of the more obvious factors that help account for differences among compared polls are question wording and question placement. Some survey items mention the presidential and vice-presidential candidates, while others mention only the presidential challengers. Some pollsters ask follow-up questions of undecided voters to ascertain whether they lean toward one candidate or another; others do not. Question order can influence responses. Normally, incumbents and better known candidates do better when the question on vote intention is asked at the beginning of the survey rather than later. If vote intention is measured after a series of issue and problem questions have been asked, respondents may have been reminded of shortcomings in the incumbent's record and may therefore be less willing to express support for the incumbent.

Comparable polls also can differ in how the sample is selected and how it is treated for analytical purposes. Some polls sample registered voters; others query adult Americans. There are differences as well in the methods used to identify likely voters. As Lipset (1980) points out, the greater the number of respondents who are screened out of the sample because they do not seem to be likely voters, the more probable it is that the remaining respondents will be relatively more Republican in their vote preferences. Some samples are weighted to guarantee demographic representativeness; others are not.

It is also possible that discrepancies among polls are not due to any of the above factors, but may simply reflect statistical fluctuations. For example, if one poll with a 4 percent sampling error shows Clinton ahead of Dole, 52 to 43 percent, this result is statistically congruent with other polls that might have a very narrow Clinton lead of 48 to 47 percent or other polls that show a landslide Clinton lead of 56 to 39 percent.

Voss et al. (1995) summarized and compared many of the methodological differences among polls conducted by eight polling organizations for the 1988 and 1992 presidential elections. Even though all eight organizations were studying the same phenomenon, there were enough differences in their approaches that polls conducted at the same time using identical questions might still get somewhat different results for reasons beyond sampling error. One feature Voss et al. examined was the sampling method—how each organization generated a list of telephone numbers from which to sample. Once the sample was selected, polling organizations conducting telephone interviews still had to make choices about how to handle "busy signals, refusals, and calls answered by electronic devices, how to decide which household members are eligible to be interviewed, and how to select the respondent from among those eligible" (Voss et al. 1995). The investigators also examined the various weighting schemes used by each survey operation to ensure a representative sample. Much of this methodological information is not readily available to the consumer of public opinion polls, and if it were many consumers would be overwhelmed by the volume of methodological detail. Yet these factors can make a difference. For example, the eight polling organizations analyzed by Voss et al. treated refusals quite differently. Some of the outfits did not call back after receiving a refusal from a potential respondent; other organizations did make callbacks. One organization generally tried to call back but with a different interviewer, but then gave up if a second refusal was obtained.

Just as different methodological features can affect election polls, they also can influence other surveys. One prominent example dealt with the widely divergent estimates of rape obtained from two different national surveys. Much of this discrepancy stemmed from the methodological differences between the two surveys (Lynch 1996). Because the poll consumer is unaware of many of the design features of a survey, he or she must assume the survey design was appropriate for the topic at hand. Then the consumer can ask whether the information collected by the survey was analyzed and interpreted correctly.

REFERENCES

Abramson, Paul R., Brian Silver, and Barbara Anderson. 1990. "The Decline of Overtime Comparability in the National Election Studies." *Public Opinion Quarterly* 54 (summer): 177–190.

Alpern, David M. 1986. "A *Newsweek* Poll: Sex Laws." *Newsweek,* 14 July, 38.

Baumgartner, Frank R., and Jack L. Walker. 1988. "Survey Research and Membership in Voluntary Associations." *American Journal of Political Science* 32 (November): 908–928.

Borrelli, Stephen, Brad Lockerbie, and Richard G. Niemi. 1987. "Why the Democrat-Republican Partisan Gap Varies from Poll to Poll." *Public Opinion Quarterly* 51 (spring): 115–119.

Clymer, Adam. 1986. "A Poll Finds 77% in U.S. Approve Raid on Libya." *New York Times,* 17 April, A-23.

Curtin, Michael. 1986a. "Celeste Leading Rhodes 48% to 43%, with Kucinich Trailing." *Columbus Dispatch,* 10 August, 1-A.

_____. 1986b. "Here Is How Poll Was Taken." *Columbus Dispatch,* 10 August, 8-E.

Dolnick, Edward. 1984. "Pollsters Are Asking: What's Wrong." *Columbus Dispatch,* 19 August, C-1.

Elving, Ronald D. 1992. "Polls Confound and Confuse in This Topsy-Turvy Year." *Congressional Quarterly Weekly Report,* 12 September, 2725–2727.

Laumann, Edward O., et al. 1994. *The Social Organization of Sexuality.* Chicago: University of Chicago Press.

Lewis, I. A., and William Schneider. 1982. "Is the Public Lying to the Pollsters?" *Public Opinion* 5 (April/May): 42–47.

Lipset, Seymour Martin. 1980. "Different Polls, Different Results in 1980 Politics." *Public Opinion* 3 (August/September): 19–20, 60.

Lockerbie, Brad, and Stephen A. Borrelli. 1990. "Question Wording and Public Support for Contra Aid, 1983–1986." *Public Opinion Quarterly* 54 (summer): 195–208.

Lynch, James P. 1996. "Clarifying Divergent Estimates of Rape from Two National Surveys." *Public Opinion Quarterly* 60 (winter): 558–619.

Michael, Robert T., John H. Gagnon, Edward O. Laumann, and Gina Kolata. 1994. *Sex in America: A Definitive Survey.* Boston: Little, Brown.

Morin, Richard. 1988. "Behind the Numbers: Confessions of a Pollster." *Washington Post,* 16 October, C-1, C-4.

_____. 1991. "2 Ways of Reading the Public's Lips on Gulf Policy." *Washington Post,* 14 January, A-9.

_____. 1994. "Don't Know Much About Health Care Reform." *Washington Post* National Weekly Edition, 14–20 March, 37.

_____. 1995. "Reading between the Numbers." *Washington Post* National Weekly Edition, 4–10 September, 30.

Morin, Richard, and John M. Berry. 1996. "Economic Anxieties." *Washington Post* National Weekly Edition, 4–10 November, 6–7.

Oreskes, Michael. 1984. "Pollsters Offer Reasons for Disparity in Results." *New York Times,* 20 October, A-8.

Phillips, Kevin P. 1981. "Polls Are Too Broad in Analysis Divisions." *Columbus Dispatch,* 8 September, B-3.

Pianin, Eric, and Mario Brossard. 1997. "Hands Off Social Security and Medicare." *Washington Post* National Weekly Edition, 7 April, 35.

Rosenbaum, David E. 1997. "Americans Want a Right to Die. Or So They Think." *New York Times,* 8 June, E3.

Schneider, William. 1996. How to Read a Trial Heat Poll." Transcript, CNN "Inside Politics Extra," 12 May (see AllPolitics Web site).

Smith, Tom W. 1993. "Actual Trends or Measurement Artifacts? A Review of Three Studies of Anti-Semitism." *Public Opinion Quarterly* 57 (fall): 380–393.

Sussman, Barry. 1985a. "To Understand These Polls, You Have to Read the Fine Print." *Washington Post* National Weekly Edition, 4 March, 37.

_____. 1985b. "Reagan's Support on Issues Relies Heavily on the Uninformed." *Washington Post* National Weekly Edition, 1 April, 37.

_____. 1985c. "Social Security and the Young." *Washington Post* National Weekly Edition, 27 May, 37.

_____. 1986a. "It's Wrong to Assume that School Busing Is Wildly Unpopular." *Washington Post* National Weekly Edition, 10 March, 37.

_____. 1986b. "With Pornography, It All Depends on Who's Doing the Looking." *Washington Post* National Weekly Edition, 24 March, 37.

Traugott, Michael W. 1987. "The Importance of Persistence in Respondent Selection for Pre-election Surveys." *Public Opinion Quarterly* 51 (spring): 48–57.

Voss, D. Stephen, Andrew Gelman, and Gary King. 1995. "Preelection Survey Methodology: Details from Eight Polling Organizations, 1988 and 1992." *Public Opinion Quarterly* 59 (spring): 98–132.

Wilcox, William Clyde. 1984. "The New Christian Right and the White Fundamentalists: An Analysis of a Potential Political Movement." Ph.D. diss., Ohio State University.

Williams, Dennis A. 1979. "A New Racial Poll." *Newsweek,* 26 February, 48, 53.

Wright, James D. 1981. "Public Opinion and Gun Control: A Comparison of Results from Two Recent National Surveys." *Annals of the American Academy of Political and Social Science* 455 (May): 24–39.

10-2

Dynamic Representation

James A. Stimson, Michael B. MacKuen, and Robert S. Erikson

The relationship between public opinion and government action is complex. In the United States, with single-member congressional districts, we often consider relationship at the "micro" level—that is, whether individual elected officials are following the wishes of their home constituencies. But the overall relationship between public preferences and government behavior, the "macro" level, is more difficult to assess. In the following essay, James Stimson, Michael MacKuen, and Robert Erikson provide a look at this relationship with the help of a creative invention. These scholars use a statistical technique to build an aggregate measure of public opinion from dozens of polls. The technique allows them to measure change in the liberalism of views expressed in the polls over several decades. Then, using similarly aggregated measures of the behavior of Congress, the president, and the Supreme Court, they evaluate the relationship between the liberalism of public opinion and the behavior of the institutions. Government as a whole proves responsive to public opinion, and Congress and the presidency prove more responsive to public opinion than the Supreme Court.

... WHAT DOES IT mean that a government represents public feelings? Responsiveness must be a central part of any satisfactory answer. Representative governments respond to—meaning act as a consequence of—changes in public sentiment. To "act as a consequence of" changes in public sentiment implies a sequence, inherently structured in time. We may say that if, by knowing about earlier changes in public sentiment, we can improve the prediction of public policy over what we could have done from knowing only the history of public policy itself, then opinion causes policy, and this is dynamic representation. ...

The *dynamic* character of representation has a second aspect. Most political decisions are about change or the prevention of change. Governments decide to change health care systems, to reduce environmental regulations, to develop new weapons systems, or to increase subsidies for long staple cotton growers. Or not. Thus, political decisions have a directional force to them, and their incremental

Source: James A. Stimson, Michael B. MacKuen, and Robert S. Erikson, "Dynamic Representation," *American Political Science Review* 89 (September 1995): 543–564. Notes appearing in the original have been deleted.

character is inherently dynamic. Further, most public opinion judgments concern change as well. The public expresses preferences for "more" or "less" governmental action across different spheres: "faster school integration," "cuts in welfare spending," "getting tougher on crime," and so on. The main difference is that public sentiment is generally more vague, diffuse, than the more concrete government action.

This understanding suggests something akin to the familiar "thermostat" analogy. The public makes judgments about current public policy—most easily that government's actions need to be enhanced or trimmed back. These judgments will change as policy changes, as real-world conditions change, or as "politically colored" perceptions of policy and conditions change. And as the simple model indicates, politicians and government officials sense these changes in public judgment and act accordingly. Thus, when public policy drifts away from the public's demands for policy, the representation system acts as a control mechanism to keep policy on course.

The question now is how. If public opinion governs, how does it find its way into the aggregation of acts that come to be called public policy.

The Mechanisms of Dynamic Representation

Start with a politician facing a policy choice. With both preferences over policy options and a continuing need to protect the electoral career from unwanted termination, the elected official will typically need to balance personal preference against electoral expediency. We presume that politicians have personal preferences for and against particular policies and also that they value reelection. Then for each choice, we can define (1) a personal ideal point in the space of policy options and (2) an *expediency point* (that position most likely to optimize future reelection changes). The expediency point might be the median voter of the relevant constituency or some similar construct. We are not concerned here about particular rules. All that matters is that the politician have a *perception* of the most expedient position.

. . . Politicians create an appropriate margin of safety: those who highly value policy formulation or who feel safe at home choose policy over security; those who face competitive challenge in the next election lean toward "expediency" and security. . . .

. . . [E]lectoral turnover stems from events that overwhelm the margin of safety that the politicians select. Campaign finance, personal scandals, challenger tactics, the framing of electoral choice—all affect outcomes. The victims come both from those who take electoral risk by pursuing policy and also from those who ignore personal preference and concentrate solely on reelection: what matters is the force of electoral events relative to the politician's expectations. . . .

To breathe life into this system, let us put it into motion to see its aggregate and dynamic implications. Assume that public opinion—global attitudes toward the role of government in society—moves over time. Immediately we can expect greater turnover as the force of public opinion augments the normal electoral shocks to upset incumbent politicians' standard calculus. Now, the changes in personnel will prove systematic: rightward shifts in public opinion will replace Democrats with Republicans, and leftward shifts Republicans with Democrats. . . .

Rational Anticipation, Turnover, and Policy Consequence

Turnover from elections works most transparently with politicians who are neither well informed (until hit on the head by the club of election results) nor strategic. But that does not look at all like the politicians we observe. The oft-painted picture of members of Congress, for example, as people who read five or six daily newspapers, work 18-hour days, and leave no stone unturned in anticipating the electoral problems that might arise from policy choices does not suggest either limited information or naïveté.

We explicitly postulate the reverse of the dumb and naïve politician: (1) elected politicians are rational actors; (2) they are well informed about movements in public opinion; and (3) they agree with one another about the nature of those movements. This was well said by John Kingdon: "People in and around government sense a national mood. They are comfortable discussing its content, and believe they know when the mood shifts. The idea goes by different names. . . . But common to all . . . is the notion that a rather large number of people out in the country are thinking along certain common lines, that this national mood changes from one time to another in discernible ways, and that these changes in mood or climate have important impacts on policy agendas and policy outcomes" (1984, 153). . . .

Elected politicians, we believe, sense the mood of the moment, assess its trend, and anticipate its consequence for future elections. Changes in opinion, correctly perceived, will lead politicians to revise their beliefs about future election opportunities and hazards. Revised beliefs imply also revised expedient positions. Such strategic adjustment will have two effects: (1) it will dampen turnover, the conventional path of electoral influence; and (2) it will drive policy through rational anticipation.

When politicians perceive public opinion change, they adapt their behavior to please their constituency and, accordingly, enhance their chances of reelection. Public opinion will still work through elections, however. When they are surprised by the suddenness or the magnitude of opinion change or when they are unable credibly to alter their policies, politicians, despite their best efforts, will occasionally face defeat at the polls. Rather more fitfully than was the case with dumb politicians, public preferences will operate on electoral institutions by changing the personnel and thus the aggregated preferences of elected officials.

But that is not the only public opinion effect. Changing policy from shifting perceptions of what is electorally expedient we will refer to as *rational anticipation*. In a world of savvy politicians, rational anticipation produces dynamic representation without need for actual electoral defeats.

Politicians modify their behavior at the margin. Liberals and conservatives do not change their stripes, but they do engage in strategic behavior either to minimize risk from movements adverse to their positions or to maximize electoral payoff from movements supportive of their positions. For example, in a conservative era, such as the early 1980s, conservative Democrats found it easier to break with their party and did it more often, while liberal Republicans found it more difficult and dangerous and did it less often. The result of such conditions can be substantial shifts in winning and losing coalitions without any change of personnel.

Moreover, such direct anticipation of the electoral future does not exhaust the possibilities. For other actors also anticipate the effects of future elections on the current behavior of elected officials. Those who advance policy proposals—bureaucrats, lobbyists, judges, and citizens—are concerned with what can be done successfully, be it administrative act, judicial decision, or legislative proposal. And other politicians—those who pursue a leadership role or advocate particular policies—may choose to push ahead of the curve, to multiply the effects of even marginal shifts in opinion by anticipating others' anticipated reactions.

The impact of rational anticipation is thus a net shift in policy outputs from the aggregation of all these smallish strategic decisions, which (responding to the same signal) tend to move all in the same direction. It should be observable as the direct response of policy to opinion change, when election turnover effects are controlled.

A Design for Assessing Representation

This two-part setup permits three possible empirical outcomes: (1) two-stage representation may occur through the mechanism of electoral turnover, where candidate success depends upon the public opinion of the moment, which is then reflected in policy behavior; (2) movements in policy acts may reflect opinion without changes in elite personnel, the rational anticipation scheme; and (3) no representation might occur if both schemes fail. The alternatives are laid out

Figure 1. The Pathways to Dynamic Representation

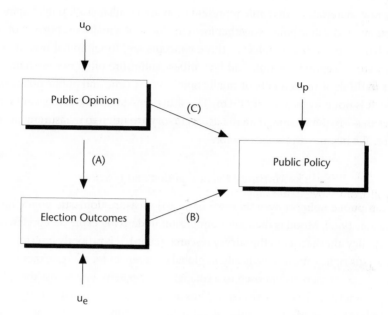

in Figure 1. There we can see three testable linkages. The first, A, is the first stage of the electoral sequence. The question to be answered is, Does public opinion affect election outcomes? The second stage, B, is not much in doubt. Its question is no cliff-hanger: Is there a difference in policy behavior between liberals and conservatives? The third linkage, C, is rational anticipation. Its question is, Does public policy move with public opinion independently of the effects of (past) elections? . . .

. . . The scheme of Figure 1 takes account of reality by positing other sets of causes of all phenomena as disturbances. The first, u_o, is the exogenous factors that account for changes in opinion. Not a focus of attention here (but see Durr 1993), they are such plausible forces as national optimism or pessimism arising from economic performance and reactions to past policies as experienced in daily life.

Elections are influenced by factors such as incumbent party performance, incumbency, macropartisanship, and so forth. Those factors appear as u_e on Figure 1. And finally, u_p captures sets of causes of public policy other than representation—such things as the events and problems to which policy is response or solution. Some of these "disturbances" are amenable to modeling, and will be. Some are irreducible, and must remain unobserved. . . .

Measurement

The raw materials of dynamic representation are familiar stuff: public opinion, elections, and public policy together form the focus of a major proportion of our scholarly activity. But familiar as these concepts are, longitudinal measures of them are (excepting elections) ad hoc at best and more often nonexistent. It is easy to think of movements of public opinion over time and public policy over time. It is not easy to quantify them. The situation—familiar concepts but novel measures—requires more than the usual cursory attention to measurement concerns. We begin with public opinion.

The Measures: Public Opinion and Elections

To tap public opinion over time we have [to] measure domestic policy mood (Stimson 1991). Mood is the major dimension underlying expressed preferences over policy alternatives in the survey research record. It is properly interpreted as left versus right—more specifically, as global preferences for a larger, more active federal government as opposed to a smaller, more passive one across the sphere of all domestic policy controversies. Thus our public opinion measure represents the public's sense of whether the political "temperature" is too hot or too cold, whether government is too active or not active enough. The policy status quo is the baseline, either explicit or implicit, in most survey questions. What the questions (and the mood measure) tap then is relative preference—the preferred direction of policy change.

Displayed in Figure 2, the *policy mood* series portrays an American public opinion that moves slowly back and forth from left (up on the scale) to right (down) over time and is roughly in accord with popular depictions of the eras of modern American politics. It reaches a liberal high point in the early 1960s, meanders mainly in the liberal end of its range through the middle 1970s, moves quite dramatically toward conservatism approaching 1980, and then begins a gradual return to liberalism over the 1980s. Note as well that the neutral point (50% liberal, 50% conservative) means something: points above 50 mean that the public wants more conservative policy. Thus, while the public's conservatism peaked in 1980, the public continued to demand more conservative policy (though by smaller margins) until 1984. (Thus we may think of our mood measure as a signal to politicians about the intensity and the direction of political pressure. It represents a demand for change.) . . .

The Measures: Policy Change

What is policy liberalism, and how can we measure it? What we observe is decisions such as congressional votes—not quite "policy." Our view is that each

Figure 2. Public Opinion over Time: Domestic Policy Mood, 1956–1993

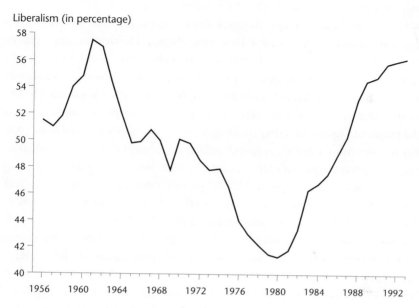

Liberalism (in percentage)

involves policy *change* at the margin. The issue as it is typically confronted is, Should we move current government policy in more liberal (expansive) directions or in more conservative ones? What we observe is who votes how. We see, for example, a particular vote in which the liberal forces triumph over conservative opponents. We take such a vote to mean that in fact the (unobserved) content of the vote moves policy in a liberal direction—or resists movement in the conservative direction.

This is a direct analogy to public opinion as we measure it. We ask the public whether government should "do more" or "spend more" toward some particular purpose. We take the response, "do more," "do less," "do about the same" to indicate the preferred direction of policy *change*. In both cases direction of change from the status quo is the issue.

Measuring this net liberalism or conservatism of global policy output seems easy enough in concept. We talk about some Congresses being more or less liberal than others as if we knew what that meant. But if we ask how we know, where those intuitions come from, the answer is likely to be nonspecific. The intuitions probably arise from fuzzy processing of multiple indicators of, for example, congressional action. And if none of them by itself is probably "the" defensible measure, our intuitions are probably correct in netting out the sum of many of them, all moving in the same direction. That, at least, is our strategy here. We will exploit several indicators of annual congressional policy output, each by itself dubious. But when they run in tandem with one another, the set will seem much more secure than its members.

Congressional Rating Scales. Rating scales are a starting point. Intended to tap the policy behaviors of individual House members and Senators, scales produced by groups such as Americans for Democratic Action (ADA) and Americans for Constitutional Action (ACA), later American Conservative Union (ACU), are now available for most of the period in question. Neither of these is intended to be a longitudinal measure of congressional action; and from a priori consideration of the properties such a measure would want, this is not how we would derive one. But if scales move similarly across chambers and scales from different organizations move in common over time, then we begin to believe that whatever it is they are measuring is probably global liberalism or conservatism of roll-call voting. Thus, as a measure of *net group rating*, we take the yearly average of the House's (or Senate's) ADA score and (100 minus) the ACA/ACU score.

Congressional Roll-Call Outcomes. The strength of the rating scales is their cross-sectional validity: they discriminate liberals from moderates from conservatives in any given year. Their weakness is longitudinal validity: we are less confident that they discriminate liberal from moderate from conservative Congresses. For greater face validity, we turn to the roll calls themselves as measures of policymaking. A quite direct measure is the answer to the questions, On ideological votes, who wins? and By how much do they win? Provided that we can isolate a set of roll calls that polarize votes along the left-versus-right main dimension of American domestic politics, measuring the degree of, say, liberalism is as easy as counting the votes. If we know which position on the vote is liberal and which conservative, then all that remains is to observe who won and by how much (and then aggregate that roll-call information to the session).

We exploit the cross-sectional strength of the rating scales (specifically, ADA) to classify roll calls. For each of the 25,492 roll-call votes in both houses for 1956–90, we classify the vote as left-right polarized or not (and then in which direction). The criterion for the classification as polarized is that the vote must show a greater association with member ADA scores than a hypothetical party-line vote for the particular members of each Congress. The intuition of this criterion is that we know we are observing a left-right cleavage when defection from party lines is itself along left–right lines—conservative Democrats voting with Republicans, liberal Republicans voting with Democrats. Although the party vote itself might be ideological, we cannot know that it is. One measure of the net liberalism of the session (for each house separately) is then simply the median size of the liberal coalition (on votes where the liberal and conservative sides are defined). A second approach to the same raw data is to focus on winning and losing, rather than coalition size. In this set of measures we simply count the percentage of liberal wins. We are observing quite directly then who wins, who loses, and by how much.

The Dramatic Acts of Congress: Key Votes. Scales of roll-call votes tell us about the overall tenor of public policy. Probably an excellent basis for inference about the net direction of policy movement, they do not distinguish between minor matters and those of enormous public consequence and visibility. Getting a good measure of "importance" presents a formidable challenge, requiring great numbers of subtle judgments about content and context. It is nonetheless desirable to have some indication of whether legislative activity produces something of import. A particular subset of legislation, the *Congressional Quarterly* "key votes" for each session of Congress, does attempt to distinguish the crucial from the trivial. The virtues of this set of votes are that it reflects the wisdom of expert observers of Congress at the time about what was important, and the measures are readily coded into liberal or conservative actions (and some that are neither).

We quantify the key votes as a combination of who wins and by how much. Accordingly, we average (1) the percentage of liberal wins and (2) the size of the liberal winning coalition. Crude, the measures nonetheless tap the issue in question, the direction of highly visible outcomes. The resulting time series are noisy (as would be expected from the small numbers of votes for each year), evincing a good deal of year-to-year fluctuation that seems meaningless. But they also show a picture of episodes of major policy change occurring exactly when expected for the Great Society (liberalism, peaking in 1965) and the Reagan Revolution (conservatism, peaking in 1981) periods respectively.

To get a sense of how legislative policy has moved over the years, look at Figure 3. [Figure 3a] presents our four measures for the House of Representatives. (To keep the eye on systematic movement, we have smoothed the graphs by taking a centered three-year moving average for each series. Note that we smooth only in this graph: we use the measured data for the statistical analysis.) It is clear that each indicator (wins, coalition size, ADA–ACA ratings, and key votes) contains both a common component and an idiosyncratic component. The lines move together, with a bit of zig and zag around the main flow. The panel for the Senate (Figure 3b) carries a similar message. Peaks of liberalism came during the early 1960s and the late 1980s, with conservatism at its height around 1980. While thus similar in outline, the patterns are not quite identical.

Presidential Policy Liberalism. The beginning point of dealing with the presidency is noting the near impossibility of direct measures of presidential liberalism from what presidents say and do. While we have an intuition about various acts and speeches, any attempt to quantify that intuition, to extract acts from the context of actions, quickly becomes hopelessly subjective. The alternative is to

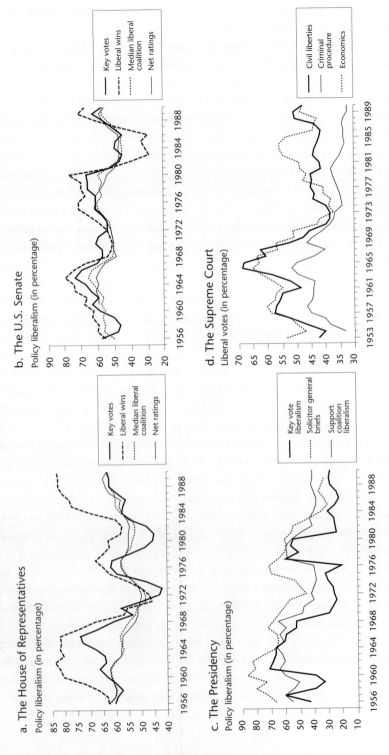

Figure 3.   Indicators of Public Policy Change in Four Parts of American Government (Three Year Moving Averages)

a. The House of Representatives

b. The U.S. Senate

c. The Presidency

d. The Supreme Court

look instead at presidents through their quantifiable records of interacting with the legislature and judiciary.

We know how often particular members of Congress support and oppose the president. And we can measure the liberalism of individual members in several ways. The most convenient of these is ADA scores, which are present for the entire period, as other comparable indicators are not. And we know that ADA ratings are very highly correlated with other ratings when available—positively or negatively—so that they can serve as a useful instrument of the underlying concept.

How then to combine these different pieces of information? A first approach is to ask the question, How liberal are the regular supporters of the president each year?, and then adopt that standard as a reflection of what the president wanted from Congress. That, however, is confounded by shared partisanship between president and member. We expect members of the president's party to be more likely to be regular supporters—independent of ideological agreement with the president's program. To deal with shared party ties as a confounding factor in presidential support, we opt instead to focus on presidential support within party. The strategy is first to divide each party into support and opposition groups based upon whether member presidential support is above or below the average for the party. The mean ADA rating of each party's "support" group is then an estimate of the president's ideological position. The opposition groups similarly measure the reverse. The measurement question then may be reduced to how such separate estimates are to be combined. For a summary measure of presidential position we perform a principal components analysis of the eight indicators (*support* vs. *oppose*, by party, by house). That analysis shows decisively that each of the eight taps a single underlying dimension. Such a dimension is estimated with a factor score and rescaled . . . to approximate the ADA scales from which it was derived.

For a second legislative presidential position measure we simply take the recorded presidential position for the key votes and compute the percentage of presidential stands each year that are liberal, where again the votes are classified by polarization with individual ADA ratings.

Presidential Interaction with the Court. With less regularity and on a quite different set of issues, presidents make their policy views known to the U.S. Supreme Court. The mechanism for doing so formally is the amicus curiae brief filed by the presidency's designated agent to the courts, the solicitor general. On over 700 occasions in the 1953–89 terms, the solicitor general went on record with the Court, arguing that the holdings of particular judicial decisions ought to be affirmed or reversed. About 90% of these briefs take positions on cases that are themselves classifiably liberal or conservative.

We employ the solicitor general briefs data as leverage to measure presumed presidential position on judicial issues. Using the direction coding from the Spaeth Supreme Court data base for the case and our knowledge of whether the solicitor general argued to affirm or reverse, we code each of the briefs as to direction—liberal, conservative, or nonideological. It is then an easy matter to produce aggregated annual scales as percentage liberal of the ideological positions taken.

A quick comparison of the presidential series with the legislative series (in Figure 3) suggests less coherence in the presidential measures. Much of the discord comes from the *Solicitor General* series (which we retain, nevertheless, for its substantive value). Note also that the presidential series is typically more conservative than the two congressional series, as we might reasonably expect from the historical party control of the two institutions.

Supreme Court Liberalism. For data we have the Supreme Court data base for the period 1953–90. From that, we can content-classify the majority position in individual cases as liberal, conservative, or neither; and from that, the lifetime liberalism or conservatism of individual justices is readily derived. Then we return to the individual cases and scale the majority and dissenting votes by the justices who cast them. This allows a content-free second classification of the majority position as liberal, conservative, or not ideological. From this we build annual measures of the major-case content categories. We have chosen four such categories—*civil rights and liberties, criminal procedure, economics,* and *other*—the number a compromise between separating matters which might in principle produce different alignments and grouping broadly enough to have sufficient cases in each for reliable annual measures.

For each measure we construct a time series consisting of the percentage of all votes cast by the justices on the liberal side of the issue, whichever that is, for the year. This focus on justice decisions, rather than aggregate outcomes of the Court, appears to produce a more moderate measure over time than the alternative. . . .

We examine the first three domains in Figure 3. There we see that the issue domains move pretty much in tandem. All domains show the famous liberalism of the Warren Court in the mid-1960s and the conservative reaction of the Burger Court. Most show a modest rebound of liberalism in the early 1980s, which then reverses from the influence of new Reagan justices.

The pattern of more substantive notice is that the *"criminal procedure"* cases produce no liberal rebound in the 1980s. This is an interesting exception, for public attitudes toward crime and criminals are themselves an exception to the growing liberalism of the 1980s (Stimson 1991). This is a case where the conservative message ("The solution is more punitive law enforcement") is still dominant. . . .

Figure 4. Global Public Opinion and Global Public Policy:
Predicted and Actual Policy

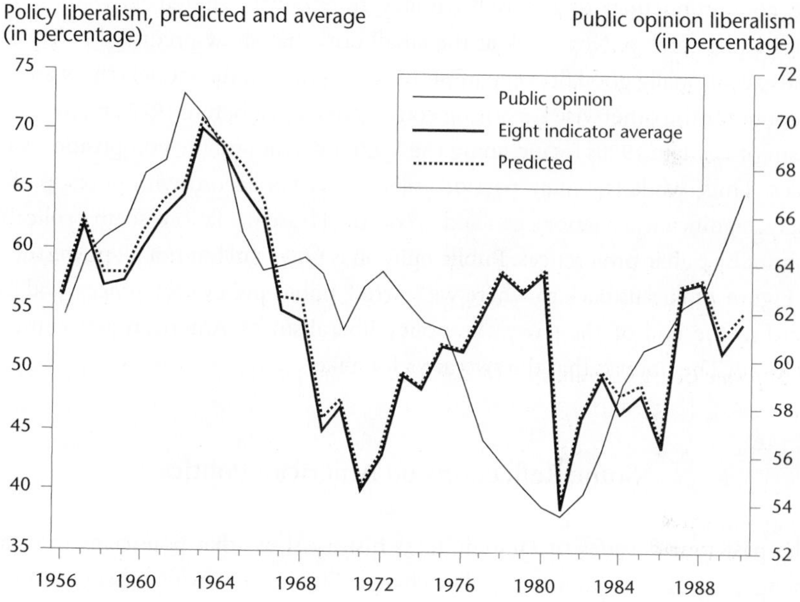

A Summary Analysis of Governmental Responsiveness

For a summation of dynamic representation we slice across the institutional structure of American politics, returning to the familiar questions, Does public opinion influence public policy? and By what process? Our combining the policy output of the four institutions is, of course, a fiction: a single national public policy
is not the average of independent branches. We "average" across different
branches to provide a rough answer to a rough question. Here we select two indicators from each of the four prior analyses (president, House, Senate, and
Supreme Court) and then estimate representation as it works on the American
national government as a whole. . . .

We get a better sense of the historical dynamic by examining Figure 4. Plotted
here are measures of public opinion, public policy and predicted policy. The first
(in the light, solid line) is public opinion, with its liberal peaks during the early
1960s and late 1980s and its conservative peak around 1980. The dark, solid line
represents policy, a simple average of our eight policy indicators. Without much
work, it is clear that the two series are basically similar: policy reflects the timing
and range of public opinion change.

Yet the two paths are not identical. Policy turned much more conservative during the late 1960s and early 1970s than the public demanded. Then, contrary to the continuing turn to the right, policy temporarily shifted leftward under Carter's leadership. Now look at the small dots that show predicted policy. . . . The exceptionally good fit is apparent. More important, the model is now able to account for the otherwise surprising conservatism just before 1972 and the liberalism of the late 1970s by including the Vietnam War and the composition variables. Thus, while the main part of policy moves in accord with public preferences, significant deviations can and do occur. Those deviations seem explicable but not by public preferences. Public opinion is powerful but not all-powerful.

Figure 4 takes us back to where we started, public policy preferences, and forward to the end of the story, the policy liberalism of American government, 1956–90. The point is that the two are a lot alike. . . .

Some Reflections on American Politics

The past four decades of United States history show that politicians translate changes in public opinion into policy change. Further, the evidence suggests that this translation varies by institution, both in the mechanisms that produce the link and in the nature of the dynamics.

Most important, dynamic representation finds strong support. Our work indicates that when the public asks for a more activist or a more conservative government, politicians oblige. The early peak of public opinion liberalism during the early 1960s produced liberal policy; the turn away from activism and the steady move toward conservatism was similarly reflected in national policy; and the recent 1980s upsurge of public demand for action was also effective (with the exception of the Court). To be sure, other things matter too. We have modeled a late 1960s shift rightward in policy (beyond that driven by public opinion) as a function of the Vietnam War's dominance over domestic political agendas. In addition, we modeled the shift leftward during the years of the Carter presidency (a shift contrary to the prevailing movement in public opinion) as a coincidence of compositional factors.

While we are confident that the basic result holds, we know that we do not yet fully understand movement in public policy. Nevertheless, the main story is that large-scale shifts in public opinion yield corresponding large-scale shifts in government action.

The link between opinion and policy is undoubtedly more complicated. While concentrating on policy response to opinion, we have seen little evidence of opinion reaction to policy. Elementary analyses generate contradictory inferences: the matter is subtle, the timing probably complex. We do know enough to assert that opinion reaction cannot explain the structural associations we uncover. We do not know enough to characterize the fuller relationship. This, of course, is a compelling subject for hard work.

Beyond the basic result, we can say that American national institutions vary in the mechanisms that produce responsiveness. It is the Senate, not the House of Representatives, that most clearly mimics the eighteenth-century clockwork meant to produce electoral accountability. When comparing the effectiveness of turnover and rational anticipation, we find that for the Senate (and also for the presidency), the most important channel for governmental representation is electoral replacement. Equally responsive, however, is the House of Representatives. Its members employ rational anticipation to produce a similarly effective public policy response, without the overt evidence of personnel change. The Supreme Court appears to reflect public opinion far more than constitutionally expected; but, in comparison, it is the institution that responds least.

Finally, the dynamics prove interesting. Each of the electoral institutions translates immediately public opinion into public policy. That is to say, when electoral politicians sense a shift in public preferences, they act directly and effectively to shift the direction of public policy. We find no evidence of delay or hesitation. The Court, not surprisingly, moves at a more deliberate speed. But equally important, rational anticipation is based not only on the long-term trends in public opinion but also on year-to-year shifts. That is to say, politicians constantly and immediately process public opinion changes in order to stay ahead of the political curve. Understanding politics well, the constitutional framers were correct in expecting short-term politics to be a fundamental part of dynamic representation.

The United States government, as it has evolved over the years, produces a complex response to public demands. The original constitutional design mixed different political calculations into different institutions so that no personal ambition, no political faction, no single political interest, or no transient passion could dominate. We now see the founders' expectations about complexity manifest in contemporary policymaking. Constitutional mechanisms harness politicians' strategies to the public's demands. In the end, the government combines both short- and long-term considerations through both rational anticipation and compositional change to produce a strong and resilient link between public and policy. . . .

REFERENCES

Durr, Robert H. 1993. "What Moves Policy Sentiment?" *American Political Science Review* 87:158–70.

Kingdon, John W. 1984. *Agendas, Alternatives, and Public Policies.* Boston: Little, Brown.

Stimson, James A. 1991. *Public Opinion in America: Moods, Cycles, and Swings.* Boulder: Westview.

10-3

America's Ignorant Voters

Michael Schudson

The meagerness of the average American's political knowledge has dismayed observers for decades. But Michael Schudson asks whether the informed citizen—meaning one who knows basic facts about government and politics—is truly the foundation of effective democracy. Reviewing the evidence, Schudson argues, contrary to conventional wisdom, that the problem is not growing worse. Moreover, voters may not recall many facts but still be able to vote in a way that reflects reasonable evaluations of candidates and parties.

EVERY WEEK, the *Tonight Show's* Jay Leno takes to the streets of Los Angeles to quiz innocent passersby with some simple questions: On what bay is San Francisco located? Who was president of the United States during World War II? The audience roars as Leno's hapless victims fumble for answers. Was it Lincoln? Carter?

No pollster, let alone a college or high school history teacher, would be surprised by the poor showing of Leno's sample citizens. In a national assessment test in the late 1980s, only a third of American 17-year-olds could correctly locate the Civil War in the period 1850–1900; more than a quarter placed it in the 18th century. Two-thirds knew that Abraham Lincoln wrote the Emancipation Proclamation, which seems a respectable showing, but what about the 14 percent who said that Lincoln wrote the Bill of Rights, the 10 percent who checked the Missouri Compromise, and the nine percent who awarded Lincoln royalties for *Uncle Tom's Cabin?*

Asking questions about contemporary affairs doesn't yield any more encouraging results. In a 1996 national public opinion poll, only 10 percent of American adults could identify William Rehnquist as the chief justice of the Supreme Court. In the same survey, conducted at the height of Newt Gingrich's celebrity as Speaker of the House, only 59 percent could identify the job he held. Americans sometimes demonstrate deeper knowledge about a major issue before the nation, such as the Vietnam War, but most could not describe the thrust of the

Source: Michael Schudson, "America's Ignorant Voters," *Wilson Quarterly*, Spring 2000, Vol. 24, Issue 2.

Clinton health care plan or tell whether the Reagan administration supported the Sandinistas or the contras during the conflict in Nicaragua (and only a third could place that country in Central America).

It can be misleading to make direct comparisons with other countries, but the general level of political awareness in leading liberal democracies overseas does seem to be much higher. While 58 percent of the Germans surveyed, 32 percent of the French, and 22 percent of the British were able to identify Boutros Boutros-Ghali as secretary general of the United Nations in 1994, only 13 percent of Americans could do so. Nearly all Germans polled could name Boris Yeltsin as Russia's leader, as could 63 percent of the British, 61 percent of the French, but only 50 percent of the Americans.

How can the United States claim to be model democracy if its citizens know so little about political life? That question has aroused political reformers and preoccupied many political scientists since the early 20th century. It can't be answered without some historical perspective.

Today's mantra that the "informed citizen" is the foundation of effective democracy was not a central part of the nation's founding vision. It is largely the creation of late-19th-century Mugwump and Progressive reformers, who recoiled from the spectacle of powerful political parties using government as a job bank for their friends and a cornucopia of contracts for their relatives. (In those days before the National Endowment for the Arts, Nathaniel Hawthorne, Herman Melville, and Walt Whitman all subsidized their writing by holding down federal patronage appointments.) Voter turnout in the late 19th century was extraordinarily high by today's standards, routinely over 70 percent in presidential elections, and there is no doubt that parades, free whiskey, free-floating money, patronage jobs, and the pleasures of fraternity all played a big part in the political enthusiasm of ordinary Americans.

The reformers saw this kind of politics as a betrayal of democratic ideals. A democratic public, they believed, must reason together. That ideal was threatened by mindless enthusiasm, the wily maneuvers of political machines, and the vulnerability of the new immigrant masses in the nation's big cities, woefully ignorant of Anglo-Saxon traditions, to manipulation by party hacks. E. L. Godkin, founding editor of the Nation and a leading reformer, argued that "there is no corner of our system in which the hastily made and ignorant foreign voter may not be found eating away the political structure, like a white ant, with a group of natives standing over him and encouraging him."

This was in 1893, by which point a whole set of reforms had been put in place. Civil service reform reduced patronage. Ballot reform irrevocably altered the act of voting itself. For most of the 19th century, parties distributed at the polls their own "tickets," listing only their own candidates for office. A voter simply took a ticket from a party worker and deposited it in the ballot box, without needing to read it or mark it in any way. Voting was thus a public act of party affiliation. Beginning in 1888, however, and spreading across the country by 1896, this system was replaced with government-printed ballots that listed all the candidates from each eligible party. The voter marked the ballot in secret, as we do today, in an act that affirmed voting as an individual choice rather than a social act of party loyalty. Political parades and other public spectacles increasingly gave way to pamphlets in what reformers dubbed "educational" political campaigns. Leading newspapers, once little more than organs of the political parties, began to declare their independence and to portray themselves as nonpartisan commercial institutions of public enlightenment and public-minded criticism. Public secondary education began to spread.

These and other reforms enshrined the informed citizen as the foundation of democracy, but at a tremendous cost: Voter turnout plummeted. In the presidential election of 1920, it dropped to 49 percent, its lowest point in the 20th century—until it was matched in 1996. Ever since, political scientists and others have been plumbing the mystery created by the new model of an informed citizenry: How can so many, knowing so little, and voting in such small numbers, build a democracy that appears to be (relatively) successful?

There are several responses to that question. The first is that a certain amount of political ignorance is an inevitable byproduct of America's unique political environment. One reason Americans have so much difficulty grasping the political facts of life is that their political system is the world's most complex. Ask the next political science Ph.D. you meet to explain what government agencies at what level—federal, state, county, or city—take responsibility for the homeless. Or whom he or she voted for in the last election for municipal judge. The answers might make Jay Leno's victims seem less ridiculous. No European country has as many elections, as many elected offices, as complex a maze of overlapping governmental jurisdictions, as the American system. It is simply harder to "read" U.S. politics than the politics of most nations.

The hurdle of political comprehension is raised a notch higher by the ideological inconsistencies of American political parties. In Britain, a voter can confidently cast a vote without knowing a great deal about the particular candidates on the ballot. The Labor candidate generally can be counted on to follow the Labor line, the Conservative to follow the Tory line. An American voter casting a ballot for a Democrat or Republican has no such assurance. Citizens in other countries need only dog paddle to be in the political swim; in the United States they need the skills of a scuba diver.

If the complexity of U.S. political institutions helps explain American ignorance of domestic politics, geopolitical factors help explain American backwardness in foreign affairs. There is a kind of ecology of political ignorance at work. The United States is far from Europe and borders only two other countries. With a vast domestic market, most of its producers have relatively few dealings with customers in other countries, globalization notwithstanding. Americans, lacking the parliamentary form of government that prevails in most other democracies, are also likely to find much of what they read or hear about the wider world politically opaque. And the simple fact of America's political and cultural super-power status naturally limits citizens' political awareness. Just as employees gossip more about the boss than the boss gossips about them, so Italians and Brazilians know more about the United States than Americans know about their countries.

Consider a thought experiment. Imagine what would happen if you transported those relatively well-informed Germans or Britons to the United States with their cultural heritage, schools, and news media intact. If you checked on them again about a generation later, after long exposure to the distinctive American political environment—its geographic isolation, superpower status, complex political system, and weak parties—would they have the political knowledge levels of Europeans or Americans? Most likely, I think, they would have developed typically American levels of political ignorance.

Lending support to this notion of an ecology of political knowledge is the stability of American political ignorance over time. Since the 1940s, when social scientists began measuring it, political ignorance has remained virtually unchanged. It is hard to gauge the extent of political knowledge before that time, but there is little to suggest that there is some lost golden age in U.S. history. The storied 1858 debates between Senator Stephen Douglas and Abraham Lincoln, for example, though undoubtedly a high point in the nation's public discourse, were also an anomaly. Public debates were rare in 19th-century political campaigns, and campaign rhetoric was generally overblown and aggressively partisan.

Modern measurements of Americans' historical and political knowledge go back at least to 1943, when the *New York Times* surveyed college freshmen and found "a striking ignorance of even the most elementary aspects of United States history." Reviewing nearly a half-century of data (1945–89) in *What Americans Know about Politics and Why It Matters* (1996), political scientists Michael Delli Carpini and Scott Keeter conclude that, on balance, there has been a slight gain in Americans' political knowledge, but one so modest that it makes more sense to speak of a remarkable stability. In 1945, for example, 43 percent of a national sample could name neither of their U.S. senators; in 1989, the figure was essentially unchanged at 45 percent. In 1952, 67 percent could name the vice president; in 1989, 74 percent could do so. In 1945, 92 percent of Gallup poll respondents knew that the term of the president is four years, compared with 96 percent in

1989. Whatever the explanations for dwindling voter turnout since 1960 may be, rising ignorance is not one of them.

As Delli Carpini and Keeter suggest, there are two ways to view their findings. The optimist's view is that political ignorance has grown no worse despite the spread of television and video games, the decline of political parties, and a variety of other negative developments. The pessimist asks why so little has improved despite the vast increase in formal education during those years. But the main conclusion remains: no notable change over as long a period as data are available.

Low as American levels of political knowledge may be, a generally tolerable, sometimes admirable, political democracy survives. How? One explanation is provided by a school of political science that goes under the banner of "political heuristics." Public opinion polls and paper-and-pencil tests of political knowledge, argue researchers such as Arthur Lupia, Samuel Popkin, Paul Sniderman, and Philip Tetlock, presume that citizens require more knowledge than they actually need in order to cast votes that accurately reflect their preferences. People can and do get by with relatively little political information. What Popkin calls "low-information rationality" is sufficient for citizens to vote intelligently.

This works in two ways. First, people can use cognitive cues, or "heuristics." Instead of learning each of a candidate's issue positions, the voter may simply rely on the candidate's party affiliation as a cue. This works better in Europe than in America, but it still works reasonably well. Endorsements are another useful shortcut. A thumbs-up for a candidate from the Christian Coalition or Ralph Nader or the National Association for the Advancement of Colored People or the American Association of Retired Persons frequently provides enough information to enable one to cast a reasonable vote.

Second, as political scientist Milton Lodge points out, people often process information on the fly, without retaining details in memory. If you watch a debate on TV—and 46 million did watch the first presidential debate between President Bill Clinton and Robert Dole in 1996—you may learn enough about the candidates' ideas and personal styles to come to a judgment about each one. A month later, on election day, you may not be able to answer a pollster's detailed questions about where they stood on the issues, but you will remember which one you liked best—and that is enough information to let you vote intelligently.

The realism of the political heuristics school is an indispensable corrective to unwarranted bashing of the general public. Americans are not the political dolts they sometimes seem to be. Still, the political heuristics approach has a potentially fatal flaw: It subtly substitutes voting for citizenship. Cognitive shortcuts have their place, but what if a citizen wants to persuade someone else to vote for his or her chosen candidate? What may be sufficient in the voting booth is

inadequate in the wider world of the democratic process: discussion, deliberation, and persuasion. It is possible to vote and still be disenfranchised.

Yet another response to the riddle of voter ignorance takes its cue from the
Founders and other 18th-century political thinkers who emphasized the importance of a morally virtuous citizenry. Effective democracy, in this view, depends
more on the "democratic character" of citizens than on their aptitude for quiz
show knowledge of political facts. Character, in this sense, is demonstrated all
the time in everyday life, not in the voting booth every two years. From Amitai
Etzioni, William Galston, and Michael Sandel on the liberal side of the political
spectrum to William J. Bennett and James Q. Wilson on the conservative side,
these writers emphasize the importance of what Alexis de Tocqueville called
"habits of the heart." These theorists, along with politicians of every stripe, point
to the importance of civil society as a foundation of democracy. They emphasize
instilling moral virtue through families and civic participation through churches
and other voluntary associations; they stress the necessity for civility and democratic behavior in daily life. They would not deny that it is important for citizens
to be informed, but neither would they put information at the center of their
vision of what makes democracy tick.

Brown University's Nancy Rosenblum, for example, lists two essential traits of
democratic character. "Easy spontaneity" is the disposition to treat others identically, without deference, and with an easy grace. This capacity to act as if many
social differences are of no account in public settings is one of the things that
make democracy happen on the streets. This is the disposition that foreign visitors have regularly labeled "American" for 200 years, at least since 1818, when the
British reformer and journalist William Cobbett remarked upon Americans'
"universal civility." Tocqueville observed in 1840 that strangers in America who
meet "find neither danger nor advantage in telling each other freely what they
think. Meeting by chance, they neither seek nor avoid each other. Their manner
is therefore natural, frank, and open."

Rosenblum's second trait is "speaking up," which she describes as "a willingness to respond at least minimally to ordinary injustice." This does not involve
anything so impressive as organizing a demonstration, but something more like
objecting when an adult cuts ahead of a kid in a line at a movie theater, or
politely rebuking a coworker who slurs a racial or religious group. It is hard to
define "speaking up" precisely, but we all recognize it, without necessarily giving
it the honor it deserves as an element of self-government.

We need not necessarily accept Rosenblum's chosen pair of moral virtues.
Indeed a Japanese or Swedish democrat might object that they look suspiciously
like distinctively American traits rather than distinctively democratic ones.
They almost evoke Huckleberry Finn. But turning our attention to democratic

character reminds us that being well informed is just one of the requirements of democratic citizenship.

The Founding Fathers were certainly more concerned about instilling moral virtues than disseminating information about candidates and issues. Although they valued civic engagement more than their contemporaries in Europe did, and cared enough about promoting the wide circulation of ideas to establish a post office and adopt the First Amendment, they were ambivalent about, even suspicious of, a politically savvy populace. They did not urge voters to "know the issues"; at most they hoped that voters would choose wise and prudent legislators to consider issues on their behalf. On the one hand, they agreed that "the diffusion of knowledge is productive of virtue, and the best security for our civil rights," as a North Carolina congressman put it in 1792. On the other hand, as George Washington cautioned, "however necessary it may be to keep a watchful eye over public servants and public measures, yet there ought to be limits to it, for suspicions unfounded and jealousies too lively are irritating to honest feelings, and oftentimes are productive of more evil than good."

If men were angels, well and good—but they were not, and few of the Founders were as extravagant as Benjamin Rush in his rather scary vision of an education that would "convert men into republican machines." In theory, many shared Rush's emphasis on education; in practice, the states made little provision for public schooling in the early years of the Republic. Where schools did develop, they were defended more as tutors of obedience and organs of national unity than as means to create a watchful citizenry. The Founders placed trust less in education than in a political system designed to insulate decision making in the legislatures from the direct influence of the emotional, fractious, and too easily swayed electorate.

All of these arguments—about America's political environment, the value of political heuristics, and civil society—do not add up to a prescription for resignation or complacency about civic education. Nothing I have said suggests that the League of Women Voters should shut its doors or that newspaper editors should stop putting politics on page one. People may be able to vote intelligently with very little information—even well educated people do exactly that on most of the ballot issues they face—but democratic citizenship means more than voting. It means discussing and debating the questions before the political community—and sometimes raising new questions. Without a framework of information in which to place them, it is hard to understand even the simple slogans and catchwords of the day. People with scant political knowledge, as research by political scientists Samuel Popkin and Michael Dimock suggests, have more difficulty than others in perceiving differences between candidates and parties. Ignorance also tends to breed more ignorance; it inhibits people from venturing into situations that make them feel uncomfortable or inadequate, from the voting booth to the community forum to the town hall.

What is to be done? First, it is important to put the problem in perspective. American political ignorance is not growing worse. There is even an "up" side to Americans' relative indifference to political and historical facts: their characteristic openness to experiment, their pragmatic willingness to judge ideas and practices by their results rather than their pedigree.

Second, it pays to examine more closely the ways in which people do get measurably more knowledgeable. One of the greatest changes Delli Carpini and Keeter found in their study, for example, was in the percentage of Americans who could identify the first 10 amendments to the Constitution as the Bill of Rights. In 1954, the year the U.S. Supreme Court declared school segregation unconstitutional in *Brown v. Board of Education,* only 31 percent of Americans could do so. In 1989, the number had moved up to 46 percent.

Why the change? I think the answer is clear: The civil rights movement, along with the rights-oriented Warren Court, helped bring rights to the forefront of the American political agenda and thus to public consciousness. Because they dominated the political agenda, rights became a familiar topic in the press and on TV dramas, sitcoms, and talk shows, also finding their way into school curricula and textbooks. Political change, this experience shows, can influence public knowledge.

This is not to say that only a social revolution can bring about such an improvement. A lot of revolutions are small, one person at a time, one classroom at a time. But it does mean that there is no magic bullet. Indeed, imparting political knowledge has only become more difficult as the dimensions of what is considered political have expanded into what were once nonpolitical domains (such as gender relations and tobacco use), as one historical narrative has become many, each of them contentious, and as the relatively simple framework of world politics (the Cold War) has disappeared.

In this world, the ability to name the three branches of government or describe the New Deal does not make a citizen, but it is at least a token of membership in a society dedicated to the ideal of self-government. Civic education is an imperative we must pursue with the full recognition that a high level of ignorance is likely to prevail—even if that fact does not flatter our faith in rationalism, our pleasure in moralizing, or our confidence in reform.

10-4

from *Culture War? The Myth of a Polarized America*

Morris P. Fiorina

Many observers of politics have asserted that Americans are increasingly polarized, particularly over cultural or social issues. That polarization, it is claimed, has intensified partisanship in the electorate and in Washington. In the following essay, Morris Fiorina challenges the assumption that Americans have become more deeply divided on cultural issues. He argues, rather, that political elites, particularly candidates for office, have become more polarized along party and ideological lines, thus changing the choices available to the voters. That, in turn, has produced a sorting of the electorate and the deceptive appearance of polarization in the mass public.

[Many observers of American politics in recent years refer] to "the 50:50 nation." During the late 1990s and early 2000s this phrase began to appear in popular discussions of American politics, as did a similar phrase, "the 49 percent nation." Such phraseology referred to the closely divided national elections of the late 1990s, when the winning party's popular vote share repeatedly came in right around 49 percent of the total vote:

• 1996 Clinton Vote	49.2%
• 1996 Republican House Vote	48.9
• 1998 Republican House Vote	48.9
• 2000 Gore Vote	48.4
• 2000 Republican House Vote	48.3
• 2002 Republican House Vote	50.9

If we consider only the two-party vote, the parties are almost exactly evenly matched nationally—50:50—or at least they were until the 2002 House elections, when the Republicans broke through that ceiling and got to 52.9 percent. Clearly, recent national elections have been exceedingly close. No presidential candidate has won a majority of the popular vote since 1988, the past three elections constituting the longest such streak since the so-called "era of indecision," when no

Source: Morris P. Fiorina, *Culture War? The Myth of a Polarized America* (Upper Saddle River, N.J.: Pearson Education, Inc., 2005), 11–26.

Figure 1. Two Very Different Close Election Scenarios

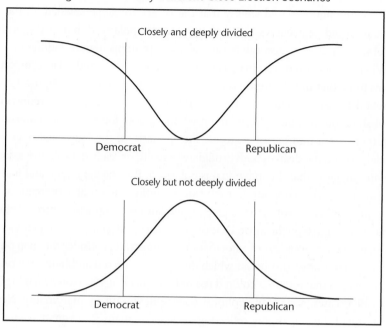

presidential candidate won a majority of the popular vote in the four elections from 1880 to 1892.

The question is what to make of these recent close elections? For most commentators, the answer is obvious: the American electorate is polarized. In the previously quoted words of the *Economist*, the close recent U.S. elections " . . . *reflect deep demographic divisions. . . . The 50-50 nation appears to be made up of two big, separate voting blocks, with only a small number of swing voters in the middle.*" The top panel of Figure 1 depicts this claim graphically. The electorate is highly polarized: a large number of "progressives" on the left support the Democrats, a large number of "orthodox" on the right support the Republicans, and very few people occupy the middle ground. With a polarized electorate like this, elections will be very close, half the voters will cheer, and half the voters will seethe, as *USA Today* asserts.

But the U-shaped distribution in the top panel of the figure is not the only electoral configuration that will produce close elections. Most obviously, consider the bell-shaped distribution in the bottom panel of Figure 1, which is the inverse of the U-shaped distribution in the top. In the lower figure most people hold moderate or centrist positions and relatively few are extreme partisans. But if the Democratic and Republican parties position themselves equidistant from the center on opposite sides, then the bottom configuration too produces close elections. In both examples the electorate is *closely* divided, but only in the top panel of the figure would we say that the voters are *deeply* divided. In the top panel it would be accurate to say that voters are polarized, but in the bottom panel we would more accurately call most voters ambivalent or indifferent.

When an election results in a near 50:50 outcome, the standard interpretation seems to be that the electorate is polarized as in the top panel of Figure 1. Why should that be the default interpretation? When an individual voter reports that he or she is on the fence (50:50) about whom to vote for, everyone understands that there are a number of plausible interpretations; the individual likes both candidates equally, dislikes both candidates equally, or really doesn't give a damn. No one suggests that the individual is polarized. But the aggregate and individual situations are analogous. In each case a continuous variable (percent of the vote/probability of voting for a given candidate) is compressed into a dichotomous variable (Republican or Democratic victory/Republican or Democratic vote), with enormous loss of information. To illustrate, consider the map on the inside back cover of this book, which differs from the red and blue map on the front cover in that a state is colored red or blue only if it was won by a margin of 55:45 or greater, a standard political science definition of marginality. Now a great deal of the map is gray, reflecting the fact that many states are marginal and not securely in the camp of one party or the other. In language analogous to that used to describe individual voters, we might call such states "ambivalent" or "uncertain."

In sum, close elections may reflect equal numbers of voters who hate one candidate and love the other, voters who like both, voters who do not care much at all about either candidate, or various combinations of these conditions. Without taking a detailed look at voter attitudes, we cannot determine whether close elections reflect a polarized electorate that is deeply divided, or an ambivalent electorate that is closely divided between the choices it is offered. So, let us take a closer look at the public opinion that underlies the knife-edge elections of the past few years. Is it as divided as election outcomes seem to suggest?

Is the Country Polarized?

> You've got 80% to 90% of the country that look at each other like they are on separate planets. (Bush reelection strategist, Matthew Dowd).

Is America polarized? Strictly speaking the question should be "has America become *more* polarized?" for that is the claim. But if the country is not polarized to begin with, the question of whether it has become more polarized is moot.

Table 1. Red Versus Blue States: Political Inclinations

	Blue	Red
Vote intention: Bush	34%	44%
Democratic self-ID	36	32
Republican self-ID	25	31
Liberal self-ID	22	18
Conservative self-ID	33	41
Moderate self-ID	45	41

Barely two months before the supposed "values chasm separating the blue states from the red ones" emerged in the 2000 election, the Pew Research Center for the People & the Press conducted an extensive national survey that included a wide sampling of issues, a number of those which figure prominently in discussions of the culture war. We have divided the Pew survey respondents into those who resided in states that two months later were to be categorized as blue states and states that two months later were to be categorized as red states. The question is whether there is any indication in these data that the election results would leave one half the country "seething" and one half "cheering," as *USA Today* reports.

Table 1 indicates that the residents of blue and red states certainly intended to vote differently: the percentage expressing an intention to vote for George Bush was ten points higher in the red states. Reminiscent of our discussion of dichotomous choices, however, the partisan and ideological predispositions underlying these voting differences were less distinct. The difference between the proportions of red and blue state respondents who consider themselves Democrats is not statistically significant, and the difference in the proportions who consider themselves Republicans is barely so—in both red and blue states self-identified independents are the largest group. Similarly, about a fifth of the respondents in both red and blue states consider themselves liberals (the four point difference is not statistically significant), and while there are more conservatives in the red states, there are more conservatives than liberals even in the blue states. In both the red and blue states the largest group of people classified themselves as moderates. In sum, while the aggregate voting patterns of red and blue states would turn out to be quite distinct in November, the underlying patterns of political identification were much less so.

Table 2 reports similar results for the group evaluations reported by residents of red and blue states. Unsurprisingly, red state residents regard the Republican Party more favorably than the Democrats, but 55 percent of them regard the

Table 2. Red Versus Blue States: Group Evaluations
(Percent very / mostly favorable toward . . .)

	Blue	Red
Republican Party	50%	58%
Democratic Party	64	55
Evangelical Christians	60	63
Jews	79	77
Catholics	77	79
Muslims	56	47
Atheists	37	27

Democratic Party favorably. Conversely, blue state residents regard the Democratic Party more favorably than the Republicans, but 50 percent report favorable evaluations of the Republican Party. Evangelical Christians are evaluated equally positively by solid majorities in both red and blue states, as are Jews and Catholics. Muslims fare less well overall and red state residents regard them lower still, but one wonders how much experience many people have with actual Muslims—especially in many of the red states—as opposed to the abstract concept of a Muslim. Finally, in a standard finding, neither red nor blue state residents like atheists: Americans do not care very much what or how people believe, but they are generally negative toward people who don't believe in anything.

Across a range of other matters, blue and red state residents differ little, if at all. Figures in Table 3 indicate that similar proportions regard the government as *almost always* wasteful and inefficient—relative to the red states, the blue states clearly are not wellsprings of support for big government. Only small minorities in either category regard discrimination as the main reason that African Americans can't get ahead—the blue states are not hotbeds of racial liberalism. Immigrants receive a warmer reception among blue state residents, but multiculturalism remains a minority position even in the blue states. Blue state residents are less likely to endorse unqualified patriotism.

On the other hand, red state residents are just as likely as blue state residents to believe that large companies have too much power and to think that corporations make too much profit—the red states are not the running dogs of corporate America. Amusingly, majorities in both red and blue states agree that Al Gore is more of a liberal than he lets on, and that George Bush is more of a conservative than he lets on—they were not fooled by all the talk about "progressives" and "compassionate conservatives." And finally—and counter to suggestions of numerous Democrats after the election—majorities in both red and blue states *strongly* disagree with the proposition that they wish Bill Clinton could run

Table 3. Red Versus Blue States: Beliefs and Perceptions:
(Percent strongly supporting statement)

	Blue	Red
Gov't almost always wasteful and inefficient	39%	44%
Discrimination main reason blacks cannot get ahead	25	21
Immigrants strengthen our country	44	32
Fight for country right or wrong	35	43
Too much power concentrated in large companies	64	62
Corporations make too much profit	44	43
Al Gore is more liberal than he lets on	55	59
George Bush is more conservative than he lets on	59	57
Wish Clinton could run again (strongly disagree)	51	61

again. Clinton was more favorably regarded in the blue states, but Clinton fatigue by no means was limited to the red states.

When it comes to issue sentiments, Table 4 shows that in many cases the small differences we have seen so far become even smaller. Contrary to Republican dogma, red state citizens are equally as unenthusiastic about using the surplus (har!) to cut taxes as blue state citizens. Nearly equal numbers of blue and red state residents think the surplus should be used to pay off the national debt, increase domestic spending, and bolster Social Security and Medicare. Contrary to Democratic dogma, blue state citizens are equally as enthusiastic as red state citizens about abolishing the inheritance tax, giving government grants to religious organizations, adopting school vouchers, and partially privatizing Social Security. Overwhelming majorities in both red and blue states favor providing prescription drugs through Medicare, and solid majorities endorse protecting the environment, whatever it takes. Neither red nor blue state residents attach high priority to increasing defense spending. Looking at this series of issue items, one wonders why anyone would bother separating respondents into red and blue categories—the differences are insignificant.

But, we have not considered the specific issues that define the culture war. Table 5 brings us to the heart of the matter—questions of religion, morality, and sexuality. The proportion of Protestants is significantly higher in the red states, of course, as is the proportion of respondents who report having a "born again" experience. There is a real difference here between the heartland and the coasts. But the significance of this difference fades when we dig deeper. Only a minority of red state respondents reports being very involved in church activities—only marginally more than those blue state respondents who report heavy involvement. A higher proportion of red state respondents report that religion is very

Table 4. Red Versus Blue States: Issue Sentiments

	Blue	Red
Should use the surplus to cut taxes	14%	14%
. . . pay off the national debt	21	23
. . . increase domestic spending	28	24
. . . bolster SS and Medicare	35	38
Favor abolition of inheritance tax	70	72
. . . gov't grants to religious organizations	67	66
. . . school vouchers for low and middle income parents	54	50
. . . partial privatization of SS	69	71
. . . Medicare coverage of prescription drugs	91	92
. . . increasing defense sepnding	30	37
Do whatever it takes to protect the environment	70	64

important in their lives, but a healthy 62 percent majority of blue state respondents feel similarly. Very similar proportions think churches should stay out of politics, and the minority of red state residents who approve of the clergy talking politics from the pulpit is slightly smaller than the minority in the blue states. Book-burners are only slightly more common in the red states. Finally, there is a clear difference in one of the major issues of the culture war, homosexuality, but probably less of a difference than many would have expected. The level of support for societal acceptance of homosexuality is ten percentage points higher in the blue states (twelve points if we add those who waffle to those who fully accept homosexuality). The difference is statistically significant, but it hardly conjures up an image of two coalitions of deeply opposed states engaged in a culture war. Opinion is almost as divided within the red and the blue states as it is between them. Significantly, this ten- to twelve-point difference on the issue of homosexual acceptance is about as large a difference as we found between red and blue state respondents in the survey. Readers can judge for themselves whether differences of this magnitude justify the military metaphors usually used to describe them.

A legitimate objection to the preceding comparisons is that they include all citizens rather than just voters. Only about half of the age-eligible electorate goes to the polls in contemporary presidential elections, and far fewer vote in lower-level elections. It is well known that partisanship and ideology are strong correlates of who votes: more intense partisans and more extreme ideologues are more likely to vote. Thus, it is possible that the *voters* in red states differ more from the *voters* in blue states than the residents do. To consider this possibility we

Table 5. Red Versus Blue States: Religion and Morals

	Blue	Red
Protestant	50%	69%
"Born again" or Evangelical Christian	28	45
Very involved in church activities	21	29
Religion is very important in my life	62	74
Churches should keep out of politics	46	43
Ever right for clergy to discus candidates or issues from the pulpit? (yes)	35	33
Ban dangerous books from school libraries (yes)	37	42
Homosexuality should be accepted by society		
Agree strongly	41	31
Agree not strongly	16	14

turn to the 2000 National Election Study which—after the election—asks individuals whether and how they voted. In 2000, the NES reported a vote distribution reasonably close to the actual national division: 50.6 percent of the respondents reported voting for Gore, 45.5 percent for Bush, and the remainder for minor candidates.

Tables 6 and 7 report differences among reported voters in the NES that are only marginally larger than those reported among all respondents in the Pew Survey. Again, the largest difference is for the vote itself. To reiterate, even if an individual feels 55:45 between the two candidates, she has to vote one way or the other. The reported vote for Bush is 54 percent in the red states versus 37 percent in the blue states—a seventeen-point gap, which is larger than the ten-point gap in vote *intention* in the earlier Pew Survey. Self-identified Democrats were significantly more common among blue state voters and self-identified Republicans significantly more common among red state voters, but in neither case does the difference reach double digits; independents and minor party affiliates were a third of the actual electorate in both categories. Self-identified liberals are more common in the blue states, but self-identified conservatives were at least as numerous as liberals in blue states. Again, moderates or centrists were the majority in both categories. An overwhelming majority of blue state voters approved of Bill Clinton's general job performance as well as his foreign policy job performance and his economic job performance, but so did a heavy, if smaller, majority of red state voters. Only minorities of both blue state and red state voters thought that one party could better handle the economy. Finally, rather than blue state residents favoring Democratic control of the Presidency and Congress

Table 6. Red Versus Blue States: Political Inclinations

	Blue	Red
Bush vote	37%	54%
Democratic self-ID*	40	32
Republican self-ID	25	34
Liberal self-ID	20	11
Conservative self-ID	24	31
Clinton job approval**	71	57
Clinton foreign policy job approval	70	63
Clinton economic job approval	81	74
Democrats better able to handle economy	35	27
Republicans better able to handle economy	24	29
Prefer unified control	24	24

 * Party identifiers include strong and weak identifiers, not independent leaners.
   Liberal identifiers are scale postions 1–2, conservative identifiers 6–7.
** Unless otherwise noted approval figures in the table combine "strongly approve"
   and "approve."

and red state residents favoring Republican control, nearly identical majorities of both prefer divided control.

Table 7 indicates that issue preferences in the two categories of states are surprisingly similar in many instances. Four in ten voters in both red and blue states agree that immigration should decrease, and seven in ten believe that English should be the official language of the United States (the proportion is actually slightly higher in the blue states). Four in ten voters in both categories put environmental considerations above employment considerations, a surprising similarity in light of the image of red states as hotbeds of clear-cutters and blue states as strongholds of tree-huggers. Narrow majorities of voters in both categories support school vouchers, and large majorities support the death penalty. In neither blue nor red states are people wildly in favor of government intervention to ensure fair treatment of African Americans in employment, and virtually identical (small) proportions support racial preferences in hiring.

Again, when we turn to the specific issues that define the culture war, larger differences emerge, but there also are numerous surprises. A solid majority of blue state voters support stricter gun control laws, but so does a narrow majority of red state voters. Support for women's equality is overwhelming and identical among voters in both categories of states. Although regular church attenders are significantly more common in the red states, similar proportions in both red and blue states believe the moral climate of the country has deteriorated

Table 7. Red Versus Blue States: Issue Preferences

	Blue	Red
Immigration should decrease*	41%	43%
Make English official language	70	66
Environment over jobs	43	42
Favor school vouchers	51	54
Favor death penalty	70	77
Government should ensure fair treatment of blacks in empolyment	57	51
Blacks should get preferences in hiring	13	14
Stricter gun control	64	52
Equal women's role**	83	82
Attend church regularly	50	65
Moral climate: much worse	26	30
somewhat worse	25	25
Tolerate others' moral views	62	62
Abortion—always legal	48	37
Allow homosexual adoption	52	40
No gay job discrimination	73	62
Favor gays in military (strongly)	60	44

* Unless otherwise noted, the figures in the table combine "strongly" or "completely agree" responses with "mostly" or "somewhat agree" responses.
**Scale positions 1–2

since 1992, and identical proportions believe that others' moral views should be tolerated. Support for unrestricted abortion is eleven points higher among blue state voters, but such unqualified support falls short of a majority, and more than a third of red state voters offer similarly unqualified support. The 2000 NES is particularly rich in items tapping people's views about matters related to sexual orientation. Here we find differences between blue and red state voters that are statistically significant, though smaller in magnitude than regular consumers of the news might have expected. A narrow majority of blue state voters would allow homosexuals to adopt children, but so would four in ten red state voters. Solid majorities of voters in both categories support laws that would ban employment discrimination against gays. Sixty percent of blue state voters fully support gays in the military, contrasted with 44 percent of red state voters. This 16 percent difference is the single largest disparity we found between the issue preferences of red and blue state voters. Perhaps Bill Clinton picked the one issue in the realm of sexual orientation that was most likely to create controversy. But the evidence supports the alternative hypothesis that Clinton's executive order polarized the electorate: according to Gallup data, popular support for gays in the military rose through the 1980s and had reached 60 percent in 1989 before plummeting in the wake of Clinton's executive order.

All in all, the comparison of blue and red state residents who claim to have voted in 2000 seems consistent with the picture reflecting comparisons of all residents of blue and red states. There are numerous similarities between red and blue state voters, some differences, and a few notable differences, but little that calls to mind the portrait of a culture war between the states.

Chapter 11

Voting, Campaigns, and Elections

11-1

from *The Reasoning Voter*

Samuel L. Popkin

Voters confront difficult choices with incomplete and usually biased informa-
tion. Many voters are not strongly motivated to learn more. Even if they want
to learn more, the information they need is often not available in a convenient
form. In the following essay, Samuel L. Popkin argues that this predicament
does not necessarily lead voters to make irrational decisions. Voters instead
rely on low-cost shortcuts to obtain information and make decisions. Popkin's
analysis can help us to better understand the role of campaigns in voters'
decision-making processes as well as other features of American politics.

IN RECENT DECADES, journalists and reformers have complained with increasing
force about the lack of content in voting and the consequent opportunities for
manipulating the electorate. And yet over the same period academic studies of
voting have begun to expose more and more about the substance of voting decisions and the limits to manipulation of voters. The more we learn about what
voters know, the more we see how campaigns matter in a democracy. And the
more we see, the clearer it becomes that we must change both our critiques of
campaigns and our suggestions for reforming them.

Source: Samuel L. Popkin, *The Reasoning Voter: Communication and Persuasion in Presidential Campaigns,* 2d
ed. (Chicago: University of Chicago Press, 1994), 212–219. Notes appearing in the original have been
deleted.

In this [essay] I summarize my findings about how voters reason and show how some modest changes which follow from my theory could ameliorate some defects of the campaign process.

I have argued . . . that the term *low-information rationality,* or "gut" rationality, best describes the kind of practical reasoning about government and politics in which people actually engage. . . . [L]ow-information reasoning is by no means devoid of substantive content, and is instead a process that economically incorporates learning and information from past experiences, daily life, the media, and political campaigns. . . .

Gut rationality draws on the information shortcuts and rules of thumb that voters use to obtain and evaluate information and to choose among candidates. These information shortcuts and rules of thumb must be considered when evaluating an electorate and considering changes in the electoral system.

How Voters Reason

It is easy to demonstrate that Americans have limited knowledge of basic textbook facts about their government and the political debates of the day. But evaluating citizens only in terms of such factual knowledge is a misleading way to assess their competence as voters.

Because voters use shortcuts to obtain and evaluate information, they are able to store far more data about politics than measurements of their textbook knowledge would suggest. Shortcuts for obtaining information at low cost are numerous. People learn about specific government programs as a by-product of ordinary activities, such as planning for retirement, managing a business, or choosing a college. They obtain economic information from their activities as consumers, from their workplace, and from their friends. They also obtain all sorts of information from the media. Thus they do not need to know which party controls Congress, or the names of their senators, in order to know something about the state of the economy or proposed cuts in Social Security or the controversies over abortion. And they do not need to know where Nicaragua is, or how to describe the Politburo, in order to get information about changes in international tensions which they can relate to proposals for cutting the defense budget.

When direct information is hard to obtain, people will find a proxy for it. They will use a candidate's past political positions to estimate his or her future positions. When they are uncertain about those past positions, they will accept as a proxy information about the candidate's personal demographic characteristics and the groups with which he or she has associated. And since voters find it difficult to gather information about the past competence of politicians who have performed outside their district or state, they will accept campaign competence as a proxy for competence in elected office—as an indication of the political skills needed to handle the issues and problems confronting the government.

Voters use evaluations of personal character as a substitute for information about past demonstrations of political character. They are concerned about personal character and integrity because they generally cannot infer the candidate's true commitments from his past votes, most of which are based on a hard-to-decipher mixture of compromises between ideal positions and practical realities. Evaluating any sort of information for its relevance to politics is a reasoning process, not a reflex projection directly from pocketbook or personal problems to votes. But in making such evaluations, voters use the shortcut of relying on the opinions of others whom they trust and with whom they discuss the news. These opinions can serve as fire alarms that alert them to news deserving more than their minimal attention. As media communities have developed, voters have the additional shortcut of validating their opinions by comparing them with the opinions of political leaders whose positions and reputations people grow to know over time.

People will use simplifying assumptions to evaluate complex information. A common simplifying assumption is that a politician had significant control over an observable result, such as a loss of jobs in the auto industry. This saves people the trouble of finding out which specific actions really caused the result. Another example of a simplifying assumption is the notion that "My enemy's enemy is my friend."

People use party identification as running tallies of past information and shortcuts to storing and encoding their past experiences with political parties. They are able to encode information about social groups prominent in the party, the priorities of the party, and the performance of the party and its president in various policy areas. This generalized information about parties provides "default values" from which voters can assess candidates about whom they have no other information. In keeping generalized tallies by issue area, they avoid the need to know the specifics of every legislative bill.

As a shortcut in assessing a candidate's future performance, without collecting more data, people assemble what data they have about the candidate into a causal narrative or story. Because a story needs a main character, they can create one from their knowledge of people who have traits or characteristics like those of the candidate. This allows them to go beyond the incomplete information they have about a candidate, and to hold together and remember more information than they otherwise could. Because these stories are causal narratives, they allow voters to think about government in causal terms and to evaluate what it will do. Narratives thus help people incorporate their reasoning about government into their projections about candidates; their assumptions "confer political significance on some facts and withhold it from others." They offer people a way to connect personal and political information, to project that information into the future, and to make a complete picture from limited information.

Finally, people use shortcuts when choosing between candidates. When faced with an array of candidates in which some are known well and some are known poorly, and all are known in different and incomparable ways, voters will seek a clear and accessible criterion for comparing them. This usually means looking for the sharpest differences between the candidates which can be related to government performance. Incorporating these differences into narratives allows them to compare the candidates without spending the calculation time and the energy needed to make independent evaluations of each candidate.

Working Attitudes

People do not and cannot use all the information they have at one time. What they use will depend in part on the point of view or frame with which they view the world; attitudes and information are brought to bear if they fit the frame. Of the attitudes and bits of information available, people tend to use those they consider important or those they have used recently. As the changes in voter attitudes entailed by the emergence of new candidates in primaries suggest, attitudes and information will also be brought to the foreground when they fit with what is *expected* in a situation. Our realizations, the thoughts that come clearly to mind, depend in part on what others say about their own thoughts and perceptions.

Thus, as options change, expectations change. If a Democrat were asked in early 1984 what he or she thought of Walter Mondale as a presidential candidate, and the reply was "He'll be all right," that response could be interpreted as coming from a nonthinking voter who was passively following a media report about the thinking of others. But the same response could also be interpreted as an indication of a complex ability to come to grips with the available choices, with issue concerns that cannot be satisfied simultaneously, and with the compromises considered necessary to reach consensus with other people. Similarly, if the same voter were asked a few weeks later what he or she thought about Gary Hart and the reply was "He's just what we need," the response could be interpreted to mean that this voter was simply following the media-reported bandwagon. On the other hand, it could be interpreted to mean that reported changes in public expectations had brought other attitudes and concerns forward in the voter's mind. As this example suggests, the information voters use depends on the reasoning they do, and the reasoning they do depends in part on their expectations. It also indicates that the way in which the content of a voter's response is interpreted depends on a theory about how voters use information and make choices. And I am convinced that any such theory must account for the "working attitudes" of voters—the combinations of feeling, thought, and information they bring to bear when they make their choices at the polls.

Why Campaigns Matter

Changes in government, in society, and in the role of the mass media in politics have made campaigns more important today than they were fifty years ago, when modern studies of them began. Campaign communications make connections between politics and benefits that are of concern to the voter; they offer cognitive focal points, symbolic "smoking guns," and thus make voters more aware of the costs of misperception. Campaigns attempt to achieve a common focus, to make one question and one cleavage paramount in voters' minds. They try to develop a message for a general audience, a call that will reach beyond the "disinterested interest" of the highly attentive, on one hand, and the narrow interests of issue publics, on the other. Each campaign attempts to organize the many cleavages within the electorate by setting the political agenda in the way most favorable to its own candidates. . . .

The spread of education has both broadened and segmented the electorate. Educated voters pay more attention to national and international issues and they are now connected in many more electronic communities—groups of people who have important identifications maintained through media rather than direct, personal contact. There are also today more government programs—Medicare, Social Security, welfare, and farm supports are obvious examples—that have a direct impact on certain groups, which become issue publics. Other issue publics include coalitions organized around policies toward specific countries, such as Israel or Cuba; various conservation and environmental groups; and groups concerned with social issues, such as abortion and gun control. Furthermore, there are now a great many more communications channels with which these people can keep in touch with those outside their immediate neighborhoods or communities. Such extended groups are not new, and modern communications technology is not necessary to mobilize them, as the abolitionist and temperance movements remind us; but the channels to mobilize such groups are more available today, and I believe that the groups they have nurtured are more numerous. When the national political conventions were first telecast in 1952, all three networks showed the same picture at the same time because there was only one national microwave relay; today, with the proliferation of cable systems and satellite relays, television and VCRs can now show over a hundred channels. Furthermore, as channels and options have proliferated, and as commuting time has increased and two-career families become more common, the proportion of people watching mainstream networks and network news is also dropping.

Over the past fifty years, as surveys have become increasingly available to study public opinion, there have been many gains in knowledge about voting and elections. There have also been losses, as national surveys have replaced the detailed community orientation of the original Columbia studies. We know much more about individuals and much less about extended networks, and we have not adequately examined the implications for society and campaigning of the transitions from face-to-face to electronic communities.

Both primaries and the growth of media communication have increased the amount of exposure people get to individual candidates, particularly the quantity of personal information they get about the candidates. This increases the importance of campaigns because it gives voters more opportunities to abandon views based on party default values in favor of views based on candidate information, and also more opportunities to shift from views based on a candidate's record to views based on his or her campaign image. Moreover, as primaries have expanded, parties have had to deal with the additional task of closing ranks after the campaign has pitted factions within the party against each other. Primaries have also changed the meaning of political party conventions. Conventions no longer deliberate and choose candidates; instead, they present the electorate with important cues about the social composition of the candidate's coalition and about the candidate's political history and relations with the rest of the party. The more primaries divide parties, the more cues are needed to reunite parties and remind supporters of losing candidates about their differences with the other party.

The Implications of Shortcuts

Recognizing the role of low-information rationality in voting behavior has important implications for how we measure and study attitudes, how we evaluate the effects of education, and how we evaluate electoral reforms. To begin with, we must acknowledge that the ambivalence, inconsistency, and changes in preference that can be observed among voters are not the result of limited information. They exist because as human beings we can never use all of what we know at any one time. We can be as ambivalent when we have a lot of information and concern as when we have little information and limited concern. Nor do inconsistency, ambivalence, and change result from a lack of education (especially civic education) or a lack of political interest. Ambivalence is simply an immutable fact of life. Economists and psychologists have had to deal with the inconsistencies people demonstrate in cognitive experiments on framing and choice: preference reversals and attitude changes can no longer be attributed to a lack of information, a lack of concern, a lack of attention, low stakes, or the existence of "non-attitudes."

The use of information shortcuts is likewise an inescapable fact of life, and will occur no matter how educated we are, how much information we have, and how much thinking we do. Professionals weighing résumés and past accomplishments against personal interviews, or choosing from an array of diverse objects, have the same problems and use the same shortcuts as voters choosing presidents. What we have called Gresham's law of information—that new and personal information, being easier to use, tends to drive old and impersonal political information out of circulation—applies not only to the inattentive and the uneducated but to all of us. We must therefore stop considering shortcuts pejoratively, as the last refuge of citizens who are uneducated, lacking in the political experience and expertise of their "betters," or cynically content to be freeloaders in our democracy.

Drunkard's Searches and information shortcuts provide an invaluable part of our knowledge and must therefore be considered along with textbook knowledge in evaluating any decision-making process. As Abraham Kaplan has noted, the Drunkard's Search—metaphorically, looking for the lost keys under the nearest streetlight—seems bothersome because of the assumption that we should begin any search rationally, in the most likely places rather than in those that are the best lit and nearest to hand. He adds, "But the joke may be on us. It may be sensible to look first in an unlikely place just *because* 'it's lighter there.' . . . The optimal pattern of search does not simply mirror the pattern of probability density of what we seek. We accept the hypothesis that a thing sought is in a certain place because we remember having seen it there, or because it is usually in places of that kind, or for like reasons. But . . . we look in a certain place for additional reasons: we happen to be in the place already, others are looking elsewhere." At least when people look under the streetlight, they will almost certainly find their keys if they are there; if they look by the car, in the dark, they are far less likely to find them even if they are there.

. . . [W]e should keep in mind the main features about how voters obtain information and reason about their political choices. The Drunkard's Search is an aid to calculation as well as an information shortcut. By telling us where to look, it also tells us how to choose, how to use easily obtained information in making comparisons and choices. As long as this is how we search and choose, people will neither have nor desire all the information about their government that theorists and reformers want them to have.

The faith that increased education would lead to higher levels of textbook knowledge about government, and that this knowledge in turn would enable the electorate to measure up to its role in democratic theory, was misplaced. Education doesn't change *how* we think. Education broadens the voter, because educated voters pay attention to more problems and are more sensitive to connections between their lives and national and international events. However, educated voters still *sample* the news, and they still rely on shortcuts and calculation aids in assessing information, assembling scenarios, and making their choices. Further, an educated, broadened electorate is a more diffuse electorate, an electorate segmented by the very abundance of its concerns. Such an electorate will be harder to form into coalitions. The more divided an electorate, the more time and communication it takes to assemble people around a single cleavage.

Since all citizens sample the news and use shortcuts, they must be judged in part by the quality of the "fire alarms" to which they respond. They must be judged in part by *who* they know and respond to, not simply by *what* they know. Furthermore, this use of fire alarms has an important implication. Since people can only respond to the fire alarms they hear, it matters how the fire alarms to which they are exposed are chosen. If it matters whether the responses to a policy or crisis are mediated electronically by Jesse Jackson and Jesse Helms, or by Bill Bradley and Robert Dole, then attention must be given to how the mediators are chosen by the networks.

11-2

Party Polarization in National Politics: The Electoral Connection

Gary C. Jacobson

A popular notion among political scientists and other observers is that national politicians have become more polarized and partisan because the electorate has become more polarized. The behavior of elected officials merely reflects the differences in the parties' electoral bases. The map of the nation's congressional districts appears to confirm this supposition. It shows that Democrats win in urban areas while Republicans win in suburban and rural areas, suggesting that a cultural divide in the American electorate has produced partisan polarization among elected members of Congress. In this essay, Gary C. Jacobson describes the polarization of the electorate and Congress but observes that the partisan polarization of Congress seems to have emerged before the polarization of the electorate. He argues that leaders in Congress contributed to the polarization of public opinion.

. . . In December 1998 the House of Representatives voted to impeach President Bill Clinton. The vote was radically partisan: all but four Republicans voted for at least one of the four articles of impeachment, and only five Democrats voted for any of them. Grant every member's claim of a conscience vote, and it becomes all the more remarkable that 98 percent of Republican consciences dictated a vote to impeach the president, while 98 percent of Democratic consciences dictated the opposite. The Senate's verdict after the impeachment trial was only slightly less partisan. Every Democrat voted for acquittal, and 91 percent of the Republicans voted for conviction on at least one article.

Research on congressional roll call voting, notably by several authors represented in this volume, makes it clear that party line voting on the impeachment issue was not an aberration, but the culmination of a trend nearly two decades old. The proportion of partisan roll call votes and party loyalty on these votes have been increasing in both houses of Congress since the 1970s, reflecting growing ideological polarization of the congressional parties. To appreciate how dramatically the parties have diverged since the 1970s, look at Figure 1, which displays the

Source: Jon R. Bond and Richard Fleisher, eds., *Polarized Politics: Congress and the President in a Partisan Era* (Washington, D.C.: CQ Press, 2000), 9–30. Notes and bibliographical references appearing in the original have been deleted.

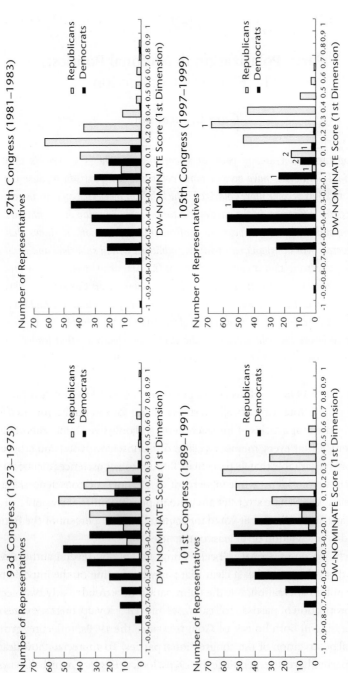

Figure 1. Ideological Positions on Roll-Call Votes

Source: Compiled by the author from Poole and Rosenthal dw-nominate Scores (http://voteview.gsia.cmu.edu.dwnl.htm).

Note: The entries are frequency distributions of Republican and Democratic members of Congress on a liberal-conservative dimension based on non-unanimous roll call votes in which 1 represents the most conservative position and −1 represents the most liberal. Each bar indicates the number of representatives falling into the specified range. For example, in the 105th Congress, sixty-two Republicans had scores between .03 and .04 on the scale.

Figure 2. Difference in Median and Mean dw-nominate Scores of Republicans and Democrats, 83d through 105th Congresses

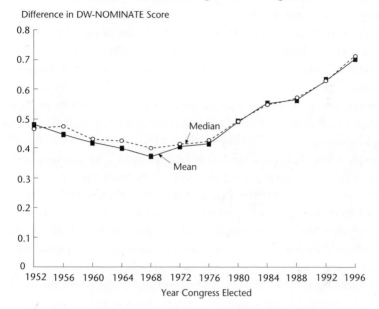

Note: The entries are the difference between the mean and the median positions on the dw-nominate scale of House Republicans and Democrats in the specified Congress. The larger the difference, the farther apart the two parties are ideologically.

distribution of House members' scores on a common measure of political ideology in selected Congresses spanning the past three decades. These scores, known as dw-nominate scores, are calculated from all non-unanimous roll call votes cast from the 80th Congress through the 105th Congress. Each member's pattern of roll call votes locates him or her on a liberal-conservative dimension ranging from −1.0 (most liberal) to 1.0 (most conservative), allowing us to compare the distribution of positions along the dimension taken by Democrats and Republicans in different Congresses.

In the 93d Congress, the ideological locations of House Democrats and Republicans overlapped across the middle half of the scale, and the gap between the two parties' modal locations was comparatively small. In the 97th Congress, the overlap was a bit less extensive but still sizable. By the 101st Congress, the parties had become noticeably more polarized. The 105th Congress, which voted on Clinton's impeachment, was the most sharply polarized of all, with not a single Republican falling below zero on the scale, and only four Democrats scoring above zero.

Trends in partisan polarization in the House over a somewhat longer period are summarized in Figure 2, which displays the difference in median and mean dw-nominate scores of House Republicans and Democrats in the Congress immediately following each presidential election from 1952 through 1996. Note particularly how dramatically the gap between the parties' average ideological locations grew in the 1990s; in the 105th Congress, the parties' medians and means were more than 0.7 points apart on this 2-point scale. According to Keith Poole and Howard Rosenthal, the first dw-nominate dimension captures, in addition to liberal-conservative ideology, the primary cleavage that distinguishes the two parties, and hence the scores also serve as measures of party loyalty. From this perspective, party unity on the House impeachment vote was simply a manifestation of a broader pattern of partisan polarization highlighted by the nearly complete disappearance of conservative Democrats and liberal Republicans (although a few moderates remain in both parties). The numbers above the columns in the last panel of Figure 1 show how many members bolted their party on impeachment. Note that all but two of the nine who defected on impeachment belong to the small set of members who still have dw-nominate scores adjacent to or overlapping those of members of the opposing party.

The Republicans persisted in their attempts to impeach and remove Clinton even though every one of the myriad national polls taken from the eruption of the Monica Lewinsky scandal in January 1998 through the end of the trial in February 1999 found the public opposed to impeachment and conviction, typically by margins of about two to one. Yet the public, like Congress, was from start to finish sharply polarized on the issue. In poll after poll, a solid majority of self-identified Republicans favored Clinton's impeachment and removal, while more than 80 percent of self-identified Democrats remained opposed. In the end, 68 percent of Republicans wanted the Senate to convict and remove Clinton, while only 30 percent favored acquittal; among Democrats, 89 percent favored acquittal, while only 10 percent preferred conviction. Members of Congress may have voted their consciences, but their consciences were wonderfully in tune with the preferences of their core supporters. Congressional Republicans acted against the manifest preferences of a majority of Americans on a highly salient issue, and they may yet pay for it in the 2000 election by losing the House and—much less likely—the Senate. But they voted the way the majority of Republican voters wanted them to.

Partisan voting on impeachment thus reflected, albeit in an exaggerated and skewed fashion, sharply divided electoral constituencies. It also reflected the power of majority party leaders in the contemporary House to enforce discipline, notably on the adoption of a rule governing the impeachment bill that did not permit consideration of a censure resolution. Moderate Republicans were left with no alternative short of impeachment. These two forces—the emergence of distinct and increasingly homogenous electoral coalitions in both parties and, in consequence, the greater willingness of members to submit to party discipline—are the chief explanations that have been offered for the broader rise in party unity and ideological divergence since the 1970s. Respect for the power of the electoral connection usually concedes causal priority to electoral change. Yet voters can respond only to the options presented by the parties' candidates. If legislative parties become more dissimilar and unified as their respective electoral coalitions become more dissimilar and homogenous, it is also true that the choices offered by more polarized, unified parties encourage polarized electoral responses.

My goal in this chapter is to review the electoral changes that both underlie and reflect the more unified and divergent congressional parties of the 1990s. The story contains few surprises, but fresh observations from the most recent elections point uniformly to a near-term future that is, if anything, substantially more conducive to partisan coherence and division, intensifying conflicts not only within the legislature, but especially—under divided government—between the president and Congress.

Most of the analysis is presented graphically, for this is the most efficient way to summarize and appreciate the various interrelated trends. I begin with some observations on changes in partisanship and voting behavior since the 1970s. Next, I show how the electoral coalitions of House Democrats and Republicans have consequently diverged. The circle is completed by an examination of how patterns of roll call voting have become increasingly predictable from electoral decisions, fulfilling one major condition for responsible party government. An ironic effect of these changes may have been to make divided government even more popular, for the parties in government have polarized much more sharply than have party identifiers in the electorate.

The Growth of Partisan Coherence in the Electorate

The consensus explanation for the rise in party cohesion in Congress since the 1970s is party realignment in the South. The short version is that the civil rights revolution, particularly the Voting Rights Act of 1965, brought southern blacks into the electorate as Democrats, while moving conservative whites to abandon their ancestral allegiance to the Democratic Party in favor of the ideologically more compatible Republicans. The movement of jobs and people to the South also contributed to larger numbers of Republican voters, who gradually replaced conservative Democrats with conservative Republicans in southern House and Senate seats. The constituencies that elected the remaining Democrats became more like Democratic constituencies elsewhere, so the roll call voting of southern Democrats became more like the roll call voting of Democrats from other regions. The southern realignment left both congressional parties with more

Figure 3. The Rise of the Republican South, 1952–1998

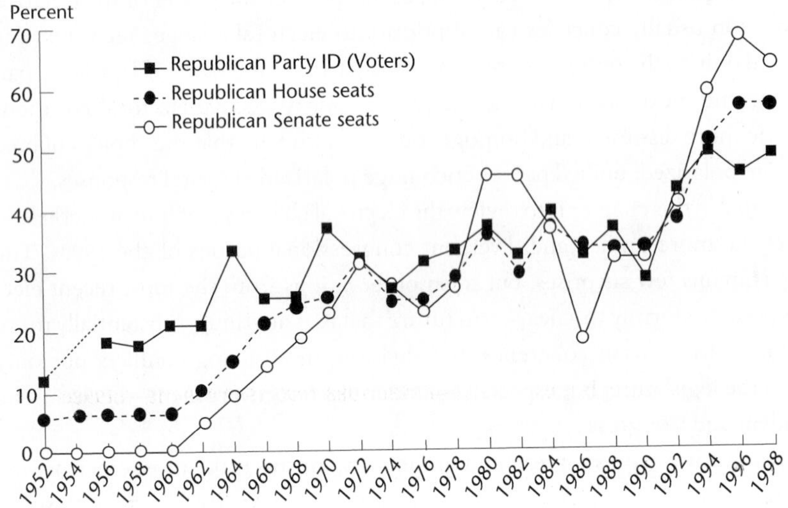

Source: National Election Studies.

politically homogeneous electoral coalitions, reducing internal disagreements and making stronger party leadership tolerable.

This analysis is certainly correct as far as it goes. The realignment of southern political loyalties and electoral habits has been thoroughly documented. Figure 3 summarizes the principal trends. As the proportion of Republicans among major party identifiers has risen, so has the share of southern House and Senate seats won by Republican candidates. Starting from almost nothing in the 1950s, Republicans now enjoy parity with the Democrats among voters and hold solid majorities of southern House and Senate seats.

Realignment in the South contributed to the increasing ideological homogeneity of the parties, but it is by no means the whole story. Other forces have also necessarily been at work, for links between ideology and party identification have grown stronger outside the South as well. Since 1972 the National Election Studies (NES) have asked respondents to place themselves on a 7-point ideological scale ranging from extremely liberal to extremely conservative. On average, nearly 80 percent of respondents who say they voted in House elections are able to locate their position on the scale. As Figure 4 shows, tau-b correlations between the voters' positions on the liberal-conservative scale and the NES's 7-point party identification scale have grown noticeably stronger since 1972 outside the South as well as within. Like other measurements of correlation, the tau-b statistic takes values from –1 (a perfect negative relationship) through 0 (no relationship) to 1 (a perfect positive relationship). In the analysis presented here

Figure 4. Correlation between Party Identification and Ideology of House Voters, 1972–1998

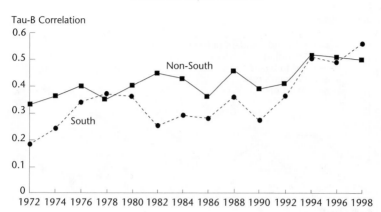

and in Figure 5, the higher the tau-b correlation, the stronger the positive relationship between party identification and the other variable of interest. The increase was steeper for southern voters, and by 1994 they had become indistinguishable on this score from voters elsewhere.

A similar pattern of growing partisan coherence within the electorate is evident in correlations between voters' party identification and positions on several of the NES's issue scales displayed in Figure 5. On every issue—ranging from the government's economic role, to race, to women's role in society, to abortion policy—the overall trend is upward, with tau-b correlations reaching their highest levels on four of the five scales in 1998. Notice that although economic issue positions are normally most strongly related to partisanship—reflecting the venerable New Deal cleavage—the steepest increases have occurred on social issues. For example, in 1980 opinions on abortion were unrelated to party identification; now we observe a substantial correlation. In 1980 only 30 percent of voters who opposed abortion under all circumstances identified themselves as Republicans; by 1998, 71 percent did so.

More generally, in 1972 the voter's positions on the various scales—ideology, jobs, aid to blacks, and women's role—predicted party identification (Republican, independent, or Democrat) with only 62 percent accuracy; in 1998 the same four variables predicted party identification with 74 percent accuracy. Clearly, citizens now sort themselves into the appropriate party (given their ideological leanings and positions on issues) a good deal more consistently than they did in the 1970s, with the largest increases in consistency occurring in the 1990s. Not surprisingly, partisan evaluations of presidential candidates, presidents, and the parties themselves have become more divergent as well.

Figure 5. Correlation between Party Identification and Issue Positions,
House Voters, 1972–1998

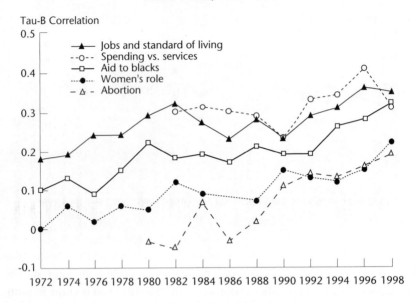

Tau-B Correlation

The Revival of Electoral Consistency

Both the southern realignment and growing ideological coherence of electoral coalitions have contributed to greater consistency in voting behavior. Among individual voters, party loyalty has risen and ticket splitting has diminished since the 1970s. Figures 6 and 7 display the pertinent data. Party loyalty in congressional elections declined from the 1950s through the 1970s but has subsequently rebounded, recovering about two-thirds of the decline. Party loyalty in presidential elections is trickier to measure, because some years have featured prominent independent or third party candidacies (specifically 1968, 1980, 1992, and 1996), while the rest have not. But even with Ross Perot drawing votes from both parties in 1996, 84 percent of partisans voted for their party's presidential candidate, a higher proportion than in any election from 1952 through 1980. If we consider as defectors only those who voted for the other *major* party's candidate, the rate of defection in both 1992 and 1996 was only 10 percent, the lowest of any election in the NES time series (1988 had the next lowest rate).

The trend in ticket splitting—voting for candidates of different parties on the same ballot—appears, not accidentally, as the inverse of the trend in party loyalty. Ticket splitting was relatively infrequent in the 1950s, grew more common through the 1970s, and since has declined to the levels last seen in the early 1960s.

Figure 6. Party Loyalty in Congressional Elections, 1952–1998

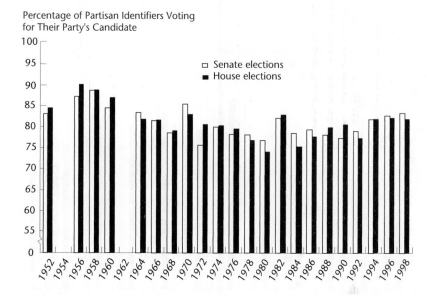

The declines since the 1970s in partisan defections and ticket splitting are probably even greater than these NES data indicate, because both phenomena have
been artificially inflated since 1978 by changes in the wording and administration
of the vote question that produce an overreport of votes for House incumbents.

An important consequence of greater party loyalty and decreased ticket splitting is that aggregate electoral results have become more consistent across offices.
For example, the simple correlation between a party's district-level House and
presidential vote shares has risen sharply from its low point in 1972, as Figure 8
indicates. Both the decrease between 1952 and 1972 and the increase since 1972
are steepest for southern districts, but the same U-shaped trend occurs in districts
outside the South as well. By 1996 the association between House and presidential voting had rebounded to a level last seen in the 1950s (.77 in the South, .85 elsewhere, and .83 overall). Similarly, a district's presidential vote predicted which
party's candidate would win the House seat with greater accuracy in the 1990s
than at any time since the 1950s. The trend toward electoral disintegration across
offices I documented a decade ago has clearly gone into reverse since then.

Diverging Electoral Constituencies

The growth in partisan coherence, consistency, and loyalty among voters has
made the two parties' respective electoral constituencies—that is, the voters who

Figure 7. Ticket Splitting, 1952–1998

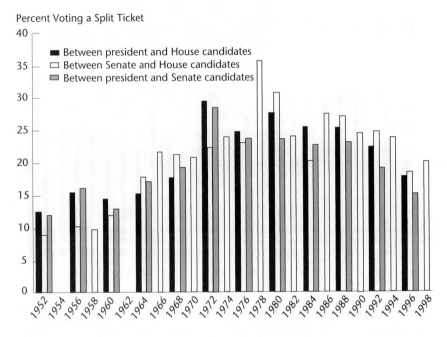

Percent Voting a Split Ticket

supported the party's winning candidates—politically more homogeneous and more dissimilar. It has also given the president and congressional majorities more divergent electoral constituencies when the branches are divided between the parties.

To begin with an elementary but telling example, according to NES surveys, 48 percent of the respondents who voted for members of the Democratic House majority in 1972 also voted for Richard Nixon; 36 percent of the voters supporting the Democratic House winners voted for Ronald Reagan in 1984; but only 27 percent of the voters supporting members of the Republican House majority voted for Clinton in 1996. The comparatively small proportion of shared electoral constituents was surely one source of Clinton's difficulties with the Republican congressional majority in a divided government.

More generally, the respective parties' electoral constituencies have diverged ideologically since the 1970s, with the parties' most active supporters moving the farthest apart. I measure differences in the ideological makeup of electoral constituencies by subtracting the mean ideological self-placement of NES respondents who voted for one set of winning candidates from the mean for respondents who voted for another set of winning candidates. Ideological divisions among activist constituents are gauged by repeating the analysis for respondents who reported engaging in at least two political acts in addition to voting during

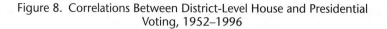

Figure 8. Correlations Between District-Level House and Presidential Voting, 1952–1996

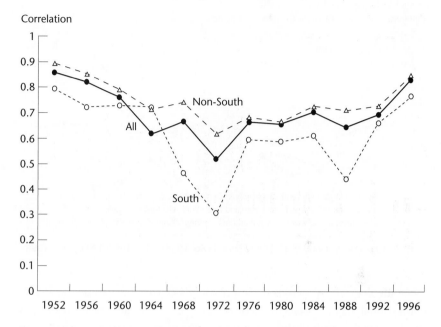

the campaign. Figure 9 displays the changes in the ideological distinctiveness of the electoral constituencies of House Republicans and Democrats and of southern and nonsouthern Democrats since 1972.

In the 1970s the ideological differences between the two parties' electoral constituencies were modest and no wider than the gap between southern and nonsouthern Democrats' electoral constituencies. By the 1990s the difference between the parties' electoral constituencies had more than doubled, to about 1.2 points on the 7-point scale, and the Democrats' regional divergence had entirely disappeared. Realignment in the South again explains only part of this change, for the gap between Republican and Democratic constituencies also grew (from 0.7 to 1.1 points) outside the South. Note also that the mean ideological difference between the parties' most active electoral constituents widened even more, nearly doubling to about two points on the scale.

Figure 10 presents the equivalent data for Senate electoral constituencies, except that entries are calculated from the three surveys up to and including the year indicated on the chart, so that data from voters electing the entire Senate membership are used to calculate in each observation. The same pattern of ideological polarization between the parties' respective electoral and activist constituencies appears, although somewhat muted, reflecting the greater heterogeneity of the Senate's larger electorates.

Figure 9. Difference in Mean Ideological Self-Placement of House Activist and Electoral Constituencies, 1972–1998

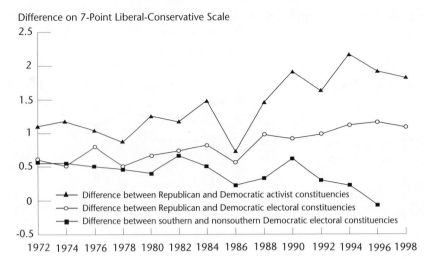

Difference on 7-Point Liberal-Conservative Scale

—▲— Difference between Republican and Democratic activist constituencies
—○— Difference between Republican and Democratic electoral constituencies
—■— Difference between southern and nonsouthern Democratic electoral constituencies

1972 1974 1976 1978 1980 1982 1984 1986 1988 1990 1992 1994 1996 1998

The ideological gap between the president's electoral constituency and the congressional majority's electoral constituency under conditions of divided government also has doubled. In 1972 Nixon voters were on average only 0.7 points more conservative than voters for the House Democrats elected that year. In 1996 the House Republicans' electoral constituency was 1.4 points more conservative than Bill Clinton's electoral constituency. The gap between the most active segment of each electoral constituency widened even more, from 1.3 points in 1972 to 2.2 points in 1996. An equivalent analysis of self-placement on issue positions tells the same story; on every issue dimension examined in Figure 5, the congressional parties' respective electoral coalitions are farther apart in the 1990s than they were at the beginning of the time series.

A discussion of changes in electoral coalitions would not be complete without confirming how profoundly the southern realignment has affected the demographic composition of the remaining Democratic coalition. Although it is not news, it is still worth highlighting just how dependent successful southern Democratic candidates are on African American voters. Figure 11 presents the pertinent data. For representatives, the entry is simply the proportion of all votes for the winning Democrat that were cast by black voters in each election year. For senators, it is the African American proportion of all votes for winning southern Democrats in the trio of elections culminating in the year listed. Therefore, the Senate entries indicate the proportion of African Americans in the electoral constituencies of all southern senators in the Congress following the specified election. Blacks were once a negligible part of the electoral constituencies of

Figure 10. Difference in Mean Ideological Self-Placement of Senate Activist and Electoral Constituencies, 1976–1998

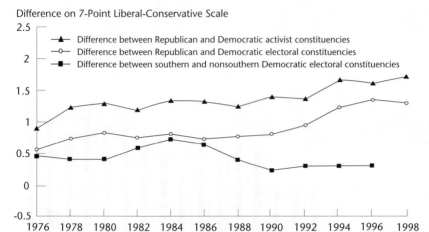

Difference on 7-Point Liberal-Conservative Scale

southern Democrats in Congress. Now they supply more than one-third of their votes. Add to this the fact that southern whites who continue to identify themselves as Democrats now share the socioeconomic profile of white Democrats elsewhere, and the nearly complete disappearance of conservative southern Democrats in Congress is no mystery at all.

Chicken or Egg?

Evidence from examination of the electorate, then, is fully consistent with the standard argument that partisan polarization in Congress reflects electoral changes that have left the parties with more homogeneous and more dissimilar electoral coalitions. When the focus of analysis is Congress, electoral change seems to be the independent variable: changes in roll call voting reflect changes in electoral coalitions. When the focus is on elections, however, it becomes apparent that causality works at least as strongly in the opposite direction: voters sort themselves out politically by responding to the alternatives represented by the two parties.

Realignment in the South *followed* the national Democratic Party's decision to champion civil rights for African Americans and the Republican Party's choice of Sen. Barry Goldwater, who voted against the Civil Rights Act of 1964, as its standard-bearer that year. Partisan divisions on the abortion issue surfaced first in Congress, then in the electorate. Electorates diverged ideologically after the parties had diverged ideologically; the divisions in Congress and among activists

Figure 11. Share of Votes for Southern Democratic Representatives and Senators Provided by African American Voters, 1956–1996

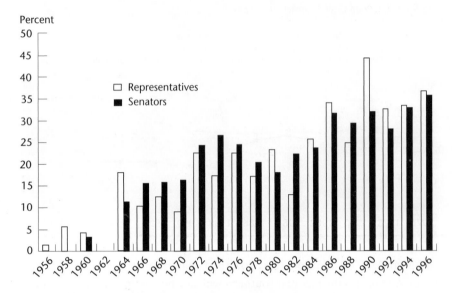

during and after the Reagan years left the two parties with more distinctive images, making it easier for voters to recognize their appropriate ideological home. Conservatives moved into the Republican ranks, while liberals remained Democrats. Notice that most of the trends among voters identified in the figures show their largest movement in the 1990s, *after* the firming up of congressional party lines in the 1980s.

This is not to say, however, that members of Congress simply follow their own ideological fancies, leaving voters no choice but to line up accordingly. As vote-seeking politicians, they naturally anticipate voters' potential responses and so are constrained by them. The Republican "southern strategy" emerged because Republican presidential candidates sensed an opportunity to win converts among conservative white southerners. Ambitious Republicans adopted conservative positions on social issues to attract voters alienated by the Democrats' tolerance of nontraditional life styles but indifferent at best to Republican economic policies. Democrats emphasized "choice" on abortion because they recognized its appeal to well-educated, affluent voters who might otherwise think of themselves as Republicans. In the budget wars of the past two decades, Democrats have vigorously defended middle class entitlements such as Social Security and Medicare, while Republicans have championed tax cuts because each position has a large popular constituency. In adopting positions, then, politicians are guided by the opportunities and constraints presented by configurations of public opinion on

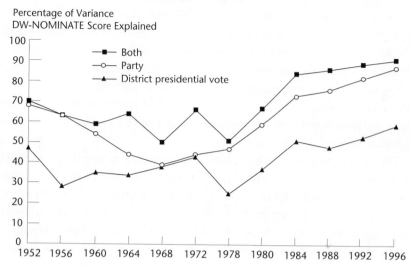

Figure 12. Variance in Roll Call Ideology Explained by District Presidential Vote and Party, 1952–1996

political issues. Party polarization in Congress depended on the expectation that voters would reward, or at least not punish, voting with one's party's majority.

In reality, therefore, the relationship between mass and elite partisan consistency is inherently interactive. Between the 1970s and the 1990s, changes in electoral and congressional politics reinforced one another, encouraging greater partisan consistency and cohesion in both. One important result is that the linkage between citizens' decisions on election day and the actions of the winners once they assume office has become much tighter. Indeed, election results predict congressional roll call voting on issues that fall along the primary liberal-conservative dimension accurately enough to meet one of the fundamental conditions for responsible party government. This is evident when we regress dw-nominate scores on two variables, party and the district-level presidential vote, and observe how much of the variance they explain. The presidential vote stands here as a serviceable if somewhat imprecise measure of district ideology: the higher the Republican share of the vote in any given election, the more conservative the district. The results are summarized in Figure 12, which tracks the proportion of variance in first-dimension dw-nominate scores explained by party and presidential vote, individually and in combination, in the Congresses immediately following each presidential election since 1952.

As we would expect from the information in Figures 1 and 2, the capacity of party to account for roll call voting on the liberal-conservative dimension declined from the 1950s to the 1970s but since then has risen steeply. The predictive accuracy of the district-level presidential vote remained lower than that of party through most of the period, reaching a low point in 1976 (a consequence of Jimmy Carter's initial appeal to conservative southerners), but then rising to its highest levels in the time series during the 1990s. The *relative* contribution of district ideology to explaining House members' positions on the liberal-conservative dimension tends to be greatest in the 1960s and 1970s, when party's contribution is lowest. Between 1976 and 1996, both variables become increasingly accurate predictors of congressional voting, to the point where by the 105th Congress, party and presidential vote account for a remarkable 91.5 percent of the variance in representatives' dw-nominate scores.

The voting patterns of House members, then, are increasingly predictable from elementary electoral variables: the party of the winner and the district's ideology as reflected in its presidential leanings (with these two variables themselves correlated in 1996 at the highest level since the 1950s). With this development, voters have a much clearer idea of how their collective choices in national elections will translate into congressional action on national issues. Because party labels are so much more predictive of congressional behavior, voters have good reason to use them more consistently to guide voting decisions.

The same circumstances that make the party label such an informative cue also deepen the dilemma faced by moderate voters, however. And, despite the growing divergence between the parties' respective electoral coalitions, most Americans still cluster in the middle of the ideological spectrum. In surveys from the 1990s, about 60 percent of House voters place themselves in one of the middle three positions on the 7-point liberal-conservative scale, down only modestly from about 68 percent in the 1970s. Polarization in Congress has outstripped polarization in the electorate, so the proportion of citizens placing themselves between the two parties has not diminished. Therefore, although the 1998 NES survey found party line voting to be near its highest level in thirty years, it also found that

- only 45 percent of voters preferred the continuation of the two-party system to elections without party labels (29 percent) or new parties to challenge the Republicans and Democrats (26 percent);
- 84 percent thought that the phrase "too involved in partisan politics" described Congress quite well (40 percent) or extremely well (44 percent);
- 56 percent preferred control of the presidency and Congress to be split between the parties, 24 percent preferred one party to control both institutions, and the rest did not care.

With elite polarization outstripping mass polarization, the advent of a central component of responsible party government—unified parties with distinct policy positions—may have had the paradoxical effect of strengthening support for divided government. The more divergent the parties' modal ideological positions, the more reason the remaining centrist voters have to welcome the moderating effect of divided government. But under divided government, the more divergent the parties, the more rancorous the conflict between the president and Congress, and rancorous political conflict is welcomed by almost no one.

The Clinton impeachment put the bitterest of partisan conflicts on full display, and the public did not find it a pretty sight. After the Senate acquitted Clinton, members of Congress, particularly on the Republican side, began looking for ways to soften the image of rabid partisanship that the impeachment had imparted. The trends examined here suggest that any success they achieve is destined to be temporary. Party divisions in Congress have increasingly sturdy electoral roots, particularly among activists, as well as strong institutional reinforcement from the congressional parties. Both parties' holds on their respective branches is tenuous, guaranteeing intense electoral competition across the board in 2000. The party that achieves the upper hand has an excellent chance of winning control of the whole federal government; if the Republicans can win the presidency, they are almost certain to capture undivided national power for the first time in nearly half a century. With so much at stake, no partisan political advantage is likely to be left unexploited. The only constraint on undiluted partisanship is the fear of losing ground by *looking* too partisan; if impeachment politics is any indication, it is not much of a constraint. All signs point to a new partisan era in national politics that is likely to continue for the foreseeable future.

11-3

from *Air Wars*

Darrell M. West

Complaints about negative advertising, manipulation of the voters, and ever-mounting costs are heard in all national, and most statewide, election campaigns. Many voters complain of being misled by campaign advertising and say that they do not receive adequate information about the candidates. Darrell West describes the strategies and mechanics of television advertising in political campaigns. West's essay reviews the criticisms of modern advertising campaigns and considers corrective measures that journalists and citizens might take.

IT WAS ONE of the most polarizing elections in American history. In the first presidential election since the September 11, 2001 terrorist attacks on New York City and Washington, D.C., Republican president George W. Bush used images of firefighters carrying victims away from the World Trade Center to explain how he was a "tested" leader who could provide steady leadership in turbulent times. At the same time, he characterized his opponent, Democrat John Kerry, as a "flip-flopper" who was unprincipled and untrustworthy. The campaign produced a commercial showing Senator Kerry wind-surfing, while a narrator asked, "In which direction would John Kerry lead? Kerry voted for the Iraq war, opposed it, supported it, and now opposes it again. . . . John Kerry: Whichever way the wind blows."

Kerry, meanwhile, attacked Bush's economic record and complained about Bush's foreign policy. One advertisement said "only Herbert Hoover had a worse record on jobs," and argued that "it's time for a new direction." Another spot showed a picture of Saudi Crown Prince Abdullah and suggested that "the Saudi royal family gets special favors, while our gas prices sky-rocket."

Groups from Swift Boat Veterans for Truth and MoveOn.org also joined in the television air wars. In a hard-hitting spot financed by the Swift Boat Veterans, a group of Vietnam War veterans challenged Kerry's Vietnam service record and

Source: Darrell M. West, from "Overview of Ads" and "Advertising and Democratic Elections" in *Air Wars*, by Darrell West (CQ Press: 2005), 1–23, 165–177. Notes appearing in the original have been deleted.

concluded "John Kerry cannot be trusted." Within days, MoveOn.org broadcast a sharp rebuttal saying, "George Bush used his father to get into the National Guard, and when the chips were down, went missing. Now he's allowing false advertising that attacks John Kerry, a man who asked to go to Vietnam and served with dignity and heroism." In the end, President Bush was reelected and Republicans increased their margin of control in the United States House and Senate. It was a dramatic conclusion to a race that attracted extraordinary press and public interest.

As illustrated throughout the campaign, advertisements are a major component of political races. In recent presidential campaigns, campaign spots accounted for around 60 percent of total fall expenditures. Commercials are used to shape citizens' impressions and affect news coverage. As such, they represent a major strategic tool for campaigners. However, not all spots produce the same result. Some ads work whereas others do not. To determine which spots are effective, analysts must look at production techniques, ad buys (the frequency and location of ad broadcasting), opposition responses, news coverage, and citizens' predispositions.

The History of Ads

From the earliest days of the Republic, communications devices have been essential to political campaigns. In 1828, handbills distributed by Andrew Jackson's supporters portrayed John Quincy Adams as "driving off with a horsewhip a crippled old soldier who dared to speak to him, to ask an alms." A circular distributed by Adams's forces, meanwhile, attacked Jackson for "ordering other executions, massacring Indians, stabbing a Samuel Jackson in the back, murdering one soldier who disobeyed his commands, and hanging three Indians."

The method, though perhaps not the tone, of communicating with the electorate has changed dramatically since 1828. Handbills have virtually disappeared. Radio became the most popular vehicle in the 1920s and 1930s. After World War II, television emerged as the advertising medium of choice for political candidates. And now, in the twenty-first century, the media marketplace has fragmented into a bewildering variety of communications channels from cable television and talk radio to late-night entertainment shows and the World Wide Web. A new Internet-based lexicon has appeared that distinguishes banner ads (large boxes that span the top of a Web site), interstitial ads (spots that flash while a Web site is being loaded), pop-up ads (spots that appear after a Web site is loaded), transactional ads (spots that allow viewers to make a purchase or request information), and rich media ads (spots that have audio, video, or motion embedded within them). Somehow, in this multifaceted situation, candidates must figure out how to reach voters who will decide key election contests.

The 1952 presidential campaign was the first one to feature television ads. In that year, each party ran television and print ads evoking World War II memories. Republicans, in an effort to support General Dwight Eisenhower and break two decades of Democratic control, reminded voters in a *New York Times* ad that "one party rule made slaves out of the German people until Hitler was conquered by Ike." Not to be outdone, Democratic ads informed voters that "General Hindenburg, the professional soldier and national hero, [was] also ignorant of domestic and political affairs. . . . The net result was his appointment of Adolf Hitler as Chancellor."

In the 1960s, television spots highlighted differences in candidates' personal traits. The 1964 presidential campaign with Lyndon Johnson and Barry Goldwater was one of the most negative races since the advent of television. Johnson's campaign characterized Goldwater as an extremist not to be trusted with America's future. One five-minute ad, "Confession of a Republican," proclaimed, "This man scares me. . . . So many men with strange ideas are working for Goldwater." Johnson's "Daisy" ad made a similar point in a more graphic manner. Along with speeches and news coverage, the visual image of a mushroom cloud rising behind a little girl picking daisies in a meadow helped raise doubts about Goldwater's fitness for office in the nuclear age, even though a firestorm of protest forced the ad off the air after only one showing.

Ads in the 1970s and 1980s took advantage of public fear about the economy. When the United States started to experience the twin ills of inflation and unemployment, a phenomenon that led experts to coin a new word, *stagflation*, campaign commercials emphasized economic themes. In 1980, Republican challenger Ronald Reagan effectively used ads to criticize economic performance under President Jimmy Carter. When the economy came roaring back in 1984, Reagan's serene "Morning in America" ad communicated the simple message that prosperity abounded and the United States was at peace.

The 1988 presidential contest was the zenith of attack politics in the post–World War II period. This campaign illustrated the powerful ability of ads to alter impressions of a candidate who was not well known nationally. Early in the summer of 1988, Massachusetts governor Michael Dukakis held a 17-percentage-point lead over his Republican rival, then Vice President George Bush. Women preferred Dukakis over Bush by a large margin, and the governor was doing well among blacks, elderly citizens, and Democrats who previously had supported Reagan.

Meanwhile, Republicans were test marketing new advertising material. Over Memorial Day weekend in Paramus, New Jersey, Bush aides Jim Baker, Lee

Atwater, Roger Ailes, Robert Teeter, and Nicholas Brady stood behind a one-way mirror observing a small group of so-called Reagan Democrats. Information concerning Willie Horton, a convicted black man who—while on furlough from a Massachusetts prison—brutally raped a white woman, was being presented, and the audience was quite disturbed. Atwater later boasted to party operatives, "By the time this election is over, Willie Horton will be a household name." Bush went on to beat Dukakis 53 percent to 46 percent.

The 1992 campaign represented the dangers of becoming overly reliant on attack ads and the power of thirty-minute "infomercials" by Reform Party candidate Ross Perot. Throughout the race, Bush used ads to attack Clinton's character and his record as governor of Arkansas. But unlike in his 1988 race, Bush did not prevail. Between the poor economy, the backlash that developed against Bush's advertising attacks, and Clinton's quick responses to criticisms, Clinton beat Bush 43 percent to 38 percent. Perot finished in third place with 19 percent, the best showing for a third-party candidate since Theodore Roosevelt in 1912.

In 1996, President Clinton coasted to reelection through the help of ads broadcast more than a year before the election. With the advice of political strategist Dick Morris, Clinton defied the conventional wisdom arguing against early advertising. He ran ads both on television and over the Internet that positioned himself as the bulwark against GOP extremism. Linking Republican nominee Robert Dole to unpopular House Speaker Newt Gingrich, Clinton portrayed the Republican Party as insensitive to women, children, and minorities and not to be trusted with important issues such as Social Security, Medicare, and education.

In 2000, Al Gore and George W. Bush ran in the closest presidential election in decades. Featuring cautious advertising that played to undecided voters, both candidates, along with outside groups, ran commercials challenging the integrity and experience of each other. Bush emphasized education reform, whereas Gore focused on health care and Social Security. One Bush ad popularly known as "RATS" featured the first use of a subliminal message in presidential campaign history when the word *RATS* was superimposed over a few frames criticizing Gore's prescription drug plan. The election even saw a remake of the infamous 1964 "Daisy" ad ("Daisy II") when a group of Texans paid for an ad with an image of a girl plucking petals off a daisy while an announcer complained that because of Clinton-Gore deals with "communist Red China" in return for campaign contributions, Democrats had compromised the country's security and made the nation vulnerable to Chinese missile attacks.

Throughout these elections, ads were a valuable lens on the inner workings of the campaign. Candidates revealed in their commercials crucial aspects of their vision, leadership style, and substantive positions. As stated by Elizabeth Kolbert, then a news reporter for the *New York Times,* "Every advertising dollar spent represents a clue to a campaign's deepest hopes and a potential revelation about its priorities."

Principles of Advertising

Strategists use the principles of stereotyping, association, demonization, and code words to influence the electorate. *Stereotypes* refer to a common portrait or an oversimplified judgment that people hold toward groups or sets of individuals. For example, Republicans are often portrayed as strong on defense, but not very compassionate toward poor people. Democrats are viewed as caring and compassionate toward the downtrodden, but overly eager to raise taxes. Because television ads are brief, generally no more than 30 seconds, campaigners evoke stereotypes knowing they appeal to voters' prejudices and commonly held views.

However, ads cannot create perceptions that do not already exist in people's minds. There must be a kernel of truth in the stereotype for these types of appeals to be effective. If people do not already think that college professors are absent-minded, nurses are caring, or car salespeople are sleazy, it is hard for election ads to play to these kinds of sentiments.

Association is based on linking a candidate or cause to some other idea or person. Politicians love to connect themselves to popular objects that are widely esteemed, while tying their opponents to things that are unpopular, controversial, or divisive. Flags, patriotism, and prominent celebrities are examples of objects with which candidates surround themselves. In contrast, opponents are pictured with unpopular causes or organizations or cast in a light that bonds them to unfavorable objects.

During the Cold War, it was popular to portray leftist-leaning candidates as communist sympathizers having allegiance to foreign powers. When Kerry received the Democratic nomination, opponents sought to tie him to controversial Vietnam War protester Jane Fonda. The Swift Boat Veterans for Truth ran an ad entitled "Friends" that asserted, "even before Jane Fonda went to Hanoi to meet with the enemy and mock America, John Kerry secretly met with enemy leaders in Paris. . . . Jane Fonda apologized for her activities, but John Kerry refuses to."

To gain greater credibility, politicians like to associate themselves with popular people such as sports heroes, astronauts, or Hollywood celebrities. These individuals come from outside the political world and often have a great deal of popularity and respect from average people. By associating with them and winning their endorsements, politicians attempt to piggy-back themselves on the high credibility these individuals have among voters in general.

Demonization is the process of turning an opponent into an evil being or satanic figure. Wartime enemies are condemned as murderers, terrorists, or barbarians. Political opponents are portrayed as extremists out of touch with the mainstream or guilty of immoral behavior. Adversaries are identified with policy actions that are widely condemned or seen as socially destructive.

An entry in an anti-Bush ad contest sponsored by the MoveOn.org Voter Fund intermingled pictures of Adolf Hitler and Bush making speeches. In a clear effort to demonize the sitting president, the spot concluded with the tagline, "What were war crimes in 1945 is foreign policy in 2003."

Meanwhile, commercials sponsored by the Progress for America Voter Fund, a conservative political action committee, attacked Kerry by showing pictures of Osama bin Laden and September 11 hijacker Mohamed Atta. The unmistakable message in these spots was that Kerry was not to be trusted with defending America's security.

As with the other principles, demonizing the opposition is a tactic that must be used carefully. There must be some believability in the specific appeal for the ad to have credibility. One cannot simply make charges that are unsubstantiated or so far out of bounds as to exceed voters' ability to internalize the charges. Demonization must bear some resemblance to the facts for this tactic to influence citizens.

Code words are shorthand communications devices that play on common stereotypes and connotations associated with particular kinds of language. Even in the limited space of thirty seconds, campaigns can use short messages to communicate broader messages to the public. Many people feel that thirty seconds is too short a period to convey much in the way of substantive themes. But during election campaigns, single words or expressions can take on enormous importance.

For example, in the 1960s and 1970s, Republicans used the phrase "law and order" to play to voter conceptions that Democrats were permissive on crime, race, and morality, whereas Republicans could be counted on to protect the social order. Democrats were paired with images and audio voice-overs of urban riots and social protests to convey complex political messages.

Democrats, meanwhile, have used a similar tactic in regard to the code word of *right wing*. Following the surprise GOP takeover of the House and Senate in 1994 and Newt Gingrich's ascension to the Speakership, Democrats played to voter stereotypes about Republicans being uncaring and insensitive. Using examples of extreme rhetoric or policy proposals that sought to slow the rate of increase in spending on various federal programs, Democrats have associated GOP candidates with unsympathetic and extremist images. Throughout the country in 2000, House Democrats used the phrase *right-wing extremists* to refer to their Republican counterparts.

Code words are powerful communications devices because they allow voters to associate particular messages with the code word. One of the most frequently used code words has been *liberal* by Republicans. In 1988, George Bush called Democratic candidate Dukakis a liberal thirty-one times in his speeches. The message got through to voters. Whereas 31 percent in May 1988 believed Dukakis was liberal, the figure rose to 46 percent by September 1988.

In 1992, Bush's use of the term *liberal* rose to sixty-two times. Similar to 1988, the word took on a number of negative meanings, such as being fiscally irresponsible, soft on crime, and dangerously out of touch with the American public. This approach allowed Bush to condemn Clinton with the single word of liberal without having to voice more detailed descriptions of the candidate's positions.

By 1996, the country's airwaves were filled with ads using the *L*-word. Dole ran ads condemning Clinton as a tax-and-spend liberal and as someone whose failed policies were liberal. In one speech in September 1996, Dole used the word fourteen times. Republican congressional candidates used the same appeal all over the country. Ads financed by the Republican National Committee criticized Democratic House and Senate candidates as "liberals," "ultra-liberals," "super-liberals," "unbelievably liberal," "embarrassingly liberal," "foolishly liberal," and "taxingly liberal."

Because of the country's changed political climate after the abortive Republican Revolution of downsizing government, though, the use of the word liberal as an epithet did not resonate with voters. As one voter in a focus group put it, the term liberal meant helping people. Others felt that "liberal is having an open mind."

This view was supported in a 1996 CBS News/*New York Times* survey asking people what they thought of when they heard someone described as liberal or conservative, respectively. The most common responses for liberal were open minded (14 percent), free spending (8 percent), high degree of government involvement (7 percent), helps people (5 percent), and pro-handouts (5 percent). The most common responses for conservative were fiscally responsible (17 percent), closed minded (10 percent), careful (8 percent), against change (7 percent), and low degree of government involvement (6 percent).

In the 2004 campaign, however, use of the *liberal* epithet returned to the campaign trail. President George W. Bush criticized Kerry for advocating a return to "massive new government agencies" with power over health care. Through an ad showing a map of a complex federal bureaucracy, Bush charged that Kerry's health care program would cause "rationing" and that "Washington bureaucrats, not your doctor, [would] make final decisions on your health." Not to be outdone, the Republican National Committee sent a mass mailing to voters in Arkansas and West Virginia accusing "liberals" of seeking to ban the Bible in order to promote policies on gay marriage.

With conservative disgust over the decision of the government in France not to support the war in Iraq, the 2004 election introduced the code word *French* to political discourse. Not only did some lawmakers seek to rename French fries as "freedom fries," Bush's Commerce Secretary, Don Evans, accused Kerry of looking "French" because he spoke the language, was cosmopolitan, and had French relatives. The National Rifle Association also associated Kerry with France by using a mailing with a French poodle wearing a Kerry campaign sweater and having a bow in its hair to condemn the Democrat's record.

As explained by Françoise Meltzer, a humanities professor at the University of Chicago, in the 2004 electoral context, "French really means un-American." It was a striking contrast to earlier periods when France was viewed favorably in the United States because it had aided the American Revolution and given America the gift of the Statue of Liberty.

How Ads Are Put Together

Production techniques for commercials have improved dramatically since the 1950s. Early ads were rudimentary by contemporary standards. Political spots often took the form of footage from press conferences or testimonials from prominent citizens. Many were of the "talking head" variety in which the candidate (or his or her supporter) looked straight into the camera and spoke for thirty or sixty seconds without any editing.

Contemporary ads, in contrast, are visually enticing. Technological advances in television and on the Internet allow ad producers to use colorful images and sophisticated editing techniques to make spots more compelling. Images can be spliced together to link visual images with one another. Animated images visually transpose one person into another in a split-second using a technique called "morphing." As we see in the next sections, catchy visuals, music, and color capture viewer attention and convey particular political messages in a variety of ways.

Visual Images

The visual aspect of advertising is the most important part of commercials. According to the old adage, a picture is worth a thousand words. Contemporary ads use graphic visual imagery to grab the public's attention and convey a message. Whereas traditional research has focused on the spoken content of ads to determine ways of conveying messages, modern analysts study both audio and visual aspects of advertising.

Candidates often attempt to undermine political opponents by associating them with unfavorable visual images. A 1990 campaign ad by Sen. Bennett Johnston, D-La., against his opponent, state representative David Duke, showed pictures of Duke addressing a Ku Klux Klan rally in the presence of a burning cross to make his point that Duke was an extremist who should not be elected to a seat in the U.S. Senate.

A similar phenomenon happened in 1996. Taking advantage of House Speaker Newt Gingrich's unpopularity, Democrats across the United States broadcast ads showing pictures of Gingrich side-by-side with Bob Dole and House and Senate Republican candidates. The message was clear: A vote for the Republican Dole was a vote for Gingrich.

In 2000, George W. Bush positioned himself as a "compassionate conservative" and frequently appeared at election rallies with retired General Colin Powell, a popular African American leader who later became Bush's Secretary of State. Bush surrounded himself in photo opportunities and ads with women, minorities, and children to convey the idea he was a different kind of Republican from Gingrich. For his part, Gore relied on pictures of him with his wife, Tipper, to communicate the idea that he was a candidate with firm values and a strong marriage. It was a way to distinguish himself from the personal scandals of the Clinton era.

In 2004, terrorism was mentioned in 13 percent of all the ads run after Labor Day. Some advertisements mentioned Osama bin Laden by name or showed pictures of him. One Republican Senate candidate in Wisconsin even invoked the visual image of a burning World Trade Center on September 11, 2001, to charge that "Russ Feingold voted against the Patriot Act and the Department of Homeland Security."

The visual aspect of campaign advertising is the one that has the most impact on viewers. The reason is simple—people remember visual images longer than they do spoken words. Images also have the advantage of creating an emotional response much more powerful than the spoken word.

CBS news reporter Lesley Stahl tells the story of a hard-hitting evening news piece broadcast on Reagan's presidency in 1984. The story claimed that Reagan had done certain things, such as cut the budget for the elderly, that were contrary to what he said he had done. Accompanying the story was a series of pleasant visual images of Reagan "basking in a sea of flag-waving supporters, beaming beneath red-white-and-blue balloons floating skyward, sharing concerns with farmers in a field." After the story aired, Stahl was surprised with a favorable telephone call from a top Reagan assistant. Asked why he liked the story, given her harsh words, the Reagan advisor explained she had given the White House four and a half minutes of positive pictures of President Reagan: "They don't hear what you are saying if the pictures are saying something different."

Visual Text

Visual text is a print message appearing on-screen, generally in big, bold letters. Printed messages on screen grab viewers' attention and tell them to pay attention to an ad. As an example, Ross Perot's 1992 ads used visual text scrolling up the screen to persuade the American public to vote for him (see Appendix for texts of memorable ads in recent elections). Spots for Clinton in 1996 used big, splashy text on screen to make the political point that Republicans wanted to "CUT MEDICARE." Dole sought to characterize Clinton as "LIBERAL" and "UNTRUSTWORTHY." In 2000, Democratic ads often noted that Texas ranked "50TH" in family health care, and Republican ads complained that Gore was guilty of "EXAGGERATIONS." Advertisers have found that memory of a message is greatly enhanced by combining visual text with spoken words and descriptive images.

Music and Sounds

Music sets the tone for the ad. Just as party hosts use upbeat music to accompany the festivities or educational institutions play "Pomp and Circumstance" to set the scene for a graduation ceremony, campaign ads use music to convey the mood of a particular commercial.

Uplifting ads use cheery music to make people feel good about a candidate. For example, the 1984 campaign featured an independently produced ad called "I'm Proud To Be an American," which used music from country singer Lee Greenwood's song by that same name. The music played over scenes of Reagan, the American flag, and cheerful scenes of happy Americans. It conveyed the message that things were good in America and people should vote for Reagan.

Conversely, somber or ominous music in an ad seeks subliminally to undermine support for the opponent. In George Bush's "Revolving Door" ad in 1988, dark and threatening music accompanied scenes of prisoners walking through a revolving door while an announcer attacked Dukakis's record on crime. The sounds of drums, the footsteps of guards on metal stairs, and threatening voices were integral to the ad's message that voters should reject Dukakis in the November elections because he was soft on crime.

Color

Color communicates vivid messages in ads. Media consultants use bright colors to associate their candidates with a positive image and grayish or black and white colors to associate opponents with a negative image. In 2000, for example, the NAACP-sponsored spot about the dragging death of James Byrd was broadcast in black and white to make the point that something dramatically different and calamitous had taken place and viewers should pay close attention.

A 1996 Dole commercial took a color videotape clip in which Clinton said if he had it to do over again, he would inhale marijuana, and rebroadcast the image in black and white to make Clinton look sinister.

The 1992 Bush campaign developed an ad called "Arkansas Record" that featured a vulture looking out over a dark and barren landscape to make its point that Clinton had poorly governed Arkansas. That year, Bush also used a low-quality grayish photographic negative of Clinton from an April 20, 1992, *Time* magazine cover to exhort voters to defeat the Arkansas governor in November. The cover with the photographic negative of Clinton was entitled, "Why Voters Don't Trust Clinton." Bush's ad juxtaposed a nice color image of himself to convey the message that voters should not vote for Clinton.

The opposite technique (going from black and white to color images) was used by Gore in his 2000 ad called "Veteran." It opened with a black and white photo of a youthful Gore in Vietnam, then shifted to color frames of Gore with his wife, Tipper.

Editing

Editing determines the sequencing and pacing of an ad. The *sequencing* of ad images refers to how images in one scene are related to following scenes. For example, the 1984 Reagan ad, "Morning in America," showed images of Reagan interspersed with scenes of Americans at work and a country at peace. The sequencing linked Reagan with the popular themes of peace and prosperity. These images were accompanied by music that enhanced the emotional impact of the ad.

The *pacing* of an ad refers to whether the visual images flow smoothly or abruptly from scene to scene. Abrupt cuts from image to image create a jarring look that tells the viewer something bad is appearing before them. Such cuts are commonly used to convey negative feelings in attack ads.

Audio Voice-Overs

Through an off-screen announcer, audio voice-overs provide a road map that knits together visual scenes. Campaign ads are composed of different pictures that convey particular points. The announcer guides viewers through these scenes to clearly communicate the message of the ad.

Typically, attack ads use male announcers to deliver blistering criticisms, but Dole made history in 1996 by using a female announcer to condemn Clinton's "failed liberal drug policies." The use of a woman for the voice-over was designed to soften any potential backlash from going on the attack and to appeal to women who were concerned about drug use and moral permissiveness in American society.

However, in 2000, both George W. Bush and Gore reverted to the historical pattern and relied most frequently on male announcers for the audio components of their ads. One exception was a Bush ad called "Compare" that used a female announcer to criticize Gore's prescription drug plan. Female narrators are used for health care ads because market research reveals that women make the preponderance of health care decisions in American households. Another exception took place in 2004 during a Bush ad known as "Wolves." This spot used the image of a pack of wolves to argue that America was surrounded by dangerous enemies. It used a female announcer to take the edge off of what was a hard-hitting attack on the opposition.

How Ads Are Financed

The financing of campaign ads has changed dramatically in recent decades. In the post-Watergate reforms of the 1970s, candidates generally paid for the bulk of advertisements out of so-called hard money contributions. These were gifts given directly to candidate organizations for voter persuasion. Campaigners would use these funds to produce and broadcast ads that were put out on the airwaves under the candidate's direct sponsorship. Both the Republican and Democrat nominees broadcast ads designed to frame the contest and set the agenda of political dialogue.

Over time, though, a series of loopholes appeared that transformed campaign ad financing. Interest groups and party organizations began to exploit a loophole that allowed unlimited amounts of money (so-called soft money gifts) to be spent on voter education and get-out-the-vote efforts. Originally created by the 1976 *Buckley v. Valeo* Supreme Court case on the post-Watergate reforms, this loophole was designed to strengthen political parties and outside groups, and allow them to mobilize and educate supporters. Donors could give whatever money they desired without being limited to the $1,000 per individual and $5,000 per organization rules for hard money contributions.

This loophole reached its zenith in the 1990s when President Bill Clinton used large amounts of soft money contributions to the Democratic National Committee (DNC) to run ads extolling his virtues and lambasting those of the Republican opposition. Rather than using the money for get-out-the-vote or party-building activities, the DNC ran commercials that were virtually indistinguishable from hard money-financed candidate spots. Republicans did the same thing through the Republican National Committee to criticize Clinton and campaign against Democratic House and Senate candidates.

The ensuing controversy over these funding practices (and a post-election investigation into Clinton's campaign spending) eventually led to enactment of the 2002 Bipartisan Campaign Reform Act (BCRA) sponsored by Senators John McCain, R-Ariz., and Russell Feingold, D-Wis. Among its key principles were the outlawing of soft money gifts at the national party level (although state party organizations still could accept these contributions), an increase in individual contributions to $2,000 per candidate per cycle, and a requirement that candidates personally appear in ads saying they paid for their commercials and took responsibility for the ad contents.

Groups still could run issue ads that talked about specific policies. For example, they could say that Republicans were harming poor people or that Democrats loved to raise taxes. But ads broadcast by these organizations in the 60 days before a general election could not engage in electoral advocacy. Groups could not criticize the policy stances of a specific federal candidate without registering as a political action committee and being subject to disclosure requirements.

The result of this legislation is a hodge-podge of rules concerning ad financing. Candidates can use hard money gifts to run advertisements, as can national party organizations. State party groups can rely on soft money contributions for political advertisements. Interest groups can spend unlimited amounts of money on issue ads without any disclosure of spending or contributors, unless in the last 60 days before a general election. At that point in the campaign, they can run ads criticizing federal candidates, but they have to disclose who paid for the spots.

Unaffected by the 2002 reform legislation are radio ads, direct mail, phone calls, and Internet advertisements. Officials focused on television ads because they form the bulk of political communications and are the technology that critics most worry about in terms of misleading voters. By restraining the most worrisome television maladies, the hope is that this reform will improve the content and tone of civic discourse. However, as discussed later in this volume, there is little evidence from 2004 that the new rules made candidate appeals any more civil.

The Impact of Ads on Voters

Ads are fascinating not only because of the manner in which they are put together but also because of their ability to influence voters. People are not equally susceptible to the media, and political observers have tried to find out how media power actually operates.

Consultants judge the effectiveness of ads by the ultimate results—who wins. This type of test, however, is never possible to complete until after the election. It leads invariably to the immutable law of advertising: Winners have great ads and losers do not.

As an alternative, journalists evaluate ads by asking voters to indicate whether commercials influenced them. When asked directly whether television commercials helped them decide how to vote, most voters say ads did not influence them. For example, the results of a Media Studies Center survey placed ads at the bottom of the heap in terms of possible information sources. Whereas 45 percent of voters felt they learned a lot from debates, 32 percent cited newspaper stories, and 30 percent pointed to television news stories, just 5 percent believed they learned a lot from political ads. When asked directly about ads in a CBS News/*New York Times* survey, only 11 percent reported that any presidential candidate's ads had helped them decide how to vote.

But this is not a meaningful way of looking at advertising. Such responses undoubtedly reflect an unwillingness to admit that external agents have any effect. Many people firmly believe that they make up their minds independently of the campaign. Much in the same way teenagers do not like to concede parental influence, few voters are willing to admit they are influenced by television.

In studying campaign ads, one needs to emphasize the overall context in which people make decisions. The same ad can have very different consequences depending on the manner in which an opponent responds, the way a journalist reports the ad, the number of times the spot is broadcast, or the predispositions of the viewer.

A vivid example is found in Kathleen Hall Jamieson's study of the 1988 presidential campaign. The effectiveness of George Bush's "Revolving Door" ad on Dukakis's crime record was enhanced by the majority culture's fears about black men raping white women and by earlier news stories that had sensationalized Horton's crime spree. Bush did not have to mention Horton in this ad for viewers to make the connection between Dukakis and heinous crimes.

This idea is central to understanding campaign advertisements. Commercials cannot be explored in isolation from candidate behavior and the general flow of media information. An analysis of thirty-second spots requires a keen awareness of the structure of electoral competition, strategic candidate behavior, media coverage, and public opinion. A variety of long- and short-term factors go into voter decision-making. In terms of long-term forces, things such as party loyalties, ideological predispositions, the rules of the game, and socioeconomic status linked to education, income, sex, race, and region affect how people interpret ads and judge the candidates. Meanwhile, there are a variety of short-term factors during the campaign that affect people. These include things such as how the media cover ads, what reporters say about the candidates, candidate strategies, and debate performance.

Generally, the better known candidates are, the less ads are able to sway voter impressions. In a situation where voters have firm feelings about campaigners based on long-term forces such as party and ideology, it is difficult for any of the short-term forces to make a difference. However, if the candidate is not well known or there is volatility in the political climate, news, ads, and debates can make a substantial difference in the election outcome.

The Structure of Electoral Competition

The structure of the electoral process defines the general opportunities available to candidates. The most important development at the presidential level has been the dramatic change in how convention delegates are selected. Once controlled by party leaders in small-scale caucus settings thought to be immune from media influence, nominations have become open and lengthy affairs significantly shaped by the mass media. The percentage of delegates to national nominating conventions selected through primaries increased significantly after 1968. From the 1920s to the 1960s, about 40 percent of delegates were selected in primaries, with the remainder chosen in caucus settings dominated by party leaders. However, after rule changes set in motion by the McGovern-Fraser Commission of the Democratic Party following the 1968 election, about 70 percent of convention delegates in each party were chosen directly by voters in presidential primaries.

Nominating reforms have required candidates to appeal directly to voters for support and in the eyes of many observers have altered the character of the electoral system. No longer are candidates dependent on negotiations with a handful of party leaders. Instead, they must demonstrate public appeal and run campaigns that win media attention. Campaigns have become longer and have come to depend increasingly on television as a means of attracting public support.

Some campaigns get far more attention than others. Citizens are more interested in and knowledgeable about presidential general election campaigns than nominating contests. Although variation exists among individual contests depending on the candidates involved, nomination races typically generate less citizen interest and less media coverage. It also is more common for candidates who are not well known to run in the primaries.

These differences in the visibility of the candidates and the extent of media coverage are important for the study of television advertisements. Because less visible races feature candidates who are not well known, ad effects on citizens' opinions of the candidates often are significant. Past research has demonstrated that television's impact is strongest when viewers have weakly formulated views.

It is easier to run ads against candidates who are not well known because there is no preexisting attitudinal profile to shield that individual against critical claims.

In addition, candidate behavior is conditioned by the rules of the game. Presidential elections in the United States are determined by a state-based electoral college. Candidates seek to assemble a majority of electoral college votes by winning targeted states. This electoral structure has enormous implications for advertising strategies. Most candidates do not run a fifty-state strategy. Instead, because many states tend to vote consistently over time, they focus on the fifteen to twenty states that swing back and forth between the two major parties.

Daron Shaw has undertaken an innovative study of electoral college strategies and found that candidates apportion their time and advertising dollars in systematic ways. According to his study, strategies center on five categories: base Republican, marginal Republican, battleground state, marginal Democratic, and base Democratic. Factors such as electoral history, size of the state's electoral vote, and current competitiveness dictate how campaigners allocate their resources. These decisions tend to be stable across presidential elections. This demonstrates the way in which electoral rules affect candidate strategies.

Advertising and Strategic Politicians

Early research downplayed the power of ads to mold public images of candidates. The pioneering study was Thomas Patterson and Robert McClure's innovative effort, *The Unseeing Eye.* Looking at both content and effects, they sought to dispel the concerns of the public and journalists regarding political commercials. Using a model of psychological reasoning based on voters' knowledge about candidates, these researchers examined whether television ads enabled voters to learn more about the policy views or personal qualities of campaigners. They found that voters learned more about the issues from the candidates' ads than from the news, because ads addressed issues whereas the news was dominated by coverage of the "horse race"—who is ahead at a given time. Popular concerns about the strategic dangers of ads were minimized as uninformed hand wringing.

The study's results also fit with the general view among election experts of the 1960s and 1970s that political strategies were not very decisive in determining election results. Researchers in the era following the 1960 publication of Campbell et al.'s classic work on voting behavior, *The American Voter,* proclaimed long-term forces, such as party identification, as the most important. Although a few scholars disputed this interpretation, many argued that short-term factors related to media coverage, candidates' advertisements, and campaign spending simply were not crucial to vote choice. For example, Harold Mendelsohn and

Irving Crespi claimed in 1970 that the "injection of high doses of political information during the frenetic periods of national campaigns does very little to alter the deeply rooted, tightly held political attitudes of most voters." Even the later emergence of models based on pocketbook considerations did little to change this interpretation. Paid ads were thought to have limited capacity to shape citizens' impressions of economic performance.

Recent decades, though, have begun to see changes in previous viewpoints. Candidates have started to use commercials more aggressively, reporters have devoted more attention to paid advertising, and ad techniques have grown more sophisticated. It now is thought that voters' assessments can change based on short-term information and that candidates have the power to sway undecided voters who wait until the closing weeks of the campaign to make up their minds. Evidence from elections around the United States suggests that ads are successful in helping candidates develop impressions of themselves.

This is particularly true when campaigners are unknown or in multicandidate nominating contests. The more strategic options that are available with the larger number of candidates involved, the more potential there is for the campaign to affect citizen judgments. One study of the New Hampshire primary by Lynn Vavreck, Constantine Spiliotes, and Linda Fowler, for example, found that a variety of campaign activities affected voters' recognition of and favorability toward specific candidates.

Furthermore, candidates no longer hold a monopoly on advertising. Political parties, interest groups, and even private individuals run commercials around election time. In fact, there are discernible differences in the percentage of attack ads run by different sources. The most negative messages involved issue ads run by interest groups. Fifty-six percent of those ads were attack oriented, compared with 20 percent of candidate-sponsored advertisements.

Because paid ads are so important in contemporary campaigns, candidates take the development of advertising strategies quite seriously. Commercials often are pretested through focus groups or public opinion surveys. Themes as well as styles of presentation are tried out before likely voters. What messages are most appealing? When and how often should particular ads be aired? Who should be targeted? How should ads best convey information?

The number of times an ad is broadcast is one of the most important strategic decisions during the campaign. Professional ad buyers specialize in picking time slots and television shows that are advantageous for particular candidates. Whereas a candidate interested in appealing to senior citizens may air ads repeatedly during television shows catering to the elderly, youth-oriented politicians may run spots on Fox Network or MTV, and minority candidates may advertise on Black Entertainment Television.

The content and timing of ads are crucial for candidates because of their link to overall success. Campaigns have become a blitz of competing ads, quick responses, and counter-responses. Ads have become serial in nature, with each ad building thematically on previous spots. Election campaigns feature strategic interactions that are as important as the individual ads themselves.

In the fast-changing dynamics of election campaigns, decisions to advance or delay particular messages can be quite important. Quick-response strategies require candidates to respond immediately when negative ads appear or political conditions are favorable. Candidates often play off each other's ads in an effort to gain the advantage with voters.

Advertising and the News Media

One of the developments of the contemporary period has been coverage of political advertising by reporters. Network news executive William Small described this as the most important news trend of recent years: "Commercials are now expected as part of news stories." Many news outlets have even launched "ad watch" features. These segments, aired during the news and discussed in newspaper articles, present the ad, along with commentary on its accuracy and effectiveness. The most effective ads are those whose basic message is reinforced by the news media.

Scholars traditionally have distinguished the free from the paid media. Free media meant reports from newspapers, magazines, radio, and television that were not billed to candidates. The paid media encompassed commercials purchased by the candidate on behalf of the campaign effort. The two avenues of communications were thought to be independent in terms of effects on viewers because of the way viewers saw them.

But the increase in news coverage of advertising has blurred or even eliminated this earlier division between free and paid media. People who separate the effects of these communications channels need to recognize how intertwined the free and paid media have become. It is now quite common for network news programs to rebroadcast ads that are entertaining, provocative, or controversial. Even entertainment shows are filled with references to contemporary politics. Journalists and entertainers have begun to evaluate the effects of campaign commercials. It has become clear that the free media provide significant audiences for television ads.

Ads that are broadcast for free during the news or discussed in major newspapers have several advantages over those aired purely as commercials. One strength is that viewers traditionally have trusted the news media—at least in comparison with paid ads—for fairness and objectivity. William McGuire has shown that the credibility of the source is one determinant of whether the message is believed. The high credibility of the media gives ads aired during the news an important advantage over those seen as plain ads. Roger Ailes explained it this way: "You get a 30 or 40 percent bump out of [an ad] by getting it on the news. You get more viewers, you get credibility, you get it in a framework."

The 2004 presidential election introduced a new category of advertisements—*phantom ads*. These are commercials that are produced and distributed to journalists but not actually broadcast. Journalists complained that Kerry released half a dozen spots on topics such as health care, taxes, and the Iraq war that were never aired. This made the ads "video news releases purporting to be substantial paid advertising," according to reporters.

Commercials in the news guarantee campaigners a large audience and free air time. Opinion polls have documented that nearly two thirds of Americans cite television as their primary source of news. This is particularly true for what is referred to as the "inadvertent audience"—those who are least interested in politics and among the most volatile in their opinions.

But there can be disadvantages to having an ad aired during a newscast. When an ad is described as unfair to the opposition, media coverage undermines the sponsor's message. The advantages of airing an ad during the news can also be lost if reporters challenge the ad's factual accuracy.

During the 2004 presidential election, though, journalists tried in vain to keep up with the onslaught of negative and misleading appeals. Both candidates pushed the envelope of factual inaccuracies. For example, Kerry accused the Bush White House of having a secret plan to reintroduce a military draft and of wanting to privatize Social Security. Bush, meanwhile, complained Kerry's health care program would create new federal bureaucracies and that Kerry thought terrorism was a nuisance like prostitution and gambling.

Reporters wrote stories criticizing the candidates for misleading and inaccurate claims, but the sheer volume of ad expenditures and campaign trail rhetoric overwhelmed press oversight. Journalists simply could not compete with the hundreds of times ads were broadcast by the candidates. Campaigners were very adroit at communicating directly with the public and ignoring critical press stories about their advertisements.

Changes in Public Opinion

Public opinion and voting behavior have undergone significant changes that are relevant to advertising. Voters are less trusting of government officials today than they were in the past. Whereas 23 percent in 1958 agreed that you cannot trust the government to do what is right most of the time, 84 percent were untrusting at the turn of the twenty-first century. A significant bloc of voters does not identify with either one of the major parties. These citizens are often the kinds of voters who swing back and forth between the parties.

The independence of American voters and the volatility in American politics unleashed by corporate downsizing and the end of the Cold War have uprooted some parts of citizen attitudes. People's impressions of short-term political events can be fluid, and the issues or leadership qualities seen as most important at any given time can change.

Each of these developments has altered the tenor of electoral campaigns and led to extensive efforts to appeal to undecided voters. Writing in the 1830s, Alexis de Tocqueville worried that the great masses would make "hasty judgments" based on the "charlatans of every sort [who] so well understand the secret of pleasing them." The prominence today of an open electoral system filled with mistrusting voters and fast-paced ads has done nothing to alleviate this concern. . . .

Democratic Expectations

Few aspects of democracy have been discussed over the course of U.S. history as much as the quality of information provided during the election process. Candidates are expected to address the subjects at stake in a given election and to indicate where they stand in regard to those matters. In fact, this information allows voters to hold leaders accountable. Failure to provide suitable material undermines the representative basis of American democracy.

As an intermediary institution, the media are expected to devote enough attention to candidates' character attributes and to the issues to help voters bridge the gaps left by candidates' communications. Not many people directly experience election campaigns. Voters are dependent on the media to help them interpret political realities. When reporters provide the type of information that educates citizens regarding the choices facing them, the election process is significantly enhanced.

However, there is disagreement over exactly how detailed the information from candidates and the media should be. The classical model of democracy calls for specific, issue-oriented material. Candidates are expected to have detailed positions on the major issues facing the country and to communicate these views clearly to voters. Issue-based voting models as well as textbook descriptions of U.S. elections emphasize the policy aspects of campaigns.

Other scholars, though, have argued that popular control can be achieved through other approaches. For example, the *party-responsibility model* uses partisanship as the means of accountability. Parties foster representation because they encapsulate general lines of thinking about major policy positions. According to this model, voters can make substantive judgments about candidates based purely on party labels. In a similar way, retrospective evaluations have become widely accepted as a means of popular control. Advocates of this system argue that the candidate's approach to issues alone is not an appropriate test because voters can be sophisticated and rational without engaging in issue-based voting. As long as leaders can be held accountable for the broad direction of government performance, democratic tenets are satisfied.

Still others have argued that knowledge about the character of potential leaders is vital to democratic elections. Elections are seen as a means of evaluating the judgment of leaders who will do the deliberating in a representative democracy. According to this perspective, assessments about leadership qualities and character are quite relevant to voters' decision making.

The emergence of thirty-second ads and short sound bites as the primary means of political communication represents a potential challenge to each of these models. Because classical democratic theory places a premium on detailed policy information, the chief danger under this model is deception and distortion by the candidates regarding their positions on issues. Ads that mislead viewers or distort an opponent's record are particularly dangerous. Numerous campaigners have used ads to create impressions of themselves that turned out to be inaccurate (including Lyndon Johnson as the peace candidate in 1964 and George Bush as the "no new taxes" man of 1988). The same logic applies to models centered on leaders' judgment. The primary danger of ads in this view is their potential to alter or reinforce citizen opinions about personal traits. In 1984, for example, Gary Hart was remarkably successful at getting people to see Walter Mondale, who had formidable Washington experience and interest group support, in a negative light as just another old-style politician currying favor with special interests.

But these are not the only consequences from advertisements. The party-responsibility model assumes that long-term party identification will protect ad viewers against excesses by candidates. Yet even this model recognizes that party attachments have shifted in recent years and that new arenas based on intraparty nominating contests have arisen. These settings are precisely where ads achieve their greatest impact. The combination of unknown candidates, volatile preferences, and shared party labels gives ads enormous influence. The emergence of independent candidates, such as Ross Perot and Ralph Nader, has put the party-responsibility model in even greater danger in regard to general elections, because party ties are less decisive in a three-way race. In these settings, advertising takes on great strategic significance. The ability to win with a plurality of the vote encourages candidates to use commercials to appeal to narrow pockets of voters.

The *pocketbook-voting model* also raises important questions. This approach appears on the surface to be the least vulnerable to ads. Because vote choice is presumed to be based on citizens' views about the economy, which are in turn rooted in people's personal experiences, ads would not seem too influential on electoral decisions. But a closer inspection reveals that even this model requires voters to assign blame for unsatisfactory performance and to assess candidates' capabilities to deal with economic matters. In 1992, for example, Bill Clinton—primarily through advertising—was able to boost public perceptions about his ability to improve the economy and to show people that he was a caring individual.

Attributions of responsibility are particularly open to media influence. Through techniques based on priming and defusing, ads can elevate or lower particular standards of evaluation. In fact, during eras of scarce resources, elections often rest on how well candidates play the blame game. Therefore, although traditional voting models diagnose the problem of advertisements quite differently, each one identifies particular dangers regarding the quality of information presented to voters and the ability of citizens to engage in informed decision making.

The Risk of Manipulation

The concerns expressed about U.S. elections did not originate with television. Writers have long complained about the dangers of outside influences on voters. Nineteenth-century reformers, for example, fought outright bribery in an era when cash payoffs to citizens in exchange for votes were quite common. The extension of voting rights in that century precipitated wild debates regarding the impact of external agents: Opponents of expanded suffrage claimed that newly enfranchised women would be unduly influenced by their husbands and that Catholic immigrants would become pawns of the pope!

Several features of democratic systems have been thought to reduce the danger of external manipulation. Foremost is vigorous electoral competition. In a two-party system in which there is equity of funding and each candidate has a reasonable opportunity to get his or her message out to the general public, voters should have enough information to protect themselves from ad distortion and manipulation. The assumption is that even though voters may not pay close attention to politics, they can garner enough material through party labels, issue information, views about the economy, or impressions of candidate qualities to reach informed decisions.

Widespread acceptance of the democratic culture by political elites is seen as providing a sufficient guarantee of fair and open competition. Self-regulation, it is said, weakens the threat from candidates and helps to ensure that election appeals are made fairly. At the same time, a variety of intermediary institutions supposedly protect citizens from overly ambitious campaigners. People can express opinions and hold leaders accountable through organizations representing their political perspectives. Parties and interest groups have been seen as the most important links in modern theories of democracy. Because these organizations facilitate the joint activity of citizens having common points of view, they are a means of bridging the gap between citizens and leaders.

The problem with this view of democracy is that its proponents have been strangely quiet about key aspects of leadership behavior. In the rush to reconcile less than optimistic views of citizens' behavior with hopes for democracy, observers have lost sight of the crucial responsibilities of candidates in the election process. Some perspectives, for example, ignore the facts that elite competition can go beyond the bounds of fair play when there is no referee to penalize players for making deceptive appeals and that partisan competition can tax public respect for our political system. With powerful advertising tools at candidates' disposal, citizens are exposed to potent and sometimes misleading campaign appeals.

In addition, problems sometimes arise in terms of equity of electoral discourse. One candidate may be better funded or have access to greater resources than others, which can create an unfair advantage. This is particularly a problem in some presidential nomination contests (such as George W. Bush versus John McCain in 2000; Bush had twice as much money as his challenger) and in House races where incumbents routinely raise and spend many times that which is available to challengers.

The decline of self-regulation by candidates' organizations would not be as problematic if a universally acknowledged body existed to protect citizens against subtle manipulation of their standards of evaluation. Unfortunately, there is no external referee with the authority to police electoral competition. Political parties and interest groups have lost some of their organizational grip on elections. Meanwhile, government agencies (such as the Federal Election Commission and the Federal Communications Commission) cannot regulate campaign appeals, because political speech is constitutionally protected.

The weakness of external regulators at a time when candidates control influential communication technologies has given candidates great incentives to attempt manipulation of voters through the airwaves. The classic problem of electoral deception involves *substantive manipulation,* whereby leaders deceive citizens about policy matters. According to Benjamin Page and Robert Shapiro, "To the extent that the public is given false or incorrect or biased information, or is deprived of important relevant information, people may make mistaken evaluations of policy alternatives and may express support for policies harmful to their own or society's interests, or in conflict with values they cherish."

If elections were primarily about public policy, substantive manipulation would remain the most dangerous threat to the political system. However, contests involve perceptions about electability and personal images as well. Many races in recent years have turned on questions of momentum, likability, and mistakes. How the game is played often has become more important than the task of setting the future course of government action.

The fact that elections generally involve short-term campaign phenomena creates another type of deception, which I call *strategic manipulation*. In this situation, efforts are made to shift impressions of the campaign in a direction favorable to particular candidates. For example, candidates often seek to influence short-term evaluations. Specifically, spot commercials can be used to alter views about an opponent's likability, they can lead to exaggerated claims regarding a contender's electoral prospects, or they can be used to change campaign dynamics and distract voters from pressing matters of the day.

There are a number of common techniques for viewer manipulation through advertising. For example, prevalent tactics include using visual trickery, condemning your opponent for a position you also hold, telling half the story, taking votes out of context, playing with definitions, and using lapses in grammar that create misleading impressions.

Television commercials are particularly problematic because they combine audio and visual technologies. Sounds, colors, and visual presentations can be used in deceptive ways, as was discussed in the opening chapter. For example, Pat Buchanan's ad consultants in 1992 occasionally sped up or slowed down George Bush's physical movements to create unfavorable impressions of the president. Independent ad producer Floyd Brown also admitted that he had doctored a 1992 ad showing President Clinton's hand raised high with Massachusetts senator Edward Kennedy's. The joint picture was faked by combining separate pictures of the men alone.

In the 1996 U.S. Senate race in Virginia, Republican senator John Warner was forced to fire consultant Greg Stevens after Stevens admitted to doctoring a photo used in a spot linking the Democratic opponent, Mark Warner, with President Clinton by replacing the head of Sen. Charles Robb with Warner's. This type of editing, which tried to link Mark Warner with other candidates said to be liberal, poses obvious problems for viewers. People may remember the visual image but not be in a position to recognize electronic chicanery.

In 2004, George W. Bush's campaign was forced to redo a commercial when ad producers were found to have doctored an ad called "Whatever It Takes." Featuring Bush talking at the Republican National Convention, the spot also showed images of Bush speaking in front of soldiers. However, a liberal Web site,

DailyKos.com, found that faces of the same soldiers appeared in several places of the crowd scene. It turned out that the ad-maker had digitally expanded the crowd by cutting and pasting the same individuals into the picture. This made it look like Bush was addressing a large group of soldiers, not the small audience that actually was present. Democrats had a field day linking this electronic deception to what it said were larger questions of truthfulness in the Bush presidency. According to Kerry's spokesman Joe Lockhart, "If they won't tell the truth in an ad, they won't tell the truth about anything else."

Strategic manipulation has not attracted as much study as substantive or symbolic manipulation, but in a media era it is a serious threat. A campaign structure that is open, volatile, and heavily dependent on media coverage gives candidates clear incentives to seek strategic advantage through doctored images or video manipulation. The rise of new technologies and the employment of professional campaign managers in the United States have broadened the range of tactics considered acceptable and given campaigners extraordinary tools for influencing voters.

Different Arenas, Different Threats

The susceptibility of voters to advertising appeals has long generated despair from political observers. Joe McGinniss's book, *The Selling of the President,* and Robert Spero's volume, *The Duping of the American Voter,* express common fears about the dangers of advertisements. But these authors failed to recognize that not all electoral arenas are subject to the same threat. The visibility of the setting makes a big difference.

The major threat in highly visible arenas, such as presidential general election campaigns, is substantive manipulation. The 1988 general election gave a textbook illustration of this danger, as the relatively unknown Michael Dukakis saw his entire campaign shattered by George Bush's successful efforts to move the campaign from past performance to flags, furloughs, and patriotism. Bush used advertising on tax and spending matters as well as crime to fill in the public profile of the relatively unknown Dukakis. The vice president was able to dominate the campaign because few voters knew much about the Massachusetts governor, 1988 was a year with a fluid policy agenda, and Dukakis did not successfully defend himself. Bush pictured Dukakis as an unrepentant liberal who was soft on crime and out of touch with the American people. To some voters, this portrait was accurate, whereas for others it was an example of image redefinition.

Similar problems arose in the 2004 presidential election. In the closing days of the campaign, both candidates made a number of debatable charges against the opponent. Bush accused Kerry of favoring a big new federal health care bureau-cracy even though there was no evidence to support this claim. Kerry, mean-while, said if Bush were reelected, he would restore a military draft and privatize Social Security, neither of which were likely to be the case. The fact that Kerry started the race with much lower visibility than the sitting president gave Bush an opportunity to paint the challenger in unfavorable ways.

Less visible electoral arenas, such as presidential nomination campaigns, are particularly vulnerable to strategic manipulation. Because they are less visible contests that are heavily influenced by campaign dynamics, they contain fewer countervailing forces than are present in presidential general elections. Democ-rats compete against Democrats and Republicans against Republicans in a sequential nominating process. In this situation, party identification is not central to vote choice. The setting limits the power of long-term forces and makes it pos-sible for short-term factors, such as advertising and media coverage, to dominate.

Senate races share some features with nominating races. These contests are susceptible to ad appeals because relatively unknown candidates compete in races that resemble roller-coaster rides. Wild swings in electoral fortunes often occur during the campaign. The absence of prior beliefs about the candidates makes advertising especially influential. It is easier to create a new political pro-file (for one's self or one's opponent) than to alter a well-defined image. Candi-dates who are the least known are the most able to use advertisements to influ-ence the public. But they also are the most susceptible to having an opponent create an unfair image of them with television ads.

Slicing and Dicing the Electorate

Campaign advertisements also pose problems for democratic elections on the systemic level. Even if ads influence voting behavior only in certain circum-stances, they have consequences for the way in which the campaign is viewed. Advertisements are one of the primary means of communication, and much of how people feel about the electoral system is a product of how campaign battles are contested.

In contemporary elections, political consultants commonly divide voters into three advertising segments based on public opinion polls and focus groups: the committed (those who are for you), the hopeless (those who are against you and about whom little can be done), and the undecided (those who could vote either way). The last group, of course, is the central target of campaign tactics.

Ads are developed to stir the hopes and fears of the 20 to 30 percent of the elec-torate that is undecided, not the 70 to 80 percent that is committed or hopeless.

Narrow pockets of support are identified and targeted appeals are made. Many Americans complain that campaign discussions do not reflect their concerns. Their complaints are legitimate. With advertising appeals designed for the small group of voters who are undecided, it is little wonder many voters feel left out.

In this system of segmentation and targeted appeals, candidates have clear incentives to identify pockets of potential support and find issues that will move these voters. Whether it is the backlash against affirmative action among white rural dwellers in North Carolina (one of the winning issues for Senator Jesse Helms in 1990) or George Bush's attacks on Clinton for his 1969 antiwar demonstrations (which did not save the election for Bush), the current electoral system encourages candidates to find divisive issues that pit social group against social group.

It is not surprising in this situation that Americans feel bad at the end of election campaigns. Candidates engage in an electronic form of civil war not unlike what happens in polarized societies. The battleground issues often touch on race, lifestyle, and gender, which are among the most contentious topics in the United States. Ads and sound bites are the weapons of choice in these confrontations. The long-term dangers of the electronic air wars are ill feelings and loss of a sense of community.

What Can Be Done

The controversies that have arisen concerning television campaign ads have produced cries for serious reform. These calls undoubtedly reflect deep frustration over the uses of advertisements in the United States. But it is far too simple to blame ads for electoral deficiencies. The problem of political commercials is as much a function of campaign structure and voters' reactions as of candidates' behavior. Structural and attitudinal changes have loosened the forces that used to restrain elite strategies. The rise of a mass-based campaign system at a time when candidates have powerful means of influencing viewers rewards media-centered campaigns.

At the same time, voters are vulnerable to candidates' messages because the forces that used to provide social integration have lost their influence. Intermediary organizations no longer control people's impressions of political reality. With the end of the Cold War, consensus has broken down on key domestic and foreign policy questions. Voters are bombarded with spot ads precisely because of their proven short-term effectiveness.

Because ads are a form of expression, they are subject to constitutional protection and thereby quite difficult to restrict. Most attempts at direct regulation have been resisted as unconstitutional encroachments on free speech. Self-monitoring efforts, such as those proposed by the National Association of Political Consultants, are of limited value. Vigorous electoral competition is the ultimate form of protection for voters, but too many times, inequity in resources tilts campaign discourse in favor of incumbents or well-funded individuals.

However, an informal mechanism in the advertising area offers voters some help: the media. Journalists who focus on deceptive or misleading commercials help the public hold candidates accountable for ads that cross the threshold of acceptability. Currently, reporters devote plenty of attention to candidates' ads but not necessarily in a way that informs citizens on important issues. For example, the media are more likely to use ads to discuss the horse race than the policy views of the candidates. But with a different approach to ad coverage, television could become a more enlightening force in U.S. elections. Journalists in the United States have an unusually high credibility with the public. American reporters are seen as being more fair and trustworthy than in other countries. A recent comparative study of five countries illustrates this point. Whereas 69 percent of the Americans surveyed had great confidence in the media, only 41 percent of Germans and 38 percent of the British gave high ratings to journalists.

Both Kathleen Hall Jamieson and David Broder have suggested that journalists should exercise their historic function of safeguarding the integrity of the election process. The media could use their high public credibility to improve the functioning of the political system. Candidates periodically make exaggerated claims in their efforts to win votes. Journalists need to look into their claims and report to voters on their accuracy.

These efforts are valuable, but journalists must go beyond fact checking to true oversight. Commercials have become the major strategic tool for the contesting of American elections. Candidates devote the largest portion of their overall campaign budgets to advertising. Their ads feature their own appeals as well as comments about their opposition.

The media have some responsibility to expose blatant manipulation, distortion, and deception, not just inaccurate use of facts. Reporters should bring to task candidates who exceed the boundaries of fair play. Unfair tactics or misleading editing needs to be publicized. Commercials that engage in obvious appeals to racism, for example, should be condemned. While it is difficult for reporters to compete with the volume of advertisements that are run in major campaigns, it remains important to have an independent check and balance on the claims of candidates for office.

Television has a special obligation because it is the medium through which most Americans receive their political news. Ad watches are especially important in spots involving race, lifestyle issues, gender, or other topics with emotional overtones. Reporters are the only major group with the credibility vis-à-vis the American public to arbitrate electoral advertising. In fact, a Gallup poll revealed that citizens would like the media to undertake an aggressive watchdog role.

There is some danger for the media in openly assuming this role. Many Americans already are concerned about what they believe is excessive influence and bias on the part of the news media. If journalists aggressively challenge candidates' statements, they may be viewed as part of the problem rather than the solution. There are increasing signs of a backlash against the media, and reporters could become subject to more stringent criticism regarding their overall influence and objectivity.

In 1991, for example, Louisiana gubernatorial candidate David Duke tried to foster antipathy toward the media through a last-minute ad directly criticizing coverage of his campaign: "Have you ever heard such weeping and gnashing of teeth? The news media have given up any pretense of fair play. The liberals have gone ballistic. The special interests have gone mad. The politicians who play up to them are lining up on cue. Principles lie abandoned and hypocrisy rules the day. I raise issues that must be discussed, and get back venom instead. Try a little experiment. Next time you hear them accuse me of intolerance and hatred, notice who is doing the shouting." George Bush attempted to build support for his 1992 reelection with the slogan, "Annoy the Media: Reelect Bush." In 1996, Robert Dole attacked the "liberal press," saying, "They don't put any anti-Clinton stories in the *New York Times*. Only anti-Dole stories in the *New York Times*."

A national survey conducted during the last week of the 2000 campaign found that 49 percent of respondents believed the media had done a good or excellent job of covering the fall presidential election, 31 percent felt the job was only fair, 11 percent thought it was poor, and 9 percent were unsure. These numbers were virtually identical to 1996, when 49 percent believed the news media had done an excellent or good job, 48 percent thought the job was only fair or poor, and 4 percent had no opinion. In 1992, 54 percent rated the media as having done an excellent or good job of covering the presidential campaign, whereas 44 percent thought the media had done only a fair or poor job.

This poll also asked in the 2000 campaign survey whether news coverage had been biased against any individual candidate. Twenty-eight percent said yes, whereas 58 percent did not feel there had been any bias. When asked which candidate had received the most biased coverage against him, 49 percent cited George W. Bush, 25 percent named Al Gore, 17 percent claimed Nader, 9 percent mentioned Buchanan, and 1 percent were unsure.

In 2004, a national survey by the Pew Research Center found that 37 percent of voters thought the press had been unfair to President Bush, while 27 percent believed the media had been unfair to John Kerry. In terms of the overall campaign coverage, 54 percent rated it excellent or good, 28 percent said it was only fair, 16 percent believed the coverage was poor, and 2 percent were unsure. When asked how much influence news organizations have on which candidate becomes president, 62 percent of voters said they believed the media had too much influence.

Despite the possible drawbacks, oversight by the media is vital enough to the political system to warrant the risk of backlash. The quality of information presented during elections is important enough to outweigh the practical difficulties facing the media. Nothing is more central to democratic elections than electoral discourse. Without informative material, voters have little means of holding leaders accountable or engaging in popular consent. By encouraging candidates to address the substantive concerns of the electorate, media watchdogs help voters make meaningful choices.

Chapter 12

Political Parties

———

12-1

from *Why Parties?*

John H. Aldrich

American political parties were created by politicians and committed citizens who sought to win elections and control legislatures, executives, and even the courts. The parties exist at local, state, and national levels—wherever elections are held for coveted offices. The system of political parties that has evolved over time is fragmented and multilayered. In the following essay, John H. Aldrich describes the nature of the political problems that parties solve for candidates and voters. As much as we may dislike partisanship, modern democracies could not, Aldrich explains, function without it.

Is the Contemporary Political Party Strong or in Decline?

The Case for the Importance of Political Parties

THE PATH TO OFFICE for nearly every major politician begins today, as it has for over 150 years, with the party. Many candidates emerge initially from the ranks of party activists, all serious candidates seek their party's nomination, and they become serious candidates in the general election only because they have won

Source: John H. Aldrich, *Why Parties? The Origin and Transformation of Political Parties in America* (Chicago: University of Chicago Press, 1995), 14–27. Notes appearing in the original have been deleted.

their party's endorsement. Today most partisan nominations are decided in primary elections—that is, based on votes cast by self-designated partisans in the mass electorate. Successful nominees count on the continued support of these partisans in the general election, and for good reason. At least since surveys have provided firm evidence, all presidential nominees have won the support of no less than a majority of their party in the electorate, no matter how overwhelming their defeat may have been.

This is an age of so-called partisan dealignment in the electorate. Even so, a substantial majority today consider themselves partisans. The lowest percentage of self-professed (i.e., "strong" and "weak") partisans yet recorded in National Election Studies (NES) surveys was 61 percent in 1974, and another 22 percent expressed partisan leanings that year. Evidence from panel surveys demonstrates that partisanship has remained as stable and enduring for most adults after dealignment as it did before it, and it is often the single strongest predictor of candidate choice in the public.

If parties have declined recently, the decline has not occurred in their formal organizations. Party organizations are if anything stronger, better financed, and more professional at all levels now. Although its importance to candidates may be less than in the past, the party provides more support—more money, workers, and resources of all kinds—than any other organization for all but a very few candidates for national and state offices.

Once elected, officeholders remain partisans. Congress is organized by parties. Party-line votes elect its leadership, determine what its committees will be, assign members to them, and select their chairs. Party caucuses remain a staple of congressional life, and they and other forms of party organizations in Congress have become stronger in recent years. Party voting in committee and on the floor of both houses, though far less common in the United States than in many democracies, nonetheless remains the first and most important standard for understanding congressional voting behavior, and it too has grown stronger, in this case much stronger, in recent years.

Relationships among the elected branches of government are also heavily partisan. Conference committees to resolve discrepancies between House and Senate versions of legislation reflect partisan as well as interchamber rivalries. The president is the party's leader, and his agenda is introduced, fought for, and supported on the floor by his congressional party. His agenda becomes his party's congressional agenda, and much of it finds its way into law.

The Case for Weak and Weakening Parties

As impressive as the scenario above may be, not all agree that parties lie at the heart of American politics, at least not anymore. The literature on parties over the past two decades is replete with accounts of the decline of the political party. Even the choice of titles clearly reflects the arguments. David Broder perhaps began this stream of literature with *The Party's Over* (1972). Since then, political scientists have written extensively on this theme: for example, Crotty's *American Political Parties in Decline* (1984), Kirkpatrick's *Dismantling the Parties* (1978), Polsby's *Consequences of Party Reform* (1983) . . . , Ranney's thoughtful *Curing the Mischiefs of Faction* (1975), and Wattenberg's *The Decline of American Political Parties* (1990).

Those who see larger ills in the contemporary political scene often attribute them to the failure of parties to be stronger and more effective. In "The Decline of Collective Responsibility" (1980), Fiorina argued that such responsibility was possible only through the agency of the political party. Jacobson concluded his study of congressional elections (1992) by arguing that contemporary elections induce "responsiveness" of individual incumbents to their districts but do so "without [inducing] responsibility" in incumbents for what Congress does. As a result, the electorate can find no one to hold accountable for congressional failings. He too looked to a revitalized party for redress. These themes reflect the responsible party thesis, if not in being a call for such parties, at least in using that as the standard for measuring how short the contemporary party falls.

The literature on the presidency is not immune to this concern for decaying parties. Kernell's account of the strategy of "going public" (1986)—that is, generating power by marshaling public opinion—is that it became more common as the older strategy of striking bargains with a small set of congressional (and partisan) power brokers grew increasingly futile. The earlier use of the president's power to persuade (Neustadt 1960, 1990) failed as power centers became more diverse and fragmented and brokers could no longer deliver. Lowi argued this case even more strongly in *The Personal President* (1985). America, he claimed, has come to invest too much power in the office of the president, with the result that the promise of the presidency and the promises of individual presidents go unfulfilled. Why? Because the rest of government has become too unwieldy, complicated, and fragmented for the president to use that power effectively. His solution? Revitalize political parties.

Divided partisan control over government, once an occasional aberration, has become the ordinary course of affairs. Many of the same themes in this literature are those sounded above—fragmented, decentralized power, lack of coordination and control over what the government does, and absence of collective responsibility. Strong political parties are, among other things, those that can deliver the vote for most or all of their candidates. Thus another symptom of weakened parties is regularized divided government, in the states as well as in the nation.

If divided government is due to weakened parties, that condition must be due in turn to weakened partisan loyalties in the electorate. Here the evidence is clear. The proportions and strength of party attachments in the electorate declined in the mid-1960s. There was a resurgence in affiliation twenty years later, but to a lower level than before 1966. The behavioral consequences of these changes are if anything even clearer. Defection from party lines and split-ticket voting are far more common for all major offices at national, state, and local levels today than before the mid-1960s. Elections are more candidate centered and less party centered, and those who come to office have played a greater role in shaping their own more highly personalized electoral coalitions. Incumbents, less dependent on the party for winning office, are less disposed to vote the party line in Congress or to follow the wishes of their party's president. Power becomes decentralized toward the individual incumbent and, as Jacobson argues, individual incumbents respond to their constituents. If that means defecting from the party, so be it.

Is the Debate Genuine?

Some believe that parties have actually grown stronger over the past few decades. This position has been put most starkly by Schlesinger: "It should be clear by now that the grab bag of assumptions, inferences, and half-truths that have fed the decline-of-parties thesis is simply wrong" (1985, p. 1152). Rather, he maintains, "Thanks to increasing levels of competition between the parties, then, American political parties are stronger than before" (p. 1168). More common is the claim that parties were weakened in the 1960s but have been revitalized since then. Rohde pointed out that "in the last decade, however, the decline of partisanship in the House has been reversed. Party voting, which had been as low as 27 percent in 1972, peaked at 64 percent in 1987" (1989, p. 1). Changes in party voting in the Senate have been only slightly less dramatic, and Rohde has also demonstrated that party institutions in the House strengthened substantially in the same period (1991). If, as Rohde says, parties in the government are stronger, and if . . . others are correct that party organizations are stronger, a thesis of decline with resurgence must be taken seriously. The electorate's partisan affiliations may be a lagging rather than a leading indicator, and even they have rebounded slightly.

A Theory of Political Parties

As diverse as are the conclusions reached by these and other astute observers, all agree that the political party is—or should be—central to the American political system. Parties are—or should be—integral parts of all political life, from structuring the reasoning and choice of the electorate, through all facets of campaigns and seemingly all facets of the government, to the very possibility of effective governance in a democracy.

How is it that such astute observers of American politics and parties, writing at virtually the same time and looking at much the same evidence, come to such diametrically opposed conclusions about the strength of parties? Eldersveld . . . wrote that "political parties are complex institutions and processes, and as such they are difficult to understand and evaluate" (1982, p. 407). As proof, he went on to consider the decline of parties thesis. At one point he wrote, "The decline in our parties, therefore, is difficult to demonstrate, empirically or in terms of historical perspective" (p. 417). And yet he then turned to signs of party decline and concluded his book with the statement: "Despite their defects they continue today to be the major instruments for democratic government in this nation. With necessary reforms we can make them even more central to the governmental process and to the lives of American citizens. Eighty years ago, Lord James Bryce, after studying our party system, said, 'In America the great moving forces are the parties. The government counts for less than in Europe, the parties count for more. . . .' If our citizens and their leaders wish it, American parties will still be the 'great moving forces' of our system" (1982, pp. 432–33).

The "Fundamental Equation" of the New Institutionalism Applied to Parties

That parties are complex does not mean they are incomprehensible. Indeed complexity is, if not an intentional outcome, at least an anticipated result of those who shape the political parties. Moreover, they are so deeply woven into the fabric of American politics that they cannot be understood apart from either their own historical context and dynamics or those of the political system as a whole. Parties, that is, can be understood only in relation to the polity, to the government and its institutions, and to the historical context of the times.

The study of political parties, second, is necessarily a study of a major pair of political *institutions*. Indeed, the institutions that define the political party are unique, and as it happens they are unique in ways that make an institutional account especially useful. Their establishment and nature are fundamentally extralegal; they are nongovernmental political institutions. Instead of statute, their basis lies in the actions of ambitious politicians that created and maintain them. They are, in the parlance of the new institutionalism, *endogenous institutions*—in fact, the most highly endogenous institutions of any substantial and sustained political importance in American history.

By endogenous, I mean it was the actions of political actors that created political parties in the first place, and it is the actions of political actors that have shaped and altered them over time. And political actors have chosen to alter their parties dramatically at several times in our history, reformed them often, and tinkered with them constantly. Of all major political bodies in the United States, the political party is the most variable in its rules, regulations, and procedures—that is to say, in its formal organization—and in its informal methods and traditions. It is often the same set of actors who write the party's rules and then choose the party's outcomes, sometimes at nearly the same time and by the same method. Thus, for example, one night national party conventions debate, consider any proposed amendments, and then adopt their rules by a majority vote of credentialed delegates. The next night these same delegates debate, consider any proposed amendments, and then adopt their platform by majority vote, and they choose their presidential nominee by majority vote the following night.

Who, then, are these critical political actors? Many see the party-in-the-electorate as comprising major actors. To be sure, mobilizing the electorate to capture office is a central task of the political party. But America is a republican democracy. All power flows directly or indirectly from the great body of the people, to paraphrase Madison's definition. The public elects its political leaders, but it is that leadership that legislates, executes, and adjudicates policy. The parties are defined in relation to this republican democracy. Thus it is political leaders, those Schlesinger (1975) has called "office-seekers"—*those who seek and those who hold elective office*—who are the central actors in the party.

Ambitious office seekers and holders are thus the first and most important actors in the political party. A second set of important figures in party politics comprises those who hold, or have access to, critical resources that office seekers need to realize their ambitions. It is expensive to build and maintain the party and campaign organizations necessary to compete effectively in the electoral arena. Thomas Ferguson, for example, has made an extended argument for the "primary and constitutive role large investors play in American politics" (1983, p. 3). Much of his research emphasizes this primary and constitutive role in party politics in particular, such as in partisan realignments. The study of the role of money in congressional elections has also focused in part on concentrations of such sources of funding, such as from political action committees which political parties are coming to take advantage of. Elections are also fought over the flow of information to the public. The electoral arm of political parties in the eighteenth century was made up of "committees of correspondence," which were primarily lines of communication among political elites and between them and potential voters, and one of the first signs of organizing of the Jeffersonian Republican party was the hiring of a newspaper editor. The press was first a partisan press, and editors and publishers from Thomas Ritchie to Horace Greeley long were critical players in party politics. Today those with specialized knowledge relevant to communication, such as pollsters, media and advertising experts, and computerized fund-raising specialists, enjoy influence in party, campaign, and even government councils that greatly exceeds their mere technical expertise.

In more theoretical terms, this second set of party actors include those Schlesinger (1975) has called "benefit seekers," those for whom realization of their goals depends on the party's success in capturing office. Party activists shade from those powerful figures with concentrations of, or access to, money and information described above to the legions of volunteer campaign activists who ring doorbells and stuff envelopes and are, individually and collectively, critical to the first level of the party—its office seekers. All are critical because they command the resources, whether money, expertise, and information or merely time and labor, that office seekers need to realize their ambitions. As a result, activists' motivations shape and constrain the behavior of office seekers, as their own roles are, in turn, shaped and constrained by the office seekers. The changed incentives of party activists have played a significant role in the fundamentally altered nature of the contemporary party, but the impact of benefit seekers will be seen scattered throughout this account.

Voters, however, are neither office seekers nor benefit seekers and thus are not a part of the political party at all, even if they identify strongly with a party and consistently support its candidates. Voters are indeed critical, but they are critical as the targets of party activities. Parties "produce" candidates, platforms, and policies. Voters "consume" by exchanging their votes for the party's product (see Popkin et al. 1976). Some voters, of course, become partisans by becoming activists, whether as occasional volunteers, as sustained contributors, or even as candidates. But until they do so, they may be faithful consumers, "brand name" loyalists as it were, but they are still only the targets of partisans' efforts to sell their wares in the political marketplace.

Why, then, do politicians create and recreate the party, exploit its features, or ignore its dictates? The simple answer is that it has been in their interests to do so. That is, this is a *rational choice* account of the party, an account that presumes that rational, elective office seekers and holders use the party to achieve their ends.

I do not assume that politicians are invariably self-interested in a narrow sense. This is not a theory in which elective office seekers simply maximize their chances of election or reelection, at least not for its own sake. They may well have fundamental values and principles, and they may have preferences over policies as means to those ends. They also care about office, both for its own sake and for the opportunities to achieve other ends that election and reelection make possible. . . . Just as winning elections is a means to other ends for politicians (whether career or policy ends), so too is the political party a means to these other ends.

Why, then, do politicians turn to create or reform, to use or abuse, partisan institutions? The answer is that parties are designed as attempts to solve problems that current institutional arrangements do not solve and that politicians have come to believe they cannot solve. These problems fall into three general and recurring categories.

The Problem of Ambition and Elective Office Seeking

Elective office seekers, as that label says, want to win election to office. Parties regulate access to those offices. If elective office is indeed valuable, there will be more aspirants than offices, and the political party and the two-party system are means of regulating that competition and channeling those ambitions. Major party nomination is necessary for election, and partisan institutions have been developed—and have been reformed and re-reformed—for regulating competition. Intra-institutional leadership positions are also highly valued and therefore potentially competitive. There is, for example, a fairly well institutionalized path to the office of Speaker of the House. It is, however, a Democratic party institution. Elective politicians, of course, ordinarily desire election more than once. They are typically careerists who want a long and productive career in politics. Schlesinger's ambition theory (1966) . . . is precisely about this general problem. Underlying this theory, though typically not fully developed, is a problem. The problem is that if office is desirable, there will be more, usually many more, aspirants than there are offices to go around. When stated in rigorous form, it can be proved that in fact there is no permanent solution to this problem. And it is a problem that can adversely affect the fortunes of a party. In 1912 the Republican vote was split between William Howard Taft and Theodore Roosevelt. This split enabled Woodrow Wilson to win with 42 percent of the popular vote. Not only was Wilson the only break in Republican hegemony of the White House in this period, but in that year Democrats increased their House majority by sixty-five additional seats and captured majority control of the Senate. Thus failure to regulate intraparty competition cost Republicans dearly.

For elective office seekers, regulating conflict over who holds those offices is clearly of major concern. It is ever present. And it is not just a problem of access to government offices but is also a problem internal to each party as soon as the party becomes an important gateway to office.

The Problem of Making Decisions for the Party and for the Polity

Once in office, partisans determine outcomes for the polity. They propose alternatives, shape the agenda, pass (or reject) legislation, and implement what they enact. The policy formation and execution process, that is, is highly partisan. The parties-in-government are more than mere coalitions of like-minded individuals, however; they are enduring institutions. Very few incumbents change their partisan affiliations. Most retain their partisanship throughout their career, even though they often disagree (i.e., are not uniformly like-minded) with some of their partisan peers. When the rare incumbent does change parties, it is invariably to join the party more consonant with that switcher's policy interests. This implies that there are differences between the two parties at some fundamental and enduring level on policy positions, values, and beliefs. Thus, parties are institutions designed to promote the achievement of collective choices—choices on which the parties differ and choices reached by majority rule. As with access to office and ambition theory, there is a well-developed theory for this problem: *social choice theory.* Underlying this theory is the well-known problem that no method of choice can solve the elective officeholders' problem of combining the interests, concerns, or values of a polity that remains faithful to democratic values, as shown by the consequences flowing from Arrow's theorem (Arrow 1951). Thus, in a republican democracy politicians may turn to partisan institutions to solve the problem of collective choice. In the language of politics, parties may help achieve the goal of attaining policy majorities in the first place, as well as the often more difficult goal of maintaining such majorities.

The Problem of Collective Action

The third problem is the most pervasive and thus the furthest-ranging in substantive content. The clearest example, however, is also the most important. To win office, candidates need more than a party's nomination. Election requires persuading members of the public to support that candidacy and mobilizing as many of those supporters as possible. This is a problem of collective action. How do candidates get supporters to vote for them—at least in greater numbers than vote for the opposition—as well as get them to provide the cadre of workers and contribute the resources needed to win election? The political party has long been the solution.

As important as wooing and mobilizing supporters are, collective action problems arise in a wide range of circumstances facing elective office seekers. Party action invariably requires the concerted action of many partisans to achieve collectively desirable outcomes. Jimmy Carter was the only president in the 1970s and 1980s to enjoy unified party control of government. Democrats in Congress, it might well be argued, shared an interest in achieving policy outcomes. And yet Carter was all too often unable to get them to act in their shared collective interests. In 1980 not only he but the Democratic congressional parties paid a heavy price for failed cooperation. The theory here, of course, is the *theory of public goods* and its consequence, the *theory of collective action*.

The Elective Office Seekers' and Holders' Interests Are to Win

Why should this crucial set of actors, the elective office seekers and officeholders, care about these three classes of problems? The short answer is that these concerns become practical problems to politicians when they adversely affect their chances of winning. Put differently, politicians turn to their political party—that is, use its powers, resources, and institutional forms—when they believe doing so increases their prospects for winning desired outcomes, and they turn from it if it does not.

Ambition theory is about winning per se. The breakdown of orderly access to office risks unfettered and unregulated competition. The inability of a party to develop effective means of nomination and support for election therefore directly influences the chances of victory for the candidates and thus for their parties. The standard example of the problem of social choice theory, the "paradox of voting," is paradoxical precisely because all are voting to win desired outcomes, and yet there is no majority-preferred outcome. Even if there happens to be a majority-preferred policy, the conditions under which it is truly a stable equilibrium are extremely fragile and thus all too amenable to defeat. In other words, majorities in Congress are hard to attain and at least as hard to maintain. And the only reason to employ scarce campaign resources to mobilize supporters is that such mobilization increases the odds of victory. Its opposite, the failure to act when there are broadly shared interests—the problem of collective action—reduces the prospects of victory, whether at the ballot box or in government. Scholars may recognize these as manifestations of theoretical problems and call them "impossibility results" to emphasize their generic importance. Politicians recognize the consequences of these impossibility results by their adverse effects on their chances of winning—of securing what it is in their interests to secure.

So why have politicians so often turned to political parties for solutions to these problems? Their existence creates incentives for their use. It is, for example, incredibly difficult to win election to major office without the backing of a major party. It is only a little less certain that legislators who seek to lead a policy proposal through the congressional labyrinth will first turn to their party for assistance. But such incentives tell us only that an ongoing political institution is used when it is useful. Why form political parties in the first place? . . .

First, parties are institutions. This means, among other things, that they have some durability. They may be endogenous institutions, yet party reforms are meant not as short-term fixes but as alterations to last for years, even decades.

Thus, for example, legislators might create a party rather than a temporary majority coalition to increase their chances of winning not just today but into the future. Similarly, a long and successful political career means winning office today, but it also requires winning elections throughout that career. A standing, enduring organization makes that goal more likely.

Second, American democracy chooses by plurality or majority rule. Election to office therefore requires broad-based support wherever and from whomever it can be found. So strong are the resulting incentives for a two-party system to emerge that the effect is called Duverger's law (Duverger 1954). It is in part the need to win vast and diverse support that has led politicians to create political parties.

Third, parties may help officeholders win more, and more often, than alternatives. Consider the usual stylized model of pork barrel politics. All winners get a piece of the pork for their districts. All funded projects are paid for by tax revenues, so each district pays an equal share of the costs of each project adopted, whether or not that district receives a project. Several writers have argued that this kind of legislation leads to "universalism," that is, adoption of a "norm" that every such bill yields a project to every district and thus passes with a "universal" or unanimous coalition. Thus everyone "wins." . . . As a result, expecting to win only a bit more than half the time and lose the rest of the time, all legislators prefer consistent use of the norm of universalism. But consider an alternative. Suppose some majority agree to form a more permanent coalition, to control outcomes now and into the future, and develop institutional means to encourage fealty to this agreement. If they successfully accomplish this, they will win regularly. Members of this institutionalized coalition would prefer it to universalism, since they always win a project in either case, but they get their projects at lower cost under the institutionalized majority coalition, which passes fewer projects. Thus, even in this case with no shared substantive interests at all, there are nonetheless incentives to form an enduring voting coalition—to form a political party. And those in the excluded minority have incentives to counterorganize. United, they may be more able to woo defectors to their side. If not, they can campaign to throw those rascals in the majority party out of office.

In sum, these theoretical problems affect elective office seekers and officeholders by reducing their chances of winning. Politicians therefore may turn to political parties as institutions designed to ameliorate them. In solving these theoretical problems, however, from the politicians' perspective parties are affecting who wins and loses and what is won or lost. And it is to parties that politicians often turn, because of their durability as institutionalized solutions, because of the need to orchestrate large and diverse groups of people to form winning majorities, and because often more can be won through parties. Note that this argument rests on the implicit assumption that winning and losing hang in the balance. Politicians may be expected to give up some of their personal autonomy only when they face an imminent threat of defeat without doing so or only when doing so can block opponents' ability to build the strength necessary to win.

This is, of course, the positive case for parties, for it specifies conditions under which politicians find them useful. Not all problems are best solved, perhaps even solved at all, by political parties. Other arrangements, perhaps interest groups, issue networks, or personal electoral coalitions, may be superior at different times and under different conditions. The party may even be part of the problem. In such cases politicians turn elsewhere to seek the means to win. Thus this theory is at base a theory of ambitious politicians seeking to achieve their goals. Often they have done so through the agency of the party, but sometimes, this theory implies, they will seek to realize their goals in other ways.

The political party has regularly proved useful. Their permanence suggests that the appropriate question is not When parties? but How much parties and how much other means? That parties are endogenous implies that there is no single, consistent account of the political party—nor should we expect one. Instead, parties are but a (major) part of the institutional context in which current historical conditions—the problems—are set, and solutions are sought with permanence only by changing that web of institutional arrangements. Of these the political party is by design the most malleable, and thus it is intended to change in important ways and with relatively great frequency. But it changes in ways that have, for most of American history, retained major political parties and, indeed, retained two major parties.

REFERENCES

Arrow, Kenneth J. 1951. *Social choice and individual values.* New York: Wiley.

Broder, David S. 1972. *The party's over: The failure of politics in America.* New York: Harper and Row.

Crotty, William. 1984. *American political parties in decline.* 2d ed. Boston: Little, Brown.

Duverger, Maurice. 1954. *Political parties: Their organization and activities in the modern state.* New York: Wiley.

Eldersveld, Samuel J. 1982. *Political parties in American society.* New York: Basic Books.

Ferguson, Thomas. 1983. Party realignment and American industrial structures: The investment theory of political parties in historical perspective. In *Research in political economy,* vol. 6, ed. Paul Zarembka, pp. 1–82. Greenwich, Conn.: JAI Press.

Fiorina, Morris P. 1980. The decline of collective responsibility in American politics. *Daedalus* 109 (summer): 25–45.

Jacobson, Gary C. 1992. *The politics of congressional elections.* 3d ed. New York: Harper-Collins.

Kernell, Samuel. 1986. *Going public: New strategies of presidential leadership.* Washington, D.C.: CQ Press.

Kirkpatrick, Jeane J. 1978. *Dismantling the parties: Reflections on party reform and party decomposition.* Washington, D.C.: American Enterprise Institute of Public Policy Research.

Lowi, Theodore. 1985. *The personal president: Power invested, promise unfulfilled.* Ithaca, N.Y.: Cornell University Press.

Neustadt, Richard E. 1960. *Presidential power: The politics of leadership.* New York: Wiley.

———. 1990. *Presidential power and the modern presidents: The politics of leadership from Roosevelt to Reagan.* New York: Free Press.

Polsby, Nelson W. 1983. *Consequences of party reform.* Oxford: Oxford University Press.

Popkin, Samuel, John W. Gorman, Charles Phillips, and Jeffrey A. Smith. 1976. Comment: What have you done for me lately? Toward an investment theory of voting. *American Political Science Review* 70 (September): 779–805.

Ranney, Austin. 1975. *Curing the mischiefs of faction: Party reform in America.* Berkeley and Los Angeles: University of California Press.

Rohde, David W. 1989. "Something's happening here: What it is ain't exactly clear": Southern Democrats in the House of Representatives. In *Home style and Washington work: Studies of congressional politics,* ed. Morris P. Fiorina and David W. Rohde, pp. 137–163. Ann Arbor: University of Michigan Press.

———. 1991. *Parties and leaders in the postreform House.* Chicago: University of Chicago Press.

Schlesinger, Joseph A. 1966. *Ambition and politics: Political careers in the United States.* Chicago: Rand McNally.

———. 1975. The primary goals of political parties: A clarification of positive theory. *American Political Science Review* 69 (September): 840–49.

———. 1985. The new American political party. *American Political Science Review* 79 (December): 1152–69.

Wattenberg, Martin P. 1990. *The decline of American political parties: 1952–1988.* Cambridge: Harvard University Press.

12-2

Partisanship and Voting Behavior, 1952–1996

Larry M. Bartels

Many Americans consider themselves to be Democrats or Republicans, and a few identify with some other party. In the late 1960s and 1970s the number of Americans willing to call themselves Democrats or Republicans declined, leading political scientists to speak of a dealignment and worry about the declining importance of parties. Then partisanship appeared to rebound in the 1990s. In this essay political scientist Larry M. Bartels describes these trends and explains the importance of partisanship for the voting behavior of Americans. He argues that party identification increased in the 1980s and 1990s and that the correlation between party identification and presidential voting increased even more. He concludes by observing that changes in the behavior of elected partisans—greater partisanship among presidents and members of Congress—may have contributed to resurgent partisanship in voting in the electorate.

THE "DECLINE OF PARTIES" is one of the most familiar themes in popular and scholarly discourse about contemporary American politics. One influential journalist has asserted that "the most important phenomenon of American politics in the past quarter century has been the rise of independent voters." . . . The most persistent academic analyst of partisan decline has argued that "For over four decades the American public has been drifting away from the two major political parties," while another prominent scholar has referred to a "massive decay of partisan electoral linkages" and to "the ruins of the traditional partisan regime."

   I shall argue here that this conventional wisdom regarding the "decline of parties" is both exaggerated and outdated. Partisan loyalties in the American public have rebounded significantly since the mid-1970s, especially among those who actually turn out to vote. Meanwhile, the impact of partisanship on voting behavior has increased markedly in recent years, both at the presidential level (where the overall impact of partisanship in 1996 was almost 80 percent greater

Source: Larry Bartels, "Partisanship and Voting Behavior, 1952–1996," *American Journal of Political Science* 44, no. 1 (January 2000): 35–50. Notes and bibliographic references appearing in the original have been deleted.

than in 1972) and at the congressional level (where the overall impact of partisanship in 1996 was almost 60 percent greater than in 1978). . . . My analysis suggests that "partisan loyalties had at least as much impact on voting behavior at the presidential level in the 1980s as in the 1950s"—and even more in the 1990s than in the 1980s.

The Thesis of Partisan Decline

Almost forty years ago, the authors of *The American Voter* asserted that

> Few factors are of greater importance for our national elections than the lasting attachment of tens of millions of Americans to one of the parties. These loyalties establish a basic division of electoral strength within which the competition of particular campaigns takes place. . . . Most Americans have this sense of attachment with one party or the other. And for the individual who does, the strength and direction of party identification are facts of central importance in accounting for attitude and behavior.

The so-called "Michigan model," with its emphasis on the fundamental importance of long-standing partisan loyalties, dominated the subsequent decade of academic research on voting behavior. However, over the same decade, changes in the political environment seemed to be rendering the "Michigan model" increasingly obsolete. By the early 1970s, political observers were pointing to the increasing proportion of "independents" in opinion surveys and the increasing prevalence of split-ticket voting as indications of significant partisan decline. By the mid-1970s, some political scientists were extrapolating from a decade-long trend to project a permanent demise of partisan politics. . . .

The "increase in the number of independents" in the 1960s and early '70s . . . — and the corresponding decrease in the proportion of the public who identified themselves as Democrats or Republicans—constitute the single most important piece of evidence in support of the thesis of partisan decline. These and subsequent trends are displayed in the two panels of Figure 1, which show the proportions of party identifiers (including "strong" and "weak" identifiers) and independents (including "pure" independents and "leaners"), respectively, in each of the biennial American National Election Studies from 1952 through 1996.

. . . The proportion of "strong" identifiers in the population increased from 24 percent in 1976 to 31 percent in 1996, while the proportion of "pure" independents—those who neither identified themselves as Democrats or Republicans nor "leaned" to either party in response to the traditional Michigan follow-up question—declined from 16 percent in 1976 to only 9 percent in 1996.

Figure 1. The Distribution of Party Identification, 1952–1996

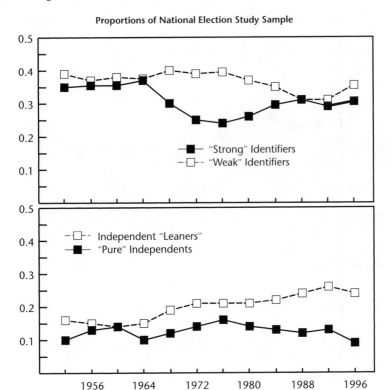

Proportions of National Election Study Sample

A Summary Measure of Partisan Voting

What significance should we attach to the shifts in the distribution of party identification documented in Figure 1? ... To the extent that our interest in partisan loyalties is motivated by an interest in voting behavior, we would seem to need (at least) two kinds of additional information to interpret the electoral implications of changing levels of partisanship. First, are the shifts documented in Figure 1 concentrated among voters or among nonvoters? Declining partisanship among nonvoters may leave the distribution of party identification in the voting booth unchanged. And second, has the electoral *impact* of a given level of partisanship declined or increased over time? Declining *levels* of partisanship might be either reinforced or counteracted by changes in the *impact* of partisanship on electoral choices.

The first of these two questions is addressed by Figure 2, which shows separate trend lines for the proportion of ("strong" or "weak") party identifiers

Figure 2. Party Identification among Presidential Voters and Nonvoters

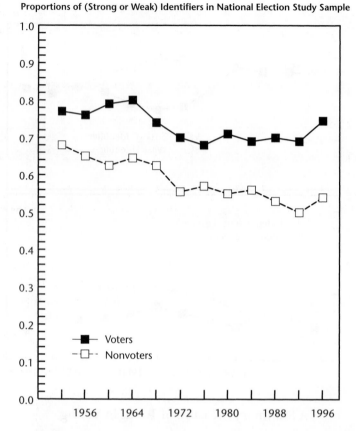

Proportions of (Strong or Weak) Identifiers in National Election Study Sample

among voters and nonvoters in presidential elections since 1952. Not surprisingly, nonvoters are less partisan than voters in every year. But what is more important to note here is that the gap in partisanship between voters and nonvoters has widened noticeably over time, from about ten percentage points in the 1950s to about twenty percentage points by the 1990s. Indeed, it appears from these results that the decline in partisanship evident in Figure 1 has been almost entirely reversed among voters: the proportion of party identifiers in the presidential electorate was 77 percent in 1952, 76 percent in 1956, and 75 percent in 1996, while the proportion among nonvoters was almost fifteen points lower in 1996 than in the 1950s. Thus, while the trend lines shown in Figure 1 suggest that the erosion of party loyalties underlying the "partisan decline" thesis has ended and probably even reversed in the last two decades, the results presented in Figure 2 suggest that these developments have been especially pronounced among actual voters.

The erosion of party loyalties among nonvoters evident in Figure 2 is of importance for any general account of the role of partisanship in contemporary American politics. It is especially important in view of evidence suggesting that declining partisanship is, at least in modest part, *responsible* for the substantial decline in turnout over the period covered by Figure 2, and that individual turnout decisions are increasingly sensitive to the strength of prospective voters' preferences for one candidate or the other, which derive in significant part from long-term partisan attachments. However, given my narrower aim here of documenting changes in the impact of partisanship *on voting behavior,* the most important implication of Figure 2 is that the distribution of partisan attachments *among those citizens who actually got to the polls* was not much different in the 1990s from what it had been in the 1950s.

Of course, the significance of partisanship in the electoral process depends not only upon the level of partisanship in the electorate, but also upon the extent to which partisanship influences voting behavior. How, if at all, has that influence changed over the four and a half decades covered by the NES data? . . . [Editors: Bartels estimates the impact of party identification on voting by taking advantage of the survey from which respondents are coded as strong Republican, weak Republican, leaning Republican, independent, leaning Democrat, weak Democrat, and strong Democrat. For each category, a statistical estimate is calculated for the effect of being in that category on voting for the alternative presidential or congressional candidates. The statistical estimate, called a probit coefficient, is averaged for the partisan categories to yield an overall measure "partisan voting." Figure 3 presents the result for elections in the 1952–1996 period.]

The Revival of Partisan Voting in Presidential Elections

. . . Figure 3 shows noticeable declines in the level of partisan voting in the presidential elections of 1964 and, especially, 1972. These declines primarily reflect the fact that Republican identifiers in 1964 and Democratic identifiers in 1972 abandoned their parties' unpopular presidential candidates by the millions, depressing the estimated effects of partisan loyalties on the presidential vote in those years. However, an even more striking pattern in Figure 3 is the monotonic increase in partisan voting in every presidential election since 1972. By 1996, this trend had produced a level of partisan voting 77 percent higher than in 1972—an average increase of 10 percent in each election, compounded over six election cycles—and 15 to 20 percent higher than in the supposed glory days of the 1950s that spawned *The American Voter.*

Figure 3. Partisan Voting in Presidential Elections

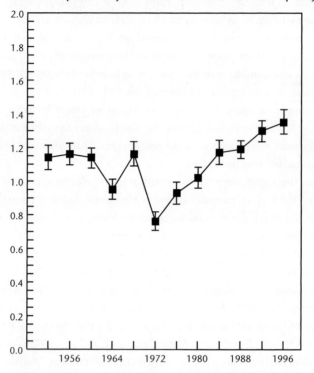

Estimated Impact of Party Identification on Presidential Vote Propensity

Note: Average probit coefficients, major-party voters only, with jackknife standard error bars.

. . . One possible explanation for the revival of partisan voting evident in Figure 3 is the sorting out of partisan attachments of southerners following the civil rights upheavals of the early and middle 1960s. As national party elites took increasingly distinct stands on racial issues, black voters moved overwhelmingly into the Democratic column, while white southerners defected to conservative Republican presidential candidates. What is important here is that many of these conservative white southerners only gradually shed their traditional Democratic identifications—and Democratic voting behavior at the subpresidential level—through the 1980s and '90s. Thus, it may be tempting to interpret the revival of partisan voting at the presidential level largely as a reflection of the gradual reequilibration of presidential votes and more general partisan attachments among white southerners in the wake of a regional partisan realignment.

As it happens, however, the steady and substantial increases in partisan voting over the past quarter-century evident in Figure 3 are by no means confined to the

Figure 4. Partisan Voting in Presidential Elections, White Southerners and White Nonsoutherners

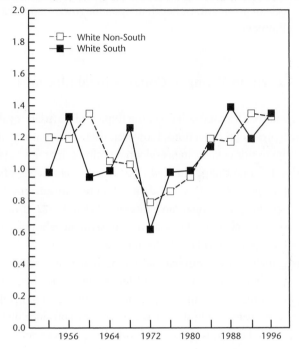

Estimated Impact of Party Identification on Presidential Vote Propensity

Note: Average probit coefficients, major-party voters only.

South. This fact is evident from Figure 4, which displays separate patterns of partisan voting for white southerners and white nonsoutherners. The trend lines are somewhat more ragged for these subgroups than for the electorate as a whole, especially in the South (where the year-by-year estimates are based on an average of fewer than 300 southern white voters in each election); nevertheless, the general pattern in Figure 3 is replicated almost identically in both subgroups in Figure 4. The absolute level of partisan voting in the 1964 and 1972 elections is only slightly lower among southern whites than among nonsouthern whites, and the substantial increase in partisan voting since 1972 appears clearly (indeed, nearly monotonically) in both subgroups.

It should be evident from Figure 4 that the revival of partisan voting in presidential elections documented in Figure 3 is a national rather than a regional phenomenon. Indeed, additional analysis along these lines suggests that the same pattern is evident in a wide variety of subgroups of the electorate, including voters under 40 and those over 50 years of age, those with college educations and those without high school diplomas, and so on. Thus, any convincing explanation of this partisan revival will presumably have to be based upon broad changes in the national political environment, rather than upon narrower demographic or generational developments.

Partisan Voting in Congressional Elections

My analysis so far has focused solely on the impact of partisan loyalties on voting behavior in presidential elections. However, there are a variety of reasons to suppose that the trends evident in presidential voting might not appear at other electoral levels. For one thing, I have already argued that the significant dips in partisanship at the presidential level evident in Figure 3 are attributable primarily to the parties' specific presidential candidates in 1964 and 1972. If that is so, there is little reason to expect those dips—or the subsequent rebounds—in levels of partisan voting to appear at other electoral levels.

In any case, analysts of congressional voting behavior since the 1970s have been more impressed by the advantages of incumbency than by any strong connections between presidential and congressional votes—except insofar as voters may go out of their way to split their tickets in order to produce divided government. Thus, it would not be surprising to find a longer, more substantial decline in the level of partisan voting in congressional elections than in the analysis of presidential voting summarized in Figure 3.

. . . Figure 5 clearly shows a substantial decline in partisan voting in congressional elections from the early 1960s through the late 1970s. Indeed, the level of partisan voting declined in seven of the eight congressional elections between 1964 and 1978; by 1978, the average impact of partisanship on congressional voting was only a bit more than half what it had been before 1964. Although the overall impact of partisanship at the presidential and congressional levels was generally similar for much of this period, the declines at the congressional level were less episodic and longer lasting than those at the presidential level.

What is more surprising is that the revival of partisanship evident in presidential voting patterns since 1972 is also evident in congressional voting patterns since 1978. While the trend is later and less regular at the congressional level than at the presidential level, the absolute increases in partisan voting since 1980 have been of quite similar magnitude in presidential and congressional elections. While partisan voting remains noticeably less powerful in recent congressional elections than it was before 1964—or than it has been in recent presidential elec-

Figure 5. Partisan Voting in Presidential and Congressional Elections

Estimated Impact of Party Identification on Presidential and Congressional Vote Propensities

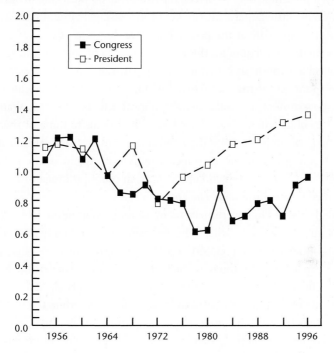

Note: Average probit coefficients, major-party voters only.

tions—the impact of partisanship on congressional votes in 1996 was almost 60 percent greater than in 1978.

An interesting feature of the resurgence of partisan voting in congressional elections documented in Figure 5 is that it appears to be concentrated disproportionately among younger and better-educated voters. For example, voters under the age of 40 were noticeably less partisan in their voting behavior than those over the age of 50 in almost every election from 1952 through 1984, but virtually indistinguishable from the older voters in the late 1980s and 1990s. Similarly, levels of partisan voting were distinctly lower among voters with some college education than among those without high school diplomas before 1982, but not thereafter. These patterns suggest that the resurgence of partisan voting reflects some positive reaction by younger and better-educated voters to the political developments of the past two decades, rather than simply a "wearing off" of the political stimuli of the 1960s and 1970s.

Discussion

If the analysis presented here is correct, the American political system has slipped, with remarkably little fanfare, into an era of increasingly vibrant partisanship in the electorate, especially at the presidential level but also at the congressional level. How might we account for this apparent revival of partisan voting?

One plausible hypothesis is that increasing partisanship in the electorate represents a response at the mass level to increasing partisanship at the elite level. "If parties in government are weakened," [political scientist Martin] Wattenberg argued, "the public will naturally have less of a stimulus to think of themselves politically in partisan terms." But then the converse may also be true: in an era in which parties in government seem increasingly consequential, the public may increasingly come to develop and apply partisan predispositions of exactly the sort described by the authors of *The American Voter.*

Why might parties in government seem more relevant in the late 1990s than they had a quarter-century earlier? The ascensions of two highly partisan political leaders—Ronald Reagan in 1981 and Newt Gingrich in 1995—may provide part of the explanation. So too may the increasing prominence of the Religious Right in Republican party nominating politics over this period. At a more structural level, the realignment of partisan loyalties in the South in the wake of the civil rights movement of the 1960s may be important, despite the evidence presented in Figure 4 suggesting that the revival of partisan voting has been a national rather than a regional phenomenon.

Regional realignment in the South and the influence of ideological extremists in both parties' nominating politics have combined to produce a marked polarization of the national parties at the elite level. By a variety of measures . . . votes on the floor of Congress have become increasingly partisan since the 1970s. . . . These changes in the composition of the parties' congressional delegations have been "reinforced by the operation of those reform provisions that were intended to enhance collective control" by party leaders in Congress, including a strengthened Democratic caucus and whip system. The new Republican congressional majority in 1995 produced further procedural reforms "delegating more power to party leaders than any House majority since the revolt against Joe Cannon in 1910."

We know less than we should about the nature and extent of mass-level reactions to these elite-level developments. However, the plausibility of a causal link between recent increases in partisanship at the elite and mass levels is reinforced by the fact that the decline in partisan voting in the electorate in the 1960s and 1970s was itself preceded by a noticeable decline in party voting in Congress from the 1950s through the early 1970s. Moreover, some more direct evidence suggests that citizens have taken note of the increasing strength of partisan cues from Washington. For example, the proportion of NES survey respondents perceiving "important differences" between the Democratic and Republican parties increased noticeably in 1980 and again in 1984 and reached a new all-time high (for the period since 1952) in 1996.

Even more intriguingly, [political scientist John] Coleman has documented a systematic temporal relationship between the strength of partisanship in government and the strength of partisanship in the electorate. Analyzing data from 1952 through 1990, Coleman found a strong positive correlation across election years (.60) between the strength of partisanship in NES surveys and the proportion of House budget votes with opposing party majorities—and an even stronger correlation (.66) between mass partisanship and opposing party majorities on budget authorization votes. While the detailed processes underlying this aggregate relationship are by no means clear, the strength of the correlation at least suggests that students of party politics would do well to examine more closely the interrelationship of mass-level and elite-level trends. . . .

12-3

Who Needs Political Parties?

Rick Valelly

Political scientists take diverging views about whether American parties are in decline and, if so, whether it is a good thing. Rick Valelly's essay is a succinct introduction to the major schools of thought. American parties, one school holds, are not in decline but rather are taking new forms. Parties are still teams of candidates for elective office, as they always have been, even if the services they provide to candidates have been transformed by new election rules and new technologies. Another school holds that the party system is failing ordinary voters by allowing campaigns to become hugely expensive undertakings run by professional consultants. According to this school, both campaign finance reform and other reforms are essential to reestablishing parties as a meaningful basis for organizing campaigns and keeping officeholders accountable. Yet a third school insists that parties have never been very important to American government.

AS THE MAJOR political parties [prepare for their national conventions], with all the usual noise, pomp, and expense, Americans can be counted on to let out a collective yawn, or maybe a grimace. But not so for political scientists. Academic experts see a lot to like—or at least a lot to study—in the American two-party system. In their considered view, a competitive party system ensures the legitimacy of opposition to government, promotes public debate about policy options, and gets citizens involved in the public sphere. The two-party system never does these things perfectly, but it does them well enough. Without it our system would collapse overnight, leaving gridlock and hyperpluralism—or so most political scientists think.

But if one looks closely at the views of those who are researching, thinking about, and writing about political parties, one finds an interesting division of opinion. One school of thought is that parties are in decline and, consequently, that we have a major problem. The public is right to be irritated. A second view holds that parties have changed dramatically but that they are just as strong as they used to be. The public ought to get used to the transformation and stop

Source: Rick Valelly, "Who Needs Political Parties?," *The American Prospect*, August 14, 2000.

griping. A third school, best articulated by David Mayhew of Yale University, is that political scientists have attributed too much importance to party dynamics. They matter, but less so than the professional literature has suggested. In this light, the public's gripes are beside the point.

To make sense of the disagreement, we must first sift through the ruins of realignment theory. For about 20 years, American government students were instructed in this line of thinking. Its concepts still echo in political punditry. But the theory died a decade ago when it became clear it wasn't explaining with any precision the events of the actual political world.

Still, it was an elegant idea. Realignment theory held that not all elections were the same. In certain highly charged elections or in a string of two or three such elections, big and lasting shifts occurred in how voters behaved. A new voter coalition would assert control over our system, determining policy outcomes for a generation. Walter Dean Burnham, the theory's best-known proponent, suggested such elections might be a uniquely American surrogate for political revolution. Before realignment, there might be a third-party challenge, protests, and even civil disorder. Eventually, ambitious politicians would pick up the pressing issues and make them their own.

With the image of periodic political renewal, there was a soothing message in all this. Realignments allowed the political system to adjust to social and political stress, and to bring those citizens who might otherwise be absorbed in personal concerns into political action. The party system periodically restored its own vitality and that of the system as a whole.

Burnham explicitly warned, however, that the party system's capacity for "peaceful revolution" was not automatic. If and when the party system lost its ability to adapt, the branches of government would lock up. Governmental remedy as both an ideal and a practice would wither. Gradually, a propensity toward broad-based oligarchy would set in. After all, the wealthy are best protected by government that is deadlocked. Simultaneously, a huge class of unmobilized people would emerge as a "party of nonvoters." Their influence on the system would necessarily be weaker.

Scholars in the "party decline" school have inherited Burnham's worry. They agree that as a party system weakens it tends to pull the rest of the order down with it. Sidney Milkis of the University of Virginia, who is close in spirit to Burnham, makes such a case in *Political Parties and Constitutional Government*, a study of the rise and development of political parties since the founding. While Milkis does not share Burnham's open distaste for markets, capitalism, and social inequalities, he does adopt Burnham's democratic nationalism. For Milkis the weakening of parties has promoted broad discontent with American government and has generated an anemic civic culture.

In Milkis's account—and this is what makes his work so provocative—the cause of party decline, and thus of public cynicism, is not the depoliticizing force of market values, as Burnham has long argued. Instead, it is the particular development of the presidency. To put Milkis's claim bluntly, FDR killed the parties when he built a government competent enough to run a welfare state. In doing that, he changed the constitutional balance that had been supported by the parties since the time of Madison, Jackson, and Van Buren. Subsequent presidents failed to reverse Roosevelt's legacy.

Party competition first emerged, Milkis argues, when James Madison and Thomas Jefferson sought to develop a political opposition to Alexander Hamilton, John Adams, and the Federalist legatees of George Washington's two-term presidency. Madison, in particular, feared for the future of federalism and the separation of powers if Hamilton's economic nationalism were left politically unchecked. Milkis takes pains to point out that there was a second Madison, one less well-known but just as important as the more familiar Madison who framed the Constitution. The first disliked parties and factions; the second had no trouble embracing them in order to save his overall institutional design. Happily for Madison, the party system that he helped to launch evolved (thanks to the genius of Martin Van Buren) into a stable contest between two large confederations of state and local parties. And happily for the system as a whole, Milkis says, the parties won the political loyalties of voters scattered across a vast geographic expanse.

Americans came to appreciate the full range of national, state, and local institutions contemplated by the founders. Voters liked their town and county governments; they valued their state institutions; and they came to treasure not only the presidency but the Senate, the House, and the Supreme Court. America's elaborate mix of national, state, and local jurisdictions and offices might never have taken hold without the early development of decentralized but nationally competitive parties. This accomplishment helps to explain the persistence of the Constitution of 1787 despite the extraordinary events of the Civil War and the Reconstruction, and the huge expansion of the republic's size.

But our party system and institutions were never particularly well-suited for strong, positive government, Milkis argues. They were good for participation and office-seeking, but not for supple macroeconomic management or the competent bureaucratic delivery of social benefits, such as old-age income security or work relief. Here Milkis carries forward a long line of thinking about party politics and public administration that dates to the work of Herbert Croly and other progressives in the early decades of the 1900s.

FDR was the first president, in Milkis's view, who was forced to cope with the lack of fit between the institutional forms given to him and new executive tasks. He keenly understood the limits of the party system he inherited, and sought briefly to do something about them, through the ill-fated 1938 "Roosevelt purge" in which New Deal liberals were encouraged to run against reactionary and conservative Democratic incumbents in Congress. He hoped to transform his party into a programmatic, responsible organization. He failed miserably.

FDR did not try again, opting instead for the independent regulatory commissions, new bureaucracies, court-packing, and executive reorganization that he or congressional liberals had already launched or planned before the purge effort. Roosevelt grasped that he could, and probably should, soft-pedal his party as an instrument of executive governance. It was too loaded with southern conservatives and stand-pat careerists. Time was short, and there was much work to be done to save liberal capitalism from its enemies within and without.

But there was a hidden price for this understandable decision. The cost to the polity, one that was not immediately obvious, was reduced voter involvement. As Kennedy, Johnson, and Nixon perfected the New Deal state, they did so on the backs of social movements, professors, experts, and government executives and lawyers. Their mission was not to revitalize the remnants of the urban machines or to reform the conservative state parties and party factions that they scorned. They made the same choice Roosevelt did. So the decentralized system of confederated parties—imagined by Madison and perfected by Van Buren—collapsed, as one ward club or county committee after another (with the notable exception of Chicago) died on the liberal vine. These local institutions were the vital foundation of voter involvement; without them voter turnout began its long decline.

Not all political scientists are alarmed by such developments. In his important 1995 work, *Why Parties?*, John H. Aldrich responds to the passing of the ward heelers by saying, in effect, "so what?" He wants us to face up to a stark proposition: The forms of parties are going to change. As he notes, trenchantly, "The major political party is the creature of the politicians. . . . These politicians do not have partisan goals per se, and the party is only the instrument for achieving them." Politicians run the parties, and they will inevitably change the ways in which parties help them to be politicians.

Aldrich is no iconoclast, to be sure. His book is deeply thoughtful, gently argued, and quite rigorous. At the heart of Aldrich's case lies an extended comparison between two party systems: the system that emerged in the North during the 1820s and 1830s and that lasted until the Civil War, and the more familiar two-party system that has structured our politics since the 1960s. The first was intensely mobilizing and generated sharp increases in voter turnout until it reached extraordinary, indeed uniquely high levels. This was also a period of "team parties," in which politicians subordinated their individual identities to the corporate identity of their party since the path to power lay through making that trade-off.

Today's parties, in contrast, are service-providing organizations. They resemble a franchise for entrepreneurs. The individual candidates of the two parties meet certain programmatic requirements related to party ideology, but in terms of campaigning they act as freelancers. They have no trouble behaving as highly competitive teams within government, particularly within the House of Representatives, but they do not cooperate with each other to rally voters. Stimulating turnout is up to an individual candidate if he or she chooses.

The point of Aldrich's contrast is not that there has been decline relative to some golden age. Instead, these are fundamentally different systems. Juxtaposed to this claim is a lucid demonstration of the central tendency of any competitive party system, regardless of differences in the campaign styles of politicians. Using simple modeling, Aldrich posits that a party system will solve pathologies that would otherwise plague politicians. Without a competitive party system, politicians could not cooperate around mutual policy gains, which can only come through repeated interaction and binding commitments that hold up across time. They would instead treat all their interactions with each other as one-shot games and thus fall prey to the non-cooperative trap epitomized by the "prisoner's dilemma."

Second, without parties' resources and their capacity to stimulate, motivate, and inform voters, politicians could never solve a major dilemma facing voters, i.e., the propensity to avoid voting and to instead "free ride" on those who take the trouble to vote out of an irrationally strong sense of civic duty. If most of us were freeriders, there could be no genuinely popular electoral system.

Third, without the partisan organization of legislatures and government, politicians could never efficiently restrict the agenda of conflict and debate to a basic set of important issues. They would instead stumble in and out of fragile log-rolls that would incorporate many unrelated items. The result would be policy immobility, rendering deliberation and participation beside the point.

Professional politicians in a democracy obviously need parties to satisfy their policy and office-seeking ambitions. But the rest of us also need parties. No parties, no "positive externalities" (in the language of welfare economics)—no streams of consistent and related policies, no agenda for public debate, and little prospect of even a modicum of voter attachment to the polity and its concerns. Thus, our current party system provides essentially the same "positive externalities," Aldrich is saying, as the earlier party system.

But a somewhat different take on the same facts is offered by Steven Schier in *By Invitation Only*. During the golden age of party politics, roughly the period from 1830 to 1890, we had something approaching a genuinely participatory democracy in this country. Today we have, in its place, a vast congeries of professionally managed "activation," that is, the stimulation and enlistment of thousands of small subsets of the citizenry in service of the ambition of an interest group or a candidate. Several kinds of professional consultancies are available to the well-heeled or the well-organized to accomplish their preferred strategy of activation: pollsters, media consultants, fundraisers, gatherers of demographic data, opposition and issue researchers, speechwriters, schedulers, and so forth. Schier catalogues them all succinctly.

The basic idea here is that parties now compete in a broad marketplace of service providers for the politically ambitious. Their historic monopoly on access to office and influence disappeared with the rise of primaries, referenda, campaign finance regulation, and a privately operated system of broadcast communications.

The loser in the shift toward a competitive market in political techniques is the mass of ordinary citizens. Following politics and getting involved in it is up to them. If they do not have the education, confidence, partisanship, or time to do so, no one will ask them. Expending resources to activate the already motivated voters is cost-effective. It is less cost-effective to pursue those who are not listed in the databases of the consultants.

In this way, the political system is a bit like the medical system: technologically advanced, expensive, and replete with a variety of coverages and exclusions. As a nation, we spend a huge amount of money on electoral politics and employ all the latest campaign techniques, but we do not get much average-voter turnout in return.

Schier's final chapter offers an exceptionally thoughtful treatment of possible cures for this state of affairs. The bottom line for reform, he suggests, is making party affiliation more salient to political candidates than it currently is. In response, politicians might have stronger incentives to cooperate with one another in mobilizing voters, rather than worrying only about their own constituency.

We should reorganize campaign finance so that parties control more resources than they do now. And the states could provide ballots that are organized as party slates. More states could do what Maine and Nebraska do, which is to allocate votes in the electoral college to whomever carries a congressional district and give the "Senate votes" to the statewide winner. These are among the most plausible reforms of the many that Schier discusses.

Could it be that such reforms overemphasize the importance of political parties to democracy? David Mayhew is the one leader of the political science profession who has consistently resisted such enthusiasms. In the course of his career, he has helped to show that political parties have little to do with whether

Congress works well, that states with weak parties are not necessarily less generous with social policies (and are sometimes more generous), and that from 1947 to 1990 divided government at the national level simply had no effect on the production of important public policy, budgetary balance, or the frequency or disruptiveness of congressional investigations of the White House or the executive bureaucracies.

It could also be the case that the party system, as Aldrich says, is not in decline but simply has acquired new forms. One might retort that the earlier system made for more active citizens. But cross-national survey research does not show that countries with party systems more like our earlier system have citizens more satisfied with how their democracy works than ours.

Nonetheless, Walter Dean Burnham was right to think as long and as hard as he did about cycles of decline and renewal in American party politics. Perhaps critical realignments never really existed, but political decline and renewal are hardly fanciful inventions of Burnham's towering intellect. They are the oldest and most important issues of political thought, going back to Aristotle.

For all their faults, political parties have been the essential foundation of both citizen involvement and citizen awareness of the issues facing a democratic polity. Perhaps nothing will come of letting our two-party system continue to become just one among many channels for citizen involvement, rather than the premier channel. It is more likely, though, that good things would come from trying, as Schier suggests, to make our party system more salient for voters and politicians than it currently is.

Chapter 13

Interest Groups

13-1

The Scope and Bias of the Pressure System

E. E. Schattschneider

In the mid twentieth century, many observers believed that James Madison's vision of America—as a multitude of groups or factions, none of which dominated the government—had been realized. E. E. Schattschneider provided an alternative view. In the following essay, which was originally published in 1960, Schattschneider argued that moneyed interests dominated mid-twentieth-century politics. In his view the dominance of moneyed interests limited the scope of government action and created a bias in the pressures placed on policymakers. Early in the twenty-first century, the issues raised by Schattschneider remain relevant to debates over the influence of organized and moneyed interests in American government and politics.

THE SCOPE OF CONFLICT is an aspect of the scale of political organization and the extent of political competition. The size of the constituencies being mobilized, the inclusiveness or exclusiveness of the conflicts people expect to develop leave a bearing on all theories about how politics is or should be organized. In other words, nearly all theories about politics have something to do with the question of who can get into the fight and who is to be excluded. . . .

Source: E. E. Schattschneider, "The Scope and Bias of the Pressure System," in *The Semi-Sovereign People* (New York: Holt, Rinehart, Winston, 1960), 20–45. Some notes appearing in the original have been deleted.

If we are able . . . to distinguish between public and private interests and between organized and unorganized groups we have marked out the major boundaries of the subject; *we have given the subject shape and scope.* . . . [W]e can now appropriate the piece we want and leave the rest to someone else. For a multitude of reasons *the most likely field of study is that of the organized, special-interest groups.* The advantage of concentrating on organized groups is that they are known, identifiable, and recognizable. The advantage of concentrating on special-interest groups is that they have one important characteristic in common; they are all exclusive. This piece of the pie (the organized special-interest groups) we shall call the *pressure system.* The pressure system has boundaries we can define; we can fix its scope and make an attempt to estimate its bias.

It may be assumed at the outset that all organized special-interest groups have some kind of impact on politics. A sample survey of organizations made by the Trade Associations Division of the United States Department of Commerce in 1942 concluded that "From 70 to 100 percent (of these associations) are planning activities in the field of government relations, trade promotion, trade practices, public relations, annual conventions, cooperation with other organizations, and information services."

The subject of our analysis can be reduced to manageable proportions and brought under control if we restrict ourselves to the groups whose interests in politics are sufficient to have led them to unite in formal organizations having memberships, bylaws, and officers. A further advantage of this kind of definition is, we may assume, that the organized special-interest groups are the most self-conscious, best developed, most intense and active groups. Whatever claims can be made for a group theory of politics ought to be sustained by the evidence concerning these groups, if the claims have any validity at all.

The organized groups listed in the various directories (such as *National Associations of the United States,* published at intervals by the United States Department of Commerce) and specialty yearbooks, registers, etc., and the *Lobby Index,* published by the United States House of Representatives, probably include the bulk of the organizations in the pressure system. All compilations are incomplete, but these are extensive enough to provide us with some basis for estimating the scope of the system.

By the time a group has developed the kind of interest that leads it to organize, it may be assumed that it has also developed some kind of political bias because *organization is itself a mobilization of bias in preparation for action.* Since these groups can be identified and since they have memberships (i.e., they include and exclude people), it is possible to think of the *scope* of the system.

When lists of these organizations are examined, the fact that strikes the student most forcibly is that *the system is very small.* The range of organized, identifiable, known groups is amazingly narrow; there is nothing remotely universal about it. There is a tendency on the part of the publishers of directories of associations to place an undue emphasis on business organizations, an emphasis that is almost inevitable because the business community is by a wide margin the most highly organized segment of society. Publishers doubtless tend also to reflect public demand for information. Nevertheless, the dominance of business groups in the pressure system is so marked that it probably cannot be explained away as an accident of the publishing industry.

The business character of the pressure system is shown by almost every list available. *National Associations of the United States* lists 1,860 business associations out of a total of 4,000 in the volume, though it refers without listing to 16,000 organizations of businessmen. One cannot be certain what the total content of the unknown associational universe may be, but, taken with the evidence found in other compilations, it is obvious that business is remarkably well represented. Some evidence of the overall scope of the system is to be seen in the estimate that 15,000 national trade associations have a gross membership of about one million business firms. The data are incomplete, but even if we do not have a detailed map this is the shore dimly seen.

Much more directly related to pressure politics is the *Lobby Index, 1946–1949* (an index of organizations and individuals registering or filing quarterly reports under the Federal Lobbying Act), published as a report of the House Select Committee on Lobbying Activities. In this compilation, 825 out of a total of 1,247 entries (exclusive of individuals and Indian tribes) represented business. A selected list of the most important of the groups listed in the *Index* (the groups spending the largest sums of money on lobbying) published in the *Congressional Quarterly Log* shows 149 business organizations in a total of 265 listed.

The business or upper-class bias of the pressure system shows up everywhere. Businessmen are four or five times as likely to write to their congressmen as manual laborers are. College graduates are far more apt to write to their congressmen than people in the lowest educational category are.

The limited scope of the business pressure system is indicated by all available statistics. Among business organizations, the National Association of Manufacturers (with about 20,000 corporate members) and the Chamber of Commerce of the United States (about as large as the N.A.M.) are giants. Usually business associations are much smaller. Of 421 trade associations in the metal-products industry listed in *National Associations of the United States,* 153 have a membership of less than 20. The median membership was somewhere between 24 and 50. Approximately the same scale of memberships is to be found in the lumber, furniture, and paper industries, where 37.3 percent of the associations listed had a membership of less than 20 and the median membership was in the 25 to 50 range.

The statistics in these cases are representative of nearly all other classifications of industry.

Data drawn from other sources support this thesis. Broadly, the pressure system has an upper-class bias. There is overwhelming evidence that participation in voluntary organizations is related to upper social and economic status; the rate of participation is much higher in the upper strata than it is elsewhere. The general proposition is well stated by [political scientist Paul] Lazarsfeld:

> People on the lower SES levels are less likely to belong to any organizations than the people on high SES (Social and Economic Status) levels. (On an A and B level, we find 72 percent of these respondents who belong to one or more organizations. The proportion of respondents who are members of formal organizations decreases steadily as SES level descends until, on the D level only 35 percent of the respondents belong to any associations).[1]

The bias of the system is shown by the fact that *even non-business organizations reflect an upper-class tendency.*

Lazarsfeld's generalization seems to apply equally well to urban and rural populations. The obverse side of the coin is that large areas of the population appear to be wholly outside the system of private organization. A study made by Ira Reid of a Philadelphia area showed that in a sample of 963 persons, 85 percent belonged to no civic or charitable organization and 74 percent belonged to no occupational, business, or professional associations, while another Philadelphia study of 1,154 women showed that 55 percent belonged to no associations of any kind.[2]

A *Fortune* farm poll taken some years ago found that 70.5 percent of farmers belonged to no agricultural organizations. A similar conclusion was reached by two Gallup polls showing that perhaps no more than one third of the farmers of the country belonged to farm organizations, while another *Fortune* poll showed that 86.8 percent of the low-income farmers belonged to no farm organizations. All available data support the generalization that the farmers who do not participate in rural organizations are largely the poorer ones. . . .

The class bias of associational activity gives meaning to the limited scope of the pressure system, because *scope and bias are aspects of the same tendency.* The data raise a serious question about the validity of the proposition that special-interest groups are a universal form of political organization reflecting *all* interests. As a matter of fact, to suppose that everyone participates in pressure-group activity and that all interests get themselves organized in the pressure system is to destroy the meaning of this form of politics. The pressure system makes sense only as the political instrument of a segment of the community. It gets results by being selective and biased; *if everybody got into the act, the unique advantages of this form of organization would be destroyed, for it is possible that if all interests could be mobilized the result would be a stalemate.*

Special-interest organizations are most easily formed when they deal with small numbers of individuals who are acutely aware of their exclusive interests. To describe the conditions of pressure-group organization in this way is, however, to say that it is primarily a business phenomenon. Aside from a few very large organizations (the churches, organized labor, farm organizations, and veterans' organizations) the residue is a small segment of the population. *Pressure politics is essentially the politics of small groups.*

The vice of the groupist theory is that it conceals the most significant aspects of the system. The flaw in the pluralist heaven is that the heavenly chorus sings with a strong upper-class accent. Probably about 90 percent of the people cannot get into the pressure system.

The notion that the pressure system is automatically representative of the whole community is a myth fostered by the universalizing tendency of modern group theories. *Pressure politics is a selective process* ill designed to serve diffuse interests. The system is skewed, loaded, and unbalanced in favor of a fraction of a minority.

On the other hand, pressure tactics are not remarkably successful in mobilizing general interests. When pressure-group organizations attempt to represent the interests of large numbers of people, they are usually able to reach only a small segment of their constituencies. Only a chemical trace of the fifteen million Negroes in the United States belong to the National Association for the Advancement of Colored People. Only one five-hundredth of 1 percent of American women belong to the League of Women Voters, only one sixteen-hundredth of 1 percent of the consumers belong to the National Consumers' League, and only 6 percent of American automobile drivers belong to the American Automobile Association, while about 15 percent of the veterans belong to the American Legion.

The competing claims of pressure groups and political parties for the loyalty of the American public revolve about the difference between the results likely to be achieved by small-scale and large-scale political organization. Inevitably, the outcome of pressure politics and party politics will be vastly different. . . .

. . . Everything we know about politics suggests that a conflict is likely to change profoundly as it becomes political. It is a rare individual who can confront his antagonists without changing his opinions to some degree. Everything changes once a conflict gets into the political arena—*who* is involved, *what* the conflict is about, the resources available, etc. It is extremely difficult to predict the outcome of a fight by watching its beginning because we do not even know who else is going to get into the conflict. The logical consequence of the exclusive emphasis on the determinism of the private origins of conflict is to assign zero value to the political process.

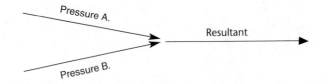

The very expression "pressure politics" invites us to misconceive the role of special-interest groups in politics. The word "pressure" implies the use of some kind of force, a form of intimidation, something other than reason and information, to induce public authorities to act against their own best judgment. [This is reflected in the famous statement by political scientist Earl Latham, in his 1952 book *The Group Basis of Politics,* that] the legislature is a "referee" who "ratifies" and "records" the "balance of power" among the contending groups.[3]

It is hard to imagine a more effective way of saying that Congress has no mind or force of its own or that Congress is unable to invoke new forces that might alter the equation.

Actually the outcome of political conflict is not like the "resultant" of opposing forces in physics. To assume that the forces in a political situation could be diagramed as a physicist might diagram the resultant of opposing physical forces is to wipe the slate clean of all remote, general, and public considerations for the protection of which civil societies have been instituted.

Moreover, the notion of "pressure" distorts the image of the power relations involved. *Private conflicts are taken into the public arena precisely because someone wants to make certain that the power ratio among the private interests most immediately involved shall not prevail.* To treat a conflict as a mere test of the strength of the private interests is to leave out the most significant factors. This is so true that it might indeed be said that the only way to preserve private power ratios is to keep conflicts out of the public arena.

The assumption that it is only the "interested" who count ought to be reexamined in view of the foregoing discussion. The tendency of the literature of pressure politics has been to neglect the low-tension force of large numbers because it *assumes that the equation of forces is fixed at the outset.*

Given the assumptions made by the group theorists, the attack on the idea of the majority is completely logical. The assumption is that conflict is monopolized narrowly by the parties immediately concerned. There is no room for a majority when conflict is defined so narrowly. It is a great deficiency of the group theory that it has found no place in the political system for the majority. The force of the majority is of an entirely different order of magnitude, something not to be measured by pressure-group standards.

Instead of attempting to exterminate all political forms, organizations, and alignments that do not qualify as pressure groups, would it not be better to attempt to make a synthesis, covering the whole political system and finding a place for all kinds of political life?

One possible synthesis of pressure politics and party politics might be produced by *describing politics as the socialization of conflict.* That is to say, the political process is a sequence: conflicts are initiated by highly motivated, high-tension groups so directly and immediately involved that it is difficult for them to see the justice of competing claims. As long as the conflicts of these groups remain *private* (carried on in terms of economic competition, reciprocal denial of goods and services, private negotiations and bargaining, struggles for corporate control or competition for membership), no political process is initiated. Conflicts become political only when an attempt is made to involve the wider public. Pressure politics might be described as a stage in the socialization of conflict. This analysis makes pressure politics an integral part of all politics, including party politics.

One of the characteristic points of origin of pressure politics is a breakdown of the discipline of the business community. The flight to government is perpetual. Something like this is likely to happen wherever there is a point of contact between competing power systems. It is the *losers in intrabusiness conflict who seek redress from public authority. The dominant business interests resist appeals to the government.* The role of the government as the patron of the defeated private interest sheds light on its function as the critic of private power relations.

Since the contestants in private conflicts are apt to be unequal in strength, it follows that *the most powerful special interests want private settlements* because they are able to dictate the outcome as long as the conflict remains private. If A is a hundred times as strong as B he does not welcome the intervention of a third party because he expects to impose his own terms on B; he wants to isolate B. He is especially opposed to the intervention of public authority, because public authority represents the most overwhelming form of outside intervention. Thus, if $A/B = 100/1$, it is obviously not to A's advantage to involve a third party a million times as strong as A and B combined. Therefore, it is the weak, not the strong, who appeal to public authority for relief. It is the weak who want to socialize conflict, i.e., to involve more and more people in the conflict until the balance of forces is changed. In the schoolyard it is not the bully but the defenseless smaller boys who "tell the teacher." When the teacher intervenes, the balance of power in the schoolyard is apt to change drastically. It is the function of public authority to *modify private power relations by enlarging the scope of conflict.*

Nothing could be more mistaken than to suppose that public authority merely registers the dominance of the strong over the weak. The mere existence of public order has already ruled out a great variety of forms of private pressure. Nothing could be more confusing than to suppose that the refugees from the business community who come to Congress for relief and protection *force* Congress to do their bidding.

Evidence of the truth of this analysis may be seen in the fact that the big private interests do not necessarily win if they are involved in public conflicts with petty interests. The image of the lobbyists as primarily the agents of big business is not easy to support on the face of the record of congressional hearings, for example. The biggest corporations in the country tend to avoid the arena in which pressure groups and lobbyists fight it out before congressional committees. To describe this process exclusively in terms of an effort of business to intimidate congressmen is to misconceive what is actually going on.

It is probably a mistake to assume that pressure politics is the typical or even the most important relation between government and business. The pressure group is by no means the perfect instrument of the business community. What does big business want? The *winners* in intrabusiness strife want (1) to be let alone (they want autonomy) and (2) to preserve the solidarity of the business community. For these purposes pressure politics is not a wholly satisfactory device. The most elementary considerations of strategy call for the business community to develop some kind of common policy more broadly based than any special-interest group is likely to be.

The political influence of business depends on the kind of solidarity that, on the one hand, leads all business to rally to the support of *any* businessman in trouble with the government and, on the other hand, keeps internal business disputes out of the public arena. In this system businessmen resist the impulse to attack each other in public and discourage the efforts of individual members of the business community to take intrabusiness conflicts into politics.

The attempt to mobilize a united front of the whole business community does not resemble the classical concept of pressure politics. The logic of business politics is to keep peace within the business community by supporting as far as possible all claims that business groups make for themselves. The tendency is to support all businessmen who have conflicts with the government and support all businessmen in conflict with labor. In this way *special-interest politics can be converted into party policy.* The search is for a broad base of political mobilization grounded on the strategic need for political organization on a wider scale than is possible in the case of the historical pressure group. Once the business community begins to think in terms of a larger scale of political organization the Republican party looms large in business politics.

It is a great achievement of American democracy that business has been forced to form a political organization designed to win elections, i.e., has been forced to compete for power in the widest arena in the political system. On the other hand, *the power of the Republican party to make terms with business rests on the fact that business cannot afford to be isolated.*

The Republican party has played a major role in *the political organization of the business community,* a far greater role than many students of politics seem to have realized. The influence of business in the Republican party is great, but it is never absolute because business is remarkably dependent on the party. The business community is too small, it arouses too much antagonism, and its aims are too narrow to win the support of a popular majority. The political education of business is a function of the Republican party that can never be done so well by anyone else.

In the management of the political relations of the business community, the Republican party is much more important than any combination of pressure groups ever could be. The success of special interests in Congress is due less to the "pressure" exerted by these groups than it is due to the fact that Republican members of Congress are committed in advance to a general probusiness attitude. The notion that business groups coerce Republican congressmen into voting for their bills underestimates the whole Republican posture in American politics.

It is not easy to manage the political interests of the business community because there is a perpetual stream of losers in intrabusiness conflicts who go to the government for relief and protection. It has not been possible therefore to maintain perfect solidarity, and when solidarity is breached the government is involved almost automatically. The fact that business has not become hopelessly divided and that it has retained great influence in American politics has been due chiefly to the overall mediating role played by the Republican party. There has never been a pressure group or a combination of pressure groups capable of performing this function.

NOTES

1. Paul F. Lazarsfeld, Bernard Berelson, and Hazel Gaudet. *The People's Choice* (New York: Columbia University Press, 1948), p. 145.

2. Reid and Ehle, "Leadership Selection in the Urban Locality Areas," *Public Opinion Quarterly* (1950), 14:262–284. See also Norman Powell, *Anatomy of Public Opinion* (New York: Prentice Hall, 1951), pp. 180–181.

3. Earl Latham, *The Group Basis of Politics* (Ithaca: Cornell University Press, 1952), pp. 35–36.

13-2

The Evolution of Interest Groups

John R. Wright

In the following essay John R. Wright provides an overview of the develop-
ment of interest groups in America. Interest groups form, Wright explains, as
a net result of two factors—societal disturbances and collective action prob-
lems. Societal disturbances create common interests for groups of individuals,
who then join forces to pursue those interests. All groups then face the collec-
tive action problem known as free riding—the tendency for group members to
benefit from others' contributions to the provision of a public good without
contributing themselves. Interest groups must find a way to encourage people
to join and contribute in order to achieve their political goals.

THE RAPID ECONOMIC and social development in the United States immediately
following the Civil War created a new and uncertain political environment for
members of Congress. Congress emerged as the dominant force in national policy making, and members' electoral constituencies became far more heterogeneous and complex than ever before. In this new and uncertain political environment, the informational needs of members of Congress were greater than at
any previous time, and it was in this environment that the American interest
group system evolved.

Although the evolution of interest groups in the United States did not begin
in earnest until after the Civil War, the groundwork for their development was
laid much earlier in several key provisions of the U.S. Constitution. These constitutional provisions have had a profound effect on the American political party
system, which in turn has had a major impact on the interest group system.

Constitutional Underpinnings

The place of special interests in American politics today is largely a consequence
of two competing political values expressed in the U.S. Constitution: a concern
for liberty and freedom of political expression on the one hand, and the desire to

Source: John R. Wright, "The Evolution of Interest Groups," in *Interest Groups and Congress,* John R. Wright
(Boston: Allyn & Bacon, 1996), 11–22. Some notes appearing in the original have been deleted.

prevent tyranny on the other. James Madison's *Federalist* No. 10 is the classic justification for the various constitutional checks and balances, which disperse power and make it difficult for any single group of citizens to control the entire government. Madison, whose thinking was strongly influenced by the English philosopher David Hume, believed that it is natural for people to differ, and in differing, to form into factions, or parties. The problem with factions, according to Madison and his contemporaries Jefferson and Hamilton, is their potential for subverting government and the public good. Factions, in Madison's words, are mischievous.

Madison's primary concern in *Federalist* No. 10 was with *majority* factions—typically, but not exclusively, political parties as we know them today—not minority factions such as contemporary interest groups. Although he recognized that minority factions could lead to disorder and conflict, Madison believed that it is the possibility of tyranny by the majority that poses the greatest threat to individual liberties. Madison did not recommend that factions be forbidden or repressed, a practice that would conflict with the fundamental values of liberty and freedom of expression, but instead that their negative tendencies be held in check and controlled through explicit constitutional safeguards.

Formal mechanisms in the U.S. Constitution for controlling majority factions include the requirements that the president be elected separately from members of Congress and that members of Congress reside in the states from which they are elected. These provisions disperse power horizontally—across national institutions of government—and vertically—from national to local political jurisdictions. Separation of the executive and legislative branches eased fears among the smaller states in 1787 that large states, which presumably would control the Congress, would also control the presidency; and geographic representation ensured that control over elected representatives would rest with local rather than national interests, thereby lessening the influence of the national government over state decisions.

These basic constitutional provisions have had a profound effect on the abilities of modern political parties to control and manage American government. Historically, control of the government has frequently been divided between the two major political parties, neither of which has been capable of exerting much discipline over its members. A single party has controlled the presidency and a majority in the U.S. House and Senate in just 43 of the 70 Congresses—61 percent—that have convened from 1855 to 1993. Even in times of single-party control of the government, voting defections within both major parties have been common. Since World War II, a majority of Democrats has voted against a majority of Republicans only 44 percent of the time on average in the U.S. House of Representatives and only 45 percent of the time on average in the U.S. Senate.

American legislators have little incentive to toe the party line for the simple reason that a cohesive majority is not required to maintain control of the government or to preclude calling new elections, as is the case in parliamentary regimes. In the absence of party discipline, American legislators look to their geographic constituencies rather than to their parties for voting cues.

Madison and his contemporaries succeeded brilliantly in designing a constitutional system to attenuate the power of majority factions, but in doing so, they also created unanticipated opportunities for minority factions to be influential. When political parties are unable to take clear responsibility for governing, and when they cannot maintain cohesion and discipline among those elected under their labels, special interests have opportunities to gain access to the key points of decision within the government. David Truman explains that when a single party succeeds regularly in electing both an executive and a majority in the legislature, channels of access "will be predominantly those within the party leadership, and the pattern will be relatively stable and orderly."[1] He notes, however, that when "the party is merely an abstract term referring to an aggregation of relatively independent factions," as in the case of the United States, then the channels of access "will be numerous, and the patterns of influence within the legislature will be diverse, constantly shifting, and more openly in conflict."[2]

One important consequence of this "diffusion of access" is that legislators will be much more accessible to interests within their local constituencies, especially *organized* interests. Simply put, interest groups will thrive in an environment in which legislators take their behavioral cues from heterogeneous constituencies rather than from cohesive political parties. E. E. Schattschneider has summed up the situation succinctly:

> If the parties exercised the power to govern effectively, *they would shut out the pressure groups.* The fact that American parties govern only spasmodically and fitfully amid a multitude of lapses of control provides the opportunity for the cheap and easy use of pressure tactics.[3]

Although the constitution makes no specific mention of interest groups, or even political parties for that matter, it has influenced the evolution of both. The weakness of the political parties in their ability to control and manage the government is an intended consequence of the efforts by the founding fathers to inhibit majority factions; the prevalence of special interests, however, is an unintended consequence of weak parties. The U.S. Constitution indirectly laid the groundwork for a strong interest group system, but that system, unlike the political party system, did not evolve right away. It took nearly 70 years from the development of the first party system in 1800 until groups began to form and proliferate at a significant rate.

Table 1. Selected Organizations and Their Founding Dates

American Medical Association	1847
National Grange	1867
National Rifle Association	1871
American Bankers Association	1875
American Federation of Labor	1886
Sierra Club	1892
National Association of Manufacturers	1895
National Audubon Society	1905
National Association for the Advancement of Colored People	1909
U.S. Chamber of Commerce	1912
American Jewish Congress	1918
American Farm Bureau Federation	1919
National League of Cities	1924

The Formation and Maintenance of Interest Groups

Although trade unions and associations have historical roots dating to the beginning of the republic, interest groups of regional or national scope as we know them today did not develop significantly until after the Civil War, and even then, pronounced growth did not really begin to take place until the late 1800s. Table 1 lists a few of the early organizations and their founding dates.

In what is known as the "disturbance theory" of interest group formation, David Truman argued that organizations will form when the interests common to unorganized groups of individuals are disturbed by economic, social, political, or technological change.[4] As society becomes increasingly complex and interconnected, Truman argued that individuals have greater difficulty resolving their differences and grievances on their own and instead must seek intervention from the government. It is at this time that political organizations will begin to take shape. Once interest groups begin to form, they will then tend to form in "wavelike" fashion, according to Truman, because policies designed to address one group's needs typically disturb the interests of other unorganized citizens, who then form groups to seek governmental intervention to protect and advance their particular interests.

The period from 1870 to 1900 was rife with disturbances favorable to the formation of interest groups in the United States. The economic, social, and political upheaval following the Civil War destabilized relationships within and between numerous groups of individuals. The completion of the railroads and the introduction of the telegraph dramatically altered communication and transportation patterns; immigration and population growth gave rise to new economic and social relationships; and commercial and territorial expansion in the

West, combined with the task of maintaining order and rebuilding the infrastructure in the South, increased demands for routine services such as post offices, law enforcement, internal improvements, customs agents, and so forth. The process of industrialization created further economic and political tensions and uncertainties. The period 1870 to 1900 witnessed three economic depressions: a major one from 1873 to 1879, a minor one in the mid-1880s, and the collapse of 1893. Overall, the period from 1870 to 1900 was one when conditions were finally right for the widespread growth of organized interests in the United States.

Margaret Susan Thompson points out that in addition to the unprecedented economic and social upheaval at the end of the Civil War, political conditions in the 1870s were also favorable to the formation of groups and, in particular, the lobbying of Congress.[5] Two factors—the ascendancy of congressional power associated with the impeachment proceedings against Andrew Johnson and the growing heterogeneity of congressional constituencies—were instrumental in the growth of congressional lobbying and interest group activity. Congress, by enacting a comprehensive program on reconstruction in 1865 over the determined opposition of the president, established political preeminence over federal policy making and, as a consequence, became the focal institution for receiving and processing the conflicting demands of many newly recognized interests. Then, as congressional constituencies diversified economically and socially, the presence of multiple and competing interests began to force legislators to develop "representational priorities."[6] Thompson notes that legislators at this time had to determine which were their "meaningful" constituencies, and organization was the critical means by which interests achieved such designation. Thompson refers to the nascent organization of interests during the 1870s as "clienteles" rather than interest groups, for even though numerous subgroups of the population began making significant demands on the government during the 1870s, there was not a great deal of formal organization then as we know it today. Still, even these nascent groups began to provide important information to members of Congress about the interests and priorities of their constituents.

One example of how interest groups formed in response to economic and political disturbances during the post–Civil War period is provided by the organization of postal workers. Even before the Civil War, the volume of mail had grown tremendously in response to the development of railroads and the resulting decrease in the costs of postage. But in 1863, another significant increase in the volume of mail occurred when Congress lowered the long-distance postage rates. This created additional strains for letter carriers and postal clerks who already were greatly overworked. Then, in 1868, the Post Office Department refused to apply the "eight-hour" law—a law enacted that same year by Congress stipulating that eight hours constituted a day's work for laborers, workmen, and mechanics—to letter carriers on the grounds that they were government employees, not laborers, workmen, or mechanics. Finally, implementation of civil service following passage of the Pendleton Act in 1883 eliminated what little political clout the letter carriers had enjoyed. Once the patronage system was eliminated, politicians lost interest in the letter carriers and no longer intervened on their behalf.

In response to these deteriorating circumstances, the letter carriers organized into the National Association of Letter Carriers in 1889. Once organized, the letter carriers had a significant advantage over the unorganized postal clerks in the competition for wages. At the time, wages for all postal workers, letter carriers and clerks alike, were provided through a single congressional appropriation to the Post Office Department, and the letter carriers used their organizational clout to claim a disproportionate share of the annual appropriation. Thus, the postal workers came under pressure to organize as well, and so in predictable "wavelike" fashion, the National Association of Post Office Clerks was established in 1894.

Changing economic, social, and political conditions are necessary but not sufficient circumstances for the formation and development of organized interests. Even when environmental conditions are favorable to the formation of groups, there is still a natural proclivity for individuals *not* to join political interest groups. The reason is that individuals do not always have to belong to political groups in order to enjoy the benefits they provide. Wheat farmers, for example, benefit from the price supports that Congress establishes for wheat even though they do not belong to the National Association of Wheat Growers (NAWG), which lobbies for price supports. Similarly, individuals do not have to belong to environmental groups in order to reap the benefits of a cleaner environment brought about by the lobbying efforts of groups such as the Sierra Club and the National Wildlife Federation. More generally, the lobbying benefits provided by groups such as the wheat growers and the environmentalists are consumed *jointly* by all citizens affected; that is, Congress does not guarantee a higher price for wheat only to farmers who have paid dues to the National Association of Wheat Growers, and it does not and cannot restrict the benefit of a clean environment only to individuals who have paid their dues to environmental groups.

Unlike lobbying benefits, which are available even to those who do not contribute to lobbying efforts, the costs of lobbying are borne only by those who actually pay their dues to political groups or otherwise participate in lobbying activities. This creates a major organizational problem, for when it is possible to get something for nothing, many individuals will rationally choose to free ride on the efforts of others. When there are thousands of wheat farmers, for example, and the annual dues to the National Association of Wheat Growers are $100 or less, individual wheat farmers might very well conclude that their single contributions are not very important, that the NAWG will manage quite nicely without their money because there are so many other wheat farmers paying dues, and that there are much better uses for the $100 in light of the fact that the government will still provide price supports for their crop. The problem for the NAWG is that if every wheat farmer reasoned this way there would be no national association, and thus probably no price supports for wheat.

Given the natural proclivity for individuals to be free riders, all organizations must provide incentives of one sort or another to induce individuals to pay dues and otherwise contribute to the collective efforts of the organization. Generally speaking, individuals do not join interest groups because of benefits that can be consumed jointly; they join because of benefits that can by enjoyed *selectively* only by those individuals who pay dues to political groups. There are three main types of selective benefits. A selective *material* benefit includes such things as insurance and travel discounts and subscriptions to professional journals and other special- ized information. A second type of selective benefit is what Peter Clark and James Q. Wilson have labelled *solidary* incentives. These, too, derive only from group membership and involve benefits such as "socializing, congeniality, the sense of group membership and identification, the status resulting from membership, fun and conviviality, the maintenance of social distinctions, and so on."[7] The third basic type of selective benefit is an *expressive* incentive. Expressive incentives are those that individuals attach to the act of expressing ideological or moral values such as free speech, civil rights, economic justice, or political equality. Individuals obtain these benefits when they pay dues or contribute money or time to an organization that espouses these values. What is important in receiving these ben- efits is the feeling of satisfaction that results from expressing political values, not necessarily the actual achievement of the values themselves.

Most organizations provide a mix of these various benefits, although different kinds of organizations typically rely more heavily on one type of benefit than another. Professional and trade associations, for example, are more likely to offer selective material benefits than purposive benefits, whereas environmental groups and other organizations claiming to lobby for the public interest rely more heavily on expressive benefits. Expressive benefits are also common in organizations relying heavily on mass mailings to attract and maintain members. Many direct mail approaches use negatively worded messages to instill feelings of guilt and fear in individuals, with the hope that people will contribute money to a cause as a means of expressing their support for certain values or else assuag- ing their guilt and fear.

That individuals are not drawn naturally to interest groups and must instead be enticed to join makes it very difficult for groups to get started. Organizations often need outside support in the form of a patron—perhaps a wealthy individual, a nonprofit foundation, or a government agency—to get over the initial hurdle of organizing collective action. In one of the leading studies on the origins and maintenance of interest groups, Jack Walker discovered that 89 percent of all citizen groups and 60 percent of all nonprofit occupational groups (e.g., the National Association of State Alcohol and Drug Abuse Directors) received financial assistance from an outside source at the time of their founding.[8] Many of these organizations continued to draw heavily from outside sources of support to maintain themselves once they were launched. Walker concluded that "the number of interest groups in operation, the mixture of group types, and the level and direction of political mobilization in the United States at any point in the country's history will be determined by the composition and accessibility of the system's major patrons of political action."[9]

In summary, the proficiency that contemporary interest groups have achieved in attracting and maintaining members has evolved from a combination of factors. Most fundamental to their evolution has been a constitutional arrangement that has not only encouraged their participation but also created unanticipated opportunities for them to exert influence. Changing economic, social, and political circumstances have also played critical roles at various times throughout American history. However, even under conditions favorable to their development, the formation and maintenance of interest groups requires leadership and creative approaches for dealing with the natural inertia that individuals exhibit toward collective activities. The number of groups continues to grow each year, however, as does the diversity of the issues and viewpoints they represent.

NOTES

1. David B. Truman, *The Governmental Process: Political Interests and Public Opinion* (New York: Knopf, 1951), p. 325.

2. Ibid., p. 325.

3. E. E. Schattschneider, *Party Government* (New York: Holt, Rinehart and Winston, 1941), p. 192.

4. David B. Truman, *The Governmental Process,* Chapters 3 and 4.

5. Margaret Susan Thompson, *The Spider Web: Congress and Lobbying in the Age of Grant* (Ithaca, NY: Cornell University Press, 1985).

6. Thompson, *The Spider Web,* pp. 130–131.

7. Peter B. Clark and James Q. Wilson, "Incentive Systems: A Theory of Organizations," *Administrative Science Quarterly* 6 (1961): 134–135.

8. Jack L. Walker, "The Origins and Maintenance of Interest Groups in America," *American Political Science Review* 77 (1983): 390–406.

9. Ibid., p. 406.

13-3

Blunt's K Street Team

Bara Vaida and Lisa Caruso

Lobbying is usually thought of as an activity of organized interests outside of Congress, the aim of which is to influence legislators to support or oppose legislation. But everyday politics in Washington is more complicated than that. In their article Bara Vaida and Lisa Caruso give an account of the relationship between House Republican leaders and the lobbying community. On many issues, particularly ones that are important to the president and top congressional party leaders, lobbyists are asked to work cooperatively in party-organized efforts to influence public opinion, shape media coverage, and round up votes on Capitol Hill. In Washington lingo, lobbyists are called "the K Street crowd" because K Street is the location, in downtown Washington, of many law, public relations, and specialized lobbying firms.

IN EARLY JANUARY 2005, the House Republican leadership's prospects for passing the Central American Free Trade Agreement [CAFTA] looked dim. Powerful interests, from the sugar industry to labor unions, lined up against the pact, and most of Washington doubted the GOP could muster enough votes to push it through.

The burden of corralling the votes fell on House Majority Whip Roy Blunt, R-Mo. Brian Gaston, his chief of staff, phoned a dozen or so of Blunt's confidants—K Street lobbyists with A—list experience on the Hill, inside the White House, and within the political parties-as he had many times before. Blunt calls them "great assets in trying to marshal whatever resources are out there to get a hard job done."

On numerous occasions, these lobbyists have helped Blunt secure the votes to pass legislation by drawing on their relationships with individual lawmakers, clients, and other Washington power brokers. To get CAFTA over the top, Blunt needed to bring 50 to 70 undecided House members into the "yes" camp.

Although the whip team could call on a broad coalition of trade groups and lobbying organizations working on the pro-CAFTA side, Blunt wanted input from the small, trusted group of informal advisers whose views he seeks on all of the big votes.

Source: Bara Vaida and Lisa Caruso, "Blunt's K Street Team," *National Journal,* November 5, 2005.

"At the time, Roy was the only guy who was talking about getting it done," said a lobbyist whom Gaston called and who didn't want to be quoted by name. "Everyone thought he was crazy. But he had a plan, and he implemented it."

Republican lobbyist Kirsten Chadwick, senior vice president at Fierce, Isakowitz & Blalock, and Democratic lobbyist Steve Champlin, vice president at the Duberstein Group, were central to executing the plan. They met weekly with the coalition to help Blunt and the House leadership line up votes. The effort included scores of lobbyists, House Republicans and Democrats who supported the trade pact, administration officials, and allies in the Senate.

On July 28, the House passed CAFTA, 217–215. The hard-fought victory underscored the effectiveness of using a coalition approach to move major legislation.

Chadwick is also among the handful of lobbyists that Blunt seeks out for strategic counsel. According to Blunt's office, the other lobbyists he is closest to are Nick Calio, senior vice president of global government affairs at Citigroup; Ed Gillespie, co-chairman of Quinn Gillespie & Associates; Steve Hart, chairman and CEO of Williams & Jensen; Gregg Hartley, vice chairman and chief operating officer of Cassidy & Associates; Susan Hirschmann, partner at Williams & Jensen; David Hobbs, president of the Hobbs Group; Dave Hoppe, vice chairman of Quinn Gillespie & Associates; Mark Isakowitz, president of Fierce, Isakowitz & Blalock; Kathryn Lehman, partner at Holland & Knight; David Lugar, director at Quinn Gillespie & Associates; Drew Maloney, partner at the Federalist Group; Dan Mattoon, co-chairman of PodestaMattoon; and Lisa Nelson, senior vice president and director of government relations at Visa USA.

Others he consults often are Ali Amirhooshmand, a vice president at Cassidy & Associates, and Samantha Cook, director of government affairs at Fierce, Isakowitz & Blalock.

Blunt does not meet with these lobbyists as a group, although all attend various sessions that the whip team organizes either to move specific bills or to discuss the party's legislative agenda.

"These are people [Blunt] has known for a long time, and he trusts their opinion and their advice," a Blunt aide explained. "They've been there in the trenches, and they know how to get things done. This is who helps us win, time and time again."

National Journal contacted everyone on the list. Some quibbled about whether they should be included in a story, and some declined to comment, but most were willing to speak about the roles they play in helping Blunt.

None, however, wanted to discuss the potential for a race to replace Rep. Tom DeLay, R-Texas, as majority leader if DeLay's legal troubles drag on, or to say whether they would support Blunt in such a race. DeLay was forced to step aside on September 28 following his indictment in Texas on campaign finance-related charges. At that time, Blunt temporarily assumed some of DeLay's duties as majority leader while continuing to fulfill his responsibilities as whip.

"I don't think that [House Speaker] Denny [Hastert, R-Ill.] or anyone else would appreciate getting calls from K Street on who should be leader," said one of Blunt's allies.

Cultivating a set of K Street "advisers" is nothing new for House leaders. But Blunt and his whip team have brought a higher level of structure and systematization to the House GOP's outreach to K Street.

Ever since the Republicans took control of the House in 1995, working with private-sector allies has been a hallmark of the party's governing strategy. Former House Republican Conference Chairman John Boehner, R-Ohio, convened a weekly sit-down with the heads of trade associations and interest groups, while DeLay, as whip, met regularly with lobbyists to round up support for votes and pushed K Street firms to hire Republicans and increase the amount of money they gave to the GOP.

The link between K Street and the GOP leadership has only grown stronger as top staffers to DeLay, former Speaker Newt Gingrich, R-Ga., and other leaders have left the Hill to join the lobbying ranks. Blunt, who as chief deputy whip under DeLay oversaw coalition efforts, has many friends on K Street. When Blunt was elected whip in 2002, he built on DeLay's success. Along with Rep. Mike Rogers, R-Mich., his deputy whip in charge of coalitions, Blunt has transformed an effective but loosely organized initiative into a formalized structure for enlisting the party's K Street allies to advance the House Republican agenda.

But the roots of the whip operation's partnership with lobbyists and outside groups go back to 1980, when now-Sen. Trent Lott, R-Miss., was elected House Republican whip. Lott was instrumental in moving newly elected President Reagan's Republican agenda through a Democratic House, said Quinn Gillespie's Hoppe, who logged 16 years with Lott, the only member of Congress to have served as whip in both the House and the Senate.

Hoppe noted that as the minority party in the House, Republicans needed Democrats' votes to pass Reagan's tax cuts and fund his defense buildup. "That involved working inside [the House] with Democrats and Republicans, working with the administration, working with outside groups . . . trying to find out where all your allies were to bring the right people to bear at the right time to get the votes you needed," Hoppe said.

It was the model used later by Democratic whips Tom Foley, D-Wash., and Tony Coelho, D-Calif., in the 1980s, Hoppe said, adding, "DeLay took it to a whole new level, and Roy Blunt has done a good job of moving it forward from there . . . [making] it a much more broad and effective operation."

Blunt and his staff now regularly consult with roughly 500 lobbyists with K Street shops, trade associations, corporate Washington offices, and interest groups, according to Blunt's office. These lobbyists meet throughout the year with Blunt, Chief Deputy Majority Whip Eric Cantor, R-Va., House GOP Conference Chairwoman Deborah Pryce, R-Ohio, and Rogers, and participate in various coalitions the whip team assembles to pass tough legislation. In 2003, Blunt also married a lobbyist who represents Altria Group, the parent company of the cigarette maker Philip Morris and the food company Kraft. Blunt's wife, Abigail Blunt, has agreed not to lobby anyone in the House, and Blunt recuses himself from Altria issues.

Separate from the coalitions created to build support for a particular piece of legislation, Blunt's inner circle of K Street advisers is a kind of "intelligence network." It acts, said one lobbyist, as an extra set of eyes and ears that provides "a lot more access to what members are actually saying to each other and not just what they are saying for public consumption."

Further, many of the lobbyists have personal relationships with lawmakers, and so can help Blunt gather the intelligence to secure a member's vote. That comes in handy for Blunt on issues such as passage of the annual budget resolution, which has no natural outside constituency that can provide the foundation for a coalition. "There are always the same four to seven issues" on the budget that are going to be controversial, such as agriculture, defense, and veterans affairs spending, a Blunt aide said. To help smooth out problems that lawmakers may have had with those issues, Blunt has tapped his network to find out what individual members might need.

Hobbs, who headed the White House office of legislative affairs after serving as chief of staff to then-House Majority Leader Dick Armey, R-Texas, describes it as "a keep-your-ear-to-the-ground kind of thing. Maybe you're shooting the breeze and you hear something, or you're at a fundraiser and have a little more time to talk and you hear something" that you can pass along.

Others, like Holland & Knight's Lehman, who until this past May was chief of staff to the House Republican Conference, said working on the Hill can be like living "inside a bubble" and the discussions with downtown lobbyists are a helpful reality check. "When you're on the Hill, you think everybody knows what you know," Lehman said. "You think everyone has access to the same information. The problem is that sometimes you just miss the obvious."

Almost all of the lobbyists work at bipartisan firms and also consult closely with Democrats on issues. Some are friends with Democratic lawmakers and provide a way for Blunt and the GOP leadership team to learn what the House Democratic Caucus is saying about a piece of legislation, or what its strategy is for opposing a measure. "We pass on intelligence on what Democrats are thinking," said Lehman.

Getting information on the Democrats is crucial because the Republican margin in the House is currently just 13; on difficult votes such as CAFTA, GOP leaders cannot count on support from all Republicans. As Mattoon, a former deputy chairman of the National Republican Congressional Committee, said, "There isn't much margin for error."

In an interview, Blunt said he knows that many people believe "there is an agenda somehow set by K Street." In fact, he said, "we reach out to K Street in the broadest possible context and [say], 'Here's what we're going to do, are you interested in getting this done or not?' And if the answer is yes, we try to figure how they can help us get that particular piece of work done."

And while lobbyists may work committees "very aggressively during the effort to get a bill ready to go to the floor," Blunt noted, "our relationship with them is almost always [after the bill is drafted], where we're really ready to get down to the hard work of getting the bill passed."

Information can also go in the other direction, helping the leadership stay on message in the media. In the weeks since Blunt took on his temporary duties as majority leader, his office has put out the word that Blunt is focused on the Republican agenda, which includes spending cuts and immigration reform.

Gaston, Blunt's chief of staff, "was eager to have it get out that the basic game plan going forward is to emphasize things that House Republicans want to emphasize and not what the White House wants or the Senate wants, but what the base wants House leaders to focus on," said the same lobbyist who didn't want to be identified.

Of course, deep ties between Blunt and his K Street confidants are good for business. Almost all of the contract lobbyists in Blunt's circle are successful rainmakers with a broad spectrum of big-name clients. Their continued access to House leaders keeps them in demand.

For the most part, these lobbyists are also reliable fundraisers for the GOP, although all emphasize that when Blunt calls for their advice, they don't discuss fundraising with him. For the 2006 election cycle, these lobbyists together had donated $267,742 to Republican candidates and parties, and $22,000 to Blunt's political action committee as of October 11, according to the Center for Responsive Politics.

The lobbyists stressed that what they get out of their close relationship with Blunt is the satisfaction of helping friends and political allies accomplish common goals, albeit ones that their clients happen to share.

"I'm happy to offer whatever advice I can and whatever intelligence I can and help pass their agenda, because it's one that I believe in," Hobbs said. Mattoon added, "We want to keep the people that we agree with on the issues in the majority."

Still, the K Street connection worries campaign finance watchdogs, who argue that such coziness gives interest groups and the business community too much influence. Blunt's ties to K Street show "how intertwined and interconnected he is with these lobbyists," said Larry Noble, executive director of the Center for Responsive Politics. "They aren't just lobbying him on bills, but are part of his inner [team of] strategists, and that gets them a leg up on everyone else."

But Blunt's aides said that they don't offer their K Street allies anything for their help—although having such access to GOP power brokers can only burnish the lobbyists' credentials and reputations.

"It's not that we're doing this big favor for them," said one Blunt aide. "They may benefit to the extent that their business is based on having good relationships [with top congressional leaders and staff] and they have good relationships with us by working with us. But there's nothing specific that they get in return."

The Group of 500

Beyond the lobbyists who are close advisers to Majority Whip Roy Blunt, R-Mo., the whip operation casts a wide net in enlisting help from allies off the Hill, as well as from Bush administration officials and sympathetic Democratic members.

Roughly 500 people from K Street lobby shops, trade associations, corporate Washington offices, and interest groups work with the whip's office, according to aides to Blunt. The whip is also the temporary majority leader.

The 500—of whom 75 to 100 are Democrats—also meet in smaller groups from time to time with Blunt; Chief Deputy Majority Whip Eric Cantor, R-Va.; Mike Rogers, R-Mich., Blunt's deputy whip for coalitions; and House Republican Conference Chairwoman Deborah Pryce, R-Ohio, to discuss the GOP agenda and offer advice.

The whip operation relies on this group of 500 to form coalitions to help move legislation. While Blunt, Cantor, Rogers, and their staffs take care of the vote-counting operation, Pryce's team is in charge of the party's message to other members and to the media. Occasionally all 500 are brought together, for instance, when top committee chairmen, or House and Senate leaders, make a presentation to the group.

Rank-and-file members and their staffs are also integral players, according to staffers to Blunt and Rogers. During the push to enact the Central American Free Trade Agreement, for example, Rep. Sue Myrick, R-N.C., worked on the textile language, and Rep. Phil English, R-Pa., addressed CAFTA's effects on Northeast manufacturers. Democratic free-traders such as Reps. Norm Dicks, D-Wash.,

William Jefferson, D-La., and James Moran, D-Va., also pitched in to round up Democratic votes.

So, too, did the chairmen of the committees with jurisdiction over the legislation, Senate leaders, and Bush administration officials—and all of their top staffers. During the run-up to the CAFTA vote, Commerce Secretary Carlos M. Gutierrez, Agriculture Secretary Mike Johanns, former U.S. Trade Representative Robert Zoellick, and his successor, former Rep. Rob Portman, R-Ohio, lobbied members directly.

These *ad hoc* coalitions help the whip team develop strategy, identify members whose votes are in play, and then work on winning those members' votes. Coalition members have their own target list, which they share with the whip team. But Blunt's office said that the whip staff never gives the coalition its official whip count.

Lobbyists also may enlist their clients to prevail upon lawmakers if a company or industry group has a large presence in a wavering representative's district.

Chapter 14

News Media

14-1

The Market and the Media

James T. Hamilton

With good reason, the news media have long been called the "fourth branch" of government. In a democracy citizens need news to monitor the perform-ance of their representatives. Conversely, officeholders and those who wish to replace them need to be able to communicate with their constituencies. More-over, with officeholders needing to coordinate with one another across the institutions that divide them, "news," as Woodrow Wilson aptly observed, "is the atmosphere of politics." The First Amendment to the Constitution rec-ognizes the news media's special role by placing freedom of the press along-side freedoms of speech and religion as deserving categorical protection from government infringement. More than in any other Western democracy, the news media developed in America as private business enterprises virtually free of government regulation or investment. Modern news, James Hamilton reminds us, is as much a product of business as it ever was. As technology cre-ates new audiences and products, the business of news has undergone signif-icant market adjustment.

Source: James T. Hamilton, "The Market and the Media," in *The Press*, by Geneva Overholser and Kathleen Hall Jamieson, eds. (Oxford University Press: 2005), 351–371. Some notes appearing in the original have been deleted.

SINCE MARKET FORCES have played the most decisive role in transforming the delivery of news, the history of the American press from the 1970s to the present is economic history. Although journalists may not explicitly consider economics as they cover the day's events, the stories, reporters, firms, and media that ultimately survive in the marketplace depend on economic factors. The decisions of producers and editors are driven by supply and demand: Who cares about a particular piece of information? What is an audience willing to pay for the news, or what are advertisers willing to pay for the attention of readers, listeners, or viewers? How many consumers share particular interests in a topic? How many competitors are vying for readers' or viewers' attention, and what are these competitors offering as news? What are the costs of generating and transmitting a story? Who owns the outlet? What are the owners' goals? What are the property rights that govern how news is produced, distributed, and sold? News is a commercial product.

News outlets that cover public affairs have always struggled with the tension between giving people what they want to know and giving them what they need to know. The low probability that any reader has of influencing the outcome of a policy debate leaves many readers "rationally ignorant" about the details of governing.[1] From an investment perspective, why learn about global warming if your actions have little chance of affecting policy? News outlets do face strong demand for entertaining news, or information that helps people in their role as consumers or workers. Some people may also express a demand for news about politics, though the set of viewers that prefers politics covered as a sport or drama may exceed that which prefers detailed analysis.

In this essay I argue that since the 1970s news coverage has shifted to an increasing emphasis on what people want to know and away from information that they may need as voters. I identify three economic factors that help account for this shift: changes in technology, product definition and differentiation, and media ownership. I will examine in detail how each has affected news content over time. I then focus on network evening news programs in a case study that demonstrates how these economic factors have shaped news coverage. After providing a snapshot of current media coverage, I conclude with a section analyzing the implications of these alterations in the ways in which news is defined, distributed, and consumed.

What's Different: Technology, Products, and Owners

Three technological changes have affected the way in which images and information have entered households since 1970: the growth of cable television; the advent of the Internet; and the increased use of satellite technology to transmit news across continents and into homes. The spread of cable television in the 1980s and 1990s and introduction of direct-broadcast satellite delivery meant that by 2003 at least 85 percent of television households subscribed to multichannel delivery systems. The average number of channels per home went from 7.1 in 1970 to 71.2 in 2001. The average number of channels viewed weekly for at least ten minutes went from 4.5 to 13.5 channels per television household.[2] This proliferation of channels meant that news on cable could focus on specific niches. Rather than attempting to garner 10 million viewers (the audience attracted by the *NBC Nightly News* in 2003), a cable news program could be successful by attracting less than 1 million viewers. The result is that cable channels can focus their products on particular types of news: sports stories on ESPN; business news on CNBC; storm data on the Weather Channel; and news that appeals to a conservative audience on FOX News Channel. Both the network evening news programs and daily newspapers have broader audiences than cable channels. If survey respondents are asked to rate themselves on an ideological scale of liberalism and conservatism, the average rating for consumers of the network evening news programs and daily newspapers is the same as the national sample average. The regular consumers of the FOX News Channel, however, have the most conservative ideological rating in the survey. Cable political shows such as *Crossfire* and *Hardball*, in contrast, attract audiences more likely to rate themselves as liberal.

The relatively small audiences of some cable news programs yield profits because of low production budgets. Since talk can be cheap, cable news programs often feature journalists acting as political pundits. Political pundits, who offer a mixture of fact and opinion, face many market constraints. Since readers have the freedom to sample and ignore stories across the portfolio of topics covered in a paper, those writing for newspapers can aim for a relatively educated audience and afford to write about topics that may not be of interest to many. Television pundits, in contrast, operate in a medium where viewers of a particular program all consume the same story. If these pundits pick topics of little interest, they risk losing viewers, who may be less educated (than newspaper readers) and more likely to search for entertainment than enlightenment from television. The result is that pundits choose different languages to talk about politics, depending on the avenue of expression.

To see these differences, consider the case of George Will, who writes a syndicated column and appears as a commentator on ABC News programming.[3] As I demonstrate in my book *All the News That's Fit to Sell*, the print George Will uses a greater variety of terms and longer words than the television George Will. When composing for a print audience, Will uses more abstract terms such as those relating to inspiration, as well as more numeric terms. He writes about groups rather than individuals, as reflected in a greater focus on core values and institutions. In television appearances, Will changes expression to comply with the greater demands for entertainment. He uses more human-interest language.

He makes more self-references. He simplifies and summarizes, and at the same time hedges his bets through qualifications (higher use of ambivalent language). His statements on television focus more on the present and emphasize motion. On television, Will offers opinions that are marked by greater activity and realism. Although George Will has developed a brand name for expression, he changes the delivery of his product to suit the audience demands and cost constraints of the medium. . . .

A second technological change affecting news markets is the spread of the Internet. Competition for attention across sites has driven the price of news on nearly all Internet sites to zero (the marginal delivery cost of the information). This explosion of free information has many ramifications. Consumption of high-quality newspapers, for example, is now possible around the world. If one looks at the top one hundred newspapers in the United States, the circulation of the top five (the *Wall Street Journal, USA Today,* the *New York Times, Los Angeles Times,* and *Washington Post*) accounted for 21.5 percent of the total newspaper circulation in 1999.[4] If you look at the links generated on the Internet by these top one hundred newspapers, however, the top five papers in terms of links (which included *USA Today,* the *New York Times,* and the *Washington Post*) accounted for 41.4 percent of the total links. In part this reflects the advantages of established brands on the Internet, since familiarity with a product's existence and reputation can lead to its consumption. . . .

The low cost of entry to placing information on the Internet has had many effects on news. The ability of news outlets, and columnists such as Matt Drudge, to post instantly during any time of the day has extended news cycles and created additional pressure on traditional news outlets to run with breaking news.[5] The lack of large investment in sites means that news provided may not be heavily edited or screened, which can give rise to a spread of rumor and gossip. The archiving of data on the Internet and easy accessibility make it easier for errors in reporting to propagate, as journalists access information collected by others and incorporate it into stories. The widespread existence of government and nonprofit Web sites lowers the cost of information generation and analysis for reporters. Journalists writing about campaign finance, for example, can readily locate data at the individual contributor level at the Federal Election Commission Web site or at Opensecrets.org. Similarly, reporters writing about the environment can use government data aggregated by the nonprofit Environmental Defense, which posts detailed pollution data by the zip code level at Scorecard.org.

Widespread use of satellite technology to beam images across the country and the world marks a third change in news reporting. During the 1970s the three evening network news programs had an "oligopoly of image," where viewers tuned in the programs in part to see the first pictures of the day's breaking stories. The deployment of satellite technology across the country, however, soon meant that local television stations had the ability to import stories quickly from other parts of the country and to go live to events in their own city. The ability of local stations to share in network feeds or tap into other sources of pictures meant that local news programs began to offer viewers images of national or international stories, which in turn put pressure on the evening news to offer a differentiated product (including more interpretative or contextual material). The existence of satellite technology also meant that international coverage could take place in real time, including the coverage of the Iraq War by embedded reporters.

These technological changes have put increased pressures on traditional news outlets to compete for readers and viewers. The growth in cable channels and cable/direct broadcast satellite subscription has eroded the market share of the network evening news programs and focused attention on retaining viewers. The network evening news programs have a core audience of faithful viewers and a set of marginal viewers, those who may tune in to the news or choose another program depending on what has happened in the world or what types of news the networks choose to focus on. News directors will select a mix of stories aimed at capturing the marginal viewers while not alienating the average or regular viewers. The result of competition from cable is a mix of stories that leaves average viewers somewhat frustrated and marginal viewers somewhat placated.

Survey data from the Pew Center for the People and the Press in 2000 show the tension between the interests of the average (i.e., regularly view) and marginal (i.e., sometimes view) consumers of the network nightly news programs.[6] A majority of the regular viewers are over fifty (54.8 percent) and female (53.9 percent). The marginal viewers are much younger. Females aged eighteen to thirty-four account for 20.6 percent of those who sometimes view the national news, and males aged eighteen to thirty-four account for 17.5 percent of these sometime viewers. In contrast, eighteen-to-thirty-four-year-old females are only 9.1 percent of the regular audience, and males of that age group only 9.2 percent of the regular viewers. These demographic differences translate into predictable and sharp differences between the interests of marginal and average viewers. Marginal viewers are not as attached to the news. When asked whether they enjoyed keeping up with the news, 68.1 percent of average viewers responded that they did "a lot" versus only 37.0 percent for the marginal viewers. A majority of marginal viewers said that they followed national or international news closely "only when something important or interesting is happening." Marginal viewers also were more likely to report that they watched the news with "my remote in hand" and switched channels when they were not interested in a topic.

What captures the interests of occasional viewers differs from the type of news favored by loyal viewers. The marginal and average viewers have the same top two news interests, crime and health, which may explain the prevalence of these news categories on the network evening news. The two sets of viewers differ markedly, however, in their interest in politics. For the average viewer of network news, news about political figures and events in Washington ranked fifth out of thirteen news types. This same category of news ranked tenth among marginal viewers. Political news about Washington was followed very closely by 28.4 percent of the average viewers, versus 12.3 percent of the marginals. Sports ranked sixth and entertainment news ranked twelfth among the regular viewers. These topics ranked much more highly among marginal viewers, who ranked them third and eighth among the thirteen news topics.

Viewers who are younger than fifty may also merit attention for another reason—they are more highly valued by advertisers. Reasons offered for why advertisers pay more for viewers under fifty include a belief that their brand preferences are not as fixed and the fact that they watch less television and hence are harder to reach. The rewards for capturing relatively younger viewers offer another reason for news directors to pay less attention to the (older) loyal watchers. One way to forge a compromise between the interests of average and marginal viewers is to cover the political issues of interest to younger viewers. The January 2000 Pew survey asked respondents to indicate the priority they attached to twenty political issues. When I examined the number of minutes or number of stories devoted on each network to these issues in 2000, I found that the higher the priority attached to an issue at the start of the year by the eighteen-to-thirty-four set, the more attention devoted over the year by the network news. The priorities of older viewers had no impact or a negative effect on coverage devoted by the networks. The survey data indicate that females in the age range care relatively more about issues such as dealing with the problems of families with children and strengthening gun control laws. Searching for marginal viewers and those valued by advertisers may thus lead the networks to talk about issues often associated with the Democratic Party. The competition generated by technology, and the influence of advertiser values, thus generate pressure to provide network stories that may give rise to perceptions of media bias. Among those identifying themselves as very conservative, 37.4 percent reported in 2000 that they viewed the national nightly network news as very biased. Among survey respondents who labeled themselves as very liberal, only 16.6 percent saw network news programs the same way.

Product Changes

In print and broadcast, there has been a substantial change in the content and style of news coverage since 1970. These product changes are numerous: a decrease in hard news (e.g., public-affairs coverage) and an increase in soft news (e.g., entertainment, human-interest stories); an increase in negative tone to cover elections; less focus on watchdog stories (e.g., those dealing with the operation of government); and an increase in the mix of opinion and interpretation in news coverage. These product changes also have many origins. Emphasis on cost cutting and profits has led to declines in international coverage. Competition across media and the pressure for product differentiation within a market have led some outlets to specialize in soft news. The drive to entertain can transform political coverage into horse-race coverage, with a focus on who is ahead in the polls and a tone that is often critical of candidates and events. In publicly traded companies, pressures to meet market earnings expectations can mean more focus on pleasing readers and viewers and less room for journalists to exercise their own news judgment. Changes in rules by the Federal Communications Commission (FCC) have reduced station worries about whether views expressed on air are "fair" and removed specific requirements that broadcasters provide a minimum amount of public-affairs coverage. In this section I describe the dimensions of news product changes since 1970. These changes in product attributes result from an interplay of demand and supply factors, though I do not attempt here to specify which factors generate particular product alterations.

Content analysis by the Committee of Concerned Journalists (CCJ) in 1998 captured broad changes in the media by examining for 1977, 1987, and 1997 one month of coverage on the three network evening news programs, each cover story during the year for *Time* and *Newsweek*, and each front-page story for the *New York Times* and *Los Angeles Times*. For this sample of 3,760 stories, the CCJ found that straight news accounts (e.g., what happened yesterday) went from 52 percent of stories in 1977 to only 32 percent in 1997. Story topics in traditional hard-news areas (i.e., government, military, and domestic and foreign affairs) went from 66.3 percent of all reports to 48.9 percent. Feature stories such as those about entertainment, celebrities, lifestyle, and celebrity crime grew from 5.1 percent in 1977 to 11.1 percent in 1997. Crime stories went from 8.4 percent to 11.4 percent and personal health from 0.7 percent to 3.5 percent. Attention also grew for stories about science (2.7 percent to 5.9 percent) and religion (0.5 percent to 3.7 percent).[7] . . .

As hard-news coverage declined, the tone of many stories about elections grew more critical. Assessing coverage of major-party presidential nominees in *Time* and *Newsweek* from 1960 to 1992, [Thomas] Patterson found that unfavorable references to the candidates grew from approximately 25 percent in 1960 to 60 percent in 1992. Studying front-page election stories in the *New York Times*, he found that in the 1960s the candidates and other partisan sources set the tone of nearly 70 percent of the articles. By 1992, journalists set the tone for the reports about 80 percent of the time. Kiku Adatto documented similar patterns of a shrinking role for the candidate and increasing role for the reporter on network television coverage of presidential campaigns. She found that in 1968 the average sound bite for a presidential candidate on the network evening news was 42.3 seconds. By the 1988 campaign this figure dropped to 9.8 seconds (and decreased further to 8.4 seconds in the 1992 general election). What replaced the words of the candidates was strategy coverage provided by reporters, who gave viewers their assessment of why the candidate was engaged in a particular strategy and how the candidate was faring in the horse race. Critical coverage also greeted the eventual winners. A study for the Council for Excellence in Government found that in the first year of the presidencies of Ronald Reagan (1981), Bill Clinton (1993), and George W. Bush (2001), coverage of the administration on network television news was negative in tone by a ratio of nearly two to one. The critical eye reporters used in covering government emerged in part from journalists' experience with government deception during both the Vietnam War and Watergate.[8] . . .

Product changes are evident too in the percentage of journalists saying that a particular media role was extremely important. In 1971 76 percent of journalists said investigating government claims was an extremely important mass media role, 61 percent said the same for providing analysis of complex problems, and 55 percent for discussing national policy. These figures dropped in 1992 to 67 percent for investigating government, 48 percent for analysis of complex problems, and 39 percent for national problems. Journalists in 1992 were much more likely (69 percent) to say that getting information to the public quickly was an extremely important role, versus 56 percent in 1971.[9]

In extended interviews with journalists, Howard Gardner, Mihaly Csikszentmihalyi, and William Damon also found that journalists were frustrated: 51 percent said changes in the media were negative, versus 24 percent indicating that the changes were positive. Sixty-four percent of the journalists they interviewed said the demands to comply with business goals in journalism were increasing, and 63 percent said there was a perceived drop in ethics and values in the media. Many of those interviewed pointed to the drive for market share as a prime force undercutting the performance of journalists.[10]

Changes in government regulation also affected the extent and kind of information provided. Prior to 1987, the FCC's fairness doctrine required broadcasters to provide free and equal time to parties that dissented from controversial views that stations chose to air. While the policy may have promoted perceptions of fairness, empirical evidence indicates that the policy may have chilled speech by discouraging stations from presenting viewpoints that might trigger demands for free response time on air.[11] Once the fairness doctrine was abolished by the FCC, the genre of informational programming immediately expanded on radio. This radio genre, which includes news programming and the talk-radio format made famous by Rush Limbaugh, became both a popular and controversial force in public-affairs debates in the 1990s.

Ownership

Change in ownership of news media outlets is a third factor affecting content. There are many theories about why ownership matters: publicly traded firms could be more likely to focus on profits than journalism properties (e.g., newspapers) owned by individuals or families; outlets owned by groups, whether a newspaper in a chain or a broadcast station owned by a network may be less likely to identify with the problems of a specific city; and the concentration of ownership in a small number of firms may crowd out a diverse set of views

Calculating how ownership has changed over time requires defining a medium and a market. Between 1970 and 1998, the number of daily newspapers declined from 1,748 to 1,489 and average circulation dropped from 62,202 to 56,183. The number of weekly newspapers, however, grew from 7,612 to 8,193 and average circulation jumped from 3,660 to 9,067. The number of cities with two or more fully competing dailies with different ownership declined from 37 in 1973 to 19 in 1996. The number of newspaper groups dropped from 157 in 1970 to 129 in 1996. In the same period, the percentage of dailies owned by chains grew from 50.3 percent to 76.2 percent and the percentage of daily circulation accounted for by these group-owned papers increased from 63.0 percent to 81.5 percent. The fifteen largest newspaper chains generated slightly more than half of the daily circulation of newspapers in the United States in 1998.[12]

At a broad level, the media have not become significantly more concentrated (in terms of the concentration of sales in a specific number of firms) over this time period. It is estimated that in terms of revenues, the top fifty media firms (which include newspaper, broadcast, cable, publishing, music, and film companies) accounted for 79.7 percent of all media industry revenues in 1986 and 81.8 percent in 1997; the share of the top four firms grew from 18.8 percent to 24.1 percent.[13] . . . One study looked at how ownership had changed between 1960 and 2000 for ten local media markets in the United States. After counting for each local market the number of broadcast outlets, cable systems, direct-broadcast satellite systems, and daily newspapers available, the study found that the percentage growth in the total number of media outlets available averaged more than 200 percent between 1960 and 2000. The percentage increase in the number of owners in the market averaged 140 percent.[14]

The actual impact of group or chain ownership in media outlets is a topic of spirited empirical debate. Reviewing the social science evidence on the impact of chain ownership on newspaper operation in 1994, Edwin Baker concluded, "Chain ownership's primary documented effects are negative. However, the findings seem tepid, hardly motivating any strong critique of chain ownership or prompting any significant policy interventions." Lisa George found that as the number of owners in a local newspaper market goes down, product differentiation between newspapers increases and the number of topical reporting beats covered in the market overall goes up. The Project for Excellence in Journalism found that in local television markets, stations affiliated with networks produced higher-quality news programs than those actually owned and operated by the networks, that stations owned by a company also operating a newspaper in the market generated higher-quality local television news programs, and that locally owned stations were not obviously superior to other stations in news production.[15]

The Changing Nature of Network News

The transformation of the network evening news programs since 1970 offers a case study of the impact of changes in technology, news definitions, and ownership.[16] In 1969 the daily debates among network news executives and reporters about what stories to include in the evening news broadcasts centered around which domestic politics and foreign policy stories to cover. Each television network was part of a media company. For each of the three networks, the founder or an early leader was still involved and identified with the operation of the organization. Network news operations were expected to generate prestige, part of which reflected back on the owners and broadcasters. The FCC routinely examined the number of hours of public-affairs programming provided when stations had their licenses renewed. A reputation for covering public affairs well in the news provided added security when licenses were up for renewal. If viewers did not enjoy the hard-news stories provided in the evening news programs, they had few other options on the dial. The average television household received seven channels. At the dinner hour more than one-third of all television households watched the network evening news. The stories they saw were news to most viewers. National news programs were not on earlier in the afternoon, and local news programs lacked the technology and time to cover national events on their own. Decision makers on network news programs felt a responsibility to provide viewers with information they needed as citizens. The large audience share and focus on politics attracted significant scrutiny of the programs, which were a frequent target of criticism from the White House.[17]

In 2000 the daily debates in network story conferences centered on whether to include domestic political stories or softer news items about health and entertainment topics. Foreign coverage was not often on the agenda, except in cases of military action. Each network was part of a publicly traded conglomerate. Network news operations were expected by corporate managers and Wall Street analysts to generate profits. The FCC no longer scrutinized public affairs coverage and license renewals were virtually assured. Television households received an average of sixty-three channels. Viewers at the dinner hour could watch sitcoms, entertainment news, sports news, and news on PBS. The three major network news programs combined captured only 23 percent of all television households. Viewers often came to the network news programs with a sense of the day's headline stories, after watching news on cable channels or local television programs containing stories and footage from around the nation. Network decision-makers felt pressure to gain ratings, which translated into a competition to discover and serve viewers' interests. Anchors and reporters were promoted as celebrities. Political criticisms of news coverage focused more on the content of cable news programs, though press critics faulted the network evening news shows for an increasing shift to soft-news stories.

To see the shift in news content, consider how the network evening news treated a consistent set of stories over time. Each year, *People* magazine selects its "25 Most Intriguing People" of the year, which consist of a set of soft-news personalities (i.e., television stars, movie actors, sports figures, persons involved in famous crimes, and royalty) and a set of famous figures from business and politics. In 1974–78, 40 percent of the soft-news personalities on the *People* list were covered in stories on at least one of the three major network evening news programs. In 1994–98, this figure rose to 52 percent. For those soft-news personalities that generated coverage over the course of the year they were listed by *People*, on ABC the "Intriguing" person averaged 9.9 stories and 1,275 seconds in coverage per year in 1974–78. This grew to 17.2 stories and 2,141 seconds of annual average coverage by 1994–98. NBC's reputation of providing more soft news than the other two networks is confirmed by its average of 25.6 stories and 3,238 seconds of coverage in 1994–98.

By many measures hard-news coverage dropped over this period. Each year, *Congressional Quarterly* identifies the key votes that take place in the U.S. Senate and House. In 1969–73, 82 percent of these major votes were covered on at least one of the network evening news programs on the day of or day after the congressional action. Yet for the period 1994–98, only 62 percent of the *CQ* votes generated network stories. A similar pattern holds for the key legislative votes identified each year by two ideological interest groups, the Americans for Democratic Action (ADA) and the American Conservative Union (ACU). The percentage of key interest-group votes in Congress that generated stories on the nightly news dropped from 64 percent in 1969–73 to 44 percent in 1994–98. The shift on the network news away from a headline service toward more background reporting is evident in the fact that those bills that were covered got more time on the evening news programs. On ABC, for example, the mean coverage length for *CQ* bills went from 117 seconds in 1969–73 to 211 seconds in 1994–98.

Statistical analysis shows that many factors contributed to these changes in coverage. *People's* intriguing personalities were more likely to be covered over the course of a year on the network evening news in the era (i.e., 1984 or later) when the FCC had deregulated much of broadcast television. Coverage of *CQ* votes declined in election years (when they were probably crowded out by campaign stories) and dropped as cost cutting became more prominent in network news operations. Interest-group vote coverage declined on each network as the percentage of households with cable increased, indicating how broadcast television shifted away from some forms of hard news as competition increased from cable. In the period 1969 to 1999, the number of network evening news stories mentioning soft-news terms such as *actor, sex,* or *movie* increased along with the percentage of households with cable. In the post-deregulation era, stories about hard-news topics such as education or Medicaid or NATO declined.

Network evening news anchors not only covered celebrities, they became them. News products have always been what economists call experience goods, which means that companies have always sought ways to signal to potential customers what today's version of events will look like in their papers or programs. The pressure for journalists to become part of the news product, however, is increasing as the number of news outlets expands. In a world of four broadcast television channels, a consumer can easily switch among viewing options to sample content. In a world where channels can number in the hundreds, sampling becomes more time-consuming.[18] If viewers recognize and enjoy watching a particular journalist on television, they may be more likely to watch a given channel because of this familiarity. The personalities of those who present the information become shortcuts for viewers to find their news niche. The changing salary rewards in network evening news programs provide evidence of how journalists have become part of the product in news.

Although network anchors deliver the news, they are rewarded in the marketplace for delivering viewers to advertisers. The salary patterns for network evening news anchors suggest that the value attached to the personal ability of these stars to deliver viewers increased markedly during the 1990s. . . . When consumers have many more choices, the value of a known commodity can increase. Network anchors become a way for channels to create a brand image in viewers' minds. If anchors become more important in drawing viewers to programs, this may translate into higher returns for anchors in salary negotiations. . . . The amount in salary that an anchor received for attracting a thousand viewing households increased from a range of $0.13 to $0.31 (in 1999 dollars) in 1976 to a range of $0.86 to $1.07 in 1999. Another way to view this is to look at the ratio of the anchor's salary to the ad price on the evening news programs. In 1976 anchors such as Walter Cronkite and John Chancellor were paid the equivalent of 28 ads per year, while in 1999 this had grown to 149 ads for Dan Rather and Tom Brokaw. The marked increase in the amount paid per viewing household, salary expressed in ad revenues, and the absolute magnitude of the salary took place in the 1990s. This was a time of declining absolute audiences, but rising importance of anchors in attracting viewers. The increased value placed on anchors is consistent with these personalities playing a growing role in attracting viewers in a multichannel universe.

Current News Markets

The expanding opportunities for individuals to consume media products has meant declining market shares for most traditional news media outlets. The percentage of survey respondents saying that they were regular consumers of a specific news outlet dropped substantially between May 1993 and April 2002 in Pew surveys: from 77 percent to 57 percent for local television news; 60 percent to 32 percent for nightly network news; and 52 percent to 24 percent for network television news magazines. Between 1994 and 2002, Pew surveys indicated drops in regular consumption from 47 percent to 41 percent for radio and 58 percent to 41 percent for newspapers. Respondents reporting regular consumption of online news grew from 2 percent in April 1996 to 25 percent in April 2002; NPR's figures also increased during that period, from 13 percent to 16 percent. In April 2002, 33 percent of survey respondents reported that they were regular consumers of cable television news. . . .

The multiplication of news outlets on cable and the Internet means [also] that an individual is more likely today than in the 1970s or 1980s to find a news outlet closer to his or her ideal news source. The creation of niche programming and content means that individuals may be more likely to find what they want. But the division of the audience into smaller groups also means that any one channel may be less likely to attract viewers, less likely to amass advertiser revenue, and hence less able to devote resources to programming. There may be a trade-off between cable channels' catering to individual topical interests and the quality of programming that can be supported by the audience size. On the Internet, the drive of competition means that price eventually equals marginal costs (zero), so sites are searching for ways to generate revenue. This means that breaking news becomes a commodity essentially offered for free. The lack of revenue may mean that sites simply repeat readily available information rather than generate their own coverage. In a study of Internet content during the 2000 presidential primaries, the Committee of Concerned Journalists found that one-quarter of the political front pages on Internet sites they studied had no original reporting.[19] The time pressure to provide news generated by the Internet and the lack of resources to do original reporting may increase the likelihood that information cascades occur. When initial news reports get facts wrong, the tendency of reporters to rely on the work of others and the quick multiplication effects can mean that bad information propagates. . . .

An additional dilemma for hard-news consumers is the economic pressures that may push some outlets away from offering the type of news they prefer. If advertisers value younger viewers and younger viewers demonstrate a higher willingness to switch channels, then broadcast programs may end up at the margins, putting more soft-news topics into previously hard-news programs. This explains in part the increased emphasis on entertainment and human-interest stories on the network news broadcasts. Media bias can also emerge as a commercial product, in at least two forms. If networks are targeting relatively younger female viewers, and these viewers express more interest in issues such as gun control and the problems of families with children, the network news programs may focus on traditionally Democratic (liberal) issues out of economic necessity. The development of niche programs on cable can also generate programs targeted at viewers with a particular ideology. The FOX News Channel. for example, attracts a relatively conservative audience and offers the cable news program with the largest audience—*The O'Reilly Factor*. The added variety arising from the expansion of cable programming means that viewers uninterested in politics can more readily avoid it. In 1996 viewers with cable who had low levels of political interest (i.e., had low levels of political information) were much less likely to watch presidential debates than viewers who had broadcast channels.[20] Those who were not interested in politics but had only broadcast television did end up watching these debates, since their options were limited. The greater entertainment options provided by cable television also appear to affect who votes. Among viewers with high interest in entertainment programming, those with cable are much less likely to vote (perhaps because they are able to avoid political programming by watching the many entertainment channels offered on cable). . . .

Changes in news markets from 1970 to today have brought new media, generated more diverse offerings, and added opportunities to find both hard and soft news. In pushing for the deregulation of broadcast television in the 1980s, FCC chairman Mark Fowler declared famously, "The public's interest . . . defines the public interest." [21] The competition for interested audiences has clearly driven many of the recent changes in journalism. Whether the aggregation of individuals pursuing the stories they want to know about yields the type of information they need to know about as citizens and voters is a question pursued further in other chapters in this volume.

NOTES

1. Anthony Downs, *An Economic Theory of Democracy* (New York: Harper Books, 1957). Downs coined the term *rational ignorance* to refer to the fact that the small probability that an individual has of influencing public policy decisions means that it may be rational to remain ignorant of current affairs, if one views information only as an instrument in making decisions and calculates the personal payoffs from keeping up with public affairs. There may still be a demand expressed for political coverage, from those who feel a duty to be informed, people who find the details of politics and policies inherently interesting, or people who derive entertainment from politics as drama, horse race, or scandal. The logic of rational ignorance may help explain why Delli Carpini and Keeter find that "despite the numerous political, economic, and social changes that have occurred since World War II, overall political knowledge levels in the United States are about the same today as they were forty to fifty years ago" (*What Americans Know about Politics and Why It Matters.* New Haven, Conn.: Yale University Press, 1996, 270).

2. For data on channel availability and consumption, see Ed Papazian, ed., *TV Dimensions 2002* (New York: Media Dynamics, 2002).

3. To study the market for pundits, I analyzed a sample of the print offerings and broadcast transcripts of fifty-six pundits in 1999 using the text analysis software DICTION. See chapter 8 in Hamilton, *All the News That's Fit to Sell,* (Princeton, N.J.: Princeton University Press, 2004).

4. For analysis of news markets on the Internet, see chapter 7 in Hamilton, *All the News That's Fit to Sell.*

5. See Kovach and Rosensteil, *Warp Speed* (New York: Century Foundation Press, 1999), and Kalb, *One Scandalous Story* (New York: Free Press, 2001), for discussions of the time pressures on journalists created by the speed of information transmission and the Internet.

6. See chapter 3 in Hamilton, *All the News That's Fit to Sell,* for an analysis of the network news audience.

7. Committee of Concerned Journalists, *Changing Definitions of News* (Washington, D.C.: Committee of Concerned Journalists, 1998), available from www.journalism.org.

8. Patterson, *Out of Order* (New York: Knopf, 1993); Adatto, *Picture Perfect* (New York: Basic Books, 1993); Council for Excellence in Government, *Government: In and Out of the News,* study by the Center for Media and Public Affairs, 2003, available at http://www.excelgov.org/displaycontent.asp?keyword=prnHomePage. Patterson's *Out of Order* also includes a discussion of distrust between reporters and politicians.

9. Weaver and Wilhoit, *The American Journalist in the 1990s* (Mahwah, N.J.: Lawrence Erlbaum, 1996).

10. Gardner, Csikszentmihalyi, and Damon, *Good Work* (New York: Basic Books, 2001).

11. Thomas W. Hazlett and David W. Sosa, "Was the Fairness Doctrine a 'Chilling Effect'?: Evidence from the Post-Deregulation Radio Market," *Journal of Legal Studies* 26, no. 1 (1997): 279–301.

12. For data on newspaper markets, see Compaine and Gomery, *Who Owns the Media?* 3rd ed. (Mahwah, N.J.: Lawrence Erlbaum, 2000).

13. Ibid.

14. Scott Roberts, Jane Frenette, and Dione Stearns, "A Comparison of Media Outlets and Owners for Ten Selected Markets: 1960, 1980, 2000" (working paper, Media Ownership Working Group, Federal Communications Commission, Washington, D.C., 2002).

15. For discussion of the impact of media ownership and concentration on content, see Peter O. Steiner, "Program Patterns and Preferences, and the Workability of Competition in Radio Broadcasting," *Quarterly Journal of Economics* 66 (1952): 194-223; Demers, *The Menace of the Corporate Newspaper* (Ames: Iowa State University Press, 1996); Bagdikian, *The Media Monopoly* (Boston: Beacon Press, 1997); McChesney, *Rich Man, Poor Democracy* (Urbana: University of Illinois Press, 2000); Jeff Chester, "Strict Scrutiny: Why Journalists Should Be Concerned about New Federal and Industry Media Deregulation Proposals," *Harvard International Journal of Press/Politics* 7, no. 2 (2002): 105–15; and Roberts and Kunkel, eds., *Breach of Faith* (Fayetteville: University of Arkansas Press, 2002). The quotation on ownership studies comes from C. Edwin Baker, "Ownership of Newspapers: The View from Positivist Social Science" (research paper, Joan Shorenstein Center on the Press, Politics and Public Policy, Kennedy School of Government, Harvard University, Cambridge, Mass, 1994), 19. See also Lisa George, "What's Fit to Print: The Effect of Ownership Concentration on Product Variety in Daily Newspaper Markets" (working paper, Michigan State University, East Lansing, Mich., 2001), and Project for Excellence in Journalism, *Does Ownership Matter in Local Television News? A Five-Year Study of Ownership and Quality*, updated April 29, 2003, http://www.journalism.org/resources/research/reports/ownership/default.asp.

16. This section excerpts and summarizes analysis from chapters 6 and 8 of Hamilton, *All the News That's Fit to Sell.*

17. In 1969 the founders or early leaders of each network still served as the chairman of the board: William S. Paley (CBS); David Sarnoff (RCA, which owned NBC); and Leonard Goldenson (ABC). For an overview of the networks that focuses on the 1980s, see Auletta, *Three Blind Mice* (New York: Random House, 1992). Data on channels per television household come from Ed Papazian, ed., *TV Dimensions 2001* (New York: Media Dynamics, 2001), which indicates (on p. 22) that averages were 7.1 for 1970 and 63.4 for 2000. Larry M. Bartels and Wendy M. Rahn, in "Political Attitudes in the Post-Network Era" (paper prepared for the Annual Meeting of the American Political Science Association, Washington, D.C., September, 2000), report that the sum of the Nielsen ratings for the three network evening news programs was close to 36 in 1970–71 and 23 in 1999–2000. For the text of Vice President Spiro Agnew's speech attacking network television news on November 13, 1969, see James Keogh, *President Nixon and the Press* (New York: Funk & Wagnalls, 1972).

18. In summer 2001 DirecTV, a digital satellite service, offered subscribers more than 225 channels (see www.directv.com). The average number of channels received in U.S. television households grew from 28 in 1988 to 49 in 1997. Households clearly have favorites among these channels. The average number of channels viewed per household, where viewing is defined as "10 or more continuous minutes per channel," was 12 in 1997. See Nielsen Media Research, *1998 Report on Television* (New York: Nielsen Media Research, 1998), 19.

19. Committee of Concerned Journalists, *ePolitics: A Study of the 2000 Presidential Campaign on the Internet* (Washington, D.C.: Committee of Concerned Journalists, 2000), available from www.journalism.org.

20. See Matthew A. Baum and Samuel Kernell, "Has Cable Ended the Golden Age of Presidential Television?" *American Political Science Review* 93, no. 1 (1999): 99–114.

21. See Hamilton, *All the News That's Fit to Sell*, 1.

14-2

Name That Source

Jeffrey Toobin

A news leak occurs when an unnamed individual in the government gives a journalist information that is subsequently published or broadcast as news. The leaker may be seeking to influence public opinion, foreclose a controversial policy alternative under consideration, embarrass a superior with damaging information, and the like. The reporter is a willing recipient because leaked information will generally be unavailable from official government sources and often makes for compelling stories. Leaks are as old as American history, but beginning with the Watergate scandal that led to President Richard Nixon's resignation in 1974, major leaks have been a regular feature of the Washington news scene. President Clinton faced the Whitewater and Lewinsky scandals, which started with leaks and led to his impeachment. News based on leaked information can have serious deficiencies. Not knowing the source or the motives that prompted him or her to contact a journalist, the reader has no way to judge the reliability of leaked news. The leak may provide critical information about a crime or, as in the case of the Libby indictment described in this essay, the leak itself might be a crime. Occasionally in such cases journalists are subpoenaed to appear before grand juries and trials to name their source. Some refuse, claiming that the Constitution's freedom of the press protects them and their sources. In the article below, New Yorker *feature writer and court watcher Jeffrey Toobin reviews the rise of leaks and the recent trend of federal courts' rejecting the news media's freedom of the press claims.*

Why are the courts leaning on journalists?

ON DECEMBER 16TH, [2005] the [*New York*] *Times*, citing anonymous government officials, reported that the National Security Agency has engaged in extensive, warrantless wiretapping of American citizens in a secret program authorized by President Bush in 2002. At a press conference three days later, the President

Source: Jeffrey Toobin, "Name That Source," *The New Yorker*, January 16, 2006.

defended the eavesdropping. "We're at war, and we must protect America's secrets," he said, adding that the Times' sources, by disclosing the program, had committed a "shameful act" that had undermined American security. By the end of December, the Justice Department had begun a criminal investigation of possible leaks of classified information to the Times. As part of the inquiry, the leaders of the investigation will almost certainly seek to interview the reporters who wrote the story, James Risen and Eric Lichtblau. The reporters may receive grand-jury subpoenas demanding their cooperation, and may face contempt charges and jail time if they refuse to comply. Thus the N.S.A. leak investigation may join a growing list of cases in which journalists, under threat of legal sanction, are being asked to identify their sources.

In the best known of these cases, Patrick J. Fitzgerald, the special counsel investigating the leak of the name of Valerie Plame Wilson, a former C.I.A. agent, subpoenaed at least six Washington journalists to appear before a grand jury last year; one, Judith Miller, who was then a reporter for the Times, was jailed on contempt charges for eighty-five days before agreeing to testify. Reporters are also being subpoenaed to testify in civil cases. Wen Ho Lee, a nuclear physicist who formerly worked at the Los Alamos National Laboratory, in New Mexico, has sued the government for improperly disclosing his name and other confidential information in the course of an espionage investigation in 1999, and in the past two years the judges in the case have issued contempt findings against Risen and Jeff Gerth, of the Times; Walter Pincus, of the Washington Post; Bob Drogin, of the Los Angeles Times; Pierre Thomas, formerly of CNN and now with ABC News; and H. Josef Hebert, of the Associated Press, all of whom have refused to testify, and ordered them to pay fines of five hundred dollars a day. An appeals court affirmed the judgment against all the reporters except Gerth, who was found to be too peripherally involved to be cited, and the journalists have asked the Supreme Court to intervene. (The fines are stayed pending the appeals.)

Steven J. Hatfill, a former government scientist who was identified in the press as a possible suspect in the anthrax investigation, has filed a similar lawsuit against the government, in connection with leaks in his case, and in December 2004, his lawyers subpoenaed thirteen news organizations for testimony. The lawyers have since withdrawn the subpoenas, while they interview government officials they suspect could be responsible for the leaks, but the subpoenas are widely expected to be reissued.

In October, Patrick Fitzgerald charged I. Lewis (Scooter) Libby, Vice-President Cheney's chief of staff, with lying to the grand jury about his conversations with reporters, including Miller, Tim Russert, of NBC, and Matthew Cooper, of Time. (Libby immediately resigned.) As Libby's lawyers prepare for his trial, which will probably take place this year, they are expected to ask to see the journalists' notes, and they may subpoena other reporters who covered the investigation. At the trial, Libby's team will try to undermine the journalists' credibility by challenging them on everything from sloppy note-taking to evidence of bias. "This guy is on trial for his freedom, and it's not his job to be worried about the rights of the witnesses against him," a person close to Libby's defense team said. "There are going to be fights over access to the reporters' notes, their prior history and credibility, and their interviews with other people. By the time this trial is over, the press is going to regret that this case was ever brought."

Media lawyers and journalism advocacy groups are alarmed by the increase in demands for reporter testimony. "Thirty-five years or so ago, reporters started getting a lot of subpoenas, and then there was a long lull," Lucy Dalglish, the executive director of the Reporters Committee for Freedom of the Press, told me. "But starting about two years ago we got this sudden pop. There are more grand-jury leak investigations. . . . "The civil cases are maybe the scariest of all," Dalglish continued. "You're talking about daily fines for contempt that last the length of a case, which could be years. That's what's really giving editors and publishers indigestion."

The subpoenas are coming at a time when the legal status of reporters is as unsettled as it has been in more than two decades. Public esteem for the media is low, and neither Congress nor the courts seem inclined to grant special protection to journalists. . . .

The last time journalists received subpoenas in significant numbers was during the early seventies. Protests against the Vietnam War were at a peak, and government officials were increasingly anxious about domestic unrest and national security. In 1972, for the first time, the Supreme Court addressed the right of journalists to protect their sources, when it decided *Branzburg v. Hayes,* a combination of four cases in which reporters had received grand-jury subpoenas. (Two of the cases involved the Black Panthers; the two others concerned drug dealers.)

Justice Byron White's opinion for the five-to-four majority began, "The issue in these cases is whether requiring newsmen to appear and testify before state or federal grand juries abridges the freedom of the press guaranteed by the First Amendment. We hold that it does not." White's opinion was a scathing dismissal of the journalists' position. "The preference for anonymity of those confidential informants involved in actual criminal conduct is presumably a desire to escape criminal prosecution, and this preference, while understandable, is hardly deserving of constitutional protection," he wrote. In short, he held for the Court that the First Amendment provides no "exemption from the ordinary duty of all other citizens to furnish relevant information to a grand jury performing an important public function." In a brief concurring opinion, Justice Lewis Powell suggested that under certain circumstances—which he defined vaguely as criminal investigations that were "not being conducted in good faith"—journalists might be justified in refusing to testify.

The reaction of lower-court judges to *Branzburg* was unprecedented in American legal history. Many federal courts simply ignored the Supreme Court's opinion. "There were some extremely capable First Amendment and mass-media lawyers who were able to spin a win out of a loss, by persuading courts to follow Powell's concurring opinion instead of White's majority opinion," Rodney Smolla, the dean of the University of Richmond School of Law and the author of "Free Speech in an Open Society," said. "Instead of citing White's rejection of the privilege, many lower courts used the Powell opinion to create a balancing test. These judges would evaluate, on a case-by-case basis, whether they thought a subpoena to a journalist was legitimate, and they wound up quashing a lot of them."

Branzburg was decided only a few months before Bob Woodward and Carl Bernstein, in breaking the story of the Watergate scandal, demonstrated the importance of protecting government whistle-blowers, and judges became reluctant to impose limits on journalists. "After *Branzburg*, you had the romance of Woodward and Bernstein, and judges saw how important confidential sources had been to uncovering Watergate," Smolla said. "They were just a lot more sympathetic to the press." Many states created shield laws, which ban or restrict subpoenas to journalists for information about their confidential sources. (The District of Columbia and all states except Wyoming now have shield laws or some form of protection for reporters, but these don't apply in federal criminal investigations or in civil lawsuits filed under federal law.) In the three decades after *Branzburg*, on the rare occasions when journalists were called into court, their lawyers, brandishing their peculiar readings of *Branzburg*, typically managed to protect them from testifying.

In 2003, however, an opinion by Judge Richard A. Posner transformed the debate over the so-called reporter's privilege. A prolific scholar and perhaps the nation's best-known federal appeals-court judge, Posner wields singular authority from his chambers, in Chicago. In *McKevitt v. Pallasch,* a case that grew out of the prosecution in Ireland of an alleged I.R.A. terrorist named Michael McKevitt, Posner took a fresh look at the Supreme Court's decision in *Branzburg*. A key government witness in the case was David Rupert, an F.B.I. informant who was widely reviled among supporters of the I.R.A.'s cause. Abdon Pallasch, a reporter for the *Chicago Sun-Times,* and several colleagues were writing a biography of Rupert, and they had tape-recorded interviews with him. McKevitt wanted his lawyers to have access to the tapes, and Rupert did not object. But the reporters wanted to keep the tapes secret, because, as Posner put it, "the biography of him that they are planning to write will be less marketable the more information in it that has already been made public."

Posner ruled that the journalists had to turn the tapes over to the defense. Reviewing interpretations of the law since 1972, Posner wrote, "A large number of cases conclude, rather surprisingly, that there is a reporter's privilege." He added dryly, "These courts may be skating on thin ice." According to Dalglish, of the Reporters Committee for Freedom of the Press, "Prosecutors and civil litigants who want reporters to testify have really felt empowered, largely, I think, because of Judge Posner. He said, 'Everybody go back and reread this case. *Branzburg* is just not there as a decision that helps the press.' "

Judicial conservatives like Posner have never held the press in especially high regard; witness his essay in the *Times Book Review* in July, in which he argued that the news media have become "more sensational, more prone to scandal and possibly less accurate." But the Fitzgerald investigation revealed a less obvious corollary: a festering hostility toward the traditional news media from the left. The role of the press in the events preceding the investigation amounted to an almost precise inversion of the whistle-blower model. In a column on July 14, 2003, the conservative commentator Robert Novak revealed that Valerie Plame was a C.I.A. operative, citing as his sources "senior administration officials." The leak may have been a politically motivated attack on Plame's husband, Joseph C. Wilson IV, who had published an op-ed piece in the *Times* a week earlier questioning the Bush Administration's assertion that Saddam Hussein's government had tried to buy uranium for nuclear weapons in Africa. As the investigation has unfolded, it has come to seem likely that several senior Administration officials, including Libby and Karl Rove, the President's top political aide, disclosed Plame's status to reporters. To some liberal critics of the Administration, and of the journalists who reported the White House officials' charges, this kind of transaction between reporter and source deserves little protection from the First Amendment. . . .

But criticism from the left and the right may not be the worst problem for reporters at the moment. Their loss of public esteem has been accompanied by the rise of a new and potentially lucrative kind of lawsuit, which is also based on news leaks. In these cases, the subject of the leak sues the federal government, and journalists are forced to testify as witnesses. So it may not be just good politics to pick fights with journalists these days; there may be money in it, too. . . . The first account of a potential scandal at the Los Alamos laboratory appeared in the *Wall Street Journal* on January 7, 1999, and Walter Pincus, of the *Washington Post*, published his first piece about the case on February 17th. In the article, headlined "U.S. CRACKING DOWN ON CHINESE DESIGNS ON NUCLEAR DATA," Pincus wrote that an F.B.I. investigation had come "to focus on an Asian American scientist at Los Alamos who had contacts with the Chinese and has since been transferred to a job outside the national security area." In a story on March 9th, Pincus identified [Wen Ho] Lee by name, as the "weapons designer . . . who was under suspicion of handing nuclear secrets to China." As with the other reporters subpoenaed in the case, Pincus's references to Lee were attributed to unidentified sources. (The *Times* also identified Lee by name in a story the same day.)

In December 1999, Lee filed his case against the federal government, making an argument . . . that the leaks to Pincus and the others constituted repeated violations by government officials of Lee's rights under the Privacy Act. [A] 1974 [law], . . . designed to prevent the unauthorized disclosure of government records[.] In such a case, the plaintiff must establish that government officials improperly disclosed information. At the time, the District of Columbia was one of the jurisdictions in which judges had interpreted the *Branzburg* case in a way favorable to journalists. Based on a 1981 ruling, plaintiffs in D.C. had an "obligation to exhaust possible alternative sources" of information—in other words, to interview possible leakers—before they could subpoena a reporter. In the past, this requirement has discouraged some litigants from pursuing journalists, or even from filing cases.

But Lee's lawyers were dogged. "We made every effort to find out the leakers without going to the journalists," Sun said. He took depositions from six employees of the Department of Energy (including Bill Richardson, the former Secretary), eight F.B.I. officials (including the former director Louis Freeh), and six officials at the Justice Department. "We came up with bubkes," Sun said. In August 2002, he started issuing subpoenas to the reporters.

Lawyers for the journalists moved to overturn the subpoenas, and, in a decision rendered on October 9, 2003, Judge Thomas Penfield Jackson issued what amounted to a cry of revulsion at cozy journalistic–source relationships in Washington: "The deposition transcripts [of the government officials] generally reveal a pattern of denials, vague or evasive answers, and stonewalling. None of the deponents, plaintiff says, has admitted to having personal knowledge of the source of any disclosures. Thus, in the absence of the serendipitous, last-minute appearance of a willing independent witness with personal knowledge of the facts, at the moment only the journalists can testify as to whether defendants were the sources for the various news stories."

Jackson ordered the journalists to testify, and last June his ruling was upheld by the D.C. Circuit Court of Appeals, in a decision that was even more dismissive of the journalists' concerns. Accusing lawyers for the *Times* reporters of being "inaccurate to a point approaching deceptiveness," the appeals court ordered the journalists (except Jeff Gerth) to identify their sources or start paying the fines. . . . Steven Hatfill's lawyers are pursuing a strategy similar to Lee's, first deposing the government officials who are suspected leakers in his case, and then, presumably, going after the reporters. The best hope for the subpoenaed journalists in both cases is that the government settles the lawsuits before the contempt rulings are affirmed.

The First Amendment instructs Congress to "make no law . . . abridging the freedom of speech, or of the press," but the Supreme Court historically has been reluctant to treat the press clause as meaningfully distinct from the speech clause. As Rodney Smolla says, "The Court has generally been unwilling to say that journalists have more rights than other citizens. Whenever the Court has had cases about access to courtrooms or disaster sites, it talks about the right of the public to be there, and journalists are just part of the public. The idea behind the cases is that everyone should be treated the same."

This principle has made it difficult for journalists to persuade courts to recognize a special privilege to protect them from testifying. "When you look at other privileges, like attorney-client or doctor-patient, they arise out of confidential relationships that have a formal quality to them, and there is a powerful and ancient interest in promoting candor," Smolla said. "If you have a journalistic privilege, it might apply to everyone a journalist meets in reporting a story, even if he has no preexisting relationship with them. The journalist can make the promise of confidentiality on the spot, as needed. The courts are loath to hand that kind of power to journalists to put information off limits."

The converse argument—that journalists should be allowed to promise confidentiality to their sources, and the courts should honor those promises—was made by Justice William O. Douglas, in a dissenting opinion in the *Branzburg* case. "A reporter is no better than his source of information," Douglas wrote. "Unless he has a privilege to withhold the identity of his source, he will be the victim of governmental intrigue or aggression. If he can be summoned to testify in secret before a grand jury, his sources will dry up and the attempted exposure, the effort to enlighten the public, will be ended. If what the Court sanctions today becomes settled law, then the reporter's main function in American society will be to pass on to the public the press releases which the various departments of government issue." . . .

This argument didn't command a majority of the Supreme Court in 1972, and, in the current political and legal environment, the most the press can probably hope for is a compromise, like the one proposed last April by Judge David S. Tatel. A Clinton appointee to the D.C. Circuit, Tatel sat on the three-judge panel that rejected Judith Miller's appeal of the contempt order against her for refusing to testify before Fitzgerald's grand jury. Like Posner, Tatel recognized that the decision in *Branzburg* essentially foreclosed the claim that the First Amendment protects journalists from grand-jury subpoenas. But Tatel went on to note that the Federal Rules of Evidence give the courts broad latitude to develop evidentiary privileges "in the light of reason and experience." It was on the basis of these rules that federal courts came to recognize privileges for clergy and attorneys. Tatel sought to determine whether journalists were also entitled to a common-law privilege, as the D.C. Circuit had recently found for psychotherapists regarding their confidential communications with their patients. "In sum," he concluded, " 'reason and experience,' as evidenced by the laws of forty-nine states and the District of Columbia . . . support recognition of a privilege for reporters' confidential sources."

But what Tatel gave Judith Miller with one hand he took away with the other. He stressed that the privilege "cannot be absolute," and, based on the evidence in her case, she was not entitled to its protection. The leak of Valerie Plame's name was a "serious matter," he argued, but the disclosure "had marginal news value. . . . Considering the gravity of the suspected crime and the low value of the leaked information, no privilege bars the subpoenas." But Tatel did cite several examples of leaks that might justify a reporter in protecting his sources. One was a 2004 story in the *Washington Post* about a "budget controversy regarding a supersecret satellite program." The story was co-written by Walter Pincus. . . .

Pincus has an idiosyncratic view of his legal predicament. He's skeptical of the notion that subpoenas to journalists necessarily have a chilling effect on sources. "My sources are not drying up," he told me. "It hasn't hurt me. There is a misconception generally about sources. When you talk about a leak, you are usually not talking about a single person handing you something. You get a little bit here, and a little bit there, and often you can't even identify the single source of a story. Anyway, most of my confidential sources are people I know extremely well. I've built up these sources over the years. Reporting in the intelligence field is talking to a lot of people. The idea that sources are people who come to you over the transom is not true in my case. And those people who come to you over the transom are often trying to plant things that turn out not to be true. My experience is that most sources you don't know personally will give you bad information."

Pincus believes that reporters are facing more subpoenas as much because of bad habits that the profession has acquired as because of an unsympathetic public and judiciary. He thinks, for example, that reporters are often too ready to grant confidentiality to their sources. "The whole subject of confidential sources has gotten mixed up between gossip, opinion, and fact," he said. "I cover intelligence, and people are really risking their jobs and perhaps their freedom by telling me information that they know is classified. That's very different from people going on background to tell you that Britney Spears is pregnant, or that Hillary Clinton shouldn't run for the Senate because it will hurt her chances of running for President. Just because someone asks for confidentiality doesn't mean you have to give it to them. And just because someone tells you something, even if it's true, doesn't mean you have to put it in the paper."

Two days before Novak revealed Valerie Plame's name in his column, an Administration official had discussed her husband's trip to Africa with Pincus. The official, to whom Pincus promised confidentiality, said that Wilson's trip had been arranged by his wife. (The official told Pincus that Wilson's wife worked at the C.I.A. but did not identify her by name.)

Miller chose to go to jail rather than cooperate with Fitzgerald; Pincus took a different tack. Rather than defy the prosecutors, as Miller did for so long, Pincus and his lawyers made a deal that would allow him both to honor his agreement with his source and to give Fitzgerald the information he requested. First, Pincus received a waiver from his source to talk to Fitzgerald, but only for the purpose of letting him answer Fitzgerald's questions. (Pincus will not identify the source publicly, except to say that it wasn't Lewis Libby.) Pincus's lawyers established that Fitzgerald's team would ask a limited number of questions about the timing and content of his interview with the source, and Pincus testified with little fanfare. (Ultimately, Miller also accepted a waiver from her source, Libby, and testified before the grand jury.) "A lot of reporters are egomaniacs," Pincus said. "Some people want a confrontation. They want us to be above the law. We're not."

The risk, of course, is that successful subpoenas of reporters will lead to more such subpoenas. As the federal appeals court in New York observed in 1999, in upholding a privilege claim by reporters for NBC, "If the parties to any lawsuit were free to subpoena the press at will, it would likely become standard operating procedure for those litigating against an entity that had been the subject of press attention to sift through press files in search of information supporting their claims." The burden of subpoenas on journalists' time, and on their employers' budgets, would be bad enough, but there would also be, as the New York court put it, "the symbolic harm of making journalists appear to be an investigative arm of the judicial system, the government, or private parties."

Pincus's accommodating approach goes only so far. With one exception, his sources in the Wen Ho Lee case have not waived confidentiality, and Pincus will continue to honor his agreement with the remaining sources, the contempt order notwithstanding. (If Pincus and the other reporters continue to defy Judge Rosemary M. Collyer, who took over the case after Jackson retired, she could order them jailed.) Today, Lee is remembered by many as a victim, who served nine months in solitary confinement after his indictment on fifty-nine counts of mishandling classified information, and was the subject of a lengthy editor's note in the *Times*, apologizing for the paper's harsh coverage of his case. But Pincus has little sympathy for Lee, arguing that the Privacy Act does not cover the kind of information that was disclosed to him, and that the substance of what he was told was made public anyway when Lee was indicted. He maintains that Lee suffered no legal damage from the news reports; although the government eventually dropped most of the charges against him, Lee did plead guilty to a felony count of copying classified documents onto computer tapes without authorization. In an opinion by Judge Collyer on November 16th, she wrote that Pincus was free to make these arguments, but only after he answers questions from Lee's lawyers in a deposition.

Pincus might be able to avoid testifying if the D.C. Circuit created a common-law journalistic privilege along the lines suggested by Tatel. If the court applies Tatel's balancing test—weighing the public benefit of the leak against the harm that the leak caused—then Pincus might not have to name his sources. "Walter accurately reported news about an important espionage investigation, with major foreign-policy implications," Kevin Baine, Pincus's lawyer, said. "That's a major benefit to the country. And there's no harm, because all the information was released by the government in a matter of weeks anyway, when Lee was indicted."

Tatel's reasoning could also help Risen and Lichtblau protect the confidentiality of their sources in the N.S.A. wiretapping story. "In the current N.S.A. situation, I think Judge Tatel's test would clearly be struck in favor of our reporters," George Freeman, the assistant general counsel at the New York Times Company, said. "This was a leak to determine whether the law was broken, and that is something that ought to be brought to the public's attention, so there can be public debate about it." . . . At the moment, however, Tatel's rule is not the law of the federal courts in Washington, D.C., much less of the United States, so the reporters have little reason to be optimistic.

Constitution of the United States

We the People of the United States, in Order to form a more perfect Union, establish Justice, insure domestic Tranquility, provide for the common defence, promote the general Welfare, and secure the Blessings of Liberty to ourselves and our Posterity, do ordain and establish this Constitution for the United States of America.

ARTICLE I

Section 1. All legislative Powers herein granted shall be vested in a Congress of the United States, which shall consist of a Senate and House of Representatives.

Section 2. The House of Representatives shall be composed of Members chosen every second Year by the People of the several States, and the Electors in each State shall have the Qualifications requisite for Electors of the most numerous Branch of the State Legislature.

No Person shall be a Representative who shall not have attained to the age of twenty five Years, and been seven Years a Citizen of the United States, and who shall not, when elected, be an Inhabitant of that State in which he shall be chosen.

[Representatives and direct Taxes shall be apportioned among the several States which may be included within this Union, according to their respective Numbers, which shall be determined by adding to the whole Number of free Persons, including those bound to Service for a Term of Years, and excluding Indians not taxed, three fifths of all other Persons.][1] The actual Enumeration shall be made within three Years after the first Meeting of the Congress of the United States, and within every subsequent Term of ten Years, in such Manner as they shall by Law direct. The Number of Representatives shall not exceed one for every thirty Thousand, but each State shall have at Least one Representative; and until such enumeration shall be made, the State of New Hampshire shall be entitled to chuse three, Massachusetts eight, Rhode-Island and Providence Plantations one, Connecticut five, New-York six, New Jersey four, Pennsylvania eight, Delaware one, Maryland six, Virginia ten, North Carolina five, South Carolina five, and Georgia three.

Source: U.S. Congress, House, Committee on the Judiciary, *The Constitution of the United States of America, as Amended,* 100th Cong., 1st sess., 1987, H Doc 100-94.

When vacancies happen in the Representation from any State, the Executive Authority thereof shall issue Writs of Election to fill such Vacancies.

The House of Representatives shall chuse their Speaker and other Officers; and shall have the sole Power of Impeachment.

Section 3. The Senate of the United States shall be composed of two Senators from each State, [chosen by the Legislature thereof,][2] for six Years; and each Senator shall have one Vote.

Immediately after they shall be assembled in Consequence of the first Election, they shall be divided as equally as may be into three Classes. The Seats of the Senators of the first Class shall be vacated at the Expiration of the second Year, of the second Class at the Expiration of the fourth Year, and of the third Class at the Expiration of the sixth Year, so that one third may be chosen every second Year; [and if Vacancies happen by Resignation, or otherwise, during the Recess of the Legislature of any State, the Executive thereof may make temporary Appointments until the next Meeting of the Legislature, which shall then fill such Vacancies.][3]

No Person shall be a Senator who shall not have attained to the Age of thirty Years, and been nine Years a Citizen of the United States, and who shall not, when elected, be an Inhabitant of that State for which he shall be chosen.

The Vice President of the United States shall be President of the Senate, but shall have no Vote, unless they be equally divided.

The Senate shall chuse their other Officers, and also a President pro tempore, in the Absence of the Vice President, or when he shall exercise the Office of President of the United States.

The Senate shall have the sole Power to try all Impeachments. When sitting for that Purpose, they shall be on Oath or Affirmation. When the President of the United States is tried, the Chief Justice shall preside: And no Person shall be convicted without the Concurrence of two thirds of the Members present.

Judgment in Cases of Impeachment shall not extend further than to removal from Office, and disqualification to hold and enjoy any Office of honor, Trust or Profit under the United States: but the Party convicted shall nevertheless be liable and subject to Indictment, Trial, Judgment and Punishment, according to Law.

Section 4. The Times, Places and Manner of holding Elections for Senators and Representatives, shall be prescribed in each State by the Legislature thereof; but the Congress may at any time by Law make or alter such Regulations, except as to the Places of chusing Senators.

The Congress shall assemble at least once in every Year, and such Meeting shall [be on the first Monday in December],[4] unless they shall by Law appoint a different Day.

Section 5. Each House shall be the Judge of the Elections, Returns and Qualifications of its own Members, and a Majority of each shall constitute a Quorum to do Business; but a smaller Number may adjourn from day to day, and may be authorized to compel the Attendance of absent Members, in such Manner, and under such Penalties as each House may provide.

Each House may determine the Rules of its Proceedings, punish its Members for disorderly Behaviour, and, with the Concurrence of two thirds, expel a Member.

Each House shall keep a Journal of its Proceedings, and from time to time publish the same, excepting such Parts as may in their Judgment require Secrecy; and the Yeas and Nays of the Members of either House on any question shall, at the Desire of one fifth of those Present, be entered on the Journal.

Neither House, during the Session of Congress, shall, without the Consent of the other, adjourn for more than three days, nor to any other Place than that in which the two Houses shall be sitting.

Section 6. The Senators and Representatives shall receive a Compensation for their Services, to be ascertained by Law, and paid out of the Treasury of the United States. They shall in all Cases, except Treason, Felony and Breach of the Peace, be privileged from Arrest during their Attendance at the Session of their respective Houses, and in going to and returning from the same; and for any Speech or Debate in either House, they shall not be questioned in any other Place.

No Senator or Representative shall, during the Time for which he was elected, be appointed to any civil Office under the Authority of the United States, which shall have been created, or the Emoluments whereof shall have been encreased during such time; and no Person holding any Office under the United States, shall be a Member of either House during his Continuance in Office.

Section 7. All Bills for raising Revenue shall originate in the House of Representatives; but the Senate may propose or concur with Amendments as on other Bills.

Every Bill which shall have passed the House of Representatives and the Senate, shall, before it become a Law, be presented to the President of the United States; If he approve he shall sign it, but if not he shall return it, with his Objections to that House in which it shall have originated, who shall enter the Objections at large on their Journal, and proceed to reconsider it. If after such Reconsideration two thirds of that House shall agree to pass the Bill, it shall be sent, together with the Objections, to the other House, by which it shall likewise be reconsidered, and if approved by two thirds of that House, it shall become a Law. But in all such Cases the Votes of both Houses shall be determined by yeas and Nays, and the Names of the Persons voting for and against the Bill shall be entered on the Journal of each House respectively. If any Bill shall not be returned by the President within ten Days (Sundays excepted) after it shall have been presented to him, the Same shall be a Law, in like Manner as if he had signed it, unless the Congress by their Adjournment prevent its Return, in which Case it shall not be a Law.

Every Order, Resolution, or Vote to which the Concurrence of the Senate and House of Representatives may be necessary (except on a question of Adjournment) shall be presented to the President of the United States; and before the Same shall take Effect, shall be approved by him, or being disapproved by him, shall be repassed by two thirds of the Senate and House of Representatives, according to the Rules and Limitations prescribed in the Case of a Bill.

Section 8. The Congress shall have Power To lay and collect Taxes, Duties, Imposts and Excises, to pay the Debts and provide for the common Defence and general Welfare of the United States; but all Duties, Imposts and Excises shall be uniform throughout the United States;

To borrow Money on the credit of the United States;

To regulate Commerce with foreign Nations, and among the several States, and with the Indian Tribes;

To establish an uniform Rule of Naturalization, and uniform Laws on the subject of Bankruptcies throughout the United States;

To coin Money, regulate the Value thereof, and of foreign Coin, and fix the Standard of Weights and Measures;

To provide for the Punishment of counterfeiting the Securities and current Coin of the United States;

To establish Post Offices and post Roads;

To promote the Progress of Science and useful Arts, by securing for limited Times to Authors and Inventors the exclusive Right to their respective Writings and Discoveries;

To constitute Tribunals inferior to the supreme Court;

To define and punish Piracies and Felonies committed on the high Seas, and Offences against the Law of Nations;

To declare War, grant Letters of Marque and Reprisal, and make Rules concerning Captures on Land and Water;

To raise and support Armies, but no Appropriation of Money to that Use shall be for a longer Term than two Years;

To provide and maintain a Navy;

To make Rules for the Government and Regulation of the land and naval Forces;

To provide for calling forth the Militia to execute the Laws of the Union, suppress Insurrections and repel Invasions;

To provide for organizing, arming, and disciplining, the Militia, and for governing such Part of them as may be employed in the Service of the United States, reserving to the States respectively, the Appointment of the Officers, and the Authority of training the Militia according to the discipline prescribed by Congress;

To exercise exclusive Legislation in all Cases whatsoever, over such District (not exceeding ten Miles square) as may, by Cession of particular States, and the Acceptance of Congress, become the Seat of the Government of the United States, and to exercise like Authority over all Places purchased by the Consent of the Legislature of the State in which the Same shall be, for the Erection of Forts, Magazines, Arsenals, dock-Yards, and other needful Buildings;—And

To make all Laws which shall be necessary and proper for carrying into Execution the foregoing Powers, and all other Powers vested by this Constitution in the Government of the United States, or in any Department or Officer thereof.

Section 9. The Migration or Importation of such Persons as any of the States now existing shall think proper to admit, shall not be prohibited by the Congress prior to the Year one thousand eight hundred and eight, but a Tax or duty may be imposed on such Importation, not exceeding ten dollars for each Person.

The Privilege of the Writ of Habeas Corpus shall not be suspended, unless when in Cases of Rebellion or Invasion the public Safety may require it.

No Bill of Attainder or ex post facto Law shall be passed.

No Capitation, or other direct, Tax shall be laid, unless in Proportion to the Census or Enumeration herein before directed to be taken.[5]

No Tax or Duty shall be laid on Articles exported from any State.

No Preference shall be given by any Regulation of Commerce or Revenue to the Ports of one State over those of another; nor shall Vessels bound to, or from, one State, be obliged to enter, clear, or pay Duties in another.

No Money shall be drawn from the Treasury, but in Consequence of Appropriations made by Law; and a regular Statement and Account of the Receipts and Expenditures of all public Money shall be published from time to time.

No Title of Nobility shall be granted by the United States: And no Person holding any Office of Profit or Trust under them, shall, without the Consent of the Congress, accept of any present, Emolument, Office, or Title, of any kind whatever, from any King, Prince, or foreign State.

Section 10. No State shall enter into any Treaty, Alliance, or Confederation; grant Letters of Marque and Reprisal; coin Money; emit Bills of Credit; make any Thing but gold and silver Coin a Tender in Payment of Debts; pass any Bill of Attainder, ex post facto Law, or Law impairing the Obligation of Contracts, or grant any Title of Nobility.

No State shall, without the Consent of the Congress, lay any Imposts or Duties on Imports or Exports, except what may be absolutely necessary for executing it's inspection Laws: and the net Produce of all Duties and Imposts, laid by any State on Imports or Exports, shall be for the Use of the Treasury of the United States; and all such Laws shall be subject to the Revision and Controul of the Congress.

No State shall, without the Consent of Congress, lay any Duty of Tonnage, keep Troops, or Ships of War in time of Peace, enter into any Agreement or Compact with another State, or with a foreign Power, or engage in War, unless actually invaded, or in such imminent Danger as will not admit of delay.

ARTICLE II

Section 1. The executive Power shall be vested in a President of the United States of America. He shall hold his Office during the Term of four Years, and, together with the Vice President, chosen for the same Term, be elected, as follows

Each State shall appoint, in such Manner as the Legislature thereof may direct, a Number of Electors, equal to the whole Number of Senators and Representatives to which the State may be entitled in the Congress: but no Senator or Representative, or Person holding an Office of Trust or Profit under the United States, shall be appointed an Elector.

[The Electors shall meet in their respective States, and vote by Ballot for two Persons, of whom one at least shall not be an Inhabitant of the same State with themselves. And they shall make a List of all the Persons voted for, and of the Number of Votes for each; which List they shall sign and certify, and transmit sealed to the Seat of the Government of the United States, directed to the President of the Senate. The President of the Senate shall, in the Presence of the Senate and House of Representatives, open all the Certificates, and the Votes shall then be counted. The Person having the greatest Number of Votes shall be the President, if such Number be a Majority of the whole Number of Electors appointed; and if there be more than one who have such Majority, and have an equal

Number of Votes, then the House of Representatives shall immediately chuse by Ballot one of them for President; and if no Person have a Majority, then from the five highest on the list the said House shall in like Manner chuse the President. But in chusing the President, the Votes shall be taken by States, the Representation from each State having one Vote; A quorum for this Purpose shall consist of a Member or Members from two thirds of the States, and a Majority of all the States shall be necessary to a Choice. In every Case, after the Choice of the President, the Person having the greatest Number of Votes of the Electors shall be the Vice President. But if there should remain two or more who have equal Votes, the Senate shall chuse from them by Ballot the Vice President.][6]

The Congress may determine the Time of chusing the Electors, and the Day on which they shall give their Votes; which Day shall be the same throughout the United States.

No Person except a natural born Citizen, or a Citizen of the United States, at the time of the Adoption of this Constitution, shall be eligible to the Office of President; neither shall any Person be eligible to that Office who shall not have attained to the Age of thirty five Years, and been fourteen Years a Resident within the United States.

In Case of the Removal of the President from Office, or of his Death, Resignation, or Inability to discharge the Powers and Duties of the said Office,[7] the Same shall devolve on the Vice President, and the Congress may by Law provide for the Case of Removal, Death, Resignation or Inability, both of the President and Vice President, declaring what Officer shall then act as President, and such Officer shall act accordingly, until the Disability be removed, or a President shall be elected.

The President shall, at stated Times, receive for his Services, a Compensation, which shall neither be encreased nor diminished during the Period for which he shall have been elected, and he shall not receive within that Period any other Emolument from the United States, or any of them.

Before he enter on the Execution of his Office, he shall take the following Oath or Affirmation:—"I do solemnly swear (or affirm) that I will faithfully execute the Office of President of the United States, and will to the best of my Ability, preserve, protect and defend the Constitution of the United States."

Section 2. The President shall be Commander in Chief of the Army and Navy of the United States, and of the Militia of the several States, when called into the actual Service of the United States; he may require the Opinion, in writing, of the principal Officer in each of the executive Departments, upon any Subject relating to the Duties of their respective Offices, and he shall have Power to grant Reprieves and Pardons for Offences against the United States, except in Cases of Impeachment.

He shall have Power, by and with the Advice and Consent of the Senate, to make Treaties, provided two thirds of the Senators present concur; and he shall nominate, and by and with the Advice and Consent of the Senate, shall appoint Ambassadors, other public Ministers and Consuls, Judges of the supreme Court, and all other Officers of the United States, whose Appointments are not herein otherwise provided for, and which shall be established by Law: but the Congress may by Law vest the Appointment of such inferior Officers, as they think proper, in the President alone, in the Courts of Law, or in the Heads of Departments.

The President shall have Power to fill up all Vacancies that may happen during the Recess of the Senate, by granting Commissions which shall expire at the End of their next Session.

Section 3. He shall from time to time give to the Congress Information of the State of the Union, and recommend to their Consideration such Measures as he shall judge necessary and expedient; he may, on extraordinary Occasions, convene both Houses, or either of them, and in Case of Disagreement between them, with Respect to the Time of Adjournment, he may adjourn them to such Time as he shall think proper; he shall receive Ambassadors and other public Ministers; he shall take Care that the Laws be faithfully executed, and shall Commission all the Officers of the United States.

Section 4. The President, Vice President and all civil Officers of the United States, shall be removed from Office on Impeachment for, and Conviction of, Treason, Bribery, or other high Crimes and Misdemeanors.

ARTICLE III

Section 1. The judicial Power of the United States, shall be vested in one supreme Court, and in such inferior Courts as the Congress may from time to time ordain and establish. The Judges, both of the supreme and inferior Courts, shall hold their Offices during good Behaviour, and shall, at stated Times, receive for their Services, a Compensation, which shall not be diminished during their Continuance in Office.

Section 2. The judicial Power shall extend to all Cases, in Law and Equity, arising under this Constitution, the Laws of the United States, and Treaties made, or which shall be made, under their Authority;—to all Cases affecting Ambassadors, other public Ministers and Consuls;—to all Cases of admiralty and maritime Jurisdiction;—to Controversies to which the United States shall be a Party;—to Controversies between two or more States;—between a State and Citizens of another State;[8]—between Citizens of different States;—between Citizens of the same State claiming Lands under Grants of different States, and between a State, or the Citizens thereof, and foreign States, Citizens or Subjects.

In all Cases affecting Ambassadors, other public Ministers and Consuls, and those in which a State shall be Party, the supreme Court shall have original Jurisdiction. In all the other Cases before mentioned, the supreme Court shall have appellate Jurisdiction, both as to Law and Fact, with such Exceptions, and under such Regulations as the Congress shall make.

The Trial of all Crimes, except in Cases of Impeachment, shall be by Jury; and such Trial shall be held in the State where the said Crimes shall have been committed; but when not committed within any State, the Trial shall be at such Place or Places as the Congress may by Law have directed.

Section 3. Treason against the United States, shall consist only in levying War against them, or in adhering to their Enemies, giving them Aid and Comfort. No Person shall be convicted of Treason unless on the Testimony of two Witnesses to the same overt Act, or on Confession in open Court.

The Congress shall have Power to declare the Punishment of Treason, but no Attainder of Treason shall work Corruption of Blood, or Forfeiture except during the Life of the Person attainted.

ARTICLE IV

Section 1. Full Faith and Credit shall be given in each State to the public Acts, Records, and judicial Proceedings of every other State. And the Congress may by general Laws prescribe the Manner in which such Acts, Records and Proceedings shall be proved, and the Effect thereof.

Section 2. The Citizens of each State shall be entitled to all Privileges and Immunities of Citizens in the several States.

A Person charged in any State with Treason, Felony, or other Crime, who shall flee from Justice, and be found in another State, shall on Demand of the executive Authority of the State from which he fled, be delivered up, to be removed to the State having Jurisdiction of the Crime.

[No Person held to Service or Labour in one State, under the Laws thereof, escaping into another, shall, in Consequence of any Law or Regulation therein, be discharged from such Service or Labour, but shall be delivered up on Claim of the Party to whom such Service or Labour may be due.][9]

Section 3. New States may be admitted by the Congress into this Union; but no new State shall be formed or erected within the Jurisdiction of any other State; nor any State be formed by the Junction of two or more States, or Parts of States, without the Consent of the Legislatures of the States concerned as well as of the Congress.

The Congress shall have Power to dispose of and make all needful Rules and Regulations respecting the Territory or other Property belonging to the United States; and nothing in this Constitution shall be so construed as to Prejudice any Claims of the United States, or of any particular State.

Section 4. The United States shall guarantee to every State in this Union a Republican Form of Government, and shall protect each of them against Invasion; and on Application of the Legislature, or of the Executive (when the Legislature cannot be convened) against domestic Violence.

ARTICLE V

The Congress, whenever two thirds of both Houses shall deem it necessary, shall propose Amendments to this Constitution, or, on the Application of the Legislatures of two thirds of the several States, shall call a Convention for proposing Amendments, which, in either Case, shall be valid to all Intents and Purposes, as Part of this Constitution, when ratified by the Legislatures of three fourths of the several States, or by Conventions in three fourths thereof, as the one or the other Mode of Ratification may be proposed by the Congress; Provided [that no Amendment which may be made prior to the Year One thousand eight hundred and eight shall in any Manner affect the first and fourth Clauses in the Ninth Section of the first Article; and][10] that no State, without its Consent, shall be deprived of its equal Suffrage in the Senate.

ARTICLE VI

All Debts contracted and Engagements entered into, before the Adoption of this Constitution, shall be as valid against the United States under this Constitution, as under the Confederation.

This Constitution, and the Laws of the United States which shall be made in Pursuance thereof; and all Treaties made, or which shall be made, under the Authority of the United States, shall be the supreme Law of the Land; and the Judges in every State shall be bound thereby, any Thing in the Constitution or Laws of any State to the Contrary notwithstanding.

The Senators and Representatives before mentioned, and the Members of the several State Legislatures, and all executive and judicial Officers, both of the United States and of the several States, shall be bound by Oath or Affirmation, to support this Constitution; but no religious Test shall ever be required as a Qualification to any Office or public Trust under the United States.

ARTICLE VII

The Ratification of the Conventions of nine States, shall be sufficient for the Establishment of this Constitution between the States so ratifying the Same.

Done in Convention by the Unanimous Consent of the States present the Seventeenth Day of September in the Year of our Lord one thousand seven hundred and Eighty seven and of the Independence of the United States of America the Twelfth. IN WITNESS whereof We have hereunto subscribed our Names,

George Washington,
President and
deputy from Virginia.

New Hampshire:	John Langdon, Nicholas Gilman.
Massachusetts:	Nathaniel Gorham, Rufus King.
Connecticut:	William Samuel Johnson, Roger Sherman.

New York:	Alexander Hamilton.
New Jersey:	William Livingston,
	David Brearley,
	William Paterson,
	Jonathan Dayton.
Pennsylvania:	Benjamin Franklin,
	Thomas Mifflin,
	Robert Morris,
	George Clymer,
	Thomas FitzSimons,
	Jared Ingersoll,
	James Wilson,
	Gouverneur Morris.
Delaware:	George Read,
	Gunning Bedford Jr.,
	John Dickinson,
	Richard Bassett,
	Jacob Broom.
Maryland:	James McHenry,
	Daniel of St. Thomas Jenifer,
	Daniel Carroll.
Virginia:	John Blair,
	James Madison Jr.
North Carolina:	William Blount,
	Richard Dobbs Spaight,
	Hugh Williamson.
South Carolina:	John Rutledge,
	Charles Cotesworth Pinckney,
	Charles Pinckney,
	Pierce Butler.
Georgia:	William Few,
	Abraham Baldwin.

[The language of the original Constitution, not including the Amendments, was adopted by a convention of the states on September 17, 1787, and was subsequently ratified by the states on the following dates: Delaware, December 7, 1787; Pennsylvania, December 12, 1787; New Jersey, December 18, 1787; Georgia, January 2, 1788; Connecticut, January 9, 1788; Massachusetts, February 6, 1788; Maryland, April 28, 1788; South Carolina, May 23, 1788; New Hampshire, June 21, 1788.

Ratification was completed on June 21, 1788.

The Constitution subsequently was ratified by Virginia, June 25, 1788; New York, July 26, 1788; North Carolina, November 21, 1789; Rhode Island, May 29, 1790; and Vermont, January 10, 1791.]

Amendments

Amendment I

(First ten amendments ratified December 15, 1791.)
Congress shall make no law respecting an establishment of religion, or prohibiting the free exercise thereof; or abridging the freedom of speech, or of the press; or the right of the people peaceably to assemble, and to petition the Government for a redress of grievances.

Amendment II

A well regulated Militia, being necessary to the security of a free State, the right of the people to keep and bear Arms, shall not be infringed.

Amendment III

No Soldier shall, in time of peace be quartered in any house, without the consent of the Owner, nor in time of war, but in a manner to be prescribed by law.

Amendment IV

The right of the people to be secure in their persons, houses, papers, and effects, against unreasonable searches and seizures, shall not be violated, and no Warrants shall issue, but upon probable cause, supported by Oath or affirmation, and particularly describing the place to be searched, and the persons or things to be seized.

Amendment V

No person shall be held to answer for a capital, or otherwise infamous crime, unless on a presentment or indictment of a Grand Jury, except in cases arising in the land or naval forces, or in the Militia, when in actual service in time of War or public danger; nor shall any person be subject for the same offence to be twice put in jeopardy of life or limb; nor shall be compelled in any criminal case to be a witness against himself, nor be deprived of life, liberty, or property, without due process of law; nor shall private property be taken for public use, without just compensation.

Amendment VI

In all criminal prosecutions, the accused shall enjoy the right to a speedy and public trial, by an impartial jury of the State and district wherein the crime shall have been committed, which district shall have been previously ascertained by law, and to be informed of the nature and cause of the accusation; to be confronted with the witnesses against him; to have compulsory process for obtaining witnesses in his favor, and to have the Assistance of Counsel for his defence.

Amendment VII

In Suits at common law, where the value in controversy shall exceed twenty dollars, the right of trial by jury shall be preserved, and no fact tried by a jury, shall be otherwise re-examined in any Court of the United States, than according to the rules of the common law.

Amendment VIII

Excessive bail shall not be required, nor excessive fines imposed, nor cruel and unusual punishments inflicted.

Amendment IX

The enumeration in the Constitution, of certain rights, shall not be construed to deny or disparage others retained by the people.

Amendment X

The powers not delegated to the United States by the Constitution, nor prohibited by it to the States, are reserved to the States respectively, or to the people.

Amendment XI (Ratified February 7, 1795)

The Judicial power of the United States shall not be construed to extend to any suit in law or equity, commenced or prosecuted against one of the United States by Citizens of another State, or by Citizens or Subjects of any Foreign State.

Amendment XII (Ratified June 15, 1804)

The Electors shall meet in their respective states and vote by ballot for President and Vice-President, one of whom, at least, shall not be an inhabitant of the same state with themselves; they shall name in their ballots the person voted for as President, and in distinct ballots the person voted for as Vice-President, and they shall make distinct lists of all persons voted for as President, and of all persons voted for as Vice-President, and of the number of votes for each, which lists they shall sign and certify, and transmit sealed to the seat of the government of the United States, directed to the President of the Senate;— The President of the Senate shall, in the presence of the Senate and House of Representatives, open all the certificates and the votes shall then be counted;—The person having the greatest number of votes for President, shall be the President, if such number be a majority of the whole number of Electors appointed; and if no person have such majority, then from the persons having the highest numbers not exceeding three on the list of those voted for as President, the House of Representatives shall choose immediately, by ballot, the President. But in choosing the President, the votes shall be taken by states, the representation from each state having one vote; a quorum for this purpose shall consist of a member or members from two-thirds of the states, and a majority of all the states shall be necessary to a choice. [And if the House of Representatives shall not choose a President whenever the right of choice shall devolve upon them, before the fourth day of March next following, then the Vice-President shall act as President, as in the case of the death or other constitutional disability of the President.—][11] The person having the greatest number of votes as Vice-President, shall be the Vice-President, if such number be a majority of the whole number of Electors appointed, and if no person have a majority, then from the two highest numbers on the list, the Senate shall choose the Vice-President; a quorum for the purpose shall consist of two-thirds of the whole number of Senators, and a majority of the whole number shall be necessary to a choice. But no person constitutionally ineligible to the office of President shall be eligible to that of Vice-President of the United States.

Amendment XIII (Ratified December 6, 1865)

Section 1. Neither slavery nor involuntary servitude, except as a punishment for crime whereof the party shall have been duly convicted, shall exist within the United States, or any place subject to their jurisdiction.

Section 2. Congress shall have power to enforce this article by appropriate legislation.

Amendment XIV (Ratified July 9, 1868)

Section 1. All persons born or naturalized in the United States, and subject to the jurisdiction thereof, are citizens of the United States and of the State wherein they reside. No State shall make or enforce any law which shall abridge the privileges or immunities of citizens of the United States; nor shall any State deprive any person of life, liberty, or property, without due process of law; nor deny to any person within its jurisdiction the equal protection of the laws.

Section 2. Representatives shall be apportioned among the several States according to their respective numbers, counting the whole number of persons in each State, excluding Indians not taxed. But when the right to vote at any election for the choice of electors for President and Vice President of the United States, Representatives in Congress, the Executive and Judicial officers of a State, or the members of the Legislature thereof, is denied to any of the male inhabitants of such State, being twenty-one years of age,[12] and citizens of the United States, or in any way abridged, except for participation in rebellion, or other crime, the basis of representation therein shall be reduced in the proportion which the number of such male citizens shall bear to the whole number of male citizens twenty-one years of age in such State.

Section 3. No person shall be a Senator or Representative in Congress, or elector of President and Vice President, or hold any office, civil or military, under the United States, or under any State, who, having previously taken an oath, as a member of Congress, or as an officer of the United States, or as a member of any State legislature, or as an executive or judicial officer of any State, to support the Constitution of the United States, shall have engaged in insurrection or rebellion against the same, or given aid or comfort to the enemies thereof. But Congress may by a vote of two-thirds of each House, remove such disability.

Section 4. The validity of the public debt of the United States, authorized by law, including debts incurred for payment of pensions and bounties for services in suppressing insurrection or rebellion, shall not be questioned. But neither the United States nor any State shall assume or pay any debt or obligation incurred in aid of insurrection or rebellion against the United States, or any claim for the loss or emancipation of any slave; but all such debts, obligations and claims shall be held illegal and void.

Section 5. The Congress shall have power to enforce, by appropriate legislation, the provisions of this article.

Amendment XV (Ratified February 3, 1870)

Section 1. The right of citizens of the United States to vote shall not be denied or abridged by the United States or by any State on account of race, color, or previous condition of servitude.

Section 2. The Congress shall have power to enforce this article by appropriate legislation.

Amendment XVI (Ratified February 3, 1913)

The Congress shall have power to lay and collect taxes on incomes, from whatever source derived, without apportionment among the several States, and without regard to any census or enumeration.

Amendment XVII (Ratified April 8, 1913)

The Senate of the United States shall be composed of two Senators from each State, elected by the people thereof, for six years; and each Senator shall have one vote. The electors in each State shall have the qualifications requisite for electors of the most numerous branch of the State legislatures.

When vacancies happen in the representation of any State in the Senate, the executive authority of such State shall issue writs of election to fill such vacancies: *Provided,* That the legislature of any State may empower the executive thereof to make temporary appointments until the people fill the vacancies by election as the legislature may direct.

This amendment shall not be so construed as to affect the election or term of any Senator chosen before it becomes valid as part of the Constitution.

Amendment XVIII (Ratified January 16, 1919)[13]

Section 1. After one year from the ratification of this article the manufacture, sale, or transportation of intoxicating liquors within, the importation thereof into, or the exportation thereof from the United States and all territory subject to the jurisdiction thereof for beverage purposes is hereby prohibited.

Section 2. The Congress and the several States shall have concurrent power to enforce this article by appropriate legislation.

Section 3. This article shall be inoperative unless it shall have been ratified as an amendment to the Constitution by the legislatures of the several States, as provided in the Constitution, within seven years from the date of the submission hereof to the States by the Congress.

Amendment XIX (Ratified August 18, 1920)

The right of citizens of the United States to vote shall not be denied or abridged by the United States or by any State on account of sex.

Congress shall have power to enforce this article by appropriate legislation.

Amendment XX (Ratified January 23, 1933)

Section 1. The terms of the President and Vice President shall end at noon on the 20th day of January, and the terms of Senators and Representatives at noon on the 3d day of January, of the years in which such terms would have ended if this article had not been ratified; and the terms of their successors shall then begin.

Section 2. The Congress shall assemble at least once in every year, and such meeting shall begin at noon on the 3d day of January, unless they shall by law appoint a different day.

Section 3.[14] If, at the time fixed for the beginning of the term of the President, the President elect shall have died, the Vice President elect shall become President. If a President shall not have been chosen before the time fixed for the beginning of his term, or if the President elect shall have failed to qualify, then the Vice President elect shall act as President until a President shall have qualified; and the Congress may by law provide for the case wherein neither a President elect nor a Vice President elect shall have qualified, declaring who shall then act as President, or the manner in which one who is to act shall be selected, and such person shall act accordingly until a President or Vice President shall have qualified.

Section 4. The Congress may by law provide for the case of the death of any of the persons from whom the House of Representatives may choose a President whenever the right of choice shall have devolved upon them, and for the case of the death of any of the persons from whom the Senate may choose a Vice President whenever the right of choice shall have devolved upon them.

Section 5. Sections 1 and 2 shall take effect on the 15th day of October following the ratification of this article.

Section 6. This article shall be inoperative unless it shall have been ratified as an amendment to the Constitution by the legislatures of three-fourths of the several States within seven years from the date of its submission.

Amendment XXI (Ratified December 5, 1933)

Section 1. The eighteenth article of amendment to the Constitution of the United States is hereby repealed.

Section 2. The transportation or importation into any State, Territory, or possession of the United States for delivery or use therein of intoxicating liquors, in violation of the laws thereof, is hereby prohibited.

Section 3. This article shall be inoperative unless it shall have been ratified as an amendment to the Constitution by conventions in the several States, as provided in the Constitution, within seven years from the date of the submission hereof to the States by the Congress.

Amendment XXII (Ratified February 27, 1951)

Section 1. No person shall be elected to the office of the President more than twice, and no person who has held the office of President, or acted as President, for more than two years of a term to which some other person was elected President shall be elected to the office of the President more than once. But this Article shall not apply to any person holding the office of President when this Article was proposed by the Congress, and shall not prevent any person who may be holding the office of President, or acting as President, during the term within which this Article become operative from holding the office of President or acting as President during the remainder of such term.

Section 2. This article shall be inoperative unless it shall have been ratified as an amendment to the Constitution by the legislatures of three-fourths of the several States within seven years from the date of its submission to the States by the Congress.

Amendment XXIII (Ratified March 29, 1961)

Section 1. The District constituting the seat of Government of the United States shall appoint in such manner as the Congress may direct:

A number of electors of President and Vice President equal to the whole number of Senators and Representatives in Congress to which the District would be entitled if it were a State, but in no event more than the least populous State; they shall be in addition to those appointed by the States, but they shall be considered, for the purposes of the election of President and Vice President, to be electors appointed by a State; and they shall meet in the District and perform such duties as provided by the twelfth article of amendment.

Section 2. The Congress shall have power to enforce this article by appropriate legislation.

Amendment XXIV (Ratified January 23, 1964)

Section 1. The right of citizens of the United States to vote in any primary or other election for President or Vice President, for electors for President or Vice President, or for Senator or Representative in Congress, shall not be denied or abridged by the United States or any State by reason of failure to pay any poll tax or other tax.

Section 2. The Congress shall have power to enforce this article by appropriate legislation.

Amendment XXV (Ratified February 10, 1967)

Section 1. In case of the removal of the President from office or of his death or resignation, the Vice President shall become President.

Section 2. Whenever there is a vacancy in the office of the Vice President, the President shall nominate a Vice President who shall take office upon confirmation by a majority vote of both Houses of Congress.

Section 3. Whenever the President transmits to the President pro tempore of the Senate and the Speaker of the House of Representatives his written declaration that he is unable to discharge the powers and duties of his office, and until he transmits to them a written declaration to the contrary, such powers and duties shall be discharged by the Vice President as Acting President.

Section 4. Whenever the Vice President and a majority of either the principal officers of the executive departments or of such other body as Congress may by law provide, transmit to the President pro tempore of the Senate and the Speaker of the House of Representatives their written declaration that the President is unable to discharge the powers and duties of his office, the Vice President shall immediately assume the powers and duties of the office as Acting President.

Thereafter, when the President transmits to the President pro tempore of the Senate and the Speaker of the House of Representatives his written declaration that no inability exists, he shall resume the powers and duties of his office unless the Vice President and a majority of either the principal officers of the executive department or of such other body as Congress may by law provide, transmit within four days to the President pro tempore of the Senate and the Speaker of the House of Representatives their written declaration that the President is unable to discharge the powers and duties of his office. Thereupon Congress shall decide the issue, assembling within forty-eight hours for that purpose if not in session. If the Congress, within twenty-one days after receipt of the latter written declaration, or, if Congress is not in session, within twenty-one days after Congress is required to assemble, determines by two-thirds vote of both Houses that the

President is unable to discharge the powers and duties of his office, the Vice President shall continue to discharge the same as Acting President; otherwise, the President shall resume the powers and duties of his office.

Amendment XXVI (Ratified July 1, 1971)

Section 1. The right of citizens of the United States, who are eighteen years of age or older, to vote shall not be denied or abridged by the United States or by any State on account of age.

Section 2. The Congress shall have power to enforce this article by appropriate legislation.

Amendment XXVII (Ratified May 7, 1992)

No law varying the compensation for the services of the Senators and Representatives shall take effect, until an election of Representatives shall have intervened.

NOTES

1. The part in brackets was changed by section 2 of the Fourteenth Amendment.
2. The part in brackets was changed by the first paragraph of the Seventeenth Amendment.
3. The part in brackets was changed by the second paragraph of the Seventeenth Amendment.
4. The part in brackets was changed by section 2 of the Twentieth Amendment.
5. The Sixteenth Amendment gave Congress the power to tax incomes.
6. The material in brackets has been superseded by the Twelfth Amendment.
7. This provision has been affected by the Twenty-fifth Amendment.
8. These clauses were affected by the Eleventh Amendment.
9. This paragraph has been superseded by the Thirteenth Amendment.
10. Obsolete.
11. The part in brackets has been superseded by section 3 of the Twentieth Amendment.
12. See the Nineteenth and Twenty-sixth Amendments.
13. This Amendment was repealed by section 1 of the Twenty-first Amendment.
14. See the Twenty-fifth Amendment.

CREDITS

1. Designing Institutions

1-1: Reprinted by permission of the publisher from *The Logic of Collective Action: Public Goods and the Theory of Groups* by Mancur Olson, Jr., pp. 1–19, Cambridge, Mass.: Harvard University Press, Copyright ©1965, 1971 by the President and Fellows of Harvard College.

1-2: Reprinted (excerpted) with permission from *Science*, December 3, 1968, pp. 1243–1248. Copyright 1968 AAAS.

1-3: Excerpted from Robert D. Putnam, "The Prosperous Community: Social Capital and the Public Life," *The American Prospect* no. 13 (spring 1993). Copyright 1993 by New Prospect, Inc.; reprinted in *Bowling Alone: The Collapse and Revival of American Community* (Simon and Schuster, 2000). Reprinted by permission. The author is the Peter and Isabel Malkin Professor of Public Policy at Harvard University.

2. The Constitutional Framework

2-1: Excerpted from the article originally appearing in the *American Political Science Review* 55, no. 4 (December 1961): 799–816. Reprinted with the permission of Cambridge University Press. Some notes appearing in the original have been deleted.

2-4: From *The Vineyard of Liberty,* by James MacGregor Burns, copyright ©1981 by James MacGregor Burns. Used by permission of Alfred A. Knopf, a division of Random House, Inc.

3. Federalism

3-1: Excerpted from James Buchanan, "Federalism as an Ideal Political Order and an Objective for Constitutional Reform." *Publius: The Journal of Federalism* 25 (Spring 1995): 19–27. Reprinted by permission of Oxford University Press.

4. Civil Rights

4-1: Adapted from the article originally appearing in *Perspectives on Politics,* 2003, Volume 3, Issue 3, pp. 557–561. Reprinted with the permission of Cambridge University Press.

4-2: Reprinted with permission. Copyright ©*The Public Interest,* no. 144, summer 2001, Washington, D.C.

5. Civil Liberties

5-1: Excerpted from Lee Epstein, ed., *Contemplating Courts* (Washington, D.C.: CQ Press, 1995), pp. 390–419. Some notes and bibliographic references appearing in the original have been deleted.

6. Congress

6-1: Reprinted with the permission of The American Enterprise Institute for Public Policy Research, Washington, DC.

6-2: Excerpted from David R. Mayhew, *Congress: The Electoral Connection* (New Haven: Yale University Press, 1974), 13–27, 49–77. Copyright 1974 Yale University Press. Reprinted by permission. Notes appearing in the original have been deleted.

7. The Presidency

7-1: Reprinted with the permission of The Free Press, a Division of Simon & Schuster Adult Publishing Group, from *Presidential Power and the Modern Presidents: The Politics of Leadership from Roosevelt to Reagan* by Richard E. Neustadt. Copyright ©1990 by Richard E. Neustadt. All rights reserved.

7-2: Excerpted from Samuel Kernell, *Going Public: New Strategies of Presidential Leadership,* 3d edition (Washington, D.C.: CQ Press, 1997), pp. 1–12, 17–26, 34–38, 57–64.

8. The Bureaucracy

8-1: From *Bureaucracy: What Government Agencies Do and Why They Do It,* by James Q. Wilson. Copyright ©1989 by Basic Books, Inc. Reprinted by permission of Basic Books, a member of Perseus Books, L.L.C. Notes appearing in the original have been deleted.

8-2: Excerpted from John E. Chubb and Paul E. Peterson, eds. *Can the Government Govern?* (Washington, D.C.: Brookings Institution Press, 1989), 267–285. Reprinted by permission. Some notes appearing in the original have been deleted

8-3: Reprinted with permission from *National Journal,* March 26, 2005. Copyright 2006 National Journal. All rights reserved.

9. The Judiciary

9-1: Scalia, Antonin; *A Matter of Interpretation.* ©1997 Princeton University Press. Reprinted by permission of Princeton University Press.

9-2: (Slightly adapted) From *Active Liberty: Interpreting our Democratic Constitution,* by Stephen Breyer, copyright ©2005 by Stephen Breyer. Used by permission of Alfred A. Knopf, a division of Random House, Inc.

9-4: Excerpted from Sarah A. Binder and Forrest Maltzman, "Congress and the Politics of Judicial Appointments," in *Congress Reconsidered,* by Lawrence C. Dodd and Bruce I. Oppenheimer (CQ Press: 2005), 13:1–13:21. Some notes appearing in the original have been deleted.

10. Public Opinion

10-1: Originally published in Herbert Asher, *Polling and the Public: What Every Citizen Should Know,* 4th edition (Washington, D.C.: CQ Press, 1998), pp. 141–169.

10-2: Excerpted from the article originally published in *American Political Science Review* 89, no. 3 (September 1995): 543–564. Reprinted with the permission of Cambridge University Press. Notes appearing in the original have been deleted.

10-3: Michael Schudson is Professor of Communication at the University of California, San Diego and author of *The Good Citizen: A History of American Civic Life* (1998) and *The Sociology of News* (2003).

10-4: Excerpt pp. 11–26 from *Culture War? The Myth of a Polarized America* by Morris P. Fiorina. Copyright ©2005 by Pearson Education, Inc. Reprinted by permission.

11. Voting, Campaigns, and Elections

11-1: Excerpted from Samuel L. Popkin, *The Reasoning Voter: Communication and Persuasion in Presidential Campaigns,* 2nd ed. (Chicago: University of Chicago Press, 1994), pp. 212–219. Copyright ©1991, 1994 by the University of Chicago. All rights reserved. Reprinted by permission. Notes appearing in the original have been deleted.

11-2: Excerpted from Jon R. Bond and Richard Fleisher, eds., *Polarized Politics: Congress and the President in a Partisan Era* (Washington, D.C.: CQ Press, 2000), pp. 9–30. Notes appearing in the original have been deleted.

11-3: Excerpted from Darrell West, from "Overview of Ads" and "Advertising and Democratic Elections" in *Air Wars,* by Darrell West (CQ Press: 2005), 1–23, 165–177. Notes appearing in the original have been deleted.

12. Political Parties

12-1: Originally published in John H. Aldrich, *Why Parties?: The Origin and Transformation of Political Parties in America* (Chicago: University of Chicago Press, 1995), pp. 14–27. Copyright © 1995 by the University of Chicago. All rights reserved. Reprinted by permission. Notes appearing in the original have been deleted.

12-2: Excerpted from Larry Bartels, "Partisanship and Voting Behavior, 1952–1996," *American Journal of Political Science.* Published with permission from Blackwell Publishing. Notes appearing in the original have been deleted.

12-3: Reprinted with permission from Rick Valelly, "Who Needs Political Parties?," *The American Prospect,* Volume 11, Number 18: August 14, 2000. The American Prospect, 11 Beacon Street, Suite 1120, Boston, MA 02108. All rights reserved.

13. Interest Groups

13-1: From *Semi-Sovereign People Re-Issue, A Realist's View of Democracy in America* 1st edition by Schattschneider. ©1975. Reprinted with permission of Wadsworth, a division of Thomson Learning: www.thomsonrights.com. Fax 800 730–2215. Some notes appearing in the original have been deleted.

13-2: Excerpt pp. 11–22 from *Interest Groups and Congress* by John R. Wright. Copyright © 2003 by Pearson Education, Inc. Reprinted by permission.

13-3: Reprinted with permission from *National Journal,* November 5, 2005. Copyright 2006 National Journal. All rights reserved.

14. News Media

14-1: From *The Institutions of American Democracy: The Press,* edited by Kathleen Hall Jamieson, copyright Oxford University Press, Ltd.—Work for hire. Used by permission of Oxford University Press, Inc.

14-2: Jeffrey Toobin is a staff writer at *The New Yorker* and the senior legal analyst at CNN.